Urbanization in Africa

Urbanization in Africa

A Handbook

EDITED BY

James D. Tarver

FOREWORD BY

Thomas J. Goliber

GREENWOOD PRESS
WESTPORT, CONNECTICUT • LONDON

Library of Congress Cataloging-in-Publication Data

Urbanization in Africa : a handbook / edited by James D. Tarver ;
foreword by Thomas J. Goliber.
p. cm.
Includes bibliographical references and indexes.
ISBN 0–313–27760–5 (alk. paper)
1. Urbanization—Africa—History. 2. Cities and towns—Africa—
Growth—History. I. Tarver, James D.
HT384.A35U73 1994
307.76′096—dc20 93–11853

British Library Cataloguing in Publication Data is available.

Library of Congress Catalog Card Number: 93–11853
ISBN: 0–313–27760–5

First published in 1994

Greenwood Press, 88 Post Road West, Westport, CT 06881
An imprint of Greenwood Publishing Group, Inc.

Printed in the United States of America

The paper used in this book complies with the
Permanent Paper Standard issued by the National
Information Standards Organization (Z39.48–1984).

10 9 8 7 6 5 4 3 2 1

Contents

Figures and Tables

FIGURES

TABLES

Foreword

In the Introduction Akin Mabogunje says that this reference book on African urbanization is designed to be a "stage setter" which assembles much of the available knowledge about African cities. The ensuing drama will be a critical one. These chapters illustrate that the economic, social, and demographic future of Africa will be increasingly a story of the cities of the continent.

Many themes bind these chapters into a coherent volume, some of which might be noted before the reader grapples with the substance of this impressive reference work. As most of the chapters in the book are country studies of the urbanization process in Africa, one perspective from which they might be read is whether the country fits the more general pattern or is an exception.

Rates of urbanization in Africa are higher than those in any place else in the world, and the rapid growth of the cities is changing what was not long ago an overwhelmingly rural region. Between 1960 and 1990, the African urban population grew at an average annual rate of about 6 percent. At that rate of growth, African cities have been doubling in size in less than 13 years. Even that number hides the higher rates in certain countries: during the 1980s the urban population of Tanzania grew by more than 11 percent per annum; of Kenya, by more than 8 percent per year. *Urbanization in Africa* is replete with examples of extremely high rates of urbanization in Africa.

Urban growth on the African continent stems from three sources: the high rate of natural increase in the cities themselves; the high levels of migration from rural to urban areas; and, to a much lesser extent, the reclassification of formerly rural areas to urban due to increases in population size or boundary changes. This observation leads to another major theme: high levels of urbanization in Africa are entwined with the slow pace of the demographic transition from high to low fertility in this region.

African birthrates and population growth rates remain the highest in the world. The Population Reference Bureau reports that in 1992 the overall total fertility rate (a close proxy for the average number of births per woman) was 6.1 in Africa as opposed to 3.4 and 3.2 births per woman in Latin America and Asia, respectively. The African population is growing at about 3.0 percent per year, a rate at which it will double in size in about 23 years. In its medium population projection, the United Nations shows the population of Africa growing from 643 million in 1990 to 1.58 billion in 2025, a pace which will add a billion persons to the African population in just 38 years.

These powerful forces of demographic change in Africa stimulate the urbanization process. Urbanization in the region has been characterized by high levels of rural-to-urban migration, in part driven by limited economic opportunities in rapidly growing rural Africa. S. I. Abumere observes that most urban growth in Nigeria can be accounted for by rural-to-urban migration. Perhaps even more striking, other authors present evidence in these essays that in several African countries natural increase in the urban areas has been a more important contributor to city growth than migration from the countryside. Philippe Antoine and Aka Kouame, for example, point out that "the principal source of population growth in Abidjan is natural growth and thus fertility."

Evidence from the Demographic and Health Surveys indicates that fertility in African urban centers remains high and this high fertility is a major contributor to the rapid expansion of the cities. For example, the 1990 Nigerian Demographic and Health Survey shows a fertility rate of 5 children per woman in urban areas (as opposed to 6.3 children per woman in rural regions). However, the current generation of young women born in African cities will likely have different social and educational experiences than their mothers. The growth of African cities has been, in part, the consequence of the extraordinary overall rates of population growth in Africa. In turn, the cities themselves are likely to be a conduit of fertility decline over time as a new generation of urban women move through their reproductive years. This is true in part because nascent African family planning programs are likely to expand first in the cities.

Another theme which emerges throughout this reference book is the tendency toward unequal distribution of the urban population within countries. African urban populations tend to congregate in a few large cities. Many countries exhibit tendencies toward urban primacy—demographic and economic dominance by a single metropolitan center. Côte d'Ivoire is cited as an example in West Africa; Tanzania, in East Africa. Similarly, African urban populations tend to congregate in certain regions of the country and are not equally distributed across the whole.

The economic context of rapid African urbanization is important. The growth of the cities is taking place against a backdrop of economic stagnation across the African continent. For example, during the 1980s, gross domestic product increased by an average of less than 1 percent per year in sub-Saharan Africa.

With the population growing by more than 3 percent per annum, gross domestic product (GDP) per capita—and African living standards—declined dramatically. (This situation has opened an interesting debate on whether economic crisis itself can be a stimulus for fertility decline in the region.)

Not only has GDP per capita declined, but industrial production fell by an average of about 1 percent per year during the 1980s. Africa is unusual. Urbanization and industrialization are not progressing together; rather rapid urbanization is taking place at a time of industrial stagnation.

With an overall poor economic performance and a lack of industrial growth, African countries have not been creating enough modern-sector jobs to absorb the growth of the urban labor force, and unemployment is often extremely high. Consequently, as is pointed out in a number of chapters in this volume, the informal sector of the economy plays a major role in the life of African cities. Philippe Antoine and Gora Mboup suggest that as much as 78 percent of the urban labor force in the Dakar area has to find employment in the informal sector. Still, what is striking about the urbanization process in Africa is how bad economic times do little to lessen the movement from the countryside to the cities. The promising lights of the city engender hopes and dreams often absent in rural African villages, and millions continue to move despite the often harsh economic realities of the urban areas.

For poor countries in times of economic crisis, an inability to provide adequate infrastructure to meet the basic needs of the burgeoning urban populations is not unexpected. As R. A. Obudho and Rose A. Obudho note in their chapter, most urban governments have difficulty just grasping the implications of a population that doubles in size so quickly. Sanitation, transport, health, education, water, energy, and a multitude of other basic urban amenities are inadequate or lacking in most African cities. Most of all, African cities are unable to provide anything approaching the needed stock of housing—hence the proliferation of slums and shantytowns and the pervasive overcrowding of urban residences.

Another issue mostly noteworthy for its near absence from the discussion is the impact of rapid urbanization on the African environment. Most urban residents still depend on fuelwood as their source of energy, and some of the most severe deforestation on the continent is taking place in rings around the cities. African urban centers do not have an adequate infrastructure to dispose of sewage, garbage, or other pollutants. Water supplies are especially at risk. Increased air pollution from vehicles and industries is also a growing problem. Cars and trucks in poor African cities are frequently of such bad quality that they send a constant spillage of emissions into the atmosphere. As Abumere notes in his chapter on Nigeria: "Luckily, Nigerians have not yet started to worry about problems of the environment. . . . Otherwise, the heaps of uncleared solid and nonsolid wastes in several Nigerian cities would have been enough to bring a government down. The same is true of the magnitudes of air and water pollution."

A "wild card" in the process of urban development is the potential impact of the AIDS epidemic on urban mortality and health systems. Millions of Africans are likely to die from this disease in the foreseeable future. Because the AIDS epidemic to date is primarily concentrated in urban areas, its impact will be most felt on city life and development. Peter O. Way, for example, observes the disproportionate impact of the epidemic on the skilled and educated labor force in urban areas.

The population explosion in Africa—the extraordinary growth in recent decades and the probable addition of another billion persons to the African population over the next 35 to 40 years—has been and will continue to be a basic reason that the postindependence social and economic development effort has not achieved success. And the final overall theme of this volume is that the population implosion—the increased concentration of Africans in the towns and cities of the continent, especially the large metropolitan areas—will be a fundamental determinant of the African future.

Thomas J. Goliber
The Futures Group

Preface

The objective of this reference book is to present the different aspects and features of urbanization in Africa, both historical and contemporary. This reference work traces urban developments in Africa from their beginning in ancient Egypt through the medieval and early modern periods and contrasts the relatively stable urbanization patterns of the colonial period with the greatly accelerated urban growth since independence. Thus, this reference book is broad in scope. For instance, there are 25 chapters by highly qualified urbanization specialists, including such prominent scholars as Akin Mabogunje, Brian J. L. Berry, Tertius Chandler, Philippe Antoine, Robert Escallier, Dennis A. Rondinelli, A. J. Christopher, and John Weeks.

The reference book is organized into three interrelated parts which portray different aspects of urbanization in Africa. Part I provides a historical overview of urbanization in Africa, beginning with its appearance in ancient Egypt. Then, the successive urban developments in Carthage, the West African empires and kingdoms, and in other areas of sustained urban development are described. Quite exhaustive references are given in each chapter.

The urbanization patterns of 15 highly urbanized countries, which were either Anglophone, Francophone, or Lusophone colonies, are presented in Part II of this reference book. Each of the 15 countries has an urban agglomeration of at least half a million inhabitants, and each of the five United Nations regions is represented. The 15 highly urbanized countries are an indication of the wide geographic coverage of this reference book.

Each of the five chapters in Part III makes a significant contribution to a clearer understanding of the urbanization process in Africa. These five scholarly special topics chapters analyze the role of urbanization policy, rural-urban and international migration, national administrative centers, and the AIDS pandemic upon urbanization in Africa. Each of these five chapters was written by an urbanization scholar.

The dedicated efforts of many individuals helped shape this reference book. For example, Tertius Chandler, Toma J. Makannah, Keith Sutton, and H. Max Miller offered many helpful suggestions in structuring *Urbanization in Africa.*

Ieda S. Wiarda, a Luso-Brazilian culture specialist, Library of Congress, and Albert Kendall, Library of Congress, assisted in language matters. John Giron, Sandra M. Laing, Sarah G. Browning, and Frederic Rondeau handled the actual translations. Joanna Lawrence did the graphic artwork.

Technical assistance was rendered by Debra C. Brown, Linda Gotay, Gloria L. Hammond, Mary Beth Lane, Diane H. Ward, Carol Winfree, and Catherine Young. Laurence Humphries, Computer Support Systems, Inc., converted several diskettes to WordPerfect 5.1.

The staff of the Sociology Department, Howard University, is due a special thanks. Dr. James T. Sabin, Executive Vice President, Greenwood Publishing Group, Inc., provided the overall guidance for this reference book, and Dr. George F. Butler, Associate Editor, Acquisitions, very carefully edited the original manuscript and supervised its completion.

Introduction: Cities and Africa's Economic Recovery

Akin L. Mabogunje

The 1970s and 1980s have been decades of traumatic economic reverses for Africa. According to the World Bank (1989), this deepening crisis for the continent

> is characterised by weak agricultural growth, a decline in industrial output, poor export performance, climbing debt, and deteriorating social indicators, institutions and environment. Agricultural output has grown annually by less than 1.5 per cent on the average since 1970, with food production rising more slowly than population. Although industry grew roughly three times as fast as agriculture in the first decade of independence, the past few years have seen an alarming reversal in many African countries where de-industrialization seems to have set in. With export volumes barely growing at all since 1970, Africa's share in world markets has fallen by almost half. [Consequently], to maintain income and investment, government borrowed heavily from abroad. Africa's long-term debt has risen 19-fold since 1970 and is now equal to its gross national product (GNP), making the region the most heavily indebted of all regions.

With such a record of overwhelming indebtedness, it is tempting to wonder where a serious assessment of the urban situation comes in for policy design in promoting Africa's economic recovery. What is the relevance at this time of another book on urbanization in Africa? What can such a book tell us that can make a difference to the agonizing strains and stresses of daily existence in African cities today?

The truth of the matter is that African cities are part of the cause and a major symptom of the economic crisis that has enveloped the continent (Santos, 1971; Bardinet, 1977; Mabogunje, 1987). Their inability to serve as veritable engines of growth and structural transformation as cities in other societies is certainly a serious element in the present equation. This inability is a function of their historical background, their colonial evolution, and their transitional characteristics within changing modes of production. To appreciate what all this entails, it is necessary to spell out first the challenge that urbanization has presented in Africa especially since the 1960s.

THE CHALLENGE OF URBANIZATION IN AFRICA

Although Africa has been described as the least urbanized of the continents with less than 30 percent of its population living in urban centers, it is generally recognized that, until recently, it was also the continent with the fastest rate of urbanization (United Nations, 1991). While this fast rate is partly a function of the initial low base, it is also a reflection of major social changes taking place within the continent. These changes relate to the impact of the colonial heritage on lives and livelihoods in even the remotest parts of the continent. This impact has taken the form of extensive peaceful conditions making life a lot more secure and encouraging wide-ranging mobility in search of improved standards of living. Initially, these streams of migrations were directed to enclave areas of colonial primary production for export whether of agricultural commodities or minerals. With time, it came to be accepted that these were the realistic niche for African countries to seek to occupy within the international division of labor (Wallerstein, 1976).

With political independence, however, and the vigorous programs of African governments to reduce the sway of ignorance and illiteracy and provide education to an increasingly large proportion of the youthful population, the direction of the migration streams showed a decisive shift to urban areas. Their composition also changed and reflected more of young school-leavers, both male and female, seeking in the cities modern types of employment different from agriculture. Thus, for sub-Saharan Africa, as the proportion of school enrollment of youths rose from 41 to 79 percent between 1965 and 1980 and dropped slightly to 73 percent in 1986, the proportion of the total population living in urban centers jumped from 14 percent in 1965 to 27 percent in 1987 (World Bank, 1989:274–278).

Urbanization thus represents a major redistribution of population in Africa. Among urban centers themselves, this redistribution showed a strong preference for the very large cities and metropolitan areas. Thus, the percentage of urban population in sub-Saharan Africa living in cities of over 500,000 rose rapidly from 6 to 41 between 1960 and 1980, and the number of such centers themselves jumped from 3 to 28 (World Bank, 1989). In other words, for a large number of young school-leavers seeking to make their fortunes in urban centers, there was little step-by-step migration from small towns to cities and on to metropolitan centers. Instead, what we have is a one-step transition from rural background to urban life with all that it entails in attitudes, modes of behavior, and styles of living.

Many of the chapters in this volume provide detailed descriptions of the urban population in most African countries. They indicate with rich statistical evidence the skewed nature of this distribution in most African countries both in terms of size and spatial location. It has been argued in the literature that this skewed distribution represented by both the primate-city phenomenon and its coastal location is not neutral with respect to the low level of economic development over vast areas of most African countries (Berry, 1971; Johnston, 1977). This pattern has consequently provoked, especially in the 1970s, discussions as to how to correct the national urban system in many of these countries (Mabogunje and Faniran, 1977).

These discussions concentrated on the need to develop countervailing urban centers which can serve as alternative magnets drawing migrants and employment-generating activities away from the primate city. The concept of growth-pole and growth center development was widely canvassed in this connection. It encouraged some countries such as Côte d'Ivoire, Tanzania, Malawi, and Nigeria to plan to move their capitals away from the coast, a task which in spite of its costs and challenging difficulties has, to a large extent, been achieved in each of the four instances mentioned. In other countries, the emphasis was to encourage the growth of small to medium-size cities which were seen as more directly vital to the need to enhance agricultural and food production (Southall, 1979).

The skewed distribution of urban population was also noticeable in the age-sex ratio in African cities (Ohadike, 1975). Initially, rural-urban migration was in most countries a predominantly male affair. This was reflected in a male-female ratio well above 1.0. With time and the most recent influx of young school-leavers, this ratio has moved closer to one. The major distortion thus remains in the age distribution with African cities being overwhelmingly cities of young people, with the aged being left behind in the rural areas or seeing those areas as more benign for their retirement from active life in the cities (Ominde, 1968).

In the earlier African urbanization studies there was considerable controversy as to the relative significance of the push-pull factors in attracting migrants to the city. This controversy would today appear of less significance since African cities, although providing some employment, have turned out to be more centers of consumption than production. Modernization was the name of the game. In order to be able to participate in the game, the Africans needed some wage employment to earn the income to pay for services provided in urban centers. These services include improved physical infrastructure such as housing, good asphalted roads, electricity, piped-water, telecommunications, and transport services. They also involved social infrastructure, especially schools for the children, hospitals and health centers, recreational facilities, and cultural amenities.

All of these were made possible by the wholesale importation of economic and productive institutions developed and nurtured in the advanced industrialized countries. Largely foreign-owned joint-stock enterprises came to be responsible for most commercial activities. They bulked and exported agricultural and other primary products while they also imported and distributed manufactured goods from the metropolitan countries. Even after independence import substituting industrialization became the fashion, it was still these largely foreign-owned corporate bodies that became the promoters and owners of these enterprises (Mabogunje, 1980).

In all of these, foreign-owned companies were assisted by foreign-owned banks which mobilized local savings and made them more easily available to these companies. Their dominance in the economy also made possible easy repatriation of profits and eventually significant capital flight from the countries.

The economic situation in most African cities was not helped by the intervention of many African governments in diverse fields of productive activities. In the flush of political independence, many of these governments sought to control the commanding heights of their national economies even when they were not doing this for ideological reasons. The inability to then manage and run these enterprises and parastatals on strictly economic lines, the inefficiencies and corruption that became characteristic of their operations, all this quickly became a major drain on the vitality of the economy. They also constituted significant elements in the international debts incurred by most of these countries. These debts have become so compound that their repayments to developed countries represent today a serious case of financial hemorrhage that has vitiated any development in both the urban and the national economies of African countries.

Even in the heyday of investment in modernization, the vast majority of rural-urban migrants could not be absorbed in terms of securing either employment opportunities or decent housing in the cities. The result was the rapid mushrooming of shantytowns on the outskirts of most African cities. These were neighborhoods self-constructed with flimsy material to protect their occupants from inclement weather and without access to water supply or other facilities of environmental sanitation. Sometimes these neighborhoods show some layout; more often than not there is no layout, and the general environmental situation is most squalid and unhygienic. In major African metropolitan centers such as Cairo, Lagos, Kinshasa, and even Nairobi, these informal settlements account for a significant proportion of the urban area and population (Stren, 1978).

In spite of the unprepossessing nature of the physical environment, these areas of the city are also the scene of robust and vigorous informal economic activities in which small producers relying on informal credit systems provide the vast majority of urban residents with many of the basic necessities of living. Indeed, according to the World Bank (1990:63), informal-sector activities account for an estimated 75 percent of urban employment in many countries of sub-Saharan Africa today.

The informal economic sector in most African cities embraces fabrication, metalworking, manufacturing, arts and crafts, repairs, trading, services, and even credit provision. It is an area of urban life whose existence has been taken seriously only since 1972 when an International Labor Office (1972) mission to Kenya could no longer dismiss it as representing the phenomenon of underemployment among most African urban residents. Since that date, numerous studies have been conducted into the operations of the informal sector and various interpretations, especially from a Marxian perspective, offered for this phenomenon (Moser, 1978). Two things, however, remain clear. One is that there is as yet no final word on our understanding of the operations and prospects of this sector; the other is that, in spite of this, the informal sector promises to be a most critical element in any attempt to put African urban and national economies back on a sound footing. In order, therefore, to appreciate better the crucial significance of the informal sector in African urbanization, it is important to provide a historical perspective to the discussion.

INFORMALITY AND THE HISTORY OF AFRICAN URBANIZATION

In spite of the fact that Africa is today the least urbanized of the continents, it is the continent with some of the oldest traditions of urbanization in the world (Childe, 1942). The first few chapters of this volume provide detailed descriptions of urbanization on the North African coast dating from ancient and medieval periods of world history. Even in sub-Saharan Africa, evidence abounds that early urbanization provided the focal points for political organizations (Hull, 1976). There is also abundant evidence that while the slave trade led to the emergence and growth of some port centers, on the whole, its impact on African urbanization was catastrophic. The slave trade saw the destruction of many African urban centers and a major reversal of the economic fortunes of vast areas of Africa. Urban centers such as Timbuktu (Miner, 1953), Bobo-Dioulasso, Kano, Mombassa, and Mogadishu, which survived this difficult period, provide evidence of economic and social organization of precolonial African cities.

By the time of the colonial adventure of European powers in the late nineteenth century, most of Africa was prostrate from the devastation of three centuries of slave trade. The economies had receded in most areas to what have been described as essentially peasant economies articulated largely through kinship relations. It was kinship that determined access to all factors of production whether it was land, labor, capital, or technical know-how. A man had to be born into a particular family to be able to have access to sizable tracts of land for farming. He had to depend on members of his nuclear or extended family for labor as well as for the acquisition of craft skills for blacksmithing, weaving, pottery, and so on. He often had to depend on his kinsmen for credit.

Although in a few parts of the continent some form of feudal structure was starting to emerge by the early nineteenth century, the well-known communal system of land ownership and the kinship nexus were characteristic of the prevailing mode of production over large parts of Africa by the time of the colonial domination.

Colonialism in Africa thus had the mission of penetrating the kinship-based traditional economies and integrating them into the global world capitalist system. However, unlike the traditional economy, capitalism as a mode of production required that every factor of production—labor, land, capital, and entrepreneurship—be assigned a price tag as if it were a mere commodity and brought to the market (Polanyi, 1957). In other words, capitalism sought to commoditize the products of all human activities, give them significance on the basis of their exchange value rather than their use value, and link the whole economy through the money nexus rather than through kinship relations. However, the task of commoditizing the whole of societal resources was a formidable endeavor. It involved turning self-employed peasants into wage-earning hired labor; turning communally owned, intermixed, nonalienable tracts of land into individually owned, alienable plots; making capital in both its mechanically embodied and nonembodied know-how forms available to all on a universalistic rather than ascriptive basis; and encouraging enterprise and entrepreneurship to strive to achieve greater profitability (Lonsdale, 1981).

Over most of Africa, the focal points of this gargantuan attempt at penetrating the traditional peasant economies and initiating the process of capitalist transformation were the urban centers. Imposition of taxation and insistence that this be paid in newly introduced money species began the process of commoditizing African labor and monetizing the African economy. To earn money to pay taxes, peasants moved into the urban centers to offer their labor for wages or brought their surplus farm produce for sale in the cities. Nowhere in Africa, however, did a totally proletariat labor class emerge which had nothing to trade on the market but its labor.

But it was with the commoditization of land as a factor of production that the inadequate transformation of the colonial economy was most evident. In countries, especially those in Western Africa, where there was no large European settler communities, very little was done to promote the commoditization of land. In colonial territories such as those in eastern, central, and southern Africa where such settler communities were well established, a strategy of carving out a large enclave of crown or state land was initiated. Within such enclaves, a thoroughgoing individualization and commoditization of land was undertaken but restricted only to the foreigners. Even where the metropolitan instructions sought to extend the process to all and sundry, the colonial administration strenuously ensured that land titling and registration were limited mainly to the settler community (Mabogunje, 1990).

One of the most significant consequences of this development was the incapacity of the Africans to fully participate in the capitalist economy. Access to credit was a central factor in such participation. Such access was guaranteed by the presentation of an indisputable registered title to a given plot of land which could be used as collateral to raise credit and enhance one's productive capacity.

By failing to transform the land situation to enable Africans to possess such indisputable claims to land, the colonial administration ensured that their participation in the colonial economy could at best be only marginal.

This situation was all the more unconscionable particularly as the Africans were not indifferent or antagonistic to such participation. Indeed, as the urbanization process proceeded and it became clear that a large influx of people other than kinsmen now had to be accommodated, the process of land individualization and land sale had begun. However, instead of providing the enabling legislative and regulatory environment that would have guided these developments in the direction of land titling and registration, the colonial administration all over Africa preferred to leave this critical transformation of the economic foundation of productive activity in Africa in limbo. In consequence, all over Africa today, the various attempts of Africans to adjust to the operations of the free market economy through negotiated individualization of land is dismissed as informal transactions in land.

Similar descriptions of informality are ascribed to the Africans' attempt to participate on their own terms in the productive sectors of the capitalist economy. Denied easy access to vital credit, the African was committed to establishing petty enterprises whether in small-scale industrial production, craft and cottage industries, trading and, of course, farming. Everywhere having no possible material security to guarantee a loan, the Africans have to fall back on traditional credit mobilization systems to enable them to achieve some modicum of sustainable operation. Even in this sector, sufficient modernizing progress was being made that if only appropriate legislative and regulatory environment were created, the economic circumstances in most African cities would have been very different from what they are presently (Haggblade, 1978).

It is thus easy to demonstrate that "informality" came to be the term applied to most attempts by Africans to transform and adjust their precapitalist mode of production to the dictates of the free market economy. It is, however, a term which hides the incompetence or indifference of the colonial and the postcolonial state in the actual task of governance and economic development. For everywhere it was recognized that well-developed economic institutions imported from Europe, whether in the form of large joint-stock trading companies, or modern industrial enterprises, or large-scale financial and banking institutions, could provide services or cater to the needs of not more than 25 percent of the population of a given African country. The remaining 75 percent consequently hoped to live and secure a sustainable, if modest, livelihood only by operating within the informal economic sector particularly in African cities and towns (World Bank, 1990:63).

Against such a historical background, the challenge of urbanization in most African countries can be seen as the challenge of dealing with "informality" as an economic process while, at the same time, promoting authentic, self-centered national development. Such a challenge entails having the right perception of the forces shaping not only the African cities and their general environmental quality but also determining the fortunes of the vast majority of urban residents who derive their livelihood from the so-called informal sector. It requires appreciating the contextual significance of those borrowed elements of modernizing societies and the need to adapt them to the realities of the African urban situation. More than this, it compels a creative evaluation of how to make African cities, especially through enhancing and developing the capacity of their informal sector, a vital and critical factor in the struggle for the economic recovery of African countries.

CITIES AND THE DECLINE TO ECONOMIC RECESSION

But the fact of the primary significance of the informal sector for African urban development was not immediately apparent in the period soon after independence when most African countries tried to show that they too had arrived on the global economic scene. At that time, the received orthodoxy was for newly independent countries to engage in import substitution industrialization as a critical strategy for promoting economic development. The logic of this strategy was that, by first manufacturing those goods for which there was a ready market, African countries could, with time and through backward integration, come more fully to exploit and develop locally available resources (Hirschman, 1957). The logic itself was unexceptionable. Where it went wrong or was being deliberately myopic was in failing to examine the composition of imports at the time and to see that no local substitution was possible for most of them in virtually all African countries.

However, once this became the accepted strategy, African countries all made a dash for importing not only the machinery and equipment but in most cases the technical know-how, the capital, and even the semiprocessed raw material required by these new factories. The products of these factories were largely nondurable consumer goods featuring beverages, leather goods, food items, and in some cases locally assembled vehicles. Indeed, much of this industrialization was no more than local assembling or bottling. Invariably, however, the imported factory had a production capacity far in excess of the needs of the individual country concerned. Almost from the very beginning, therefore, inadequate capacity utilization had dogged the fortunes of most of these factories. This situation became even more critical when it is recognized that most of these factories were established on the basis of loans proffered either on a multilateral or bilateral government-to-government basis or directly through private foreign financial arrangements. Paying back these loans while at the same time seeking foreign exchange to keep buying the needed industrial raw material and spare parts was to constitute the bane of most African economies in succeeding decades, leading Rweyemamu (1973) to describe the whole process as one of "perverse capitalist industrial development."

In the meantime, because of the heavy import dependence of this strategy, port cities became the preferred location for industrial development. Since, for obvious reasons, these were often also the preferred location of colonial administrations especially in those countries without large European settler populations, these cities became at once the capital city, the port city, and the nascent industrial center of most African countries. In the case of those countries of relatively large European settlement, their choice interior location such as Nairobi, Harare, Lusaka, and Johannesburg served the same purpose even when it was not a port. Consequently, the trend to a primate-city urban system was initiated, and large, single metropolitan urban development became the order of the day in most African countries. A number of the contributions to this volume are concerned with describing in detail how most countries in Africa reached this situation. Apart from being differentiated on the geographical basis of whether the cities are in north or sub-Saharan African, countries have been categorized on the size of their urban agglomerations whether these were largely above a half million but less than one million or whether at least one city had already passed one million.

Everywhere and irrespective of their size, African metropolitan centers became the scene of conspicuous and unwarranted consumption. Here were to be found the latest models of gadgets and automobiles which became veritable status symbols. Here, the elite indulged their tastes for food and other fares which they had cultivated while still students abroad and which bore no relation to the resource profile of the local ecology. A good example of this is the dominance of wheat bread in the diet of the urban population, a development which has been described as "the wheat trap" and which compels many African countries to spend a significant amount of their foreign earnings on paying for the massive import of a commodity which can never become a staple diet for the majority (Andrae and Beckman, 1985).

This high propensity to import in order to support both the productive and the consumptive capacity in African cities was clearly not likely to be sustainable over the medium to long run. In no time at all, foreign debts began to pile up (Hughes, 1979). Capacity utilization in most of the industries which had absorbed much of the countries' foreign earnings and which was even at the best of times not particularly high began to drop to most uneconomic levels. Everywhere, African cities began to exhibit glaring evidence of economies seriously in recession. Infrastructural facilities could hardly be maintained in a fit condition of repair, and the delivery of most urban services became erratic and subject to serious shortages (Stern and White, 1989). Health-care and educational standards dropped dramatically. Modern housing could no longer keep up with the rate of rural-urban migration, and the extent of self-constructed shantytowns expanded rapidly.

What with all these seemingly negative developments, urban life did not collapse in most African countries. Indeed, it tended in most cases to show a perverse "buoyancy" especially in its informal sector, prompting Green (1981) to opine that this sector, locally known as "magendo," is the dominant submode of production in Africa. For most of the new migrants to the city, it is this sector that guarantees them a shelter over their heads; it is this sector that ensures that they have any employment at all; and it is this sector that makes it possible for them to have any income and any claims on consumption goods in the city. More than anything else, therefore, the future of most African cities can be said to depend inexorably on what is done to ensure that this sector of the urban economy becomes progressively more productive and more entrepreneurial.

CONCLUSION

In evaluating the basis of the present collapse of African economies, the World Bank (1989:3) had this to say:

> The post independence development efforts failed because the strategy was misconceived. Governments made a dash for "modernization" copying, but not adapting, Western models. The result was poorly designed public investments in industry; too little attention to peasant agriculture; too much intervention in areas in which the state lacked managerial, technical and entrepreneurial skills; and too little effort to foster grassroots development. This top-down approach demotivated ordinary people whose energies most needed to be mobilized in the development efforts.

This misconceived strategy of development equally applies to African urbanization whose dynamics and real essence remain seriously misunderstood. Within African cities, African governments continue to copy rather than adapt appropriate models of governance and promote wide-ranging and sustainable economic development.

Yet, before our very eyes the people themselves are evolving institutions and erecting social structures to facilitate and mediate their access to various factors of production, notably, urban land, credit, and technical know-how. The experience in Nigeria with the rapidly growing number of community banks which have been based on traditional community development associations is a case in point (Nigeria, 1990). So are the *banques populaires* of Rwanda. Nonetheless, unless governments move in to legitimatize these institutions, restructure them in a manner to align them more easily with the mainstream of free market economic activities in the country, and provide some regulatory oversight which enhances while not impeding their growth and innovativeness, such institutional development may never take place, and national economic recovery may be stalled.

Attempts to mobilize the energies of the masses in African cities can hardly succeed if serious attention is also not paid to issues of governance. To ensure greater participation and increased willingness to pay for services, the governance of African cities has to be shorter on bureaucratic procedures and longer on democratic participation and accountability. People must know what they are paying taxes for. The linkage between tax revenue generation and the quantum and quality of service delivery must be highly transparent. How to achieve a highly realistic level of popular participation is also a function of activating and adapting institution arrangements which are meaningful to the masses rather than simply copying Western models of doubtful authenticity.

Clearly, there is need for a new paradigm of urban development in Africa (Mabogunje, 1991). There is a lot that must be done if cities are to become significant factors in African economic recovery. There is also a lot that we still need to know about urban society and the urban economy in most African countries if policy formulation is to be based on realistic empirical knowledge. The imperative of providing increased research has never been so compelling as at present. The present reference work on urbanization in Africa thus provides a useful takeoff point for this new generation of studies. It helps to set the stage by bringing together much of what we know presently about the situation of African cities.

REFERENCES

Andrae, Gunilla, and Bjorn Beckman. 1985. *The Wheat Trap: Bread and Underdevelopment in Nigeria.* London: Zed Books.

Bardinet, Claude. 1977. "City Responsibilities in the Structural Dependence of Sub-industrialized Economies in Africa." *Antipode: A Radical Journal of Geography* 9:43–48.

Berry, Brian J. L. 1971. "City Size and Economic Development." In *Urbanization and National Development,* edited by Leo Jacobson and V. Prakash, 111–155. Beverly Hills: Sage.

Childe, V. Gordon. 1942. *What Happened in History.* London: Max Parrish.

Green, Reginald. 1981. *Magendo in the Political Economy of Uganda: Pathology, Parallel System or Dominant Sub-mode of Production.* Institute of Development Studies, Discussion Paper No. 164. Brighten: University of Sussex.

Haggblade, Steve. 1978. "Africanization from Below: The Evolution of Cameroonian Savings Societies into Western-Style Banks." *Rural Africana* 2:35–55.

Hirschman, A. O. 1957. *The Strategy of Economic Development.* New Haven: Yale University Press.

Hughes, Helen. 1979. "Debt and Development: The Role of Foreign Capital in Economic Growth." *World Development* 7:95–112.

Hull, R. W. 1976. *African Cities and Towns before the European Conquest.* New York: Norton.

International Labor Office (ILO). 1972. *Employment, Incomes and Equality: A Strategy for Increasing Productive Employment in Kenya.* Geneva: ILO.

Johnston, R. J. 1977. "Regarding Urban Origins, Urbanization and Urban Patterns." *Geography* 62:1–8.

Lonsdale, John. 1981. "States and Social Processes in Africa: A Historiographical Survey." *African Studies Review* 24:139–225.

Mabogunje, A. L. 1980. *The Development Process: A Spatial Perspective.* London: Hutchinson.

———. 1987. *The End of the Beginning: Reflections on the Development Crisis in Sub-Saharan Africa.* Harvard Africa Lecture. Cambridge: Harvard University Press.

———. 1990. *Perspective on Urban Land and Urban Management Policies in Sub-Saharan Africa.* Washington, D.C.: World Bank, Africa Technical Infrastructure Division.

———. 1991. "A New Paradigm for Urban Development." *Proceedings of the World Bank Annual Conference on Development Economics 1991.* Washington, D.C.: World Bank.

Mabogunje, A. L., and A. Faniran, eds. 1977. *Regional Planning and National Development in Tropical Africa.* Ibadan: Ibadan University Press.

Miner, Horace. 1953. *The Primitive City of Timbuktu.* Princeton: Princeton University Press.

Moser, C. O. N. 1978. "Informal Sector or Petty Commodity Production: Dualism or Dependence in Urban Development." *World Development* 6:1041–64.

Nigeria, Federal Republic of. 1990. *Community Bank Prospectus.* Lagos: Community Bank Implementation Committee.

Ohadike, P. O. 1975. "The Evolving Phenomena of Migration and Urbanization in Central Africa: A Zambian Case." In *Town and Country in Central and Eastern Africa,* edited by David J. Perkin, 126–144. London: Oxford University Press.

Ominde, S. H. 1968. *Land and Population Movements in Kenya.* London: Heinemann.

Polanyi, Karl. 1957. *The Great Transformation: The Political and Economic Origins of Our Time.* Boston: Beacon Press.

Rweyemamu, Justinian Z. 1973. *Underdevelopment and Industrialization in Tanzania: A Study of Perverse Capitalist Industrial Development.* Nairobi: Oxford University Press.

Santos, Milton. 1971. *Les Villes du Tiers Monde.* Paris: Genin.

Southall, A., ed. 1979. *Small Urban Centers in Rural Development in Africa.* Madison: University of Wisconsin.

Stren, Richard E. 1978. *Housing the Urban Poor in Africa: Policy, Politics and Bureaucracy in Mombasa.* Berkeley: University of California Press.

Stren, Richard E., and Rodney R. White, eds. 1989. *African Cities in Crisis: Managing Rapid Urban Growth.* Boulder, Colo.: Westview Press.

United Nations. 1991. *World Urbanization Prospects 1990.* New York.

Wallerstein, Immanuel. 1976. "The Three Stages of African Involvement in the World Economy." In *The Political Economy of Contemporary Africa,* edited by Peter C. W. Gutkind and Immanuel Wallerstein, 135–263. Beverly Hills: Sage.

World Bank. 1989. *Sub-Saharan Africa: From Crisis to Sustainable Growth—A Long-Term Perspective Study.* Washington, D.C.: World Bank.

———. 1990. *Poverty: World Development Report 1990.* Washington, D.C.: World Bank.

Part I

Urbanization in Africa: A Historical Overview

1

Urbanization in Ancient Africa

Tertius Chandler

The development of urbanization in the ancient historical period is traced in this chapter to approximately A.D. 500. By the end of this early era urbanization had appeared in four major regions of Africa: Egypt, Cush (Nubia), Abyssinia (Ethiopia), and Carthage. Chapter 1 presents the major features of the urbanization process in ancient Africa. The second chapter will be devoted to the African urban developments which appeared after A.D. 500.

This reference book, of course, is about urbanization in Africa. However, in a few instances urbanization in Mesopotamia, China, and the Americas is mentioned strictly for comparative purposes, as urbanization appeared at different times in different places.

Human beings learned long ago to live in villages for security and comradeship while growing grain, raising livestock, and tending fruit trees. Such villages were indeed small. Even Jericho, the only one with an ancient wall, had fewer than a thousand inhabitants.

The advance to a city was a quantum leap in both size and role. The role was partly political, to direct the activities of many farms and villages. This event can be dated. The first listed pharaoh, Menes, has been placed by Richard Parker (1971) at c.3110 B.C. Indeed Menes's time can be fixed even closer, for 3114 B.C. marks Menes's victory that unified Egypt. Still earlier were Egypt's two calendars, a solar and a lunar one. These coincided with the start of Pakhons, the water month every 1,505 years. One such occasion was in 3285 B.C. It was then that the calendars came into existence. Since all pharaohs were regarded as gods, the gods that antedated them were also rulers (Harris, 1991). These early gods were Atum, Ra, Shu, Osiris, Horus, and Hapi, in direct line, not counting brothers who were gods also. Ra became the supreme sun god, so it is plausible that the calendars were invented during his time. There were five generations between him and Menes, which correspond to the difference between 3285 and 3114 B.C.

Ra was undoubtedly a village headman, who recognized the need to forecast yearly overflows of the Nile. That annual event brought water and fertile soil and was Egypt's great blessing but drowned unwary people, creating the need for a solar calendar. Once the 365-day cycle was discovered, it was counted by making daily notches on a stick.

The next advance involved the writing of words. Egyptian priests told Plato this advance was made by Thoth, apparently Menes's son Athothis. Names for Menes (Men, Aha, Narmer) have been found in excavations. So the legend told to Plato is probably correct.

With writing, Menes organized an effective administration and sent instructions to other places. Thus cities were born as capitals. Menes's hometown was Abydos, near the Nile at 26 degrees north. Abydos kept its ceremonial importance for centuries, and many pharaohs were buried there. But Menes, having conquered the north, made his capital well downriver at Memphis, on solid ground just short of the shifting Nile Delta. It was an excellent location and is where Cairo stands today.

As king and god were the same, it's not surprising that religion played a profound role in Egyptian life. Religion brought respect to the royal family. This was a time of total union for church and state, and the pharaoh was wholly dominant. "His divine powers permeated the entire realm." As for Menes, who may have formally established this religion, he became the god Amon, whose temples became the richest of all.

Was there any religion before Ra-worship? Perhaps not. Despite all that has been written about primitive religion, the evidence is not convincing. Early villages probably had shamans, who healed when they could and lamented when they couldn't. There were probably hallowed trees, groves, and animals; celebrations of New Year, spring, and the fall harvest, and fertility rites—but these all honored nature, the world of the living. There were prehistoric burials with material possessions, but people could bury someone with his fondest possessions and still consider him mystically alive. Even the rare finds of red-painted bones amount to little more than reminders that they were once associated with life. The case for primitive piety can be considered unproved. Religion may be one of the first social inventions of the city (Metz, 1991).

What is certain is that the murder of Ra's son, Osiris, by his brother, Set (Satan), was not accepted by Egyptians as involving real death. Instead, Osiris was believed to preside over a judgment seat deep below ground, consigning good souls to the care of Ra up in the sky, and bad souls to some rather uncomfortable place underground. This faith was a good deal milder than the Christianity and the Islam that followed. No crusades were ever fought in its name.

MESOPOTAMIA

The earliest writing of the Sumerians in the Tigris-Euphrates valley of Mesopotamia is now datable to about 3100 B.C., contemporary with Egyptian writings. Since Edmond Sollberger (1954–55), the earlier datings of Sumerian dynasties have been dropped.

Denise Schmandt-Besserat (1978) called attention to simple scratch marks on pots, possibly trade marks, in Mesopotamia as early as 3600 B.C., but these are not words. Similar marks may exist under Egypt's delta mud.

There are several linguistic hints of contact with Egypt, and all of them suggest that Egypt was the place of origin. Sidney Smith (1922) traced *Asari,* the surname of Babylon's god Marduk, to Osiris. If Marduk was a son of Osiris, he belonged to the clan of Ra. Moreover, this means that the Tiamat of Sumerian legend may have originated in Egypt.

Also, the Babylonian god of writing was Nabu or Nebo, which is simply the Egyptian word *nebi,* "prince." So an Egyptian prince—Marduk or Tiamat—appears to have introduced writing into Sumerian Mesopotamia. Along with it came the appearance of cities. Osiris himself may have founded Assur, the early capital of Assyria. And his son, Horus, may have been the founder of Ur, another very old place.

CHINA

Compared to Africa, China's urban development was definitely late, and came from the west along with its sculpture and bronze. Both of the early known urban centers in China were capitals of the reforming emperor Pan Geng, who, if we accept the standard date of 1050 B.C. for the end of his dynasty, reigned from 1330 to 1302 B.C. He moved from Ao (now Chengzhou) to Anyang. On the basis of its area, Ao had 320 hectares and about 32,000 people. Anyang, on the basis of its 5,000 soldiers, had at least 30,000 inhabitants. Perhaps Pan Geng may have built both cities. Regardless, they were the first in China and about the same size. Even kings were unknown in China before 2300 B.C., and their capitals were apparently small.

THE NEW WORLD

Urbanization appeared in the New World much later than in Africa. The oldest city in the Americas was Tiahuanaco in Peru, 12,930 feet above sea level on a nearly barren windswept plain high amidst the Andes. Rafique Jairazbhoy (1974) claims that it was built in about 1180 B.C. by Rameses III. Large American cities rose only after Ptolemy III's admiral, Maui, came to America in 231 B.C. (Fell, 1976).

EGYPT AFTER MENES

So great was the role of capital cities that secondary Egyptian towns were hardly needed and remained small. For well over a thousand years there were no city walls in Egypt, unlike Mesopotamia. Egypt's ramparts were her deserts and the sea. Thus, Mircea Eliade's bizarre theory, that city walls were symbolic tributes to the gods, seems highly unlikely (Mumford, 1961).

Only after the Hyksos occupation did city walls appear in Egypt. It was at this time that Homer referred to Ares, who conquered Egypt in about 1208 B.C., as "the blood-stained stormer of walls."

Gordon Childe was struck by the lack of important inventions during the last 3,000 years B.C. He blamed this on the rulers' complacency and the laborers' servility (Mumford, 1961). The whole population, from pharaohs on down, seemed to have been generally content with the status quo and even proud of it.

New professions appeared, notably merchants, bankers, and government officials such as clerks, irrigation engineers, and architects. Gold ingots came into use as a crude form of currency around 1400 B.C. But handling heavy ingots, literally worth their weight in gold, was difficult. A good deal of business was conducted by barter, or done on credit with mutual purchases largely canceling each other. Those who loaned money charged up to 100 percent annual interest.

Precious items included jade, probably from Badakhshan in easternmost Afghanistan, and lapis lazuli from the Pamir region north of there. These imports prove the existence of a trade route to China.

In Egyptian cities, the most impressive buildings were temples and palaces. Imhotep, vizier around 2780 B.C., was a renowned architect who built with stone instead of sun-dried bricks. An example of his work was the first pyramid at Saqqarah, west of Memphis. Here Imhotep made a temple with fluted columns, much like those made later in Greece, and decorated the walls with scenes of people and wildlife. This happy motif was one that remained popular until the coming of Islam.

At Abydos, priests organized theatrical plays portraying Osiris's life. These Egyptian plays inspired the early Greek and Roman plays, which in turn inspired the plays of Duke Ercole of Ferrara in 1486. These same plays inspired Shakespeare a century later in England.

Memphis

"The oldest and most royal of cities," Memphis was the capital of Egypt for a long time, from 3114 until 2173 B.C. (Thompson, 1988). Egypt was the most prestigious country for nearly one thousand years. The pyramids, built near Memphis, remain one of the most famous tourist attractions in the world. Other buildings were generally made of mud brick and weathered away (United Nations, 1990).

Memphis is the Greek pronunciation of Mnnfr, meaning "pyramid city of Pepi II." Pepi constructed no pyramids, but was the last ruler of importance in early Memphis. His reign was prosperous and lasted 90 years, nearly a world record.

Memphis was adjacent to the Nile in the early days and had protective dykes to prevent overflow during the flooding season. The city produced linen, metalware, glass, and with timber from Asia became Egypt's shipbuilding center.

Thebes and Avaris

For a generation after the dynasty at Memphis collapsed, the capital of Egypt was Heracleopolis, 60 miles south of Memphis. Then Upper Egypt broke away, when Lord Intef of Thebes declared himself free. About 2040 B.C., Lord Intef's line, under Mentuhotep II, took northern Egypt, and reunited the country. This dynasty ruled prosperously, as did the next.

Thebes's Egyptian name was Waset, and it was the Greeks who called it Thebes. When Egypt's capable XII dynasty finally faded away, a century of chaos and outside rule followed. The Hyksos, who were outsiders, came from Asia. According to Manetho, they came peacefully, but even so maintained something new for Egypt—a huge armed camp with walls. This was Avaris, located in the delta. When the Egyptians revolted and expelled the Hyksos a century later, they destroyed Avaris and its records. Except for its strong walls, it can hardly be described.

Even under the Hyksos, a black-skinned Egyptian governed Upper (south) Egypt, and it was his descendant that revolted in 1557 B.C. and ousted the Hyksos completely. Thebes was again the capital. For 150 years thereafter, the pharaohs frequented Memphis, which was a convenient location for their campaigns, like the one in which they took Syria-Palestine from the Hyksos.

Yet Thebes was not neglected. From about 1500 B.C., the pharaohs were buried in tombs located in the cliffs west of the Nile, opposite Thebes. These were ornate tombs, and nearly all rulers were buried there until 1100 B.C. Senmut created one of the finest tombs here for Queen Hatshepsut. The site of these tombs is now called Deir el-Bahri, "monastery by the river," named for a nearby monastery.

Around 1400 B.C., Pharaoh Amenhotep III, or his Vizier Amenhotep, son of Hapu, realized that the Hyksos were soundly beaten and ruled Egypt with a policy of peace. The family relocated to Thebes where the temples and palaces grew larger and more numerous. Thebes's heyday was from 1580 to 1160 B.C.

Foreigners were settled at Thebes as a result of the wars. Pharaoh Amenhotep III commented on his vast Amon temple: "It is surrounded by villages of Syrians, inhabited by the children of chieftains." He hoped to keep his Asian province pacified.

Amarna

Pharaoh Akhnaton, Amenhotep III's son, founded a new capital midway between Thebes and Memphis, calling it Akhetaton. Now it is called by its modern name, Amarna. Akhnaton founded the new capital in 1370 B.C. and moved there the next year. His purpose was to get away from the numerous priests at Thebes, whose influence he was trying to break.

Changing City Sizes

A clue to the size of an ancient Egyptian city such as Thebes may be found in the 10,000 men exempted from taxation around 1995 B.C. (Harris, 1990). They were priests or soldiers, probably both. A reasonable ratio of 6 citizens per soldier or priest equals 60,000 people for Thebes, which is not unreasonable. Ur in Mesopotamia was of similar size.

For Avaris, Manetho stated that it covered 10,000 arurae. Ten arurae make about one hectare, and 100 people per hectare is a reasonable density for ancient cities. Avaris was the first city to reach a population of 100,000, and it was largely due to the vast extent of Hyksos power.

For Amarna, F. Griffith (1924) estimated a population of 30,000 on the basis of its buildings. That size is comparable to Mycenae or the capital of China but somewhat smaller than the Hittite capital.

Rameses III, probably the most powerful and certainly the most venturesome pharaoh, made a population census at the end of his reign in 1160 B.C. The people were largely rural. However, it was noted that the people of Karnak were included under the census count for Medinet Habu, another residential part of Thebes (Breasted, 1906). This figure of 62,626 may have included some farmers though we assume it is Thebes's urban population. In any event, it approximates the 60,000 already estimated for the city back in 1995 B.C., an earlier period when Thebes was strongly ruled.

Egypt went into a long decline which lasted five centuries. Sheshonk, the Shishak of the Bible, asserted himself in Palestine after Solomon died, and laid out the world's largest royal square at Thebes. Around 850 B.C., Nineveh, the Assyrian capital, passed Thebes in size. It had immense walls and a population, plausibly stated in the Bible, of 120,000.

After several periods of strife, Egypt was again free in 404–343 B.C., and Memphis was the main city. Julius Beloch (1886) estimated its population then at 100,000. Toward 100 B.C., when its importance declined, Memphis had an inhabited area, including temples, of 600 hectares, indicating a population of about 60,000.

Alexandria—Greek Period

Alexander the Great of Macedon entered Egypt in 332 B.C. after defeating a Persian army in Asia. He had been hailed as a liberator since the Persian rule had been intolerant. During his short stay in Egypt, he founded Alexandria as an oceanside seaport. While visiting the village of Rhacotis in January 331 B.C., Alexander laid out the large city of Alexandria (Cummings, 1940). Like all his cities, it was named for himself. Alexandria grew rapidly and changed Egypt profoundly, restoring its dignity while bringing Greek rule.

When Alexander died, Ptolemy, his governor in Egypt, became ruler. During Ptolemy's reign 30,000 Jews were brought from Palestine to Alexandria. They became Greek-speaking and translated the Torah (abbreviated Old Testament) into Greek; this version is called the Septuagint because it was done by 70 (actually 72) translators. Around 60 B.C., Diodorus claimed a free population (few were slaves) of 300,000, a reasonable estimate judging from its large army. Through the third century B.C., Alexandria vied with Patna, India, as the largest city in the world, while Carthage ranked third. Two of the three largest cities in the world were in Africa.

Roman Period

It was at Alexandria that Caesar met and romanced Cleopatra, the young, probably blonde, queen of Egypt. With Caesar dying, Cleopatra made an attempt to unite Rome and Egypt by flirting with Anthony. When Anthony lost a civil war with Augustus, Egypt became a mere Roman province, exploited like the rest.

Yet Alexandria remained a great city. Its 300,000 people made it larger than Antioch, the empire's third largest city. Augustus abolished the city's democracy and its elected city council, but did allow self-rule in the Jewish quarter. Alexandria had five quarters, and the Jewish people lived in two of them. In the year A.D. 38 the Emperor Caligula tried to force the Jews into one crowded quarter; a riot broke out and he decided to let matters be. The Jews accounted for approximately 30 percent of Alexandria's 300,000 inhabitants, which made Alexandria the largest Jewish city in the world, as well as the largest Greek city. Its common speech at that time was Greek (O'Connor, 1990).

In 215, the mad Emperor Caracalla killed every male of arms-bearing age. A generation later its population was said to be down by half. In 270, Queen Zenobia of Palmyra in Arabia took Alexandria by siege and half its people died. Probus quickly retook it. Judging from the adult male census taken after Byzantine rule ended, the population of Alexandria was 94,000—scarcely a third of its Ptolemaic peak.

CUSH (NUBIA)

Up the Nile from the first to the sixth cataracts stretches Cush, the land of blacks. Greeks and Romans called it Ethiopia. Byzantines called it Nubia. Now it is Sudan, Arabic for "blacks." Though many confuse this land with present-day Ethiopia, it is not.

The first Cushite capital was Kerma. Pharaoh Thutmost I (d. 1501 B.C.) conquered it and advanced to the third cataract. Located here were the Napata and Amon temples staffed with Egyptian priests. Much later in time, the same Napata created its own dynasty. Its kings, Kashta in 742 B.C. and Piankhy in 721 B.C., took Egypt.

Taharqa, Piankhy's son, became the most famous of the Cushites (or Nubians, as they are generally called). According to Strabo, he ruled Egypt, fought Assyria, conquered north-coastal Africa, and then went into Spain. His reign marked the peak of Cushite power. However, it is unlikely that Napata ever grew as large as Thebes. Though Taharqa built at Napata, he was generally busy elsewhere. With Taharqa's expulsion from Egypt by Esarhaddon in 664 B.C., the great period of Napata ended (Metz, 1991).

In 591 B.C., Psammetichus II of Egypt invaded Cush and sacked Napata. The Cushite king rebuilt it, but for safety's sake relocated his capital upriver 200 miles and 2 cataracts to Meroe (Shinnie, 1967). This is not to be confused with modern Merowe, the town that later developed from Napata's ruins. Meroe was located right above the Nile's junction with the Atbara. There, in Pliny's time, the desert gave way to green vegetation and forests due to yearly rainfall. Elephants and rhinos were common. It was a more desirable place for a city than Napata, as well as safer from northern attack. However, commerce with the north did continue. Items of Greek and Roman origin in the graves at Meroe prove this. Further evidence came from Juvenal. He wrote about the superstitious women who made trips to Meroe for lustral water and sprinkled it in the Isis temple at Rome. Another trade advantage for Meroe was that it was located on a caravan route to the Red Sea. This was good for trade with Sheba and India.

Meroe's residential quarters are gone as the people, then as now, lived in huts of brick or straw. Chairs were used at least by the royalty, and a folding stool was found in a commoner's grave. Meroe had at least six temples. Jacques Houdaille (1981) has plausibly estimated its population at 30,000. A rash raid on Roman Egypt in 23 B.C. led to a reprisal by Petronius, who destroyed Napata a second time (around A.D. 300 Cush ceased to exist).

ABYSSINIA (ETHIOPIA)

Another black African country with a rather historical urban perspective was Abyssinia. For 3,000 years it was known by this name and then became Ethiopia in 1930. Its dynasty came from Sheba in Arabia, and its people are a dusty fusion of Arab and Negro. Its Christian religion was brought by a Roman merchant and since 1270 has been linked to the Coptic Church in Egypt. This church has always appointed the Abyssinian high priest. The rise of Islam has isolated this tenacious and mountainous nation to an extraordinary degree, almost causing a condition of collapse.

This area has had several noteworthy cities (Kasarda and Parnell, 1992). Only one was a seaport, and that was Adulis in Ptolemaic and Roman times; the city traded with India and at least indirectly with China. Aksum or Axum, founded about 900 B.C. by the king of that name, was capital until perhaps A.D. 600 and apparently again around 1400–1545, when it had 11 churches and about 33,000 inhabitants. Lasta, an early medieval capital, was probably small. Gonder was a city of European medieval type, quite unique in tropical Africa. It was quite large, around 72,000 in population. It fell on hard times, especially when attacked by fanatical Moslems from Sudan in 1887, and all but one of its 44 churches were wrecked beyond repair. The city had lost all importance in government and commerce earlier, as had other towns. City building revived in Abyssinia only when the great Menyelik II founded Addis Ababa in 1892.

CARTHAGE

Halfway between the Nile and Gibraltar, the African coastline thrusts out toward Sicily, only 80 miles away. There stood Carthage; the name originated from Qart Hadasht and meant "new city." The old city from whence it sprang was near Tyre, the most active port of the seafaring Phoenicians. Carthage, like Tyre, was located on an island in the sea and united to the mainland by a narrow ribbon of land.

According to a likely legend, Carthage was founded in 814 B.C. by Princess Elissa, when fleeing her tyrannical brother, Pygmalion, Lord of Tyre. She was usually known by her jolly nickname Dido, meaning "refugee." The legend of her romance with Rome's founder, Aeneas, is untrue as he lived three centuries before her time.

Each year Carthage sent a religious tribute to the god of Tyre, but the city was free. It is likely that this freedom began when Nebuchadnezzar of Babylon conquered Tyre in 573 B.C. Soon after, Carthage became dominant in the west Mediterranean when it took Sicily around 550 B.C. and Corsica in 536 B.C. Under Mago, Carthage's fleet took Sardinia, and then the Balerics (Charles-Picard and Charles-Picard, 1961), where Mago founded Port Mahon. In 509 B.C., Mago made a commercial treaty with Rome. He and his descendants ruled Carthage from then on, winning the election to head the army every year, exactly as Pericles did later in Athens.

The Greek city Syracuse violated its allegiance to Carthage with a naval victory in 480 B.C. As a result, Carthage prevented the eastern nations from traveling to the Atlantic, while Athens blocked Carthage from trading east. So, though still busy merchants, Carthaginians drew into themselves.

Carthage grew to be many times larger than Tyre. She rivaled Syracuse and Athens in the fourth century B.C., and rivaled Alexandria and Rome (and distant Patna) in the third century. Carthage's empire, except for a brief hold on Spain, was not large, at most one-third of the Maghreb, or about one-thousandth of Africa. This included Tunisia, Libya, and part of Algeria, in each case excluding the desert oases. Strabo credited Carthage with a population of 700,000; that might fit for the whole African country. The city itself may never have surpassed 200,000.

Carthaginians spoke Phoenician. Romans shortened that to Punic. Hence the wars of Rome versus Carthage are known as the Punic Wars. The wars started when some mercenary soldiers, called Mamertines, seized Messina in Sicily. A brutal bunch, the Mamertines ravaged the countryside, but were consequently beaten by the Syracusans. Some Mamertines then called upon Rome for help, while others appealed to Carthage. The Mamertines were quickly eliminated, but then the Romans and Carthaginians quarreled over which would hold Messina. Thus they slid into a bitter, all-out contest, well described by Polybius. The wars lasted 264–241, 218–201, 149–146 B.C. In one encounter, Hamilcar was almost victorious until Rome unexpectedly gained control of the sea. In another, Hannibal entered Italy over the Alps with elephants and routed several Roman armies, but in the end, he was defeated when double-crossed by his Numidian ally Massinissa at the battle of Zama in 202.

Only the third Punic War directly touched Carthage. Urged by an elderly senator, Cato, the Romans launched the war without provocation. By the terms of the previous peace treaty, Carthage had been forbidden to arm. She now armed quickly as the Roman fleet came in for a siege. The city's population can be gauged by the measures taken for defense. The foundries of Carthage produced 30,000 fighting men. At a desperation ratio of 5 people per soldier, this signifies a population of just about 150,000.

The siege at first failed. But in 147 B.C., the Romans placed young Scipio in command, adoptive grandson of the victor at Zama. He tightened the blockade, and in 146 B.C., Scipio's men broke through and took the city, house by house. After the fighting ended, only 50,000 inhabitants were alive. These were sold into slavery. The city was flattened, the site cursed, and resettlement forbidden. Towns under Carthage were small; according to Diodorus, they were not over about 1,000 in population (Charles-Picard and Charles-Picard, 1961).

Just a century later in 46 B.C., Julius Caesar, during a civil war, defeated Pompey's followers close to where Carthage had stood. Impressed by its secure harbor, he revived the city by settling poor Roman citizens. This urban colony prospered. As local people drifted in from the countryside, Punic once more became the spoken language. Statues were made for early heroes, such as Hannibal. Temples were again dedicated to the old god Melkarth. In 14 B.C., Carthage displaced Utica as the provincial capital. By A.D. 100, with 100,000 people, Carthage stood second only to Rome in the western part of the Mediterranean basin (Abun-Nasr, 1975).

In 439, Gaiseric the Vandal, after leading his Germanic tribe from Spain into Africa, took Carthage by surprise without losing a man. It became his capital. To head off possible reconquest, he built a fleet. With this he took Sicily, Sardinia, Corsica, and the Balearics—as ancient Carthage had done. He raided the shores of Spain, Italy, and Greece. At a time of one coup after another at Rome, he sailed there in 455 and met no resistance.

In 523, the Byzantine emperor, Justinian, sent his young general, Belisarius, against the Vandals to make Catholicism the brand of Christianity there. Belisarius did this brilliantly, even putting down his own troops when they revolted in 533. From then, Carthage was capital of the Byzantine province until it fell to the Moslem Arabs in 698. It then faded away. Carthage's first era of greatness had lasted over 600 years; its second and last era of greatness lasted over 700 years. Its role is now held by Tunis.

SUMMARY

Urbanization appeared in ancient Egypt around 3200 B.C. when Abydos, Pharaoh Menes's home, became the first city with about 20,000 inhabitants. Then, Pharaoh Menes founded Memphis in 3114 B.C. and by 3000 B.C. it had reached a population of 30,000. Egypt then became the most highly urbanized country in the world at various times. By 320 B.C. Alexandria, the city founded by the invading Greek general, was the largest city in the world with 300,000 residents. The Persians, Greeks, Romans, and Byzantines exploited and plundered Egypt during the ancient period. At the beginning of the medieval period the Arabs were poised to conquer Egypt and establish their Moslem domination of that country.

The ancient Cush culture which evolved from Egypt around 1500 B.C. disappeared around A.D. 300. It was never highly urbanized as Meroe, its last capital city, had about 30,000 inhabitants. Abyssinia (Ethiopia) was somewhat more urbanized even though its ancient capital city of Aksum, founded about 900 B.C., had only about 30,000 inhabitants. Carthage, the most prominent city of northwest Africa, was founded by the Phoenicians in 814 B.C. It formed an empire of its own like a city-state and progressed through trade with Rome and Greece as well as by the long-distance trans-Saharan trade. It reached its peak population of 200,000 before it was destroyed by the Romans in 146 B.C.

The population of the early African urban centers fluctuated widely. These ancient Egyptian cities were primarily religious centers and subject to frequent attacks from invaders who not only conquered them but often destroyed their cities.

REFERENCES

Abun-Nasr, Jamil. 1975. *A History of the Maghrib.* Cambridge: Cambridge University Press.

Beloch, Julius. 1886. *Die Bevölkerung der Griechischen-Römischen Welt.* Leipzig: Duncker and Humblot. Reprint New York: Arno Press, 1979.

Breasted, James H. 1906. *Ancient Records of Egypt.* Chicago: University of Chicago Press.

Charles-Picard, Gilbert, and Colette Charles-Picard. 1961. *Daily Life in Carthage at the Time of Hannibal.* New York: Macmillan.

Cummings, Lewis. 1940. *Alexander the Great.* Boston: Houghton Mifflin.

Fell, Barry. 1976. *America BC*. New York: Quadrangle/The New York Times Book Company, Inc.

Griffith, F. 1924. "Excavations at El-Amarnah, 1923–24." *Journal of Egyptian Archaelogy* 10:299–305.

Harris, Geraldine. 1990. *Ancient Egypt*. New York: Facts on File.

———. 1991. *Gods and Pharaohs from Egyptian Mythology*. New York: P. Bedrick Books.

Houdaille, Jacques. 1981. "Colloque sur la Démographie de l'Afrique." *Population* 36:1191–92.

Jairazbhoy, Rafique. 1974. *Ancient Egyptians and Chinese in America*. Totowa, N.J.: Rowman and Littlefield.

Kasarda, John D., and Alan M. Parnell. 1992. *Third World Cities*. Newbury Park: Sage.

Metz, Helen Chapin, ed. 1991. *Egypt: A Country Study*. Washington, D.C.: Library of Congress, U.S. Government Printing Office.

Mumford, Lewis. 1961. *The City in History*. New York: Harcourt, Brace and World.

O'Connor, David. 1990. *Ancient Egyptian Society*. Pittsburgh: Carnegie Museum of Natural History.

Parker, Richard. 1971. "The Calendars and Chronology." In *The Legacy of Egypt*, edited by John R. Harris, 13–26. Oxford: Clarendon Press.

Schmandt-Besserat, Denise. 1978. "The Earliest Precursor of Writing." *Scientific American* 238:50–59.

Shinnie, P. 1967. *Meroe*. London: Thames and Hudson.

Smith, Sidney. 1922. "The Relation of Marduk, Ashur, and Osiris." *Journal of Egyptian Archaeology* 8:41–44.

Sollberger, Edmond. 1954–55. "Sur la Chronologie des Rois d'uret quelques problèmes connexes." *Archiv Fur Orientforschung* 17:10–48.

Thompson, Dorothy J. 1988. *Memphis under the Ptolemies*. Princeton: Princeton University Press.

United Nations. 1990. *Population Growth and Policies in Mega-Cities, Cairo*. Population Policy Paper No. 34. New York: United Nations.

2

Urbanization in Medieval and Early Modern Africa

Tertius Chandler

The early ancient urbanization that began in Egypt continued at an unsteady pace during the medieval and modern periods despite oppressive foreign rule, exploitation, and deadly plagues. Although Carthage was destroyed by the Romans, urbanization gained momentum in the Maghreb region of Northwest Africa, initially by the Romans and later in Morocco by the Berbers in medieval days. Also, large medieval kingdoms appeared in the Sudan and Guinea coast areas of West Africa, resulting from long-distance trans-Saharan trading. The east coast of Africa was colonized by Asians who founded relatively small cities. In addition, several scattered urban settlements appeared in Africa at different times; some flourished while others were abandoned.

The patterns of urbanization and urban development during the medieval and early modern periods will be presented chronologically in this chapter for each of the major regions of Africa, with some overlapping in the two periods. The medieval period is assumed to have started in Africa about A.D. 500 and lasted until 1500. The early modern period extends from 1500 to about 1950 at the beginning of independence. Actually, the modern period in Africa began with the Portuguese colonization of Cape Verde in 1462.

EGYPT: THE MOSLEM PERIOD

Amr took Egypt in 640 in a bold raid for Islam, Mohammed had been dead eight years at that time. Many still believed his announcement that God's coming was at hand. So had the Jewish followers of Jesus believed back in A.D. 33, thus founding the Christian church. Christianity and Islam therefore should have been friendly sects, as Mohammed hoped, but wars between them quickly turned the two into bitterly divergent religions. The effect of this hostility isolated Africa from Europe. Trade continued, but on a reduced scale and with the fear of holy-war piracy on both sides.

Egypt usually had two sizable cities and the Maghreb generally had one. Under the Moslem Arab Caliphate, these conditions remained. In Egypt, Alexandria continued as one major city, but the capital was Fostat (Abu-Lughod, 1971). Fostat was built by Amr in 640 as his army camp for besieging Memphis (Muir, 1907). In Tunisia, Carthage declined to a mere village while a new capital arose 80 miles south and 40 miles inland from the sea at Qairawan. Founded by the Arab general Oqba about 670, Qairawan means "caravan" and was derived from the camel caravans that brought the city's goods.

In 643, Amr reopened the old Nile-Suez Canal which began at Fostat. He won over the Christian population by leaving their churches unmolested and by reinstating the Coptic patriarch whom the Byzantines had driven into hiding. After Amr, the next governor of Qairawan forbade the Christians to wear turbans, setting them apart from Moslems. Despite this and despite having to pay poll taxes, very few Christians converted to the Islam religion.

A few of the Arab tribes moved to Egypt, but the area basically remained Christian. The main Arab infusion came from the escort of soldiers that each new governor brought, about 10,000 for each governor. Nearly all stayed at Fostat, and thus it quickly became an Arab city. In 800, Tunisia became independent of the caliph at Bagdad, and between 827 and 878 its Aghlabid kings conquered nearly all Sicily. Qairawan, to judge from the size of its Raqqada suburb, rose to a population of about 100,000, rivaling Alexandria and Fostat in size (Chandler, 1987).

Even before Tunisia and further to the west, free Moslem countries had begun arising in Africa; capitals were at Tahert in Algeria, Sijilmesa in far-southern Morocco, and in Fez.

Egypt shook off the rule of Bagdad in 868 under the governor's viceroy, Ahmed Ibn Tulun. Ahmed was known as Ibn Tulun. In 876 to 878, this young Turk, barely 40 years old, built the Tulunid Mosque at Fostat. Thanks to Ibn Tulun, Egypt was once more a free country for the first time since Cleopatra. Judging from the size of Tulun's standing army of 64,000, Fostat probably had over 150,000 people (Chandler, 1987). By this time, Fostat was called Misr, which became the Arabic name for all of Egypt. In 885, an earthquake killed 1,000 people in Misr and a massacre wiped out Alexandria's people in 928. Medieval Egypt's main port was then Tinnis, with Damietta second, both of these located in the eastern part of the Nile Delta.

Far down the African east coast, a Persian named Ali founded Kilwa in 976. Kilwa never surpassed a population of about 30,000, but around 1300–1450 under a new dynasty of Arabs from Yemen, it ruled Sofala and thus controlled the east African export trade of ivory and gold. Prospering well, Kilwa's rich citizens wore silks and dined off porcelain from China. The poor wore glass beads, along with their locally woven cotton clothes.

Later on, a second dynasty of Tunisia, the Fatimids, eventually took Egypt and made Cairo the new capital.

Cairo

The Fatimid general, Jawhar, took Egypt in 969 and gained popularity by forbidding his troops to loot Fostat (Metz, 1991). He established a new city called Kahira, which is pronounced Cairo in English. The city included palaces for the Fatimid royal family who arrived in 974 from Tunisia. The Fatimid king had been known to live simply in Tunisia, but in Cairo he had a palace with a golden throne, 4,000 rooms, and 18,000 servants.

The early Fatimid period at Cairo was active with the construction of mosques and naval docks. Most of the lower administrative staff continued to be Christian Copts. In 994, the second Fatimid, who had a Christian wife, chose a Christian as a vizier.

In 1013, the ruinous sack of Cordova left Cairo and Fostat, with about 135,000 people. Cairo was now the largest city in all Islam and about fifth in the world behind Kaifeng, Constantinople, Angkor, and probably Kyoto (Chandler, 1987).

Mostansir had the longest reign of any Moslem, 1036–94. During his time, the Persian traveler Nasir-Khosraw visited Cairo and wrote that it had 20,000 households with "Misr" (Fostat) nearly as large. This urban area had a population of about 185,000 people, which is nearly treble Thebes's size and approaching Alexandria's size under the Ptolemies.

In 1062, the Turk and Berber soldiers won a scuffle over the black units who had fled from Cairo toward Nubia. This ended 17 years of black dominance. Under competent kings—Saladin, Adil, and Kamil—Cairo grew to a population of about 300,000, rivaled by only one city anywhere, Hangchow in China with 320,000 people (Chandler, 1987).

Cairo under the Mamelukes

In 1250, the rule of the Mamelukes began, not so much a dynasty as a series of kings, each taking power by force. All had been slaves (*mamluk*), most had been born outside of Egypt, had been seized, and then sold to serve as slave soldiers. Slaves formed the entire army which was stationed at or near Cairo.

Most of the Mamelukes were Turks. Their first rulers came from a Nile island and were called Bahri ("by the water") Mamelukes. Their average reign would be only five years. Yet several reigns were substantial, and this would be the greatest building era of medieval Egypt, especially at Cairo.

During Nasir's reign (1293–94, 1298–1308, 1310–41) Cairo saw its medieval peak. The historian Maqrizi said that Cairo had 12,000 shops. There were 35 major marketplaces, 3 of them set up by Nasir. The city expanded in all directions. In 1313, Nasir declared the new lands created by the shifting Nile to be open for settlement, and in 1325, he constructed a canal to hasten settlement.

About 1315, Cairo must have surpassed Hangchow as the world's largest city—the first time an Egyptian city had achieved that distinction since ancient Thebes two thousand years before. By the end of Nasir's reign, according to the modern expert Janet Abu-Lughod (1971), Cairo had about 500,000 people. Its 494 mosques would be appropriate for such a figure. It was nearly the size of ancient Rome at its peak and half of Bagdad's at its peak.

Soon after Nasir's death, in 1348–49, the bubonic plague killed nearly 200,000 people in Cairo (Abu-Lughod, 1971). Whole districts were never reoccupied. By 1400, Cairo had lost one-third of its population and dropped to the third largest city in the world, behind Nanking and Vijayanagar.

Cities tend to attract talent, sometimes from smaller cities. Thus Maimonides came to Cairo from Cordova. And so in 1383, Ibn Khaldûn came to Cairo from Tunis.

There was an invasion by Selim, sultan of the rising nation of Ottoman Turks of Turkey. Selim overthrew Qansuh in Syria in 1516 and occupied Cairo in 1517. For the next three centuries, Egypt was a province of Turkey, and Cairo's role declined sharply.

Cairo under Turkey

At least one Turkish governor did well, Suleiman the Eunuch who ruled 1524–34. He annexed Aden and Yemen to the Turkish empire and tried to unite the Moslem kings of western India in order to oust the newly arrived Portuguese spice traders. Suleiman's interest in Cairo continued after his retirement, when he built a mosque there.

Cairo remained the biggest city in Africa, but its external influence seems to have been only military. It was home base for Ozdemir's army, which in 1557 overran Tigre in Abyssinia (Ethiopia). From Cairo, Governor Sinan, around 1570, reconquered Yemen and Tunis for Turkey. In 1598, some 10,000 citizens of Cairo moved to Yemen.

In 1600, the city had perhaps 200,000 people and had dropped to about ninth among the world's cities (fourth in 1550) (Chandler, 1987). Open fields separated it from its port Bulaq and from Fostat.

As the crusading spirit died down, European nations opened consulates at Cairo: first came the Venetians in late Mameluke times, then the French, English, and Dutch. A few tourists came too. By 1798, Cairo, with a clustered population around 175,000, was one of the world's largest cities but had been stationary for two centuries (Table 2.1). It seemed as if nothing interesting had ever happened there.

Table 2.1
Largest Cities of Africa at Various Dates, 1100–1900

(Population in Thousands)

1100		1200		1300	
Marrakesh	150	Cairo	200	Cairo	400
Cairo	150	Fez	155	Fez	200
Fez	125	Marrakesh	150	Damietta	100
Tinnis	110	Damietta	100	Marrakesh	75
Bougie	50	Qus	50	Tlemsen	70
Qus	50	Rabat	50	Alexandria	65

1400		1500		1600	
Cairo	360	Cairo	400	Cairo	200
Fez	150	Fez	130	Marrakesh	125
Damietta	90	Tunis	65	Fez	100
Mali	50	Gao	60	Algiers	75
Oyo	50	Oyo	60	Kazargamu	60
Tlemsen	50	Kano	50	Zaria	60

Table 2.1 (Continued)

(Population in Thousands)					
1700		1800		1900	
Cairo	175	Cairo	175	Cairo	595
Algiers	85	Tunis	90	Alexandria	314
Fez	80	Oyo	80	Ibadan	204
Gondar	72	Algiers	73	Johannesburg	173
Meknes	70	Katsina	70	Tunis	156
Tunis	69	Alkalawa	50	Cape Town	148

Source: Tertius Chandler. 1987. *Four Thousand Years of Urban Growth*. Lewiston, N.Y.: St. David's University Press.

EARLY SUDAN URBANIZATION

Dongola

A Byzantine (Late-Roman) emissary, Longinus, converted the Nobatae to Christianity in 580. But they found themselves cut off when the Arabs took Egypt in 640 and brought in their relentless Moslem faith. Within two decades the Arabs began levying slaves as an annual tribute from the Christian kingdom. This kingdom became known as Dongola for its capital near the Nile's third cataract.

The excavator of Dongola estimated that the area had a population of 30,000. The Moslems under King Nasir of Egypt took Dongola in 1317, and later Egyptian campaigns finished the country off by 1400. Aloa, another Christian kingdom further south, lasted about a century longer.

Funj

From 1504 the dominant people in this area were the Funj, blacks with Arabic speech acquired from the Shebans in Ibrahim's migration. They converted to Islam, and this gave them immunity from the Egyptian slave-raiding holy wars. However, in 1821, Moslem Egypt conquered them regardless. Their capital, Sennar, judging from its circumference, probably had a peak population slightly over 30,000 (Poncet, 1814).

The Egyptians made Khartoum the provincial capital, and after 80 years of Egyptian rule, this city too had reached a population of 30,000 by 1900. The history of this region for over 2,000 years is rather impressive although the way of life seems to have changed little.

MAGHREB REGION OF NORTHWEST AFRICA

Although the Phoenician settlement of Carthage was the dominant ancient urban center of North Africa outside Egypt, other immigrant groups had also colonized North Africa before the Christian era. For example, the Greeks settled in Cyrene about 630 B.C. And the Berbers probably came to Northwest Africa thousands of years ago from either Canaan, Syria, or Yemen.

After Carthage fell, it became a province of the Romans and was partially revived by Julius Caesar. Roman colonists were settled in the area, and they produced large quantities of grain and olive oil which were exported to Rome. So, the Roman colony greatly prospered until a severe economic crisis occurred, Vandals from Spain conquered the area, and the Western Roman Empire itself collapsed in 476. No major urbanization developments in Northwest Africa occurred until the Berbers created the vast Almoravid Empire around A.D. 1000.

Medieval Morocco became an important region for cities. Earlier towns there had been prosperous but small with the main one being Volubilis. Fez, Morocco's first Moslem capital, was founded in 789, by Idris, an Arabian refugee with 3,000 Berber families, which is about 15,000 inhabitants. He extended his power to Tlemsen, but was then murdered in 791, leaving behind an infant son. Idris II took in Arab refugees from the revolts in Spain and Tunisia. Afterwards, Fez was mainly Arab-speaking, unlike the Berber countryside. Thus Fez became different from the rest of Morocco.

Rival capitals arose at Meknes nearby, and at Sijilmessa further south at the edge of the Sahara desert. In the next century, Fez was generally ruled by the Fatimids of Tunisia or by Arab Spain. Ibn Yasin formed a group called Almoravids (''monks''). This Arab crossed the Sahara with a Berber chief and gathered his followers on an island on the upper Niger River. With this army, his general took Sijilmessa in 1053. Attempting further conquests, the general and Ibn Yasin were slain. Under Joseph (Yusuf), better known as Ibn Tashfin (''sun of Tashfin''), the movement swept over Morocco. Fez was taken and its 30,000 people killed, but it soon recovered and prospered even more than before. In the west over 200 miles from Fez, Ibn Tashfin built his capital Marrakesh and surrounded it with a wall.

Ibn Tashfin was an approachable man. He lived plainly in a tent, ruled thriftily, and avoided levying taxes on income or business. The result was prosperity. His empire was said to have 1,900 *jami* mosques, implying a population around 17 million. Among his cities, Marrakesh, Fez, and Seville had probably over 100,000 people each (Chandler, 1987).

The general Abd-el-Momin besieged Marrakesh in 1130 and took it in 1147, allowing a massacre in which Marrakesh's population dropped by 70,000 people (Deverdun, 1959). Yet he kept the capital there, so it soon recovered. The dynasty he founded was the Almohads (''unitarians,'' stressing belief in just one God).

During the years 1170–80, at a time of division and decline in China, Marrakesh may have been the largest city in the world. Jacob I of Morocco was called ''the conqueror'' for his victory in Spain over the Castilians in 1195. His base for fleets was Rabat. There he built a wall enclosing an area of 450 hectares, big enough to hold 45,000 people. It did not fill up, but along with its cross-river suburb, Sale, its urban area may have reached 50,000 by 1199 when Jacob died. Jacob the Conquereor had also extended Marrakesh's walls until they took in an area of 1,300 hectares. The city was rather densely settled, and its population has been plausibly estimated at 150,000. Fez once again became the capital city. Its Lord Jacob II, better known as Abu Yusfu (''father of Joseph''), took Marrakesh, thus founding the Merinid line (1269–1471). Fez had an excellent location: astride a river near hills, at the best natural crossroads in the land, south of Spain, north of a pass for the Sahara, and on the main route from Algeria to west Morocco.

Fez had weavers, cobblers, and jewelers scattered throughout the city—there was no zoning—while merchants used the pilgrimage to trade as far as Egypt. Fez's population in 1300 was probably over 200,000 (Martineau, 1953).

Concurrently, a dynasty of Moroccan origin, the Hafsids (1236–1535), ruled with considerable ability at Tunis. Between them and Morocco was a small kingdom centered at Tlemsen. These three held all the Maghreb in the later Middle Ages, Tunis and Tlemsen having populations of about 65,000 at their medieval peaks.

Moroccan urban history declined after 1400. The traveler Ibn Battuta found Marrakesh no longer the capital and largely in ruins around 1350 as did Leo Africanus (1896) around 1515. Restored to the rank of capital and well ruled from 1525 to 1603, it revived to a population of 120,000. In 1591, King Ahmed "the conqueror" sent an army across the desert and destroyed the Songhai Empire, making little Timbuktu a Moroccan city. However, gaining control of the gold route merely corrupted the dynasty. The country fell into decay as surely as Spain did with the wealth of Peru. The population of Marrakesh by 1700 was down to 25,000.

Jewish refugees, from Spain in 1492 and from Portugal in 1497, and Moslems fleeing from Spain kept Fez's population over 100,000 until about 1600. Then the decline continued. Ismail, in his long reign (1672–1727), brought temporary glory to Meknes. But in 1799 a severe epidemic of plague probably pushed Fez below 50,000.

Mohammed XVI, who finally brought order into the country, built a new port at Mogador in 1760–70. He also took Mazagan, the last Portuguese-held post along the Atlantic Moroccan seaboard. No impressive population increases occurred until the arrival of the French in 1907.

NIGER BASIN OF WEST AFRICA

Urban developments appeared in the late ancient and early medieval periods in the Sudan and Guinea coast areas of the Niger Basin, with the Ghana kingdom being founded in the fifth century A.D. The Mali Empire superseded Ghana, and the much larger Sonhay Empire succeeded Mali in the Sudan area of West Africa.

Gao

Other than Nubia and Abyssinia, there was a long absence of towns in the black-inhabited regions of Africa. "Their homes," wrote Yaqubi in 871, "are just huts of grass. They have no cities."

When the Sheba kingdom was overthrown in Yemen, Arabia, in 590, its prince, Ibrahim, trekked with 722 fellow Arabs to Lake Chad and ruled in peace (Palmer, 1928). He impressed the blacks with his horse, his spear, his clothes, and perhaps above all, his Jewish ideals which included the Golden Rule.

His descendant Taras ruled wisely. Hamdani in the tenth century called him "the ancestor of the Nubas, the Zaghawa, the Zanj, and Negroes generally." Zanj meant most of Africa's east coast. Zaghawa would be *za*-Gao-*wa*, "king of Gao's people." Mohallabi, in the same century, wrote that Gogo ruled to the border of Abyssinia, adding: "It was the Zaghawa who are responsible for the existence of Kaukau (Gogo, Gao) as a political unit.'' Hamdani confirms that the Zaghawa were Yemenite Arabs. The rise of small seaports in east Africa at this time may be Taras's work—almost surely that of his dynasty.

In Taras's time, two cities appeared within the Bornuese Empire, Kukia and Gao, both along the mid-Niger, around the year A.D. 690. These may have been bases to defend against the rapidly expanding Moslem Arabs.

Taras left three sons. One ruled Gao; another, Idris, founded Masina upriver; and Solomon, still further west, founded Walata, the forerunner of Ghana (Palmer, 1928). Walata prospered, and its successor city Ghana (not to be confused with the modern country) even more, until it eventually had a population of 30,000 (Maquet, 1962). The city was sacked in 1076 and then completely destroyed in 1240. In 790, at Ghana, the line of white Arabs was displaced by a dynasty of blacks.

In 767 another city was founded, this time with buildings of stone. This was Jenne, a bit further up the Niger beyond Masina. Jenne became the entrepôt for gold from the mines of western Africa. Gao continued to be largest of all. The well-known writer Khwarizmi in 832 called its nation ''the greatest and most powerful kingdom of the Sudan'' (the Sahel or lands just south of the Sahara, stopping just west of modern Sudan). Similarly, Yaqubi called Gao the greatest city in the Sudan. Merchants crossed the Sahara to trade there. More came from Egypt or Algeria than from Morocco. One merchant's son born at Gao, Abu Yazid, married a princess from Bornu and led a heretical revolt that almost overthrew the powerful Fatimid dynasty of Tunisia in 943–47.

Mahmud Kati later wrote about Gao: ''The region south of Timbuktu . . . was formerly inhabited by the Beni Israel: seven princes descended from the king of Israel, each prince possessing 12,000 horsemen.'' Kati's seven princes are successive generations of kings at Gao. Seven generations fit neatly between 690 when Gao was founded and 890 when it fell to the black Songhai lords of Kukia. The 12,000 horsemen were royal cavalry, posted at the capital and, at 6 per soldier, represented a population of 72,000. Gao may have been larger than Thebes had ever been.

Jabar may have ruled Zaghawa/Bornu quite far into the eighth century. There seems to be a gap after him. Then the kings are recorded regularly, beginning with Dugu 784–835 and Fune 835–893.

Gao, from 890 under the black Songhai, continued to prosper. Edrisi, about 1150, referred to Gao's busy trade in salt from across the Sahara. A bit further up the Niger, the city of Mali became the center of an empire, and in 1324 its general, Sagmandia, took Gao. But in 1335 Prince Ali Kolon, held as a hostage, escaped and revived the Songhai kingdom at Gao. Songhai expanded vigorously under Sonni Ali and then Mohammed Askia, and in 1500 absorbed Mali altogether, soon ruling to the Atlantic Ocean near Senegal. Songhai, briefly dominating most of the Hausa states around 1515, had a peak population of perhaps 7 million, making it the twelfth most populous country in the world (behind

China, Turkey, Vijanagar, Delhi, Japan, Germany, Bengal, France, and maybe Spain, Persia, and Inca Peru).

A recent writer (Mauny, 1961) has concluded that Gao had 75,000 people in 1585. Around this time a squabble over the salt mines in the northern Sahara led to an invasion by Ahmed IV of Morocco. The battle took place in 1591 near Gao. Hopelessly outmatched, the Songhai warriors laid down their spears and sat on their shields. They were gunned down. A Moorish garrison took over Gao and exploited the declining city until 1680, when it was overrun by Tuaregs from the nearby desert. By 1854, there were only 300–400 occupied huts left. Now a minor town, Gao has two monuments from its past, a mosque tower and the tomb of its farthest conqueror Mohammed Askia.

Mali, Hausas, and Fulani

Cities other than Gao were founded as a result of Ibrahim of Sheba's entry with Arabs into central Africa. There were Masina, Ghana, Mali, and Jenne. Another was Bussa, near the confluence of the Niger and its main tributary, the Benuwe. Its people still keep the tradition that it was founded about A.D. 600 by Kisra. Kisra was Khosraw, and Persian in name; he was probably from the Persian army that helped Ibrahim's father regain his throne of Sheba in 570.

About A.D. 999, on the north-Nigerian plain just above the Benuwe, seven Hausa-speaking city-states were created: Kano, Rano, Katsina, Zaria, Zamfara, Daura, and Gober. Seven other Hausa states arose later. The original seven stemmed from the grandsons of Abu Yazid, the merchant's son who married a princess from Bornu and nearly overthrew the Moslem Fatimid dynasty in Tunisia.

In 1235, under Sundiata's rule, Mali became the capital of a kingdom that extended over the upper Niger Basin. By 1300, this kingdom extended to the Atlantic. In 1307 its king, Abubekr II, sailed west with 2,000 ships and never returned. His successor Musa (Moses) made a grand pilgrimage east to Mecca. His retinue was 12,000 men, suggesting a likely population of 60,000 for his capital. As late as 1515, when Mali was no longer capital, over 6,000 families lived there, just over 30,000 people (Africanus, 1896). In 1545, Mali was sacked for a week for revolting against Songhai. This and the Moorish conquest of 1591 ended its prosperity.

Timbuktu, the most famous of the Niger-bank cities, was settled in 1077, and had one main mosque in the 1200s, two in the 1300s, and three in the 1400s. For a while, around 1515, it was the Songhai king's residence. Its three main mosques, its number of militia, and its area, all point to a population of about 27,000.

In Bornu itself, the capitals were located near Lake Chad. Two of them, Manan and Njimi, were not as large as Gao. A traveler described Njimi as only "a large village." The next capital, Garoumele, 1392–1472, was barely three miles in circumference. But Ali Ghajideni's new capital, Nkazargamo or Kazargamu, 1472–1806, was six miles in circumference and reported to have 50,000 people. Around 1600 it must have had 60,000.

Among the Hausa cities, Kano was nearly 11 miles in circumference, and Katsina 13 miles. Katsina was estimated at nearly 100,000 at its peak, but around 1670–1760 had about 75,000. Zaria was raised to greatness in the 1500s by its relentless crusading queen, Amina, who was the scourge of pagan states to the south. She kept raiding for slaves, and in 1825 Zaria had 50,000 inhabitants. From 1764, the strongest Hausa state was the northernmost one, Gober or Gobir.

The Fulani dynasty of Sokoto conquered every Hausa state and destroyed Bornu's capital, even though all except Gober were already Moslem. The Fulani also overthrew and destroyed Gober's capital, Alkalawa, a place of 50,000; it overthrew Borgu, an ancient pagan kingdom west of the Niger and converted it to the Moslem religion. Despite a heavy influx of slaves taken in war, Sokoto remained rather small. It had about 33,000 people when Heinrich Barth (1857–58) was there in 1850.

After the Moroccan power waned along the middle Niger around 1670, Kulubali created a pagan kingdom on the upper Niger at Segu with a population of 30,000. The Niger, formerly without cities, came to have many in the 25,000–75,000 class.

Yorubas

West of the lower Niger, just outside its drainage area, live the Yorubas. They've been there since Ibrahim of Bornu's time and they remember the migration—90 days' march westward from Arabia. They recall too an effort to regain the homeland, which must have been the Sheban exile Amr's campaign that actually ousted Mohammed's newly arrived Moslems from Yemen for six months in 632.

The Yorubas have remained in their new home ever since. Their earliest capital was Ife, but from about 1200 it was Oyo almost continuously (except in the 1500s). Then the crusading Fulani frightened the Yorubas into abandoning Oyo in 1839. Oyo, also called Katunga, had 60,000 people at this time.

Yoruba life was generally peaceful and humane. There was a king, but his rule seems to have been comparatively light. Slavery hardly existed. Women had high status as in Sheba. A Yoruba woman could marry her choice, even if a princess wanted to marry a commoner, and a wife could not be divorced without legal cause. Polygamy existed among the Yorubas, sometimes suggested by the first wife. There was no writing, and education consisted of learning useful skills from the parents. Seldom anywhere has a society been so peaceful and harmonious.

In 1797, after several quiet centuries, the monarchy hatched a palace plot. The nineteenth century featured warring states of which Ibadan and Abeokuta became the most successful. Around 1850 missionaries found these two cities with 60,000 inhabitants each while Ogbomosho had 45,000. A good many Yoruba places were over 20,000; they had stockades and contained many farms that furnished food in case of long siege. The British, by a little fighting and by adept negotiation, ended the wars in 1893, leaving the way of life untouched.

EAST AFRICA

Shi'ites from Oman and Sunni Muslims from Shiraz in the Persian Gulf colonized areas from Mozambique to Somalia in the eighth and ninth centuries. The Shirazi were credited with founding Kilwa and Mogadishu. The Bantus, Omani, and Shirazi lived peacefully in the coastal towns. Kilwa was an important shipping center on the Tanzanian coast founded in A.D. 976 and probably had about 30,000 inhabitants when the Portuguese arrived in about 1500.

The Merina probably migrated from Borneo to Madagascar in the first millennium B.C. about the same time as the emigrants from South Arabia and Yemen settled in Ethiopia.

Great Zimbabwe prospered for nearly a thousand years, but after reaching a peak population of perhaps 35,000 to 40,000 after 1440, it was virtually abandoned by 1500. Zimbabwe (Great Zimbabwe) is the largest and most impressive of southerly Africa's 200 stone towns (Fagan, 1965). The site was inland and occupied early.

Finds of coins from India and Malaya indicate that Zimbabwe was once a thriving place. Recent similar finds show that other small places (all seaports) were developed at the same time. These, along with Gao and others in westerly Africa, were the first urban places in Negrodom beyond Nubia. Taras of Bornu, the founder of Gao, lived to about the year 717, so he likely laid out Zimbabwe. But Zimbabwe's main builder was probably Taras's granddaughter, Queen Arteit, as "She gave birth to . . . the Nubas, the Zenj, the Zaghawa, and negroes in general." It was her base for resistance against Moslem slave raiders along the east African coast.

What sort of city was Zimbabwe? Located 200 miles south of the Zambezi, it is approachable by a tributary. The built-up areas were partly on a plain and partly set among the granite rock outcroppings of a hill. Walls up to 14 feet thick surround its main parts. So far it resembles 200 other similar sites but was by far the largest. Covering 300 hectares, it can easily have had 30,000 inhabitants, an extraordinary number for that time and region.

As trade grew via the ports of Sofala and Kilwa around the year 1350, Zimbabwe grew to its peak size and maintained it for a century (Drakakis-Smith, 1992). After that, wars wrecked it and by 1500 it was deserted. The word *zimbabwe,* "lion's home," signified "capital" and was applied to other walled places as well. Thus the royal pomp discussed by Barreto in 1552 refers to the current capital of Monomotapa, not to the Zimbabwe site.

SOUTHERN AFRICA

Although the Portuguese navigator Bartholomeu Dias was the first to circumnavigate the Cape of Good Hope in 1487–88, the Dutch made the first settlement there in 1652 at the Cape of Good Hope to provide a stopover for ships traveling to the Indian Ocean. The colony passed permanently to the British in 1806 when Cape Town had 16,400 inhabitants. Now, the Cape urban agglomeration has over 1.9 million inhabitants.

ENTREPÔTS FOR THE SLAVE TRADE

Some late medieval and early modern African population centers existed either entirely or mainly for the purpose of conducting trade in African slaves. They appeared because of slaving as either their sole or their primary function. Slaving was carried on from early times, but no continent has suffered as Africa from the highseas slave trade between 1442 and 1894.

The start was not so bad. A Portuguese brought some Moors home from Africa. Prince Henry, "the navigator," told him to take them back. The captain did, but he returned with other blacks in exchange. These became house servants and were well treated. But soon Negroes (as the blacks were then always called) were being picked up regularly to work the sugar plantations; first in the Cape Verde Islands and later in Haiti, Brazil, and throughout the Americas generally. Eventually an estimated 12 million were taken from Africa in Christian-owned ships and another 7 million in Moslem ships headed for Asia.

Even though the slave trade's demographic effect was negative, it accelerated the development of ports where few existed. The main Portuguese port on the Guinea coast was Elmina (São Jorge da Mina) from 1477 until the Dutch took it in 1637. Elmina was not a city but a pickup site on an offshore island with a strong fort.

From 1481 the Portuguese traded at Benin, a capital at the mouth of the Niger River. They bought slaves from the native King Ozolua in exchange for muskets. Ozolua, in turn, used the muskets to raid nearby tribes and took more slaves to sell. Benin became a place of 60,000 with a dreadful public display of human sacrifice which was stopped by a British military expedition in 1897.

In 1484 the Portuguese reached the Congo (Zaire) River. Soon they converted the local king Affonso, who in 1512 offered this advice: "In our kingdom there should no longer be any trade or export in slaves." However, being without muskets, the king could not enforce his wishes. Thus, he compromised and allowed the Portuguese to take their slaves well upriver, away from his capital.

Then King Affonso grew rich. His capital Mbanza (officially São Salvador) grew until it had 12 churches and an estimated 10,000 huts, indications of a population around 40,000. However, Jagga tribesmen destroyed Mbanza during a war, 1565–68, and it never really recovered.

Loanda (now Luanda) was founded about that time and rose to a population of 30,000 by the year 1600. Though meant to be the center for Portuguese slave trading, Loanda fell and became deserted around 1700 (Balandier, 1968). By 1850 it had recovered somewhat with a population of 14,000.

The Portuguese took the east coast African seaports Kilwa and Mombasa in 1505, and eventually exported East Africans as slaves. A Turkish admiral took Mombasa in 1587, but it was too remote to hold. The Arab king of Oman took both ports in 1698 and held them.

The Cape of Good Hope Colony, founded by the Dutch in 1652, counted 1,107 slaves in its first census of 1707. There were a few Malay house servants and nearly 30,000 slaves when the British took possession in 1806. Cape Town itself had 9,400 slaves. Cape Town started out as a water and supply port for Dutch ships going to the East Indies but under British rule grew into a small city of 26,000 by 1851.

The Dutch collected slaves along the Guinea coast. There the native chiefs, Osai Tutu of Ashanti and Guaja Trudo of Dahomey, built sizable kingdoms by trading slaves for muskets. The slave ports, Elmina off Ashanti and Popo and Whydah in Dahomey, were small places of 4,000–20,000, existing for the one industry: slaving. These places were hot, rainy, and unhealthy—certainly not desirable sites.

Finally Thomas Clarkson's great antislavery movement ended the British slave trade, which by then was the greatest portion of worldwide slave selling. In 1807 the trade began to fade away, and by 1889 the various Western nations abolished slavery altogether.

Algiers

The greatest slave port of all time was in the Mediterranean. Algiers was a small fishing town when Turkey took it from Spain in 1508. In 1520, the Turkish sultan, Selim, appointed Khayreddin governor there, sending him ships and 2,000 Janissary soldiers. Khayreddin was called Barbarossa by his enemies because of his red beard.

There was intense bitterness in the western Mediterranean at that time because of recent wars—Christians had ousted Moslems from Spain—and because of the Christian efforts (both Portuguese and Spanish) to gain footholds in north Africa in Ceuta and Oran (North Africa).

Khayreddin's business was slave raiding, both at sea and on European shores. He made captives galley slaves and others were sold at Algiers. He took Tunis from Spain in 1534 but lost it the next year. He won an indecisive victory over the Spanish-Papal-Venetian fleet. To this day, he is considered Turkey's greatest naval hero. After Khayreddin, the governors of Algiers briefly occupied Fez, the capital of Morocco, and Turkey dominated the whole southern shore of the Mediterranean.

Algiers, however, was almost independent. Tunis and Tripoli were also generally free centers for corsairs. Christians made similar raids from Malta and

Leghorn. But the Moslem slaving was on a larger scale, and Algiers dominated that market. Algiers concurrently did a sizable amount of legitimate commerce. The city traded with Christians and especially the French with whom Turkey had an alliance. By 1600, counting its 15,000 slaves, Algiers was a city of 75,000 people.

The early governors were ex-Christians, captured on corsair raids and trained as Moslems. They were, with one exception, reported as just and competent until 1586. At that time the sultan began selling the governorship to the highest bidder, and Algiers, though still prosperous at sea, fell into disorder.

In 1588, Algiers was the base for 35 galleons, ships that moved mainly by oars. The shipbuilders were all resident Christians, and the Turkish Empire did not insist on Moslem faith. Now, when the corsairs took booty, the galley slaves, Christian or Moslem, received a full share. Such was Algiers, outpost of the Turkish Empire.

Emperor Charles V led an unsuccessful attack on Algiers in 1541. In 1606, the Dutch pirate Simon De Danser transferred his activities from Marseille to Algiers, where he taught the residents to build ships for open-water sailing rather than rowing. Using such ships, the pirates of Sallee raided the shores of Iceland in 1627. By 1634, Algiers's population had grown close to 100,000, which included 25,000 slaves.

Algerian slave catching naturally led to reprisals. In 1682, Renau, with a French fleet, bombarded Algiers with mortars until it yielded French captives. Admiral Decatur of the United States forced similar terms on Algiers in 1815. Finally in 1830 the French conquered the city, ending its pirating days.

Zanzibar

The entrepôt of the nineteenth-century East African coastal slave trade was Zanzibar. Said, the ruler of Oman, shifted his capital in 1832 from Muscat to Zanzibar Island, lying off of what is now Tanzania. There he encouraged the Arab slave trade. He also settled at Zanzibar the first sizable group of laborers from India, both Moslems and Hindus.

The Arabs pushed inland from Mombasa in search of ivory and slaves. Men, women, and children were seized during raids on defenseless villages at night and marched under the whip to the coast to be sold at markets in Zanzibar. The Arab slavers set up a base inland at Tabora about 1830 and another one at Ujiji on Lake Tanganyika about 1840. Ironically, this slave trade was made possible by British help to Said early in his reign. Britain had outlawed slave trading in 1807. In 1824, William Owen and an English captain occupied Mombasa, at its own request, to stop the slaving. Owen asked his government to annex Mombasa to control the situation. It refused. In 1834 and in 1838, he repeated his request, but British officials again refused, adhering to the 1822 treaty signed with Said. Here is an instance when adherence to the letter of the law resulted in immense damage.

By 1870, Zanzibar was exporting 20,000 slaves annually. With 60,000 inhabitants, it was by far the largest city in eastern Africa south of Egypt. The slavers tended to be men of dark skin with Arab blood in their paternal ancestry. Their homes were in Zanzibar. The most famous one, Tippu Tib, had a large palace, later used as a hospital. In 1890, Zanzibar at last became a British protectorate. And in 1892–94, a Belgian, Baron Dhanis, crushed the Arab slavers in central Africa. A long nightmare ended.

SUMMARY

The Greeks and Romans occupied North Africa in pre-Christian days. However, the more recent European colonization of Africa began in the fifteenth century with the Portuguese settlement of Cape Verde in 1462 and in São Tomé and Príncipe in 1483. The major cities in the medieval and early modern periods were Fez with about 200,000 inhabitants in 1170–80; Marrakesh with 150,000 in 1200; Tunis with 65,000 inhabitants in 1500; Algiers with 100,000 in 1634; and Meknes with a population of 200,000 in 1727. Even though colonial administrations established new ''European'' cities in Africa and built railroads to the interior regions, there was comparatively little urbanization during the colonial period, certainly not compared to the rapid urbanization of African cities since independence.

REFERENCES

Abu-Lughod, Janet. 1971. *Cairo*. Princeton: Princeton University Press.

Africanus, Leo. 1896. *The History and Description of Africa*. Vol 3. London: Haluyt Society.

Balandier, Georges. 1968. *Daily Life in the Kingdom of Kongo: From the Sixteenth to the Eighteenth Century*. London: Allen and Unwin.

Barth, Heinrich. 1857–58. *Travels and Discoveries in North and Central Africa*. New York: Harper and Brothers.

Chandler, Tertius. 1987. *Four Thousand Years of Urban Growth*. Lewiston, N.Y.: St. David's University Press.

Deverdun, Gaston. 1959. *Marrakech des Origines à 1912*. Rabat: Editions Techniques Nord-Africaine.

Drakakis-Smith, David, ed. 1992. *Urban and Regional Change in Southern Africa*. London: Routledge.

Fagan, Brian M. 1965. *Southern Africa During the Iron Age*. New York: Praeger.

Maquet, Jacques. 1962. *Afrique, les Civilisations Noires*. Paris: Horizons de France.

Martineau, Gilbert, ed. 1953. *Nagel's Morocco: Travel Guide*. Paris: Nadel's Publishers.

Mauny, Raymond. 1961. *Tableau Géographique de l'Ouest Africain au Moyen Age*. Dakar: IFAN.

Metz, Helen Chapin, ed. 1991. *Egypt: A Country Study*. Washington, D.C.: Library of Congress, U.S. Government Printing Office.

Muir, William. 1907. *The Caliphate*. Edinburgh: J. Grant.

O'Connor, David. 1990. *Ancient Egyptian Society*. Pittsburgh: Carnegie Museum of Natural History.

Palmer, H. Richmond. 1928. *Sudanese Memoirs*. London: Frank Cass & Co.

Parker, Richard. 1971. "The Calendars and Chronology." In *The Legacy of Egypt*, edited by John R. Harris, 13–26. Oxford: Clarendon Press.

Petrie, W. M. Flinders. 1905. *A History of Egypt*. London: Methuen.

Poncet, C. J. 1814. "A Journey to Abyssinia." In *A General Collection of the Best Voyages and Travels in All Parts of the World*, edited by John Pinkerton, 61–107. London: Longman, Hurst, Rees, Orme, and Brown.

Schmandt-Besserat, Denise. 1978. "The Earliest Precursor of Writing." *Scientific American* 238:50–59.

Smith, Sidney. 1922. "The Relation of Marduk, Ashur, and Osiris." *Journal of Egyptian Archaeology* 8:41–44.

Sollberger, Edmond. 1954–55. "Sur la Chronologie des Rois d'uret quelques problèmes connexes." *Archiv Fur Orientforschung* 17:10–48.

Thompson, Dorothy J. 1988. *Memphis under the Ptolemies*. Princeton: Princeton University Press.

United Nations. 1990. *Population Growth and Policies in Mega-Cities, Cairo*. Population Policy Paper No. 34. New York: United Nations.

3

Urbanization during Colonial Days in Sub-Saharan Africa

A. J. Christopher and James D. Tarver

The colonial period extended from 1462 when the Portuguese colonized Cape Verde until the colonies obtained their independence. Libya obtained its independence in 1951, and Zimbabwe in 1980.

While the colonial powers founded new "European" cities and connected them to interior areas with railroads, relatively little sustained urbanization actually occurred in the colonial period. Several major urban developments of at least 50,000 inhabitants appeared for the first time in 26 countries at different times during the colonial period. South Africa was the first and most highly urbanized of these. The discovery of diamonds around 1870 and gold in 1886 led to rapid population growth and urbanization, as urbanization there was the most advanced of all African colonies. In the approximately 60 years that followed, another 25 African colonies began their urban development on a somewhat more modest scale before attaining their independence. Most colonies got their independence in the 1960s, and by 1970 36 of the 48 sub-Saharan colonies were independent republics. Urbanization in colonial South Africa will be presented first, followed by urban developments in the other colonies of sub-Saharan Africa.

URBAN DEVELOPMENT IN COLONIAL SOUTH AFRICA

South Africa lacked any indigenous urban tradition, and it was therefore only in the colonial period that urbanization was formulated. A permanent European colonial presence was commenced in 1652 when the Dutch East India Company established a supply base at Cape Town. Subsequently, European settlers and Asian slaves were introduced to work at the base. Most significantly, Cape Town was laid out as a town, rather than remaining merely a fortified camp, as were most contemporary European bases on the continent. Thereafter other towns were founded as a colony of European settlement was created in South Africa, more particularly in the nineteenth century. Thus parallels may be drawn with the other European overseas enterprises in the Americas and Australasia. However, the white colonists and their descendants never outnumbered the indigenous African population, although it was only in the twentieth century that the latter entered the cities in any substantial numbers.

DUTCH COLONIAL TOWNS

The Dutch East India Company established a refreshment station, with the primary object of supplying passing company ships plying between the Netherlands and the Dutch possessions in Indonesia. According to the initial plan, fresh fruit and vegetables were to be grown by company servants, and fresh meat purchased from the indigenous inhabitants. Thus the initial sector of the settlement consisted of a fort and garden. However, the original intentions were not fulfilled, and the company released some of its employees to become free settlers in 1657. In the same year the government began the importation of slaves from Asia to work on the agricultural enterprises and serve as artisans in the developing town (Elphick and Giliomee, 1979).

Cape Town was the only urban settlement of any size throughout the period of Dutch rule. In 1806 when the British occupied the colony permanently, the town contained some 16,400 inhabitants, including 6,400 Europeans, 9,400 slaves, and 600 indigenes. It was a tightly organized town with narrow streets (13 or 20 meters in width), and small blocks and individual plots (700 square meters) which exhibited many similarities with the plan of a contemporary European town. Building regulations early in the eighteenth century banned thatched roofs, and architectural styles therefore followed those of other colonial Dutch towns in the East and West Indies (Fransen and Cook, 1980). The castle and public buildings, including the hospital, slave lodge, church, and Government House, were concentrated on the southeastern side of the town and adjacent to the original company garden (Figure 3.1).

In the interior of the colony few towns or villages were established in the Dutch period. The government had founded the village of Stellenbosch in 1679 as part of the agricultural settlement program (Smuts, 1979). However, rural European settlement beyond a distance of 60 kilometers from Cape Town was sparse, based on extensive stock farming and hence offering few opportunities for trade or the provision of services (Guelke, 1976). By 1806 only six settlements outside Cape Town could be regarded as urban. They were of two forms, the small market and service centers in the western Cape and the planned government administrative towns of Graaff-Reinet and Uitenhage in the eastern Cape. In the former case either the government had established a seat for a magistrate or the Dutch Reformed Church had built a church. The settlements were small and

Figure 3.1
Cape Town in the Eighteenth Century

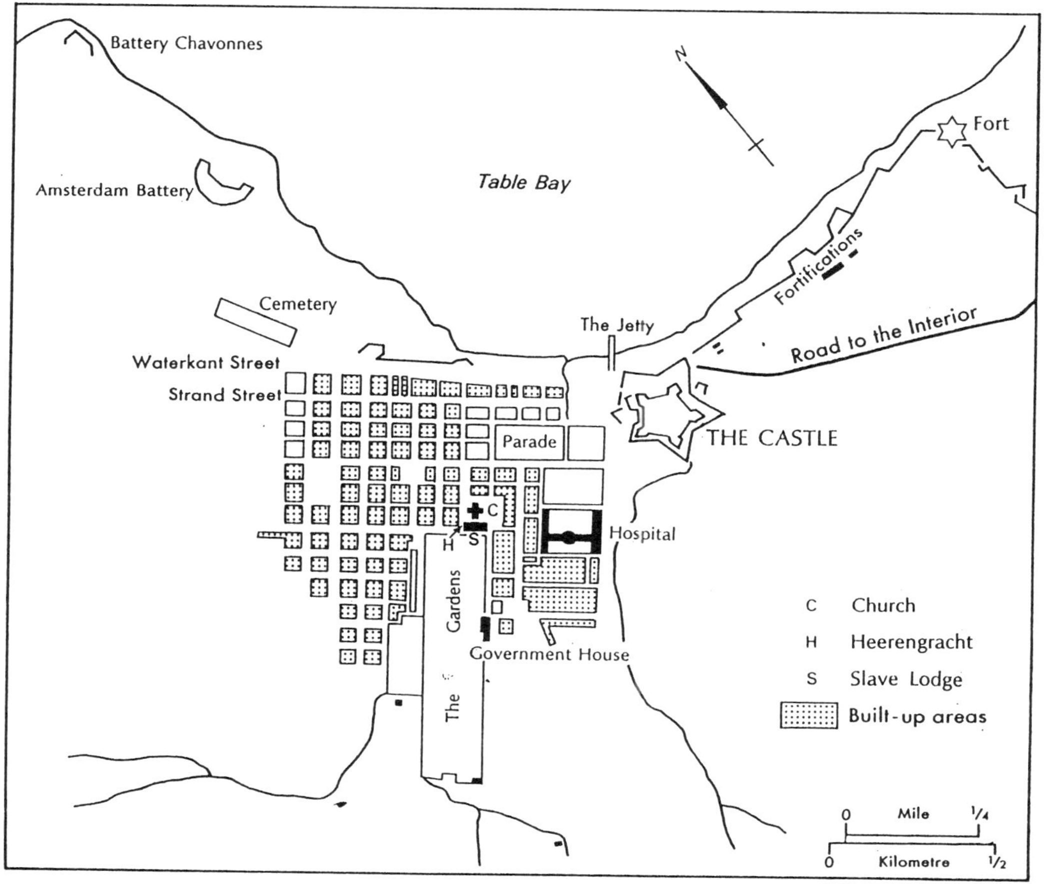

dependent upon the farming communities around them. In the latter case large plots (0.8 hectares) were supplied with irrigation water, permitting intensive cultivation. The provision of extensive common grazing lands around the towns enhanced the agricultural component, allowing for a high degree of self-sufficiency deemed to be necessary on the frontier of European settlement. The towns were therefore often rural in appearance, with thatched-roof farmhouses lining the streets.

URBANIZATION IN THE NINETEENTH CENTURY

Urban development in the period from the final British occupation in 1806 to the establishment of the Union of South Africa in 1910 was more rapid (Christopher, 1976). Large numbers of towns were founded for a variety of reasons, but comparatively few developed into major population centers. Thus, in 1911 only 14 towns exceeded a population of 20,000 people, and only two, Johannesburg and Cape Town, exceeded 100,000 inhabitants. The majority of towns were still extremely small. In 1911, of the 329 places classified as urban in the census, almost half (151) recorded populations of under 1,000 inhabitants. Furthermore, only a quarter of the total population of the country was urbanized by 1911. This was a race-selective process as over half the European population lived in urban areas by this date, but only an eighth of the African population of the country (South Africa, 1912).

The Port System

Urban development took several forms. Within a colonial system linked to the international market, the port network was of prime significance and was extended with the foundation of a series of towns to handle the expanding volume of trade. Competition between them resulted in the emergence of four major ports and a couple of minor sites (Clark, 1977). The ports controlled the communication system with the interior, initially through the construction of the graded road system in the first half of the nineteenth century and then the railway network in the second half.

Until the first decade of the twentieth century Cape Town retained its primacy as the largest city, as the capital of the major political unit in the subcontinent and the port closest to the metropolitan power in Europe. The city underwent substantial change as a result of increased trade levels, notably after the exploitation of diamonds and gold in the 1870s and 1880s boosted the South African economy. Growth was slow in the first half of the nineteenth century, and by 1855 the population of the city and suburbs was only 32,000. In the following 50 years growth was far more rapid, with 180,000 inhabitants enumerated in 1904. Extensive new suburbs were occupied commencing with the building of District Six in the 1830s which coincided with the freeing of the slaves. By 1910 a line of suburbs extended some 20 kilometers southwards toward the naval base at Simonstown (Picard, 1969). The range of built environments varied from tightly packed terraced housing, with small backyards, to extensive mansions in grounds of several hectares. Industrial development, boosted by the railway workshops in the 1860s, resulted in the emergence of a diversified economy. At the same time port facilities were expanded through the construction of harbor works and land reclamation from the sea. The development of the regular steamship liner service with England in the 1850s enhanced the position of Cape Town as the port of entry for passengers and high value goods.

Other ports were laid out along the South African coastline as the interior was colonized. There were few natural harbors, estuaries, or navigable rivers to select, so the development of the ports involved substantial reclamation or dredging works. Port Elizabeth was fortified in 1799 but only organized as a town in 1815 (Christopher, 1987). Durban was founded in 1835 and East London in 1848. These were able to compete successfully with their rivals and develop trade lines with the interior. The wool boom of the 1840s and 1850s resulted in Port Elizabeth's becoming the premier port for bulk exports (Mabin, 1986a). However, in the 1890s, with the construction of the railways, Durban exploited its position as the closest port to the Witwatersrand towns (Davies, 1963). Port Elizabeth thus fell from fourth to ninth place in the urban hierarchy between 1904 and 1911.

Administrative Towns

The British administration was more intent on controlling the interior of the colony than the Dutch East India Company had been. This involved not only a military presence on the frontiers with potentially hostile indigenous polities, but closer supervision of the European farming population. Added imperatives were the rising levels of population and prosperity as commercial farming was developed in the interior, and the move toward independence by the Dutch-speaking farmers beyond the Cape colonial border.

The British colonial government in the Cape founded several new towns to serve as administrative, commercial, military, and religious centers. Towns were viewed as an essential part of European civilization and primarily catered for the needs of the expanding white population. Although only numbering 27,000 in 1806, the white population of South Africa expanded rapidly to reach 140,000 in 1855 and numbered some 1.3 million in 1911. Significantly, half this total was then urbanized. In addition, missionary societies were encouraged to found settlements to promote the Christianization of the indigenous population. Garrison towns were established on sensitive frontiers. The Dutch-speaking emigrants from the Cape Colony in the 1830s and thereafter took town-planning concepts developed in the Cape with them into the Transvaal, Orange Free State, and Natal (Laband and Haswell, 1988). The British annexed Natal in 1843, and the subsequent administration similarly developed an urban-based colonization program.

The towns thus established were of two basic types. Those conceived as being primarily commercial and administrative in function were usually laid out with relatively small plots (less than 0.4 hectare) and limited common grazing land. In contrast, those conceived as serving an agricultural function were more generously planned on the model of late eighteenth-century Graaff-Reinet, often with large irrigated plots. Towns were also laid out to accommodate settlers on land development schemes, and to serve as sites for the Dutch Reformed Church's quarterly communion services. All these reflected the growth of the European colonial population and the increasing urban bias of the colonial states.

Nineteenth-century town-planning design was fixed on the basic colonial grid plan of streets intersecting at right angles (Christopher, 1976). In the early part of the century towns were planned with vistas symbolically closing upon prominent public buildings such as the church or magistracy, but later in the century plans became more utilitarian. Public open spaces were prominent in the landscape, notably in the form of market and church squares, and in some of the larger centers, botanical and pleasure gardens. The constraints noticeable in the Dutch planning of Cape Town were abandoned as the availability of space was appreciated by town planners. Apart from the ports and mining towns, nineteenth-century towns in South Africa were thus characterized by remarkably low densities of population.

Mining Towns

The development of mining had a profound effect upon the economy of South Africa, through the injection of capital and the attraction of urban immigrants from Europe. Small copper mining enterprises were undertaken in the northwestern Cape in the 1850s, but it was the discovery of diamonds in the vicinity of the future city of Kimberley which ushered in the new era. Kimberley was the first industrial town in South Africa. Its plan was irregular and population highly mobile. The mining opportunities attracted both European and African diggers. Production was soon concentrated in the hands of a few, and finally one financial institution. Owing to the nature of the product, control of the workings was essential to guard against illicit diamond dealing. Control was extended by forcing the African, but not the European, workers to live in segregated barrack-like compounds (Mabin, 1986b). The mining company, in this case De Beers, thus determined the form of the settlement with a European mine workers' village and African barracks (Figure 3.2). This imposed residential isolation was so profitable for the mine owners in reducing the costs of labor that it was emulated on the later gold and coal mines of the Transvaal.

The transformation of the urban pattern of South Africa came in 1886 with the discovery of a major gold reef on the Witwatersrand in the southern Transvaal (Van Onselen, 1982). The Transvaal government proclaimed a series of towns along the line of the outcrop, and private individuals did the same as mining activity was extended. The initial towns were laid out in small city blocks with

Figure 3.2
Kimberley in 1900

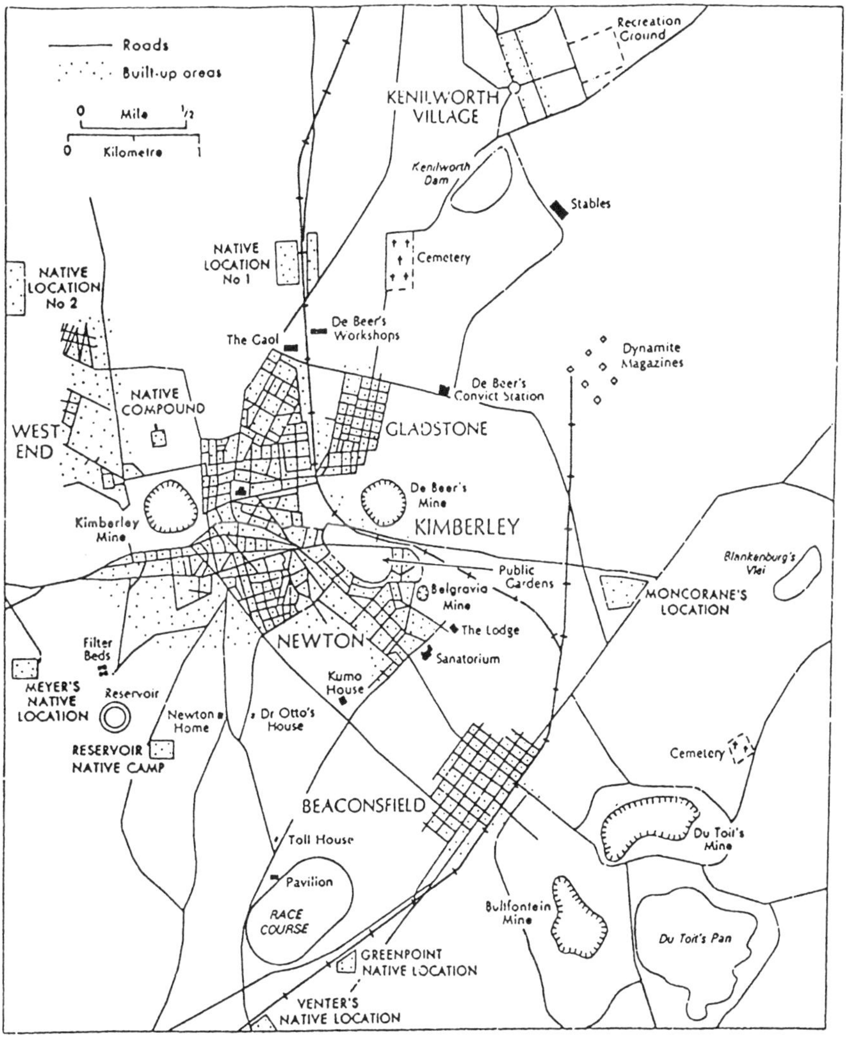

small plots, narrow streets, and restricted public buildings and open spaces. It has been suggested that this was done in the official expectation that they would be temporary, as previous gold mining camps had been (Shorten, 1970). The mines proved to be the richest in the world and capable of substantial extension as new mining techniques were developed, more particularly deep-level mining.

Owing to the expensive nature of mine development, mining was concentrated in the hands of a number of large enterprises which established a series of extensive, virtually self-contained settlements in the 1890s, recruiting mine labor from throughout southern Africa.

Twenty-five years after the foundation of the Witwatersrand towns, Johannesburg had become the largest city in South Africa, and the entire urban system had been radically transformed. The initial cramped mining town had developed into a complex settlement of almost 240,000 inhabitants by 1911. New more affluent suburbs were laid out on the ridge to the north of the original town, while poorer working-class white suburbs were laid out south of the mining area. Within the mining land, the mines were organized with their distinctive pattern of separate European housing estates and African compounds. Locations for the African, Indian, and colored populations were organized separately, adjacent to the industrial area. However, after the bubonic plague outbreak, much of the African population was moved some 20 kilometers from the city center to Klipspruit, the precursor of modern Soweto.

It is a measure of the dominance which the Witwatersrand had begun to exercise over the urban system that six of the eleven largest towns in South Africa in 1911 were situated within the agglomeration. The railway network constructed in the 1890s had ensured that it became the focus of the communication system, and it was symbolic that the headquarters was housed in Johannesburg, together with the major financial institutions of the country, not in the political capitals of Cape Town or Pretoria. Thus the entire space economy of the country was reversed from a series of coastal cores to a single interior core (Browett and Fair, 1974).

The construction of the railway network profoundly affected other aspects of the urban pattern of the country. The majority of lines were built for long-distance trade and passenger traffic. Thus many towns were bypassed and secondary transshipment stations had to be created. Those with a station were boosted at the expense of others which did not, so encouraging the differential growth of the towns. Other towns were built to service the railways at line junctions or boosted through the establishment of workshops.

URBAN SEGREGATION IN COLONIAL SOUTH AFRICA

South Africa has been universally condemned for the policy of apartheid adopted by the National party after 1948, but the origins of the policy go deep into the colonial period and indeed into the early English colonial experience (Christopher, 1983). Before 1910 the four colonies adopted differing policies toward the management of multiethnic urban populations (Christopher, 1988). These profoundly affected the form of the towns and cities and also the composition of the urban populations.

The administration of the Cape Colony was nominally color blind, with a franchise open to all people satisfying basic income or property qualifications. However, in a number of sectors distinctly racially based laws were enacted. The first was the provision of missionary settlements for the indigenous or freed slave populations. Accordingly, in Port Elizabeth a separate suburb, or location, for the indigenous population was laid out in 1834. Separate villages for African and colored people were also established in the smaller towns. The second was the promulgation of regulations in 1847 that separate municipal locations for the African population be established on the margins of towns in the eastern part of the colony. The third was the provision of mine compounds for the African mine workers at Kimberley. Official segregative tendencies were given a boost by the outbreak of bubonic plague in Cape Town and Port Elizabeth in 1901–2. The ensuing outbreak of the ''sanitation syndrome'' which affected the white population resulted in the establishment of new state-controlled African locations several kilometers from the centers of the two cities (Swanson, 1977).

The Natal government, by contrast, adopted a more racially restrictive regime. African domestic workers were housed by their employers on their own properties and control exercised to prevent unemployed Africans from staying in the towns (Swanson, 1976). Barracks were established to house African staff employed by the Natal Government Railways and the Durban Harbour Board, as well as, in Durban, day laborers and industrial workers. Few African families migrated to the towns in the colonial period, and the African population was thus overwhelmingly (93 percent) composed of single African males.

In the Transvaal and Orange Free State the republican governments of the nineteenth century adopted rigidly racial constitutions. Only whites could become citizens and only citizens could own land. Thus in theory African and other people of color were confined to locations on the margins of the white-occupied towns. However, although the Orange Free State enforced such regulations quite rigorously, the Transvaal administration did not. Accordingly, in many Transvaal towns with a substantial agricultural base, African workers were housed on their employers' plots. The compound system in the mining settlements has previously been discussed.

The colonial settler population was also of diverse origins, including a prominent Indian component, particularly in Natal after 1860. Although most Indians arrived in the colony as indentured workers, generally destined for the sugar plantations, others came as free settlers and supplied services to their own community. However, Indian traders increasingly competed successfully for the white and African trade, establishing shops in the white central business districts. Although barracks were built for Indian laborers in the main towns of Natal, the remainder of the Indian community lived among the white population. Racially inspired moves were made as early as the 1890s to restrict Indians from purchasing properties in perceived white suburbs. It was white settler pressure upon Indian business interests in central Durban which prompted Gandhi to settle in Durban in the 1890s and become involved in politics (Swan, 1985).

In the Transvaal, Indians were highly restricted, but allowed to purchase properties in limited officially defined areas. In several towns separate Indian bazaars were laid out on the edge of the white town, although only in a few cases was the Indian population forcibly moved into the bazaars. Within the gold mining settlements, only whites were permitted to purchase property, with a few limited exceptions. The restrictions were imposed by statute and covenants written into suburban title deeds. However, limited numbers of Indian traders established businesses in the city center. Total exclusion was achieved by the Orange Free State government, which banned all Indians from its territory in 1890.

The mixed origin, colored, population was subject to varying degrees of control and hence segregation. In the Cape and Natal no disabilities were placed upon the community, and it was integrated with the white population. However, it was noted that economic status and skin color were related, with the poorer suburbs being darker in complexion than the richer suburbs. In the Transvaal colored people were housed in a series of separate locations intended to be racially exclusive (Parnell, 1991). The Orange Free State administration confined colored people to the African locations.

South African towns and cities at Union in 1910 were thus highly segregated (Christopher, 1990). If segregation levels are examined for the 1911 census as a summary of the differing segregation experiences of the colonial urban populations, then the range is particularly significant (Figure 3.3). The white and colored populations of the western Cape were not segregated by the standards of current American definitions, but other groups in other regions were highly segregated by the same measure (Massey and Denton, 1988). The Orange Free State towns in particular exhibited high levels of segregation for the white and African populations, with the eastern Cape towns approaching the same levels of separation.

URBAN DEVELOPMENTS IN OTHER SUB-SAHARAN COLONIES

Sustained urban developments appeared during the colonial period in some colonies for the first time before independence in sub-Saharan Africa. Here, urbanization in Ghana and Nigeria was excluded from the analysis since they first experienced definite urbanization in precolonial days, and Ethiopia and Liberia were excluded because they were not considered European colonies even though the Italians invaded Ethiopia and occupied it from 1936 to 1941.

Table 3.1 identifies each of the 26 countries that underwent major urbanization during the colonial period with the name of the capital city of each country specified. Cape Town had the largest 1950 urban agglomeration of all sub-Saharan capital cities which underwent urbanization in the colonial period.

Dakar and Antananarivo were the next largest colonial urban agglomerations with 180,000 to 220,000 inhabitants in 1950. Because of its deep harbor, Dakar became the capital of Senegal in 1904. The Kinshasa, Luanda, and Harare urban agglomerations were the next largest capital cities with 100,000 and 170,000 inhabitants in 1950. Agglomerations with 1950 populations of 60,000 to 90,000 inhabitants included Maputo, Nairobi, Dar es Salaam, Abidjan, Port Louis,

Figure 3.3
White Index of Segregation, 1911. The index is measured on a scale from 0 (no segregation) to 100 (total segregation).

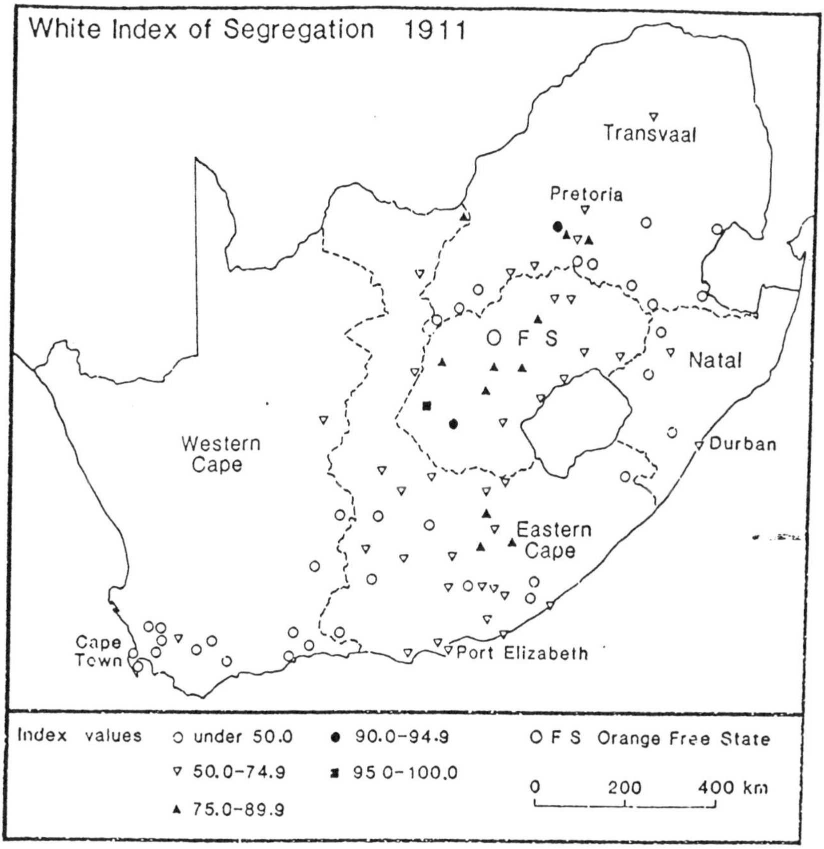

Brazzaville, and Bamako. Those colonial urban agglomerations with 1950 populations of at least 50,000 inhabitants included Bujumbura, Freetown, Mogadishu, and Kampala.

In addition, there were a number of smaller urban agglomerations with less than 50,000 inhabitants in 1950; Bangui, Porto-Novo, Conakry, Ndjamena, Niamey, Ouagadougou, Yaoundé, Lomé, and Lusaka.

Population gains in sub-Saharan Africa began to increase after World War II, and urbanization accelerated rapidly. For example, by 1950 there were over 14 million inhabitants living in the urban areas of the countries in which the colonial capital cities of sub-Saharan Africa were located. About 2.5 million of these inhabitants resided in the national capitals. Therefore, over 80 percent of the urban residents in sub-Saharan Africa lived outside the urban agglomerations of capital cities in 1950. By the time these countries attained their independence,

Table 3.1
Urbanization of Sub-Saharan African Colonies during the Colonial Period: Agglomerations That Reached 50,000 before Independence

Urban Agglomeration	Country	Date of Independence	Estimated Population	
			1950	Independence
Cape Town	South Africa	1910	618,000	160,000
Dakar	Senegal	1960	223,000	366,000
Antananarivo	Madagascar	1960	180,000	250,000
Kinshasa	Zaire	1960	173,000	451,000
Luanda	Angola	1975	138,000	669,000
Nairobi	Kenya	1963	87,000	275,000
Harare	Zimbabwe	1980	110,000	590,000
Maputo	Mozambique	1975	91,000	532,000
Dar es Salaam	Tanzania	1961, 1963	78,000	180,000
Abidjan	Côte d'Ivoire	1960	59,000	180,000
Port Louis	Mauritius	1968	65,000	135,000

Brazzaville	Congo	1960	60,000	130,000
Bamako	Mali	1960	60,000	130,000
Bujumbura	Burundi	1962	50,000	70,000
Freetown	Sierra Leone	1961	50,000	100,000
Mogadishu	Somalia	1960	50,000	90,000
Kampala	Uganda	1962	50,000	150,000
Bangui	Cen. Afr. Rep.	1960	40,000	90,000
Porto-Novo	Benin	1960	40,000	60,000
Conakry	Guinea	1958	39,000	100,000
Lomé	Togo	1960	40,000	80,000
Ndjamena	Chad	1960	40,000	80,000
Niamey	Niger	1960	30,000	60,000
Ouagadougou	Burkina Faso	1960	30,000	60,000
Yaoundé	Cameroon	1960	30,000	70,000
Lusaka	Zambia	1964	30,000	150,000

Source: Compiled from United Nations, 1989, 1991.

many of their national capitals had more than doubled their populations. By the date of their independence the colonial capitals had 5.2 million inhabitants, a gain of more than 110 percent since 1950.

The urban agglomerations that experienced the largest population gains in this period were located in countries which obtained their independence at comparatively late dates—those that had spent the longest time in colonial status since 1950. For example, Zimbabwe was the last African country to obtain its independence in 1980.[1] The urban agglomeration of Harare grew from 110,000 inhabitants in 1950 to 590,000 in 1980, a gain of 480,000, or nearly 440 percent in 30 years. Both Maputo and Luanda, capitals of Portuguese colonies that obtained their independence in 1975, had population gains of 490 and 380 percent, respectively, during the 1950–75 period.

Lusaka had a 400 percent gain and Kinshasa had a 160 percent increase in its urban agglomeration. Kinshasa's pre–World War II population growth depended largely upon shipping and trade by rail and water on the Congo River. After the war European demand led to increases in industrialization and population. Abidjan had a 205 percent population increase during its 1950–60 colonial days. It became a capital city in 1934 in a country that was undergoing rapid economic development.

Nairobi gained 216 percent during its 1950–63 colonial period. In 1905 the British East Africa administration shifted the capital from Mombasa to Nairobi. Dar es Salaam was another urban agglomeration with more than a 130 percent population increase from 1960 to its independence. It was a small town when the Portuguese arrived in the sixteenth century and was the capital of Tanzania until recently. Most urban agglomerations of less than 50,000 inhabitants in 1950 doubled their populations by the time they became capital cities of independent nations.

In sub-Saharan Africa, urban population growth was much more rapid after than before independence. During the colonial period, pass laws kept most Africans from residing in the white European cities in many areas of Africa. These strict prohibitions, of course, disappeared after independence except in South Africa. This freedom of movement changed the racial composition of cities and quickly led to rapidly mounting urban populations.

Migration has been a major factor in the urban population increases, particularly from the outlying rural areas and villages where most poor natives made their living from subsistence agriculture. As the African colonies obtained their independence, movement to cities accelerated greatly. With the huge exodus out of the agricultural areas, Africa has had the highest rate of urbanization of all major regions in the world. Certainly the rate of population growth in Africa's urban areas has outstripped the rate of industrialization as rural Africans have sought the amenities of cities.

SUMMARY AND IMPLICATIONS

Colonialism had a very profound effect upon South Africa, both through the length of time that the country was under European control and through the numbers of European settlers who migrated to the country. Indeed in the second half of the nineteenth century it was the urban opportunities offered, not land, which attracted European settlers to South Africa. So strong was the impact of this settlement that alone of the African states, decolonization in the twentieth century involved the transfer of political power to the white settler community. As the region lacked an indigenous urban tradition, the colonial cities were thus built by Europeans for Europeans. The concept of the urban areas as "the domain of the white man" was only challenged when African urbanization accelerated after World War I. The result was the creation of a new form of city, distinguished from its colonial predecessors by greater rigidity and coercion. The foundations of the apartheid city had nevertheless been laid in the colonial period.

Early in the colonization of Africa, Europeans ended slave raids. Then, largely after World War II, modern health and medical care was introduced and applied to curb various health problems and plagues. The opening of European markets provided new jobs for Africans. With these developments and new opportunities, the African population grew rapidly and continues to increase rapidly. Cities throughout Africa have experienced very rapid gains, especially since attaining their independence when Africans were permitted to move freely into cities without restrictions from Europeans.

The general consensus is that most African urban agglomerations will continue to increase for some time but perhaps not on the same scale as in the past 40 years. In many cases, these rapid population gains have outstripped available jobs and made it impossible for cities to provide adequate municipal services. Slums, called shantytowns, bidonvilles, and musseques have risen and created severe sanitation problems. Nevertheless, the large urban agglomerations in Africa have attracted millions of migrants and will continue to do so because they offer many amenities unavailable in rural villages.

NOTE

1. Urbanization existed in pre-colonial Zimbabwe from about the thirteenth until the seventeenth century, then it abruptly ended until it began again in the colonial period. Urbanization also occurred along the eastern coastal area at trading centers from Mogadishu to Sofala. For example, Kilwa, founded in 975, was a small urban center of about 30,000 inhabitants when the Portuguese arrived. However, the populations of these trading centers fluctuated with their fortunes.

REFERENCES

Browett, T. G., and T. J. D. Fair. 1974. "South Africa, 1870–1970: A View of the Spatial System." *South African Geographical Journal* 56:111–120.

Christopher, A. J. 1976. *Southern Africa: Studies in Historical Geography*. Hamden, Conn.: Archon.

———. 1983. "From Flint to Soweto: Reflections on the Colonial Origins of the Apartheid City." *Area* 15:145–149.

———. 1987. "Race and Residence in Colonial Port Elizabeth." *South African Geographical Journal* 69:3–20.

———. 1988. "Roots of Urban Segregation: South Africa at Union 1910." *Journal of Historical Geography* 14:151–169.

———. 1990. "Apartheid and Urban Segregation Levels in South Africa." *Urban Studies* 27:421–440.

Clark, E. A. 1977. "Port Sites and Perception: The Development of the Southern and Eastern Cape Coast in the Nineteenth Century." *South African Geographical Journal* 59:150–167.

Davies, R. J. 1963. "The Growth of the Durban Metropolitan Area." *South African Geographical Journal* 45:15–43.

Elphick, R., and H. Giliomee, eds. 1979. *The Shaping of South African Society 1652–1820*. Cape Town: Longman.

Fransen, H., and M. A. Cook. 1980. *The Old Buildings of the Cape*. Cape Town: A. A. Balkema.

Guelke, L. 1976. "Frontier Settlement in Early Dutch South Africa." *Annals of the Association of American Geographers* 66:25–42.

Laband, J., and R. Haswell, eds. 1988. *Pietermaritzburg 1838–1988: A New Portrait of an African City*. Pietermaritzburg: University of Natal Press.

Mabin, A. 1986a. "The Rise and Decline of Port Elizabeth 1850–1900." *International Journal of African Historical Studies* 19:275–303.

———. 1986b. "Labour, Capital, Class Struggle and the Origins of Residential Segregation in Kimberley 1880–1920." *Journal of Historical Geography* 12:4–26.

Massey, D. S., and N. A. Denton. 1988. "Dimensions of Residential Segregation." *Social Forces* 67:281–315.

Parnell, S. 1991. "Sanitation, Segregation and the Natives (Urban Areas) Act: African Exclusion from Johannesburg's Malay Location, 1897–1925." *Journal of Historical Geography* 17:271–288.

Picard, H. W. J. 1969. *Grand Parade: The Birth of Greater Cape Town 1850–1913*. Cape Town: C. Struik.

Shorten, J. R. 1970. *The Johannesburg Saga*. Johannesburg: John R. Shorten.

Smuts, F., ed. 1979. *Stellenbosch: Three Centuries*. Stellenbosch: Stellenbosch Town Council.

South Africa. 1912. *Census of the Union of South Africa 1911*. U. G. 32–1912. Pretoria: Government Printer.

Swan, M. 1985. *Gandhi: The South African Experience*. Johannesburg: Ravan.

Swanson, M. W. 1976. "The 'Durban System': Roots of Urban Apartheid in Colonial Natal." *African Studies* 35:159–176.

———. 1977. "The Sanitation Syndrome: Bubonic Plague and Urban Native Policy in the Cape Colony 1900–1909." *Journal of African History* 18:387–410.

United Nations. 1989. *Prospects of World Urbanization, 1988*. Population Studies No. 112. New York: United Nations.

———. 1991. *World Urbanization Prospects 1990*. Population Studies No. 121. New York: United Nations.

Van Onselen, C. 1982. *Studies in the Social and Economic History of the Witwatersrand 1886–1914*. London: Longman.

4

The Growth of Africa's Urban Population

Robert A. Obudho and Rose A. Obudho

As a formal field of inquiry, the serious study of urbanization in Africa is little more than three decades old (O'Connor, 1982, 1983; Obudho and El-Shakhs, 1979; and El-shakhs and Obudho, 1974). During this time, particularly in the post-1960s, many scholars conducted social surveys of urban centers, examined the effects of urbanization upon Africans, and studied the relationship between urbanization and economic development. Until the 1970s, most studies were concerned primarily with the development of urbanization in major urban centers, particularly the large urban centers. In the 1950s, G. T. Trewartha and W. Zelinsky (1954:144) estimated that only 8.5 million people lived in urban centers with 5,000 or more inhabitants and concluded that the relative numerical insignificance of urban dwellers did not warrant a detailed discussion. Horace Miner (1967:1) analyzed the situation carefully when he said that "Africa is the least urbanized of continents, but this demographic fact belies the new importance of African cities. A decade ago the continent was a colonial patchwork and Africans a powerless people. Today the caucus of independent African nations has a third of the votes in the General Assembly in the United Nations. At home, African leaders . . . are the holders of the economic, military, and political power of the new nations. . . . Here is the center of commerce, the seat of government, the source of news and innovation and the point of contact with the outside world. As in other modernizing nations of diverse peoples, the emergence of national cultures in African countries is overwhelmingly an urban phenomenon."

The rate of urbanization certainly accelerated in the late 1960s and early 1970s. The urbanization patterns have changed so greatly within the last 30 years with regard to the pace and scale that scholars have recognized the importance of studying the urbanization theories within the context of African countries (El-Shakhs and Obudho, 1974).

This chapter traces the growth, nature, and extent of urbanization processes and urbanism in Africa, especially its demographic nature. Certainly the demographics of urbanization growth and urbanization are manifestations of more fundamental structural changes in the national economies undergoing their transformations from agrarian to industrial societies. Thus, demographics cannot be logically separated from the associated economic, sociocultural, and political factors. Obviously, many insights regarding the evolution of urbanization trends can be gained from a thorough analysis of the patterns of urban growth and distribution.

PRECOLONIAL URBANIZATION

The earliest urban centers in Egypt appeared about the same time as the urban centers in the Euphrates. Some of these centers were destroyed during the Persian, Roman, and other conquests of the region. During the first to the third centuries A.D., new urban centers were established by the Romans in and around Rabat, Moulay Idriss, Tangier, Tunis, Algiers, and Bizerte in northern Africa. In the eighth to the eleventh centuries, many Muslim urban centers were founded in eastern and western Africa as well as in other parts of northern Africa. The majority declined because they were associated with divine kingship. However, most African urban centers were founded from the early sixteenth to the late nineteenth centuries, occurring along with large waves of international migration and European trade with Africans.

It is important to distinguish between the ''old'' and the ''new'' forms of urban centers, between precolonial and postcolonial urbanization. Although not noted for its ancient urban centers, precolonial Africa had a number of indigenous centers, especially on the northern coast of Africa, western Africa, and in parts of central, eastern, and southern Africa (Hance, 1970:1209–219). A full chronological account of precolonial urbanization in Africa is given in Chapters 1 and 2 of this book by Tertius Chandler and described by William A. Hance (1970); R. W. Hull (1976); Allen Howard (1975:247–270); Salah El-Shakhs and R. A. Obudho (1974); R. A. Obudho and Salah El-Shakhs (1979); and P. Vennetier (1970).

The precolonial urban centers were not of the same stage in ''urbanness'' as the modern urban centers because the former still maintained their traditional forms, function, and structure while the latter possessed features of an ''urban place'' in the Western sense of the term. The medieval urban centers in Sudan, Savanna, Central Africa, and along the coast of East Africa appeared around the tenth century. They were closely associated with Islam, which brought marketing and trade routes, and resulted in the building of urban centers. Thus, the urban centers in the Sudan and on the eastern and central African coast combined Islam and traditional African elements. In the Guinea Coast of West Africa and the Great Lakes of East and Central Africa, urban centers were based upon the divine rule of a king. Most centers were ephemeral because they were built of impermanent materials and closely associated with an individual king or emperor. In northern Africa especially, Europe helped build early trading posts and forts by creating trade routes that influenced the urban morphology before colonization. During the early stages of colonization, Europeans penetrated the interior parts by caravan routes which hastened the decline or disappearance of the majority of precolonial African urban centers. The surviving precolonial centers merged as a form of "colonial settlement" with essentially two central business districts—one traditional and the other modern.

COLONIAL URBANIZATION

Colonial rule resulted in some important urban centers. These centers were founded between the sixteenth and twentieth centuries as either new colonial settlements to serve as administrative and trading centers or as upgraded precolonial centers. Other centers were created in the exploitation of mineral resources, and other centers emerged as national and provincial capitals of their respective countries, regional markets, and transport networks. Colonial administrations established peaceful conditions, introduced money economies that linked Africa to world markets, and increased agricultural production and industrial development, thereby stimulating the growth of urban centers in Africa.

Colonial administrators usually linked the interior with roads and railways, and important mineral fields became nodal points. Towns such as Kumasi (gold), Jose (tin), Enugu (coal), and Katanga (copper and diamonds) reflect the importance of minerals in the growth of new urban centers. The coastal urban centers of East Africa such as Mogadishu, Mombasa, Sofala, Kilwa, and Dar es Salaam had a long history of settlement by Arab immigrants from the Middle East.

Early European urbanization in sub-Saharan Africa began with small forts, trading posts, and railway stations in the sixteenth century. These early settlements included Rufisque, Senegal; Kayes, Mali; Bissau, Guinea-Bissau; Lagos, Nigeria; Luanda and Benguela, Angola; Cape Town, Republic of South Africa; Conarky, Guinea; Sekondi, Cape Coast; and Accra, Ghana. Most urban centers in the interior were founded during the last quarter of the nineteenth century and the first quarter of the twentieth century when many sub-Saharan centers were established as important centers (Hance, 1970:209–219). With few industrial jobs in the early stages of their development, these newly founded centers acted as magnets to the rural population.

Originally, the population of the colonial African centers was young and predominantly male (Caldwell, 1969:21). The male domination continued until the beginning of the postcolonial era when Africans were allowed to reside in the urban areas. The postcolonial era, therefore, represents a very important stage in African urbanization.

POSTCOLONIAL URBANIZATION

Africa remains essentially on the frontiers of urban explosion and spatial transformations as witnessed by the rest of the world during the twentieth century. The continent still has a few large urban centers, primarily in northern and southern Africa. Except for northern and southern Africa, the continent is at the threshold of an urban transformation of major proportions. Tropical Africa, for example, provides almost unparalleled opportunities to see "cities in the making" (O'Connor, 1983:16). The ingredients for such transformation are minimal levels of urbanization, low degrees of urban concentration, high and increasing rates of population and urban growth, uneven distribution of population and resources, increasing efforts of national integration, and highly centralized political systems. Such conditions point toward spatial polarization with increasing urban concentration and widening regional inequalities.

Despite the generally low levels of urbanization, Africa is experiencing the highest rates of urbanization in the world, averaging 4.6 percent per annum. The annual average rate of urbanization in Africa is not expected to decrease to 3 percent until after the year 2025. Although Africa is the least urbanized of the continents, its urban growth will continue to be the most rapid in the world.

Whereas urban growth rates have been falling secularly both in the world as a whole and in less developed countries (LDCs) in general, this is not the case in Africa as a whole (Obudho, 1985). The urban population in Africa increased from 33 million (15 percent) in 1950 to 176 million (32 percent) in 1985, and it is likely to reach 903 million (59 percent) by 2025. Low levels of urbanization are characteristic of most regions of Africa. In 1980, 29 percent of Africa's population lived in urban areas.

The rates of growth of urbanization combined with high population growth rates will ensure a dramatic increase in Africa's urban population. The urban population will increase from 129 million in 1980 to more than 765 million by 2025, at which time over 52 percent will be living in towns and cities.

The level of urbanization in Africa increased from 15 percent in 1950 to 29 percent in 1980. The number of African urban dwellers rose from 135 million in this same period, and it is likely to reach 227 million by 1990, 362 million by 2000, and 865 million by 2025, a dramatic increase in Africa's urban population. Already southern Africa is mostly urban, while in eastern and western Africa, only 20–25 percent of the population live in urban areas. By the year 2020, approximately 60–70 percent of the population of northern and southern Africa is expected to be living in urban centers while eastern and western Africa are projected to have 40–50 percent. The average annual growth rate of urban populations in eastern and western Africa is, however, the highest in the continent, although the rates for both are declining. In northern and southern Africa, natural population increase will be the dominant factor in the growth of urbanization, while in western and eastern Africa, which have some of the fastest-growing urban centers in the world, rural-urban migration will be the most significant factor in urban growth.

The high rate of urbanization poses grave developmental problems for governments and the peoples concerned. The high rate of growth is mainly due to rural-urban migration, to high urban natural increase, and to an expansion of urban boundaries, as well as to interethnic wars. Also, nonspatial factors have significant impacts on the form, rates, nature, and extent of urban growth, such as nonspatial policies which include fiscal, industrial, defense, equalization, and agricultural and immigration policies. This indicates that governments should place great importance on the evaluation of urban impacts by the agencies responsible for such policies and, where necessary, formulate urban development policies that realistically assess the effects of nonspatial national policies.

Urbanization must be ranked as one of the world's most fundamental and radical changes in the twentieth century. The world's population living in urban centers will have jumped from a mere 13 percent around the turn of the century to over 50 percent by its end. For the first time in history, the majority of the world population will be living in urban areas. The impact of such radical spatial and occupational population shifts will be acutely felt in Africa.

Should the urbanization trends continue as expected, the situation in Africa will become particularly critical; the continent is the poorest of the LDCs and cannot manage effectively a growing urban population and the resulting socioeconomic concentration. Regardless, rapid population and urban growth are likely to occur in the poorest areas, and Africa is moving toward an urban transformation of major proportions. Its spatial impacts and consequences are likely to be highly uneven among countries as well as urban centers within the urban settlement systems. The largest urban centers will continue to grow faster than medium-sized and small urban centers. Indeed urban centers with one million inhabitants are likely to triple in size over the period. Africa is expected to have 64 urban centers with one million in population by the end of the century.

The excessive concentration of large urban centers already prevails with varying degrees. By 2025, Africa will probably have four supercities with over five million in population each (Cairo, Kinshasa, Lagos, and Nairobi). The sheer size, pace of growth, and relative geographical distribution of the major urban concentrations should underscore their economic and political impacts on interactions and interdependencies within their countries.

This growth would not present a serious problem should it occur only in small and intermediate-sized urban centers (Obudho and Aduwo, 1990:51–68). This growth, however, will be in primate urban centers. For example, Cairo, the capital and primate urban center in Egypt, is the largest city in Africa with a 1970 population of about 5.6 million. The United Nations Economic Commission for Africa estimates that Cairo will be over 15 million in 2000. Similarly high rates of population growth will occur in Lagos, Kinshasa, Alexandria, El-Giza, Algiers, Casablanca, Addis Ababa, Johannesburg, Cape Town, and Rand (United

Nations, 1989). The combination of low levels of urbanization and high rates of urban growth makes the formulation and implementation of sound national urban policies very critical to the economic and social development in Africa.

In 1950 there were only 16 countries with urban centers of 100,000 or more inhabitants. Now there are 125 centers with at least 100,000 population having a total population of 27.6 million people. Over the 20-year period, urban centers reaching the 100,000 threshold accounted for the highest percent of the total population in urban centers with 20,000 or more inhabitants. In addition, there are some 609 urban centers with at least 20,000 inhabitants with a total population of 76.3 million. Northern Africa has the largest number with a total population of 25.3 million inhabitants (Table 4.1). Most centers with at least 20,000 inhabitants are concentrated in the 20,000–50,000 size group accounting for about 57 percent of all centers of this size but only 13 percent of the total population (Table 4.2).

Large urban centers play an important role in urbanization which is closely related to their primary function in many African countries. In most cases the growth rates of these principal urban centers are exceptionally high. The tendency in Africa is for national urbanization to favor large urban centers. A special aspect of the development of large urban centers is the emergence of centers of a million population, which are increasing in number. In 1950, Cairo-Giza-Imbaba and Alexandria were the only two urban centers in Africa that had a million inhabitants. Johannesburg and Casablanca joined the group in 1960. By 1970 and 1980, the numbers increased to 8 then 19, respectively, with the majority of these urban centers in sub-Saharan Africa. By 1990 and 2000, it is projected that there will be 38 and 59 such centers, respectively (Table 4.3). In 1950, the total population of these centers was 3.5 million, and it went to 36.2 million in 1980. By the end of this century, the millionaire urban centers will likely have a population of 153.6 million.

The unprecedented increase in Africa's urban population and its immediate growth prospects have ominous economic and social implications for employment, education, and health. Unless positive spatial planning measures are taken, this rapid urban proliferation could certainly exacerbate the prevailing ills associated with the rapid expansion of spontaneous settlement (Obudho and Mhlanga, 1988).

NATIONAL AND REGIONAL VARIATIONS

Low levels of urbanization are characteristic of most regions except in northern and southern Africa. However, projections indicate that middle, western, and eastern Africa will be more than 50 percent urbanized by 2025.

Northern Africa

Northern African countries have passed various stages of urban growth and decline. Except for Sudan, all are highly urbanized. About a quarter of the total

Table 4.1
Regional Urbanization Trends in Africa, 1980–2020 (in Millions)

	1980		2000		2020	
Region	Population	Percent	Population	Percent	Population	Percent
Eastern	21.5	15.1	77.5	32.0	206.0	42.6
Middle	16.4	31.6	43.9	51.4	95.3	61.7
Northern	43.0	39.9	88.8	50.6	154.1	63.0
Southern	16.3	49.6	33.2	60.9	59.5	71.0
Western	32.0	22.2	96.7	34.9	250.8	50.0
Total	129.3	27.0	340.1	42.3	765.6	52.2

Table 4.2
Size Distribution of Africa's Urban Centers with 20,000 Inhabitants by Regions (in Numbers)

Size Group (in '000s)	Eastern	Central	Northern	Southern	Western	Total
1 million+	1	1	5	4	1	12
500-1 million	4	1	-	3	5	14
100-500	18	15	42	12	38	125
50-100	25	15	34	8	27	109
20-50	35	47	132	40	95	349
Total	83	80	213	67	166	609

Source: Compiled from United Nations Economic Commision for Africa, 1980.

population in 1960 lived in urban centers of at least 20,000, and the proportion in centers of 100,000 population was 13 percent. The country with the highest percentage of urbanization in 1980 was Algeria (61), closely followed by Sahrawi (53), Libya (52), Tunisia (52), Egypt (45), and Sudan (25), the only country in the region with less than the African average of 29 percent in 1980. The maximum concentration of cities occurs in Morocco, where 80 percent of the urban population live in centers of at least 100,000 inhabitants. In Egypt the proportion was 77 percent.

The northern African region has 213 centers with at least 20,000 inhabitants with almost half in Egypt. Cairo-El Giza-Imbaba is the most populous center, followed by Alexandria, Casablanca, Algiers, and Tunis. Of all North African countries, the one with the highest annual average 1980 to 1985 growth rate was Libya (6.5 percent), followed by Algeria (5.4 percent), and Morocco (4.9 percent). These high urban growth rates are expected to decline by 2025 mainly due to a greater urban natural increase than rural to urban migration.

Western Africa

Western Africa, like northern Africa, has an indigenous African tradition. The most remarkable example is the so-called African metropolis which developed a complex pattern of rural-urban interdependence (Peel, 1980:269–277; Gugler and Flanagan, 1978). In addition, a number of old, established precolonial centers

Table 4.3
Africa's Urban Agglomerations of a Million Inhabitants, 1990 and 2000

Agglomeration	Population (millions)		Rank (World)		Annual Growth Rate (Percent) 1985-1990	Percent of Total Population, 1990
	1990	2000	1990	2000		
Abidjan	2.2	3.5	103	80	5.4	18.1
Accra	1.1	1.5	247	221	2.3	7.3
Addis Ababa	1.9	3.1	120	92	4.7	3.8
Alexandria	3.7	5.1	46	44	3.4	7.0
Algiers	3.0	4.5	67	52	4.1	12.2
Cairo	9.0	11.8	15	18	2.6	17.2
Cape Town	2.3	3.2	91	85	3.6	6.5
Casablanca	3.3	4.6	62	50	3.8	12.8
Dakar	1.5	2.3	168	139	4.2	20.4
Dar es Salaam	1.7	3.1	112	94	3.9	16.3
Durban	1.1	1.3	225	250	1.4	3.0

Table 4.3 (Continued)

Agglomeration	Population (millions)		Rank (World)		Annual Growth Rate (Percent) 1985-1990	Percent of Total Population, 1990
	1990	2000	1990	2000		
East Rand	1.1	1.4	242	239	1.4	3.2
Ibadan	1.3	2.0	191	161	3.4	1.2
Johannesburg	1.7	2.0	136	154	1.2	4.9
Khartoum	1.9	3.2	118	87	4.8	7.7
Kinshasa	3.5	5.5	53	38	4.6	9.9
Lagos	7.7	12.9	21	13	5.6	7.1
Luanda	1.7	2.9	135	104	5.8	17.1
Nairobi	1.5	2.7	167	113	5.7	6.3
Rabat	1.1	1.5	252	216	3.7	4.3
Tunis	1.6	2.2	149	139	3.7	20.0

Source: Compiled from United Nations, 1990.

such as Kano and Kumasi prospered in West Africa for many years. However, most centers in Anglophone and Francophone West Africa were established during the colonial period. The degree of urbanization in western Africa is less than in northern or southern Africa, but greater than in eastern and central Africa. In 1980, the Côte d'Ivoire had the relatively largest urban population (38 percent), followed by Ghana (36 percent), and Mauritania (36 percent). According to the latest estimates, there are 44 urban centers in western Africa with 100,000 or more inhabitants. Lagos has the largest population in the region with 2.5 million (1980), and 22 of the remaining centers have populations over 200,000.

The urban growth rate is highest in Senegal, followed by Nigeria, Ghana, Côte d'Ivoire, and Sierra Leone.

Middle Africa

Historically, this region had the lowest level of urbanization in Africa (Parker, 1975). Since 1965 the rate of urbanization has increased, and by 1980, 85 percent of the residents lived in urban areas. Since 1961, high rates of urbanization have occurred in Gabon, Burundi, Congo, Zaire, and the Central African Republic. In 1980 the Central African Republic (41 percent) had a high proportion living in urban centers, and in all other countries the percentage was more than the African average of 29 percent. Only Angola, Cameroon, Central African Republic, Chad, Congo, Gabon, and Zaire have urban centers exceeding 100,000. Of 18 urban centers in the region, 11 are in Zaire, with the largest city of Kinshasa having a population of about 3.1 million in 1980. The second largest is Katanga (1.1 million in 1980).

Eastern Africa

Eastern Africa has the lowest level of urbanization (12 percent) despite the fact that it is one of the most densely populated regions in Africa (Obudho, 1983, 1986). The highest level of urbanization in 1980 was in Djibouti (74 percent), followed by Réunion (55 percent), and Mauritius (52 percent).

Most eastern African countries are basically agricultural with very few large-scale industrial or mining bases (Hutton, 1972; Kanyeihamba and McAuslan, 1978; and Soja and Weaver, 1976). The annual rate of urban growth for eastern Africa is one of the highest in Africa; between 1960 and 1980, the average annual rate of increase was over 6 percent.

With a mere 5 percent of its population in urban centers, eastern Africa is the least urbanized of all regions. Like western Africa, urbanization is high in Djibouti, where 58 percent live in urban localities with 20,000 or more inhabitants, followed by Réunion (45 percent) and Mauritius (30 percent). There are 16 urban centers in eastern Africa having 100,000 or more inhabitants, and these are located in 10 countries. The urban centers with the largest 1980 populations are Addis Ababa (1.7 million), followed by Nairobi (1.3 million), and Dar es

Salaam (1.1 million). Thus, urban primacy is clearly a distinct feature of urbanization in this region.

Southern Africa

Thirty-five percent of the 1965 population of South Africa was living in urban centers with 20,000 or more inhabitants. Moreover, 75 percent of South Africa's population was in urban centers in 1985. Johannesburg (1.8 million in 1980) is one of the eight African urban centers with more than a million inhabitants, and the Republic of South Africa also has the four most populous urban centers in southern Africa—Cape Town (1.5 million), Durban (1.1 million), and East Rand (1.2 million). Urbanization in southern Africa is high because of large industrial bases and mining activities in the region. However, the rate of urbanization is high in the relatively low urbanized countries of Botswana and Namibia. With the recent political independence of Namibia its urbanization pattern will probably accelerate in the future.

URBAN GROWTH AND RURAL STAGNATION

The degree of urbanization and the rate of growth of the urban population in Africa vary considerably from country to country and from one region to another. Each subregion has been treated separately and comparisons made between regions. Except for western and northern Africa, urbanization is essentially a twentieth-century phenomenon and basically a product of Africa's colonial history (Steel, 1961:253). The southern region has the highest rate of urbanization; the northern region has the longest tradition of urbanization; the western region and parts of the middle region have the longest trend of urbanization; and the eastern region is the least urbanized despite its long history of coastal urbanization.

Africa's future urban population increases will come more and more from natural increase than from rural-urban migration. Obviously, the influx of large numbers into African urban centers puts an added strain on basic urban services and facilities. At the same time, it also tends to stagnate development in rural areas because the young and the educated have left in the rural-urban migration exodus. Nevertheless, most Africans continue to live in rural areas, deriving their livelihood from various forms of agriculture that range from subsistence farming to the production of commercial crops.

The rate of urbanization has especially affected the major urban centers. The role of large cities has been primate and parasitic in that they have continued to attract rural inhabitants and other development activities at the expense of other areas. These centers have, therefore, become the sites of a wide variety of social, economic, and environmental problems including marginality since their excessive growth occurred at the expense of smaller urban centers and rural areas. As a consequence of this biased development, the influx of rural people to urban areas creates many practical administrative difficulties in planning and implementing local public services.

The policy problems that have beset Africa since independence are severe and can be identified everywhere, being accompanied by a conspicuous failure to predict and plan for urban growth. Most urban governments have simply been unable to grasp the implications of a population that doubles every nine years. Overconcentration has compounded the problems, as many new central institutions have assumed or claimed more responsibility than they can handle. The consequence has been hypertrophy at the center and atrophy at the local level.

Most urban residents earn low incomes and cannot pay for basic services and facilities provided in urban centers. Unless positive planning measures are taken, the rapid increase of those in poverty is likely to exacerbate the prevailing ills associated with the rapid expansion of slums and squatter settlements.

The present rate of population growth in Africa is about twice as high as in industrial Europe in the nineteenth century. The recent experience of other developing areas suggests that Africa is in the early phase of accelerating population growth (Coale, 1968:186).

Despite the fact that the majority of African countries are predominantly rural, most urban centers will increase faster than their social amenities. The reasons for the high rural to urban migration and overurbanization, according to J. Barry Riddel (1975:271), include the "wage differential thesis, bright lights hypothesis, . . . the lure of labour recruiters, the new and extended transportation networks and the vehicles which ply them, land hunger, and the population pressure." This knowledge about urbanward migration has not been applied to social, physical, and economic planning.

CONCLUSION

The policies of the colonial authorities, influenced as they were by an industrial culture, created two rather distinct regions—the urban areas and the country. The pattern continued after independence, when

> various national governments started building upon the foundation of the development strategy initially laid by the colonial. . . . were heavily concentrated in the towns to the neglect of rural areas. Thus, increasingly, the economies of these countries were marked by the uneasy coexistence between the rural, agriculture, low productivity, and the urban, industrial, high productivity sectors. The export-oriented development path and the concentration of massive investment in a few cities were a major cause of regional inequality which in turn paved the way for migration. In such a situation, the choice facing the migrant with respect to the decision to migrate and where to go is, therefore, largely predetermined by the overall development strategy, in the sense that the location of productive activities virtually determines the intensity, pattern and direction of migration. (Adepoju, 1977:215)

Programs of rural deconcentration or planning from below have been advocated by Obudho (1982:1–7). Supposedly the agglomeration of industrial and commercial activities in a few centers maximizes economic benefits under conditions of economic "takeoff." In countries with vast land areas such as Algeria, Sudan, and Zaire, the development of growth points away from the primate urban centers that bring urban amenities closer to remote rural dwellers. The question becomes really one of priorities, of whether the most important objective is industrialization, equitable distribution of government-provided facilities across the nation, the rapid advancement of the few, or the most gradual but ultimately most momentous progress of the many, the achievement of modernization along Western lines or the creation of the African synthesis, taking the best from elsewhere when appropriate but building on an African foundation (Obudho and El-Shakhs, 1979). African planners and government officials must choose between the two development strategies, namely, the growth pole strategy, advocating the center-down approach, and the agropolitan approach, essentially a bottom-up approach emphasizing territorial integration and inward planning with a system of "selective spatial closure" (Mehretu and Campbell, 1982:91–110; Friedman, 1982:3–20; Obudho and Aduwo, 1990). Obviously, the most effective development approach appropriate for Africa is that from below, because it allows for self-reliance, spatial equity, local participation, devolution, and territorial integration.

Certainly, African spatial planners must first seriously consider the improvement of the welfare of people in the rural informal sector, then second, concentrate on the urban informal sectors. Perhaps one of the best ways to achieve this development strategy is to concentrate planning in the small and intermediate-sized urban centers (Obudho and Aduwo, 1990). Before these small centers can succeed as "mini" growth centers for the rural areas, there must be a fundamental change in the relationship between the small and intermediate-sized urban centers and their umland. Without this change any extension of the urban hierarchy to the lower levels may simply increase the exploitation of the rural people (Southall, 1979; Baker, 1990).

A policy of encouraging development at the metropolitan levels without distributing development planning at small or intermediate-sized urban centers will only magnify rural-urban migration, a situation that all spatial planners are trying to avoid. The critical role of development planning should be that of developing urban centers as marketing centers rather than administrative centers. The overriding criteria for the organization and planning of the formation of urban centers in space should be where it would be possible to install social amenities to serve the rural population.

REFERENCES

Adepoju, A. 1977. "Migration and Development in Tropical Africa: Some Research Priorities." *African Affairs* 76:210–225.

Baker, Jonathan. 1990. *Small Town Africa: Studies in Rural-Urban Interaction.* Uppsala: Scandinavian Institute of African Studies.

Caldwell, J. C. 1969. *African Rural-Urban Migration: The Movement to Ghana's Towns.* New York: Columbia University Press.

Coale, Ansley J. 1968. "Estimates of Fertility and Mortality in Tropical Africa." In *The Population of Tropical Africa,* edited by John C. Caldwell and Chukuka Okonjo, 179–186. New York: Columbia University Press.

El-Shakhs, Salah, and R. A. Obudho. 1974. *Urbanization, National Development and Regional Planning in Africa.* New York: Praeger.

Friedman J. 1982. "Regional Planning for Rural Mobilization in Africa." *Rural Africana* N.S., 12–13:3–20.

Gugler, J., and W. Flanagan. 1978. *Urbanization and Social Change in West Africa.* Cambridge: Cambridge University Press.

Hance, William A. 1970. *Population, Migration and Urbanization in Africa.* New York: Columbia University Press.

Howard, Allen. 1975. "Pre-colonial Centres and Regional Systems in Africa." *Pan African Journal* 8:247–270.

Hull, R. W. 1976. *African Cities and Towns before the European Conquest.* New York: Norton.

Hutton, J. 1972. *Urban Challenge in East Africa.* Nairobi: East Africa Publishing House.

Kanyeihamba, G. W., and J. P. W. B. McAuslan. 1978. *Urban Legal Problems in East Africa.* Uppsala: Scandinavian Institute of African Studies.

Mehretu, Assefa, and David J. Campbell. 1982. "Regional Planning for Small Communities in Rural Africa: A Critical Survey." *Rural Africana* 12–13:91–110.

Miner, Horace. 1967. "The City and Modernization: An Introduction." In *The City in Modern Africa,* edited by Horace Miner, 1–20. New York: Praeger.

Obudho, R. A. 1982. "Planning From Below or Above in Africa: An Introduction." *African Urban Studies* 13:1–7.

———. 1983. "National Urban Policy in East Africa." *Regional Development Dialogue* 4:87–110.

———. 1985. *Demography, Urbanization, and Spatial Planning in Kenya: A Bibliographical Survey.* Westport, Conn.: Greenwood Press.

———. 1986. "The Spatial Structure of Urbanization and Planning in East Africa." In *Urban Systems in Transition,* edited by J. G. Borchert, I. S. Bourne, and R. Sinclair, 171–193. Amsterdam/Utrecht: Netherlands Geographical Studies.

Obudho, R. A., and G. O. Aduwo. 1990. "Small Urban Centres and the Spatial Planning in Kenya." In *Small Town Africa: Studies in Rural-Urban Interaction,* edited by Jonathan Baker, 51–68. Uppsala: Scandinavian Institute of African Studies.

Obudho, R. A., and Salah El-Shakhs. 1979. *Development Urban Systems in Africa.* New York: Praeger.

Obudho, R. A., and C. E. Mhlanga. 1988. *Slum and Squatter Settlement in Africa: Towards A Planning Strategy.* New York: Praeger.

O'Connor, Anthony M. 1982. *Urbanization in Tropical Africa: An Annotated Bibliography.* Boston: G. K. Hall.

———. 1983. *The African City.* London: Hutchinson.

Parker, D. J. 1975. *Town and Country in Central and Eastern Africa.* London: Oxford University Press.

Peel, J. D. Y. 1980. ''Urbanization and Urban History in West Africa.'' *Journal of African History* 21:269–277.

Riddel, J. Barry. 1975. ''Population Migration and Urbanization in Tropical Africa.'' *Pan African Journal* 8:271–285.

Soja, Edward W., and C. E. Weaver. 1976. ''Urbanization and Underdevelopment in East Africa.'' In *Urbanization and Counterurbanization,* edited by Brian J. L. Berry, 233–266. Beverly Hills: Sage.

Southall, Aidan. 1979. *Small Urban Centers in Rural Development in Africa.* Madison: African Studies Program, University of Wisconsin.

Steel, R. W. 1961. ''The Towns of Tropical Africa.'' In *Essays on African Population,* edited by K. M. Barbour and R. M. Prothero, 249–278. New York: Praeger.

Trewartha, G. T., and W. Zelinsky. 1954. ''Population Patterns in Tropical Africa.'' *Annals of the Association of American Geographers* 44:135–162.

United Nations. 1980. *Patterns of Urban and Rural Population Growth.* New York.

———. 1982. *Estimates and Projections of Urban, Rural and City Populations, 1950–2025: The 1980 Assessment.* New York.

———. 1986. *Urban and Rural Population Projections 1950–2025: The 1984 Assessment.* New York.

———. 1989. *Prospects of World Urban Urbanization.* New York.

United Nations. Economic Commission for Africa. 1980. *Demographic Handbook for Africa.* Addis Ababa.

Vennetier, P. 1970. *Les Villes De l'Afrique Noire.* Paris: Masson.

5

Urbanization during the Postcolonial Days

H. Max Miller and Ram N. Singh

The African colonies obtained their independence between 1910 and 1980. Although urbanization was well underway in some colonies before they achieved their independence, urbanization has greatly accelerated only since that time. Only two African cities had reached a population of at least one million by 1950, the Egyptian cities of Cairo and Alexandria. Casablanca, Morocco, was the next largest agglomeration with around 710,000 inhabitants, and Cape Town, South Africa, followed with about 620,000 (Tables 5.1, 5.2). Of the sub-Saharan countries that began their major urbanization in the colonial period, Dakar (Senegal) and Addis Ababa (Ethiopia) had the most populous urban agglomerations in 1950, about 210,000 to 220,000 inhabitants. The Antananarivo and Kinshasa agglomerations had reached 170,000 to 180,000 population and Luanda and Harare had agglomerations of 100,000 to 140,000 inhabitants (Table 5.1). Thus, by 1950 the urban agglomerations of six newly urbanized areas in sub-Saharan Africa had attained a population of 100,000 inhabitants or more.

After independence the urban agglomerations in the capital cities of another 12 countries reached at least 50,000 inhabitants: Botswana, Cape Verde, Djibouti, Gabon, Gambia, Guinea-Bissau, Mauritania, Mauritius, Namibia, Réunion, Malawi, and Rwanda. That left only eight African countries with urban agglomerations with fewer than 50,000 inhabitants: Comoros, Equatorial Guinea, Lesotho, St. Helena, São Tomé and Príncipe, Seychelles, Swaziland, and Western Sahara.

Table 5.1

Urbanization of African Countries during the Postcolonial Period: Agglomerations That Reached 50,000 Inhabitants by 1950

Urban Agglomeration	Country	Date of Independence	Estimated Population		
			1950	Independence	1990
Cape Town	South Africa	1910	618,000	160,000	2,310,000
Dakar	Senegal	1960	223,000	366,000	1,492,000
Addis Ababa	Ethiopia	----	209,000	-------	1,891,000
Antananarivo	Madagascar	1960	180,000	250,000	675,000
Kinshasa	Zaire	1960	173,000	451,000	3,505,000
Luanda	Angola	1975	138,000	669,000	1,717,000
Nairobi	Kenya	1963	87,000	275,000	1,503,000
Harare	Zimbabwe	1980	110,000	590,000	851,000
Maputo	Mozambique	1975	91,000	532,000	1,588,000
Dar es Salaam	Tanzania	1961,1963	78,000	180,000	1,657,000
Abidjan	Ivory Coast	1960	59,000	180,000	2,168,000
Brazzaville	Congo	1960	60,000	130,000	630,000

Bamako	Mali	1960	60,000	130,000	661,000
Bujumbura	Burundi	1962	50,000	70,000	246,000
Monrovia	Liberia	----	50,000	-------	668,000
Freetown	Sierra Leone	1961	50,000	100,000	690,000
Mogadishu	Somalia	1960	50,000	90,000	718,000
Kampala	Uganda	1962	50,000	150,000	689,000
Bangui	Cen. Afr. Rep.	1960	40,000	90,000	725,000
Porto-Novo	Benin	1960	40,000	60,000	213,000
Conakry	Guinea	1958	39,000	100,000	1,296,000
Lomé	Togo	1960	40,000	80,000	514,000
Ndjamena	Chad	1960	40,000	80,000	728,000
Niamey	Niger	1960	30,000	60,000	583,000
Ouagadougou	Burkina Faso	1960	30,000	60,000	413,000
Yaoundé	Cameroon	1960	30,000	70,000	768,000
Lusaka	Zambia	1964	30,000	150,000	985,000

Source: Compiled from United Nations, 1989b, 1991.

Urban agglomerations are comprised of central cities and surrounding urbanized areas.

Table 5.2
African Urban Agglomerations with an Estimated Population of One Million or More Inhabitants in 1990

Urban Agglomerations	Population (in Millions) for Selected Years				
	1950	1970	1985	1990	2000
Cairo/Giza	2.41	5.33	7.92	9.04	11.83
Lagos	.29	2.03	5.83	7.71	12.89
Alexandria	1.04	1.99	3.11	3.68	5.11
Casablanca	.71	1.51	2.66	3.21	4.56
Kinshasa	.17	1.37	2.78	3.51	5.52
Algier	.44	1.32	2.46	3.03	4.53
Cape Town	.62	1.11	1.93	2.31	3.18
Addis Ababa	.21	.73	1.49	1.89	3.13
Khartoum	.18	.66	1.53	1.95	3.16
Abidjan	.06	.55	1.65	2.17	3.53
Luanda	.14	.46	1.28	1.72	2.87
Tunis	.47	.74	1.36	1.64	2.25
Accra	.25	.74	.98	1.10	1.50
Tripoli	.11	.40	1.54	2.06	3.16
Dar es Salaam	.08	.39	1.17	1.66	3.13
Nairobi	.09	.53	1.13	1.50	2.72
Dakar	.22	.60	1.21	1.49	2.28
Conakry	.04	.32	.96	1.30	2.26
Maputo	.09	.37	1.09	1.59	3.14
Rabat	.17	.50	.89	1.07	1.52
Ibadan	.43	.75	1.12	1.33	1.95

Source: Compiled from United Nations, 1991.

URBAN POPULATION CHANGE IN AFRICA DURING INDEPENDENCE

The rural population had been relatively immobile during colonial days, for Africa was the least urbanized region in the world in 1950, with only 15 percent of its inhabitants living in urban centers (United Nations, 1989b). During the colonial period Africans were forbidden to live permanently in the cities of eastern and southern Africa. European administrators were, of course, in charge of municipal governments and services, and the number of African laborers

Table 5.3
Urban Population Estimates and Projections of Africa, by Region, 1950–2025

Region	Urban Population (000)			Percentage of Total Population Living in Urban Areas		
	1950	1980	2025	1950	1980	2025
Africa	32,249	132,533	911,735	15	28	57
Northern Africa	12,667	42,816	181,981	25	40	66
Eastern Africa	3,405	21,605	254,138	5	15	47
Middle Africa	3,747	16,098	122,328	14	31	64
Southern Africa	5,972	15,627	59,123	38	48	74
Western Africa	6,457	36,387	294,165	10	26	58

Source: Compiled from United Nations, 1991.

needed fluctuated from one colony to another from time to time. Most workers employed by municipal governments and private companies were housed in dormitory-like quarters in compounds and were considered as transients rather than permanent city dwellers (Muwonge, 1980). Europeans forbade other eastern and southern Africans to reside permanently in cities.

In contrast, Africans in the indigenous West African cities during the colonial period purchased urban property, erected city homes, and migrated freely between rural and urban areas (Gugler and Flanagan, 1978). However, the typical cities of colonial origin in eastern and southern Africa were considered "European cities" and regarded as "White Man's Country" in which Africans had no right to permanent settlement (O'Connor, 1983).

When the African colonies obtained their independence, movement to cities increased sharply. Urbanization was greatly accelerated by the movement of millions from the rapidly deteriorating agricultural sector where most migrants lived in rural villages. Frequent droughts, coupled with overgrazing, soil erosion, and other conditions that adversely affected crop and livestock production were factors contributing to millions of rural migrants leaving for urban areas. Under the pressures of poverty and unemployment, millions were forced into slums in urban areas. Recent estimates of the percentage of the population living in the shantytowns of 20 major African cities range from 30 percent in Nairobi to 90 percent in Addis Ababa (Obudho and Mhlanga, 1988).

With the huge exodus out of the agricultural areas, Africa had the highest rate of urban development of all regions in the world. For example, the number of urban Africans increased from 32 million in 1950 to about 133 million in 1980 (Table 5.3). In 1990, the number of African agglomerations with at least one million inhabitants had increased to 21 from 2 in 1950 (Table 5.2). In addition to these large metropolises, there are probably an equal number with half a million inhabitants. Most are capital cities strategically located in coastal sites (Christopher, 1985).

The urban areas had much larger population gains after independence than before. For example, the number of inhabitants in the urban agglomerations of the capital cities increased more than 110 percent between 1950 and the date of their independence. However, the population of the urban agglomerations of the capital cities increased approximately 430 percent between 1950 and 1990. For the entire 40-year period since 1950, the number of inhabitants in the sub-Saharan urban agglomerations of the national capitals increased more than 10 times. The urban population outside the capital cities grew rapidly too, about 5 times since 1950—about half that of the urban agglomerations. The major noncapital cities include Johannesburg, Douala, Lubumbashi, and Mombasa.

In numerical terms the population of the urban agglomerations of the capital cities in sub-Saharan Africa increased from 2.5 million in 1950 to over 27 million in 1990, a gain of about 25 million or 1,017 percent during the 40-year period (Table 5.4). Moveover, the urban population in these same countries residing outside these urban agglomerations increased nearly 60 million, over 510 percent. This is truly a major redistribution and concentration of the population unequalled on any other continent in such a short period of time.

Africa is the most rapidly growing continent in the world, and its large primate cities are experiencing relatively large population increases. While some of its urban agglomerations will probably reach an equilibrium in the future, most will likely continue their rapid growth as they absorb rural migrants.

MIGRATION INTO THE MAJOR CITIES SINCE INDEPENDENCE

Part of the rapid urban population growth since independence is a result of an excess of births over deaths, or natural increase. However, the migration of persons in outlying areas has brought millions of new residents to the large urban agglomerations. One method of assessing the contribution of migration to urban population growth is to examine the relative importance of lifetime migration. In this context migration into Africa's major cities may be analyzed in terms of the place of birth of the urban inhabitants. Every urban resident born outside the city, whether within that country or in some other country, is considered a migrant. Therefore, both internal and international migrants into cities are included. The migration rate of each city was calculated using the percentage of inhabitants born outside the city as determined by population censuses except in the Republic of South Africa. Lifetime migration patterns of cities will be examined for the following three geographic areas of Africa: sub-Saharan Africa excluding South Africa, North Africa, and the Republic of South Africa.

Table 5.4
Urban Inhabitants Living In and Outside the Urban Agglomerations of Sub-Saharan Africa, 1950–90 (in Millions)

Major Regions	Urban Population of Countries with Capital City Urban Agglomerations	Population in Urban Agglomerations of Capitals	Other Urban Population	Total Urban Population	Urban Agglomerations of Capitals	Other Urban Population
Eastern Africa	2,271	791	1,480	33,997	9,070	24,927
Middle Africa	3,650	481	3,169	25,770	8,073	17,697
Southern Africa	5,898	618	5,280	20,991	2,310	18,681
Western Africa	2,187	571	1,616	17,214	8,030	9,184
Total	14,007	2,461	11,546	97,972	27,483	70,489

Source: Compiled from United Nations, 1989b, 1991.

Table 5.5
Percentage of the Total Population Born Outside of Each West African City, 1950–63

City	Country	Year	Percent of Population Born Outside City
Abidjan	Ivory Coast	1963	61
Accra	Ghana	1960	53
Lagos	Nigeria	1950	60
Bamako	Mali	1961	53
Cotonou	Benin	1961	66
Dakar	Senegal	1960	51
Lomé	Togo	1961	51
Ouagadougou	Burkina Faso	1962	38
Bobo-Dioulasso	Burkina Faso	1959	44
Bathurst[1]	Gambia	1962	38

[1]Bathurst was founded in 1816 by the British. In 1973 this capital city was renamed Banjul.

Sub-Saharan Africa Excluding South Africa

Since independence the major population centers of West Africa have attracted comparatively large numbers of migrants (Table 5.5). In the 1950–60 period around half of the urban inhabitants had been born outside the cities and in Abidjan, Lagos, and Cotonou at least 60 percent were lifetime migrants born outside the cities. Apparently, migration accounted for two-thirds of Nigeria's overall urban population growth between 1952 and 1963 (Mabogunje, 1977).

After 1970 the relative magnitude of the population movements into the major cities of sub-Saharan Africa increased (Table 5.6). Prior to this time about half of the city residents were lifetime migrants into the cities. By 1970, an average of 60 percent of the inhabitants of the 14 major cities in Table 5.6 were born outside the cities. In 1979 nearly three out of every four Nairobi inhabitants had migrated to that city during their lives. Also, in 1976 over 70 percent of Bamako's residents were migrants from outside the city.

Obviously, the large metropolises in sub-Saharan Africa depend heavily upon black migrants for nearly two-thirds of their population growth. The European pass laws no longer hinder their movement to cities, and some of the stability and security once offered by rural villages has disappeared. The migration patterns of Zimbabwe, Botswana, and other countries indicate that about half of the migrants to sub-Saharan Africa's rapidly growing population centers come from rural areas.

Table 5.6
Lifetime Migration into Selected Cities in Sub-Saharan Africa, 1970–83

City	Country	Year	Total Population of city	Number Born outside city	Percent Born outside city
Nairobi	Kenya	1979	827,775	615,942	74
Dar es Salaam	Tanzania	1978	757,346	484,803	64
Abidjan	Ivory Coast	1975	703,313	487,105	69
Harare	Zimbabwe	1982	621,100	417,190	67
Bamako	Mali	1976	419,239	295,983	71
Antananarivo	Madagascar	1975	406,366	56,700	14
Bulawayo	Zimbabwe	1982	396,500	257,730	65
Mogadishu	Somalia	1975	350,000	176,050	50
Yaoundé	Cameroon	1976	291,071	192,942	66
Blantyre	Malawi	1977	219,011	114,972	52
Ouagadougou	Burkina Faso	1975	172,661	94,282	55
Lomé	Togo	1970	148,300	70,700	48
Lilongwe	Malawi	1977	98,718	11,644	12
Banjul	Gambia	1983	44,188	17,109	39
	Total		5,455,588	3,293,152	60

Source: Compiled from censuses of population of each country.

Table 5.7
Lifetime Migration into the Cities of North Africa, 1955–71

City	Country	Year	Percent Born Outside City
Cairo	Egypt	1960	38
Alexandria	Egypt	1960	29
Giza	Egypt	1960	21
Greater Khartoum	Sudan	1955-56	48
Tripoli	Libya	1964	23
Benhazi	Libya	1964	16
Tunis	Tunisia	1966	34
Casablanca	Morocco	1960	32
Casablanca	Morocco	1971	32
Rabat	Morocco	1960	28
Rabat	Morocco	1971	32

Source: Compiled from censuses of population of each country.

North Africa

Since the 1960s, approximately a third of the population growth in the major North African cities has been a result of migration (Tables 5.7 and 5.8). Accordingly, lifetime migration into the major cities of North Africa has been substantially less than into the cities of sub-Saharan Africa. In North Africa the relative number of migrants to Giza and Rabat increased after 1960, but the comparative number to Cairo and Alexandria declined. Moreover, Cairo and Alexandria had considerably lower rates of in-migration than the largest cities in sub-Saharan Africa. Rabat and Sale were the only two North African cities in which lifetime migration accounted for as much as half of the urban population growth (Table 5.8).

Obviously, many factors are responsible for the differences predominantly in the migration patterns of whites to North African cities and the movement of blacks to the cities of sub-Saharan Africa. First, in 1950 at the onset of independence, the North African cities were much more highly urbanized than cities in sub-Saharan Africa, except for a few in West Africa whose origin predated European colonialism. Consequently, lifetime migration and population growth has been much more rapid in the major sub-Saharan African cities than in the North African cities. Second, other factors such as instability in rural areas and declines in the agricultural economy have probably resulted in a greater volume of lifetime migration to the cities of sub-Saharan Africa than to those in North Africa.

Table 5.8
Lifetime Migration into the Cities of North Africa, 1976–84

City	Country	Year	Total Population of city	Number Born outside city	Percent Born outside city
Cairo	Egypt	1976	5,018,779	1,377,658	27
Alexandria	Egypt	1976	2,303,539	431,676	19
Giza (Urban)	Egypt	1976	1,358,686	608,093	45
Casablanca[1]	Morocco	1982	2,139,206	854,064	40
Rabat	Morocco	1982	518,616	262,964	51
Sale	Morocco	1982	289,391	148,667	51
Tunis[2]	Tunisia	1984	775,600	272,730	35
Sfax[2]	Tunisia	1984	577,200	26,980	5
Oran[1]	Algeria	1977	484,287	223,651	46
	TOTAL		13,465,304	4,206,483	31

Source: Compiled from censuses of population of each country.

[1]Figures apply to the agglomerations of Casablanca and Oran.

[2]Figures apply to the governorats of Tunis and Sfax.

Republic of South Africa

The South African population censuses regularly obtain information on the country of birth of individuals. However, it is impossible to determine whether city residents are born inside or outside urban areas. Consequently, the patterns of urbanization and migration in South Africa must be examined in a somewhat different perspective than for North Africa and sub-Saharan Africa.

A period of rapid population growth and urbanization in South Africa followed the discovery of diamonds and gold. For example, the population of Johannesburg, founded in 1886 in the Witwatersrand range of gold deposits, increased from about 155,000 in 1904 to over 600,000 in 1946. Cape Town, the other dominant South African city, and one of the two national capitals, experienced population gains from 179,000 in 1904 to nearly 385,000 in 1946.

The total population of the five most populous cities increased consistently until 1970, when they reached a peak of slightly more than 3 million. During this time the African population continued to increase gradually until 1970, when more than 800,000 lived in the five cities (Table 5.9). They represented only 25 to 30 percent of the total population of these cities throughout this period even though they comprised more than two-thirds of the total population of South Africa.

Under the Group Areas Act over 620,000 blacks were evicted from their homes in these five cities after 1970, which may be considered an out-migration rate of 76 percent. By 1985 Africans comprised only 7 percent of the total population of Cape Town, Durban, Johannesburg, Port Elizabeth, and Pretoria combined, contrasted to 30 percent in 1946 and 1951.

Obviously, the provisions of the Group Areas Act and the recent Free Settlements Act prohibit Africans from living in cities in designated white areas (Pirie, 1983; Platzky and Walker, 1985). Certainly, these laws have hampered urbanization and resulted in population declines in four of the five most populous cities (Tomlinson, 1988; Mare, 1980). Only Cape Town had a larger population in 1985 than in 1970.

SUMMARY AND IMPLICATIONS

During European colonization urbanization occurred in only a nominal way. With the coming of independence and stagnation in the agricultural sector, migration to cities increased substantially, resulting in Africa's having the highest rate of urban population growth of all regions in the world.

After 1950 the patterns of urbanization and migration differed considerably in three different areas of Africa. About 60 percent of the recent population growth of the major cities in sub-Saharan Africa was attributed to lifetime migration; about one-third of the population growth of the major cities in North Africa was due to lifetime migration; and forced out-migration from the major cities in the Republic of South Africa accounted for black population losses of

Table 5.9

Total Population of the Five Most Populous Cities in South Africa by Color, 1904–85

		Population		
Year	Total	Whites	Africans	Percent African
1904	486,253	268,721	108,526	22
1911	591,460	297,348	145,311	25
1921	771,129	390,386	202,147	26
1936	1,243,943	619,227	339,239	27
1946	1,672,408	796,603	509,009	30
1951	1,908,738	862,272	573,834	30
1960	2,216,329	969,815	611,578	28
1970	3,026,279	1,239,461	813,569	27
1980	2,842,140	1,352,560	260,920	9
1985	2,759,190	1,243,467	193,266	7

Source: Censuses of Population.

The five cities are Cape Town, Durban, Johannesburg, Port Elizabeth, and Pretoria.

about 75 percent since 1970. Certainly, cities in these three areas of Africa reflect contrasting and divergent migration patterns.

The relative magnitude of the population movements into the major cities of sub-Saharan Africa like Nairobi and Abidjan seems very high. Nevertheless, in some of the very large megacities with millions of inhabitants, migration has also contributed more than natural increase to population growth. For example, at the beginning of the 1980–90 decade, 55 percent of the residents of Seoul and Delhi had been born outside of each respective city (United Nations, 1986a, 1986b). The stagnation and deterioration of employment opportunities in the agricultural sector in small towns and villages have obviously stimulated the large movements to the major centers in Africa.

Most African countries are concerned with spatial distribution problems, particularly primate city population growth and rural out-migration (United Nations, 1989a). For example, over 60 percent of the African governments have adopted policies to reduce the rate of primate city growth, and more than half adopted policies to encourage the growth of small towns and intermediate cities. Moreover, many countries are promoting growth centers and countermagnets. Although many countries have formulated different policies and programs to correct the distribution imbalance, generally they have proven ineffective.

One scholar suggests that development investments should be located in such a way to reduce an excessive concentration of population and productive activities in large primate cities. In order to accomplish this objective, he proposes policies to promote investment in physical infrastructure, marketing, small-scale manufacturing, and agroprocessing in secondary cities and towns (Rondinelli, 1985).

Ellen M. Brennan and Harry W. Richardson (1986) indicate that urban and rural problems are interrelated so closely that both sound rural and sound urban policies must be adopted. They suggest a number of wide-ranging policy measures, a few of which are the following: the adoption of new urban management methods, training methods, and procedures, the creation of new urban jobs at low per-job costs, credit schemes, the provision of basic industrial services, the promotion of viable public utility agencies, and the greater adoption of housing policies through site and service projects.

REFERENCES

Brennan, Ellen M., and Harry W. Richardson. 1986. "Urbanization and Urban Policy in Sub-Saharan Africa." *African Urban Quarterly* 1:20–42.

Cairo Demographic Centre (CDC). 1973. *Urbanization in Some Arab and African Countries*. Research Monograph Series, No. 4. Cairo: CDC.

Christopher, A. J. 1985. "Continuity and Change of African Capitals." *Geographical Review* 75:44–57.

Gugler, Josef, and William Flanagan. 1978. *Urbanization and Social Change in West Africa*. Cambridge: Cambridge University Press.

Mabogunje, Akin L. 1977. "The Urban Situation in Nigeria." In *Patterns of Urbani-*

zation: Comparative Country Studies, edited by Sidney Goldstein and David F. Sly, 2:569–641. Dolhain (Belgium): Ordina Editions.

Mare, Gerry. 1980. *African Population Relocation in South Africa.* Johannesburg: South African Institute of Race Relations.

Muwonge, Joe Wamala. 1980. "Urban Policy and Patterns of Low-Income Settlement in Nairobi, Kenya." *Population and Development Review* 6:595–613.

Obudho, Robert A., and Constance C. Mhlanga, eds. 1988. *Slum and Squatter Settlements in Sub-Saharan Africa.* New York: Praeger.

O'Connor, Anthony. 1983. *The African City.* New York: Africana Publishing Company.

Pirie, G. H. 1983. "Urban Population Removals in South Africa." *Geography* 68:347–349.

Platzky, Laurine, and Cherryl Walker. 1985. *The Surplus People: Forced Removals in South Africa.* Johannesburg: Ravan Press.

Rondinelli, Dennis A. 1985. "Population Distribution and Economic Development in Africa: The Need for Urbanization Policies." *Population Research and Policy Review* 4:173–196.

Tomlinson, Richard. 1988. "South Africa's Urban Policy: A New Form of Influx Control." *Urban Affairs Quarterly* 23:487–510.

United Nations. 1986a. *Population Growth and Policies in Mega-cities, Seoul.* Population Policy Paper No. 4. New York.

———. 1986b. *Population Growth and Policies in Mega-cities, Delhi.* Population Policy Paper No. 7. New York.

———. 1989a. *World Population Trends and Policies: 1989 Monitoring Report.* New York.

———. 1989b. *Prospects of World Urbanization, 1988.* Population Studies No. 112. New York.

———. 1991. *World Urbanization Prospects 1990: Estimates and Projections of Urban and Rural Populations and of Urban Agglomerations.* Population Studies No. 121. New York.

Part II

Urbanization in Selected Countries

6

Algeria

Keith Sutton

Algeria entered the 1990s with about half of its rapidly growing population living in urban centers. Three population censuses since independence in 1962 permit a detailed analysis of the country's urbanization trends despite the perennial problems of defining an "urban" center and of assessing the true population of an administratively underbounded capital city. While the population of the urban metropolis of Algiers now exceeds two million, the presence of strong regional centers such as Oran and Constantine, inherited from colonial times, recently has tended to reverse the dominance of the macrocephalic primate city of Algeria. Indeed, a major program of building new rural service centers, or "socialist villages," has markedly strengthened the lower ranks of the urban hierarchy. In contrast, a lack of metropolitan planning for Greater Algiers, together with a neglect of the emerging inner-city problems of the precolonial and colonial cores of the metropolises, has probably contributed to their slower population growth.

RECENT URBANIZATION IN ALGERIA

Algeria's long colonial experience (1830–1962) altered the urban system. The colonial extractive economy dictated the pattern of urbanization whereby port cities began to dominate the hierarchy. European populations—Italians, Spaniards, and French—dominated the major cities. Interior towns were increasingly resource sites, military control points, and more recently, places for an expanded European agriculture. Historic interior towns, such as Tlemcen, retained their integrity but declined, bypassed by the colonial economy and deprived of craft industries in the face of competitive European imports (Abu-Lughod, 1976).

Figure 6.1
Population Growth, Urban and Rural, 1886–1987

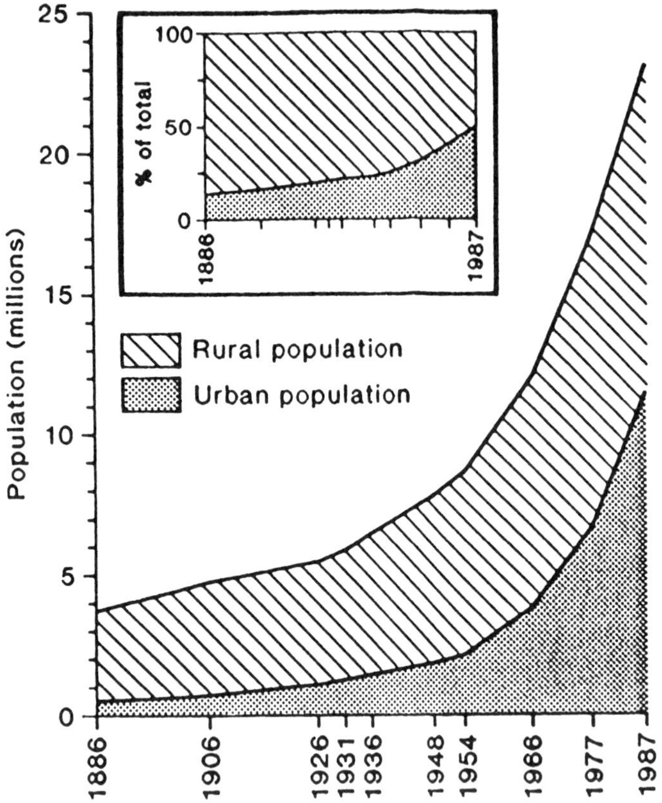

Thus the present urban patterns were established during the colonial period. With decolonization came the need to reorder the urban system after this false start.

The 1954–66 intercensal period was one of rapid urbanization, including the rapid departure in 1962 of the largely urban European population of about one million (Troin, 1987; Cote, 1988; Lesbet, 1990). This upsurge of urbanization between 1954 and 1966 stands out prominently (Figure 6.1). Because the rural population also grew, the urban population increased less sharply from 25 in 1954 to 31 percent in 1966 (Table 6.1). If the European population is excluded from the 1954 data, then the rate of urbanization of the 1954–66 indigenous Algerian population was close to 10 percent per annum (Troin, 1987:151). The French army's policy of *regroupement,* whereby up to 3.5 million were cleared from their rural home areas to more concentrated settlements (*centres de re-groupement*) or directly to nearby towns, was a major factor in this late 1950s

Table 6.1
Growth of Algeria's Urban Population, 1886–1987

Census Year	Urban Population (millions)	Percentage of Population Urbanized
1886	0.523	13.9
1906	0.783	16.6
1926	1.100	20.2
1931	1.248	21.1
1936	1.432	22.0
1948	1.838	23.6
1954	2.150	25.0
1966	3.700	31.4
1977	6.840	41.0
1987	11.440	49.7

Source: Compiled from Office National des Statistiques, 1988a.

urbanization push (Cornaton, 1967). Many stayed in the new *centres* or moved to other towns after the end of hostilities. This wartime trauma had a major and permanent effect on Algeria's settlement pattern (Sutton, 1981a). A further impetus to rural-urban movement was the postindependence economic development strategy with its emphasis on industrialization, especially in the coastal cities of northern Algeria.

By 1977 the urban population had nearly doubled as it had increased at a rate of 5 percent per annum compared with a total population growth rate of 3 percent. Whereas the top-down industry-focused development strategy continued to attract migrants from rural areas, the number of urban agglomerations increased markedly from 95 in 1966 to 211 in 1977, which superficially appeared to be exponential urban growth. Earlier in the century censuses restricted the definition of *urban* to the more Europeanized *communes de plein exercice*. Consequently, the 1936, 1948, and 1954 censuses excluded certain agglomerations in southern Algeria such as Béchar (18,090 in 1954), Ghardaia (14,073), and Touggourt (17,380) from the "urban" population. Table 6.2 illustrates this difficulty by focusing on changing census definitions of *urban* (Mokkadem, 1989).

The 1977–87 period witnessed a strengthening of the urban network, with the

Table 6.2
Changing Definitions and Subdivisions of Algeria's Urban System, 1966–87

		Number of Agglomerations
1966 Census	Urban	66
	Semi-Urban	29
	TOTAL	95
	(Plus 44 semi-rural agglomerations)	

1977 Census		1987 Census	
Urban Strata	67	121	agglomerations
Sub-Urban Strata	29	68	
Semi-Urban	49	175	
Potential Semi-Urban	55	58	
Unclassified	11	25	(1987 - all are *chef-lieux* of *daira*)
TOTAL	211	447	agglomerations

Source: Compiled from 1987 census.

211 urban agglomerations in 1977 increasing to 447 by 1987, thus reclassifying hundreds of thousands of people as urban. This in part stemmed from repeated administrative restructuring whereby the 15 *wilayate,* or regions, were increased to 31 *wilayate* in 1974 and to 48 in 1984. The number of administrative centers, or *dairate,* increased from 90 to 160, then to 207, all serving to spread urban functions to hitherto semiurban or even rural agglomerations (Office National des Statistiques, 1988). As well as the urban population rising to 11.44 million by 1987, about half of the total population, the number of cities of 100,000 or more increased from 4 in 1966 to 15 by 1987. The capital, Algiers, grew more slowly in 1977–87, to 1.5 million in a restricted definition of the agglomeration, or to 2.16 million in a more generously defined built-up area. Also the 1987 census classified a further 440 agglomerations as semirural, with a total of 1.69 million inhabitants. These are obviously potential new urban centers in the next census.

THE EFFECT OF URBANIZATION ON THE URBAN HIERARCHY

Compared with its Maghreb neighbors, Algeria's urban hierarchy has a relatively low level of urban primacy. G. H. Blake (1971) noted that in spite of the size of Algiers (898,000 in 1966), the presence of two other large cities in Oran and Constantine, together with several medium-sized towns, served to keep Algeria's primacy to a relatively low level for a developing country. Algiers in 1966 had 8 percent of the country's population and 22 percent of its urban population, hardly indices of macrocephalic urban primacy. Tunis and Tripoli were much more dominant with 34 percent and 43 percent of their countries' mid-1960s populations. However, Blake anticipated a greater primacy in Algeria, noting that within a radius of 100 kilometers of Algiers a dozen or so urban centers had grown at very high rates and that the region contained half of the country's urban population.

Algiers's urban primacy increased by 1977. Its restricted area's population of 1.523 million represented 22 percent of Algeria's urban population, but if one more realistically added 15 suburban communes, Greater Algiers accounted for 26 percent of the urban population (Troin, 1987;160). The population of the second city, Oran, amounted to 61 percent of that of Algiers in 1954, had slipped to 36 percent in 1966, and to only 32 percent by 1977. Algiera's dynamism has steepened the upper end of Algeria's rank size rule.

Before the 1987 census results were released, Dennis Rondinelli (1988) detected a reversal of urbanization trends in Algeria. His general conclusion was that the dominance of the capital Algiers was low and declining. He indicated that the strong growth in Algeria's secondary cities accounted for this trend. In 1987 the agglomeration of Greater Algiers had grown to only 2.16 million people, comprising only 19 percent of Algeria's urban population. This was a lower level of primacy than elsewhere in the Maghreb, with Tunis (33 percent), Casablanca (27 percent), and Tripoli (57 percent) all being much more dominant. The three large regional metropolises of Oran, Constantine, and Annaba maintained their rankings from second to fourth in the hierarchy between 1977 and 1987. Below them, interior towns such as Batna, Chlef, Biskra, and Béchar rose in rank, often at the expense of coastal or Tell towns such as Mostaganem, Blida, Sidi-bel-Abbès, and Skikda (Office National des Statistiques, 1988:110).

Algeria has shared in the strong urbanization as many African countries. It has maintained a better balanced rank-size urban hierarchy but not an increasing capital city primacy. In fact, the 1987 rank-size curve is no steeper than the 1966 curve at the upper end and is decidedly less steep at the lower end between ranks 50 and 100.

SOURCES OF URBAN POPULATION GROWTH

Migration

Migration data in Algeria are poorly collected and then belatedly published. If a town or region's population is increasing significantly faster than the national population growth rate (3 percent per annum, 1966–77; 3 percent, 1977–87), then in-migration is assumed to account for the difference.

Prior to independence much of the urban population was European. In Algiers in 1954 only 30 percent of the population were Algerian, and 42 percent lived in shantytowns (Lesbet, 1990). With the departure of the Europeans in 1962 came a massive influx of in-migrants, especially to the capital, attracted by the prospect of homes and jobs, both being vacated chaotically by the European settlers. The urbanized shantytown dwellers remained in their shanties while rural-urban migrants occupied the vacant dwellings, known as the *biens vacants*. There were 102,195 such *biens vacants,* homes and flats, European in style and ill-suited to the inward-looking traditional housing needs of rural in-migrants. Compared with a low rural exodus of 24,000 a year, 1936–54 (Troin, 1987:165), between 1962 and 1972 nearly 2.5 million rural folk moved to urban centers. Many had been evacuated into *centres de regroupement* by the French army. About one-third of those displaced, or about 800,000 people, moved on to settle in towns at the end of hostilities in 1961–62. Later in the 1960s rural exodus settled down to a lower annual rate of about 130,000, or about 1.7 million rural-urban migrants between 1966 and 1977 (Cote, 1988:219). This represented 1 percent per year of the rural population migrating in 1966–77 compared with less than 1 percent per year in 1936–54 (Troin, 1987:165).

After the upheavals of the war of independence, steady rural-urban migration resulted from a continual crisis of Algerian agriculture and a vigorous policy of industrialization focused initially on coastal cities. Strong economic and social disparities between town and country were increasingly recognized by rural folk. Only 20 percent of the government investments was going to rural areas. An agrarian reform for production cooperatives in the 1970s was a failure, and the policy reversed toward the privatization of landholdings, until the mid-1980s price policies worked against rural producers. However, some success was achieved in bringing basic services to rural areas. A national development strategy of "industrializing industries" focused investment over successive national plans in heavy industrial poles such as Annaba, Skikda, and Oran-Arzew. Urban life became synonymous with progress and modernism. Yet urbanization outstripped industrialization. While only 240,000 industrial jobs were created in 1966–77, employment multipliers in the construction industry and in the service sector boosted the urban economy and, through extensive commuting zones, furthered urban-rural interaction. As regional development policies, especially from the mid-1970s, sought to spread industrial and service employment growth to small interior centers, the attractive pull of such regional agglomerations intensified when that of an increasingly congested Algiers was waning.

Probably the most remarkable feature of the 1987 census data was the unexpectedly slow growth rate of coastal metropolises, especially the *wilaya* of Algiers which increased by only 0.7 percent per annum in 1977–87, compared with 5 percent per annum in 1966–77. Indeed, this indicated out-migration from the congested capital city region. An analysis of the 1977 census data of the dates of arrival of in-migrants from their respective regions suggested a decline in the growth of Algeria (Prenant, 1987, 1989). Annual migration to Oran and Algiers had dropped, respectively, from 68,545 in 1962–66 to 37,444 in 1967–

69, 40,713 in 1970–73 and to 46,269 in 1974–77, all suggesting no acceleration in migration after independence. Moreover, increasingly Algiers's in-migrants came from the rest of the *wilaya* of Algiers, confirming a reversal of earlier migration trends. Out of a national total of 580,780 people who changed *wilaya* of residence since 1977, the Algiers *wilaya* had a net loss of 120,734 migrants, which does not include children below the age of ten. Contrastingly, the other coastal *wilayate* like Oran (+ 12,519) and Mostaganem (+ 10,354) had modest net migration gains. Skikda *wilaya* had a loss of 5,242, and Annaba (+ 1,861) and Constantine (+ 586) were practically stationary.

By the 1980s the negative aspects of Algiers's congestion, lack of dwellings, and high rents were discouraging in-migration and diverting it to peripheral and often detached suburbs and to interior towns. The "crisis of dwellings" especially hit Algiers. During the decade 1978–88 a total of 71,478 dwelling units a year were constructed in Algeria. Despite being three times the 1966–77 construction, it was woefully inadequate. Population growth alone required 68,000 new dwellings a year. However, the deficit of dwellings stood at 700,000 units in 1986. Many Algerian families were without dwellings and lived in overcrowded flats with parents or other relatives. Algeria increasingly became unattractive, and many families moved to other towns or became long-distance commuters from the peripheries of the Algiers region.

By the late 1980s the rural exodus seems to have been halted or even reversed. A considerable house-building boom in the countryside together with better services, especially schools and rural electrification, and more widespread ownership of cars, vans, and television sets reduced markedly rural isolation and linked rural folk into urban networks while they remained in their rural dwellings. A new phenomenon of retirement migration from Algerian and French cities is beginning to lessen and even reverse traditional rural-urban migration (Troin, 1987:171). The 1987 census reveals 71,378 in-migrants to Algeria from a 1977 residential location abroad. Some may be retirement migrants.

Natural Increase

The last two intercensal periods, 1966–77 and 1977–87, have been characterized by a natural increase of the urban population exceeding rural-urban migration. Indeed, urban natural population growth was high in the 1966–77 period when rural-urban migration was also at its peak (Troin, 1987:167). By 1977–87 there was growing evidence of regional disparities in natural population growth (Sutton and Nacer, 1990). By 1987 crude birth rates in the 48 *wilayate* ranged from 24 per thousand to 42 per thousand around a national rate of 34 per thousand (ONS, 1989b:15). The lowest birthrates occurred in the coastal and highly urban *wilayate*. The highest birthrates were in less urban Saharan or eastern Algerian *wilayate*.

The low birthrates in the coastal metropolises, together with low or even negative migration rates, account for their slow overall growth rates (Table 6.3).

Table 6.3
Birth Registrations and Birthrates in Selected *Wilayate*, 1985–88

Wilaya	1985	1986	1987	1988	Crude birthrate 1987 (per thousand)
Algiers	45,390	42,451	43,267	40,089	25.6
Oran	25,940	24,440	24,849	24,582	26.7
Blida	22,071	20,081	20,216	20,776	28.8
Annaba	15,147	14,057	13,739	14,643	30.1
Boumerdés	21,084	19,420	19,728	19,339	30.3
Tipaza	19,627	17,399	17,264	16,182	27.8

Source: Compiled from Office National des Statistiques, 1988, 1989b.

Some *wilayate* had fewer births after 1985, suggesting that urban-focused family planning campaigns and the increased participation by women in employment and higher education were affecting fertility. The shortage of accommodation in Algiers had an impact on household formation and delayed new families. The fertility decline reduced the number of children in primary school in the Algiers *wilaya* from 278,576 in 1984 to 263,585 in 1985, and in Oran from 152,734 to 147,992 (Ministère de la Planification et de l'Aménagement du Territoire, 1984–85).

Reclassification of Areas

The number of urban centers steadily increased at each postindependence census. The urban system went from 211 agglomerations in 1977 to 447 in 1987, with a proportion of the 1977 rural population being counted as urban without changing their place of residence. The average size of each urban agglomeration decreased from 39,800 in 1966 to 31,700 in 1977 and to 25,600 in 1987 (Mokkadem, 1989). These 236 new urban centers in 1987 generally had less than 10,000 inhabitants. The 236 newly defined urban centers in 1987 contained 16 percent of the urban population, or 1.85 million people (Office National des Statistiques, 1988:34–51). Approximately 40 percent of the 1977–87 increase in Algeria's urban population is as a result of reclassifying rural centers as urban. This high proportion makes intercensal comparisons difficult.

Some large towns grew by absorbing adjacent agglomerations. Thus Béchar merged with two secondary agglomerations, Skikda absorbed Stora, and Adrar incorporated five neighboring secondary agglomerations, 1977–87 (Office National des Statistiques, 1988:108).

Socialist Villages

A recent source of urbanization in Algeria has been the construction of 400 widely scattered socialist villages built from 1973 through to the early 1980s as part of the agrarian reform program to provide much needed dwellings and service infrastructure in the redistribution of land. The ambitious program of 1,000 socialist villages was never achieved. Most villages were of the primary type with a minimum range of services including a commercial center of five or six shops, a primary school, a clinic, and a mosque. Their essential feature was their highly concentrated settlement morphology resembling an urban housing estate rather than an Algerian village (Sutton, 1987). The houses were built to modern urban standards, but their new agricultural residents often lacked the means to farm properly.

The socialist villages have come in for much criticism. Few of the villages have enough people to qualify as urban, but they do have concentrated settlements and an urban ethos.

REGIONAL PATTERNS OF URBANIZATION

Regional variations in levels and rates of urbanization are quite marked in Algeria. The proportion of the population in urban centers varies from below 30 percent in several northern and often mountainous *wilayate,* to above 80 percent in the four *wilayate* of Algiers, Oran, Constantine, and Annaba (Figure 6.2). Above-average levels of urbanization also prevail in eastern Algeria; south of Oran; the Saharan fringes and the northern Saharan *wilayate* of Ghardaia, Ouargla, and Béchar; some long-established traditional urban communities such as the M'zab with its renowned pentapolis, or five towns; and the Tlemcen region. Elsewhere, modern mining and hydrocarbons-related urbanization has strongly affected the settlement pattern in the mineral-rich Tébessa *wilaya* and the oilfields *wilaya* of Ouargla.

Many interior urban centers displayed much stronger population growth between 1977 and 1987 than the main northern and coastal metropolises. Rapid growth occurred in the main towns of the interior Hauts-Plateaux, except for Sétif (Table 6.4). Elsewhere towns in the Northern Tell had about the same growth rate as the national population. In contrast, all metropolises had slower growth than the national rate, indicating out-migration. In contrast an acceleration of growth rates has been experienced in the Hauts-Plateaux belt.

The more rapid population growth in the towns of the Hauts-Plateaux region in 1977–87 suggests that the planning strategy of the *Options Hauts-Plateaux* has succeeded in attracting population. As part of the First Five Year Plan, 1980–

Figure 6.2
Percentage of Population Urban, 1987

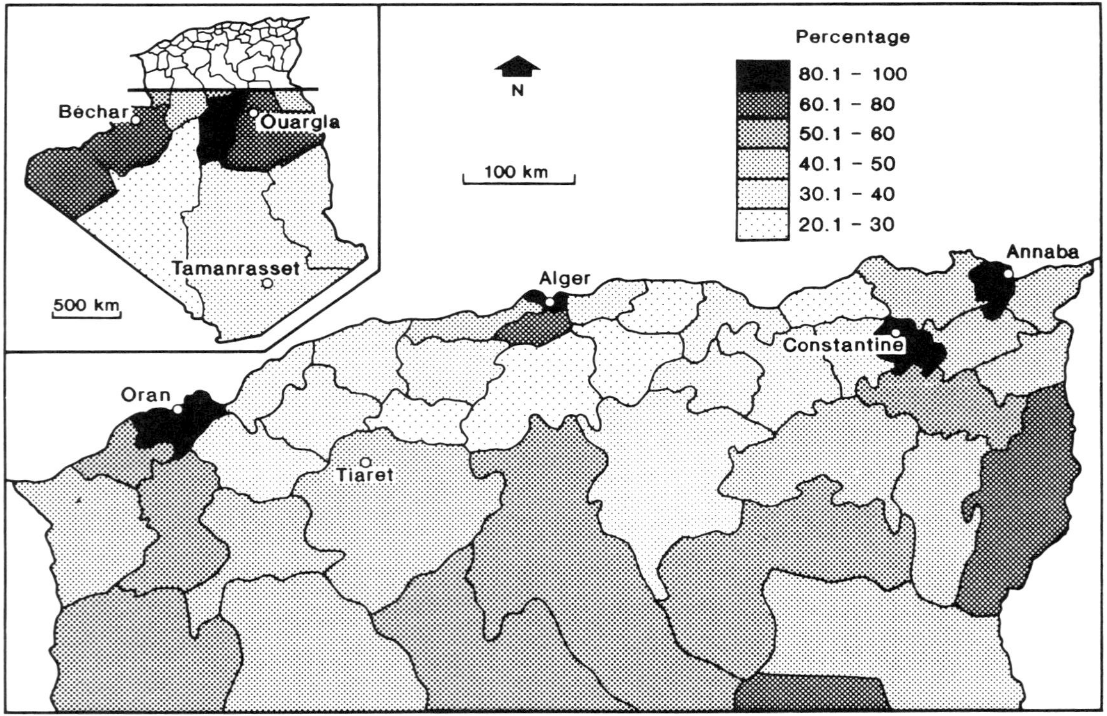

Table 6.4
Population Growth of the Main Towns and Cities, 1977–87

	Population 1987	Percentage Growth 1977-87
Main metropolises		
Algiers	1,507,241	11.3
Blida	170,935	17.3
Oran	628,558	26.9
Constantine	440,842	27.5
Annaba	305,526	22.5
Hauts-Plateaux and Sahara		
Batna	181,601	76.7
Sétif	170,182	31.2
Biskra	128,281	66.6
Tébessa	107,559	76.1
Béchar	107,311	89.7
Tiaret	95,821	79.9
Rest of Northern Tell		
Sid-bel-Abbès	152,778	35.2
Chlef	129,776	66.5
Skikda	128,747	35.9
Mostaganem	114,037	34.1
Bejaia	114,534	54.9
Tlemcen	126,882	43.4

Source: Compiled from Office National des Statistiques, 1988.

84, this *Options Hauts-Plateaux* promoted a broad east-west band of interior *wilayate* as a counterweight to the coastal urban-industrial poles. Strong urban growth will contribute to an additional 1.5–2 million inhabitants in the interior region by 1995. The factors of congestion diseconomies and urban-focused family planning contributed to the slowdown in population growth rates in the northern metropolises. There was a population stagnation of the inner quarters of Algiers as all inner communes experienced population declines in 1977–87. There was an aggregate decline of 12 percent for central Algiers (Prenant, 1989).

The inner communes of central Algiers experienced population increases in 1966–77 of 27 to 41 percent. These 1966–77 figures had prompted planners to predict a population of 2.3 million for Greater Algiers by 1990 and of 2.9 million by 2000. Algiers's primacy has not proved so dominant, and both eastern and western Algeria have well-structured urban hierarchies (Figure 6.3). The Oran region owes much to colonial urbanization while the Constantine-Annaba-Skikda region stems largely from postindependence industrialization and regional development policies. In contrast the center and interior regions are understructured, though the increase in local administrative centers stemming from two administrative restructuring exercises in 1974 and 1985 boosted urban functions of centers such as Oum-el-Bouaghi, Djelfa, and Naama.

POPULATION GROWTH IN SUBURBS AND SLUMS

From studies of Cairo, Rabat-Sale, and Tunis, Janet Abu-Lughod (1976) developed a model structure of the morphology of the North African city with six components: (1) the medina core; (2) the modern appendage; (3) the rapidly proliferating uncontrolled settlements; (4) peripheral suburbs; (5) a rural fringe; and (6) transitional working-class zones.

Greater Algiers partly conforms to Abu-Lughod's model, but with a greater emphasis on *cités* of high-rise flats rather than villas in the recent suburbs. As with regional variation in recent urbanization, the different components of Algiers's urban morphology fared somewhat differently between the burgeoning suburbs and the slums of the inner Casbah core and the intermediate shantytowns.

The periphery of Algiers has been the scene of the most rapid population growth with suburban communes like Bab Ezzouar, Bordj El Kiffan, and Cheraga contributing numerous new *cités*—housing estates (Table 6.5). In 1966–77 the inner suburbs had this same dynamism as Algiers's Hussein-Dey (+49 percent) and El Harrach (+101 percent) and the northwest Bologhine Ibnou Ziri and Bouzareah (together +67 percent). By the 1980s the wave of suburban dynamism moved further to centers like Rouiba, Reghaia, Sidi Moussa, and even Bougara south of the Mitidja Plain (Figure 6.4). In such suburbs numerous housing estates, modelled on the French *grands ensembles* approach, were constructed during the 1970s and 1980s.

The estates in the slums lack services, and the public spaces between blocks are strewn with rubbish. Few flats are owned as most residents hope to move

Figure 6.3
Algeria's Urban System in 1987

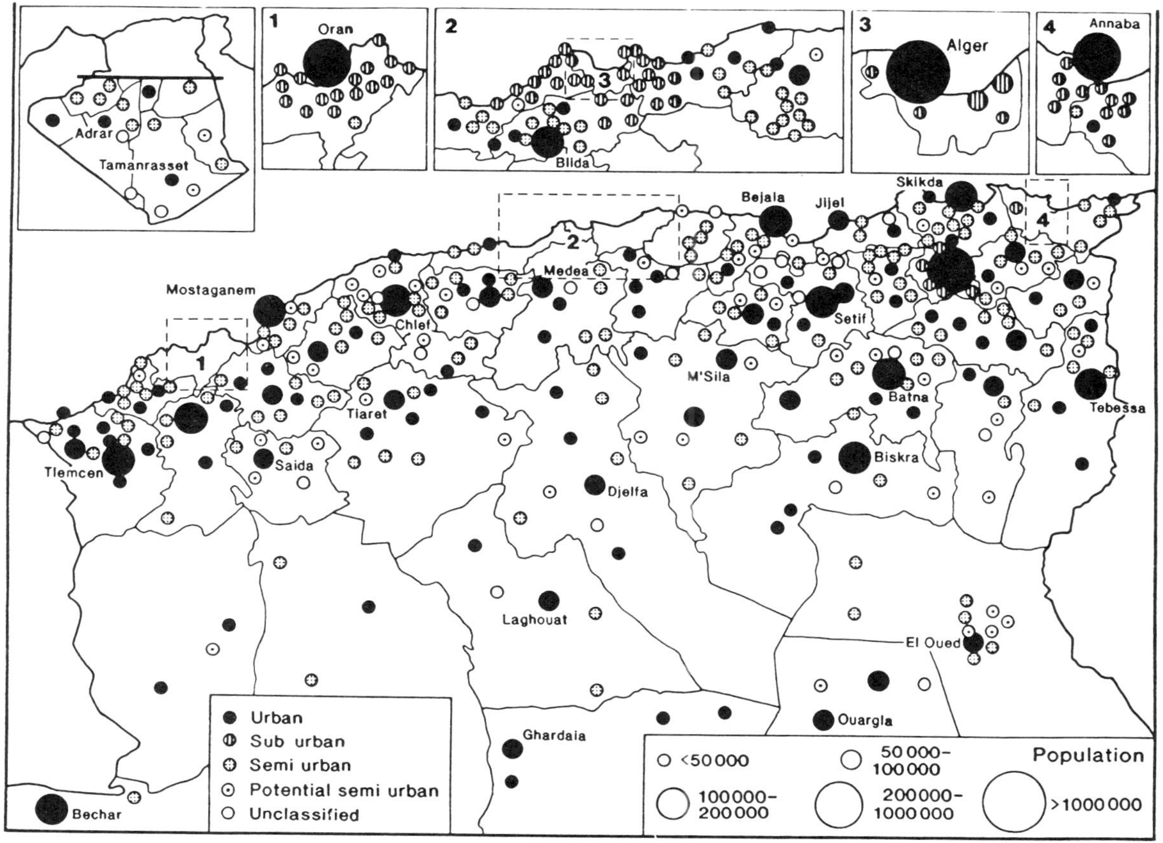

Table 6.5
Population Decline and Stagnation in Inner Algiers, 1977–87

Areas	Population 1977	1987	Percentage Change 1977-87
Algiers City	1,523,000	1,507,000	-1.1
Inner Core	676,000	555,000	-17.9
Outer Core	847,000	952,000	+12.4
Periphery	393,000	599,000	+52.4
Algiers Metropolis	1,916,000	2,106,000	+9.9
Communes of the Inner Core			
Alger Centre	122,105	106,560	-12.7
Sidi M'hamed	124,771	105,966	-15.1
Bab El Oued	121,489	105,374	-13.3
Casbah)	116,398	60,061)	-0.9
Oued Koriche)		56,230)	
El Madania)	146,017	52,520)	-17.1
Hamma Anassers)		65,522)	
Central Algiers	630,780	555,233	-12.0

N.B. After appreciating serious undercounting in Algiers in 1977 the census authorities issued higher adjusted figures for 'Algiers City' but this was not disaggregated for individual communes. Hence the 630,780 figure for Central Algiers is adjusted upwards to 676,000 for the same area of the Inner Core higher in the table.

Sources: Compiled from CNERU, 1983; Office National des Statistiques, 1987.

Figure 6.4
Urban Population Growth Rates, 1977–87

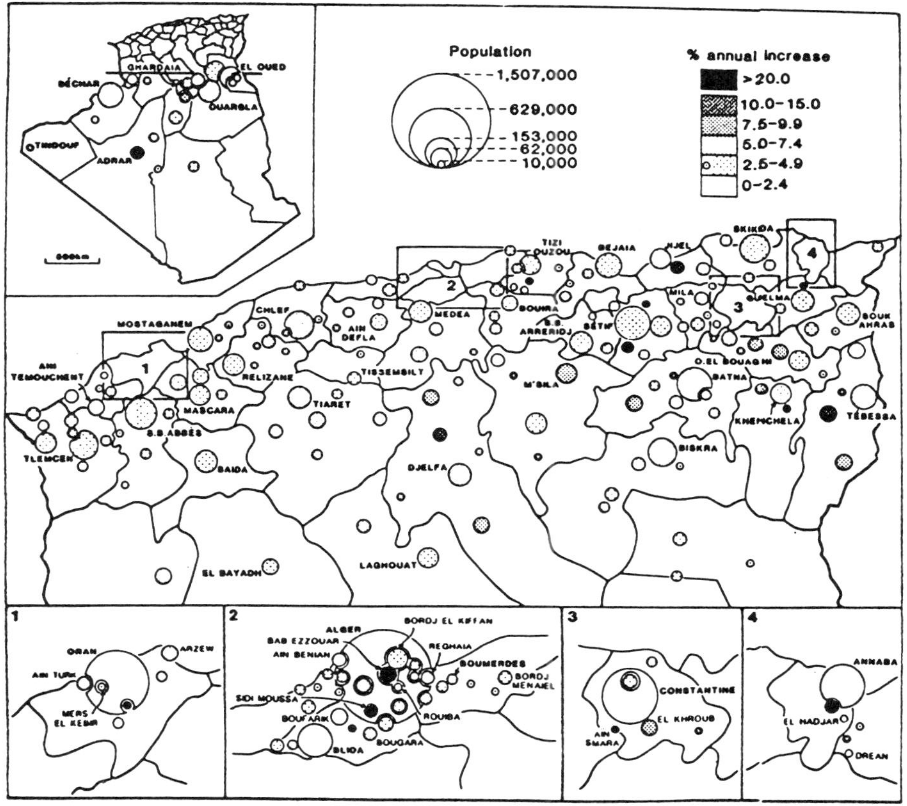

to a better accommodation in a more agreeable urban environment. However, such *cités* now dominate the urban periphery of most cities, as from the 1970s to the late 1980s about 420,000 flats were built in hundreds of estates (Cote, 1988:263–265).

The slum areas of Algerian cities are of two main types: the shantytowns, or *bidonvilles,* and the precolonial medina cores. The first shantytown appeared in Algiers in 1922, and the local name *bidonville,* meaning hovels made from flattened petrol cans or *bidons,* was coined in 1934. The 13 *bidonvilles* in 1938, accommodating 5,000 people, increased to about 90 by 1954, with 86,500 inhabitants. Though they were initially located on the edge of the built-up area, urban sprawl incorporated many *bidonvilles* into the urban fabric. By 1954 concentrations of shanties were found at El Harrach and Hussein-Dey, adjacent to recent suburbs and areas of industrialization. Sixteen *bidonvilles* exceeded 1,000 inhabitants (Descloitres, 1961). According to the 1960 census, 150,000 people lived in shanty dwellings in Algiers, plus another 112,000 in similar traditional dwellings of a "summary" nature. Nearly half of the non-European population of Algiers on the eve of independence were living in shantytowns.

With the availability of abandoned European dwellings after independence, many *bidonvilles* disappeared, and the 1966 census counted only 10,703 people in 2,223 *bidonville* huts or *barques.* Algiers's *bidonville* population grew again during the late 1960s as the rural-urban exodus expanded to about 150,000 people in the mid-1970s (Benatia, 1980). A 1982 survey estimated 126,000 people in *bidonvilles* in the Kouba, Hussein-Dey, and El Harrach districts. Elsewhere *bidonvilles* were found around Annaba being especially prolific and linked to rural-urban in-migration to jobs associated with the El-Hadjar steelworks (Brule and Mutin, 1982:51).

Despite the fairly high incomes of some workers authorities embarked on a major clearance program with occupants of *bidonvilles* being returned to their regions of origin in 1983. Again in the mid-1980s an Algiers city cleanup operation sought to expel shantytown dwellers to their places of origin and bulldoze their shanty dwellings. Only selective expulsions were undertaken because many were city employees and construction workers essential to the capital city (Lesbet, 1990:270–271).

The second major type of slum area is the increasingly degraded medina or casbah which declined from its precolonial focal role to little more than an immigrant reception center. From the 1930s rich families began moving to the suburbs of European towns, a trend which accelerated around 1950. Poor in-migrants moved into *fondouks* or *oukalas,* multifamily lodging houses. Thus began the processes of densification; *taudification,* or degeneration into slums; and *oukalisation,* or subdivision of houses.

A new urbanization trend is the "spontaneous suburbs" of private self-built or *autoconstruction* housing which has mushroomed around cities and towns. This type of urbanization lies between the *bidonvilles* and the formal housing estates developments. Often constructed without building permits, the new houses are usually on land legally owned. Older examples may resemble vernacular medina houses, while newer houses are built in modern styles with garages and on properly laid-out estates. Such *autoconstruction* provides 25 percent of the dwellings in Constantine and as many as 40 percent in Souk Ahras and 60 percent in Batna. Apparently *bidonvilles* are often found in inverse proportion to *autoconstruction*.

ADEQUACY OF HOUSING AND SOCIAL SERVICES TO URBAN RESIDENTS

On independence the French abandoned over 100,000 dwellings, mainly in the large cities. These *biens vacants* accommodated the first influx of in-migrants and caused the government to give a lower priority initially to housing than to industrial investment and job creation. Consequently, there was an increase of 400,000 dwellings in the housing stock during 1966 to 1978, but also of 1.1 million in the number of jobs (Lesbet, 1990:257). By 1970 the building industry was industrialized. Fifty heavy prefabrication units were set up with a capacity of 35,000 dwelling units a year. However, they functioned at only one-third of their capacity. So foreign companies were asked to construct housing projects.

By the 1980s new measures emphasized private building plots to increase the capacity of the housing stock. Local authorities sold land to private citizens especially when grouped into housing cooperatives. While the target of 100,000 building plots was never reached, this private housing initiative produced low-density housing of about 50 dwellings a hectare.

The switch to privatization in housing included an attempt to sell public housing units to tenants. While good detached houses were readily purchased, flat dwellers preferred to continue to pay modest rents, and the policy failed. While the Caisse Nationale d'Épargne (CNEP) exists to provide loans for house purchases, its funds are underused. Indeed, throughout the 1970s state finances available for housing were three times higher than expenditures (Lesbet, 1990:267).

The lack of cement and other construction materials, shortages of skilled building workers, and difficulties in keeping within budgets because of high costs contributed to the shortfall in the building of new dwellings. In 1982, the government estimated a national shortage of 1.2 million dwellings, half in urban areas, without including the dilapidated medina houses or inadequate *bidonville* dwellings in need of renovation or upgrading (Brule and Mutin, 1982:50). With a population growth requiring 68,000 new dwellings a year, 1.5 million new units are probably needed. This deficit is 2 million if the occupancy is reduced to seven persons per dwelling.

The urban housing crisis affects surrounding rural areas which are commuter hinterlands. Most are employed in nearby urban and industrial jobs and are illegally occupying rural dwellings, after switching from state agricultural to urban-based jobs (Brule and Mutin, 1982:52). The housing crisis thus finds an expression in extensive commuting zones around cities and especially industrial poles.

CHANGING EMPLOYMENT AND LABOR MARKETS IN THE MAJOR CITIES

Since colonial times Algiers has been the major center of industrial activity. Its industrial quarters adjacent to and east of the port area have been supplemented since the 1960s by new industrial estates on the periphery of the metropolitan area, at Rouiba and Reghaia to the east and at Sidi Moussa to the south. While remaining the main industrial center of employment, the Algiers region has been neglected in the national industrial development strategy which has located heavy industrial plants in the hydrocarbons, petrochemicals, steel-making, and phosphatic fertilizer in other coastal poles such as Oran-Arzew, Skikda, and Annaba. From the late 1970s a switch in emphasis to lighter industrial development has incorporated a subsidiary regional development objective of spreading state industrial activities to smaller cities and interior regions such as Sétif, Guelma, and Tiaret. Nevertheless, certain consumer industries have located in and around Algiers with the result that the capital continues to stand out in industrial employment (Brule and Mutin, 1982:60; Nacer and Sutton, 1987).

Some decentralization occurred since 1970 as many small towns became administrative centers of new *wilayate* or newly created *dairate* and acquired related tertiary activities for the first time.

While regional dispersions were made by the government and the private industrial sector in favoring the interior, the four largest cities and Northern Tell account for 70 to 75 percent of the proposed private development. The top-ranking *wilayate* are Algiers, Oran, Boumerdes, and the eastern industrial suburbs of Algiers and Blida (Sutton, 1989).

INCOME AND WAGES IN THE CAPITAL CITY

The expenditure data of households from a 1979–80 sample survey show the per head expenditures in Greater Algiers decidedly higher than in the countryside and in villages (CNRES, 1982). Higher living standards were reflected by the higher consumption of bread, rather than *semoule* (for couscous), meat, chicken, eggs, and milk in Algiers. Such higher consumption levels in 1979–80 indicate higher incomes in Greater Algiers than in rural areas, but also higher costs of living, higher rents, greater congestion costs. Rural self-subsistence practices narrow the gap of living standards and reduce the attraction of Greater Algiers to potential migrants.

POLICIES ON URBANIZATION AND REGIONAL DEVELOPMENT

As a country with a series of national development plans and a strong state-controlled industrial and commercial sector, Algeria has not hesitated to advance policies to influence and direct the location of investment, both public and private, of economic activity, and of urban growth. Policies seeking to influence urbanization trends have fallen into two categories. First, policies to boost regional urban centers through regional development programs have generally been oriented toward lagging, interior regions. Second, policies to restrict the growth of Algiers have sought to manage its inevitable sprawl and deal with its problems of congestion and inner-city degradation.

Initially colonial policies favoring coastal regions were continued with heavy industrial investment in the coastal *pôles de croissance* of Arzew, Skikda, and Annaba. This resulted in some deconcentration from Algiers. By the late 1960s Special Programs had been launched, each for a specified lagging region. Ten of these, from 1966 until 1973, were mainly focused on interior regions and incorporated social as well as economic objectives (Sutton, 1981b). The service function and labor markets of the main towns in each program's region were boosted. By the mid-1970s the Special Programs approach was replaced by a policy of *Plans Communaux de Développement* (PCD) to diffuse development through enabling local authorities to initiate and implement local projects to develop their resources and meet the basic needs of their inhabitants. Thus 704 communes or local authorities were integrated into this enlarged development planning system. Additional programs were established for 200 most impoverished communes. Furthermore, the government established *Plans de Modernisation Urbaine* (PMU) for the main towns experiencing demographic and economic growth. Such special allocations went to 39 selected towns to promote drinking water, sewerage, urban renewal and redevelopment, and municipal buildings. This was necessary for towns chosen as regional administrative centers in 1974 when the number of *wilayate* increased from 15 to 31. Between 1975 and 1982 the local projects policy program amounted to 40.5 billion dinars, of which 20.4 billion dinars had been effectively spent by 1982 on social infrastructure.

Regional industrial investment was covered by another area of policy, the *Petites et Moyennes Industries* (PMI) program. Despite some failings, this PMI program carried a regional bias toward rural and underindustrialized zones and attempted to spread industrial development, and with it urban growth, away from the coastal poles of heavy industry. By 1979 there were 30 interior towns benefiting from industrial deconcentration and regional industrial poles in the High Plains (Mutin, 1985). The PMI program had 240 industrial units functioning throughout Algeria by the end of 1981, with another 440 units underway.

The First Five Year Plan (1980–84) added a new regional planning initiative with its *Options Hauts-Plateaux,* which sought to promote a band of interior regions stretching east-west across eight *wilayate*. The program was aimed at an additional 1.5 to 2 million people in the region by 1990–95 and for its share of Algeria's work force to increase from 22 percent to 27 percent (MPAT, 1980).

The Second Five Year Plan (1985–89) continued this regional planning strategy, and the 1987 census suggested favorable results. On the basis of 1966–87 population trends Hauts-Plateaux's 1987 population was expected to reach

5,264,000 to 5,424,000. The 1987 census recorded 5,637,000 people in this zone, and Hauts-Plateaux urban centers were among the most rapidly growing towns (Table 6.4).

Rondinelli (1988) suggested that the *Options Hauts-Plateaux* policy be combined with a promotion of secondary cities. By 1980, Algeria possessed six secondary cities, and was one of only six countries in Africa with more than five secondary cities. In order for the "decentralized concentration" of investments to succeed, there is a need for intermediate-sized cities with sufficient concentrations of people with large hinterland markets mutally reinforcing urban and regional development. Within the interior Hauts-Plateaux zone there existed four cities in excess of 100,000 people in 1987 capable of meeting Rondinelli's criteria for secondary city rank. Indeed, Taieb (1981) advocated the promotion of interior cities with populations of 300,000 to 500,000 to achieve threshold sizes adequate to offer sufficient opportunities to divert migration flows. By giving enlarged cities strong regional administrative functions of *wilayate,* real counterweights to the coastal metropolises could be established.

Parallel with this evolving regional development strategy, there have been several attempts to restrict the growth of Algiers. Greater Algiers has been the object of three *plans directeurs d'urbanisme* (PUD), none of which has been put into effect.

The 1987 census results suggest that the plans for Algiers have been partly based on false premises of rapid growth for a primate capital city. Actually, Algiers and the other three main cities have grown more slowly than the smaller urban centers.

SUMMARY AND IMPLICATIONS

Writing in 1976 about urbanization in North Africa from Morocco to Sudan, Abu-Lughod (1976:200–201) stated that allometric growth is "still the dominant pattern" and that "net migration is going almost exclusively into the capital." This was because it "has been virtually impossible to achieve noticeable reversals during decolonization." While this generalization was valid for Algeria during its first decade of decolonization until the mid-1970s, since then allometric, primate-city dominated urban growth has not continued to be the pattern. Moreover, the 1980s have seen a reversal of population and urbanization trends of the 1970s (Sutton and Nacer, 1990).

The growth anticipated in CNERU's 1983 plan for the inner quarters of Algiers proved to be overly optimistic as all communes of the inner core declined in population in 1977–87 (Table 6.5). Nevertheless, the dynamism of Algiers extended beyond the built-up area to the outer suburbs and to the commuter towns and villages of the Mitidja Plain and beyond. The four region *wilayate* of Algiers, Blida, Boumerdes, and Tipaza contained 3.65 million people in 1987, compared with 2.58 million in the two spatially similar *wilayate* of Algiers and Blida in 1977, an increase of 42 percent.

Rather than primate city allometric growth, the regional dimensions of Algeria's recent urbanization are proving significant. The counterweights of the Oran-Arzew-Mostaganem urban-industrial axis and Annaba-Skikda-Constantine triangle have continued to limit the degree of polarization of people and economic activity in the capital city. Also increasingly the dynamism of interior Hauts-Plateaux and northern Saharan towns has contributed to a more balanced urban system and diverted rural-urban migration away from its earlier coastal urban poles.

Within-city trends have included the functional, social, and even physical decline of precolonial medinas, inner-city problems of land use and traffic congestion, the development of massive housing estates, and, most recently, the chaotic sprawl of self-built housing, now of the middle class whereas earlier it had consisted of the shantytowns of the poor and those denied access to the housing market.

The post-1980 changes in Algeria's political and economic strategies away from state centralized planning toward economic liberalization and increased private-sector initiative may reverse the 1980s trends. A more laissez-faire approach to the location of investment and jobs by the rehabilitated private sector may combine with further *autoconstruction* in unplanned suburban extensions around Algiers, Oran, and other established urban poles to reintroduce the allometric urban growth tendencies of the 1960s and 1970s. The plans to constrain the growth of Greater Algiers established by Comité Permanent d'Etudes de Développement, d'Organisation et d'Aménagement de l'Agglomération d'Alger and CNERU and the *Schéma National d'Aménagement du Territoire* (1986) with its strategy of promoting still more the towns and regions of the Hauts-Plateaux and the northern Sahara are readily available.

REFERENCES

Abu-Lughod, J. 1976. "Developments in North African Urbanism: The Process of Decolonization." In *Urbanization and Counterurbanization,* edited by B. J. L. Berry, 191–212. Beverly Hills: Sage.

Benatia, F. 1980. *Alger: agrégat ou cité?* Algiers: Société Nationale d'Édition et de Diffusion.

Blake, G. H. 1971. "Urbanization in North Africa." *Tijdschrift voor Economische en Sociale Geografie* 62:190–196.

Brule, J. C., and G. Mutin. 1982. "Industrialisation et urbanisation en Algérie." *Maghreb-Machrek* 96:41–66.

CNERU (Centre d'Étude et de Recherche en Urbanisme). 1983. *Alger PUD. Options et Schémas—Rapport de Synthèse.* Algiers: CNERU.

CNRES (Commissariat National aux Recensements et Enquêtes Statistiques). 1982. *Dépenses de Consommation des Ménages Algeriens.* Algiers: CNRES.

Cornaton, M. 1967. *Les Regroupements de la Decolonisation en Algérie.* Paris: Les Éditions Ouvrières.

Cote, M. 1988. *L'Algérie ou l'espace retourne.* Paris: Flammarion.

Descloitres, R. 1961. *L'Algérie des bidonvilles.* Paris: Mouton.

Lesbet, D. 1990. "Algeria." In *Housing Policies in the Socialist Third World,* edited by K. Mathey, 249–273. London: Mansell.

Mokkadem, A. 1989. "L'Urbanisation en Algérie." *Revue Statistiques (ONS)* 23:1–5.

MPAT. 1980. *Rapport General. 1er. Plan Quinquennial 1980–1984.* Algiers: Ministère de la Planification et de l'Aménagement de Territoîre.

———. 1984–85. *Fiches Signaletiques des Wilayate.* Série Statistiques Regionales. Donnees 1984–85. Algiers: Ministère de la Planification et de l'Aménagement de Territoîre/Office National des Statistiques.

Mutin, G. 1985. "Industrialisation et urbanisation en Algérie." In *Citadins, Villes, Urbanisation dans le Monde Arabe aujourd'hui,* 87–113. Tours: Centre d'Etudes et de Recherches sur l'Urbanisation du Monde Arabe.

Nacer, M., and K. Sutton. 1987. "Regional Disparities and Regional Development in Algeria." In *The Socialist Third World, Urban Development and Territorial Planning,* edited by D. Forbes and N. Thrift, 129–168. Oxford: Basil Blackwell.

ONS. (Office National des Statistiques). 1988. "L'Armature Urbaine 1987." *Les Collections de Statistiques* 4. Algiers: ONS.

———. 1987. "Premiers resultate provisoires du recensement genéral de la population et de Habitat 1987." *Collections Statistiques* 16. Algiers: ONS.

———. 1989b. "Démographie algérienne Édition 1989." *Collections Statistiques* 17. Algiers: ONS.

Prenant, A. 1987. "Un épouvantail: l'hypertrophie d'Alger. Mythes et Réalité." *Cahiers de GREMAMO* (Groupe de Recherches sur le Maghreb et le Moyen-Orient, Université Paris VII) 5:81–112.

———. 1989. "Quelle est la population d'Alger?" *Les Cahiers d'URBAMA* 2:25–29.

Rondinelli, D. 1988. "Giant and Secondary City Growth in Africa." In *The Metropolis Era,* vol. 1: *A World of Giant Cities,* edited by M. Dogan and J. D. Kasarda, 291–321. Newbury Park and London: Sage.

Sutton, K. 1981a. "The Influence of Military Policy on Algerian Rural Settlement." *Geographical Review* 71:379–394.

———. 1981b. "Algeria: Centre-Down Development, State Capitalism and Emergent Decentralization." In *Development from Above or Below,* edited by W. B. Stohr and D. R. F. Taylor, 351–375. Chichester: Wiley.

———. 1987. "The Socialist Villages of Algeria." In *The Middle Eastern Village,* edited by R. Lawless, 77–114. London: Croom Helm.

———. 1989. "Conflict between the Growth of Greater Algiers and Algeria's Regional Development Policies." *Les Cahiers d'URBAMA* 3:5–39.

Sutton, K., and M. Nacer. 1990. "Population Changes in Algeria, 1977–87." *Geography* 75:335–347.

Taieb, M. 1981. "Le développement des régions intérieures en Algérie." *Cahiers de l'Aménagement de l'Espace* 13:39–62.

Troin, J.-F. 1982. "Vers un Maghreb des villes en l'an 2000." *Maghreb-Machrek* 96:5–18.

———. 1987. *Le Maghreb. Hommes et Espaces.* 2nd ed. Paris: Armand Colin.

7

Angola

Filipe R. Amado, Fausto Cruz, and Ralph Hakkert

This chapter starts with a historical perspective of colonial urban development in Angola, as the main feature that shaped the urban system before and after independence (Massiah and Tribillon, 1988:Chapter 2). In 1575, a Portuguese ship anchored in the bay beside the Island of Goats, now called the Island of Luanda. When Paulo Dias de Novais disembarked, the ship's crew sought an appropriate place to build a church and there, on a portable altar, a mass was said. One year later, in 1576, Dias de Novais founded the port of Luanda, which was to become the outlet for one of the largest slave export operations on the continent (Thornton, 1980). The village expanded and 30 years later, in 1605, acquired the prerogatives of a town. The colonial and postcolonial history of Angola can be divided into several stages:

- slave traffic (1520–1885);
- wars of military occupation (1885–1910);
- development of capitalism (1910–61);
- war of independence (1961–75);
- period since independence (1975–present).

A historical analysis shows the existence of a certain parallel between these historical periods and the so-called economic cycles, determined by the main export products:

- cycle of slaves, wax, and rubber (1892–1910);
- cycle of diamonds and corn (1917–45);
- coffee cycle (1946–72);
- petrol cycle (from 1973 until the present).

From these historical periods and their underlying economic cycles, one may infer that the twentieth century is of special importance for the urbanization process, for despite the early foundation of Luanda and shortly afterwards Benguela (founded in 1584 and rebuilt in 1617), the Angolan cities were of very little importance prior to 1900, as is true for most African cities (Gregory, 1988:372). The Angolan economy in the twentieth century reflected important national and international events. By World War I, it was characterized by stagnation, as the rubber cycle had ended, without being immediately substituted by another cycle.

The predominance of a few coastal towns is related to the period when resources were taken through ports which also served as colonial administrative centers. This dominance was accentuated by the market system of domestic economic organization. The traditional economic base in most urban areas was agriculture. As the Portuguese pacified the country and brought it under their rule, a major administrative effort was directed at growing export crops, beside subsistence crops for local consumption and trade. This economic development created an urban system. The development of the urban system was linked to advances in the construction of the country's three most important railways:

- the Benguela Railway, from Benguela to Luanda and further east into southern Zaire;
- the Malange Railway, from Luanda to Malange, connecting with the Benguela Railway at the border; and
- the Moçâmedes Railway, from Menongue to Lubango and Namibe in the south.

The Benguela Railway, whose construction started in 1903, gave access to all the constituent municipalities. The creation of Huambo (Nova Lisboa) in 1912, by a simple administrative decree, was a direct consequence of the railway construction, whereas Kuito (Silva Porto) gained importantly. These three subsystems of rail and road connections conditioned the economic transactions and relations between regions. The road network allowed regional relations, but only in areas under the influence of these railroads, which served as regions because of their socioeconomic interactions.

During World War I, the most important development in the colonial economy was the ever-rising prices of imported products. The period between the wars was likewise characterized by stagnation, but also by events such as a profound economic and financial crisis from 1921 until 1928, the collapse of the Banco Nacional Ultramarino and its substitution by the Banco de Angola (1926), proclamation of the Indigenous Labor Code (1928), forceful installation of fascism in Angola and proclamation of the Colonial Act (1930), the great world crisis (1929–33), and locust plagues in 1932, 1934, and 1935.

Economic recovery started in 1931 when the balance of trade began to close with positive figures, and from 1932 on the state budgets were systematically balanced as a consequence of the financial policies of the Salazar government. Nevertheless, foreign exchange problems continued until 1941. The excessive burdens imposed on the population were heavy until 1927 when they diminished, but grew thereafter. Between the two wars, the nascent capitalist structures were consolidated, with the expulsion of peasants from their land.

From 1939 to 1945, the Angolan economy failed to register growth of any importance, contrary to exceptional developments in some African countries. Despite price increases of raw materials (except "goods of the conditioned economy" exported to Portugal), the terms of trade deteriorated greatly, accompanied by a vertiginous increase of freights and insurance, to the point where imports declined in volume. Portugal became practically the only commercial partner of Angola, for in 1943, 74 percent of all Angolan imports originated there.

From 1946 to 1960 the coffee cycle was produced by contract labor. The Korean War (1950–53), brought a boom in coffee prices and contributed enormously to the enrichment of the colonial bourgeoisie who made the housing industry prosper, particularly in Luanda. As elsewhere in Africa (Amin, 1974), the inequalities between small- and large-scale agriculture, between rural and urban, came to the forefront. Due to coffee, this period experienced some growth, as the export volume grew by 11 percent per annum and imports by 10 percent per annum. However, coffee prices fell suddenly, and Angola again faced years of foreign exchange problems after 1957.

During the coffee cycle the urbanization process began to accelerate in the northern region of the country, particularly in Luanda. While the urbanization process had been gradually molded by the economic cycles, it was the coffee cycle that kindled the urban explosion in Angola. According to Ilídio do Amaral (1978), the urban population doubled during the 1950s, going from 248,000 (6 percent) to 512,543 (11 percent). A contributing factor was the increased influx of white *colonos,* whose number increased from 78,826 in 1950 to 172,529 in 1960, and who settled predominantly in the cities. They were unskilled and semiskilled workers, and some engaged in administration, overseas trade, and other commercial activities.

From 1961 until 1973 was the struggle for independence. Exports in current prices increased 18 percent per annum and imports 14 percent per annum. Minerals accounted for an increasing share of exports. In 1973 petrol surpassed coffee as the major export commodity, initiating the petrol cycle and making the Angolan economy increasingly dependent on foreign trade. In 1966, exports accounted for 26 percent of the gross national product (GNP), but by 1970 the figure had risen to 32 percent. Agriculture, which occupied 85 percent of the population, contributed only 12 percent of the gross domestic product (GDP) (1971) and declined 3 percent per annum from 1966 until 1971.

The 24 district capitals had historically been the centers of concentration of the continuous industrial, administrative, and service activities. As such they were the primary poles of attraction for urban-to-rural migration. They attracted large numbers of Africans, but offered very unstable livelihoods based on unskilled and irregular employment, petty trade, and activities in the informal sector. As a result, migration led to the growth of central and peripheral squatter settlements.

The overseas white settlement continued, even as the threat of decolonization became imminent. By 1970 Angola had a sizable European population of about 270,000. Approximately 62 percent lived in cities, as did 62 percent of the population of mixed descent, but only 11 percent of the African population. Luanda alone had a European population of 126,233 in 1970, up from 55,567 in 1960. This expansion of the dominant population group during one decade caused a real estate boom in the city; most of Luanda as it is known today was constructed during the 1960s. Although Europeans constituted less than 5 percent of the total population, about a quarter of the urban population was white. Employers, who constituted 3 percent of the active population, were mostly Portuguese, as were the 100,000 qualified workers, who constituted 3 percent of the active population.

Table 7.1 depicts the evolution of the population and urbanization from 1930 until 1990. It shows that by 1970, urbanization, defined as the proportion of the population living in agglomerations of 2,000 or more, had increased to 14–15 percent, from 6 percent two decades earlier. The overall population density was less than five inhabitants per square kilometer and the distribution very unbalanced: over 90 percent lived in the western portion of the country, occupying less than 50 percent of its total area (Dilolwa, 1978).

At the turn of the twentieth century there existed only two cities in Angola: Luanda and Benguela (Amaral, 1978). Then, Luanda had only about 20,000 inhabitants. Around 1850, Benguela barely passed 3,000, and at the turn of the century it had not yet reached 10,000 inhabitants. The evolution of Huambo, Kuito, Lobito, Lubango, Malange, and Namibe to city size dates from 1900 to 1940. By 1940 Angola counted eight cities, with a total population of 61,000 in Luanda and a total of 68,000 in the remaining seven. There were 16 in 1960, and 24 in 1970 (Table 7.2). As the number of cities increased, so did the relative importance of Luanda. The 4-city primacy index for Angola grew from a modest 1.31 in 1930 and 1.38 in 1940 to 2.12 in 1950, declined marginally to 2.00 in 1960, and increased again to 2.93 in 1970. The 11-city primacy index in 1970 was even slightly higher, namely 3.14.

Aggravated by the war of independence in the 1960s, migrations were a common phenomenon in Angola: to the neighboring countries, a rural exodus from the Central Planalto to the coffee areas and the coast. Cities at the focus

Table 7.1
Evolution of Population and Urbanization, 1930–90

Year	Total Population (Amaral/INE)	Urban Population (Amaral/INE)	Proportion Urban	
			UN	Amaral/INE
1930	3,343,500			
1940	3,738,010	201,000		5.4 percent
1950	4,145,266	248,000	7.6 percent	6.0
1960	4,840,719	512,543	10.4	10.6
1970	5,673,046	789,300	15.0	13.9
1975	6,520,000	1,183,100	17.8	18.1
1980	7,722,000	1,731,100	21.0	22.4
1985	8,753,900	2,574,300	24.5	29.4
1990	10,020,000	3,703,600	28.3	37.0

Sources: Compiled from INE, 1987; United Nations, 1991b; and Amaral, 1962, 1978.

Table 7.2
Population of the Major Cities, 1940–70

City	1940	1950	1960	1970
Luanda	61,028	141,647	224,540	475,328
Huambo	16,288	28,296	38,745	61,885
Lobito	13,592	23,897	50,164	59,528
Benguela	14,243	14,690	23,253	40,996
Lubango	8,521	11,654	15,086	31,674
Malange	5,299	9,473	19,271	31,599
Kuito	4,671	8,840	5,606	18,941
Namibe	4,926	8,576	7,693	12,076
Cabinda			4,635	21,124
Saurimo			3,092	12,901
Uíge			6,251	11,972
Tômbua			5,943	8,235
Sumbe			4,820	7,911
N'Dalatando			5,571	7,342
Mbanza-Congo			3,525	4,002
Cáala				8,894
Gabela				6,930
Cubal				6,672
Camacupa				5,740
Menongue				3,023
Waku-Kungo				2,784
Negage				2,548
Luena				2,539
Ganda				2,538

Sources: Compiled from INE, 1987.

of capital accumulation and productive life attracted large numbers from the hinterland. Laborers were drawn into these centers as a consequence of job opportunities created by expanding manufacturing and a large commercial and service sector to meet the needs of traders and consumers. People transplanted from rural areas to the anonymity of the towns had to adjust to modern living conditions, internalizing the values, norms, and modes of behavior which characterized Western patterns of society and culture. Hundreds of Angolans succeeded in accommodating or coping with these increased cultural demands, in search of a lifestyle commensurate with their aspirations. The rapid growth of cities suggests a net transfer of people to urban areas associated with changing and perceived economic and social opportunities between rural and urban sectors. Indeed, urbanization in Angola evolved under conditions of dominant colonial economic policies that affected the traditional modes of Portuguese socioeconomic organization, in which migration exerted not only direct, but also indirect effects, by modifying the family patterns and age composition of the cities.

POSTCOLONIAL URBANIZATION TRENDS

The Lack of Adequate Data

Despite their deficient quality, the Portuguese colonial censuses of 1940, 1950, 1960, and 1970 constitute the longest uninterrupted series of decennial censuses anywhere in the continent, and provide a reasonably accurate picture of regional population trends. Unlike the other former Portuguese colonies, which managed to continue the sequence in 1980 or 1981, Angola had to postpone its 1980 census until 1983, when the population of the Province of Luanda was enumerated. In 1984, similar enumerations were carried out in the provinces of Cabinda, Zaire, and Namibe. In the remaining provinces, however, the military situation had deteriorated to the point where a complete enumeration was no longer possible. Consequently, only the provincial capitals and a few accessible areas in the interior were covered. Even these data were never completely processed: complete census tabulations exist of the aforementioned provinces and the *municípios* of Uíge, Negage, and Lubango, but the Istituto Nacional de Estatística (INE, National Statistical Institute), with assistance from United Nations Fund for Population Activities, has just begun the processing of the remaining census returns.

A useful source of information on urban problems is the survey on household consumption patterns carried out by the Ministry of Planning, with support from UNICEF, in the periphery of Luanda, in early 1990 (UNICEF, 1990). UNDP has recently started a project with the INE to improve basic statistics, including some small-scale surveys, and UNFPA plans to sponsor a series of demographic and health surveys in the near future.

The Population Division of the United Nations (1991a) estimates the 1990 population of Angola at 10.02 million and the rate of increase from 1985 to

1990 at 2.7 percent per annum. The urban growth rate during the same period is estimated at 5.6 percent per annum and the rural growth rate at 1.7 percent per annum, with an overall 28 percent of the population living in urban areas in 1990, up from 10 percent in 1960, 15 percent in 1970, and 21 percent in 1980 (United Nations, 1991b). The Population Reference Bureau (1986) cities an urbanization index of 25 percent for 1985. For the capital Luanda, the United Nations (UN) gives a population of 1,717,000 in 1990, with a growth rate of 5.8 percent per annum for the period from 1985 to 1990.

Angolan demographers generally consider these national and urban growth rates to be seriously underestimated. Because no complete national census has been conducted since 1970, the United Nations, in its population projections, does not consider any data collected after independence. Instead, its projections are based on a constant total fertility rate (TFR) of 6.40. Fertility analyses of the 1983–84 census returns, from provinces where censuses were carried out, even the capital Luanda, consistently have TFRs exceeding 8.0. Based on the partial returns of the 1983–84 census and using mathematical extrapolations where such results were not available, the Angolan National Institute of Statistics (INE, 1987) prepared urbanization estimates in Angola, which suggest that in 1990 37 percent of the Angolan population lived in cities, considerably more than the UN estimate of 28 percent. Despite the lower overall proportions of urban population predicted by the UN, its estimates of the population of Luanda, at least until 1995, are on the high side. Whereas the 1983 census of the Province of Luanda (98 percent of which was urban) enumerated a total population of 923,842, the UN estimated the population of the City of Luanda at 948,000 in 1980 and 1,284,000 in 1985. Based on census figures, INE elaborated 1,544,400 in 1990 and 1,994,200 in 1995, compared with the UN forecasts of 1,717,000 and 2,257,000, respectively.

Issues of Urbanization after Independence

Rural to urban migration constitutes one of the most serious problems of urbanization in Angola. In the case of Angola, the migration to the cities is not generally brought about by the search for employment, as the peasant population does not have the basic skills which would allow it to work in the city. Migration occurs due to the search for basic services which can be found only in the cities. In this context, an extremely important component of internal migration is the forced migration of political and other refugees motivated by the civil war that attracted migrants to the cities, at first gradually and later at an accelerated pace. As a result, migratory movements in the 1980s differed from those of the 1940s.

On the eve of independence, Angola faced the challenge of economic recession and a history of colonial underdevelopment, particularly a critical shortage of trained manpower to replace Portuguese employers and technicians, most of whom left the country. Government attempts to escape this background of deprivation were preempted by the outbreak of an extended civil war and military aggression. Two decades of military insecurity and physical disaster condemned thousands to forced rural-urban migration and exile in neighboring countries. Then, in these years of threats and economic hardship in rural areas, cities attracted thousands of people. The long-drawn conflict and the disastrous upheavals which it has entailed, particularly in the countryside, contributed to the uncontrolled and anarchic growth of cities, which became places of refuge and assistance.

The State Secretariat of Social Issues officially estimates the number of displaced persons at 648,000. Apart from this group, which is being attended to in centers especially created for this purpose, another 406,000 in the rural areas are qualified as "rural inhabitants affected by the war situation," and 447,000 as "refugees to the urban areas," who do not receive any special assistance. It is expected, somewhat unrealistically, that the latter group will return to their rural residences as soon as the military situation allows. In addition, by the end of 1990, another 310,000 Angolans had sought refuge in Zaire, 98,000 in Zambia, 40,000 in Namibia, and 1,200 in other neighboring countries.

The urbanization process has been extended by severely deficient living conditions. Besides Luanda, the private economic and administrative centers of Malange, Huambo, Benguela, and Lobito are the main urban agglomerations, whose populations range from 150 to 300 thousand inhabitants (Figure 7.1).

The structure of the urban labor market changed profoundly, as attempts to create a centrally planned economy did not produce the desired results. In the 1960 census, the activity rate of the population of Luanda over age 10 was 64 percent. By 1983, it had fallen to 36 percent (55 percent for men and 16 percent for women). In Uíge (urban population of 58,305 in 1984) and Lubango (95,915), economic participation was even lower: 32 percent and 25 percent, respectively. According to preliminary results from the Luanda household expenditure survey (UNICEF, 1990), which used a less restrictive definition of economic activity, the Luanda labor force totaled 835,000, divided among the following categories: 4 percent in public administration, 14 percent in state enterprises, 7 percent in private or mixed enterprises, 17 percent self-employed, 52 percent unemployed, and 5 percent in other categories.

Commerce suffered in Luanda with only 19,646 active workers enumerated in 1983 compared to 19,399 twenty-three years earlier in 1960. A large parallel circuit arose to serve needs unattended by the official outlets in the formal sector (Morice, 1985). At present, in Luanda an estimated 78 percent of all basic consumption goods are acquired through these parallel markets (*candonga*), as the official distribution systems are increasingly incapable of providing for either private consumption or the needs of the productive sector. Chronic shortages of raw materials, equipment, spare parts, and other supplies have become a common part of life in the Angolan cities. Also, the parallel market has created substantial income differentials. The UNICEF survey indicates that the real consumption per adult equivalent of Luanda families in the highest income decile differed by a factor 9 from that of the poorest decile.

Figure 7.1
Provincial Divisions and Main Angolan Cities and Towns

While Angola is one of the most sparsely inhabited countries of Africa, it is rapidly urbanizing. Since 1975, there has been a growing gap in housing needs, with a current shortage estimated at 370,000 units for urban Angola. Deprived of adequate maintenance, the existing housing stock has undergone deterioration and decay, while construction on officially allotted plots in areas which should accommodate the waves of new migrants has been minimal. The cities experienced the adverse effects of rapid urban growth and change: congestion, pollution, unemployment, inadequate social services, delinquency, and the growth of slums and squatter settlements on the urban fringes. The lack of urban plans further aggravated the acute problems, particularly in Luanda.

LUANDA: A PROCESS OF DISURBANIZATION

A Demographic Analysis of Contemporary Growth in Luanda

Table 7.3 depicts the growth of Luanda until 1974, when the city had approximately 600,000 inhabitants. During 1940 to 1970, the average annual growth rate reached 7 percent, practically doubling the population each decade.

Table 7.3
Luanda: Population, 1818–1974

Year	Population
1818	4,490
1845	5,605
1881	11,172
1898	20,106
1930	50,588
1940	61,028
1950	141,647
1960	224,540
1970	480,613
1974	590,000

Sources: Compiled from INE, 1987.

The Population Division of the United Nations (1991b) extrapolated the population of Luanda, based on 1950–70 data to 1,284,000 in 1985, 1,717,000 in 1990, 2,257,000 in 1995, and 2,866,000 in 2000. This extrapolation does not include the estimated 120,000 Portuguese settlers living in the capital who fled the country at independence. The National Statistical Institute (INE, 1987) population forecasts of the Province of Luanda are 1,155,100 in 1985, 1,544,400 in 1990, and 1,994,200 in 1995. Finally, Luis Filipe S. Colaço (1991), who used an appropriate demographic projection methodology based on the 1983 census returns, forecasted a population of 1,590,000 for 1990, expected to increase to 2,200,500 by 1995.

Although the direct impact of migration from the rural areas on the urban infrastructure has been dramatic, it is often forgotten that it contributes at least half of the city's growth in the 1980s, and most of the increase after independence should be attributed to natural increase, conditioned by the indirect consequences of migration. Net migration rates are high, but not higher than during the 1960s. Amaral (1968:63) mentions that around 1960, Luanda had a crude birthrate (CBR) of 26 per 1,000 and a crude death rate (CDR) of 13, giving a natural increase of 1.33 percent per annum. This seems too low; with a CBR this low and the age structure of that date, the TFR should have been 3.57 children per woman. Probably, the birth register was underenumerated, for alternative sources (Salazar, 1987) indicate a TFR of at least 4.03. It is reasonable to assume that the CBR was from 29 to 34 per 1,000, implying a natural increase of 1.6–2.1 percent per annum. Since the growth rate was about 6.3 percent per annum, this implies an enormous expansion due to migration, on the order of 4.2–4.7 percent per annum.

An analysis of the 1983 census returns by INE (Salazar, 1987), using William Brass's method, yielded a TFR (Total Fertility Rate) of 8.81 children per woman. Our analysis, based on the Ansley Coale–James Trussell method, with a more conservative choice of the P/F ratio, yielded a slightly smaller result of 8.11 children per woman. P/F ratios relate parity to current cumulated fertility and indicate whether an underenumeration of births has occurred during a reference period. Trussell's method for infant and child mortality measurement gives an estimated life expectancy of 51 years for both sexes, 50 for men and 52 for women. The 1983 age structure suggests a short-term CBR of 59 per 1,000 and a CDR of 15 per 1,000, implying a natural increase of 4.4 percent per annum. If current fertility and mortality were to continue, without migration, the long-term growth rate would be 3.85 percent per annum with the remaining 0.55 percent due to the transitional effects caused by the unbalanced age and sex structure, which in turn are indirect effects of migration.

The large rise of natural increase since 1960 is not due to an improvement of health conditions but instead, to the much higher fertility of the African population which occupied the city after the Portuguese settlers left. Using Mortara's method on numbers of children ever born in the 1983 and in the 1960 censuses, the INE study found a 74 percent fertility increase in 1983 over 1960.

To this fertility increase, one should add a smaller effect caused by modifications in the age and sex composition of the population. Like many colonial cities in Africa and Asia (Ward, 1985), Luanda in 1960 had a heavily biased sex structure, with 57.7 percent men and 42.3 percent women. In the reproductive age group, from ages 15 to 49, the imbalance was particularly strong, with a sex ratio of 154 men per 100 women. Consequently, women of prime childbearing ages (15–39) constituted only 18.9 percent of the population. The predominance of men in the city has not entirely disappeared after independence, and it seems likely that the 1983 figures actually understate this phenomenon to some extent.

The proportion of women of prime childbearing ages is slightly higher than in 1960. The population of Luanda in 1983 is younger than it was in 1960, with a decline of the proportion over age 50 from 6.6 to 3.9 percent. These factors, together, account for another 10 percent increase of the rate of natural increase.

In-migration to Luanda is relatively easy to quantify, as the 1983 census gives a total of 34,578 inhabitants with a declared residence outside the province one year before the census date, and 182,175 within five years before the census, whereas 171,255 declared having moved to Luanda during the past five years. The differences between these data are more likely to result from definitional problems than from fluctuations in the annual rate of in-migration. Thus, the number of in-migrants during the year preceding the census should be 34,500 to 42,500, and the in-migration rate from 37.5 to 47.5 per 1,000.

Only 35 to 40 percent of Launda's population consisted of natives of Luanda or Bengo Province, which until 1978 formed one administrative unit. This suggests a continuity of migration to Luanda. The differences between the distributions refer mostly to the gradual decline of the percentage of foreign born, the increase of the proportion of migrants from the north of the country, and the relative decrease of the number of natives from Kwanza Sul, Huambo, and Bié.

Although migrants to Luanda greatly outnumber those leaving the city, the out-migrants cannot be entirely ignored. Its estimation poses some problems, due to the small number of areas outside Luanda. The following list gives the number of migrants for the five-year period preceding the census between Luanda and areas where census operations were carried out:

From Cabinda to Luanda: 18,524

From Zaire to Luanda: 5,399

From Namibe to Luanda: 129

From Uíge to Luanda: 27,425

From Huíla to Luanda: 459

From Luanda to Cabinda: 575

From Luanda to Zaire: 187

From Luanda to Namibe: 618

From Luanda to Uíge: (550)

From Luanda to Negage: (108)

From Luanda to Lubango: (1,281)

The parentheses refer to the fact that the census in the provinces of Uíge and Huíla was limited to the municipalities of Uíge, Negage, and Lubango. Unfortunately, these municipalities constitute only a small portion of their provincial populations. Therefore, to consider the number of in-migrants from Luanda in these municipalities representative of provincial figures causes severe underestimation. An alternative is to prorate these numbers to the estimated provincial populations in 1983, yielding 5,241 in-migrants in Uíge and 9,991 in Huíla. This, in turn, may be somewhat overestimated, as it seems likely that in-migrants from Luanda would be disproportionally concentrated in the major cities. At best, one may conclude that out-migration from Luanda was somewhere around 6.4–32.0 percent of the in-migration, resulting in an out-migration rate of 2.5–15.0 per 1,000.

Summarizing these tentative results gives the following decomposition of Luanda's 1983 growth rate:

Long-term natural increase (intrinsic growth rate):	3.85 percent
Natural increase due to the current age structure:	0.55 percent
In-migration:	3.75–4.75 percent
Out-migration:	−0.25–1.50 percent
Total:	6.65–8.90 percent

These geometric growth rates may be converted to exponential growth rates of 6.44–8.53 percent.

Social Aspects of the Growth of Luanda

The negative aspects of Luanda's rapid population growth have been widely publicized in such terms as "the city is no longer urban" or "the city has become a *musseque* (shantytown)." These same types of stories appeared in old chronicles and registers of the second half of the nineteenth century.

In 1974, most Europeans and persons of mixed descent, an estimated 335,000, left Angola for Portugal. In Luanda, the departure of about 120,000 Portuguese was accompanied by a massive influx of Angolans from the *musseques* into the city center, where they rapidly occupied the houses and apartments abandoned by their European residents. Subsequently, the anarchy of war drove thousands of people from rural areas into shantytowns on the edge of the city. Population mobility took the form of migration in stages, from rural areas to small towns, then to Luanda.

Within six years, Luanda was transformed in size and ethnic composition, as it experienced a veritable transfusion of population. Complexes of high-rise apartment blocks and houses taken over from European residents and ill-adapted to the needs, resources, and social organization of their new occupants—mainly long-term urban residents—were rapidly overcrowded and fell into disrepair. Clustered throughout the city, the proportion and growth of the *musseques* increased dramatically, and as new ones sprang up on the periphery, the majority of their dwellers, particularly recent rural migrants, new urbanites, poor, illiterate, with few skills or resources, strongly influenced by rural customs and values, remained poorly integrated into the urban way of life.

An analysis of the relationship between urbanization and migration in the context of Angola's situation reveals that migration has brought about essential changes, but in the common sense of "rurbanization" of the city, denoting a blending of rural and urban cultural traits and patterns (Stren, 1986). Sociologically, it is a way of life, a subnational community with a set of norms and values characterized by deprivation, illiteracy, diseases, epidemics, personal and social disorganization, deviant behavior, and marginality. The city of Luanda is no longer urban, but has become sub-urban, in the sense of the Portuguese word *subúrbio*. People are there, but do not belong to it, just living there without adjustment. Under these circumstances, they have "(dis)urbanized" the city.

They did not invade it; they took refuge there. Because more than 80 percent of the city's inhabitants don't have urban customs, the result was a break with everything that makes a city.

In Luanda a large gap exists between rural and urban values, attitudes, aspirations, and goals, even as people of widely differing cultural backgrounds and social organizations interact. When people move into areas and disrupt established institutions and social structures, the disruptions lead to social and psychological dislocations and dissatisfaction. In the end, a process of assimilation occurs by which the various cultural differences gradually disappear.

With regard to the role of migration in the urbanization process, other major social implications may be inferred: (1) migration patterns in Angola have evolved through a complex combination of factors; (2) the determinants and consequences of rural-urban migration vary according to the specific social and cultural context, but certainly lead to urban growth; (3) because of environmental stress, readjustment to rapid urban change can be unprecedented, with disorganizational consequences; and (4) when a large gap exists between the characteristics and behavior of urban residents, the city changes in the common sense of "rurbanization" when most inhabitants are newcomers from rural areas.

URBAN PLANNING ISSUES

During the colonial period, the political and administrative division of Angola had as its objective the political administration of the territory. There was little interest in basic health services or primary education, as there was no compatibility between the political administration and these services.

The government policy with respect to the massive influx of rural migrants into Luanda has been laissez-faire: at no point has it intervened in the process. On the other hand, little has been done to adapt the existing urban infrastructure to the ever-increasing number of users, or even to maintain the capacity already installed. Not infrequently, government technicians hold the view that massive rural-urban migration and its consequences in the urban areas, such as the growth of the informal sector, are somehow "abnormal" and that these phenomena will disappear when political stability returns.

Consequently, the massive transfer of population from the countryside to the city has provoked severe problems which interfered with social and economic reconstruction. The environment has deteriorated dangerously in the last decade. Limited health care, poor housing, and unsanitary living conditions have increased the incidence of malaria and frequent outbreaks of cholera. These problems are compounded in high population densities in *musseque* areas like Rangel and Vila Operário, in the range from 250 to 350 inhabitants per hectare. The housing shortage, estimated at 160,000 for Luanda alone, is of serious concern. Urban transportation is severely inadequate, leaving large segments of the population with no access to services. Between 1981 and 1987, the number of urban buses in service declined 77 percent, and the number of passengers served by

87 percent (United Nations Development Program/World Bank, 1989). To provide an alternative, private cars have been authorized (Processo 500) to serve as taxis, charging about 40 times as much as the largely symbolic price of the bus fare. The transportation problem in turn is partly responsible for the high degree of labor absenteeism in government firms and institutions.

The water supply system of Luanda has deteriorated due to years of neglect. In other cities, like Huambo, it became inoperative several years ago. The acutely deficient public educational system contributes to low enrollment. After an initial increase soon after independence, gross enrollment ratios for the country as a whole started declining in 1979, from 69 percent in 1981–82 to 52 percent in 1987–88, for the 6–14 age group. The number of classrooms available for basic education declined from 18,955 to 10,392 in the same period, and the number of teachers from 43,899 to 31,367. The list of indicators of stagnation and decay could be continued almost indefinitely.

The first Master Plan for Luanda was prepared in 1942, under the Colonial Act of 1933, suggesting segregated residential development of European and native quarters. In 1962 a Town Planning Bureau was created to integrate the various racial, ethnic, and economic groups, including the integration of the *musseques* into the overall development strategy. In 1971, a French consulting firm was contracted to produce a Comprehensive Urban Development Plan, which was widely criticized as an instrument of the colonial administration for safeguarding the privileges and services available to the white settlers, based on a concept of spatial and functional segregation. Nevertheless, it provided the *musseque* population with limited access to some services and employment opportunities. The *musseques* were to be organized as reception areas for newly arrived migrants and residential areas for the rest of the African population (Mendes, 1988). After independence, and with Cuban assistance, the National Directorate of Physical Planning elaborated a new plan (Ministério de Construção e Habitação, 1979), based on the following elements:

1. Expansion of green areas;
2. Adjustment of the new housing development areas to those already foreseen;
3. Relocation of the airport and alternative uses of its present area;
4. Development of a commercial and an industrial port;
5. Reorganization of the railway system and construction of a subway; and
6. Preservation and productive use of the coastal landscape.

None of these plans were ever implemented. A new Urban Development Plan is beginning to be elaborated, with support from the World Bank. Among other things, the 1979 plan was unrealistic in that it greatly underestimated the potential growth of the city, whose population was projected to be only 1,650,000 by the year 2010. It has been suggested that, in order to be successful, the new plan should be modest and cumulative in scope, avoiding the grand schemes of earlier planning efforts, which cannot function in a context of uncontrolled growth, deficient information, and weak administrative capacity.

After a period of political turmoil immediately following independence, during which construction came to a standstill, the building of residential housing was resumed with Cuban and Council for Mutual Economic Assistance in 1977, at a rate of 250 dwellings per year, too little for the present need of 16,000 units per year in Luanda. The program, which consisted largely of the construction of small four-to-six floor apartment buildings, was criticized for several reasons (Mendes, 1988), such as lack of adaptation of the basic layout to typical family sizes and other local circumstances, dependence on imported building materials, and poor organization of the construction process. With respect to typical family sizes, Angola is completely different from Cuba. According to preliminary results from a survey in the periphery of Luanda (UNICEF, 1990), the median number of persons per household was 7.5, but the median number of bedrooms only 2.5. In practice, however, the building of small apartment complexes has been the *de facto* housing policy, as little or nothing has been done to implement alternative approaches, such as slum upgrading programs, or the construction of other kinds of public housing (Galil-Lewin et al., 1990).

After 1985, investment in Luanda housing fell off to almost zero in 1987. Apart from the consequences of the civil war, the general deficiencies in economic management associated with an ineffective central planning approach, high prices of imported building materials, the lack of definition of housing priorities and policies, limited technical capacity, lack of local autonomy of the executing agencies, including lack of locally generated revenues, and the absence of community involvement in the definition and execution of policies are problems that have plagued the construction sector. Consequently, the public housing available is still largely comprised of 127,800 units (in all of Angola, most of which are in Luanda) left behind by their Portuguese occupants in 1975. Unlike some provincial delegations, the Housing Directorate in Luanda is not in a position to administer its housing stock, due to a lack of strategies and priorities, qualified personnel, funds, and logistic support. No inventory is kept, and a substantial number of the tenants, many of whom belong to the middle- or upper-income brackets, do not pay rent because control and enforcement instruments are lacking. Even rents that are collected are 5–10 times lower than the typical private-sector rents paid for much poorer housing in the *musseques,* and do not even begin to pay for repairs and preventive maintenance that would be necessary if the existing housing stock were kept up.

To help meet the housing needs of the city, site and service schemes are being officially developed by the Urban Development, Land Survey, and Cadastral Services, which annually distribute about 1,200 plots, a fraction of the 10,000 applications received, a small fraction of the number needed. Bureaucratic and other obstacles, which may take years to resolve, are responsible for the small number of plots distributed. Once a plot is actually delivered, the leasing conditions are extremely favorable. Nevertheless, in practice land transactions are mostly the domain of the illegal but well-established informal land market, where the price of a standard construction plot, depending on size and location, may vary from $1,500 to $7,500. At present, the expansion of Luanda's housing stock takes place almost exclusively through this kind of self-help construction, most of it in the *musseques,* which housed about a third of Luanda's population at the turn of the century, about half just before independence, and at present nearly two-thirds. However, as the chances of eviction from the land, even when illegally obtained, are minimal, residents tend to invest in their homes, and consequently the quality of construction is fairly good.

Luanda's water supply system dates from 1888 and at the time served only 15 percent of the population. A new system was implanted in 1953, capturing water from the Bengo River, with a total capacity of 60,000 cubic meters per day. As this soon became insufficient, a second system, with a capacity of 70,000 cubic meters, was installed in 1971, and expanded to 140,000 cubic meters in 1981. The actual supply is far inferior to the installed capacity of 200,000 cubic meters, due to lack of equipment and poor maintenance. In several areas, the water supply has ceased altogether. In other areas, it is frequently interrupted. Its mean volume amounts to about 140,000 cubic meters per day, compared to an estimated demand of 450,000, which is expected to increase to 600,000 by the year 2000. There are plans to upgrade the existing network, with support from the French government, but these reforms will serve mostly the middle-class areas. As yet, there are no plans for expanding the network in the *musseques.* Yet, according to a survey carried out in 1989 among 250 households in the Sambizanga area, lack of sufficient drinking water is generally perceived as the major problem of the urban infrastructure (Galil-Lewin et al., 1990).

Luanda has no sewage system. In the 1960s, septic tanks in the city were connected to the drainage network for storm-water. This, added to poor maintenance, led to the decay of the network, the flooding of lower zones, and poor sanitary conditions, which are partially responsible for the annual cholera epidemics. Inadequate drainage also aggravated the problem of erosion in some areas. In the *musseques,* storm-water drainage practically does not exist, resulting in flooding and pools of stagnant and contaminated water, which are breeding grounds for mosquitoes and malaria. Refuse collection also deteriorated to critical levels during the 1980s, to the extent that the empty terrains next to some apartment buildings in the city center turned into virtual garbage dumps. In 1989, the Provincial Commissariat contracted a foreign company with German and Philippino management, for about $5 million per year, to collect about 75,000 cubic meters of refuse each month from containers placed on the public driveways (Galil-Lewin et al., 1990). Most of the *musseques* do not benefit from these services.

Despite the apparent incapability of Luanda to solve its basic problems of urban infrastructure, the national planning strategy suffered from an excessive concentration of resources in the capital. To constitute an urban system as such in Angola should be a strategic priority, conjugating natural resources, existing infrastructure, and the political and administrative infrastructure to be created, so that the urbanization process may proceed on a solid economic basis, to promote development. Therefore, the definition of the regional urban subsystem, in which the basic services (education and health) are defined, could be an investment in order to stabilize the flight of population from the countryside to the city, while it would at the same time contribute to agricultural development. Otherwise Luanda may continue to grow at present rates for at least another decade.

REFERENCES

Amaral, Ilídio do. 1962. *Ensaio de um estudo geográfico da rede urbana de Angola.* Lisboa: Junta de Investigações do Ultramar, Estudos, Ensaios e Documentos 97.

———. 1968. *Luanda: estudo de geografia urbana.* 2a Série, no. 53. Lisboa: Memória da Junta de Investigações do Ultramar.

———. 1978. "Contribuição para o conhecimento do fenómeno de urbanização em Angola." Separata de *Finisterra. Revista Portuguesa de Geografia* 13:43–76.

Amin, Samir. 1974. *Modern migrations in Western Africa.* London: Oxford University Press.

Bettencourt, José de Sousa. 1965. "Subsídios para o estudo sociológico da população de Luanda." *Boletim do Instituto de Investigação Científica de Angola* (Luanda) 2:83–130.

Colaço, Luis Filipe S. 1991. *Angola: projecções da população 1990–2010.* Luanda: Ministry of Education.

Dilolwa, Carlos Rocha. 1978. *Contribuição à história económica de Angola.* Luanda: Imprensa Nacional de Angola.

Galil-Lewin, A. C., T. Chana, and A. Torres. 1990. *Housing and Squatter Upgrading in Luanda, Angola.* Luanda: United Nations Development Program Mission Report.

Gregory, Joel. 1988. "Migrations et urbanisation." In *Population et sociétés en Afrique au Sud du Sahara,* edited by Dominique Tabutin, 369–395. Paris: l'Harmattan.

INE (Instituto Nacional de Estatística). 1987. *Projecção da população do país por províncias para o período 1970/85.* Boletim Demográfico 4. Luanda: INE.

Massiah, Gustave, and Jean-François Tribillon. 1988. *Villes en développement.* Paris: La Découverte.

Mendes, Maria Clara. 1988. "Slum Housing in Luanda, Angola: Problems and Possibilities." In *Slum and Squatter Settlements in Sub-Saharan Africa: Toward a Planning Strategy,* edited by Robert A. Obudho and Constance C. Mhlanga, 231–243. New York: Praeger.

Ministério da Construção e Habitação. 1979. *Esquema preliminar do Plano Director da Cidade de Luanda.* Luanda: Ministério da Construção e Habitação, Direcção Nacional de Planificação Física.

Morice, Alain. 1985. "Commerce parallèle et troc à Luanda." *Politique Africaine* 17:105–120.

Mourão, Fernando de Albuquerque. 1988. *Continuidades e descontinuidades de um processo colonial, através de uma leitura de Luanda.* São Paulo: Tese de Livre Docência University of São Paulo.

Population Reference Bureau (PRB). 1986. *World Population Data Sheet 1985*. Washington, D.C.: PRB.

Salazar, Julia. 1987. *Estimativa da fecundidade da Província de Luanda efectuada através dos dados do censo-1983*. Documento de Trabalho 2. Luanda: INE.

Stren, R. 1986. "The Ruralization of African Cities: Learning to Live with Poverty." In *Coping with Rapid Urban Growth in Africa*, edited by R. Stren and C. Letemendia, iii–xxi. Montreal: Centre for Developing Area Studies, McGill University.

Thornton, J. 1980. "The Slave Trade in Eighteenth Century Angola: Effects on Demographic Structures." *Canadian Journal of African Studies* 14:417–427.

UNICEF. 1990. *Luanda Household Budget and Nutrition Survey*. Preliminary Report. Luanda: UNICEF.

United Nations. 1991a. *World Population Prospects 1990*. Population Studies 120. New York: United Nations, Dept. of International Economic and Social Affairs.

———. 1991b. *World Urbanization Prospects 1990: Estimates and Projections of Urban and Rural Populations and of Urban Agglomerations*. New York: United Nations, Dept. of International Economic and Social Affairs.

United Nations Development Program/World Bank. 1989. *Angola: análise económica introdutória*. 2 vols. Relatório 7283-ANG. Luanda: UNDP.

Ward, Kathryn B. 1985. "Women and Urbanization in the World-System." In *Urbanization in the World-Economy*, edited by Michael Timberlake, 305–323. New York: Academic Press.

8

Congo

Gabriel Tati

The search for a balanced pattern of urban growth and regional development has become one of the dominant concerns of the policies undertaken by the Congo authorities. In the Congo urban population growth is considered a threat because of its high level (ORSTOM/AGECO, 1987). As early as 1965, with its degree of urbanization estimated at 31 percent, the Congo was at the top of the French-speaking African countries classified according to their degree of urbanization (United Nations, 1991).

Since the independence of the country in 1960, the massive settling of social, economic, administrative, and cultural infrastructures in urban areas has been accompanied by a high growth of urban population. Although no major change in the number of principal towns has occurred since 1960 (there were four in 1960 and six in 1990), the urban population has increased nearly fivefold in the period 1960–84. Besides, in that period only two towns, Brazzaville, the political capital, and Pointe-Noire, the commercial capital, have seen their importance grow. Both remain by far the most important towns since the independence of the country.

The urban evolution prevailing in the Congo is of concern when the size of the total population of the country is considered. In 1984, there were a total of 1,909,248 inhabitants whereas the urban population was 992,809. The rapid urban growth has generated a lot of social and economic problems for town management; it is therefore difficult for planning to achieve a balanced regional development (ORSTOM/AGECO, 1987). The authorities are attempting to solve these problems, and that concern obviously requires a very good knowledge of the urban dynamics, particularly of its sociodemographical angle, which has not yet been the subject of extensive investigations. The urban population is increasing rapidly at 6.7 percent a year; the high urban growth is explained by a massive in-migration into the urban area. That in-migration is related to the progressive modernization of the economic activity in the towns, which widely offer urban residents many possibilities to participate in the national division of labor.

Urbanization is not solely demographic concentrations but also the manifestation of access possibilities to social services, to housing, and to economic participation. This chapter will focus on certain aspects of that manifestation related to economic participation in the major town, Brazzaville, because of its importance in the total urban population.

Moreover, the pattern of urban growth since the independence of the country reveals the lack of asserted policies to bring under control the process of urbanization. We shall revert to these considerations in the last section of the chapter regarding the diverse urbanization policies implemented.

The data upon which this chapter is based come from two censuses (1974 and 1984), two surveys (1960 and 1973), and other research works related to urban issues in the Congo and in Africa.

URBAN POPULATION AND URBANIZATION

Urbanization is a process which refers to the demographic evolution within a given administrative or geographic space comprised by a set of towns. In the Congo particularly, the concept of town is still not defined correctly because the geographical space known as the urban area by the administrative authorities sounds more like a political agreement or procedure than an objective view of the urban reality. Apart from the four towns created by the ex-colonizer power, two others have been declared "towns" by decree.

These six towns are, in rank order, Brazzaville (the political and administrative capital of the country), Pointe-Noire (harbor town with commercial activities), Loubomo (a former railway station which has become progressively an important town though its population size is still small), N'kayi (an agri-industrial town with a small population), Ouesso and Mossendjo (two small towns with a very low modern economic activity except traditional agriculture). The two latter were included as urban in the period 1974–84. Since the country won independence in 1960, Brazzaville and Pointe-Noire have been the only towns in which important demographic gains have been observed, as shown by their urban growth rates (Table 8.1).

Urban Growth from 1960 to 1984

Since 1960 the urban growth rate has increased rapidly. In the 1960–74 period the urban growth rate was 6.6 percent, and in the second period, 1974–84, the rate was 6.8 percent, a very small increase. However, that evolution has not

Table 8.1
Growth Rates of Town Populations, 1960–84

Town	Period	
	1960 - 1974	1974 - 1984
Brazzaville	6.4	6.6
Pointe-Noire	5.3	7.4
Loubomo	6.0	5.4
N'kayi	9.5	2.3
Mossendjo	-	1.9
Ouesso	-	2.6
Total	6.6	6.8

been experienced in the same way by each of the main towns, for there are obviously some disparities between towns. Brazzaville and Pointe-Noire have experienced an increase in their demographic growth rate (more important for Pointe-Noire), whereas Loubomo and N'kayi experienced a decline in their rate of population growth.

The significant increase in the resident populations of the two major towns, Brazzaville and Pointe-Noire, can be explained by the fact that before independence, they were the center of industrial, administrative, commercial, and political activities. Since independence, the macroeconomic, commercial, and social policies undertaken by the political authorities have remained in favor of those two towns and have widely contributed to their important demographic gains.

The degree of urbanization, indicating the percentage of the country's population living in urban areas, was 27 percent in 1960 and 38 percent in 1974 (Table 8.2). In 1984 the percentage was 52 (the two small towns Ouesso and Mossendjo being included). With regard to the evolution of the urbanization, Congo stands above the average for central Africa (United Nations, 1991).

Besides, projections of urban population calculated over the period 1990–2005 (Tati, 1989) reveal that 55 percent of the whole country's population will live in urban areas. Because of the projected high level of urbanization, like Colombia or Mexico, the Congo will face many economic and social problems.

The major town of the country, Brazzaville, has played an important role in the high level of urbanization since 1960, with the share of the whole country's

Table 8.2
Degree of Urbanization for Each Town since 1960

	Year			Annual variation Percent	
Town	1960	1974	1984	1960-74	1974-84
Brazzaville	16	23	31	3	3
Pointe-Noire	8	11	15	1	4
Loubomo	2	2	2	2	2
N'kayi	1	2	2	6	-1.8
Ouesso					
Mossendjo					
Total	27	38	52	2	3

population living in that city increasing steadily to 31 percent in 1984. The demographic imbalance in the urban structure implied by its weight is evident. In that city has lived 60 percent of the total urban population since 1960.

Pointe-Noire's share of the total population of the country rose from 8 percent in 1960 to 15 percent in 1984. It is very likely that its economic function, primarily related to the oil industry, has contributed greatly to its expansion.

The two major cities are experiencing rapid demographic expansions, but the situation is different for the four others. Their small sizes range between 11,000 and 50,000 inhabitants and reflect their small contribution to the urban growth of the country. Those towns on the whole have only 6 percent of the total population.

Without taking into account all aspects of the country's economy, we have to point out that demographic imbalance within the urban area reflects the macroeconomic orientations and others mentioned above. The two larger towns are centers of the country's industrial activity. Besides, public and administrative services have been concentrated there just like the school structure (secondary schools, grammar schools, and the sole university in the country). If we refer to the closed links which exist between population mobility and variation in the size of urban agglomeration, then localization of economic and social country infrastructures in the urban area plays an essential role in the positive demographic dynamic of the two main towns while its effect is negative in the dynamics of the four others.

Those links are also related to the sources of urban growth since the towns have to be considered not only by the increases in their residents but by links existing between that growth and demographic and administrative aspects such as fertility, mortality, and migration in the urban area. Those aspects form the essentials of the components of urban growth (Goldstein and Sly, 1979). An analysis of these aspects provides an understanding of the dynamism of the urban phenomenon and its components (United Nations, ECA, 1989).

Source of Urban Growth

Previously, it was shown that in the Congo the process of urbanization is characterized on one hand by a rapid urban growth and, on another, by a concentration of the urban population in the bigger cities, Brazzaville and Pointe-Noire. That urban configuration has not changed much since independence as far as the number of important cities.

In other respects, the measurement of the aggregate demographic growth between 1974 and 1984 indicates a rate of 3.5 percent per year for the whole country. The natural increase is estimated at 2.6 percent, and consequently, the share of the growth to be attributed to migration (internal and international) is 1.1 percent. If the international migrants settle to a great extent in the urban areas, the relatively high level of the urban growth, 6.8 percent between 1974 and 1984, could primarily be the outcome of the net migration between towns and rural areas and of natural increase. The hypothesis can be tested by estimating the contribution of each urban growth component mentioned earlier.

The influence of migration on the evolution of the urban growth is difficult to accurately measure. It is the same thing for the natural increase. That difficulty relies on the lack of adequate data of good quality. It is true that demographic data are still poor for a great number of African countries, and Congo is in that situation. For that country, demographic indicators are provided by two censuses, two surveys which have covered the urban area, and also by estimations by international organizations such as United Nations, World Health Organization (WHO), International Labor Organization (ILO), or United Nations Children's Fund (formerly United Nations International Children's Emergency Fund) (UNICEF). Nevertheless, those data can provide good estimates of demographic indicators if they are adjusted.

Before determining the contribution of each of those components in the urban growth, let us examine, at a first stage, a general view of the evolution of each since 1960.

Evolution of the Natural Increase in Urban Areas

The levels of natality in 1960, 1974, and 1984 indicate a high birthrate in the urban area (Table 8.3). The data show respectively birthrates of 45, 42, and 44 percent (Tati, 1989). Until 1974, urban natality was lower than the rural rate of

Table 8.3
Crude Birthrates for Areas and Towns since 1960

	Year		
Town and area	1960	1974	1984
Brazzaville	53	43	43
Pointe-Noire	48	34	44
Loubomo	52	44	46
N'kayi	40	46	27
Ouesso	-	-	43
Mossendjo	-	-	39
Urban area	45	42	44
Rural area	50	50	40
Total	47	46	42

50. However, in 1984 the urban natality is relatively higher than the rural rate of 40, whereas the average for the whole country was 42.

The high birthrates explain to a great extent the high percentage of young adults among the urban population. Such a high birthrate could be attributed to an improvement of health services, to a relative rising living standard, and to the launching of public health programs in the towns (mainly the two bigger towns). It could also be the result of a social behavior which consists in attributing a positive value to a high number of children and of the urban immigration from rural areas since it brings important numbers of people able to procreate.

Significant differences in the birthrates are likewise observed throughout the six main towns. Fluctuations from one town to another are quite remarkable. The town of N'kayi experienced a drop in its birthrate (46 percent in 1974 and 27 percent in 1984).

Life expectancy at birth increased from 50 years in 1974 to 53 years in 1984, a gain of three years in the intercensal period. That gain resulted from social policies which improved health conditions in the country. As mentioned above for urban fertility, those health policies have affected only the urban area, particularly the two main towns.

Migration in Urban Areas

The rural migrants count for 57 percent of the whole urban population. Migration toward the main towns remained important from 1960 to 1984 (Tati,

Table 8.4
Components of Urban Growth and Their Contribution (Percent)

	1974 - 1984		1960 - 1974	
Component	Value	Percent	Value	Percent
Total urban growth	491737	100	301538	100
Effect of area inclusion in urban area	26408	5	0	0
Net migration	331688	68	244246	81
Natural increase	133641	27	38292	19

1987). About 50 percent of the residents are migrants. The two largest towns attracted more migrants than the four others, particularly in the last five years before the 1984 census. The second most important city, Pointe-Noire, appears to be developing a greater attractiveness than the political capital. Pointe-Noire, with its harbor and its oil industry, could stand at first rank in terms of attractiveness. Another fact to be pointed out is the in-migration coming from rural areas and outside of the country. It appears obvious that the first has been by far the more important since 1960.

Finally, the urban population has changed greatly since 1960 because of migration into the two bigger towns, the favored destinations for rural-urban migrants. Those streams reflect the permanent imbalance in the localization of economic activities and equipment.

As urban growth appears closely linked with rural depopulation, we must try to determine quantitatively the contribution of migration and natural increase to urban growth.

The three components of urban growth are net migration, natural increase, and area reclassification. To determine the share of each is always a difficult task because of the lack of accurate data in many African countries. Nevertheless, for the Congo, it is possible to estimate net migration in 1974 to 1984 using a method described by the United Nations (1971). In the measurement of each component one can estimate the net migration (m) between censuses. Then, an estimate of the natural increase can be made. This method shows that from 1974 to 1984, natural increase accounted for 27 percent of urban growth; net migration, 68 percent; and area reclassification, 5 percent (Table 8.4).

In 1974, there is no information about the out-migration of urban residents to rural areas. However, the in-migration can be obtained from data provided by the 1974 census. Those data indicate that if we neglect the out-migration of urban to rural inhabitants and use the same method as for 1984 data, net migration contributes 81 percent and natural increase contributes 19 percent.

The relatively large contribution of net migration to overall urban population growth overshadows that of natural increase. Its contribution would be higher if its direct and indirect impacts on urban fertility had been taken into account. However, the relative percentage of migration decreased and that of natural increase rose between 1974 and 1984.

Migration has steadily increased since 1960, resulting in more people living in urban areas. However, urban growth also results from natural increase, reflecting a high level of natality and a decline in mortality, especially under 15 years of age.

URBAN SPACE OCCUPATION: CHARACTERISTICS OF THE URBAN LAND MARKET AND OF HOUSING

Access to the soil in Congolese cities reflects the competition to acquire a private house which reflects in turn the phenomenon of densely populated areas. Both large cities are experiencing rapid growth.

Access to the soil is preferably oriented toward areas still empty for many reasons: swamps, landslides, frequent inundations. People look in this way to take advantage of the fact that uninhabited areas are near the "center" of the city. They reduce the acute problem of transport and get nearer to urban social services. The occupation densities of plots increase twofold or even tenfold in some districts including danger zones, as P. Haeringer (1982) also notes for the quarters of the Abidjan city (Côte d'Ivoire). "Popular urbanization" (informal settlements) appearing in both the periphery and the center of the town reflects the competition for the soil in which urban residents are constantly involved (Mashabela, 1990). The acquisition of one's house is a great concern of all Congoleses living in urban areas.

HOUSING MARKET IN THE URBAN AREA

Two simple indicators of housing tenure are presented: the ratio P/L and the ratio P/P + L, where P indicates the number of owners, L the number of renters, and L + P the potential demand of lodgings. The concerned population is of household heads whose ages range from 15 to 65 (people who are economically active).

The census of 1974 reveals that there are two owners for one renter on average (ratio P/L). The demand for housing is satisfied at 62 percent (ratio P/P + L). In the population of owners, in-migrants are overwhelming (for there are six in-migrants for each nonimmigrant).

In 1984 the ratio P/L, calculated from the census data, falls to just over 1, and the demand is only 54 percent satisfied (ratio P/P + L). We can also calculate the two cities Ouesso and Mossendjo, recently included in the urban area, where there are as many owners as renters in each of the four other cities.

The levels of the ratios reveal the keen competition among nonowner urban residents to acquire a home and their likelihood of doing so. We can predict that in cities, and particularly in the two bigger towns of the country, the horizontal expansion of the urban boundaries has increased greatly since 1984, and some renters have become homeowners. Parallel to the peripheral extension of cities, the growing "informal habitat" in the danger zones has to be considered too. Permanent conflicts over the past few years could be evidence of the "informal habitat" proliferation.

ASPECTS OF URBAN LIVING CONDITIONS

The peripheral extension of urban land is not always accompanied by a supply of adequate social services (education and health, for instance) compatible with the size of the population. It is impossible to evaluate accurately the adequacy of the supply of housing and social services and the demand from Congo urban residents.

Characteristics of Housing

The overwhelming majority of urban households do not live in a house that offers minimum comfort. Precarious building materials, sources of energy for the cooking and lighting that are costly and harmful to the environment, low or nonaccess to drinking water, and archaic lavatories are the dominant aspects of the living conditions of urban residents. However, the decline noted in 1984 in the level of those ratios since 1974 expresses an improvement in living conditions.

An improvement may have come from the oil boom that the country experienced between 1974 and 1984, which stimulated the development of several small informal and formal economic activities generating revenues. But the overwhelming majority of urban residents are living in dwelling units that reflect deep poverty.

Supply of Health Services

The supply of health services is unevenly allocated throughout the urban area. In 1979, for instance, 27 percent of the total hospital beds were at Brazzaville, and 15 percent of the total of medical structures in 1981 were in that town. The dominant weight of Brazzaville in the urban area could explain that imbalance. Besides, data on Brazzaville (from Ministry of Health, 1982) reveal that while its rate of population growth was 6.6 percent, the growth rate of medical structures was 3.9 percent in the period 1974–84, thus satisfying about 59 percent of the demand. Moreover, there is a shortage of hospital beds, nurses, and physicians (World Bank, 1992).

There is a scarcity of health staff in the cities. The number of nurses declined between 1965 and 1987. Besides, because of the economic crisis the country has faced since 1985, recruitment of medical staff has stopped even though the urban population is growing rapidly, 7 percent annually.

Health problems in urban areas are aggravated by the poor living conditions of the overwhelming majority of urban residents. The consumption of polluted water causes amoebiasis, with the number of cases reported each year being about 2,000 (Ministry of Health, 1986). As for severe diarrhea, it strikes each year about 25,000 individuals, usually very young children (Ministry of Health, 1981).

Gaining access to health services and acquiring decent housing remain difficult tasks for the majority of urban residents. That difficulty has been reinforced over the past few years by budget reductions the government has adopted in health care. Those budget restrictions are the result of structural adjustment of the economy and have affected other spheres such as education (UNESCO, 1991).

Education

Broadly speaking, the Congo educational system has experienced a significant and steady development since independence. The average annual increase in the number of students was about 7 percent (Ministry of National Education, 1986). The importance of schooling in Congo is reflected, on the one hand, by the high presence of young people (under 20 years old) in school and, on the other hand, efforts by authorities to give each child a basic education. One of the characteristics of those efforts has been for a long time a quasi-free education in Congo. The combination of both elements has increased the enrollment rate for children aged 6 to 14 from 88 percent in 1961 to 94 percent in 1974, setting Congo at the top of African countries (Ministry of Plan, 1976). In 1984, that rate dropped to 86 percent. The decline may be explained by a cut in education spending which occurred early in the 1980s. Although notable differences remain between the educational patterns of girls and boys, there is no doubt that the schooling policy undertaken by authorities, from 1960 to 1984, allowed many children to acquire a basic education. After 1984, many things changed in the schooling policy because of the economic crisis. Among these was increased fees.

Just like health, education is primarily an urban phenomenon, mainly in the two bigger cities. For instance, of the 11 grammar schools of the country, Brazzaville possesses 5 including one technical grammar school. Each of the other cities has one grammar school except Pointe-Noire which has, in addition, a technical grammar school. Besides, in each town there are primary and secondary schools. The sole university of the country is at Brazzaville. If we consider an indicator such as the rate of children attending school, we observe that for urban children from 6 to 14 years old, that ratio was 76 percent in 1974 whereas it was 56 percent in 1984, a decline of percentage points. The rate of non-attending school was 12 percent in 1974. It seems surprising to observe such levels. The explanation lies primarily in the high level of school desertion by children (22 percent in 1974) and in the number who repeat a year (28 percent on average). To that must be added the insufficiency of classrooms and schools for a steadily growing number of pupils. For instance, in 1981, children who repeated a year represented 57 percent of those enrolled in all of the grammar schools of Brazzaville. From 1974 to 1984, the number of children enrolled in the grammar schools of that city increased 18 percent per year. That increased the number of pupils per classroom (on an average of 80 pupils per teacher in 1984).

It is particularly in Brazzaville and Pointe-Noire where problems of satisfying educational demands are emerging with acuteness. With a demographic growth rate close to 7 percent and a young population, each city is continually faced with the problem of chronic insufficiency of school establishments and equipment. Then, there is necessity to establish new schools in the peripheral zones more and more away from the center of the city.

Higher education is exclusively at Brazzaville. The enrollment rate in higher education for young people between 20 and 25 fluctuated between 3 and 7 percent in 1986. Since 1986, an inclination toward a stabilization of that rate at 7.2 percent was observed.

Some educational subjects such as economics and law are experiencing a plethoric number of students in comparison with the capability of those branches to receive students. Classrooms, teachers, and educational equipment are not enough. From 1978 to 1981, the two education branches experienced a 28 and 23 percent annual increase, respectively, in the number of students (Ministry of National Education, 1981). In the teaching quality sphere, general and theoretical teaching is privileged to the detriment of technical and professional teaching, the necessity for which has become more and more urgent over the past few years. Demand for technical and professional education is growing, but university structures do not meet it. The insufficiency of those structures and the inadequacy of several education branches cause young people to go to foreign countries (especially Europe) to study in fields which they consider more appropriate for their future. Statistics from the Ministry of National Education show that in 1981 about half of the students of higher education were studying in foreign countries. That could be an indicator of the insufficiency, both qualitative and quantitative, of the higher educational system in the Congo.

THE LABOR FORCE IN THE URBAN AREA

The rapid increase of the Congo population creates an acute problem of employment, especially in urban areas. Massive streams of migrants are motivated by the economic attraction of cities which must offer jobs to a working population growing rapidly. A positive correlation is then observed between the labor force and the total urban population although it is unequally distributed throughout cities.

The Urban Labor Force

From 1974 to 1984, the urban labor force increased from 128,423 to 275,978 individuals, an average growth rate of 8 percent. The urban working population has therefore doubled in ten years.

The percentage of the urban working-age population between 15 and 65 years old increased from 32 percent in 1974 to 36 percent in 1984. The percentages of those actually employed were respectively 24 percent and 34 percent, an increase of 42 percent in that period. A significant increase of the labor force can be explained by the growth of the whole urban population and by the revival of economic activities in 1974–84, especially in the two large towns.

There were approximately four males for every female in the 1974 urban labor force. By 1984 there were only two males per female employed in the urban area. The working population is very unequally distributed within the six main towns of the country. For example, Brazzaville alone has about 60 percent of the whole urban working population and 30 percent of the whole country. Moreover, if we exclude the oil production which is taking place in another city, the economic activity of Brazzaville reflects considerably that of the whole country.

The Labor Force of Brazzaville: Occupational Characteristics

The working population refers to the date of each census. The concept of profession (or occupation) refers to the actual work performed. The most predominant occupations are in sales, or as commercial workers, craftsmen, unskilled workers, and drivers of transport engines. The administrative staff stands just after those categories. An important fact is that these occupational characteristics have not changed since 1974.

In the category of salespersons and commercial staff, the fact that women are more numerous (65 percent) could be a sign of the changing commercial activities in the city.

In the city of Brazzaville some residents are engaged in agricultural activity, fishing, hunting, and forestry. They represent 7 percent in 1974 and 4 percent in 1984 of the whole working population. The decline can be explained by a progressive integration of them in the other activities.

The occupational structure of Brazzaville's labor force reveals that it is widely involved in economic activities not requiring a given qualification such as those related to the modern industrial sector. Occupational characteristics of that labor force reveal rather the high domination in that city of the informal sector and, as far as the modern sector of economy is concerned, the one of public services.

The Industrial Activity of Brazzaville City

An examination of the industrial structure of Brazzaville reveals that in 1974 and 1984 the percentage of the working population in industrial activities was, respectively, 25 percent and 20 percent. Industrial activity is essentially dominated by the manufacturing industry including food-processing and beverage industries (including breweries), the textile industry, and the wood-processing industry. The last includes people who set up their own business in the informal sector such as carpentry. Also, one can find a few industrial firms, with variable size, oriented to the production of tobacco (cigarettes), the production of plastic commodities, the production of shoes, and the production of diverse commodities (soap, lubricants, cement, painting, etc.). Overall, the manufacturing industry in Brazzaville employed 14 percent of the whole really working population in 1974, but only 9 percent in 1984.

The building industry and public works sector experienced a significant growth in 1979–85 due to important investments in urban construction. The aim of that stream of investments was to give Brazzaville a modern aspect. A vast building program, ministry offices, and city road network, has been undertaken. That process can be perceived through the evolution of the number of persons involved in that sector. From 6 percent in 1974 they represented 9 percent in 1984 of the total employed labor force of the city. However, since 1985 the building industry has probably experienced a loss due to the economic crisis.

The industries of electricity generation, gas production, drinking water supply, and mining employ only 1 percent each of the working population.

The number of persons employed in the manufacturing industry of the city of Brazzaville declined 36 percent in 1974–84. The number of persons employed in community, social services, and private services increased 6 percent in the same period. Those service activities accounted for 35 percent of the working population employed in 1974 and 37 percent in 1984. Brazzaville has become more and more an administrative city (oil activity being wholly at Pointe-Noire) whose economic activities are oriented toward public, specialized, and similar services. Economic functions have, therefore, increased the working population of Brazzaville in the branch of services whereas the opposite occurred in the manufacturing industry.

The industrial sector has been greatly set back by the fall in the oil prices, which has disrupted the labor market throughout the Congo and particularly in Brazzaville.

Employment in Brazzaville: Salaried Work in the Services

The focus in this section will be on paid workers and employers. The share of independent workers or paid workers in each group of occupations is useful for assessing the economic dynamism of the city resident population. It is broadly admitted that the more informal an economy is, the more independent workers constitute the majority of the working population. In an opposite case, it is thought that the more an economy is inclined toward modernism, the more paid workers in the formal sector dominate the working population. The economy of

Brazzaville is dominated by public services, so we expect that paid workers will be more important than independent workers.

In 1974 paid work dominated for the occupation groups related to executives, technicians, and staff of scientific occupations, regardless of the sex of workers. The same situation applied to the group of administrative staff.

Among transport and communication workers, 85 percent are salaried; among workers in services, 91 percent; and among skilled workers and craftsmen, only 52 percent. Independent workers included commercial workers and salespeople (85 percent of them were working for their own interest), farmers (83 percent), and skilled workers, craftspeople (artisans), and unskilled workers (39 percent).

It is important to stress that salaried workers in the city of Brazzaville represent 57 percent of the working population whereas independent workers represent 39 percent. As for the employers, they represent less than 1 percent of the population.

In 1984 the distribution of paid and independent workers in the city of Brazzaville, according to the occupation practiced, showed a lower concentration than in 1974. For paid workers, we find 50 percent were unskilled and skilled nonagricultural workers. In the other occupations, the percentage of paid workers ranged from 9 percent to 18 percent and, as in 1974, independent workers were more numerous among unskilled and skilled nonagricultural workers, representing about 60 percent of that category.

Of the employed population in 1984, paid workers represented 46 percent and independent workers, 18 percent. Compared with the 1974 ratio, there was a relative decline for these two categories of workers. That decline can be explained by an important spatial mobility among paid and independent workers who should have perhaps changed their city of residence. Both growing service activities and changes in migration could explain the domination of paid workers among the city working-age employed population.

The number of paid workers (salaried) indicated by the available data does not reveal completely the numerous ways by which Brazzaville residents achieve their incomes. For instance, there is a general practice there (just as in other cities) of letting houses (rental housing) in order to obtain a secondary or principal income. In the city of Brazzaville the percentage of renters moved from 34 percent in 1974 to 41 percent in 1984. These renters allow house owners (salaried or not) to obtain secondary or principal incomes.

To face the fall of receipts drawn from oil exports, the government has resorted to wage freezing. On the whole, the low wage level did not increase in 1985–90. Since 1985, the general standard of wages and income remained under a lower purchase power for urban residents because of growing inflation.

Social and economic deterioration has resulted in urgent problems caused by a rapid and noncontrolled urbanization such as the one the country has experienced since 1960.

SUMMARY AND IMPLICATIONS

The concerns raised by urbanization in the Congo lie primarily on the speed and the shape of the urban growth. The urban population is increasing at a high rate (about 7 percent per year) and is concentrated in two cities. Besides, this growth derives essentially from migratory streams constituted, to a great extent, by young countrymen coming to live in town for many reasons. One of the consequences of that migration is that since 1960, the rural population has experienced a steady decrease (73 percent in 1960, 62 percent in 1974, and 48 percent in 1984 of the total population) in addition to aging. Shortages of crops are increasingly emerging. The situation is particularly acute, for it is not being accompanied by a steady introduction of new technical methods to improve agricultural yields. Supplying food to cities such as Brazzaville and Pointe-Noire is becoming more and more difficult because of the rapid demographic growth and the weakness of the national agricultural sector.

Moreover, these two cities are experiencing a social evolution which is raising some concerns: proliferation of slums and squalid shantytowns (inside and at the periphery of the city), deterioration and inadequacy of public and social services, excessive shortage of lodgings, and urban transports which do not satisfy the demand. Most acute, in addition, the unemployment level, already high between 1974 and 1984 (about 19 percent), experienced a significant increase since 1985, on account of economic difficulties at the national level.

There is also an absence of a strong urbanization or regional planning policy. Authorities have paid little attention to the pressing need to adopt aggregate strategies in order to halt the rapid and imbalanced urbanization. One can note a very fine attitude of "noninterference" from authorities. As a matter of fact, in this process of urbanization, a confrontation constantly looms, bringing into political conflict authorities and popular actions which do not usually take into account official urban management schemes.

Because of such situations, these small towns have become places of relay for rural migrants toward big cities. Their inhabitants are, steadily and in mass, leaving on account of the very low level of development prevailing in those small towns. Despite some punctual governmental actions, their decline is becoming more and more marked and is also being accompanied by high urban growth and depopulation.

REFERENCES

Goldstein, S., and David F. Sly. 1979. *The Measurement of Urbanization and Projection of Urban Population*. Dolhain, Belgium: Ordina Editions.

Haeringer, P. 1982. "Le phénomène suburbain." Unpublished paper. Office de Recherche Scientifique D'outre Mer. Brazzaville, Congo.

Mashabela, Harry. 1990. *Mekhukhu: Urban African Cities of the Future*. Johannesburg: South African Institute of Race Relations.

Ministry of Health. 1981. *Health Statistics Yearbook,* Brazzaville, Congo.

———. 1982. *Health Statistics Yearbook.* Brazzaville, Congo.

———. 1986. *Health Statistics Yearbook.* Brazzaville, Congo.

Ministry of National Education. 1981. *Schooling Statistics Yearbook.* Brazzaville, Congo.

———. 1986. *Schooling Statistics Yearbook.* Brazzaville, Congo.

Ministry of Plan. 1976. *The Economic and Social Situation of the Congo From 1960 to 1974.* Brazzaville, Congo.

Office de Recherche Scientifique D'outre Mer/Association des Geographes Conbolais. 1987. Proceedings of the Scientific Meeting on the Brazzaville, Congo. Development of the City of Brazzaville (25–28 April 1986).

Tati, G. 1987. "L'activité économique au Congo (d'après le recensement de 1984). Analyse critique." Working paper. Institut de Formation et de Recherche Demographiques.

———. 1989. "Quelques aspects et implications démographiques de l'urbanisation au Congo (1960–1984)." Thesis of DEA in demography presented at the Demography Institute of Paris.

UNESCO. 1991. *Education Statistics Yearbook.* Paris: UNESCO.

United Nations. 1971. *Methodes de mesure de la migration interne.* Série A/47. New York: United Nations.

———. 1979. *Methods of Projecting Urban and Rural Populations.* Handbook no. 8. New York: United Nations.

———. 1991. *World Urbanization Prospects 1990.* Population Studies 121. New York: United Nations.

United Nations, Economic Commission for Africa. 1989. *Patterns, Causes, and Consequences of Urbanization in Africa.* Addis Ababa.

United Nations, Educational, Scientific, and Cultural Organization. 1991. *Statistical Yearbook 1991.* Paris.

World Bank. 1992. *World Development Report 1992.* New York: Oxford University Press.

9

Côte D'Ivoire

Philippe Antoine and Aka Kouame

Côte d'Ivoire is one of the most highly urbanized African countries. In fact, out of its 10.8 million inhabitants in 1988, 4.2 million lived in cities, representing 40 percent of the population. This urbanization process is relatively recent, and only began in the 1950s. Until the beginning of the twentieth century, Côte d'Ivoire was forsaken by European merchants. There were very few coastal settlements (Assini, Grand-Lahou, Grand-Bassam). In the country's interior, a few cities served as stopovers for caravans (Bondoukou, Kong). Côte d'Ivoire became a French colony in 1893, but for the most part in theory only as a large part of the territory remained "uncontrolled" (Rougerie, 1972). The colonization process brought military and administrative posts to the country's interior. Simultaneously there was the need to facilitate the gathering and export of agricultural products.

The first cities resulted from these two administrative and economic necessities, and most cities today are circles or old trading posts (Kipre, 1985). The first urban network since Abidjan would be designated along the railway line: Agboville, Dimbokro, Bouaké, Ferkéssédougou. Between 1904 and 1945 urban growth remained relatively moderate, approximately 2 to 3 percent annually. The settlement of cities resulted from European colonization (administrators, merchants, forest and agricultural exploiters and their families) and by the migration of natives of Côte d'Ivoire and migrants of other African countries, occupying subaltern posts in administration and commerce or becoming workers in public utility fields.

The development of the urban network began with the valorization of the colony. This led to the opening of the port of Abidjan (the piercing of the Vridi

Canal, finished in 1950, gave the capital its deep water port) and the extension of the road network from the east to the west, which were the privileged zones of the plantation economy, and the prolongation of the railway track up to Ouagadougou in 1955. The latter particularly facilitated the progression of the Burkinabé labor force toward the public utility works, forest exploitation, and coffee and cocoa plantation zones. The movements brought on by these activities led to a level of urbanization of 15.4 percent on the eve of independence (Koffi, 1991). In 1960, coffee, cocoa, and wood represented 50 percent, 23 percent, and 17 percent respectively of export values. The port of Abidjan rapidly became the main point of export activities. All lines of communication converged toward the new capital. To these port activities was joined the demand for a labor force for large equipment work, housing construction, and service and commercial activities. In the interior of the country, even though urban growth was significant, there were only 10 cities of over 10,000 inhabitants on the eve of independence.

During the 20 years following independence, Côte d'Ivoire's model for development depended on the diversification of agricultural exports (palm oil, banana, pineapple, cotton, sugar cane, etc.) and on a policy for industrialization aimed at satisfying the markets of the interior. At the time of its independence, there were 60 factories and French capital controlled 92 percent of the production (Dubresson, 1989). A double process followed: the substitution of imports and the transformation of local products intended for export, supported by some state agencies. In 1980 industrial activity furnished one quarter of the gross domestic product (GDP), and over the period 1960–80 the growth rate of the manufacturing industry was about 13 percent annually. This tendency was reversed at the beginning of the 1980s, production stagnating (even regressing in 1983 and 1984). The scale of the urban network changed; the number of cities of more than 10,000 inhabitants jumped from 20 in 1965, to 44 in 1975, to 57 in 1988 (Dubresson, 1989; Chaleard et al., 1990). Nonetheless, the urban network remained in imbalance, two out of every three cities being located in the south of the country, and Abidjan remaining predominant despite government attempts, in the 1980s, to engage a policy of decentralization and municipalization. This policy was completed in 1983 by the decision to transfer the capital from Abidjan to Yamoussoukro (in the center of the country). However, it must be noted that, nearly 10 years later, the ministries and embassies still remain in the old capital. Industrial production equally remains concentrated in this city, which furnished 72 percent of manufacturing production in 1979, as opposed to 56 percent in 1965 (Dubresson, 1989). Despite the slowing of its growth, Abidjan was home to 45 percent of the country's urban population in 1988, whereas only 38 percent of the urban population resided there in 1965. Sixty percent of jobs in the secondary sector and 75 percent in the modern tertiary sector are concentrated in Abidjan (Koffi, 1991). But since large numbers of migrants are attracted to Abidjan because of the concentration of industrial activities and of employment, it is not certain whether the investments implemented in the different sectors of urban development (employment, housing, health, education, transportation) could respond to the aspirations of all of the townspeople. The object of this study is to render an account of the mechanisms which led to this "disequilibratory" urbanization, its modalities, and its consequences on the living conditions of urban populations, notably that of the city of Abidjan.

After having seen the modalities of the country's urban growth and the relative weight of natural and migratory growth, we will analyze the evolution of settlement and habitation in Abidjan then look at the evolution of the labor force and of revenue, before drawing a schedule for a population policy in the field of urbanization.

THE DEMOGRAPHIC COMPONENTS OF URBAN GROWTH

Even having declined during the last decade, urban population growth has been very strong since the late 1950s. The average annual growth rate of the urban population was 8.1 percent from 1965 to 1975 (Ahonzo et al., 1984:28) and 5.4 percent between 1975 and 1988 (Ba, 1991:14). Despite the fluctuation in growth from one decade to the next, the level remained very high. Growth was particularly strong in the city of Abidjan, where the annual rate rose to 11 percent (as opposed to 7 percent for the other urban centers) toward the end of the 1970s, and 4 percent between 1984 and 1988. This strong urban growth was the result not only of the combined effects of the balance of migration and of natural increase but also of the reclassification of cities.

Migratory Growth

Migration is a very highly intensive phenomenon in Côte d'Ivoire. In fact, the country has experienced significant international immigration since its independence because of an open-border policy and the economic prosperity enjoyed during the first two decades of its history. This immigration has occurred in as strong a significance for rural destinations as for urban destinations (51 percent and 49 percent respectively in 1978) (Ahonzo et al., 1984:82). According to census data, the foreign population in Abidjan represented 44 percent of the city's population in 1955, 39 percent in 1975, and 37 percent in 1988. According to the same sources, the two most important communities of origin of immigrants are Burkina Faso (275,000 persons in 1988) and Mali (166,500 persons the same year). The relative proportion of the first group declined compared to 1975, suggesting the hypothesis of returns or of orientation toward secondary cities for certain Burkinabé. Other nationalities are particularly represented in Abidjan, origins mentioned according to their numerical importance: Guinea (58,000 persons in 1988), Ghana, Nigeria, Benin, Togo, and Senegal (23,500). The diversity of origins underlines the scope of Abidjan's hinterland. Regarding the non-African population, it has strongly declined from 25,250 in 1975 to 22,120 in 1988.

Even in the country's interior, the population experienced intense geographic mobility due to the orientation of development policy favoring cities (notably Abidjan). Intense migratory movements occurred, on the one hand, from rural zones toward the secondary urban centers and Abidjan and, on the other hand, from the secondary urban centers toward Abidjan. Thus in 1978 migration exchanges between the different strata resulted in a negative balance for the rural areas—favoring Abidjan and other cities—which was compensated by the surplus registered by rural areas over foreign. The balance was positive for the intermediate cities to the detriment of the rural and foreign spheres, but negative with Abidjan. Abidjan registered a positive balance with all other strata for a net balance of 87,621 persons (Kouame, 1987).

Migration contributed a very important part of urban growth. One can even say that it was the most important source of urban population growth in Côte d'Ivoire toward the end of the 1970s. In fact, in 1978 it accounted for 62 percent and 54 percent of the respective population growth of the city of Abidjan and of other interior cities. The annual migration growth rates were then 7 percent and 4 percent, respectively. For Abidjan, the net rate of internal migration was 4 percent and that of international migration was 3 percent. For the interior cities, the rate was 2 percent in both cases (Ahonzo et al., 1984).

Over the course of the last decade, this share has weakened. Migratory growth represented no more than 27 percent of the total growth of the city of Abidjan, for a net migration rate of merely 0.8 percent. The city even registered a negative migration balance with other regions of the country (rural areas and secondary urban centers, being 0.7 percent). The 0.8 percent positive migratory growth was due to exchanges made with the exterior favoring Abidjan. Abidjan's annual growth rate was merely 4.8 percent, and the average annual growth rate between 1975 and 1988 was 5.6 percent. This represents a drop nearly in half as compared to the rate at the end of the 1970s.

Detailed data are unavailable for the secondary urban centers, but all indicators suggest that the intermediate urban regions have maintained their growth rhythm and that migration has probably played an important role. In fact, the average annual population growth rate of the interior cities between 1975 and 1988 was 7.1 percent, whereas the natural growth rate in these regions was only 3.3 percent in 1988.[1] Considering an annual growth rate of 7.1 percent for the year 1988,[2] one can deduce that the migration balance was around 3.8 percent for the intermediate urban regions, which is about the same level as that observed at the end of the 1970s. The intermediate urban regions thus would take the relay from the city of Abidjan in receiving migrants coming from the countryside and probably from abroad, following the economic crisis which has lashed out at Côte d'Ivoire's economy for over ten years. This implies that the crisis will affect Abidjan even more than the other interior cities. This seems most likely seeing that most economic activity and foreign investments, which have certainly been exhausted since the crisis, were concentrated at Abidjan. Secondary urban centers, where economic activity was largely dominated by the informal sector

Table 9.1
Components of Population Change in Abidjan, 1978 and 1988

	1978	1988
Total Growth	10.9 percent	4.8 percent
Natural growth	4.1	3.5
Migratory growth	6.8	0.8
Internal migration	4.0	0.7
International migration	2.8	1.5

Sources: Ahonzo et al., 1984; 108 for 1978. Data for 1988 was calculated from results obtained at the seminar on the diffusion of the 1988 census.

in the past (Dureau, 1987), probably offer a greater potential for sustenance than Abidjan for migrants. Experience has shown them to be more attracted to this type of activity.

Natural Growth

In 1978 the natural growth rate was 4.1 percent for the city of Abidjan and 3.4 percent for the secondary urban centers. Its contribution to urban population growth was 38 percent in Abidjan and 46 percent in all other cities, important although less so than migratory growth. In 1988 the natural growth rate for the population of Abidjan was evaluated at 3.5 percent. This level has declined compared to the previous period. However, thanks to an important drop in the balance of migration, natural growth now constitutes the principal factor in urban growth, being 73 percent of the total growth rate of 4.8 percent.

The drop in the level of natural growth translates into a reduction in the variation between natality and mortality in the urban regions. This occurred in spite of the fact that mortality has continued to drop during the last years in these regions (Table 9.1). Fertility has registered a relatively important drop in urban regions, as opposed to rural regions, where its level seems to have increased. Thus the phenomenon has maintained a constant overall level for the whole country (Table 9.2). The crude birthrate, evaluated at 51 per thousand in intermediate urban zones and 50 per thousand in Abidjan, has dropped to 42 per thousand in both cases. The total fertility rate has declined from 6.4 to 5.1 in the intermediate urban zones, and from 5.6 to 4.7 in Abidjan over the same period. This drop is relatively important when one considers that fertility had remained at a high and constant level over a long period of time in Côte d'Ivoire.

Table 9.2
Mortality and Fertility Rates in the Côte d'Ivoire, 1978–79 and 1988

Geographical Zone and Rate	Rate per 1,000	
	1978-79 Survey	1988 Census
Côte d'Ivoire		
Crude birthrate	49	48
Crude death rate	17	13
Total fertility rate	6.8	6.8
Rural zones		
Crude birthrate	48	52
Crude death rate	20	16.1
Total fertility rate	6.9	7.0
Urban zones		
Crude birthrate	51	42
Crude death rate	14	9.3
Total fertility rate	6.4	5.1
Abidjan		
Crude birthrate	50	42
Crude death rate	9	7.5
Total fertility rate	5.6	4.7

Sources: Abbas, 1991; Djédjé, 1991.

This can be attributed to increases in the proportion of educated women within the female population (Kouassi, 1991:12). In fact, differential analysis by schooling level and place of residence has predicted a much lower fertility level among women having attained at least a secondary schooling. The fertility drop can also be explained by the adoption, in urban zones, of new behaviors favorable to a reduction in family size. In fact, it has been observed that fertility levels have remained higher in rural areas than in urban areas regardless of schooling. The seminar for diffusion of the 1988 census results concluded a trend toward uniformity of certain behaviors of urban women because they would have had quasi-identical access to a certain number of social services, including family planning services. Urbanization will thus be a strong determining factor of differential fertility in Côte d'Ivoire because it will generate "modern" behaviors regarding procreation (Abbas, 1991:21).

The Evolution of the Urban Network

The 1980s were characterized by a slowing of urbanization. Perspectives led to foresee an urbanization ratio of about 50 percent in 1988. Now census results give a rate of 40 percent (Chaleard et al., 1990). Nevertheless, the analysis can vary according to the perception one makes of the city. According to the Census Bureau, Côte d'Ivoire has 68 cities by a double criterion: having over 5,000 inhabitants, and having at least half of the heads of households engaged in nonagricultural and nonartisan activities. However, according to town planners, these criteria exclude small cities, and according to them the urban population is around 5 million (46 percent of the total population), of which 68,500 persons reside in cities of 4,000–10,000 inhabitants.

Abidjan has maintained its preeminent position. The country's second city, Bouaké (85,000 residents in 1965 and 333,000 in 1988), has seen a lower rhythm of growth. Hopes for reequilibrium put into Yamoussoukro have not been crowned a success, despite sustained demographic growth between 1975 and 1988 (9 percent annually). The city had 110,000 inhabitants in 1988 as opposed to 35,500 in 1975; however, it has not taken Abidjan's relay. The same goes for San Pedro, the country's second port, which also should have attracted numerous migrants. Its population increased from 31,606 in 1975 to 70,611 in 1988. Abidjan thus remains by far the most important city in Côte d'Ivoire.

THE GROWTH OF ABIDJAN

The Stages of Spatial Growth

Abidjan became Côte d'Ivoire's third capital after Bingerville, the second, and Grand-Bassam, where the European population was decimated at the end of the nineteenth century by an epidemic of yellow fever. It would not be until November 28, 1920, that the decision would be taken to transfer the capital from Bingerville to Abidjan, a city where it was hoped a comfortable association would arise between the new capital and the port. Although the transfer of the capital was effectuated as of July 1, 1934, the capital/port association would not be completed until 1950 with the opening of the Vridi Canal. As of this era the city's development would be crystallized around portal activities, and Abidjan would have spectacular demographic growth, becoming at the same time the principal industrial and commercial center of the country, and of all the subregion.

Its population, estimated at merely 1,400 inhabitants in 1912 and 17,500 in 1934, increased to 65,000 inhabitants in 1950 and 180,000 in 1960. Enumerating

950,000 residents in 1975, the city's population was evaluated at 1,934,000 inhabitants at the last census in 1988. Since 1950 and until the end of the 1970s, the city grew at a rate of 10 percent annually. This growth, we have already seen, is primarily the result of internal and international migration. Parallel to these external exchanges, the city was also subject to important internal mobility. Hence in 1978–79, 200,000 persons changed their dwelling (representing 31 percent of the population).

Population growth profoundly modified the distribution of inhabited sites. Before colonization, several Ebrié villages spotted the space today covered by the agglomeration.

Various studies undertaken since the 1955 census permit an apprehension of the evolution of the population by large geographical areas. Until 1980, the agglomeration consisted of 12 districts and numerous localities attached to the Bingerville subprefect (Abobo, Yopougon, Ebrié villages). The definition of spatial limits of these different units varied from one organization to the other. Since 1980, the city of Abidjan has been divided into 10 municipalities (Law no. 801182 of October 17, 1980).

Three big stages, three scale changes characterize Abidjan's spatial growth, according to the distinction brought out by P. Haeringer (1977): the colonial town, for which development occurred during the period 1912–50; the portal town, where growth occurred between 1950 and 1970; and the new perimeter, which has been receiving a large part of Abidjan's population since 1970. We will consider, one after the other, these three urban entities.

Côte d'Ivoire's capital since 1934, the colonial town owes its essence to the railway. From 1930 to the postwar period, the city contained only three districts: the Plateau, Treichville, and Adjamé. The Plateau was the administrative center and European district, divided from the other two African districts, from the north by military camps and from the south by the lagoon; these two obstacles plainly separated it from the ''popular'' Treichville and Adjamé districts. The urban hold then covered 600 hectares, and in total included hardly more than 60,000 inhabitants in 1950. Despite spatial expansion of the city, the two ''popular'' districts continued to attract residents, and regular human settlement continued there up until the 1970s. Since the rhythm of growth has slowed down substantially the last few years, fewer and fewer new migrants arrive there. The population of these districts has increased from 98,300 in 1955 to 241,452 in 1988.

The agglomeration's current physiognomy will be outlined starting from 1948, at the time of the preparation of the urban plan, better known under the name Badani Plan (1952), which marked the passage from being the administrative town to the port and industrial city.

The development of the port and opening of the Vridi Canal, along with the subsequent expansion of several districts, the second stage in the agglomeration's development, was accompanied by an economic takeoff. The 1952 urban plan, which combined appropriation of land and road outlines, accentuated the partitioning of the districts: industrial zones in the southwest and residential district in the northeast. The new projected residential zones sketched certain current districts: North Adjamé, Cocody, Marcory, Koumassi. The Plateau affirmed its role as the city's administrative and commercial center.

This allotment of urban functions entailed serious disequilibriums in the distribution of population and workplace, responsible for the intensification of daily commuting. The priority granted to prestigious urban planning did not permit the release of the financial means necessary to brake the occupation of the island of Petit-Bassam, which nevertheless is hardly propitious to human settlement due to poor natural conditions for drainage. The "port city" was thus the result of urbanization of a large part of Petit-Bassam Island, and of a portion of the coastline toward Port-Bouet, and of the occupation of new residential zones, principally to the north and to the east of the Plateau.

During this period, the city's expansion and settlement particularly affected the south of the agglomeration and, paradoxically, areas that were least easily developed. Urban dwellers seem to have searched for proximity to their work places, principally located on Petit-Bassam. The population of the latter was 80,500 inhabitants in 1963, attaining 408,500 in 1975 and 608,000 in 1988.

Next, the explosion of the city outside its limits would entail the conquest of new spaces on the continental Plateau. Until 1955, the agglomeration was limited to a radius of 4 kilometers, and the urbanized surface attained 1,350 hectares. In 1970, the radius had doubled, and constructed areas covered around 6,000 hectares. Starting from this date, new urbanization poles appeared, contained within a radius of 10 kilometers, with the exception of Abobo, distanced at 12 kilometers from the Plateau.

The new perimeter was the product of a sustained demographic growth. Urban space would win over the continental Plateau after the 1970s. Certain districts were born under a more or less planned form, such as Yopougon, the Riviera, or Deux Plateaux. Others like Abobo would arise from illegal occupation of the land. In 1990, several districts composed the new perimeter: Yopougon, located on the Banco Plateau, experienced mass urbanization, including evolving allotments in the north and numerous inexpensive housing programs constructed by state agencies in the south. An industrial zone was created with the aim of reequilibrating the distribution of activities and creating work poles in the agglomeration's northern part. This commune grew from 99,000 inhabitants in 1975 to 374,500 in 1988.

Abobo, which some thirty years earlier was merely a modest concentration of dwellings around the station, quickly developed to become, along with Yopougon, one of the capital's two most important communes, seeing its population grow from 143,000 inhabitants in 1975 to 401,200 in 1988. Illegally constructed courtyard habitation dominated for a long period, but Abobo has since experienced important restructuring, and in certain sectors the outfits have been considerably improved.

The residential population of this third rim surpassed one million inhabitants in 1988. Its annual rhythm of growth slowed from 12.1 percent over the period 1975–84 to 4.5 percent for 1984–88, a rate slightly greater than that for the whole agglomeration. The perimeter's limits expanded; urban planners tended to draw long-term development plans for a radius of over 30 kilometers, with the agglomeration reaching Bingerville to the east and Anyama to the north. With the inclusion of these peripheral extensions, 160,175 persons are added to the agglomeration (including the population of urban centers like Bingerville or Anyama). The size of the agglomeration in the larger sense is thus approximately 2,100,000 inhabitants, according to urban planners' evaluations (DCGTX, 1989).

The colonial town constituted for several years the quasi-exclusive core of settlement in the agglomeration; thus, in 1963, 67 percent of the city's population was credited to this central entity, whereas currently 12.4 percent of the population resides in these central districts. Having already experienced negative growth, the zone is now undergoing a moderate growth rate of 2.9 percent.

However, very quickly, since the 1970s the population distribution between the perimeters was deeply modified to attain a momentary equilibrium toward 1973. Since then, a major portion of the population has tended to reside more and more at the city's current periphery (34 percent of the population in 1975; 56.3 percent in 1988).

The periphery's rhythm of annual growth was particularly high between 1963 and the end of the 1970s, clearly setting the pace in all the perimeter, and the periphery grew at a rate barely greater than that of the agglomeration. Finally, at the fringes, toward Bingerville and Anyama, the population grew faster, at a rate of 6 percent annually.

The sustained growth in the number of inhabitants, despite a multiplication of urbanized areas (1,350 hectares in 1955, 12,000 hectares in 1980), had as corollary a reduction in the availability of land per resident, which declined from 108 square meters in 1955 to 77 square meters in 1980. The city's expansion coincided with a rarefaction of inhabitable space. The concentric organization left room for a structure leaning on several poles. But the disequilibrium grew between the north of the city, which included a majority of inhabitants, and the Plateau, the island of Petit-Bassam, and the almost island of Vridi, where remained concentrated most salaried employment of the so-called modern sphere of activity.

Population and Housing in the Area of Abidjan

The concentric growth of the city was accompanied by an accumulation of strata of population and housing. The colonial town rested on a dualism of blacks (Adjamé and Treichville) and whites (the Plateau), characterized by different types of housing according to the district. The city's successive expansions also included diverse settlements. But the concentric superposition gives today a relatively complex urban landscape, always in full mutation under combined effects of evictions, renovations, development, and the transformation of the functions of certain districts.

Still, housing constitutes a good witness of the agglomeration's diversity, and despite its imperfections, the typology of housing permits a better comprehension of Abidjan's complexity. The choice of typology always arises from a certain arbitrariness, in particular in the field of housing where, quite often, the body's characterization takes into consideration diverse analytical, juridical, economic, morphological, and sociological elements. Since 1960, planning departments have proposed diverse typologies founded, at the same time, on construction's juridical status and of the equipment's economic criteria.

Most of the typologies retained at Abidjan refer to the one elaborated in 1963 by the 1965 SEMA publication and differentiated in four large categories:

1. Residential housing: habitation of European origin, constituted of colonial-type villas. This habitation experienced during the 1970s a certain expansion and takes social symbol functions.
2. Economic housing: implemented by mostly public real estate agencies, and constituted of either single dwellings or continuous habitational units (group housing).
3. Evolutive housing: constituted the oldest form of habitation adopted by the people of Abidjan, named as such because it could progressively evolve with successive construction of new buildings in the midst of the courtyard, or with the construction of new levels on the roofing in existing balconies. This type of habitation, sitting on a parcel of land 40 meters by 40 meters, is thus characterized by a progressive denseness.
4. Shanty housing: concerns the precarious constructions, illegally implanted and located outside of official lots. This category regroups different natured constructions but is where the shanties predominate. The last two types concern the greatest proportion of housing: courtyard housing (Antoine et al., 1987).

This typology, although sometimes too limited, presents nonetheless the advantage of continuity, and permits a diachronic analysis. The residential housing, well represented for over a long period of time in the Plateau, at Marcory, in Zone 4, and at Cocody, has been forsaken little by little in favor of Cocody's extensions: Deux Plateaux to the north and the Riviera to the east. The economic boom of the 1970s permitted the creation of a habitation of important standing (5.9 percent of the population in 1963, 8.4 percent in 1979), favored by excessive amounts for rent. The crisis, the departure of numerous expatriates and the discontinuation of free housing for numerous higher-class employees, had important repercussions on this type of habitation, all the more that the individual villas were abandoned in favor of small dwellings offering more security. Currently 4.2 percent of the population lives in this type of habitation.

Modern economic housing frequently takes the form of large developments including numerous dwellings in street-level bands. The main areas concerned are the north part of Abidjan, Port-Bouet, Koumassi, Marcory, and the heart of Cocody; but the archetype of this habitation is primarily found in the northwest, in Yopougon, where 35 percent of the population resides in this type of housing. This modern habitation houses in particular natives of Côte d'Ivoire with regular salaries at their disposal (civil servants, wage earners in the modern sector). Paradoxically, large family sizes perpetuate in this type of housing. Thus in 1963 its average household size was 5.7 (whereas the average in Abidjan was 3.9 persons), which attained 7.5 persons in 1975 (against 5.5 for the city's average) and 6.5 persons per household in 1988 (as opposed to 5.4 for the whole of the agglomeration).

Despite all the construction efforts during the 1970s (real estate agencies produced 20 percent of the constructed park), this habitation never sheltered more than a quarter of the population, and the program's termination as of 1979 checked its growth. The relay of public agencies by private agencies in the supply of housing in this type of habitation and in the habitation of average standing could have probably relaunched growth; however, it is not certain that these dwellings were accessible to the masses. There, as in other forms of capital, the pricing level rendered social housing inaccessible to those for whom it was initially intended, and in the 1970s these dwellings became the property of the middle and upper classes. Whatever policies followed, one has the impression that the same result ended up in most large African cities: the system for financing low-cost housing construction and building plots contributed to the enrichment of a clientele benefiting from the transfer of capital for the land. All over one remarks a pattern of exclusion of access to the land and to housing for the masses (Antoine et al., 1987). A status change is currently operating: numerous rental housings (17,000) are being put on sale by the real estate agencies. Certain occupants of these lodgings are among the principal victims of the crisis like wage earners aligned on public remuneration, or license holders of diverse enterprises. They must then proceed to sublet a part of their dwelling in order to continue rent payments (Blanc et al., 1991; Soumahoro, 1992).

Treichville and Adjamé are the oldest districts of evolutive housing. They densified little by little, and many courtyards possess a multileveled habitation. This type of habitation was equally found in most districts, but since the mid-1970s, Abobo (in the north) constituted the most vast area of the agglomeration's evolutive housing. The spectacular growth of evolutional habitation in this district responded to the wishes of many of Abidjan's residents of having more land available for residential use. The intraurbanal flux toward this periphery was maintained, even intensified during the 1979–85 period, since the population of this type of habitation grew from 190,000 to 280,000 persons in the parish. This type of habitation sheltered nearly 60 percent of the population. Its relative gain between 1979 and 1988 was the result of a simultaneous termination in low-cost housing projects and a drop in precarious housing in accordance with the progress of urbanization and the integration of the "evolutive" category of these habitations once they were allotted (DCGTX, 1989).

The average household size in these dwellings hardly evolved since 1975: it went from 5.5 to 5.3 in 1988, but it has increased with respect to 1963: 3.9

persons. All strata of the population are represented in this type of habitation, which represents a great heterogeneity: one can say that "the popular are in the court, but all of the court is not popular" (Antoine et al., 1987). The courtyard habitation receives a large proportion of foreigners, workers from the informal sector, and merchants. The courts are increasingly saturated, and their overpopulation can breed many disputes among neighbors. New courtyard conceptions appear: this concerns clearly individualized dwellings in the midst of one common rental courtyard, in particular at the periphery (Soumahoro, 1992). These constructions are made by individuals inspired from the habitation model by bands of economic operations. This new conception of the courtyard corresponds in particular to the expectations of the young generations born in the city and practicing in the tertiary sector.

Shanty housing is still largely represented in Abidjan, but it is for this type of habitation that definitional ambiguities are most numerous. Sometimes the juridical criteria predominate, and one can find solid, high-quality houses classified in this category. But it is mostly the shanties which comprise this type of habitation. One of its major characteristics is the poor hygienic conditions which prevail: greatest density (600 inhabitants per hectare, as opposed to 450 in the economic housing), the absence of toilets in the dwellings, and the lack of running water (9 percent of these dwellings have running water). A higher incidence of contagious diseases can equally be found, as well as a greater level of juvenile mortality (Antoine et al., 1987). Nonetheless, with the extent of the crisis, the social composition of the abridged habitation's population is tending more and more to resemble that of the evolutive housing.

The population residing in precarious housing was estimated at 37,000 persons in 1963 (or 14 percent of the city's population). In 1973 over 20 percent of the population resided in this type of habitation, despite the expulsions and the resettlements of the shantytown of Port-Bouet in 1969. The portion of the population residing in this desultory habitation decreased in accordance with policies of clearances or of restructurations. In 1988, an estimated 285,000 persons resided in shanty housing (13.6 percent of the population) (DCGTX, 1991).

Contrary to widespread opinion, shanty habitation is not the appanage of only foreigners (principally the Birkinabè). With the accentuation of the crisis, more and more natives of Côte d'Ivoire are living in precarious housing. Thus in the oldest slum of Abidjan, that of Vridi Canal which goes back to the beginning of the twentieth century, a recent survey revealed that 43 percent of owners of shanties are Côte d'Ivoire natives, and among them 83 percent effectively live there on site (YapiDiahou, 1992). The policy has evolved, in particular since Abidjan's municipalization: the bulldozer policy has been replaced by negotiation under the influence of different financial backers including the World Bank. Restructuring has endeavored to prevent the risks of social explosion, and has permitted the integration of numerous districts to the city (YapiDiahou, 1992).

Abidjan remains above all a city of tenants: four out of five residents of Abidjan are tenants. The highest rates are registered in evolutive housing (83 percent). The development of a rental market responded to a function of reception of migrants, of whom a large number sought to save money with the objective of later acquiring a house in their neighborhood of origin. A quarter of the tenants were housed by the state, but since 1980 this type of rental has ceased. The state now seeks to aid in the accessibility of proprietorship. Currently, courtyard rentals are covered in a bracket going from 5,000 to 25,000 CFA francs which is relatively high compared to the price of modern economic housing, and compared to the level of salaries.

The Adequacy of the Supply of Social Services in Abidjan

From the preceding it stands out that, despite the efforts provided by the public authorities in the urban project framework, the greatest number of housing problems could not have been resolved except with the development of courtyard habitation. In fact, although covering 46 percent of investments over the period 1973–77, public real estate agencies could offer only 23 percent of all housing as opposed to the 70 percent provided by courtyard habitation, which accounted for but 17 percent of investments (Antoine et al., 1987:145). However, even if courtyard habitation offers shelter to the majority of urban dwellers, it only partially affirms its habitational function due to the degradation of the indoor and outdoor environment of the lots in which their inhabitants live.

Indeed, in these parts of the city of Abidjan, sanitation infrastructures are practically nonexistent. Inside the dwellings, kitchens and sanitaries are collective—when the latter are available—and the water gates drain by various individual systems which do not always offer the desired security (Dubresson and Manou-Savina, 1985)—excepting recently built evolutive districts where a modern courtyard habitation has developed copying the model of modern economic housing (Soumahoro, 1992). Households have access to drinkable water and electricity only from peddlers, legal or illegal, who draw profits from the equipment of nearby districts. In the outdoor environment, substandard equipment is generally found in evolutive housing districts, whereas the infrastructures and collective equipment are nonexistent in the shanty housing districts. With the exception of the older evolutive districts (Treichville and Adjamé) recently allotted, there exists not a single drainage network for consumed water (Dubresson and Manou-Savina, 1985). Overpopulation compounds with the substandard equipment, which leads to overcrowded courtyard housing. This habitation's very mediocre hygienic conditions reverberate on the health of children, especially those of age to play in the courtyard's immediate environment. This is particularly true in shanty housing where juvenile mortality has risen to 115/1,000, as opposed to 47/1,000 in evolutive housing and 20/1,000 in economic housing (Antoine et al., 1987).

Since the beginning of the 1980s, projects aiming for the improvement of sanitational services in the evolutive districts have been initiated with the cooperation of the World Bank and United States Agency for International Development (USAID). They concerned the emergence of a connection of all municipalities in these districts to the general sanitation network and to the potable water network existing in low-cost and standing habitation districts. The obtained results were mitigated for the good reason that the popular housing zones did not have the means to assume the necessary costs for the connection of individuals to the public network put in place in their districts (Dubresson and Manou-Savina, 1985). Thus, according to results of the 1986 survey on the standard of living, 37 percent of households did not have flush toilets, and 52 percent of households did not have any interior faucets for their supply of potable water.

The variations in juvenile mortality observed earlier also translate into differential access to sociosanitary services according to the type of habitation as well as the insufficiency of these services with respect to the population's needs; and this in spite of a non-negligible concentration of the sociosanitary infrastructure in Abidjan. Indeed, all three of the country's university hospitals are in Abidjan, as well as nearly 60 percent of high-level medical personnel and 41 percent of paramedical personnel from urban public hospitals, for a total strength of 659 (full-time) physicians and assimilated professionals and 2,105 paramedics respectively in 1989. At the same time, in the private sector 52 out of the 64 (full-time) physicians and assimilated professionals accounted for resided in Abidjan, along with 213 of the 240 paramedics. Estimating the population of Abidjan at 2 million in 1989, this entails rates of only 2 physicians and 5 paramedics per 10,000 inhabitants of Abidjan, despite the concentration of medical personnel. Abidjan also accounted for 26 percent of urban hospital beds in 1989, or 2,570 beds; this translates into only 1.3 beds per thousand residents (République de Côte d'Ivoire, 1989). And this does not account for the patients the university hospitals receive coming from all other regions of the country. Incidentally, the established dysfunctions and the sometimes prohibitive costs render access to health care difficult for the majority of the population (Antoine et al., 1987). In a general way, health services are suffering from a case of obstruction and degradation stemming from the deterioration of certain types of equipment, and from the insufficiency in the supplying of medicines (République de Côte d'Ivoire, 1991).

With respect to education, one also realizes that the considerable efforts implemented did not adequately face the demand. Thus, despite the noteworthy progress in the construction of elementary schools in the different districts, the ratio of students per class remains at a high level. So in 1988, the average ratio for the whole city was 50, with a maximum at Abobo (59 students per class) and a minimum at Cocody (38) and the Plateau (37). These numbers were much higher in public education, with an average of 55 overall, and a maximum of 69 for Abobo and a minimum for Cocody (43) and the Plateau (40). In secondary schooling the results were hardly better. The number of students per class was even higher, at an average of 64 for public education. The high level of this ratio translated into an increasingly reduced accessibility in the educational system, and such at all levels. A reduction in the primary admission rate, a bottleneck at different transitory levels, and drops in the rates of school attendance were also observed (République de Côte d'Ivoire, 1991). In Abidjan, the school enrollment rate for children of 6 to 11 years of age was no greater than 67 percent in 1986 (République de Côte d'Ivoire, 1988a:29).

These observations on health and education are also valid for the transportation sector concerning demand which, with demographic pressure, has not ceased to rise. And this despite the fact that Abidjan possesses a roadway network and a public transportation park unique to the subregion (the rate of motorization has reached 22.4 percent for the whole country [Bonnamour, 1991], which signifies that it must be much higher in Abidjan). Despite considerable population growth, the bus fleet decreased between 1980 and 1987 from 1,751 to 1,208 (République de Côte d'Ivoire, 1988b).

ECONOMIC ACTIVITY, EMPLOYMENT, AND THE STANDARD OF LIVING IN URBAN CÔTE D'IVOIRE

Recent Trends in Urban Economic Activity and Employment

With considerable contributions of the two components of demographic growth, strong urban growth reverberates on that of the labor force in the short term as well as in the long term. Thus in the period between the last two censuses (1975–88), the urban population of age of economic activity increased by 6.5 percent, growing from 1,213,670 to 2,245,325. In applying these numbers to the rates of economic activity observed as 44.8 percent and 43.8 percent in 1975 and 1988 respectively, one obtains an average growth rate of the labor force of 6.2 percent annually for that period.

Over the same period urban employment, measured by the volume of the employed urban labor force, grew by 5.4 percent. This is slightly inferior to that of the labor force. The compared evolution of these two aggregates thus reveals the existence of distortions in the urban labor market.

Indeed, according to the results of the 1988 census, the unemployment rate was very high, reaching 16 percent in Abidjan and 12 percent for all urban areas. The level of urban unemployment is thus double that of 1975, when the numbers were 8.8 percent and 6.3 percent, respectively.

The high level of unemployment is in fact merely the tip of the iceberg of the urban labor market's problems. It also includes some very important qualitative distortions. In fact, the relatively fast growth of urban employment is attributable more to development of the informal sector than to development of the formal sector. Because of this weak yield in the formal sector, growth in urban employment corresponds more to a hypertrophy of the job market than to a real development in employment. Thus underemployment is very high. This has led to an equivalent urban unemployment rate of 23.8 percent in 1985 (Kouame, 1987). Added to the observed unemployment, which was then at 6.2 percent, a rate of 30 percent was estimated for the underutilization of human resources in

1985 in the urban areas. This level could have increased in 1988 if one takes into account the greater level of unemployment at this date.

The Evolution of the Structure of Urban Employment

In a recent analysis of the structure of the job market in Côte d'Ivoire, the recorded strong urban growth led to a restructuring of this market which involves henceforth a nonstructured agricultural sector (NSAS), an informal nonagricultural sector (INAS), and a "modern" sector (MS) (Kouame, 1987). The informal and formal sectors are essentially found in urban areas, whereas the agricultural sector's activities are concentrated in rural zones. Urban employment can be subdivided into formal or modern employment and informal employment. These two types of urban employment experienced a high growth rate over the period 1965–85. Yet the informal sector experienced a much greater growth rate (11.9 percent annually) than the modern sector (7.2 percent annually). Because of this growth, the informal sector, whose share of the job market was merely 6.7 percent in 1965, offered nearly as many jobs as the "modern" sector in 1985 (13 percent as opposed to 14 percent). In reality, the formal sector experienced a drop in strength over the first half of the 1980s. This is at least such as we have already observed elsewhere on the evolution of the private and parapublic formal labor sector (Kouame, 1987). More rapid development of the informal sector will occur subsequent to the growing incapacity of the modern sector to satisfy employment demands. The high level of the rate of unsatisfaction even led to a decline in the inquiries at the employment office (Office de la main d'oeuvre de Côte d'Ivoire, OMOCI). This could be translated into workers' disillusionment over "modern" employment. Many of them would rather direct themselves into the informal sector than wait for a hypothetical job in the formal sector as they have done in the past.

Characteristics of the Informal Sector

If the informal sector is able to offer so many jobs, it is because its functional conditions enable it to do so. The weak yield which it characterizes is due to the use of high labor force–intensive techniques. This labor force is composed of a majority of apprentices and family aides. It accounts for very few wage earners. The use of labor force–intensive techniques is also due to the fact that workers in the informal sector are mainly illiterates who receive their training on the job, that is, in conditions which are not always favorable to the improvement of production techniques.

Because of the lack of qualifications, most workers in the informal sector can be found in the tertiary sector, in particular in the commercial sector, which demands few qualifications. Thus in 1985 workers in the informal sector were distributed with 66 percent in the tertiary sector and a rivaling 34 percent in the secondary sector, the proportion in the primary sector being negligible. This

Table 9.3
Structure of the Urban Informal Sector, 1978 and 1985

Type of Sector	1978	1985
Primary	-	-
Secondary	32.9	34.3
Tertiary	67.1	65.7
Total	100.0	100.0

Sources: République de Côte d'Ivoire, n.d., b; Binet, 1982.

Table 9.4
Evolution of the Structure of Modern Employment, 1974, 1979, and 1984

Type of Sector	1974	1979	1984
Primary	25.0	11.5	16.4
Secondary	41.4	50.3	40.1
Tertiary	33.6	38.2	43.5
Total	100.0	100.0	100.0

Source: République de Côte d'Ivoire, n.d., a.

distribution of the informal sector's labor force between sectors of activity has not varied greatly with respect to what it was in 1978 (67 percent in the tertiary and 33 percent in the secondary sector) (Table 9.3).

The Structure of the Formal Sector

Employment in the formal sector is divided between the civil service, the parapublic sector, and the "modern" private sector. Since data are unavailable on the civil service, we will limit our discussion to employment in the parapublic and private sectors.

Study of the evolution of the structure of private and parapublic employment from 1974 to 1984 reveals a progressive increase in the tertiary sector's share. The relative importance of the primary sector declined in 1979 then increased in 1984. This climb occurred due to the substantial drop in industrial employment which accounted for the majority of jobs in 1979 (Table 9.4). The industrial sector seems thus to have been the most affected by the economic crisis which has crossed the country since the end of the 1970s.

Household Income and Standard of Living

The average household income in Abidjan reached 128,000 cfa francs in 1988. This level represents a drop in comparison with that of 1985, which was 178,000 cfa francs, thus probably reflecting a worsening of the economic crisis. Despite this crisis, which started at the end of the 1970s, average household revenue experienced continuous growth until 1985. It was 55,000 and 70,000 cfa francs in 1963 and 1978, respectively. This trend probably reflects that of salaries. Indeed, the minimum salary experienced a considerable increase between 1970 (5,830 cfa francs) and 1978 (24,912 cfa francs) and then between 1978 and 1985 (33,274 cfa francs) to subsequently stagnate at the 1985 level henceforth (Blanc et al., 1991; DCGTX, 1989). In the modern private and parapublic sector, average income went from 29,000 cfa francs in 1971 to 60,000 cfa francs in 1979 and then 96,000 cfa francs in 1984 (République de Côte d'Ivoire, n.d., a). At the civil service, annual income of the scale's 100 index grew from 255,000 cfa francs in 1978 to 280,000 cfa francs in 1984 (République de Côte d'Ivoire, 1983). We do not have data for the period after 1985, but indications lead us to believe that there was a stagnation, even a drop, in salaries in the modern sector; the level observed at the civil service in 1984 is the same as that of 1981. If nominal salaries experienced such an evolution over the recent period, one can ask what it was for real incomes for the entire period after 1960.

Relying on the evolution of the consumer price index, it is feared that even the considerable growth in observed incomes before 1985 did not necessarily lead to a betterment in the standard of living—on the contrary. In fact, using 1963 as a base, the index rose to 309 in 1978, 543 in 1985, and 685 in 1988. The levels of observed incomes in 1978, 1985, and 1988 would have thus been widely inferior to that of 1963 once the prices had been fixed. Thus, the level of the real average household income in Abidjan would have been only 33,000 cfa francs in 1985. This corresponds to a considerable drop in the household standard of living compared with what it was in 1963. And all this excludes consideration that the averages so calculated hide enormous disparities which have induced the impoverishment of a larger and larger fringe of the population.

In fact, the distribution of revenues according to different criteria including sector of economic activity, nationality, and housing type, reveals enormous inequalities. In 1978, the results of the budget-consumption presurvey showed differentials in the level of income between the modern and informal sectors. Income levels were 44,610 cfa francs against 16,000 cfa francs in production and 54,000 cfa francs against 33,000 cfa francs in commerce for the formal and informal sectors respectively (Ministère de l'Économie et des Finances, 1980). These numbers also reveal the existence of differences according to whether one is engaged in production (industry or crafts) or in commerce within each sector

(Ministère de l'Économie et des Finances, 1980). These latter variations were also observed from surveys on the labor force in the modern private and parapublic sector. The 1984 results indicated a greater average salary in the tertiary (123,900 cfa francs), followed by the secondary (90,200 cfa francs), and finally the primary (only 40,000 cfa francs) sectors. This hierarchy was observed for the other years during which this same survey was held (1971, 1973–74, and 1979). Disparities were also observed according to socioprofessional categories, as one would have expected, and national groups. In the latter case, non-Africans, who represented only 4 percent of wage earners, drew 27 percent of the wage bill. Meanwhile, natives of Côte d'Ivoire accounted for 68 percent and 60 percent, and Africans non-native to Côte d'Ivoire were at 28 percent and 13 percent, respectively. This gives average monthly salaries of 634,000, 88,000, and 49,000 in 1984 for each national group, respectively (République de Côte d'Ivoire, no date a). These inequalities were maintained in 1988 (Koffi, 1991). They were also observed in accordance with the type of housing. In 1988, average monthly household income reached 555,000 in residential housing, 185,000 in economic housing, 90,000 in evolutive housing, and 62,000 in shanty housing for a global monthly average of approximately 128,000 cfa francs (DCGTX, 1989: 58). With such inequalities, it is not surprising to confirm the strong concentration of revenues revealed by the previously cited 1978 survey. In Abidjan, 20 percent of the richest households disposed of 50 percent of revenues whereas the poorest 50 percent received only 23 percent (Ministère de l'Économie et des Finances, 1980).

POPULATION POLICIES RELATING TO URBANIZATION IN CÔTE D'IVOIRE

Until recently, Côte d'Ivoire had no explicit population policy. All that was known on the question related to the government of Côte d'Ivoire's opposition to broad family planning programs (Nortman, 1982). The government policy of advocating a strong demographic growth through high fertility was also inimical to the health of mother and children. It is also known, since the United Nations surveys on population policies, that the government is not satisfied with the current spatial distribution of the population and the continued intensity of foreign immigration. However, these are the results of options that the government itself retained at the beginning of the 1960s. They consisted of encouraging foreign African and non-African immigration and the simultaneous displacement of natives of Côte d'Ivoire from the rural zones toward urban areas and from the savanna to the forest zones.

In fact, it might not have been explicit, but a sound population policy existed in Côte d'Ivoire. It was integrated into the global development policy and consisted in furnishing the qualified and nonqualified labor force the economic structures lacking in the beginning of the 1960s (Kouame, 1987), taking into account the direction of the economic policy. Foreign immigration would have helped resolve the scarcity of short-term labor whereas high fertility, in conjunction with the development of education, would have, in the long run, offered a local qualified and nonqualified labor force to the production apparatus. The production of this abundant labor force would also have aided a reduction in the costs of labor so as to attract foreign investments for the development of the industrial sector. In maintaining a very low remuneration for peasant work (Toure, 1985), the government encouraged the rural exodus of young educated natives of Côte d'Ivoire as to increase the supply of labor in the cities, particularly in Abidjan where industrial activity was concentrated. African immigration of the labor force would have thus compensated the departure of rural youth. But certain perverse effects of this policy (particularly the orientation of half of the African immigration toward the cities and the strong intensity of the rural exodus) led to greater than expected urban growth at the same time as it created a shortage of labor in the rural zones, according to predictions by F. Binet (1982).

This favorable direction for strong demographic growth and accelerated urbanization assumes that arrangements had been taken to create conditions for a successful insertion of inhabitants of the cities and particularly Abidjan. This implies the creation of a sufficient number of jobs, the production of adequate habitation, and the supply of social services to the urban populations without neglecting the rural populations. Just like the population policy, the housing and employment policies were entirely integrated into the global development policy (Antoine et al., 1987; Kouame, 1987). The pursued goals were to create modern housing and employment for the greatest number of people. This had not been possible, as was seen in previous sections. The only remaining option for the government of Côte d'Ivoire was to reorient its policies. This seems to have been done, but again within the framework of a global strategy for development.

Côte d'Ivoire's new model for development now really rests on the World Bank's new strategy to redress the African economy on the basis of structural adjustments and revalorization of human resources. Côte d'Ivoire's new population policy is included in the development of human resources, which also deals with health, education, and employment. Unfortunately, this policy has not yet been sufficiently detailed so as to know exactly what the implications will be on urbanization. However, a will to reduce the strong population growth can be noted, in acting on fertility and foreign immigration simultaneously (République de Côte d'Ivoire, 1991). It is especially intended to control fertility by the expansion of family planning services. Because the actual source of population growth in Abidjan is natural growth and thus fertility, this measure could contribute to a considerable reduction in the city's growth. A drop in fertility has already occurred in Abidjan as in other cities, where access to family planning services has become increasingly extensive, with the activities of the Ivorian Association for Family Well-Being (Association Ivorienne de Bien-Etre Familial, AIBEF) essentially being concentrated in urban zones for the time being. We have also seen that the economic crisis would have entailed a reorientation in the migration flow toward secondary urban centers; measures relative to internal migration could be useful if taken in order to maintain this tendency with the aim of unblocking the city of Abidjan. To this effect, the decentralization policy in course, if it offered possibilities for the development of economic activities and particularly for the informal sector in the intermediate urban zones, could play here an important role. Concerning habitation, the government has resolved, following pressure from the World Bank, to lay aside prestige investments which reduced its capability to offer decent housing to a greater number of people. In this perspective, the state's tasks are reduced significantly, and a greater role is accorded to the municipalities for the management and maintenance of urban spaces and to the private sector for housing construction. Nonetheless, the state expects to dominate urban expansion with minimal equipment of new spaces so as to avoid the development of precarious housing. The minimal equipment implies a reduction in norms with respect to previous practice (Antoine et al., 1987). The totality of these measures (a reduction in urban growth which would imply such for the demand for housing, social services, etc.; a reduction in the norms for construction which would probably entail a more significant supply of housing) could, if the objectives were reached more than just partially, lead to an improvement in the standard of living in urban zones.

CONCLUSION

Côte d'Ivoire experienced very strong urban growth over the first two decades of its history (1960–80). This growth was particularly strong for the city of Abidjan. During the last decade (1980–90), urban growth has slowed considerably, and Abidjan was the most affected. This did not hinder it from remaining, by far, the country's most important city. Investments that could have helped in the development of the city of Bouaké were instead detoured to benefit Yamoussokro and San Pedro, thus impeding the former from becoming a real pole for development in the country's center. Abidjan has maintained its weight despite the will for decentralization and urban planning. It would be preferable that this tendency continued without in any way creating a shortage in the labor force in the rural zones. If this were the case, it could be assumed that Abidjan's problems in housing, social services, equipment, and employment would be transferred to the secondary cities. Thus particular attention must be paid to these problems for all measures taken to maintain this tendency. The decentralization of the application of the urban policy could only contribute to the real improvement of urban standards of living if it aims, among other goals, to resolve these problems.

NOTES

1. These rates were calculated from data taken from Ba (1991).
2. Abidjan's average annual growth rate between 1975 and 1988 was 5.6 percent, and

its annual growth rate observed in 1988 was 4.8 percent. The divergence between these two rates is thus minimal.

REFERENCES

Abbas, S. 1991. *Fécondité.* Séminaire national de présentation des résultats du recensement général de la population et de l'habitat de 1988, Abidjan.

Ahonzo, Etienne, B. Barrere, and P. Kopylov. 1984. *Analyse de la situation démographique de la Côte d'Ivoire à partir des données existantes.* Abidjan: Direction de la Statistique, Ministère de l'économie et des finances.

Antoine, P., A. Dubresson, and A. Manou-Savina. 1987. *Abidjan "côté cours."* Paris: Karthala-Orstom.

Ba, I. 1991. *Répartition spatiale de la population.* Séminaire national de présentation des résultats du recensement général de la population et de l'habitat de 1988. Abidjan.

Binet Giannoni, Francoise. 1982. *Bilan national de l'emploi en Côte d'Ivoire: analyse retrospective, situation actuelle et projections dans les differents milieux et secteurs d'activites.* Paris: Republique francaise, Ministere des relations exter ieures, Cooperation et développement, Service d'etudes du développement.

Blanc, B., et al. 1991. *Habitat économique: Modernisation et promotion sociale à Abidjan,* Rapport de recherche Université de Montréal. Institut d'urbanisme.

Bonnamour, L. 1991. "Le transport urbain en Afrique au sud du Sahara." *Afrique contemporaine* 158:14–29.

Chaleard, J. L., O. Dembele, and A. Dubresson. 1990. *Villes, villages et recensement de Côte d'Ivoire: "Qui est fou?"* Institut de Geographie Tropicale (IGT)—Office de la Recherche Scientific et Technique Outre Mer (ORSTOM).

DCGTX (Direction et contrôle des grands travaux). 1991. *Abidjan, perspectives à long terme.*

Djédjé, L. 1991. *Mortalité.* Séminaire national de présentation des résultats du recensement général de la population et de l'habitat de 1988, Abidjan.

Dubresson, A. 1989. *Villes et industries en Côte d'Ivoire.* Paris: Karthala.

Dubresson, A., and A. Manou-Savina. 1985. "Dossier Abidjan." *Cités africaines,* 3:32–35. Paris: janvier-mars.

Dureau, F. 1987. *Migration et urbanisation, le cas de la Côte d'Ivoire.* Paris: Orstom.

Haeringer, P. 1977. "Occupation de l'espace urbain et péri-urbain." *Atlas de Côte d'Ivoire.* Ministère du Plan-ORSTOM-IGT.

Kipre, P. 1985. *Villes de Côte d'Ivoire, 1893–1940.* Vols. 1 and 2. Abidjan-Dakar: Nouvelles Editions Africaines (NEA).

Koffi, A. 1991. *Planning and Management in Large Cities: A Case Study of Abidjan, Côte d'Ivoire.* Centre de Recherche Architecturale et Urbaine (CRAU). Abidjan: Université d'Abidjan.

Kouame, A. 1987. "De la pénurie à la sous-utilisation de la main-d'oeuvre: un essai sur la problématique des ressources humaines en Côte d'Ivoire." Ph.D. diss., Université de Montréal, Montréal, Canada.

Kouassi, L. 1991. *Les caractéristiques socio-économiques de la population.* Séminaire national de présentation des résultats du recensement général de la population et de l'habitat de 1988, Abidjan.

Ministère de l'Économie et des finances. 1980. *Résultats définitifs de la pré-enquête budget-consommation, 1978.* Abidjan: Direction de la Statistique.

Nortman, Dorothy. 1982. *Population and Family Planning Programs; a Compendium of Data through 1981.* New York: Population Council.

Républic de Côte d'Ivoire. 1983. *Annuaire statistique du travail.* Abidjan: Direction de l'emploi, Ministère du travail et de l'ivoirisation des cadres.

———. 1988a. *Résultats définitifs, enquête permanente auprès des ménages.* Abidjan: Ministère du plan, Direction de la statistique.

———. 1988b. *Memento chiffré de la Côte d'Ivoire, 1986–87.* Abidjan: Ministère du plan, Direction de la statistique.

———. 1989. *Annales de la santé.* Abidjan: Ministère de la santé publique et de la population.

———. 1991. *Project de déclaration de politique de développement des ressources humaines.* Abidjan: Comité de suivi et de la valorisation des ressources humaines.

———. n.d., a. *Enquête sur la main-d'oeuvre, 1984: principaux résultats.* Abidjan: Office National de la Formation Professionnelle.

———. n.d., b. *Enquête sur le secteur informel, 1985: principaux résultats.* Abidjan: Office National de la Formation Professionnelle.

Rougerie, G. 1972. *La Côte d'Ivoire.* Paris: PUF.

Societé d'Ecomonie et de Mathématiques Appliqués. 1965. *Étude socio-économique de la zone urbaine d'Abidjan.* Rapport n° 4: L'habitat en 1963. Paris.

Soumahoro, C. 1992. *L'habitat locatif populaire à Abidjan: un secteur du logement en évolution.* Montréal: Communication à la 5 ème Conférence internationale de recherche sur l'habitat.

Toure, A. 1985. *Les Petits Métiers à Abidjan.* Paris: Karthala.

YapiDiahou, A. 1992. "Nationalités, ethnies, emplois et bidonvilles à Abidjan. La question des facteurs et des déterminants." In *Maîtriser le développement urbain en Afrique sub-saharienne,* edited by Emile Lebris and H. Girhnitrapaml, 705–716. Paris: Orstom Ponty.

———. n.d. *Les détenteurs coutumiers, les citadins et l'Etat dans la course pour l'accès au sol urbain à Abidjan.* Abidjan.

10

Egypt

Mohamed El-Attar

Egypt, known today as the Arab Republic of Egypt, is a territorial rectangle occupying the northeast corner of the African continent. Its total area is about 386,900 square miles (1,002,00 square kilometers). Egypt is bordered by the Mediterranean Sea in the north, the Sudan in the south, Libya in the west, and the Red Sea, Saudi Arabia, Jordan, and Israel, in the east and northeast. Egypt has always been a nodal point of routes between Europe and colonies in Asia and the southern parts of Africa due to its prominent geographical location and the Mediterranean coastline which stretches about 620 miles. In the east, its coastline on the Red Sea and the Gulf of Aqaba is about 1,835 miles.

Egypt consists of 25 governorates: four of which are frontier governorates (El-Wadi El-Gedid, Matrouh, Red Sea, and Sinai) and four are entirely urban governorates (Alexandria, Cairo, Port Said, and Suez). Cairo, Alexandria, and Giza are the governorates with the largest concentrations of urban population. Their populations in 1986 were reported to be (in million) 6.1, 2.9, and 1.9, respectively, accounting for 10,803,344 persons or 51 percent of the total urban population. The Greek historian Herodotus stated in the fourth century B.C. that "Egypt is a gift of the Nile." To wit, seven of the nonfrontiers governorates are located in part in the Nile Valley where there is a narrow strip of vegetation as it streams northward through their desert environment. At Cairo, the river starts to form its delta, intensifies its agriculture, and increases its population density, exerting great pressures on residential and agricultural lands. A basic fact about Egypt is the impossibility of increasing its cultivable land in an amount that absorbs the increase in its population (El-Attar, 1990). Thus, while the total area of Egypt is 386,900 square miles, about 96 percent (48,205,049) of Egypt's total population (50,455,049) in 1986 was packed into 3.6 percent (14,000 square miles) of the total area. The remainder of the area is desert. The Nile cuts its way through the desert dividing it into two parts: the Western Desert, which is arid; and the Eastern Desert, which is characterized by *Wadis* fringed by "rugged mountains."

Egypt's population, always growing albeit unevenly over parts of the country, has historically shown most rapid growth in and around Cairo, the capital city, and other capital cities of the surrounding governorates. This has been a function of the growth in the total population, transportation, and a decent level of social organization.

The flow of population from countryside to urban centers is merely a response to expected economic opportunities and urban attraction (El-Attar, 1990; WGPGED, 1986; Yap, 1977; Todaro, 1980; Schultz, 1971; Rempel, 1981; Greenwood, 1969, 1971, 1978). This exodus from rural areas is related to the shortage of farmland and lack of the comforts of life found in the city: running water, good housing conditions, paved streets, lights, recreation facilities, health centers, and, in general, all that country people aspire to have but cannot attain in rural areas. Many of the crucial problems which Egypt faces and wishes to solve are related to the absolute size of its population and to the pattern of urban population growth and concentration. The ramifications of this process tend to impair the quality of life in the urban centers. Densely populated urban areas suffer from unemployment, poor transportation, crime, alienation, and many other related factors that give rise to environmental imbalance and regional disparity in development and welfare. Specifically, the impact of the transfer of population from the rural areas to the nation's capital and other urban centers in Egypt has resulted in overurbanization with its dysfunctional consequences in Cairo and surrounding areas (Goldstein, 1987; El-Attar, 1990; Ibrahim, 1982; Abu-Lughod, 1969).

DATA ON URBANIZATION

The major source of data for this study is the Egyptian population censuses. Initially, knowledge on urbanization in Egypt, as in most developing countries (DC), has been limited primarily by available statistics. Egypt is one of the few developing countries which has a long history of population censuses. The modern and regular censuses began in 1882.

Definition of urban population represents a stumbling block which impedes national and international comparability (Goldstein and Sly, 1975a; Eldridge 1956). Although the undertaking of modern censuses in Egypt began in 1882 (the eleventh of which was taken in 1986), definition of the urban population was first introduced in the eighth census in 1960. A similar urban definition in the vital statistics had been in use for almost a decade before the 1960 population census. The vital statistics definition considers as urban the "big cities namely Cairo and Alexandria" and urban governorates, "chief towns of provinces and districts'' (Department of Statistics and Census, 1962: ix). Thus, the 1960 census definition meant not only the same definition that the vital statistics utilized but almost exactly the same administrative delineated areas.

Essentially, urban areas in Egypt constitute the four urban governorates mentioned above, the capitals of the rest of the governorates, the capitals of *marakez* (the administrative districts to which a governorate is divided) (Department of Statistics and Census, 1963:3), along with cities, towns, and their administrative subdivisions (Sayed and Zaky, 1985; El-Attar, 1990). This indicates that the urban definition in Egypt is determined by administrative rather than demographic or quantitative criteria.

APPROACH AND METHODS OF STUDY

The study of urbanization requires different approaches, data, and measures for its assessment because it represents multifaceted phenomena (Goldstein and Sly, 1975b; Lampard, 1965). Specifically, E. E. Lampard (1965) delineated three conceptions of urbanization: ''the behavioral, the structural, and the demographic.'' H. T. Eldridge (1956) viewed urbanization in terms of demographic and structural processes. The demographic approach requires an investigation of the changes in urban population, increase in numbers and size of urban localities, and population concentration and redistribution. The structural approach stresses the variations in the occupational structure of employment and technological changes as a vehicle to or an indicator of transportation advances, educational changes, and the like (Wander, 1975). This study adopts the demographic approach as a major mean for the investigation. The following measures are utilized (Arriaga, 1975): (1) The extent of urbanization; (2) the ratio of urban (U) to rural (R) population; (3) growth of population in cities of 100,000 or more inhabitants in terms of city average, ''rank-size rule,'' and index of primacy; (4) the redistribution index; and (5) population concentration index.

Degree of Urbanization

E. Arriaga (1975) defines the degree of urbanization as ''the absolute or relative number of people who live in what are defined as urban places.'' Table 10.1 indicates that in 1907, slightly over one-sixth of Egypt's population lived in urban areas, and by 1986 about 44 percent did. Between those two dates the urban percentage increased with the taking of each census without reversals regardless of political events or economic conditions. In the meantime, while the size of population in the 79 years between 1907 and 1986 had quadrupled (4.3), the urban population (slightly more than 21 million) had increased elevenfold by 1986. Moreover, the urban population increased by 997 percent, from 1,930,137 in 1907 to 21,173,436 in 1986, compared with 331 percent in the total population (from 11,189,978 to 48,205,049). The growth of the urban population of Egypt as a proportion of the total population proceeded at equal

Table 10.1
Percentage Distribution of Urban and Rural Population and Urban-to-Rural Population Ratio in Egypt, 1907–86

Census Year	Urban	Rural	Total		Ratio U/R
			Number	Percent	
1907	17.2	82.8	11,189,978	100	0.2
1917	22.6	77.4	12,718,255	100	0.3
1927	26.9	73.1	14,177,864	100	0.4
1937	28.2	71.8	15,920,694	100	0.4
1947	33.5	66.5	18,966,767	100	0.5
1960[a]	38.0	62.0	25,984,101	100	0.6
1966[b]	40.5	59.5	29,724,099	100	0.7
1976	43.8	56.2	36,626,204	100	0.8
1986[c]	43.9	56.1	48,205,049	100	0.8

[a]Excluding nomad population.

[b]Excluding frontier population.

[c]Excluding temporary emigrants totalling 2,250,000.

Source: Compiled from CAPMAS, 1987, except for 1917 which is an interpolation.

pace (almost) until 1976, after which it tapered off. Table 10.1 indicates that while the country is still predominantly rural (56.1 percent in 1986), the urban population in the 1986 census had surpassed that of the 1976 census by only a tenth of a percent (from 43.8 to 43.9, respectively). The insignificant increase in the percentage of urban population must not be considered as an indicator of stabilization in Egypt's urbanization. The excess of temporary emigration (2.25 million persons or 4.5 percent) in 1986 over that of 1976 (1.4 million persons or 3.7 percent) is a major contributor to the small increase between the two censuses (CAPMAS, 1987).

Urban-to-Rural Ratio (U/R)

The ratio of urban to rural population is another measure of the degree of urbanization. It differs from the proportion urban in a sense that it shows the number of urbanites per number of ruralites in Egypt, whereas the proportion urban gives the portion of the urban population as a percentage of the total population. Table 10.1 indicates that during a period of 79 years (from 1907 to 1986) the U/R increased from 21 to 78 urbanites per every 100 ruralites. Despite the inherent limitations of this measure (Gibbs, 1966, 1968a, 1968b; Jones, 1967, 1968; Mitra, 1968; Shryock et al., and Associates, 1976), it has the advantage to trace the historical path and specify the pace of urbanization in a given country. Table 10.1 indicates the equality of the ratio in the two censuses of 1976 and 1986 (0.78 for each). Whether this equality is to be considered the beginning of a stabilization in the process of urbanization in Egypt's urban growth is to be determined by the 1996 population census. In view of the sizable labor emigration as documented by the two censuses of 1976 and 1986, the tapering off in the growth of urban population may be spurious and interim (CAPMAS, 1987; El-Attar, 1990).

Extended Cities

Extended cities have been the characteristic of the city of Cairo and the contiguous cities of administrative centers, subregions, and villages. Since the end of World War II, there has been an increasing trend for Cairo to extend habitably and regionally to include territory essentially rural in character. Table 10.2 indicates that between 1976 and 1986 the population of the city of Cairo increased 19 percent. However, the Cairo Urban agglomeration increased 30 percent between 1975 and 1985 (United Nations, 1991). The population share contributed by each component is categorized into eleven centers, three of which are the result of new habitat in the city of Giza, *Markaz* El-Giza, and the town of Shubra El-Khema. On the other hand, the intercensal rates of growth of governorate population from 1966 to 1976 and 1976 to 1986 (Table 10.3) indicate that the population of the city of Cairo had a stable population during 1966 to 1986 whereas the nation's population growth rate rose from 2.0 to 2.7 percent between 1966–76 and 1976–86, respectively. The corresponding rates for the contiguous governorates of Giza (3.8 and 4.3), Kalyubia (3.3 and 4.0), and Fayum (2.0 and 3.0) are high with the exception of the governorates of Port Said, Suez, Ismailia, and Frontier governorates which experienced massive out-migration during the belligerent relations between Egypt and Israel during the years from 1967 to 1979.

City Average

The average city size in a country, in the sense of the statistical expectation of the considered cities, is another measure of the degree of urbanization (Arriaga, 1975). This measure is computed by different methods, depending on the nature of the available data. Since the available data for this study are for cities of 100,000 or more inhabitants, a restricted expectation (Arriaga, 1975) is computed as follows:

Table 10.2
Regional Population Components of Greater Cairo, 1976 and 1986

Region	Population			
	Number		Change	
	1976	1986	Number	Percent
City of Cairo	5,074,016	6,052,836	978,820	19.3
City of Giza	1,230,446	1,870,508	640,062	52.0
Markaz El-Giza	94,169	127,789	33,620	35.7
City of Shubra El-Khema	394,223	710,794	316,571	80.3
Town of Badrasheen	26,992	40,159	13,167	48.8
Town of El-Hwamdiah	48,030	73,060	25,030	52.1
Some villages in El-Saf	32,367	47,292	14,925	46.1
Town of Shebeen El-Kanater	25,505	35,519	10,014	39.3
Markaz El-Khanka	154,572	251,645	97,073	62.8
Markaz Kalyub	184,432	272,172	87,740	47.6
El-Kanater El-Khairia	145,726	218,546	72,820	50.0
Some villages in Shebeen K.	39,802	53,540	13,738	34.5
Total	7,450,280	9,753,860	2,303,580	30.9

Source: Compiled from CAPMAS, 1987.

$$RE = \text{Sum}\,(A_iC_i) \,/\, P \tag{1}$$

where *RE* is the restricted expected value of city size, A_i is the actual city population, C_i is controlled city population (where cities with population over one million are restricted to one million), and *P* is the total population in the country. The summation is from *1* to *n*, where *n* is number of cities in each census.

Table 10.4 gives the cities of 100,000 or more inhabitants in the censuses of 1960, 1966, 1976 (CAPMAS, 1978), and municipal counts and United Nations estimates for 1986 (United Nations, 1990). Utilizing Tables 10.1 and 10.4 and formula (1) produced the following four expectations for city size: 200,674; 228,863; 256,118; and 258,509 for 1960, 1966, 1976, and 1986, respectively. The changes in these indices indicate a descending growth amounting to 14.05,

Table 10.3
Intercensal Growth Rates of Governorate Population in Egypt, 1966–86

Governorate	Population Census			Growth Rates	
	1966	1976	1986	1966-76	1976-86
Cairo	4,219,853	5,074,016	6,052,836	1.8	1.8
Alexandria	1,801,056	2,317,705	2,917,327	2.5	2.3
Port Said	282,977	262,760	399,793	-0.7	4.2
Suez	264,098	193,965	326,820	-3.1	5.2
Ismailia	344,789	353,975	544,427	0.3	4.3
Behera	1,978,889	2,464,445	3,257,168	2.2	2.8
Damietta	431,596	576,326	741,264	2.9	2.5
Kafr El-Sheikh	1,118,495	1,407,160	1,800,129	2.3	2.5
Gharbia	1,901,117	2,293,240	2,870,960	1.9	2.2
Dakahlia	2,285,332	2,737,306	3,500,470	1.8	2.5
Sharkia	2,107,971	2,617,938	3,420,119	2.2	2.7
Menoufia	1,458,048	1,710,849	2,227,087	1.6	2.6
Kalyubia	1,211,764	1,680,837	2,514,244	3.3	4.0
Giza	1,650,381	2,416,659	3,700,054	3.8	4.3
Fayum	935,281	1,141,879	1,544,047	2.0	3.0
Beni Suef	927,910	1,110,132	1,442,981	1.8	2.6
Menia	1,705,602	2,054,105	2,648,043	1.9	2.5
Asyut	1,418,164	1,697,422	2,223,034	1.8	2.7
Suhag	1,689,397	1,924,814	2,455,134	1.3	2.4
Kena	1,470,812	1,709,299	2,252,315	1.5	2.8
Aswan	520,567	618,518	801,408	1.7	2.6
Frontier Gov.	351,759	262,854	565,389	-2.9	7.7
Total	30,075,858	36,626,204	48,205,049	2.0	2.7

Source: Compiled from CAPMAS, 1975, 1986, 1987.

Table 10.4
Cities of 100,000 or More Population, Egypt: 1960–86

City	1960	1966	1976	1986
Alexandria	1,516,234	1,801,056	2,317,705	2,893,000
Cairo	3,348,779	4,219,853	5,074,016	6,052,836
Suez	203,610	264,098	193,965	265,000
Port Said	245,318	282,977	262,760	382,000
Damanhur	126,600	146,079	170,633	226,000
Mhalla El-Kubra	178,288	225,323	292,114	385,000
Imbaba	136,429	-	-	-
Ismailia	116,302	144,163	145,930	236,000
Kafr El-Dwar	-	-	146,248	194,000
Mansura	151,192	191,459	259,387	358,000
Shebin El-Kom	-	-	102,805	136,000
Shubra El-Khema	-	172,902	394,223	710,794
Tanta	184,299	229,978	228,324	374,000
Zagazig	124,417	151,186	202,675	274,000
Assyut	127,485	153,956	213,751	291,000
Aswan	-	127,594	144,654	196,000
Beni-Suef	-	-	117,910	163,000
Faiyum	102,064	133,616	166,910	227,000
Giza	262,218	571,249	1,230,446	1,857,508
Kena	-	-	-	142,000
Menia	-	112,580	146,366	203,000
Sohag	-	-	102,914	141,000
Total All Cities	6,823,235	8,928,069	11,913,736	15,707,138
Restricted Index	200,674	228,863	256,118	258,509

Source: Compiled from United Nations, 1964, 1974, 1990; and from CAPMAS, 1978.

11.91, and 0.93 percent for 1960–66, 1966–76, and 1976–86, respectively. The small magnitude of change in the index of 1976 to 1986 may be related to the use of estimated values for 1986.

The Rank-Size Rule

The "rank-size rule" is another index for measuring the extent of concentration in cities. This measure was pioneered by F. Auerbach (1913) and extensively elaborated on later by G. K. Zipf (1941). It has been utilized by many researchers (Stewart, 1947; Duncan, 1957; Shryock et al., 1976; Arriaga, 1975). Considering a set of cities, J. Q. Stewart (1947:462) states the formula for this measure in a general format of which the following is an example:

$$r^n s_r = L \quad (2)$$

where L is the population of the largest city in a set of cities of a given country, S_r rank of rth city, and n is a positive exponent which is to be determined. The value of n is an indicator of a city population concentration. Specifically, "the greater the value of n, the greater the concentration of population in the largest cities relative to the smallest cities" (Arriaga, 1975:59). Applying the necessary data from Egypt, the computed indices formed slowly decreasing values for n of 1.454, 1.418, 1.365, and 1.298 for the years 1960, 1966, 1976, and 1986 for cities of 100,000 or more inhabitants. Inclusion of cities of 50,000 or more in 1976 produced an index of 1.315, which is smaller than 1.365. These indices represent a high degree of concentration in large cities.

The Index of Primacy

The index of primacy relates to the notion of the "primate city" which M. Jefferson described as the most influential city in the country in terms of political, economic, and population dominance. It is our hypothesis that the index of primacy in Egypt is of high magnitude and that its immensity decreases in size from one census to another indicating thereby a diffused effect of the city of Cairo. The test of this hypothesis is readily available from the data on the rank-order size of the cities in Egypt. The primacy index (PI) is defined as the ratio of the population of the city of Cairo weighted by the magnitude (m) of the summation of (1/r) divided by the total population of cities of 100,000 or more inhabitants. In symbols:

$$PI_n = (m)(P_r) / \text{sum}(P_{r+1}) \quad (3)$$

where r = 1, 2, 3, . . . n; n = number of cities under consideration and/or the highest rank attained in each group which amounted to 14, 16, 20, and 21 in

1960, 1966, 1976, and 1986, respectively; and m = sum of (1/r) where the first term begins with r = 2. The calculations for 1960 are as follows:

$$m = 1/2 + 1/3 + \ldots + 1/14 = 2.25$$
$$PI_{14} = (2.25)\ (3{,}348{,}779)\ /\ 3{,}474{,}456 = 2.169$$

The m values for 1966, 1976, and 1986 are 2.379, 2.544, and 2.688, respectively. The corresponding three primacy indices are 2.132, 1.887, and 1.685 for 1966, 1976, and 1986, respectively. These indices measure the concentration of population in Cairo in relation to the rest of the cities of 100,000 or more population. Slightly higher values for these indices are obtained when the number of cities is held constant to 14 cities in the four periods for purpose of comparability. The following gives each index versus its restricted counterpart: (2.169–2.169), (2.132–2.125), (1.887–1.877), and (1.865–1.606) for 1960, 1966, 1976, and 1986, respectively.

The four indices indicate greater population concentration in the city of Cairo amounting to more than twice the size of population concentrated in the rest of the cities of 100,000 or more inhabitants in 1960 and 1966. The magnitude of the index declined to less than two in 1976 and 1986, implying a decrease in the concentration effect of the city of Cairo. This is a natural consequence of many factors among which are the labor emigration to the Arab oil-producing nations, the establishment of regional institutions of higher education, and decentralization of some government activities (El-Attar, 1990).

The Redistribution Index

To examine whether the process of population redistribution was general or differentiated to all governorates, one may utilize an index which measures the degree of population dispersion among all the governorates (Eldridge, 1964). This index is created by dividing 100 by the number of governorates in the country. For the purpose of this study, the frontier governorates are excluded, and this limits the number of governorates to 21. When this ratio (100/21 = 4.76) is subtracted from the percentage of the population in each governorate to the total population, the positive sum of the differences yields the value of the index. If equal numbers of individuals were contained in each governorate, the value of the index would be zero. The upper limit of the index in this study is 95.24 and would occur if the entire population of the 21 governorates were packed in one governorate. The obtained indices for seven censuses indicate the percentage of the country's population that would need to be redistributed in order to attain population equality in all governorates. The seven indices from 1927 to 1986 are given below:

Census	**Index**
1927	23.6

1937	23.1
1947	23.0
1960	22.9
1966	22.6
1976	22.9
1986	22.4

The indices indicate a slight decline of 1.2 percentage points over 39 years, from 23.6 in 1927 to 22.4 in 1986. Put differently, in 1986 it would have required the redistribution of 1.2 percent of the population to regain the level of concentration of 1927.

Given the differentials in governorate land areas, it becomes clear that equal population sizes in all governorates would represent a very unbalanced population distribution. Alternatively, it would be essential to utilize another index that takes simultaneously the areas of the governorates and the size of their populations into consideration. The concentration index fulfills these objectives.

Index of Concentration

The index of concentration (CI) is another measure of population concentration which E. M. Hoover (1941, 1951) has utilized in his studies of population "redistribution," mobility, and industry location in the United States. The formula for computing the CI (Duncan et al., 1961) is as follows:

$$CI = 1/2 \text{ the absolute sum } ({}_jP_i - A_i) \quad (4)$$

where ${}_jP_i$ = the percentage of population in the ith governorate in the jth census; $i = 1, \ldots, n$ and $j = 1, \ldots,$ m; and n and m are the number of governorates (21 in this study) and censuses (seven), respectively.

A_i = the percentage of the area in square kilometers in the 1976 population census. Governorates constitute stable geographic and administrative units for purposes of this analysis, especially in view of the adjustment or revision of boundaries which census authorities undertake for purposes of comparability. The CI measures population dislocation in the country and explains the percentage of a nation's population which would be shifted from their current location in order to bring relative distribution equality among populations and areas of all regional units under study.

The CI of the governorate populations in these censuses shows an increase in the value of the index in each census year since 1927 until 1976, from 25.06 to 27.04. The value of the index has decreased slightly in 1986 to 27, a trend which is consistent with the rank-size rule. When one ignores the governorates of Gharbia, Menoufia, Assyiut, and Souhag, whose share has been growing at a declining rate, one finds that the value of the index has been dominated by the share of the following governorates: Cairo, Alexandria, Giza, and Kalyubia. While the share of these four governorates to the index increased from 51.3 percent in 1927 to 90.8 percent in 1986, the share of Cairo began to decline from roughly 52 percent in 1966 to 49 and 45 in 1976 and 1986, respectively. Alexandria showed a decline of almost one percentage point between 1976 and 1986. While the share of these two oldest and largest urban governorates began to decline, that of the governorates of Giza and Kalyubia continued to increase steadily for Giza and with some fluctuation for Kalyubia.

CONCLUSIONS AND IMPLICATIONS

Egypt continued to be predominantly rural until 1907, when 17 percent of its population resided in urban areas. It was only after the turn of the first decade of the twentieth century that the population began to inhabit the new cities of Port Said, Ismailia, and Suez and to concentrate in the cities of Cairo and Alexandria and the capitals of the governorates. On the other hand, the growth of Cairo and all other cities in Egypt has not evolved from technological developments but rather from concentration of political and governmental activities, financial functions, business and trade services, and college and university education. This is what Gideon Sjoberg describes as "cities without industry" (Gist, 1961:660).

Primacy or Counter Primacy

Additionally, investigation of the unevenness of city population growth and concentration indicates that the urbanization patterns in Egypt still reflect the existence of "primacy" condition. However, there is a tendency for this primacy to diffuse with time, a phenomenon which Colin Clark (1967) calls "oligarchy" or "counter primacy." The decrease in primacy indices since 1960 relates to the increase in the interaction between man and the environment. A more advanced degree of organization and technology will be needed if the effect of primacy is to cease and/or diffuse at a greater pace (Lampard, 1965). Other studies have documented that primacy approaches a rank-size form as development and extent of urbanization prolong (Berry, 1964, 1967; Clark, 1967).

The decline in population growth rates of the largest two urban governorates of Cairo and Alexandria and the increase of those of the contiguous governorates of Giza and Kalyubia expound the explanation of the rank-size rule. Studies on lifetime migration (El-Attar, 1990; Sayed and Zaky, 1985) indicate that the contiguity of Giza and Kalyubia has been "instrumental" to their significant population growth where the lifetime net migration rates in 1976 were 19.1 and 4.4 percent for Giza and Kalyubia, respectively. Although the corresponding data for 1986 are not available, the data on hand (CAPMAS, 1990) indicate a decline in the lifetime in-migration rates for the four governorates in 1986. These rates (in percentage) are compared with their 1976 counterparts as follows (1976 first): Cairo (27.2 v. 20.3), Alexandria (18.6 v. 14.1), Giza (23.4 v. 19.2) and Kalyubia (12.9 v. 13.4).

Rural vs. Urban

It should be noted that irrespective of the administrative reclassification of rural-urban types of residence (Nassef, 1973), intergovernorate migration flow has been dominated in the past by the movement of population from rural areas to urban centers to the extent that rural-urban differentials in population growth are basically a function of internal migration (El-Attar, 1990). This pattern disappears with the specification of migration streams. In their analysis of lifetime migration streams for the intercensal decade 1966–76, Sayed and Zaky (1985:74–77) found that "the share of the rural-urban stream was the minimum among all other streams," and expected, accordingly, a decrease in such stream and an increase in the "urban-rural migration" in the future. They relate this decrease to (1) the international emigration of Egyptians to the oil-producing Arab countries, (2) migration by stages, and (3) areas defined "administratively" as urban which actually maintain rural characteristics. The 1986 census data on Greater Cairo and other 1986 migration data partially support H. A. A. Sayed and H. H. M. Zaky's statement as reflected in the decrease in the growth rate of the city of Cairo proper and the lifetime in-migration rate. Further analysis of 1986 migration data and the allocation of 2.25 million persons who work in the Arab countries is needed for conclusive judgment.

In a country like Egypt, one is reluctant to imagine an immediate, exciting urban future without solving some of the current difficult problems. If Egypt's past urban trend (that is, that before 1976, when it was halted by temporary emigration to the oil-producing Arab countries) continues into the future, one would expect some extremely serious problems to occur. Such problems range from lack of food and healthy water to inadequate transportation and substandard housing, substandard health care systems, and inefficient educational services. Alleviating this suffering requires highly productive efforts on the part of the people and the government, and above all, sufficient foreign exchange funds. The latter is impossible to attain since supplies of natural resources are limited or nil. In such a situation, international assistance and subsidies are needed. Moreover, the urban land is a scarce natural resource, and this makes "two-dimensional land-use planning . . . out-of-date," so "three-dimensional plans" (Perloff, 1967) and prudent conservation policy for agricultural land are to be entertained. Data of the World Bank (WB) indicate that the average annual growth rate of gross domestic production (GDP) has declined from 6.8 percent during 1965–80 to 5.7 percent during 1980–88 (World Bank, 1990). On the other hand, cereal imports increased from approximately 3.9 to 8.5 million metric tons in 1974 and 1988, respectively. These data show that the agricultural base needed to support urban growth is inadequate in Egypt. The urban population increased from 38 percent in 1960 to 44 percent in 1986. An enlightened urbanization requires a socioeconomic and demographic development which constitutes high technology level and low population growth (Berry, 1961). In fact, Berry (1961:585) concluded that "different city size distributions are in no way related to the relative economic development of countries . . . (and that) primacy is not confined to lesser developed countries."

REFERENCES

Abu-Lughod, J. L. 1969. "Testing the Theory of Social Area Analysis: The Ecology of Cairo, Egypt." *American Sociological Review* 34:198–212.

Arriaga, E. 1975. "Selected Measures of Urbanization." In *The Measurement of Urbanization and Projection of Urban Population,* edited by S. Goldstein and D. F. Sly, 19–87. Dolhain, Belgium: Ordina Editions.

Auerbach, F. 1913. "Das Gesetz der Bevolkerungskonzentration." *Petermanns Mitteilungen* 59:74–76.

Berry, B. J. L. 1961. "City Size Distribution and Economic Development." *Economic Development and Cultural Change* 9:573–588.

———. 1964. "Cities as Systems within Systems of Cities." In *Regional Development and Planning,* edited by J. Friedman and W. Alonso, 116–137. Cambridge, Mass.: MIT Press.

———. 1967. *The Geography of Market Centers and Retail Distribution.* Englewood Cliffs, N.J.: Prentice-Hall.

———. 1971. "City Size and Economic Development: Conceptual Synthesis and Policy Problems, with Special Reference to South and Southeast Asia." In *Urbanization and National Development,* edited by L. Jakobson and V. Prakash, 111–155. Beverly Hills: Sage.

CAPMAS (Central Agency for Public Mobilization and Statistics). 1975. *Statistical Yearbook 1952–1974.* Cairo: Nahdet Misr Press.

———. 1978. *Statistical Yearbook 1952–1977.* Cairo: NAHDET MISR Press.

———. 1986. *Statistical Yearbook 1952–1985.* Nasr City, Cairo: CAPMAS.

———. 1987. *The General Census of Population, Housing and Establishments, 1986, Preliminary Results* (in Arabic). Nasr City, Cairo: CAPMAS.

———. 1990. "Distribution of Egyptian Population by Governorate of Birth and Governorate of Residence, Age, and Sex, Table 45," mimeographed (in Arabic). *Personal Communication.*

Clark, Colin. 1967. *Population Growth and Land Use.* New York: St. Martin's Press.

Department of Statistics and Census. 1962. *Vital Statistics,* vol. 1: *1959.* Cairo: General Organization for Government Printing Offices.

———. 1963. *1960 Census of Population,* vol. 2: *General Tables.* Cairo: S. O. Press.

Duncan, O. D. 1957. "The Measurement of Population Distribution." *Population Studies* 11:27–45.

Duncan, O. D., R. P. Cuzzort, and B. Duncan. 1961. *Statistical Geography, Problems in Analyzing Areal Data.* Glencoe, Ill.: Free Press.

El-Attar, M. 1990. "Egypt." In *International Handbook on Internal Migration,* edited by C. B. Nam, W. J. Serow, and D. F. Sly, 103–124. Westport, Conn.: Greenwood Press.

Eldridge, H. T. 1956. "The Process of Urbanization." In *Demographic Analysis,* edited by J. J. Spengler and O. D. Duncan, 338–343. Glencoe, Ill.: The Free Press.

———. 1964. "Demographic Analysis." In *Population Distribution and Economic Growth, United States, 1870–1950, Vol. III, Demographic Analysis and Interpretations,* edited by H.T. Eldridge and D.S. Thomas, 3–318. Philadelphia: The American Philosophical Society.

Gibbs, J. P. 1966. "Measures of Urbanization." *Social Forces* 45:170–177.

———. 1968a. "Further Observations on 'Measures of Urbanization.' " *Social Forces* 46:400–405.

———. 1968b. "Reply to Jones and Mitra." *Social Forces* 47:222–223.

Gist, N. P. 1961. "Cities without Industry." *Economic Development and Cultural Change* 9:660–662.

Goldstein, S. 1987. "Forms of Mobility and Their Policy Implications: Thailand and China Compared." *Social Forces* 65:915–942.

Goldstein, S. and D. Sly, eds. 1975a. *Basic Data Needed for the Study of Urbanization.* Dolhain, Belgium: Ordina Editions.

———. 1975b. *The Measurement of Urbanization and Projection of Urban Population.* Dolhain, Belgium: Ordina Editions.

Greenwood, M. J. 1969. "The Determinants of Labor Migration in Egypt." *Journal of Regional Science* 9:283–290.

———. 1971. "Regression Analysis of Migration to Urban Areas of a Less-Developed Country: The Case of India." *Journal of Regional Science* 11:253–262.

———. 1978. "An Econometric Model of Internal Migration and Regional Economic Growth in Mexico." *Journal of Regional Science* 18:17–31.

Hoover, E. M. 1941. "Interstate Redistribution of Population, 1850–1940." *Journal of Economic History* 1:199–205.

———. 1951. "Internal Mobility and the Location of Industry." In *The Growth of the American Economy* (2nd ed.), edited by H. F. Williamson, 739–765. New York: Prentice-Hall.

Ibrahim, S. E. 1982. *A Critical Review of Internal Migration in Egypt.* Research Monograph v. Cairo: Population and Family Planning Board.

Jefferson, M. 1939. "The Law of the Primate City." *Geographical Review* 29:226–232.

Jones, F. L. 1967. "A Note on 'Measures of Urbanization' with a Further Proposal." *Social Forces* 46:275–279.

———. 1968. " 'Measures of Urbanization': Further Discussion." *Social Forces* 47:216–220.

Lampard, E. E. 1965. "Historical Aspects of Urbanization." In *The Study of Urbanization,* edited by P. M. Hauser and L. F. Schnore, 519–554. New York: John Wiley.

Mitra, S. 1968. " 'Measures of Urbanization': A Comment." *Social Forces* 47:220–221.

Nassef, A. 1973. "Internal Migration and Urbanization in Egypt." In *Urbanization and Migration in Some Arab and African Countries,* Research Monograph Series No. 4. Cairo Demographic Centre. Cairo: S.O.P. Press

Perloff, H. S. 1967. "Modernizing Urban Development." *Daedalus* 96:789–800.

Preston, S. 1979. "Urban Growth in Developing Countries: A Demographic Reappraisal." *Population and Development Review* 5:195–215.

Rempel, H. 1981. *Rural-Urban Migration and Urban Unemployment in Kenya.* Luxembourg, Austria: International Institute for Applied Systems Analysis.

Sayed, H.A.A., and H.H.M. Zaky. 1985. "Rural-Urban Migration in Egypt." Chapter 8 in *1984 Annual Seminar,* 165–192. Cairo: Cairo Demographic Centre.

Schultz, T. P. 1971. "Rural-Urban Migration in Columbia." *Review of Economics and Statistics* 53:157–163.

Shryock, H. S., J. S. Siegel, and Associates. 1976. *The Methods and Materials of Demography.* Condensed Edition by E. G. Stockwell. New York: Academic Press.

Stewart, J. Q. 1947. "Empirical Mathematical Rules Concerning the Distribution and Equilibrium of Population." *Geographical Review* 37:461–485.

Todaro, M. 1980. "Internal Migration in Developing Countries: A Survey." In *Population and Economic Change in Developing Countries,* edited by R. E. Easterlin, 361–402. Chicago: Chicago University Press.

United Nations. 1964. *Demographic Yearbook 1963.* New York: United Nations.

———. 1974. *Demographic Yearbook 1974.* New York: United Nations.

———. 1980. *Patterns of Urban and Rural Population Growth.* New York: Population Division, United Nations.

———. 1990. *Demographic Yearbook 1988.* New York: United Nations.

———. 1991. *World Urbanization Prospects 1990.* New York: United Nations.

Wander, H. 1975. "Basic Data Needed for the Study of Urbanization: An Examination of Data on the Urban Population in the Censuses of Selected Countries." In *Basic Data Needed for the Study of Urbanization,* edited by S. Goldstein and D. F. Sly, 33–69. Dolhain, Belgium: Ordina Editions.

WGPGED (Working Group on Population Growth and Economic Development). 1986. *Population Growth and Economic Development: Policy Questions.* Washington, D.C.: National Academy Press.

World Bank. 1990. *World Development Report 1990.* New York: Oxford University Press.

Yap, L. 1977. "The Attraction of Cities: A Review of the Migration Literature." *Journal of Development Economics* 4:239–264.

Zipf, G. K. 1941. *National Unity and Disunity.* Bloomington, Ind.: Principia Press.

11

Ethiopia

Habtemariam Tesfaghiorghis

Ethiopia has one of the lowest levels of urbanization in Africa. This is due to historical factors, mainly the lack of peace and stability which characterizes its past and current history, as well as the low level of development. Historically, there were numerous civil wars between rival regional kings or chiefs; religious wars from the thirteenth to the sixteenth century between Moslem sultanates and Christian monarchies; tribal invasions and wars, the Oromo migration from the southeast into traditional highland Ethiopia in the sixteenth and seventeenth centuries; and external aggressions by the Turks, the Dervishes (from Sudan), the Egyptians, and the Italians (Luther, 1958:9–22; Lipsky, 1962:7–26; Pankhurst, 1965:61–68). These wars, which occupied most of Ethiopia's history from the fall of the Aksumite Empire following the rise of Islam in the seventh century A.D. to the end of the nineteenth century, resulted in urban depopulation and destruction of towns, cultural and religious institutions, decline of trade and prosperity, and an isolation of the country from the outside world. The effect of wars is a lack of continuity in the growth of established urban centers, constant shift of capital towns with every rising king, lack of development of a tradition of urbanization, and lack of external (especially European) influence on urbanization.

Modern Ethiopia, excluding Eritrea, emerged toward the end of the nineteenth century when Emperor Menelik II incorporated territories in the southeast, south, and west under his rule (Luther, 1958:18; Ullendorff, 1960:93–94). By contrast, Eritrea was an Italian colony from 1890–1941, then under British administration from 1941 to 1952, federated with Ethiopia from 1952 to 1962 under a United Nations arrangement, and was annexed into Ethiopia in 1962. The political and socioeconomic changes in the twentieth century had an important impact on the development of urbanization. The Italian invasion and occupation of Ethiopia in 1935–41 saw the development of modern urban centers and expansion of urban populations in both Ethiopia and Eritrea. The postindependence developments under the centralized government of the feudal and partly capitalistic monarchy of Emperor Haile Selassie, 1941–74, saw the most rapid urban population growth. On the other hand, the war policies, the repression, the movement-restricting policies, the rural and urban land reforms, and the massive resettlement of the rural population for strategic and redistribution purposes of the military government of Ethiopia from 1974 to 1991 adversely affected the steady development of urbanization in Ethiopia in general, and in Eritrea in particular.

However, a new political change simultaneously occurred in both Ethiopia and Eritrea at the end of May 1991 following the overthrow of the military government in Ethiopia and the defeat of the Ethiopian army in Eritrea, which will have profound repercussions on the future development of urbanization as well as on the other facets of social and economic life. These political changes are the establishment of a transitional government committed to democracy, addressing the problem of nationalities, Eritrea's right to self-determination through a referendum, and disbanding the war policies of the previous governments. The change in Eritrea in May 1991 ended Africa's longest independence war after 30 years, with Eritreans emerging as victors. The provisional government of Eritrea, established following the military victory, has a formidable task of rebuilding the destroyed economy, rehabilitating urban infrastructure and reconstructing destroyed towns, and overseeing the political independence of Eritrea through a United Nations supervised referendum within two years to complement its military victory. In this chapter, Eritrea and Ethiopia are treated as one country, although Eritrea will soon become an independent country.

HISTORICAL ORIGINS OF URBANIZATION

Ethiopia has no long history of urbanization. The nature of urbanization in the history of the country is clearly summed up by R. Pankhurst's (1965:60) observation that "Ethiopia was traditionally a rural country with small villages and isolated homesteads rather than large urban conglomerations. In various parts of the country, however, there were throughout recorded history several important cities and towns, as well as numerous villages large and small." Mesfin W. Mariam (cited in Rafiq and Hailemariam, 1987:187) states also that the general absence of urbanization is one of the most remarkable facts in the long history of Ethiopia. He comments that "the three prominent capitals of Aksum, Lalibela and Gonder are but brief episodes in the long and essentially rural history of the country."

The ancient cities and towns of Ethiopia developed primarily as indigenous administrative capitals of kingdoms, though some of them served as religious centers and trading centers. While the ancient cities of Aksum and Lalibela also served as holy places and places of pilgrimage, the old town of Harer also served as a trading center. Some of the important ancient cities and old towns in recorded history which still exist include Aksum, Lalibela, Harer, Gonder, and Adwa. While few of the old towns continue to be important, the demographic, political, and economic importance of many of these towns has diminished.

Aksum, the first ancient city, was the capital of the Aksumite Empire, which flourished from the first to the seventh century A.D. The Aksumite kingdom reached a high level of civilization as manifested from the architectural achievements found in the magnificent obelisks and archaeological discoveries. Though Aksum today is a medium-sized urban center under 20,000 population and a provincial capital in Tigray, it still continues to be the holy Christian city. Aksum ranks among the oldest towns of Africa which still exist, along with others such as Alexandria, Tripoli, and Constantine (which was founded about A.D. 313) (Hance, 1970:212). The Aksumite Empire crumbled following the rise of Islam in the seventh century, and nothing of comparable civilization took its place. There are no further records of historical achievements, no monuments, coins, or relics dating from a later period to indicate that a cultural continuity had been maintained (Luther, 1958:11).

As the importance of Aksum declined, the towns of Lalibela, Gonder, and Harer were founded in different parts of the country. Lalibela was founded as the capital of the Zagwe Dynasty during the eleventh and thirteenth centuries. Lalibela is the site of the famous monolithic churches of Lasta hewn from solid rocks. Lalibela, which is today a small provincial capital in Welo region, continues to be a holy place and a center of tourist attraction and pilgrimage. The city of Gonder was founded as the capital city of Gonder Empire during the reign of Emperor Fasiladas in 1632–67. Gonder was the first to experience European contact and influence on its development. The Portuguese influenced construction in Gonder from 1650 to 1867 (Hance, 1970:213), and the monolithic castles of that period are centers of attraction. Gonder had an estimated population of 80,000 during the seventeenth and eighteenth centuries. But its population declined greatly in the nineteenth century from looting and establishment of another capital resulting from civil wars and the decline of the imperial government in the late eighteenth and early nineteenth century. The sacking of the city by Dervishes in the early nineteenth century was detrimental to trade and prosperity and resulted in a further decline in its population (Pankhurst, 1965:61). Today Gonder is the fourth ranking urban center in the country and capital of Gonder region, which derives its livelihood from administrative and social services, trade, and limited manufacturing.

Harer was the capital of a Muslim state until it became part of the country in 1885. Harer, which rose in the seventh century (Hance, 1970:212), was the old established trading center in the eastern highland of the country. It is today the seventh largest urban center, the capital of Harerge region, and a coffee market. Adwa, to the east of Aksum, was for a long time the most important urban center in Tigray. Adwa, capital of Tigray at that time, was the center of Tigray's wealth and power and had an estimated population of 8,000 during its relative peace in the first decade of the nineteenth century. Its population, however, had been decimated by civil war in the first part of the nineteenth century, and by the Egyptian wars of the 1870s and fighting with the Italians in 1895–96 (Pankhurst, 1965:63), which also decimated other towns of Tigray. Adwa is a famous battleground which saw the defeat of the Italians in 1896 and now is a medium provincial capital in Tigray.

The development of urbanization in Ethiopia is thus recent. Most of the important urban centers in Ethiopia were founded during the latter part of the nineteenth century and the early part of the twentieth century. These urban centers expanded during the Italian occupation, and continued to experience faster growth during the post-Italian developments. These modern urban centers include Addis Ababa, the capital city, founded as capital by Emperor Menelik II in 1888; Asmara, established as the capital of the Italian colony of Eritrea in 1889; Desie, founded in the second half of the nineteenth century; Mekele, founded as the capital of Emperor Yohanes in 1871–89; Dire Dawa, founded in 1904; and Nazareth, Debre Zeit, and Akaki, established in the first half of the twentieth century.

Although administrative activities initially played a role in the development of modern major urban areas during the Italian occupation and the postliberation period, greater growth was due to industrial developments, the growth of commercial activities, and road, rail, and air services. This is particularly true in the growth of Addis Ababa, Asmara, and Dire Dawa, where most of the country's manufacturing activities are concentrated. The development of manufacturing industries and transport links was responsible for the fast-growing towns of Akaki and Nazareth, towns in the southern vicinity of Addis Ababa, and Bahr Dar in Gojam. Akaki, on the outskirts of Addis Ababa, is home to many light industries including textile and food processing. Nazareth has a range of service and commercial activities, a sugar factory, and is an important transport link on the Addis Ababa–Djibouti railway as well as the Addis Ababa–Aseb major highway. It also has road links with Harerge, Arsi, and Shewa regions. Bahr Dar has a textile factory, two colleges of higher education, and service activities.

The ancient towns had small and fluctuating populations, and with the exception of Gonder, have small populations today. Only the modern cities of Addis Ababa and Asmara and the large urban centers such as Dire Dawa and Nazareth have large populations. The modern towns flourished after the first quarter of this century and more so after 1950, due mainly to the disproportionate concentration of manufacturing, trade, and service activities; infrastructural and social services; and administrative services. Addis Ababa, a metropolitan city with one million inhabitants in 1984, has developed from essentially a village at the beginning of this century. W. Thesiger (1988:43) described Addis Ababa in 1909 as consisting of "a series of scattered villages grouped on hillsides with open, uncultivated spaces. Menelik's palace crowned the largest hill; nearby a jumble of thatched huts and some corrugated-iron-roofed shacks clustered round the large open market. Nowhere were there any proper roads."

There is limited information about historical population estimates of towns. There are Italian sources in the 1930s, especially the *Guida dell' Africa Orientale,* which gave population estimates of towns of the Italian colony of Eritrea from the 1931 census as well as for 1938, and population estimates for Ethiopian towns during the Italian occupation of Ethiopia from 1936 to 1941. The Eritrean towns, Asmara, Masawa, Keren, Dekemhare, Mendefera, and Aseb, had significant Italian populations when Eritrea was an Italian colony from 1890 to 1941. In the case of Asmara, more than 50 percent of its 1938 population were Italians living in the European quarter of the city set apart from the natives.

Estimates of population size of the ancient towns do not exist for most of their history. Except for Gonder, maximum population estimates of the ancient city of Aksum and other towns do not exist. The earliest available population estimates of towns date from those of Alvarez in the sixteenth century, Peru Pais in the seventeenth century, James Bruce in the eighteenth century, and others of the nineteenth and early twentieth centuries. R. Pankhurst (1965) compiled population estimates of towns based on accounts of travelers, members of diplomatic delegations and missionaries from the seventeenth to the nineteenth centuries, as well as from reliable Italian sources of the 1930s. These two sources plus sample survey and census results starting from the mid-1960s were used to compile the population estimates displayed in Table 11.1.

The recency of urbanization in Ethiopia can be appreciated from an examination of the population size of selected towns over time. The population of modern towns has shown a dramatic growth, while the population of the old towns has declined and stagnated. While some reliance can be put on the earlier population estimates made by the Italian sources in the 1930s, the earlier estimates are not as reliable as they are based on impressions.

GROWTH OF URBAN AREAS AND POPULATION

Between 1970 and 1984, there was a rapid growth in both the number of urban areas and their population. The number of urban areas with 2,000 or more inhabitants increased from 185 in 1970 to 339 in 1984, and the urban population grew from two to four million. Large increases in the number of urban areas have occurred in all size-classes except areas with populations of 100,000 or more. There remain only two cities, but soon Dire Dawa, with a little under 100,000 population in 1984 (Table 11.1), will join their ranks. The growth in the number of urban areas was dramatic in the small and medium-sized towns with populations under 20,000, which almost doubled in number for every size-class. The most remarkable growth is further demonstrated by the emergence of 10 urban centers of 50,000–99,999 population in 1984 from none in 1970.

There is a sizable difference in population size between the largest city and the second largest city, and between the second largest city and the third largest

Table 11.1
Historical Population Estimates of Towns: Seventeenth–Twentieth Centuries

Town	17th-18th	19th	1938	1965-66	1970-71	1984
Addis Ababa	-	40,000	300,000	443,700	683,500	1,412,600
Asmara	-	6,000	98,000	137,000	192,000	275,400
Dire Dawa	-	-	20,000	48,800	60,900	98,100
Gonder	80,000	5,000	14,000	35,000	35,300	80,900
Nazareth	-	-	-	26,400	39,200	76,300
Dessie	-	-	36,000	39,100	45,900	68,000
Harer	-	35,000	45,000	41,200	44,900	62,200
Mekele	-	15,000	12,000	22,200	28,000	61,600
Jima	-	-	15,000	29,400	41,900	61,000
Bahr Dar	-	1,400	-	11,900	22,300	54,900
Akaki	-	-	-	10,500	17,300	54,100
Debre Zeit	-	-	-	21,200	27,800	51,100
Debre Markos	-	2,000	10,000	20,700	27,100	39,800
Asela	-	-	500	13,400	17,200	36,700
Awasa	-	-	-	5,500	13,200	36,200
Wonji	-	-	-	-	-	35,400
Shashemene	-	-	-	7,500	11,900	31,500
Aseb	-	5,000	8,000	10,700	-	31,000
Nekemte	-	-	10,000	12,200	16,200	28,800

Debre Berhan	-	2,000	3,000	8,700	14,900	25,800
Keren	-	3,000	9,700	-	-	6,100
Soddo	-	-	10,000	10,400	11,700	24,600
Dila	-	-	800	10,900	12,900	23,900
Jijiga	-	-	11,000	4,000	-	23,200
Arba Minch	-	-	-	2,800	5,900	23,000
Goba	-	-	3,000	-	11,000	23,000
Aksum	200h	200	10,000	13,400	12,800	17,800
Masawa	-	5,000	15,200	15,200	-	15,400
Debre Tabor	-	5,000	9,000	6,800	7,700	15,300
Adwa	300h	8,000	6,000	12,500	15,700	13,800
Metu	-	-	-	4,100	5,300	12,500
Mendefera	-	500	4,600	9,800	-	12,200
Dekemhare	-	-	12,800	8,100	-	7,300
Lalibela	-	3,000	3,000	-	-	5,200
Ankober	-	10,000	3,000	-	-	1,000

Notes:

- estimates not available

h estimate of number of houses

The figures given under the 1965-66 and 1970-71 periods refer in the case of Addis Ababa respectively to the 1961 and 1967 censuses, for Asmara to the 1963 Survey and 1968 Census, and for Nazareth to 1964 and 1970 surveys.

Source: Compiled from CSO, 1968, 1974, 1977, 1984.

urban center. As of 1984, Addis Ababa was a classic primate city with a population of 1,412,600, five times that of the population of Asmara, 275,400. In turn, Asmara's population was about three times that of Dire Dawa. However, after the third ranking urban center, the size differences between successive ranking major urban areas were comparatively small. Gonder, the fourth ranking, had a population of 80,900; the fifth ranking, Nazareth, had 76,300.

Thus, the urban population is concentrated in Addis Ababa. Its primacy in the urban hierarchy is clearly evident from the primacy index of 3:1 based on the first four largest urban areas.

Despite substantial increases in the number of urban localities and urban population, their distributional patterns by size-class of localities have remained almost the same (Table 11.2). The urban areas are concentrated in small-sized localities. Unlike the negatively skewed distribution of urban areas, the urban population distribution was positively skewed. The relatively few urban centers with 20,000 or more inhabitants were the residence of more than 60 percent of the total urban population. Moreover, the two cities of 100,000 or more inhabitants accounted for 40 percent of the total urban population. The two cities together accounted for 71 and 61 percent of the total population in centers of 20,000 or more in 1970 and 1984, respectively. Addis Ababa alone accounted for 48 percent in 1970 and 51 percent in 1984 of the urban population living in localities of over 20,000 population, clearly indicating its primacy in the Ethiopian urban hierarchy.

DEGREE OF URBANIZATION

Urban Concept and Definition

The concept of urbanization embodies social, economic, and demographic processes and changes whereby an increasing proportion of a country's population lives in urban areas.

The majority of Ethiopian towns are small-sized, and their economic activities are not readily distinguishable from their surrounding rural areas. There is as yet no official national urban definition in Ethiopia, thus some agencies adopt their own working definitions. There were municipal towns in Ethiopia before the military government's takeover in 1974. Since then most towns have been replaced by the formation of *Kebeles* (Urban Dwellers' Associations). The Central Statistical Office (CSO) since 1970 has used a working urban definition of a locality of 2,000 or more inhabitants. On the basis of this definition, it has been publishing town population estimates in its annual Statistical Abstracts from 1970 to 1982, but in the 1983 and 1984 issues, it included only 322 towns accorded urban status by the Ministry of Housing and Urban Development. Urban status is determined by using criteria combining formation of *Kebeles*, population size, income, infrastructural facilities, and economic viability of the localities.

Table 11.2
Distribution of Number of Towns and Population by Size-Class of Towns: 1970 and 1984

Size-class Population	Towns	1970 Population	Percent of Population	Towns	1984 Population	Percent of Population
2,000-4,999	109	36,130	15.5	197	611,100	13.8
5,000-9,999	44	295,906	12.7	77	522,296	11.8
10,000-19,999	18	248,934	10.7	39	531,258	12.0
20,000-49,999	12	415,630	17.8	14	398,264	9.0
55,000-99,999	-	-	-	10	668,946	15.2
100,000+	2	1,014,260	43.3	2	1,687,960	38.2
Total	185	2,337,860	100.0	339	4,419,824	100.0

Source: Compiled from CSO, 1977; and Population Census, 1984.

According to these criteria, there were 322 towns, 25 with less than 2,000 inhabitants.

Obviously, the process of according urban status is arbitrary and is not yet completed. In order to maintain comparability with CSO's definition of towns and also to take account of the definition of the Ministry of Housing and Urban Development, Habtemariam Tesfaghiorghis (1986:160) arrived at 370 urban areas in Ethiopia in 1984. These included the 322 localities accorded an urban status plus another 48 localities with 2,000 or more inhabitants not accorded an urban status.

Urbanization Level

Ethiopia is a least urbanized country. The first-ever 1984 Population and Housing Census of Ethiopia showed that the existing official population estimates substantially underestimated the rural population by 29 percent, and overestimated the urban population by 19 percent (Tesfaghiorghis, 1986:160). The proportion of the total population residing in urban areas was estimated to be 8 percent in 1970 and 11 percent in 1984. If the definition is limited to only large urban centers of 20,000 or more inhabitants, then the degree of urbanization in 1984 drops to 7 percent. These figures depict the low level of urbanization in the country.

Both the degree and trend of urbanization in Ethiopia were very low by world and African standards. According to the national practices of defining urban, the percentage urban in Africa in 1985 was 31 percent (United Nation, 1989: 5). The degree of urbanization for Ethiopia was even much lower than the regional average for Eastern Africa (19 percent), which is Africa's least urbanized region.

REGIONAL DISTRIBUTION OF URBANIZATION

The regional distribution of urbanization is highly uneven with the degree of urbanization by regions varying from 5 to 22 percent, being under 10 percent in most regions (Figure 11.1). Shewa, the region surrounding Addis Ababa, was the most highly urbanized region in the country with 22 percent of its population living in urban areas. It accounted for 47 percent of the country's urban population.

The three major urban centers of Akaki, Debre Zeit, and Nazareth lie within 120 kilometers on the major southern highway and railway leading to Addis Ababa, starting with the industrial town of Akaki on the outskirts of Addis Ababa. The other towns of Shewa with populations of 20,000 to 49,999 are north of Addis Ababa, Debre Berhan (130 kilometers), and south are Wonji (120 kilometers) and Shashemene (250 kilometers).

Eritrea is the second most highly urbanized region, with 15 percent of its population living in urban areas and accounting for 9 percent of the total urban

Figure 11.1
Regional Distribution of Urban Localities: Ethiopia, 1984

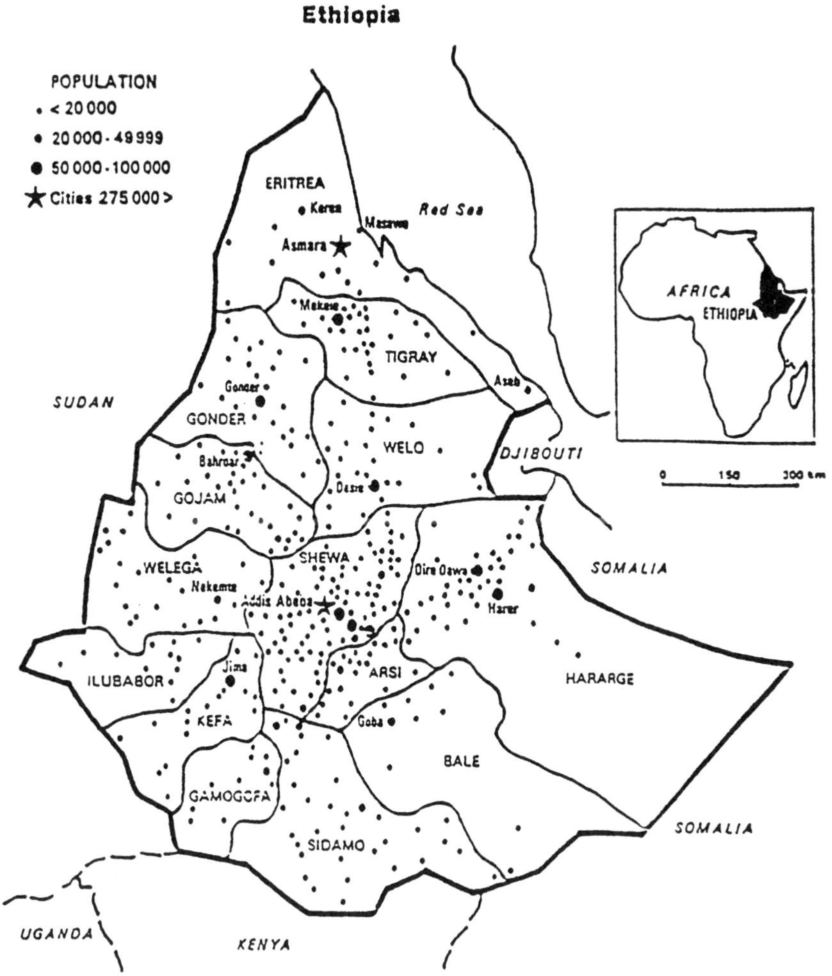

population of Ethiopia. Asmara, the capital of Eritrea, is the largest city. Other significant Eritrean towns are Keren and the port towns of Aseb and Masawa.

Tigray, with 10 percent urban, has the third highest level of urbanization. Although Aksum and Adwa were the historically important towns of Tigray, their importance today is overshadowed by Mekele, the capital and major urban center. The combined urban population of Shewa, Eritrea, and Harerge accounted for 63 percent of the total Ethiopian urban population.

There were 305 urban centers in 1984 with populations under 10,000. Also, there were 65 urban areas with populations of 10,000 and over which were unevenly distributed between the regions.

A comparative analysis of the regional growth of urbanization by M. Rafiq and A. Hailemariam (1987:189–191, 200) indicated relatively slow urban population growth in Eritrea, Tigray, Welo, and Harerge, and a more rapid urban growth in Bale, Gojam, Arsi, Gonder, Gamo Gofa, and Welega. The urban growth rate of 2 percent for Eritrea was 50 percent lower than the 5 percent national average. There have been substantial increases in the number of urban localities in all regions. In Eritrea no new urban localities appeared, and no rural localities were reclassified as urban, resulting in a slow growth of the urban population. The growth of urban localities was uneven in the other regions. The highest growth of urban localities was in Gojam, Bale, Arsi, Kefa, Shewa, and Harerge (Rafiq and Hailemariam, 1987:200).

URBAN POPULATION GROWTH RATES

For the country as a whole the annual urban population growth rate over 1966 to 1984 was 5 percent, which represents a decline from the high growth of the 1960s. In fact, the urban population growth rate was 7 percent per annum between 1966 and 1970 and 4 percent between 1970 and 1984. The 1978 Manpower and Housing Survey also indicated a decline in annual urban population growth from 5 percent between 1970 and 1978 to 4 percent between 1978 and 1984.

High growth rates occurred among urban areas with 20,000–49,999 population, and low growth rates occurred among small urban centers under 10,000 inhabitants. The previously high growth rates for Addis Ababa and Asmara have not continued, with the rate for Asmara dropping from 7 percent between 1963 and 1968 to 2 percent between 1968 and 1984. Urban areas with populations of 50,000 to 99,999 had gains of about 5 percent between 1966 and 1978 but only 4 percent per annum between 1978 and 1984.

High annual rates of population growth occurred in urban centers that had recently been designated new regional capitals (Arba Minch, Awasa, and Metu) and in newly developed centers of manufacturing industries and other economic activities (Akaki, Bahr Dar, Nazareth). For example, the large population increase of Kombolcha was due to the construction of a new textile factory as well as its function as an important transport link with the major urban areas of Addis Ababa, Dessie, and Aseb. Other urban centers with high rates of growth in 1966–70 were Fiche, Debre Berhan, and Shashemene and, recently, Robi, due to the opening of state farms in its vicinity.

A DEMOGRAPHIC AND SOCIOECONOMIC PROFILE: ADDIS ABABA

Addis Ababa has grown from a small village when founded as the capital of Emperor Menelik II in 1888 to be a dominant metropolitan city of one million people in 1984. It is situated on a plateau at an altitude of 2,408 meters covering an area of 222 square kilometers. Its high altitude results in a pleasant climate of an average annual maximum temperature of 23 degrees and a minimum of 11 degrees centigrade. It has an annual rainfall of 1,161 millimeters (CSO, 1984:7–22). Addis Ababa is a dominant political center, a seat of many international bodies and embassies, as well as an important administrative, commercial, transport, and manufacturing center.

Population

The city has experienced rapid population growth, increasing from 443,700 in 1961 to 1,412,600 in 1984. The sex structure of the city shows female predominance with 93 males for every 100 females in 1984. The excess of females over males was concentrated in the migrant ages 10–34 years and at ages 50 and over. The city's population is young; 43 percent of the total were youths under 15 years of age and those under 20 years comprised 55 percent. Of the total population aged 15 years and over, 39 percent were single and 44 percent were married (Tesfaghiorghis, 1990:82–91). The percentage single among the population aged 15 years and over has increased from 25 percent in 1967 to 39 percent in 1984, while the proportion married has declined from 57 to 44 percent (OPHCC, 1987:3–20).

The city is inhabited by numerous indigenous nationalities with foreigners constituting less than 1 percent of the total population. The major ethnic group is the Amaras (49 percent of the total population), followed by a substantial number of Gurages (18 percent) and Oromos (17 percent). Other groups are from Eritrea and Tigray (9 percent). The numerous ethnic minorities constituted 5 percent. The percentage born of mixed Ethiopian nationalities was only 1 percent. In terms of the language usually spoken at home, 89 percent reported the official language, Amharic, the language of the Amaras. Addis Ababa is mainly a Christian city made up of 86 percent Copts, 2 percent other Christians, and 11 percent Moslems.

Education

The enrollment ratio of the primary school age population was 69 percent and 35 percent for the secondary school age population. The city has a high literacy status: 82 percent of all persons aged 10 years and over were able to read and write (89 percent of males and 76 percent of females). However, the educational attainment is relatively low: 56 percent of the literate population had primary education (grades 1–6), and only 5 percent had postsecondary education. Nevertheless, the city is the center of learning as it has the largest of the three universities of the country, and outstanding secondary and vocational schools.

Economic Activity

Forty-five percent of the city's working-age population (aged 15 years and over) was economically inactive. Of this total, 29 percent were homemakers, mostly women (99 percent). The overall labor force participation rate for those 15 years and over was 55 percent. The female labor force participation was 37 percent, compared to 74 percent for males. The overall labor force participation of females aged 10 years and over rose from 24 percent in 1967 to 32 percent in 1984 while the rates for males declined from 71 to 61. The unemployment rate in 1984 was 11 percent. Nevertheless, an ILO African Employment Report (UNECA, 1989:25–27) found that 24 percent of Ethiopia's urban youth aged 15–24 were unemployed in 1984.

The 1984 occupational profile of the city's employed population was as follows: 29 percent were production and related workers and equipment operators; 26 percent service workers; 14 percent sales workers; 11 percent professional, technical, and related workers; 9 percent clerical and related workers; 8 percent laborers and unclassified workers; 2 percent administrative and managerial workers; and 1 percent agricultural workers. Compared to men, females were overrepresented as service workers and clerical and related workers, while comparatively few were in the high status occupations and production and transport equipment operators.

Addis Ababa is predominantly an administrative, service, and commercial city rather than an industrial/manufacturing city. Its total employment from manufacturing was only 13 percent, compared to 65 percent in the major industrial towns of Akaki, Dire Dawa (29 percent), and Bahr Dar (24 percent). The 1984 Census collected not only the occupation of employed persons, but also the industry and economic activity in which they were engaged. The distribution of employed persons by industry and economic activity was as follows: 26 percent in public administration and social services; 20 percent in wholesale and retail trade; 13 percent in manufacturing; 7 percent in transport, communication, and related work; 3 percent in construction; and 2 percent in banks, insurance and business services (OPHCC, 1987:131–137).

About 40 percent of Addis Ababa's work force is government employees, 31 percent private organization employees, 25 percent own-account workers, 2 percent employers, and 2 percent unpaid family workers and others. The informal sector employment is substantial, as reflected by the share of own-account workers. Females accounted for only 27 percent of the total self-employed.

Housing Conditions

Over 80 percent of the houses in the city were made of wood and mud walls; 93 percent had corrugated iron sheet roofs; and another 3 percent had thatched roofs. The main ceiling of houses was made of fabrics, but one-half of all houses were without ceilings. The flooring was such that 51 percent of the dwellings had earth/mud floors, 34 percent had wood tiles, and only 12 percent had cement/concrete, plastic tiles, or cement tiles (OPHCC, 1987:297–326). Nevertheless, the city's housing units were well equipped with electricity and piped water: 90 percent of all housing units had electricity and 92 percent had piped water, though only 4 percent had a tap inside the house, and a further 26 percent had private taps and 22 percent shared taps inside the compound.

The bathing and toilet facilities were inadequate. Eighty-six percent of all housing units had no bathing facilities. Nine percent had private bathtub or shower facilities, and another 4 percent had shared bathing facilities. Whereas 29 percent of all housing units had no toilet facilities, 12 percent had flush toilets, 15 had a dry pit toilet, and 42 percent had a shared dry pit toilet. The city has no sewage system. Despite adequate provision of clean piped water and electricity, the city has poor housing. An estimated 85 percent of the city's population lived in slums and informal settlements in 1980 (Oberai, 1989:188). The condition of housing units in 1978 was such that 24 percent either had to be demolished or required extensive and expensive maintenance and only 27 percent were reported to be in good condition. The units were also overcrowded with a person-room ratio of three (Hadgu, 1987:23).

The possession of communication items was such that 63 percent of all housing units had radio, 18 percent had television sets, and 16 percent had telephone sets. Only 33 percent owned their houses; the rest mainly rent their housing units from the *Kebeles*.

PROSPECTS FOR URBAN POPULATION GROWTH

Ethiopia has experienced rapid urban population growth over the last two decades, with the urban population growing 7 percent per annum between 1966 and 1970 and by 4 percent between 1970 and 1984. Although there has been rapid urban population growth, most of the increase occurred in the primate city, Addis Ababa, and in other major urban centers.

Despite the concentration of urban population, infrastructure, and manufacturing in Addis Ababa, the city's residents do not enjoy high living standards. Only one-half of the working-age population are employed, and educational levels are very low. People live in miserable housing conditions with inadequate toilet and bathing facilities.

The rapid growth of urban population between 1966 and 1984 took place under relative peace and stability. The growth of urban centers, which started during the Italian occupation, gained momentum during postliberation administrative, commercial, and manufacturing developments which are necessary conditions for steady development of urbanization. However, urban development and population growth in Eritrea was hindered by the 30-year independence war.

The decline and stagnation of Dekemhare, Masawa, and other Eritrean towns are testimonies to their destruction by the war and their depopulation following blanket bombing of towns, villages, and farms; mass atrocities and arrests; and the consequent fleeing of the population to Sudan and other countries. The destruction and depopulation of Eritrean towns inflicted by the Ethiopian army was also extended to the northern towns of Ethiopia, as these towns and surrounding rural areas were the battlegrounds of the civil war, particularly since the mid-1980s. A substantial proportion of the Eritrean and Ethiopian populations are refugees in foreign countries as a result of wars, droughts, and famines.

The Ethiopian military government, under its slogan "Everything to the War Front," committed most of the resources of the country, human and nonhuman capital and budget to the execution of its many wars. There were hardly any resources left for developing new manufacturing industries or updating old machinery or improving the basic needs of the people. The change in ideologies from that of the feudal and partly capitalist monarch to that of the socialist government resulted in de-emphasis of urbanization and associated socioeconomic deterioration of urban areas in favor of villagization and massive rural-resettlement programs.

As the historical accounts show, wars were responsible for the absence of urbanization for a long period. In the aftermath of wars and economic crises in which Ethiopia finds itself today, it is difficult to foresee steady urban development in the near future. Although peace and stability are being established following the overthrow of the military dictatorship in May 1991, immediate recovery of urban development and urban growth seems impossible for some time. Reconstruction of destroyed towns as well as rehabilitation of urban infrastructure and services requires great effort and time. In the immediate future following the restoration of peace, the urban population growth rate in Ethiopia may not be significantly different from that of the rate of natural increase. On the other hand, urbanization in Eritrea is expected to grow faster than that of Ethiopia owing to the return of tens of thousands of Eritrean fighters and substantial numbers of refugees following the defeat and expulsion of the occupying army. Future urban growth in Ethiopia can come about through restoration and continuation of peace and stability, economic recovery, favorable ideology, and favorable external economic factors.

REFERENCES

CSO (Central Statistical Office). Ethiopia. 1968. *Survey of Major Towns in Ethiopia.* Addis Ababa.

———. 1974. *The Demography of Ethiopia.* Addis Ababa.

———. 1977. *Analysis of Demographic Data of Urban Areas Covered during Urban Survey, Second Round, 1969–1971.* Addis Ababa.

———. 1980. *Population, Labor Force and Housing Characteristics of Seventeen Major Towns: Results of Manpower and Housing Survey, 1978.* Addis Ababa.

———. 1984. *Ethiopia: Statistical Abstract.* Addis Ababa.

Hadgu, Bariagaber. 1987. "The Role of Demographic Information for Planning for Urban Growth and Development in Ethiopia." Paper presented to a Seminar-cum-Workshop on Development Planning and Demographic Analysis: The Case of Ethiopia, Addis Ababa, October–November 1987.

Hance, W. A. 1970. *Population, Migration, and Urbanization in Africa.* New York: Columbia University Press.

Lipsky, G. A. 1962. *Ethiopia: Its People, Its Society, Its Culture*. New Haven: Hraf Press.

Luther, E. W. 1958. *Ethiopia Today*. Stanford: Stanford University Press.

Ministry of Labor and Social Affairs. Ethiopia. 1987. "Role of Demographic Information/Knowledge in Employment and Education Planning." Paper presented to a Seminar-cum-Workshop on Development Planning and Demographic Analysis: The Case of Ethiopia, Addis Ababa, October–November 1987.

Oberai, A. S. 1989. "Rapid Population Growth, Employment and Housing in Mega-cities in Developing Countries." In *21st International Population Conference,* 2:187–200. New Delhi, India, September 20–27, 1989, International Union for the Scientific Study of Population.

OPHCC (Office of the Population and Housing Census Commission). Ethiopia. 1984. *Ethiopia: 1984 Population and Housing Census Preliminary Report*. Addis Ababa.

———. 1987. *Population and Housing Census of Ethiopia, 1984: Analytical Report on Results for Addis Ababa*. Addis Ababa.

Pankhurst, R. 1965. "Notes on the Demographic History of Ethiopian Towns and Villages." *Ethiopian Observer* 9:60–83.

Rafiq, M., and A. Hailemariam. 1987. "Some Structural Aspects of Urbanization in Ethiopia." *Genus* 43:183–204.

Tesfaghiorghis, Habtemariam. 1986. "The Growth of Urbanization in Ethiopia, 1966–1984." *Eastern Africa Economic Review* 2:157–167.

———. 1990. "Fertility and Infertility in Ethiopia." Ph.D. diss., Australian National University.

Thesiger, W. 1988. *The Life of my Choice*. Glasgow: Fontana/Collins.

Ullendorff, E. 1960. *The Ethiopians: An Introduction to Country and People*. London: Oxford University Press.

UNECA (United Nations Economic Commission for Africa). 1989. *Patterns, and Causes and Consequences of Urbanization in Africa*. Addis Ababa.

United Nations. 1989. *Prospects of World Urbanization, 1988*. Population Studies, No. 112. New York.

Wood, A. P. 1985. "Population Redistribution and Agricultural Settlement Schemes in Ethiopia." In *Population and Development Projects in Africa,* edited by J. I. M. Clarke, M. Khogali, and L. A. Kosinski, 84–111. Cambridge: Cambridge University Press.

12

Kenya

Robert A. Obudho

Among the world's less developed countries (LDCs), Kenya's population is known to be increasing rapidly. Also, this is particularly true with the urbanization process. In the last two decades the urban population of Kenya has been growing within the range of 6.5 to 8.0 percent per annum (Table 12.1). This is twice as fast as the average of all LDCs. Whereas urban growth rates have fallen secularly, both in the world and in LDCs in general, this is not yet the case in Kenya (Obudho, 1983, 1984, 1985).

The mortality decline in Kenya has resulted in a rapid population increase. For example, infant mortality declined from an estimated 184 deaths per thousand in 1948 to 76 deaths per thousand in 1986. This decline has boosted the population size since a large number of children were added to the population. This is in addition to the contribution of fertility, which is high and stable. The mortality decline has been attributed to the rapid socioeconomic development realized in the country, especially as it relates to education, agriculture, and most important, the availability and accessibility of medical facilities. However, the mortality decline has not been uniform across the country. The regions which still experience high infant mortality, in the range of 200 deaths per 1,000 births, are South Nyanza District, Siaya District, Lamu District, and Kilifi District.

Kenya is still very rural in character, a trend that will tend to decrease by the year 2025. The bulk of Kenya's urban population increase is, and will continue to be, due to rural-urban migration and urban natural increase. Obviously, this influx of people into urban centers will put an added strain on basic services and facilities. At the same time, it may also stagnate the development of the rural areas as the young and educated join the rural-urban migration exodus. The

Table 12.1
Rural and Urban Population of Kenya, 1948–79 (Populations in Thousands)

				Annual Rate of Growth		
Year	Rural	Urban	Total	Rural	Urban	Total
1948	5,120	286	5,406	-	-	-
1948-62	-	-	-	3.2	6.6	3.4
1962	7,910	671	8,636	-	-	-
1962-69	-	-	-	3.2	6.4	3.3
1969	9,861	1,082	10,943	-	-	-
1969-79	-	-	-	2.8	7.9	3.4
1979	13,018	2,309	15,327	-	-	-

Source: Compiled from Kenya Population Censuses 1948, 1962, 1969, and 1979.

majority of Kenya's population continue to live in the rural areas which derive their livelihood from various forms of agriculture. These forms range from subsistence to commercial farming.

Kenya has one of the highest rates of urbanization in East Africa. The current rate of urban population growth and its attendant problems are some of the major issues confronting policy makers today. The problem is further compounded by the lack of knowledge regarding the extent and nature of urbanization in the country. The purpose of this chapter is to discuss in detail the changing urbanization process in Kenya.

In brief, this phenomenal growth in urbanization can be explained by a number of factors: the high rate of rural-urban migration; a generally high rate of urban natural population growth rate; the expansion of boundaries in the urban centers; and a combination of the above factors. However, not all areas in Kenya have experienced this phenomenal growth in urbanization. Instead, there are regional variations in the extent to which urbanization has occurred in different areas, and this keeps on changing from time to time. This chapter looks at these variations in its attempt to explain the factors which influence the changing urbanization process in Kenya.

It is apparent that relatively little information and few insights are available concerning this phenomenon. Such insights and information are important as a means to suggest how urban growth can be regulated, coordinated, or structured at the urban center or national level. However, before doing this, it is important to understand the previous patterns of urban growth in Kenya.

The process of urbanization in Kenya is still an evolving phenomenon. However, it has proceeded at a tremendous pace in the last few decades, especially after political independence. In 1948 only one Kenyan of every twenty lived in the urban centers; by the turn of the century, this is expected to rise overwhelmingly. One of every three Kenyans will be living in an urban center by the year 2000.

HISTORICAL NATURE OF URBANIZATION

Urbanization in Kenya has a long history in the coastal region, but a short history in the interior part of the country (Obudho, 1983, 1984, 1985). Urbanization as part of Kenya's development process has its root in the pre-colonial period. A close analysis of this period suggests that certain central places could be described as urban centers, even by contemporary standards. These were in the form of caravan towns, periodic markets, collection points, and ethnic centers. However, these centers were weakly organized, ethnic oriented, and most certainly inexpensively managed. They were also scattered all over the territory, from Mumias in the lake region, to Kikubulyu and Kwavi settlements in the Mombasa-Kamba area. It was these centers that acted as nodes from which the colonial authorities established themselves (Obudho, 1975, 1982, 1983).

Although the advent of colonial rule in Kenya saw the activities of these urban centers increase, the spatial organization of urbanism in Kenya was in effect determined by the infrastructure developments of the umlands. More specifically, the Mombasa-Kisumu railway "established the general urbanization pattern in Kenya, fostering the growth of important centers at key points along the route" (Soja, 1968:29). Hence Kibwezi became the next resting place before ascending to the highlands. Nairobi's growth was so rapid that within a few years the colonial administrative center was moved from Mombasa to Machakos then to Nairobi. This administrative step was the "first official step in Nairobi's emergence as the principal metropolis of all eastern Africa" (Miller, 1971:414).

The interior parts did not have an urban tradition, by Western definition, until the colonial period. The pattern which exists today predominantly reflects the development of British colonization and trade rather than the traditional African population and agricultural patterns. Urban agglomerations in the form of trading centers were founded along the coast of Kenya as early as the ninth century A.D. However, rapid urbanization has a relatively recent history in Kenya.

The urban population growth has been increasing since independence. This share of the urban population increased from .8 percent in 1962 to over 18 percent in 1991. Urban population has grown faster than total population, which registered an annual growth rate of about 3.4 percent between 1948 and 1979 and an estimated 4.1 percent between 1979 to 1992, one of the highest rates in the world. The growth of urban population in Kenya can be seen by looking at the number of urban centers in different size groups over space and time. At the time of the first Kenya population census in 1948 there were 17 urban centers with an aggregate population of 286,000 (Table 12.1). The urban population was concentrated in Nairobi and Mombasa (83 percent of the urban population) with the majority of urban dwellers being non-Africans. By 1962, the number of urban centers had doubled to 34 and the urban population had increased to 671,000 people with an annual growth of 6.6 percent per annum. From 1948 to 1962, the secondary urban centers recorded the highest increase. The growth of urban centers, both in number and population, accelerated after independence when the Africans were allowed to migrate and reside in urban areas without restriction.

According to the 1969 and 1979 population censuses, there were 48 and 90 urban centers, respectively. During the 1962–69 intercensal period, the urban population doubled. The population grew from 670,950 in 1962 to 1,079,908 in 1969, growing at the rate 7 percent per annum. In the 1969 census, there were 48 urban centers with a total population of 2,000 or more inhabitants, thus representing an increase of 14 urban centers since 1962. Thus, in 1969, Nairobi and Mombasa accounted for 70 percent of the total urban population. The overall level of urbanization had risen to 10 percent, compared to 8 percent reported in 1962. The 1979 census indicated 90 urban centers with an urban population of 2.3 million. The urban population grew at the rate of 8 percent per annum during the 1969–79 intercensal period. During the 1962–79 intercensal period, the increase in urban centers took place in all size groups, but the increase of 14 percent per annum was in the 20,000 to 99,999 size group, followed by the 10,000 to 19,999 size group with 7 percent per annum. The third highest record increase was in the size groups of 2,000 to 4,999, underscoring the importance of secondary urban centers in Kenya's spatial structure. Urban centers with over 100,000 people and centers between 2,000 to 4,999 inhabitants grew almost at the same rate of 6 percent per annum, respectively, showing the primacy slowing of Nairobi (Obudho and Taylor, 1979). Considering the urban centers of 2,000 or more, the 1979 census shows that 36 percent of the total population lived in urban centers of 500,000 or more and 51 percent in urban centers of 200,000 or more. This represented just over half of the total population for urban centers of 2,000 or more. The three major urban centers of 100,000 or more people accounted for 60 percent of the total population of 2,000 or more. At the time of the 1979 census, therefore, three-fourths of the total population were in 11 urban centers of 30,000 or more. Some 88 percent were to be found in centers of 20,000 or more (Tables 12.2, 12.3, and 12.4). However, they are deceptive because of expanded urban boundary changes during the census period.

After adjusting for these boundary changes, the growth rates for Nakuru (6 percent), Thika (6 percent), Kakamega (6 percent), Nyeri (5 percent), and Kisumu (3 percent) emerge. Boundary expansions in Machakos and Meru were so great that apparent growth rates are meaningless. The annual intercensal rates of growth certainly were influenced by boundary changes in the case of Kisumu, Meru, Eldoret, Nyeri, Kisii, Kericho, and Bungoma. Even when we allow for boundary changes, the urban population of the intermediate urban centers in-

Table 12.2
Percent of Urban Population in Kenya, 1950–2025

Year	Percent of Urban Population
1950	5.6
1955	4.2
1960	7.4
1965	8.6
1970	10.2
1975	12.0
1980	14.2
1985	16.7
1990	19.2
1995	22.7
2000	26.2
2005	29.9
2010	33.8
2015	37.8
2020	41.8
2025	45.7

Source: Compiled from United Nations, 1991.

creased sharply during the intercensal period. The rate of annual increase of all urban centers during 1969–79 was over 10 percent per annum except for Nairobi, Mombasa, Nakuru, Thika, Malindi, and Nanyuki. These urban centers, whose annual increases were below 10 percent, are the ones whose percentage share of urban population over the years has been the highest. The population of other urban centers grew 16 percent per annum while their share of urban population increase went from 5 percent in 1948 to 29 percent in 1979, or doubling in the last decade.

The rate of urban population growth in Kenya between 1948 and 1979 is even more exaggerated in the case of the African population. At the time of the 1948 census 65 percent of the total urban population were Africans. By 1962 this population had risen to 70 percent. At the end of the 1969 census, with the

Table 12.3
Number of Urban Centers by Size, Kenya, 1948, 1962, 1969, and 1979

Size	1948	1962	1969	1979
100,000	1	2	2	3
20,000-99,999	1	2	2	13
10,000-99,999	2	1	7	10
5,000-9,000	3	11	11	22
2,000-4,999	10	16	26	42
Total	17	32	48	90

Source: Compiled from Kenya Population Censuses 1948, 1962, 1969, and 1979.

exception of Eldama Ravine and Marsabit, all urban centers reported sharp declines in the percentage of non-Africans.

Urbanization in Kenya is proceeding at a rapid pace. Population census results from 1948, 1962, 1969, 1979, and 1989 (Table 12.4 and 12.5) show that between the census years the growth in urban areas increased substantially, averaging 5 percent between 1962 and 1969 and reaching 8 percent between 1969 and 1979. This has increased the urban population from 10 percent of the total in 1969 to 15 percent in 1979. Based on the last intercensus trends, the urban population is expected to reach 28 percent by the year 2000. At that time there will be 8.6 million people living in urban areas, almost twice the current urban population.

The results of the last census show that Kenya was relatively successful in diverting urban growth to secondary urban centers, thus promoting regional equity and avoiding excessive population concentration in Nairobi and Mombasa. Although high by international standards, the intercensus growth rates in Nairobi (5 percent per annum) and Mombasa (3.5 percent per annum) were significantly lower than those in the secondary towns. The average growth rate for secondary urban centers was 7 percent per annum. This provides a striking contrast to experience elsewhere in Africa where the principal urban centers bear the brunt of urban expansion.

The Kenya government's policy of supporting agriculture and emphasizing the development of secondary urban centers has been acknowledged as appropriate and has received the support of the international donor community. Consequently, a major share of investment in infrastructure over the past ten years has gone to rural areas and to the development of rural-urban and national

Table 12.4
Urban Population of Kenya and Percent Urban by Size, 1948, 1962, 1969, and 1979 (Population in Thousands)

Size	1948		1962		1969		1979	
	No.	Percent	No.	Percent	No.	Percent	No.	Percent
Over 100,000	119	43	523	70	756	70	1,322	57
20,000-99,999	85	30	62	8	80	7	568	25
10,000-99,999	29	11	44	6	91	8	140	6
5,000-9,000	20	7	70	9	72	7	154	7
2,000-4,999	23	9	49	7	83	8	123	5
Total	276	100	748	100	3,082	90	2,307	100
Percent Urban	5.1		7.7		9.9		14.6	

Source: Compiled from Kenya Population Censuses 1948, 1962, 1969, and 1979.

transport linkages. During this period, urban transport infrastructure received little attention. The government's main concern in the urban area has been to promote its spatial development policy and work toward fulfilling basic needs in terms of health, nutrition, education, housing, social services, and water. The major value of the implied spatial strategy is that it is drawing the secondary urban centers into the economic development process and supporting rural development by providing service centers close to agricultural activity.

Secondary urban centers can be classified into two types: (1) existing urban centers and (2) small, rapidly expanding communities. Between 1969 and 1979 the population of the existing urban centers increased by 7 percent, whereas the overall expansion was measured at 8 percent. During this period the number of classified urban communities increased from 47 to 90. The proportion of the population living in urban centers exceeding 100,000 fell from 70 to 57 percent over the intercensal period. This change was offset by an increase from 7 to 25 percent in urban centers with a population range of 20,000 to 100,000. This trend continued in the 1980s with the pro-rural development policies and the neutral stance regarding investment in Nairobi and Mombasa. Despite this policy, it is clear that Nairobi and Mombasa will continue to play a dominant role in

Table 12.5
Population of Urban Centers, Kenya, 1979 and 1989

Urban center	1979	1989
Nairobi	827,775	1,346,000
Mombasa	341,148	465,000
Kisumu	152,643	185,100
Nakuru	92,851	162,800
Machakos	84,320	116,100
Eldoret	50,503	104,900
Nyeri	35,753	88,600
Meru	70,439	78,100
Thika	41,324	57,100
Kitale	28,327	53,000
Kakamega	32,025	47,300
Kisii	29,661	44,000
Kericho	29,603	40,000
Malindi	23,275	35,200
Bungoma	25,161	29,100
Webuye	17,963	25,700
Nanyuki	18,986	24,500
Muranga	15,290	21,000
Homabay	7,489	20,000
Embu	15,986	18,000
Nyahururu	11,277	13,900
Kerogoya	5,776	13,300
Busia	5,266	12,200
Voi	7,397	11,700
Kapsabet	2,945	11,500
Kitui	4,402	8,700
Kabarnet	3,621	8,600

Table 12.5 (Continued)

Urban center	1979	1989
Kiambu	3,669	4,400
Vihiga	-	4,300
TOTAL	1,984,875	3,051,100

Source: Compiled from Kenya Population Census, 1989.

the economy and that urban areas generally will continue to grow at a faster pace than the national population. The infrastructure needs of Nairobi and other main urban centers will increase significantly as they expand.

In general, the rate of urban natural increase tends to be reduced by a predominantly male population in the urban areas, and better access to social economic amenities (i.e., family planning services). An analysis of the urban population in Kenya shows that men are generally in the majority, and most are in the early adulthood to early maturity years. Over the intercensal period 1962–69, 65 percent of the total immigrants to Nairobi were age 15–30, and about two-thirds of them were males. About 18 percent of Nairobi's African population growth can be attributed to the resident African population in 1962, with the remaining 82 percent being migrants and their children.

REGIONAL VARIATION OF URBANIZATION

The degree of urbanization in Kenya varies by regional natural resource endowments, proximity to the central transportation network, and the patterns of the previous colonial development. The regional urbanization pattern shows that the urban population is concentrated in regions which have experienced intense resource development. These regions include some districts in Western Province and Nyanza Province. In the arid and semiarid north and northeastern parts of the country, urban centers are confined to scattered markets or administrative centers (Kenya, 1978).

This state of affairs has gone on for a long time, but the trend of regional variation has changed slightly. Based on the 1969 census, the Central Highlands region had 63 percent of the urban centers and 43 percent of the urban population. The coastal region was second in population and the western region second in number of urban centers. The Masai-Northern region was the least urbanized of all. Historically, the least urbanized areas have received few non-African settlements while the non-Africans who settled in the central region developed a diversified urban economic base, which helped sustain a larger number of urban centers than in other regions. Apart from this, the region has remained one of the most densely populated in Kenya, hence creating urban centers with large population concentrations.

The Rift Valley Province has a relatively high level of urbanization. In 1979, it comprised 21 percent of the total population of Kenya and had about 15 percent of the total urban population. Within the provinces the differential urbanization by district shows a dispersed pattern (Obudho, 1986:385–399).

Apart from Elgeyo Marakwet, most districts have at least one urban center. Nakuru District, with about 39 percent of the provincial urban population, is the most urbanized district, followed by Uasin Gishu (15 percent) and Kericho (11 percent), while the remaining districts have shares of less than 10 percent of the total provincial urban population.

Central Province has a comparatively low level of urbanization. In 1979, the province had 15 percent of the nation's total population and only 5 percent of the total urban population. The leading district is Kiambu, with about 42 percent of the total provincial urban population. The town of Kiambu has grown fast and acts as an industrial satellite, attracting the overspill of industries from Nairobi. In 1979, 34 percent of the total urban population of the province was in Thika (41,324), and 30 percent in Nyeri town (35,753). Kirinyaga District is the least urbanized, with only 6 percent of the total provincial population.

Coast Province is the second most urbanized province in the country after Nairobi. In 1979 it had 9 percent of the total population of Kenya and 18 percent of the total urban population of the country. The distribution of urban population within the province shows a wide gap between Mombasa and the smaller urban centers. Mombasa alone accounted for nearly 84 percent of the population in the province. The major reason for this is the unique location of Mombasa as a major East African port. It contributes immensely towards the economy of the country and the precolonial nature of the urbanization process of that region (Obudho and Obudho, 1988).

The level of urbanization in the Eastern Province is substantially less, partly because the main transportation network touches few settlements on the periphery of the province. These are Meru, Embu, Kitui, and Machakos. Whereas the province had 18 percent of the total population of the country in 1979, its urban population was only 10 percent. The two major urban centers in this province, Machakos and Meru, accounted for 44 percent and 30 percent of the total provincial urban population, respectively.

In the Western and Nyanza provinces the degree of urbanization is very low. While the Western Province accounted for 12 percent of the total Kenyan population in 1979, its urban population was only 5 percent of the total urban population in the country. The distribution of the urban population in the Western Province shows a more or less even pattern with the three district headquarters of Kakamega, Busia, and Bungoma, each having just over 20 percent of the provincial urban population. Kakamega, the provincial headquarters, accounted for a little higher share of urban population (30 percent) compared to Bungoma and Busia, each contributing 24 percent of the provincial urban population. Nyanza Province had 9 percent of the total urban population of Kenya despite its 17 percent share of the total population of the country.

The North-Eastern Province is the least urbanized province. Though the land is expansive, being an arid and semiarid region, it is less developed. In 1979, the province accounted for only 2 percent of the population in Kenya. The three district headquarters of Garissa (14,076), Mandera (13,126), and Wajir (6,384) are small urban centers accounting for 22 percent, 21 percent, and 10 percent of the provincial urban population, respectively.

Due mainly to the influence of the two large cities of Nairobi and Mombasa, the national proportion of urban population was 15 percent in 1979. About 25 percent of the districts had urban proportions of less than 10 percent.

DEMOGRAPHIC CHARACTERISTICS OF URBAN AREAS

One way of looking at and understanding the urban dynamics in Kenya is by examining the demographic characteristics of the urban areas. More than 50 percent of the total urban population are males, giving a sex ratio of 122 males for 100 females. Since there are more females than males in the total population of Kenya, males can be said to be more urbanized than their female counterparts. However, the Lamu, Marsabit, Mandera, and Wajir districts had larger proportions of urbanized females than males in the 1979 census.

The following urban areas reported sex ratios of less than 100: Machakos (95), Busia (91), Lamu (99), Moyale (98), Msambweni (99), Njoro (98), Siaya (90), Bura (95), Luanda (86), Sololo (98), Oldonyiro (92), Baragoi (83), Wamba (86), Kendu (87), Kimilili (99), and Kargi (97). While various factors contribute to these low sex ratios vis-à-vis Nairobi, a major factor is the inclusion of the rural population, which has more females than the respective urban areas. The only other plausible reason is that such small urban centers are basically rural in their characteristics.

Another way of looking at the urban demographic dynamics in Kenya is by analyzing the age-sex ratio. Kenyan urban centers are overwhelmingly male except in age categories under 15 (the youth), where the sexes are nearly equal in number. Male dominance for all the urban centers increased by age categories until 49 years (the limit of active working age), at which time there is a slight drop in the ratio. This is very high for the Kenyan average since the ages 20 to 49 are dominated by females in most urban centers. However, urban centers in Kenya still continue to develop new characteristics which should be watched more closely during the future.

The child-woman ratio of the urban population (defined as population under 5 years per 1,000 females aged 15–49) is 731, which is high compared to that of other LDCs. However, such data should be handled with caution, bearing in mind that the 1979 census was undertaken during the school holidays when most children stayed with relatives in the urban areas. Moreover, variations exist insofar as various urban centers are concerned. The large urban centers, however, seem to be more male dominated than the smaller ones. This is more so in the 15–49 age group where males dominate, with the exception of such centers as Eldoret, Bungoma, and Maralal.

There is a general predominance of the age group 15–49 in all urban centers with the relative unimportance of the children (0–14 years) and the aged (50 years and over). This trend is also exhibited in the general population. However, in the urban areas this trend can mainly be explained by the ability of this more mobile group to migrate to the urban areas in search of better prospects.

One of the most important indicators of urbanization among Kenyans is the degree to which various racial and ethnic groups have intermarried. The urban centers in Kenya have been cultural and demographic frontiers where people of different ethnic and cultural backgrounds settled, and for the first time in their lives have come to learn and contend with the customs, traditions, and norms of one another. Ethnic identity in a predominantly rural country such as Kenya is very important in understanding not only the pattern of the urbanization process but also the population mobility in general.

Geographically, the population in Kenya has shown the greatest mixing in the urban centers of the Western Region, the Central Highlands, and a few parts of the Coastal Region. The mixing process has encouraged migration from rural to urban areas, and from the less developed parts to the developing areas of Kenya. Ethnic and racial heterogeneity is greater in the larger urban centers and/or developing areas than in the rural areas and/or the lagging regions. In Kenya, there is a strong tendency for ethnic or racial groups to retain links with traditional homelands through circular migration. This is one of the major problems facing the urban centers today, especially because most residents remit their financial or other gains to the rural areas and consider the urban areas only as temporary homes.

Analysis of ethnic distributions in Kenya shows that the mixing of diverse people is one of the most important roles that urbanization has played in transforming the country's landscape. In general, the Central Bantu (Kikuyu, Embu, Meru, Mbere, Kamba, and Tharaka) accounted for more people (40 percent) in urban centers than any other ethnic or racial group. The Western Bantu (Luhya, Kisii) are the second most highly urbanized group, but among individual ethnic groups, the Kikuyu, Luo, Luhya, and Kamba dominate. District and provincial migration is a major factor to be noted in the urbanization process, hence urban residence is almost always in conformity with the ethnic-oriented settlement patterns. Urban areas of the Western Region, for example, are dominated by the Nilotic Luo (32 percent), followed by the Western Bantu (28 percent), the Central Bantu (15 percent), and the Asians (13 percent). In the Central Highlands, however, urban settlement is dominated by the Central Bantu (53 percent).

FUTURE URBANIZATION PATTERNS

The most alarming aspect of urbanization in Kenya is its rapidity rather than the relative sizes of the urban and rural populations. This trend of affairs is likely to continue and may well accelerate if measures are not taken to control it. The primary factors of urban population growth are urban natural population growth, rural-urban migration, boundary expansion, and the emergence of new market centers. These four factors have operated together to produce the observed rate of population growth in urban centers in Kenya. If the government is to formulate effective urban population policies, it will be necessary to take into consideration, either directly or indirectly and separately or in unison, all of the factors.

The urban population growth rate is likely to decrease slightly in the future. Based on the 1969–70 growth rate it is estimated that the total population of those living in urban areas will increase from 2,307,000 in 1979 to about 8,600,000 by the year 2000. There is likely to be a much faster growth of urban centers other than Nairobi and Mombasa whose primacy roles will decrease if the growth rate follows the 1969–79 pattern, which seems most logical. More important is the fact that the small and intermediate urban centers' role is likely to increase tremendously with over 50 percent of the urban population. The rate of emergence and growth of new urban centers is likely to be lower; hence by the year 2000, it is estimated that they will have only 6 percent of the urban population.

Apart from North-Eastern, Central, Nyanza, and Western regions, all other regions may experience a slight decrease in their urban growth rates during the period 1991–2000. In general, the percentage of the people living in urban areas is likely to increase from 15 percent in 1979 to 28 percent in the year 2000.

The projected growth rate is somewhat similar to the growth rate in the ten-year period 1979–89. During this period, the urban population increased from 2.3 million to 4.3 million. The urban centers had risen in numbers from 90 in 1979 to 172 in 1989 (Kenya, 1989). By 1992, these centers are expected to increase to a total of 240 while the urban population is projected to be 5.2 million people.

The urban population is, however, expected to increase overwhelmingly by the turn of the century. Thus, it is projected that 9 to 10 million Kenyans will be living in urban centers by the year 2000. This represents about 26 to 29 percent of the total population. Put in ratios, this means that one out of every three Kenyans will be living in urban areas by the turn of the century. Taking 1969 as the baseline year, it is projected that by the year 2000, the urban population will have increased by 500 to 700 people every day. The process of the urbanization is therefore proceeding much faster than the country's national planners are prepared to admit and, consequently, seriously plan for. Rather than execute plans, the government seems to create general policies and strategies on urbanization, policies and strategies which, more often than not, cry out for details and specifics.

CONCLUSION

Urbanization in Kenya is almost entirely a twentieth-century phenomenon and is mainly a product of British colonization. Decolonization of Kenya led to the establishment of the first towns in the interior of the country. During the postcolonial period, however, a new spatial system began to emerge. The rate of urbanization in Kenya has been increasing rapidly since independence. This is evidenced by gains in both the urban population and the number of urban centers. Until recently, the level of primacy was very high with all the socio-economic activities concentrated in the two main cities of Nairobi and Mombasa. This has led to a number of developmental and/or urbanization problems in these urban centers. This also led to the top-down approach in planning. It is therefore suggested that urban growth be diverted to secondary urban centers. The results of the last population census showed that Kenya has been relatively successful in diverting urban growth to secondary urban centers, thus promoting regional equity and avoiding excessive population concentration in Nairobi and Mombasa.

Planning from below is particularly important and appropriate for Kenya, whose central places were developed at the turn of the century and are still dangerously oriented toward the former colonial countries. Planning models that emphasize planning at the local or grass-roots level, rather than at higher order centers, could be devised.

REFERENCES

Johnson, G. E., and W. E. Whitelaw. 1972. *Urban-Rural Income Transfers in Kenya: An Estimated Remittance Function.* Nairobi: University of Nairobi, Institute for Development Studies.

Kenya, Republic of. 1970. *National Development Plan 1970–1974.* Nairobi: Government Printer.

———. 1974. *National Development Plan 1974–78.* Nairobi: Government Printer.

———. 1978. *Human Settlement in Kenya: A Strategy for Urban and Rural Development.* Nairobi: Government Printer.

———. 1986. *Economic Management or Renewed Growth.* Sessional Paper Number 1 of 1986. Nairobi: Government Printer.

———. 1989. *National Development Plan 1989–1993.* Nairobi: Government Printer.

———. 1991. *Kenya Population Census, 1989.* Nairobi: Ministry of Economic Planning and Development.

Miller, C. 1971. *The Lunatic Express: An Entertainment in Imperialism.* New York: Ballantine Books.

Obudho, R. A. 1975. "Urbanization and Urban Development in Kenya: An Historical Appreciation." *African Urban Notes* Series B 1:1–56.

Obudho, Robert A. 1982. "Planning from Below or Above in Africa: An Introduction." *African Urban Studies* 13:1–7.

———. 1979. "The Nature of Kenya's Urban Demography." *African Urban Studies* 4:83–103.

———. 1983. *Urbanization and Development Planning in Kenya.* Nairobi: Kenya Literature Bureau.

———. 1984. *Nairobi, Kenya: A Bibliographic Survey.* Monticello, Ill.: Vance Bibliographies.

———. 1985. *Demography, Urbanization and Spatial Planning in Kenya: A Bibliography Survey.* Westport, Conn.: Greenwood Press.

———. 1986. "A Multivariate Analysis of Kenya's Urban Systems." *Geojournal* 13:385–399.

———. 1988. "Urbanization National Development and Planning in Kenya." Paper presented at the First International Conference on Urban Growth and Spatial Planning, Nairobi, December 13–17.

Obudho, R. A., and D. R. F. Taylor. 1979. *Spaital Structure of Development: A Study of Kenya.* Boulder, Colo.: Westview Press.

Obudho, R. A., and G. O. Aduwo. 1990. "Small Urban Centers and Spatial Planning in Kenya." In *Small Town Africa: Studies in Rural-Urban Interaction,* edited by Jonathan Baker, 51–68. Uppsala: Scandinavian Institute of African Studies.

Obudho, R. A., and Rose A. Obudho. 1988. *Precolonial Urbanization in East Africa.* No. 88/10. Nairobi: Urban Center for Research.

Soja, E. W. 1968. *The Geography of Modernization in Kenya: A Spatial Analysis of Social, Economic and Political Change.* New York: Syracuse University Press.

United Nations. 1991. *World Urbanization Prospects 1990.* Population Studies 121. New York: United Nations.

13

Libya

Saad Kezeiri

Libya has been one of the most remarkable African countries, combining a progressive foreign policy, a domestic political revolution, and extraordinary economic growth over the last two decades. At independence in 1951, Libya was characterized by three distinct parts: urban centers, rural areas with settled agriculture, and rural areas dominated by the tribes with unsettled agriculture. The average per capita income was below $50 per annum, capital formation was zero or less, and there was an absence of skilled labor and experienced entrepreneurship. These and other obstacles to development led Benjamin Higgins to state that "if Libya can be brought to a stage of substantial growth, there is hope for every country in the world" (El Wifati, 1987:157).

The discovery and rapid exploitation of Libya's oil reserves during the 1960s brought a dramatic transformation in the country's fortunes. Today Libya is one of the wealthiest nations in the world. Oil wealth transformed this deserted and sparsely populated country, bringing dramatic demographic changes. Today Libya is one of the most urbanized countries in Africa and in the entire world. In 1990 an estimated 90 percent of the total population lived in urban centers with more than 2,000 inhabitants (Kezeiri, 1990).

The Libyan population has become polarized on the two major cities, Tripoli and Benghazi, accentuating the country's spatial and structural dualism. In spite of Libya's having one of the highest rates of natural increase in the world, its labor market suffers from an acute manpower shortage. The country has been forced to import a growing number of foreign workers, who have further accentuated the urban concentration of the population. Conscious of the undesirable consequences of urbanization and the continued polarization of population and investment, the state had to intervene.

PROBLEMS OF DEFINITION

One of the most difficult problems facing Libyan urbanization scholars is that of defining an urban center, due in part to the shortcomings of the population data from the 1954, 1964, 1973, and 1984 censuses (Kezeiri, 1984).

The 1954 census of population, for example, identified only nine urban settlements: two were Tripoli and Benghazi, and the other seven urban centers were small towns with populations under 20,000 inhabitants: Ejdabiah, Derna, El Merj, Ez Zawiyah, Suq el Gumah, and Tobruq.

In 1964 there were only six urban settlements—Tripoli, Benghazi, Derna, Tobruq, Ejdabiah, and Sirte (Government of Libya, 1966). In 1966, however, separate figures were published that classified every settlement with more than 2,000 inhabitants as urban regardless of its function. The 1973 census of population divided the country into 46 *Baladiyat* (municipalities) and 156 *Fur Baladiyat* (submunicipalities). Each *Fur Baladiyah* was subdivided into *Mahalat* (quarters). All settlements with an "urban development plan" were defined as urban regardless of their function and size (Ministry of Planning, 1977). On the basis of the 1973 census, 189 settlements were identified as urban and 474 settlements as rural. The 1973 census failed to recognize a large number of urban centers simply because they did not have urban development plans and considered some parts of towns such as El Merj as rural and others urban.

The United Nations in 1976 defined urban Libya as the total populations of Tripoli and Benghazi *Muhafadat* (provinces) and the urban parts of the *Mutassarifiat* (subprovinces) of El Beida and Derena (United Nations, 1977). This definition, however, underestimated the true proportion of urban dwellers since it excluded some small urban centers in the 10,000–20,000 inhabitants range and the 5,000–10,000 range. Many of these centers clearly perform urban functions of considerable importance (Blake, 1979).

The 1984 census of population divided Libya into 24 *Baladiyat* and used the same definition of an urban area used in the 1973 census of population (Secretariat of Planning, 1985). On the basis of the 1984 census, 268 settlements were identified as urban and 406 settlements as rural (Table 13.1). Also the 1984 census failed to recognize a large number of urban centers simply because they did not have urban development plans. Since there is no agreement about the appropriate criteria to adopt, the objective definition of towns and cities remains a basic problem that must be faced by all researchers.

Using both the size of the population and the function of the settlement as criteria from the 1984 census, all settlements in Libya (Table 13.2) were classified into four major categories:

1. Cities—the three metropolitan areas of Tripoli, Benghazi, and Misurata.
2. Intermediate towns—eleven towns with populations above 30,000 inhabitants.

Table 13.1
Distribution of Urban and Rural Settlements by *Baladiyat* Based on the 1984 Census

Baladiyat (municipalities)	Number of Urban Settlements	Number of Rural Settlements	Total
Tobruq	3	14	17
Derna	6	21	27
Jabel Akhdar	7	25	32
El Fatah	5	20	25
Benghazi	29	29	58
Ejdabiah	6	14	20
Sirte	12	19	31
Souf Ejeen	1	16	17
Kufra	1	5	6
Misurata	15	9	24
Zliten	9	11	20
El Khums	16	16	32
Tripoli	55	8	63
El Aziziah	18	1	19
Ez Zawiyah	22	19	41
Tarhuna	7	14	21
Negat El Khms	22	14	36
Gherian	4	44	48
Yefren	6	29	35
Ghdams	6	22	28
Sabha	6	4	10
El Shate	8	16	24
Urbari	2	14	16
Murzuq	2	22	24
Total	268	406	674

Source: Compiled from the Libya Census, 1985.

Table 13.2
Urban Centers of Libya with 20,000 or More Inhabitants in 1984

Rank	Centers	Population
1	Greater Tripoli (a)	990,690
2	Greater Benghazi (b)	442,860
3	Greater Misurata (c)	131,030
4	Ez Zawiyah	91,600
5	Sebha	69,150
6	El Beida	66,020
7	Ejdabiah	65,270
8	Tobruq	62,500
9	Derna	60,980
10	El Merj	43,500
11	Zliten	39,950
12	El Khums	38,170
13	Sirte	35,280
14	Sabratah	30,220
15	Tarhuna	29,750
16	El Aziziah	29,310
17	Bani Walid	28,650
18	El Ajelat	28,250
19	Sorman	27,040
20	Zwarah	21,600
21	El Jmail	21,160
22	Brak	20,360

Notes:

(a) Greater Tripoli, including Tajura, Janzur, and Gasr Ben Ghashier.

(b) Greater Benghazi, including Sidi Khalifa, Beninah, Bu Atni, Gwarsha, and Garyounis.

(c) Greater Misurata, including El Zarwag, Gasr Ahmed, and El Marsa

Source: Compiled from the Libya Census, 1985.

3. Small towns.
4. Villages and hamlets.

Some 79 settlements within the population range 2,000–30,000 were considered small towns because of the nature of the data. The reasons for lowering the definition of an urban settlement to 2,000 inhabitants is to include some urbanizing villages and other regional centers.

A number of settlements with more than 2,000 inhabitants have not been classified as urban. In some cases more than 50 percent of the active population are engaged in agriculture and agriculture-related activities. Other *Mahalat* and *Fur Baladiyat,* as an area unit used to tabulate the population data in the 1984 census, do not correspond to an individual settlement, so it was impossible to extract statistics relating only to that settlement.

Certainly it is very difficult to define urban centers in Libya because the Census Department fails to apply an area unit to existing boundaries of the towns. Researchers should be aware of the limitations and inconsistencies in the urban population data of Libya.

URBAN GROWTH

Libya has had a long and distinguished record of urbanism going back to Greek and Phoenician times. Despite the changing fortunes of individual towns and cities, urban life somehow has always managed to retain its vitality. Like many other African countries, Libya has been subject to rapid urban growth, the rate of which has been very fast since the 1960s.

Estimates vary about the rate of growth of Libya's urban population during the first half of the twentieth century. M. Attir, for example, calculates an average annual urban growth rate of 4 percent for this period (Attir, 1983). A. M. Misrati, on the other hand, suggests an annual growth rate of the urban population of 8.1 percent per annum in 1911–54, indicating that the very low growth rate of the total population was due to casualties of the Libyan-Italian War, World War II, and the high rate of migration to neighboring countries. The rapid growth of the urban population was the result of the worsening economic situation in rural areas (Misrati, 1983).

Despite the population censuses of 1954, 1964, 1973, and 1984, there were widely differing estimates of the rate of urban growth due to the different definitions of the urban population adopted by various authors.

M. Alawar stated that in the absence of a rural classification of the population in the 1954 census, the urban population would normally be determined by occupational criteria. Thus, he calculated a 1954 urban population of 235,000 (25 percent of the total population); in 1964, 385,239 (also 25 percent of the total population); and in 1973, 46 percent (Alawar, 1982).

Misrati identified nine centers with more than 5,000 inhabitants in 1954 as urban, with a total population of 270,000 or 25 percent of the total population. Using urban planning surveys, he identified 14 towns with populations of more than 5,000 inhabitants in 1966, giving an urban population of 674,000 or 40 percent of the estimated total. He indicated that between 1954 and 1966 the urban population increased by 8 percent per annum while Libya's total population increased by 3.7 percent per annum. In 1973, 62 percent of the population was urban, and the average annual rate of growth between 1966 and 1973 exceeded 11 percent, almost three times the rate of total population growth (Misrati, 1983).

G. H. Blake considered all settlements with populations of over 5,000 inhabitants as urban centers and calculated that 56 percent of Libya's population lived in such settlements in 1973. Comparing 1966 and 1973 figures, he determined that the average annual urban growth rate was 16 percent (Blake, 1979).

According to Attir, the urban population living in settlements of 5,000 inhabitants or more increased from 25 percent in 1954 to 40 percent in 1964 and from 60 percent in 1973 to 81 percent in 1980. The annual average urban growth rate between 1966 and 1978 was 7 percent (Attir, 1983).

Using the population of the ten most important urban centers identified as the chief towns of the ten *Muhafadat,* M. Atallah and M. Fikry estimated that the urban population increased from 31 percent in 1954 to 34 percent of the total in 1964, giving an average annual growth rate of 6 percent (Atallah and Fikry, 1972).

In 1954 only 25 percent of Libya's inhabitants lived in places of 2,000 population and over. This increased rapidly to 46 percent in 1964, 69 percent in 1973, then to 78 percent in 1984. In 1984, about 70 percent of the total population lived in settlements with 10,000 inhabitants or more. The number of urban centers rose from 9 in 1954 to 18 in 1964 to 46 in 1973 and reached 93 in 1984 (Figure 13.1).

Libya's population increased at an average annual rate of 4.2 percent between 1973 and 1984, and the urban population grew at an annual average rate of 8 percent. The rates of population and urban growth in Libya are among the highest in Africa and can be expected to continue in the future.

The growth of the Libyan urban centers since the 1950s resulted from a natural increase in the population, rural-to-urban migration, the presence of foreign workers, and the transformation of many rural centers to urban status.

Blake claims that the high rate of natural increase is a more significant factor in urban growth than migration (Blake, 1974). A. Toboli, on the other hand, stresses the major importance of migration in the urbanization of Libya (Toboli, 1974). Janet Abu-Lughod emphasized that the high rates of growth in North African cities were largely due to natural increase with the exception of Cairo and Tripoli, the latter because of its role as a reception center for skilled manpower (Abu-Lughod, 1976). This remarkable change in urban development of Libya since 1950 is largely due to the discovery and subsequent exploitation of

Figure 13.1
Urban Centers in Libya, 1984

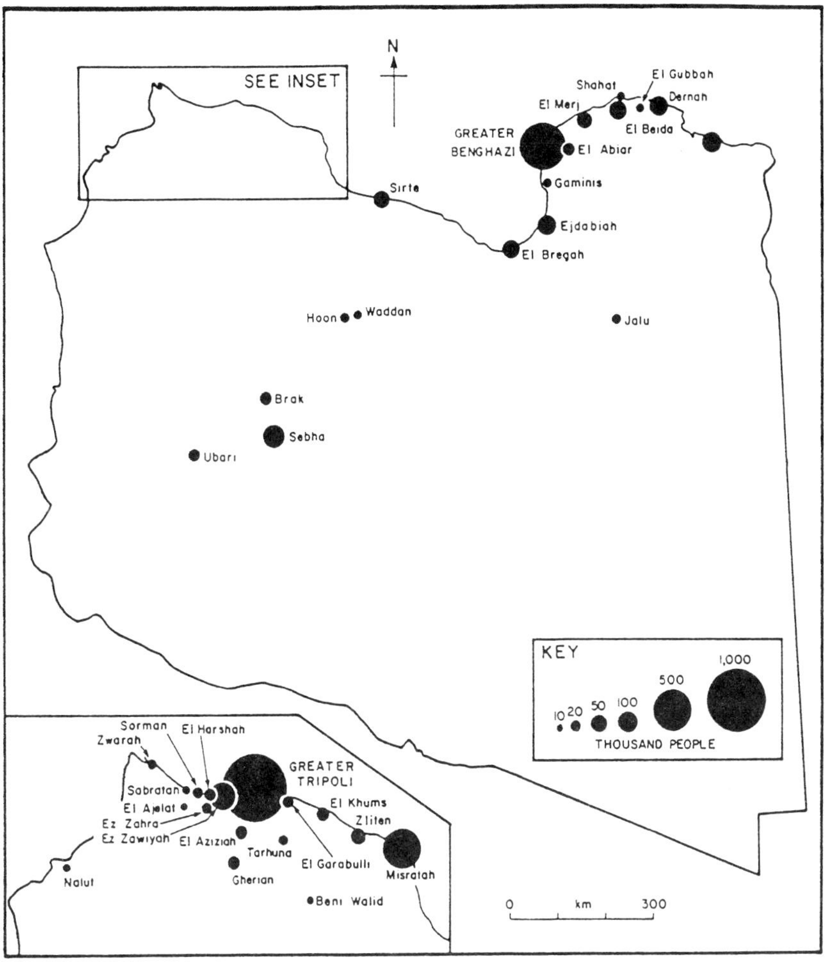

oil. The high rate of urbanization could also be attributed to the inhospitable environment, which favors the concentration of population in towns and cities along the Mediterranean Coast.

URBAN PHYSICAL CHANGE

Physical changes have occurred in Libya's urban centers both qualitatively and quantitatively as a result of the massive development initiated by the state. Major physical changes such as new administrative complexes, schools, and housing projects have occurred in selected urban centers in Libya between 1966 and 1980, and more are expected by the year 2000. Misurata's built-up area in

1980 was almost twelve times its size in 1966 while Tripoli's was five times its size in 1966.

ANALYSIS OF THE SETTLEMENTS SYSTEM

Libya's settlement pattern is marked by a high degree of primacy and extreme spatial disparities among regions. In 1973 the Benghazi region (northeast) had a relatively well balanced settlement hierarchy where Benghazi city, intermediate towns, small towns, and villages make up effective functional units. However, by 1984 Benghazi city had become increasingly dominant. In the Tripoli region (northwest), the pattern of location and settlement reflects the overly strong dependence upon Tripoli city. The size distributions of settlements in 1954, 1964, 1973, and 1984 are all characterized by a high degree of primacy, being defined as the ratio of the population of the largest settlement to the combined population of the four largest settlements (Figure 13.2).

When measured by the proportion of the population of the four largest cities residing in the largest city, the degree of primacy of Libya's settlement pattern is deceptively low (El Shakhs, 1975:371–386). Because the Libyan settlement pattern is basically polarized on Tripoli and Benghazi, primacy measures are meaningful only within each of the two subsystems, where such values become considerably higher. In fact, if Tripoli and Benghazi were removed from the city-size distribution analysis, Libya's pattern of settlement would show hierarchical qualities similar to George Zipf's "Rank-Size Rule." In fact, five distinct levels of hierarchical groupings can be identified.

Rapid urban growth has been unequally distributed in the Libyan urban system. Tripoli and Benghazi, the two primate cities of the former provinces of Tripolitania (northwest) and Cyrenaica (northeast), the two major port industrial, commercial, administrative, and educational centers, have become increasingly predominant. After World War II, Tripoli had about 100,000 inhabitants and Benghazi 60,000. By 1964 they had doubled to 213,000 and 137,000, respectively. By 1973 they had more than doubled again to 615,000 and 266,000 respectively, and by 1984 they jumped to 990,690 and 442,860, respectively.

Together Benghazi and Tripoli comprised 50 percent of the total population. Tripoli contained 35 percent of the total urban population of Libya and 57 percent of the total urban population of its region. Benghazi contained 16 percent of the total urban population of the country and 51 percent of the total urban population of its region. The two cities provide more than three-fifths of service-sector employment. Their overwhelming importance in employment and urban growth has overshadowed the growth of other towns.

The dramatic economic changes in Libya have increased the polarization of population concentration of Tripoli and Benghazi. Tripoli stands on the edge of the rich agricultural area of the Gefara Plain, and Benghazi is near the richest oil fields. Both are located on the most important routes from the interior to the Mediterranean Coast and are on the major coastal highway. These transport

Figure 13.2
Rankings of Libya's Urban Centers, 1954–84

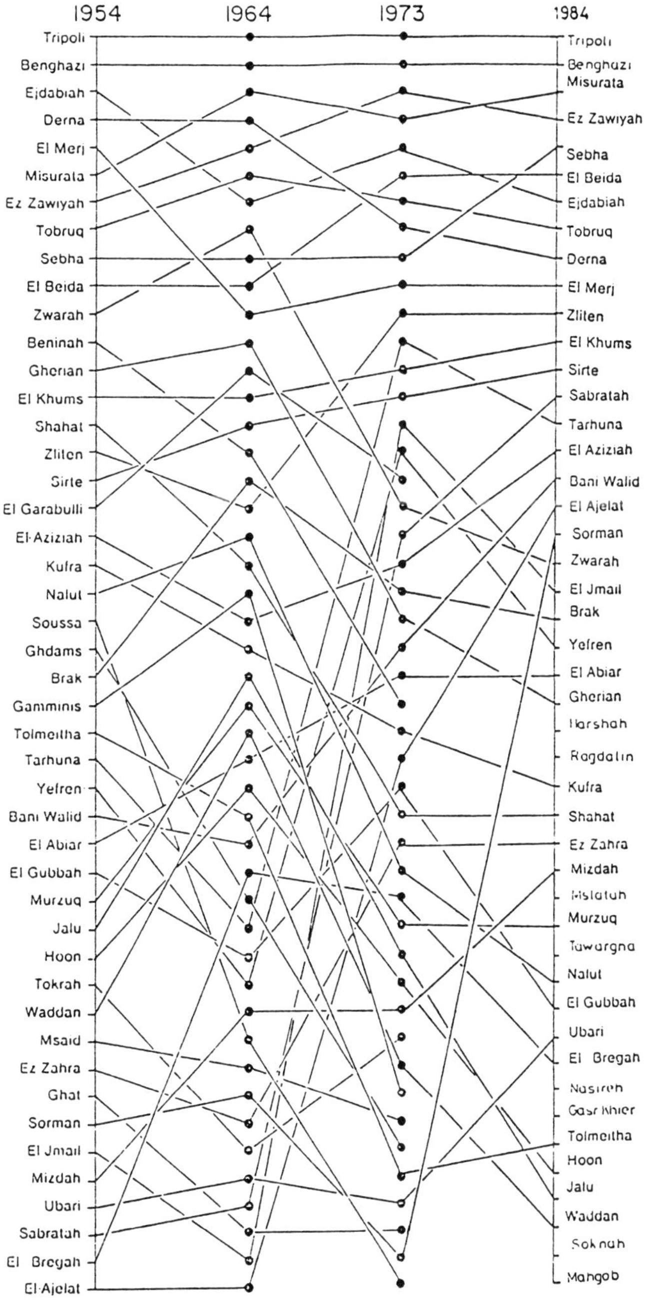

patterns have encouraged a major potential for urban development within these areas, just as the Mediterranean served them throughout Libya's long history (Alawar, 1982).

STATE INTERVENTION

Many related factors have caused dramatic changes in the population of towns, one dominant factor of which is the state interventionist policies and the role of the government.

In Libya, as in most developing countries, the burden of economic and social development falls squarely upon the government. It is the government which must stimulate industrial and urban development, build infrastructure, and establish welfare programs. The government is responsible for decisions concerning all aspects of urbanization, land use, urban location, legislation, economic stimulation, and population redistribution; thus the state can be described as both the engine of development and purveyor of amenities. The participation of the government in the development of this oil-rich state has increased progressively with the growth in oil revenue so that today the state has become the dominant factor in the economy. By 1967 the public sector had grown dramatically and was more important than the private sector; and by 1982 the private sector had vanished with the wide-scale nationalization of all economic and social activities.

State intervention in Libya resulted in the growth of most towns and resulted in several changes in population, changes in functions, and changes in the built-up areas in towns. The significance of the state as an external growth factor in the development of Libya's towns is very clear. The stimulus in Libya is due to the fact that Libya was one of the poorest nations, if not the poorest, during the 1950s. When oil was discovered in the 1960s, the wealth was heavily concentrated in the two major cities of Tripoli and Benghazi where the private sector as an internal growth factor played a significant role in the development of those two cities. There the private sector invested mainly in commercial enterprises and in housing. The role of the public sector in the towns of Libya was negligible during this period.

Although the private sector flourished during the early years of the revolution, mainly in Tripoli and Benghazi, its contribution to total investment was nevertheless small, with the public sector playing an ever-increasing role in the country's development program. By the late 1970s the government had begun to dismantle the private sector progressively so that by the early 1980s even small retailing outlets were nationalized and replaced by large state-owned and state-run supermarkets. By 1984 there were very few opportunities for private investment in the Libyan economy, mainly in the agricultural sector, and the state played a dominant role in all aspects of the country's economy. Two aspects of state intervention were considered in this study, town planning and regional planning and their impact on shaping the towns and restructuring the urban system.

Although many African cities and towns have been generally neglected from the planning point of view, Libya is one of the exceptions. The need to intervene and to plan in Libya stems from several factors, notably rapid population increase, urbanization and polarization of populations in Tripoli and Benghazi. Uncontrolled growth of these centers has created severe imbalance in population distribution among different regions. All this meant that the government had to plan for the increasing population, providing schools, houses, hospitals, jobs, and leisure amenities by means of urban and regional planning. The government is committed to the reduction of inequalities between regions and has tried to offset this high degree of spatial imbalance by channelling oil revenues into extensive improvement and expansion of infrastructures.

TOWN PLANNING

The roots of town planning in the country go back to the Italian era (1911–42). The Italian invasion and the establishment of colonial rule introduced a new phase of urbanization in Libya. New extensions were built to the precolonial centers, in which wide streets, roads, and piazzas were laid out, gardens and parks were established, and multistory buildings, modern shops, markets, schools, hospitals, and churches were erected. Urban development plans were prepared for Tripoli, Benghazi, Derna, Misurata, El Merj, and Zwara; for the first time modern European planning concepts were applied in Libya such as the creation of ''Cittagiardina'' or the garden city (Kezeiri, 1983). The Italian occupation resulted in the dominance, both spatially and visually, of colonial-style townscapes. The new urban development undertaken by the Italians represented the first modern departure from the traditional urban fabric of the Arab world.

In 1966, five years after the first oil was exported from Libya, the Ministry of Planning and Development initiated an extensive urban planning program designed both to regulate urban expansion and to make the benefits of the country's newfound wealth accessible to as many citizens as possible (Blake, 1979). Four separate contracts were awarded to four consultants for the preparation of the master and layout plans. By 1970, the four consultants had prepared 29 master plans, and 148 layout plans that covered the whole country by inventory reports. These documents still provide valuable information on the urban scene in Libya. The planning horizon for the master plans extended some 20 years into the 1980s. Considering the detailed nature of the plans and the spectacular rate of change brought about by oil revenues, such a time span was probably too long. The master plans of 1967–68 were not, in fact, the first major urban plans attempted in Libya since independence. In 1963, the small town of El Merj had been devastated by an earthquake, and a master plan for the reconstruction of a new town was published in 1964. The new town, located about four kilometers to the west of the ruined site, was subsequently built, closely following the master plan.

In 1964 the government decided to build a new capital at the small market town of El Beida with 12,000 inhabitants. In 1966 Doxiadis Associates prepared the master plans for El Beida, providing for a city of 50,000 inhabitants in the first phase and a future extension for a possible 100,000 inhabitants.

Although the physical plans themselves were instrumental in bringing modern services, such as sewage systems, fresh water, and electricity, and attempting to rationalize road systems and urban land use, and without the broad guidelines laid down in the plans, the physical expansion of Libyan towns would have been uncontrolled and chaotic in the 1970s and 1980s. However, they have major weaknesses, such as overlooking the possibility of adapting traditional urban styles to the needs of the modern world. Moreover, the government found it necessary to elaborate new plans for all settlements in the country up to the year 2000.

These new physical plans prepared by foreign consultancy companies were set within a framework established by three important documents: the work of an Italian consultant on settlement; the National Physical Perspective Plan, which was prepared by the government with the help of a technical team from the United Nations (Secretariat of Municipalities, 1979); and the Terms of References for Regional and Master Plans, which was prepared by the Secretariat of Municipalities (Secretariat of Municipalities, 1977). In this way the new physical plans became one of the tools by which the government began planning for the economic social development of the country to the year 2000. Libya was divided geographically into four main regions: Benghazi and Jabel Akhdar; Tripoli and the western coastal districts; Sebha, including much of what was generally termed the Fezzan; and Khalij, stretching from the Gulf of Sirte to Kufra (Figure 13.3). Within this regional planning context, physical plans were formulated and designed up to the year 2000.

The government commissioned for the second time Doxiadis Associates to undertake the development plan for the Benghazi Region and to prepare 11 master plans and 55 layout plans (Doxiadis Associates, 1979). For the Tripoli Region Polservice was commissioned to prepare 24 master and 55 layout plans. Speerplan of West Germany undertook the study, planning and mapping all settlements in El Khalij Region with the cooperation of Finnmap of Helsinki (Speerplan, 1980). Finnmap, another consultant firm, also carried out work in Sebha Region. The government also commissioned several separate consultants to prepare master plans for a number of new towns.

REGIONAL PLANNING

Before 1973 the Libyan government used sectoral planning as a tool for overall economic growth. In recent years, however, there has been an increasing awareness of the negative aspects of the continued polarization of population and investment, and development plans have stressed the need to achieve greater rural-urban and regional balance. The importance of the spatial dimension in the development process was acknowledged when a Spatial Planning Department

Figure 13.3
The Major Regions of Libya

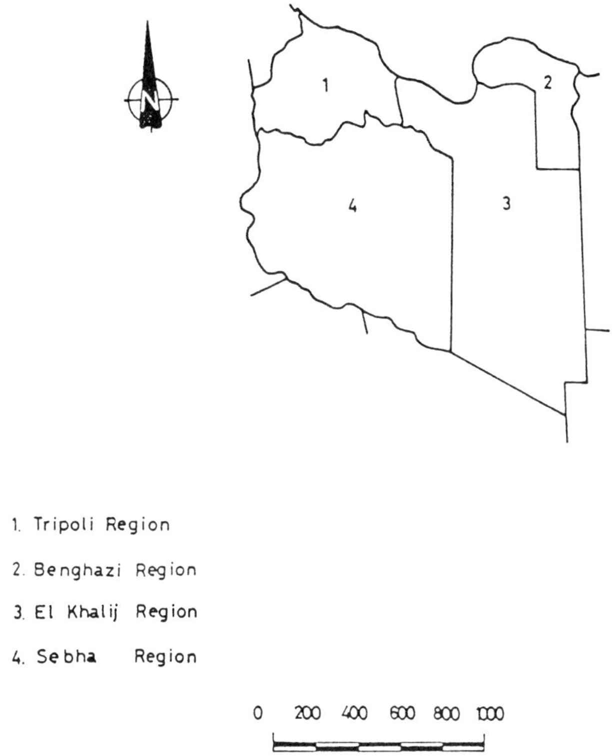

was established in the Ministry of Planning in the early 1970s and the government commissioned Italconsult to prepare a study of the entire Libyan settlement system. Produced in 1976, the Italconsult study for the first time looked at the entire settlement system, identified those settlements recommended to be upgraded or downgraded, suggested the creation of new settlements to become new growth poles, and established priorities for the future development of economic, technical, and infrastructure programs.

Analyzing the trends and policies in 1976, Italconsult outlined the main problems concerning the country's spatial development. It indicated that both the existing and the planned location of industrial projects tended to polarize growth in a restricted number of towns; employment opportunities in manufacturing created in large cities would have to compete with higher paying job opportunities in other urban occupations. The communication and distribution system was insufficiently developed to afford effective and agile flows within regions. While substantial improvement was planned for the main national highways, progress on the development of a complementary system of feeder roads had been slow and incapable of serving new agricultural projects. Port traffic had been excessively centralized on the congested Tripoli and Benghazi harbors. Serious gaps persisted in the existing distribution of social services throughout the country, and the predominant role of the two major metropolitan centers gave rise to many problems. A greater number of small villages needed more effective provision of basic social and technical infrastructure and general improvement of living conditions. The lack of economic and social opportunities in rural areas increased large-scale rural out-migration and gravitation toward the largest urban centers. Shortage of water was acute in the more settled regions of the country and could become a crucial negative factor within the next decade with serious repercussions on any program to boost agricultural or industrial production. Finally many areas lacked capable leadership at different levels.

The Italconsult team made the following recommendations:

1. The existing eastern and western urban subsystems should be integrated by the creation of a star-shaped main communication network focussed on a large new city to be created in the Sirtic Gulf.
2. The middle rank cities should be upgraded, particularly the regional capitals, by decentralized industrial strategy and location of specialized social, commercial, and administrative facilities.
3. Twenty-four new growth centers should be created to exploit untapped resources, absorb excess population, settle new lands, and integrate the settlement network.
4. One hundred and fifty-nine villages which lacked natural, economic, and physical resources essential for future development and improvement of living conditions should be downgraded and their population eventually resettled.

The Libyan government, through its various secretariats, *Baladiyat,* and agencies, and with the collaboration of the United Nations team in Tripoli, studied the recommendations of Italconsult. Some of the main recommendations were incorporated in the National Physical Perspective Plan (NPPP) published in 1979 as the guide for future development at the national, regional, and local scale as a means of securing coordinated spatial planning (Kezeiri and Lawless, 1986).

The plan places no limits on the growth of Tripoli and Benghazi, which will continue to dominate the urban system in the year 2000. However, below the level of the two major centers a certain restructuring of the urban system is proposed. Three intermediate towns are scheduled for rapid growth, notably Misurata but also Ez Zawiyah and Sebha. Eight small towns have been selected for development as second rank centers. With the exception of Hoon, Bani Walid, Brak, and Waddan, all the small towns scheduled for development as second and third rank centers lie on the primary coastal axis.

The major features of the proposals incorporated in the spatial model recommended by the NPPP are now being implemented. An ambitious project to pipe water from aquifers in the interior to the primary development axis along the Mediterranean coast has been completed. In November 1983 the Libyan government signed a U.S. $3.300-million contract with South Korea's Dong Ah Construction Industrial Company to lay a massive man-made river from the Sahara Desert to the Mediterranean coastal regions. The water will be gathered from wells around Tazerbo and Sarir. The second phase of the project, the construction of a 400-kilometer pipeline from Hasawna to Tripoli, began in 1989.

The development of the coastal area between Ejdabiah and Misurata has already begun by locating major industrial developments at El Bregah and in the new town of Ras Lanuf and Gasr Ahmed. El Bregah is experiencing a dramatic transformation from a small dormitory settlement for workers at the oil terminal to a major heavy industrial center and the city of Libya's new technical university. Ras Lanuf, the site of Mobil Oil's crude petrochemicals center, is a new town constructed 17 kilometers west of the petrochemicals complex and was planned to house some 15,000 people. The new town of Gasr Ahmed is located 9 kilometers to the east of Misurata and 3 kilometers from the harbor. It is being built to house workers from the nearby steel complex. Another new town is being constructed at Kufra north of the existing town of El Jof on the secondary axis linking Ejdabiah and Kufra. It will house 2,000 people, most workers in the agricultural project nearby.

New modifications have been incorporated into the NPPP by the promotion of the small town of Sirte to become the First Administrative Center for the Jamahiriya.

CONCLUSION

Oil wealth transformed Libya from a poor and backward society in which the majority of the inhabitants were nomadic or seminomadic to a country experiencing rapid urbanization.

During the 1960s to 1980s the rate of urban growth was among the highest in the world. Certainly the level of urbanization will continue to rise in the future. Indeed, Libya appears to be experiencing a transformation toward the urbanization of the whole society.

Eagerness to become modern in the shortest period of time and increasing wealth have contributed to the development of an unbalanced pattern of urbanization. In a very short time Libyan towns expanded rapidly, creating "instant urban environments" designed and executed by foreign consultants and companies. Unfortunately, it will take longer to resolve the problems of social adaptation and adjustment for their inhabitants.

The absence of a coherent overall policy for urban growth in the country before the 1970s has resulted in costly mistakes and, above all, in missed opportunities for national development planning. Only recently has integrated planning been given serious consideration. A positive attempt has been made to produce a more balanced distribution of resources through the reorganization of the settlement system by economic and administrative decentralization. A major weakness in this strategy is that no limitations are placed on the growth of Tripoli and Benghazi.

It remains to be seen whether such decentralization policies can counter the existing trend toward the two big cities. The need to take some of the pressure off Tripoli and Benghazi and move in the direction of decentralization can best be achieved by limiting the growth of the two big cities and at the same time encouraging the growth of those centers already experiencing strong growth.

REFERENCES

Abu-Lughod, Janet. 1976. "Development in North African Urbanism: The Process of Decolonization." In *Urbanization and Counterurbanization,* edited by B. Berry, 191–211. Newbury Park: Sage.

Alawar, M. 1982. "Urbanization in Libya: Present State and Future Prospects." In *Social and Economic Development of Libya,* edited by E. G. H. Joffe and K. S. Mclachlan, 331–353. London: Means Press.

Atallah, M. and M. Fikry. 1972. "Le phénomène urbain en Libya, problèmes juridiques et sociaux." *Annuaire de Afrique du Nord* 11:79–103.

Attir, M. 1983. "Libya's Pattern of Urbanization." *Ekistics* 300:157–162.

Blake, G. H. 1974. "Urbanization in North Africa: Its Nature and Consequences." In *The City in the Third World,* edited by D. S. Dwyer, 67–80. London: Macmillan.

———. 1979. "Urbanization and Development Planning in Libya." In *Development of Urban Systems in Africa,* edited by R. A. Obudho and S. El Shakhs, 99–115. New York: Praeger.

Doxiadis Associates. 1979. *Existing Conditions in Benghazi Region.* Report No. 5. Athens.

El Shakhs, S. 1975. "Urbanization and Spatial Development in Libya." *Pan-African Journal* 8:371–386.

El Wifati, B. 1987. "Agricultural Development and Its Future in Libya." In *The Economic Development of Libya,* edited by Bichara Khader and Bashir el Wifati, 157–182. London: Croom Helm.

Government of Libya. 1966. *The 1964 Census of Population.* Benghazi (In Arabic).

Kezeiri, S. K. 1983. "Urban Planning in Libya." *Libyan Studies* (London) 14:9–15.

———. 1984. "The Problems of Defining a Small Urban Center in Libya." *Libyan Studies* (London) 15:143–148.

Kezeiri, S. K. and I. Lawless. 1986. "Economic Development and Spatial Planning in Libya." *Orient,* German Journal for Politics and Economics of the Middle East No. 1:69–87.

Ministry of Planning. 1977. *The 1973 Census of Population.* Tripoli (In Arabic).

Misrati, A. M. 1983. "Land Conversion to Urban Use: Its Impact and Character in Libya." *Ekistics* 300:183–194.

Secretariat of Municipalities. 1977. *Terms of References for Regional and Master Plans for the Socialist People's Libyan Arab Jamahiriya.* Tripoli.

Secretariat of Municipalities and Secretariat of Planning and United Nations Technical Co-operation Physical Planning Project. 1979. *National Physical Perspective Plan 1981–2000.* Tripoli.

Secretariat of Planning. 1985. *Preliminary Results of the 1984 Census of Population.* Tripoli (In Arabic).

Speerplan. 1980. *Existing Conditions in Elkhalij Region.* Frankfurt.

Toboli, A. 1974. "Urban Growth and City-Size Distribution in Libya." *Economics and Business Review* (Benghazi) 11:22–23.

United Nations. 1977. *Demographic Yearbook, 1976.* New York.

14

Mali

Sekouba Diarra, Aka Kouame, Richard Marcoux, and Alain-Michel Camara

Mali, like most countries in the Sahelian region, is generally known for its rural and pastoral populations. To this day, a large majority of the Malian population lives in nonurbanized regions, living from agriculture, livestock, and fishing. Yet the territory which Mali presently occupies witnessed the development of some of the oldest cities on the African continent, Djene and Segou, to name but two. Both played, at one time, major roles in the history of Africa, but they may have lost their political and economic importance. The city of Bamako, however, has progressed considerably. What was in 1921 a small town of less than 15,000 inhabitants grew to a population of more than 800,000 in 1992.

Mali's relatively low urbanization rate (22 percent in 1987) hides a very important phenomenon of urban growth. Because of incomplete statistics, only the urban growth since the mid-1970s can be fully presented. At the same time an analysis of the Malian capital will be made, notably in relation to questions linked to the habitat and economic activity.

MALI'S URBAN PHENOMENON

For a long period, Mali was the center for important commercial contacts due to the prosperity of its great empires and kingdoms, like the empires of Mali and Songhoi, the kingdoms of Macina and Bambara of Segou. For a long time, celebrated cities like Tombouctou, Gao, Djene, and Segou radiated both on a cultural and commercial level. Their prestige was known well beyond the borders of Mali.

The majority of these empires owed their wealth to commercial contacts (gold trade, ostrich feather trade, and salt trade) which extended into Europe and the Middle East. Trans-Saharan and interregional commerce were directly linked to the urban network. The cities were areas for transshipment or storage as they were located between different climatic and/or cultural regions. Among these cities were Kumbi, Timbuktou, Niani, and Tekrur. Many have disappeared (as is the case with Niani, which was the capital of the Malian empire) or have sustained a considerable decline (as is the case of Timbuktou).

During the colonial period, the influence which commerce with Europe and the Americas had on the development of the cities increased. With the growing importance of maritime transport, coastal cities experienced a growth in their political and economic roles which served as a detriment to the interior cities. The cities located in Mali's territory witnessed a slowing of their growth to the profit of the coastal cities like Abidjan and Dakar. Nevertheless, an urban network is taking shape. Mali's colonial cities developed primarily in the regions where production for exportation occurred as well as along the circulation routes which linked these regions to the Dakar and Abidjan ports. The introduction of the cultivation of peanuts in the Kayes region; the building of the Dakar-Bamako-Koulikoro railroad in 1905; as well as the introduction and cultivation of cotton in southern Mali around Sikasso and Bourgouni have largely contributed to the urban structure now in present-day Mali.

DEMOGRAPHIC ASPECTS OF URBANIZATION IN MALI

Urbanization and Urban Hierarchy

Following its independence, the new Republic of Mali began an inquiry into the demographics of its territory. This survey estimated an urban population of 416,000 in 1960, making up 12 percent of Mali's sedentary population. However, as with many other countries, changes in the concepts and definitions of the urban milieu make such comparisons difficult in time. Thus, only the census information from 1976 and 1987 provides strict comparisons. The analysis of urbanization in Mali will be limited to these two population censuses.

In 1987 there were 21 more urban centers than in 1976 (Table 14.1). In 1987 these new centers were the residences of more than 140,000 individuals. The total urban population went from 1,076,829 in 1976 to 1,690,289 in 1987, an increase of 57 percent. The urbanization rate, which was 17 percent in 1976, reached 22 percent in 1987, still a relatively low level of urbanization.

Between 1976 and 1987, the size structure of the urban centers was modified considerably. There was a sharp rise in the number of urban centers of 5,000 and 10,000 inhabitants. This resulted in a major reduction in places with less than 5,000 inhabitants, from almost a third of all urban centers in 1976 to a little more than a tenth of all 1987 centers.

The population of the capital city of Bamako—a disporportionately large

Table 14.1
Evolution of the Urban Population of Mali by Size, 1976–87

SIZE	URBAN CENTERS 1976 NO.	PERCENT	URBAN CENTERS 1987 NO.	PERCENT	POPULATION 1976 NO.	PERCENT	POPULATION 1987 NO.	PERCENT
under 5,000	19	33	11	14	64,950	6	37,425	2
5,000 - 10,000	21	36	46	59	141,463	13	308,404	18
10,000 - 50,000	15	26	16	20	332,429	31	343,161	21
50,000 - 100,000	2	3	5	6	118,748	11	343,024	20
100,000 - 500,000	1	2	--	--	419,239	39	--	--
500,000 and over	--	--	1	1	--	--	658,275	39
TOTAL	58	100	79	100	1,076,829	100	1,690,289	100

Source: Compiled from Mali Censuses, 1976 and 1987.

primate city—in 1976 and 1987 is much larger in size than the other centers. Thirty-nine percent of Mali's urban population live in the capital city of Bamako.

From 1976 to 1987 the urban hierarchy for most cities did not change except for Kayes, Sikasso, Gao, San, and Tombouctou (Table 14.2). Kayes, which held fourth place in 1976, ranked sixth in 1987, while Sikasso and Gao moved up one rank. San and Tombouctou, which held ninth and tenth place respectively in 1976, experienced population gains mainly from a massive exodus of Tombouctou's rural inhabitants toward the commune during the years of drought (1984 in particular). Thus, the population of Tombouctou's commune almost doubled between 1976 and 1987. The massive exodus of nomadic populations from the Tombouctou and Gao regions and of the Dogons from the Mopti Region account for most of the population increase of Sikasso.

The Evolution of Bamako

One of the earliest accepted estimates of the population of Bamako in modern times is 37,000 inhabitants in 1945 (Meillassoux, 1965:127; Villien-Rossi, 1966:294; Bleneau and Cognata, 1972:26). Thus, from the end of World War II to 1958, Bamako grew at a relatively slow pace. The period from 1958 to 1961 was definitely the most important period of growth as the Bamako population increased by 53,000 within two and a half years (Table 14.3). This growth may be explained by the self-determination achieved by the "Sudanese Republic" to the benefit of the city of Bamako. Also, the collapse of the Federation of Mali in August 1960 led to the massive return of Malians living in Senegal.

Bamako's growth diminished considerably in the 15-year period following

Table 14.2
Urban Hierarchy in Mali in 1976 and 1987

1976		1987	
CITY	POPULATION	CITY	POPULATION
Bamako	419,239	Bamako	658,275
Segou	65,426	Segou	88,135
Mopti	53,322	Mopti	74,771
Kayes	49,431	Sikasso	73,859
Sikasso	46,503	Gao	55,266
Gao	30,863	Kayes	50,993
Koutiala	27,156	Koutiala	48,698
Kati	24,831	Kati	34,315
San	23,378	Tombouctou	31,962
Tombouctou	19,166	San	30,772
Kita	17,492	Kita	22,914
Bougouni	17,410	Bougouni	22,374
Koulikoro	16,133	Koulikoro	20,795

Source: Compiled from Mali Censuses, 1976 and 1987.

Table 14.3
Evolution of the Population of the City of Bamako, 1945–87

YEAR	POPULATION	PERIOD	AVERAGE ANNUAL RATE OF CHANGE
1945	37,000	1945-1958	5.7
1958	76,200	1958-1961	23.2
1960-61	129,300	1961-1966	4.7
1965-66	161,300	1966-1974	8.5
1974	317,400	1974-1976	10.7
1976	419,239	1976-1987	4.5
1987	658,275		

Source: Compiled from the Mali Censuses, 1976 and 1987, and from early estimates.

independence. The politics put forth by President Modibo Keita's government was against the rural exodus, a phenomenon it considered a hindrance to the harmonious development of the country. Concrete measures were taken to halt departures: institution of obligatory travel visas, the diffusion on national radio of messages condemning the rural exodus, and stricter surveillance of travel routes (Bleneau and Cognata, 1972:35).

Following the mid-1960s, the annual growth rate surpassed 10 percent from 1974 to 1976. Two events partially explain this phenomenon. On one hand, the political events of 1968 led to the overturning of the regime in power. As a result, the new government promoted liberalization which favored the development of commerce in the capital (Bleneau, 1976). Finally, the severe drought during the early 1970s contributed to the demographic growth of the Malian capital, for numerous people, unattached and in families, moved to Bamako hoping to find work. Finally, during 1976 to 1987, the capital's growth rate returned to its preindependence level.

The internal growth patterns experienced by the capital show that the population of the newer areas and villages of the district grew much faster than those of the older areas. Essentially, the peripheral communes absorbed most of Bamako's demographic growth. As such, the two communes located in the center made up 44 percent of the district's population in 1976, and yet housed only 31 percent of Bamako's residents in 1987.

Demographic Structure and Components of Urban Growth

Between 1976 and 1987, the age structure of the urban population remained more or less the same and differed little from the structure of the rural population. Thus, both populations have 45 percent under the age of 15. However, the urban population has a higher percentage of females.

Mali's urban population growth may be explained partly by natural growth, partly as a result of migratory exchanges, and partly by the inclusion of new urban centers. The two censuses give estimates of the different components of the demographic growth. Table 14.4, for example, shows that the country experienced an increase in the birthrate along with a noticeable decline in the death rate. Thus, the natural growth rate of Mali's population rose from 2.51 percent in 1976 to 3.70 percent in 1987. There was a major reduction in mortality rates in rural areas, combined with an increase in birthrates resulting in an increase in the rural natural growth rate of more than 1 percent. Mali's urban regions experienced minor changes with small reductions in the birthrates and death rates.

By using the average calculated birthrates and death rates, it is possible to estimate the intercensal migratory balance in each of the areas of Mali. Using these calculations, the growth of Mali's urban population was as follows: 72 percent was due to the surplus of births over deaths, and the new urban centers contributed 23 percent and finally, leaving the migratory balance as only 5

Table 14.4
Mali's Population Growth Indicators from 1976 to 1987, by Type of Residence

	MALI	RURAL	URBAN	BAMAKO
1976 Census				
Crude birthrate	4.31	4.30	4.40	4.36
Crude death rate	1.81	1.95	1.13	0.84
Natural increase rate	2.51	2.35	3.27	3.52
1987 Census				
Crude birthrate	4.96	5.14	4.33	4.05
Crude death rate	1.26	1.39	0.82	0.61
Natural increase rate	3.70	3.75	3.51	3.44

Source: Compiled from Mali Censuses, 1976 and 1987.

percent. Bamako, which had no changes in its boundaries in this period, owed 75 percent of its growth to natural increase while migratory exchanges accounted for the rest of its demographic growth. Thus, Mali's urbanization process was achieved mainly through natural increase during 1976–87.

URBAN HABITAT, INFRASTRUCTURES, AND SERVICES

Mali's urban growth has had important consequences upon the demand for lodging and urban services. Here we shall examine the housing conditions in Mali and housing construction in Bamako since independence and finally the basic urban infrastructure in the capital.

Living Conditions: Building Quality, Occupation, and Amenities

Project housing is predominant in Mali's urban environment and particularly in Bamako where it represents 9 out of 10 households. The detached house and the apartment block, which are found in several African cities, are only marginally in Mali, and even less in Bamako where less than 5 percent of the households live.

Project housing is the predominant type in Mali's urban areas, but the construction materials used for residential buildings is decidedly different in Bamako. In the urban areas outside of Bamako more than 70 percent of inhabited lodgings have walls made from banco, a mixture of mud and straw (80 percent in rural areas), and another 6 percent are constructed from wood or straw. In Bamako, less than a third of households live in these types of construction, while "hard" and "semi-hard" materials are used in almost 70 percent of all dwellings.[1]

The superior quality of construction in Bamako is also notable in the roofing materials used since 95 percent of Bamako's households use tile and cement while the use of banco is predominant in all other cities (57 percent). Finally, cement or tile flooring is used in 85 percent of the capital's housing while clay is used in the majority of the other cities.

Bamako also differs from Mali's other cities and rural areas in its form of ownership. Almost 43 percent of Bamako's households are tenants, while tenants comprise less than 30 percent of Mali's other cities and less than 2 percent in rural areas.

Less than 21 percent of Bamako's households have running water. Two-thirds of those in Bamako and other cities use wells found either in the yard or in the neighborhood. Finally, we know that only 7 percent of Bamako's households have flushing toilets (République du Mali, 1990). One can imagine the risk of contamination that exists due to the fact that most wells are located near the latrines.

Less than 30 percent of Bamako's households use electricity, with two-thirds using lanterns, and this figure rises to 80 percent in other cities. Finally, more than 85 percent of all urban households use wood as their principal fuel. Gas and electricity are used very infrequently in food preparation in Mali.

Housing Production in Bamako

The urban demographic growth of Mali has been accompanied by an important increase in the demand for housing. One noted aspect of Mali's urban milieu is that of growth in the size of households. The average size of urban households went from 4.9 in 1960 to 5.5 in 1976, then to 6 persons in 1987 (Marcoux, 1990). This phenomenon, which M. Lututala (1988) called urban implosion, has been found in only a few African countries (Locoh, 1988). Perhaps the growth in the number of dwellings may have been less than the growth in the number of household members. The number of dwellings has gone from 25,700 in 1960 to 74,106 in 1976, then to 105,394 in 1987. During 1976–87 the number of dwellings in Bamako increased 42 percent while the district's population increased 57 percent. In spite of these changes in the structure of households, Bamako's demographic growth was accompanied by a sharp increase in dwellings. The construction in Bamako is typically one-story dwellings which results in urban sprawl. Thus, Bamako's urbanized surface went from 3,100 hectares in 1976 to 5,000 hectares in 1983, an annual increase of 7 percent (DPU, 1984:210). The expansion occurred primarily in the southern part of the city with the riverbank getting almost half of the 31,000 new households. Only 22 percent of Bamako's population resided in the area in 1976.

From independence to 1983, public authorities opened more than 2,380 hectares of land for housing, 86 percent of which was prepared during the first 16 years following independence. The amount of territory opened by the state for habitation went from 1,900 hectares from 1960 to 1976 to 310 hectares during the next seven years. Since the state was unable to meet the demand created by the arrival of new families, private initiative had to prepare the terrain. As a result, during these two periods, the private sector increased its role from 31 percent to 72 percent. Legal preparation by the private sector accounted for only 10 percent of all allotments during the 1960–83 period. Spontaneous and clandestine allotment accounted for almost 60 percent of the land opened in 1976–83.

The second type of intervention involves the construction of housing and the infrastructures on the lot. As S. Dulucq notes, the actions of the state in the development of housing "are so sporadic that it is possible to enumerate them" (1989:108). The public sector directly contributed to the construction of less than 1,000 dwellings during 1960–83. When compared to other African cities, this figure is extremely low. For example, in Dakar such firms as Société Immobilière du Cap-Vert and the Office des Habitations à Loyers Modérés constructed about 20,000 dwellings from 1960 to 1980, and 22 percent of Abidjan's population resided in dwellings built by realty companies in 1979 (Antoine et al., 1987).

Urban Infrastructures and Social Structures in Bamako

The 1987 census demonstrates the weak level of development of the urban infrastructures. Only 21 percent of Bamako's households have a faucet, and even in areas served by the aqueduct system, less than 75 percent of all water needs are met at the end of the dry season. When the reservoirs located in the higher areas become exhausted, households located farthest from the aqueduct must wait until night time, after peak hours, to obtain their water. Over the past years water has been provided to an average of 650 new customers per year (Ballo et al., 1990).

Most housing projects use wells in yards due to the long waiting period and the high cost of connection to the system. However, these bored wells are very shallow (on average 2 to 10 meters), which exposes the water to the risk of contamination. Perhaps it should be prohibited to drink Bamako's well water (Ballo et al., 1990:22).

Bamako does not have a wastewater treatment plant. Most of its wastewater evacuation infrastructure was built during colonialism and has become inefficient given the rapid demographic growth. Now, most areas use the gutter systems to dispose of wastewater. However, less than 6 percent of the gutters were functional (Ballo et al., 1990). In Bamako's areas of spontaneous development, where no infrastructure exists, disposal of dirty water directly into streets or cesspools in yards creates a risk of contamination to surrounding wells.

Thirty percent of the households use electricity. Thus, considerable effort needs to be made to provide all households with electric power and a water supply.

Mali had one of the lowest rates of motorization in Africa in 1988, with 3.6

vehicles for every 1,000 inhabitants, compared to 17.1 in Senegal and 22.4 in the Côte d'Ivoire (Bonnamour, 1991). In the mid-1980s, Bamako had approximately 140 kilometers of paved roads. Recently the network of paved roads has worsened, with the repaving of certain roads having stopped completely (DPU, 1984:316). However, during the past few years substantial work has been done through the Urban Project as downtown roads have been rebuilt and a second bridge constructed in 1992.

Bamako, like most other national capitals, has health services and education superior to such services in the rest of Mali. Nevertheless, in 1987 there were 24,380 people per dispensary and 14,961 per pharmacy in the district. With 227 educational establishments, in 1987 Bamako had 2,900 students per school.

ECONOMIC ACTIVITY, EMPLOYMENT, AND HOUSEHOLD STANDARD OF LIVING

Bamako's Recent Tendencies in Activity and Employment

Bamako's activity rate rose from 25.2 percent to 26.5 percent from 1976 to 1988.[2] In spite of the increase, economic activity has remained at a relatively low level, especially for women, who registered important gains from 7 percent to 10.2 percent while the economic activity rate of men dropped from 43.2 percent to 42.6 percent.

The activity rates were based on the population aged 10 and older (Table 14.5). This partially accounts for the low rates. Should only individuals 15 to 54 years of age be used, the activity rate would be 84.8 percent for men and 17.7 percent for women, giving an average activity rate of 49.1 percent for the total population 15–54 years old.

Bamako's active manpower increased from 105,779 in 1976 to 167,337 in 1988, an annual growth rate of 4 percent. Also, the occupied active manpower—which measures employment volume—went from 96,623 to 140,906, which corresponds to an annual growth rate of 3.2 percent. Thus, there is a stronger growth in the active population than in employment. Nevertheless, important quantitative imbalances are in Bamako's job market. First, Bamako has a high unemployment rate of 12.8 percent, which is higher than that of the entire urban area of Mali (10.2 percent). Young Bamako workers were particularly affected in 1988, 24 percent of the 20–24 age group and 30 percent of the 25–29 age group respectively.

This high unemployment rate is not surprising when one considers the low satisfaction rates of applicants in modern employment. The number of applications has declined. This implies worker disillusionment about modern employment, which steers them toward the nonregistered or informal sector.

The high unemployment rate also eliminated jobs in the public sector due to programs aimed at structural adjustment. In effect, from 1985 to 1990, the state eliminated 2,915 jobs, with only 1,556 workers reintegrated (République du

Table 14.5
Labor Force Participation Rates by Age and Sex, 1988, and Total Activity Rates, 1976 and 1988

AGE GROUP	MALE	FEMALE	TOTAL
10-14	11.8	5.5	8.7
15-19	87.2	14.0	25.0
20-24	61.3	16.2	40.7
25-29	83.7	19.3	48.6
30-34	96.6	25.0	59.7
35-39	97.3	21.8	61.1
40-44	97.8	16.0	56.4
45-49	97.9	10.9	59.0
50-54	90.0	17.1	86.8
55-59	63.5	14.9	44.2
60-64	44.3	6.3	28.8
65 & over	36.2	6.7	23.2
TOTAL (1988)	42.6	10.2	26.5
15-54	84.8	17.7	49.1
TOTAL (1976)	43.2	7.0	25.2

Source: République du Mali, 1988; 6 and 10.

Mali, 1988:2). The job market also suffered qualitative imbalances linked to the precariousness of employment, particularly in the informal sector, which was linked to an oversupply of manpower. There were positions that could not be filled due to a lack of qualified workers.

Activity Structure

In 1988 there was a predominance of production workers in the testing sector with two-thirds of all employed workers. Industry, manual work, and construction are included in the secondary sector, which employs 27 percent of all occupied workers. Agriculture and raising livestock are the main activity of only 7 percent of the workers in Bamako.

A few major changes in the primary and secondary sectors occurred between

1976 and 1988. For example, agriculture and poultry farming declined by half between 1976 and 1988. Also, there was a small increase in transport, commerce, banking, insurance, and administration, accompanied by a noticeable drop in other services. In the secondary sector, only manual or handiwork had a significant gain. This suggests that the increase in the secondary sector is mainly due to gains in the informal production sector.

Certainly, job creation during the period was largely due to the informal sector, for its job creation rate was twice that of the formal sector (République du Mali, n.d., c). Moreover, of the 350,000 urban jobs available in 1987, three-quarters were in the informal sector (Wane, n.d., OCDE/CILSS, 1989:86). The 1989 survey showed that the informal sector accounted for 78 percent of the jobs (République du Mali, n.d., b). Essentially the informal sector provides employment in urban areas.

The Characteristics of Informal Activity

Working conditions lend themselves to the informal sector. These conditions are determined by the orientation of the activity and its productivity as well as by the composition of the manpower.

First, the informal sector is comprised primarily of required service units with transformation or manufacturing aimed at local markets (Wane, n.d., OCDE/CILSS, 1989:24). Informal activities are also dominated by commerce and services. Indeed in 1978 only 15 percent of those in the informal sector worked in production (handicrafts). Yet this subsector produced the highest added value within the sector, which makes it very competitive in certain markets like woodworking and metalworking, mechanics, electricity, and construction (OCDE/CILSS, 1989).

One important feature of Bamako's informal sector is the presence of an important agricultural sector within it. Agriculture is practiced by 15 percent of Bamako's occupants, or 21,000 people (République du Mali, 1988). Often it is secondary to formal employment or other nonregistered activities, being practiced primarily as a means of providing for family consumption.

Despite its size, the informal sector barely contributes to the gross national product (GNP), representing only 5 percent of it (Wane, n.d.). Definitely, one can attribute this sector's abundance of manpower to its low productivity as it is comprised essentially of family members and apprentices (27 percent of workers), employers and independent workers (55 percent) (République du Mali, n.d., b:32). Also, females represent 55 percent of the workers in the informal sector.

The Structure of Formal Employment

The majority of the workers in the formal sector are employees. Among employees, 40 percent work in private enterprise, 42 percent in administration, and 18 percent in cooperatives and other nongovernmental organizations (République du Mali, n.d., b:30). There has been a decline of salaried employment in administration since 1986, when 59 percent of the formal sector workers were in this field. In 1981, administration accounted for 61 percent. This progressive decline is a result of a 1983 decision to reduce the number of employees in the public service under the structural adjustment program, with the employees declining from 46,151 in 1986 to 41,488 in 1989 (République du Mali, n.d., b). In the future, the private sector and the parapublic sector must provide the majority of the formal-sector jobs.

Industry plays an important role in providing formal employment in both the private and parapublic sectors, even though this importance declined during the mid-1980s. Among the other branches of the formal sector, only commerce has seen a considerable increase, as its relative proportion has almost doubled. In absolute terms all sectors experienced increases in their manpower in real values during 1968–86.

Formal employment outside of administration indicates a high proportion in the parapublic sector. Since the 1980s this sector has declined due to personnel cuts. The private sector, which represented only 37 percent of formal jobs outside administration in 1986, had an average annual growth of 6 percent between 1968 and 1986 compared to 63 percent and 1 percent, respectively, for the parapublic sector. Consequently, Bamako's future employment problems are likely to depend more and more on the formal sector, as the parapublic sector weakens and government continues to reduce employment in the public sector. However, the very small size of the formal sector (only 3.4 percent of the entire active urban population) (OCDE/CILSS, 1989:90) suggests that these problems will remain since the number of jobs it is likely to create will be insufficient to meet the needs of the rapidly growing urban population. Thus, the informal sector will continue to play a major role in job creation in Bamako. However, this sector will probably not be able to greatly raise revenues and living conditions within the urban milieu.

Revenue and Household Living Conditions

The average monthly income of Bamako's households in 1983 was estimated at 62,000 cfa francs (DPU, 1984). This corresponds to a 20 percent increase since 1979. However, the top 10 percent of the households earned 36 percent of the total revenues while the lowest 36 percent earned only 12 percent (DPU, 1984). More than half of the households have incomes less than the median of 40,000 cfa francs. In fact, 68 percent of the households had less than the average incomes, and their collective income represents only 34 percent of the total compared to 66 percent for the 32 percent of households with above-average income.

The inequalities are related to a certain number of household characteristics such as size and number of active workers as well as the type of habitat and the occupational status of members of the dwelling. Of course, the large households have higher total incomes, and the majority of the low-income families were concentrated in spontaneous housing areas while those with higher incomes were in areas of high- and middle-standing housing. Also, homeowners earned the highest incomes, while those with the low incomes were usually tenants. Heads of households earned about 75 percent of the household income through their primary and secondary activities, with 55 percent coming directly from salaries.

Prospects for the Future: Population Policy and Urbanization

Since 1963 public authorities have been forced to look at an urban development policy integrated with the national economic and social development plan. The development and urbanization plan was created essentially for the purpose of improving the quality of life and limiting the disorder of the urbanization phenomenon. For all practical purposes, this has been a failure.

In May 1991 Mali adopted its first definite population policy (République du Mali, n.d., c). Urbanization was a key preoccupation in the elaboration of this policy. This is not because of the actual urban growth rate, but rather because of size of rural-urban migrations which were feared would result from the progressively deteriorating socioeconomic and ecological conditions in rural areas. Internal migration and the spatial distribution of the population prompted Mali to launch a new population policy. Policy makers assumed that populations with Mali distributions created environmental problems as well as problems in living conditions in areas of urban concentration, like Bamako. Among these problems are housing, infrastructure, employment, and social services. The following six measures were proposed to help alleviate these problems:

1. Elaboration of an operational national policy on the zoning and development of territory.
2. Reinforcement of the basic development policy and the improvement of rural living conditions.
3. Promotion of mid-sized cities based on a policy of decentralization and deconcentration of socioeconomic activities.
4. Elaboration and implementation of a training and information program for migrants.
5. Short- and middle-term rehabilitation of traditional nomadic channels and a long-term program for the sedentarization of them.
6. Elaboration and implementation of a program for migrant departure zones.

It is difficult to distinguish among some of the objectives, except 4 and 5. In effect, objectives 2, 3, and 6 could be considered as part of the first objective. These objectives have appeared in most development plans in Africa without any concrete result. Neither revenues nor living conditions have experienced any real improvement in rural areas or in secondary cities. On the contrary, conditions have worsened due to the unjust allocation of public resources and successive disasters.

The envisioned measures may become inoperative, unless the population policy is integrated in its entirety in the global development policy, which means taking and putting into effect measures that affect the socioeconomic variables at the root of certain forms of demographic behavior while at the same time acting simultaneously upon these. It is important to note that rural-urban migration due to natural disasters is an uncontrollable phenomenon in Africa's development.

Urbanization is also affected by other aspects of the new policy. These are primarily measures affecting natural growth and more specifically fertility. For example, Mali's urban growth was due primarily to natural growth, accounting for 72 percent in other cities and 75 percent in Bamako, which could be explained by the high fertility level and the falling mortality rate.

Controlling fertility is one of the objectives of the new population policy. This objective is to be accomplished through the promotion of family planning and is one of the key elements of the population policy. It is projected that a contraceptive rate of 60 percent will be achieved by the year 2020, and this service will be offered primarily in maternal and child health centers. Since these centers are concentrated in urban areas, no doubt the urban population will be the first to benefit from family planning. Already a small decline in the birthrate has occurred in the urban areas whereas in the rural areas the birthrate rose from 1976 to 1987.

For an eventual reduction in urban growth rates to improve living conditions, it will be necessary for other measures such as employment, housing, and social service to become effective. Measures taken by the urban project could improve housing. However, since these projects began in the early 1980s, living conditions have not changed greatly for the majority of Bamako's residents. Job creation depends on the dynamics of the economy. The privatization process taking place in most countries of the subregion hopefully will lead to economic growth. The budget cuts which the structural adjustment program have imposed upon the government are not likely to improve social services.

CONCLUSION

Mali has experienced a relatively rapid urbanization over the last few decades. This expansion, particularly in Bamako, can be explained mainly by natural growth, with migration playing a small role. However, migration may become a major factor should the socioeconomic situation of the countryside continue to diminish. In Bamako, where most of the investment has been made, living areas are underequipped, and the absence of an urban infrastructure is notorious. For example, sanitation conditions of dwellings outside the newly built areas are deplorable. These areas are densely populated, particularly in the older central area of the city.

The situation is similar in the job market, for the young educated adults are the hardest hit by unemployment; and most workers are in the informal sector, where production and incomes are low. Measures to improve the living conditions of city dwellers should not only reduce the pressures on the existing infrastructure and services but should also improve them. The policy implies a reduction of the rate of urban growth, an improvement of living conditions and social services, and job creation. Finally, the Mali urbanization policy must be based upon a better understanding of the movements of its population. In order for the planning and execution of these programs to be effective, it is important that sufficient relevant information be available.

NOTES

1. This result corresponds with those obtained during the household inquiry which took place in 1983 under the Mali Urban Project (DPU, 1984:266–267).

2. The data used in this section come from the reports on the inquiry into "employment and unemployment in the district of Bamako" (1988) and the inquiry "informal sector" (1989). See respectively République du Mali (1988) and République du Mali (n.d., b).

REFERENCES

Antoine, P., A. Dubresson, and A. Manou-Savina. 1987. *Abidjan "côté cours"*. Paris: Karthala-ORSTOM.

Ballo, A., S. Diallo, G. Pallier, and S. Traore. 1990. *L'eau à Bamako.* Limoges: Presse de l'Université de Limoges et du Limousin.

Bleneau, D. 1976. "Démographie bamakoise." *Etudes maliennes* 19:1–36.

Bleneau, D., and G. La Cognata. 1972. "Evolution de la population de Bamako." *Etudes maliennes* 3:26–46.

Bonnamour, L. 1991. "Le transport urbain en Afrique au sud du Sahara." *Afrique contemporaine* 158:14–29.

DPU (Direction du Projet Urbain). 1984. *Programmation décennale des investissements. Etude du développement urbain de Bamako.* Bamako: Banque Mondiale-Groupe-Huit-BCEOM-SNED.

Dulucq, S. 1989. "Mali: Bamako." *Les investissements publics dans les villes africaines, 1930–1985,* sous la direction de S. Dulucq et O. Goerg, 107–113. Paris: l'Harmattan, collection "Villes et entreprises."

Locoh, T. 1988. "L'analyse comparative de la taille et de la structure des ménages." *Actes du deuxième congrès africain de population, Dakar, 1988,* Union Internationale pour l'Etude Scientifique de la Population 2:17–40.

Lututala, M. 1988. "Aspects démographiques de l'urbanisation en Afrique: la dynamique de la croissance due aux migrations et au mouvement naturel." *Actes du deuxième congrès africain de population, Dakar, 1988,* Union Internationale pour l'Etude Scientifique de la Population UIESP 2:1–16.

Marcoux, R. 1990. "Structure démographique des ménages en milieu urbain africain: analyse des tendances, études du cas malien et approches conceptuelles." *Actes de la conference sur le rôle des migrations dans le developpement de l'Afrique,* Nairobi: Union for the African Population Studies (UEPA) 1:199–213.

Meillassoux, C. 1965. "The Social Structure of Modern Bamako." *Africa* 35:125–142.

Organization de Coopération et de Développement Economiques/Comité Inter-Etats de lutte contre la Sécheresse au Sahel. 1989. *Etude du secteur privé.* Bamako: United States Agency for International Development.

République du Mali. 1988. *Enquête sur l'emploi et le chômage dans le district de Bamako—Avril 1988.* Bamako: Minsitère de l'emploi et de la fonction publique et de l'emploi. Office de la main-d'oeuvre, Projet Programme des Nations Unies pour le Développement/Bureau international du Travail.

———. n.d., a. *Bamako. Recensement 1958.* Enquête démographique 1960–61. Bamako: Service de la statistique.

———. n.d., b. *Enquête sur le secteur informel, 1989.* Bamako: Ministère du Plan, Direction Nationale de la Statistique et de l'informatique, Programme des Nations Unies pour le Dévelopment/Banque Mondiale.

———. n.d., c. *Déclaration de la politique nationale de population du Mali.* Bamako: Ministère du plan et de la coopération internationale, Direction nationale de la planification.

Villien-Rossi, M.-L. 1966. "Bamako, capitale du Mali." *Bulletin de Institut Fondamental d'Afrique Noire* 28:249–380.

Wane, H-R. n.d. *Les variables démographiques dans les plans de développement du Mali,* document de travail, Centre d'Etudes et de Rechenches Sur la Population pour le Développement (CERPOD) de l'Institut du Sahel.

15

Morocco

Robert Escallier

At the beginning of the twentieth century, rural society dominated the political, social, and economic life in Morocco. Cities were relatively unimportant, having only 7 percent of the population; the urban centers were few (27) and of modest sizes. Only one ranked among big cities: Fez, with around 100,000 inhabitants. Near the end of this century, the picture is very different: almost one out of every two Moroccans resides in town. The urban framework has grown considerably, to more than 250 urban centers. Dominated by the coastal conurbation Casablanca-Rabat-Kenitra of four million people, it includes some thriving regional cities. The centers of power have moved. They have acquired a strategic place of their own in the modern nation's politics due to the crucial stake they represent.

The marked modification of Morocco's population distribution and the passing from rural to urban have occurred along with the political, economic, and social changes imposed by recent history, colonization and independence, the forces of the market, and recent modernization. Urbanization of the Moroccan society is visible everywhere, even though a great inequality subsists between the ''central'' regions and some ''peripheral'' spaces that were, until recently, poorly integrated with the geosystem and little affected by the urban economy. The numerous signs it projects are not unequivocal or without ambiguity and contradiction and justify this question: Is urban growth the result of an internal necessity, an adjustment between a productive structure and the spatial distri-

Translated from the original French text by John Giron.

bution of the population, or is it the troubled expression of alienation caused by the forced disruption of exogenous modernization too difficult to assimilate and to control?

URBANIZATION: A CONSTRAINING ENVIRONMENT

In spite of the crisis involved in feeding people in economic difficulties caused by opening of the international market, the Moroccan cities remained, until the founding of the protectorate in 1912, structural places with a strong sociospatial cohesion.

With the assertion of a new logic and a new space development, the new city (the colonial ''villeneuve'') imposed its power of commanding and rejected on the margin the medina, particularly in the urban centers located in the heart of the colonial mechanism of domination and control. The colonial urbanization model, whose logic was based on the extroverted character of the modern economy, was distinguished by the strong spatial selection of the urban occurrence and the downgrading of traditional cities (Fez, Marrakesh, Sale) abandoned in part by the new relational flows. As traumatizing as was colonialism, urbanization nevertheless took place at a moderate rhythm, and cities then maintained a certain amount of control over their growth.

World War II started a more complex period rich in upheaval. The unstructuring-restructuring mechanism greatly accelerated, and the constraints weighing on the future of cities became considerably heavier.

DEMOGEOGRAPHY AND THE DEMOGRAPHIC EXPLOSION

Morocco retains a dynamic demographic behavior characteristic of the Arabic cultural pattern, with the natural annual growth rate estimated at 2.76 percent during 1971–82, and it continued at 2.4 percent in 1987. The demographic transition is distant from its term. The low variant population projections show from 34 to 35 million inhabitants in the year 2007, with the Moroccan population having multiplied seven times within one century. Certainly, the quantitative threshold toward which Morocco is moving is problematic.

Indeed the drop in fertility is very much involved in urbanization in Morocco, particularly in the urban environment (the synthetic index is 2.85 children per woman compared to 5.97 in the rural environment in 1987). However, the Moroccan city still confronts a strong endogenous growth (1.8 percent in 1987).

Through migration, cities have won a growing part of the country villages' natural population increase (about two-thirds in the period 1960–82 but nearly 75 percent by 1987). However, the rural population has increased steadily, and the number working in agriculture has more than doubled in the last sixty years. In fact, the occupational density of agricultural land has increased noticeably, and rural overpopulation affects a large number of regions. Thus, the rural density growth happened without a noticeable increase of agricultural productivity. It is useless to insist here on the reasons of this negative evolution: durability of nonegalitarian agrarian structures, lack of interest from the authorities concerning traditional agriculture, poor technical training, the seizure of the rural areas by the cities, and the situation made inferior for the fellah (farmer or small land owner).

Thus, the rural society crisis and the demographic pressure crisis combined have generated powerful migratory currents that have attracted large numbers of uprooted country people to the cities. Cities with limited production potentials, unable to integrate thousands of newcomers, have been subjected to the serious effects of neo-urbanization.

Urban population growth comes from two divergent sources: a strong endogenous growth from natural increase and migration from the country. Thus, urban growth becomes very difficult to control. In just a few years the urban population has doubled: from 3.4 million in 1960 to 8.75 million in 1982 (Table 15.1). The urban population projection for the year 2000 is nearly 17.5 million inhabitants (United Nations, 1989). However, as delicate as it is to manage, the urban question in North Africa is far remote from the massive problems facing the urban areas of the nations of black Africa.

URBAN INFLATION AND THE EXPLOSION OF NEEDS

Population growth increases various needs because of unsatisfied demands and the unfulfilled aspirations of families for their consumer well-being. New perceived needs are not being met in spite of the undeniable economic well-being during the last few decades, and of achievements in such sensitive domains as health, education, and habitations that remained incomplete and neglected. Thus, the gap between the necessities and unattained family needs is the source of tensions, and the concentration of the population in the city has resulted in intense social and cultural perturbations.

The city expresses the ambiguity and the distressing modernity of these tensions. The fundamental needs and the desires of city dwellers make the government one of the main suppliers of family needs. However, the economic crisis and the policy of thrift inspired by the Fonds Monetaire International (FMI) (reducing public subventions and stopping the hiring in public services) have limited the financial resources of the state-the-purveyor, and the basic needs have gone unmet. The explosions of normalized and unsatisfied needs are met by shortages and frustrations, obviously.

MAJOR ECONOMIC FACTORS

Morocco's industrial policy is not comparable in scope and in continuity with those of other countries of North Africa. However, one cannot underestimate the degree of industrialization accomplished in the framework of national plan-

Table 15.1
Urban Population of Morocco, 1900–2000

Year	Number of Inhabitants (in Millions)	Average Annual Percentage Increase	Rate Urbanization
1900	.42		8.0
1914	.65	3.18	11.0
1926	.98		12.5
1936	1.45	3.71	15.1
1952	2.65		25.0
1960	3.40	3.18	28.4
1971	5.40		35.0
1982	8.75	4.40	43.0
1990	12.20		48.5
2000	17.50	3.93	55.8

Source: Compiled from United Nations, 1989; CERED, 1987.

ning, thanks to a powerful public sector. Industrial production represents an important part of the gross product (about 37 percent), and the ratio of industrial workers has progressed from 14 percent in 1960 to 25 percent in 1987. In spite of indisputable success and the broadening of the productive base, many questions remain about its future. The ambitious planning of economic diversification has not been entirely achieved, integration has not progressed satisfactorily, the control of the domestic market is incomplete, and technologic dependence remains.

Spectacular projects have been preferred over more diffuse ones carried out on a smaller scale and capable of using the available city manpower. The recent transformations have reinforced the urban economy's fundamental tendencies dominated by commercial transactions and speculation, rather than reinforcing the productive sector. The land rent levied on fellahs has always been a source of profit for the city bourgeoisie.

Land appropriation remains a pillar of the local towns' wealth and power, giving a foundation to the bourgeoisie's desire to reinvest the profit of the land they own into more lucrative activities such as trade and land speculation. A distinct example in the speculation is the Middle-Atlas region involving the bourgeoisie of Fez.

Hypertrophy of business activities is a consistent aspect of the urban economy. The measures to liberalize foreign trade and to encourage foreign investment reinforced these "commercial" orientations.

In fact, the noticeable increase of trading activities (import, export, wholesale, and luxury business) went hand in hand with the increase in the service business (financial institutions such as banks and insurance companies) and the areas of accommodations, transportation, and communication. This expansion, and its related perspectives, led to optimization, through the economic process, of a situation of intermediaries, and a mechanism whose harmful effects are well known: inflation, lowering the purchasing power, and greater social disparities.

In the domain of real estate the speculative tendencies are very intense. Its place has become essential in the capital development strategy of many groups: from the institutional people to the migrant workers. For the holders of capital, real estate investments are tools of fast profit, especially when the pressures of the real estate market are strong. Housing shortages favor the permanent game of the actors in the real estate power.

Real estate investments in urban and suburban zones are matchless. The price increase of a square yard of building property is superior to the rate of inflation. The gap between the increase of building costs and the rise of salaries for workers widens continuously, while the speculative behavior of supplies and retention of stock remain poorly impeded. Finally, the attractiveness of real estate speculation is so overwhelming because government intervention is minimal due to the economic crisis and the national debt.

Although attempts have been made to create land reserves, it was impossible to control the market, and those who dealt in real estate took advantage of this situation. The private ventures that cater to the needs of urban masses are more and more extralegal, as the clandestine housing development caught by the expansion fever overflowing the periphery of cities like Sale, Fez, and Tetouan demonstrates. Migrant workers tend to flood the urban economy and participate in its speculative movement. Many studies have viewed international immigration in the regions of departure. Also studies have sought to determine the effect of real estate investments on the activities of the building industry and public workers and the small related private businesses.

The tendencies that have been detected help explain the tertiary character of the urban economy and the growing discrepancy between production and demographic development. This is confirmed by food supply dependencies even in Morocco where agriculture maintains solid traditions, which proves that more and more cities can survive detached from the productive context of the rural world.

THE MOROCCAN URBAN SYSTEM

Demosocial Foundations of Urbanization

Until the seventies urbanization was mainly the growth of the Atlantic towns which were in the first ranking of the urban hierarchy. Since then, smaller towns have experienced faster rates of growth, while some peripheral semirural zones, considered backward, are having astonishing urban explosions.

The spatial enlargement of the urban agglomerations and the rapidity of the urbanization process emanate from various factors. The government is intervening, anxious to apply programs of regional integration and social control. The administrative remodeling and the intensification of the network have created new economic and social dynamics and have given birth to new types of city-to-country interrelationships. The modernization of regional spaces has encouraged diversification of activities for small and medium-sized towns.

Greater fluidity of spaces (caused by the opening of regions) has led to the expansion of centers with strong trade nuclei and with marketplaces (*souks*), roads, and built-up areas.

International industry and tourism do not represent dynamic vectors for regional urbanization. However, external migration was a remarkable stimulant for these regions and cities. The good fortune of the return of migrant guest workers abroad means the expansion of construction and work-related building, the opening of new businesses, the implantation of private services and better equipment, transformation of centers brutally facing the effects of modernization, and new patterns of consumption. Urban explosion is everywhere spectacular, in the plain of Souss as well as in the mountains of Rif.

Urbanization, with intensification of trading and domination of rural elements by city groups, has transformed rural society. The loss of consistency of the social body has induced the blooming of migratory currents toward the cities.

Table 15.2
Net Migration from the Country to the Cities, 1900–87

Period	Average Annual Volume	Percentage of Rural Population
1900-1912	7,800	1.6
1912-1926	11,400	2.2
1926-1936	17,300	3.0
1936-1952	29,000	4.3
1952-1960	45,000	5.6
1960-1971	86,000	9.5
1971-1982	123,000	11.4
1987	271,000	17.0

Source: Compiled from EDN, 1990.

Migration and Urbanization

There are few city dwellers who do not have recent country ancestry. The rural roots of city dwellers are major data of the economic and social reality of cities. The new way to adapt to city living involves a radical change.

In terms of flow, the acceleration of the rural exodus was spectacular in 1987, as nearly ten times as many moved annually during the years 1936–52 (Table 15.2). For example, the National Demographic Survey of 1986–88 gave a city-country movement of 271,000 people for 1987, a remarkable figure that would cancel many hypotheses and analyses. The rural society crisis deepens each year and leads to the brutal loss of large fractions of the rural population to cities. Thus, the rural immigration rate has sharply progressed from an annual average of 11 percent between 1971 and 1982 to 17 percent in 1987 (Table 15.3).

The rate of urban growth is probably faster than anticipated in the urban population projection of 3.6 percent for the years 1987–92 (CERED, 1986) in spite of the decline of fertility. In fact, Morocco has registered again at the end of the eighties (as in 1936 to 1952) a preponderantly exogenous form of urban growth. Will the 1993 census reinforce those tendencies, whose implications would be severely significant for all life circles?

Complex Patterns of Urban Growth

The rural exodus remains the major migratory flow, representing 41 percent of all movements. This fact should not overshadow the emergence of a new,

Table 15.3
Moroccan Migrants in the Year 1987

Origin	Urban	Rural	Destination Morocco	Foreign	Total
Urban	290,000	103,000	393,000	45,000	438,000
Rural	374,000	148,000	522,000	26,000	548,000
Morocco	664,000	251,000	915,000		
Foreign	27,000	5,000	32,000		
Total	691,000	256,000	947,000		

more complex migratory system which demonstrates that a superior level of sociospatial organization has been attained. Morocco has entered a new phase in the transaction of spatial mobility corresponding to the blooming of new ordinary forms of mobility: migration between cities (nearly a third of migrants in 1987), descending or lateral migration, movement tied to life cycles (migration of retirees) to emphasize the interdependence of spatial mobility with the other forms of social mobility (occupational, matrimonial).

The diversity of migratory flows implicates one of the urban dynamics, as it induces the acquisition of new characters of "being in a city" up to the smaller centers where the ferments of social recomposition are stirring.

Economic Foundations of the Urban System

Graft traditions and colonial heritage are not negligible, but with independence in the seventies, government action brought a noticeable transformation in industrial structures. While maintaining the former options (agricultural foodstuff), the will for development of the industry for exportation is asserting itself.

Both the improvements in technical capabilities of the Atlantic ports (Casablanca, Mohammedia, Safi) and the creation of the new port for phosphate at Yorf-Lafsar are efforts to build an important sector of the chemical industry.

In attempts to spread industries nationally, the government plans called for building more than 30 industrial complexes in the 1980s. In spite of the advantages granted foreign investors, the industrial space in Morocco has not been restructured. It remains a phenomenon without any real diffusion effects and incapable of stimulating the regional surroundings. Without any significant intensification of interindustrial exchanges, some sectors of industry are operating only because of their imports.

The industrial Casablanca-Kenitra urban compound remains the only large industrial park. In a space of about 2,000 square kilometers are reunited two-thirds of the industrial production and nearly 70 percent of the industrial employment, mainly in the Casablanca-Mohammedia area (more than 150,000 jobs and 2,200 firms in the early nineties).

INCREASED COMPLEXIFICATIONS OF THE NATIONAL ECONOMIC SYSTEM

The integration of the Moroccan economy with the world market is assisted by the progress of technology and industry in meeting the consumer's demand. This leads to the greatest complexity of the spatial structure by its modernizing activities. Its intervention acts in the direction of seeking economic efficiency for helping the firms. That means that measures must be taken to optimize the chances of the market. Thus, the modernization of circulatory infrastructures allows firms to broaden and unify their market altogether. Thus, the jacking-up of the state bureaucracy particularly the central services, reinforces the impulse of the state control apparatus. In this domain, its action favors the mechanism of economic concentration: the weight of Casablanca, the metropolis, in finance, industry, and commerce. By the same token, to satisfy the population's demands for various services and equipment, the state must favor a better regional integration and seek a better spatial justice. Thus, it must become the distribution agent of decultural modernity. The proliferation of administrative districts—16 provinces in 1959, 34 provinces and prefectures in 1977, and 57 in 1991—vastly complicates the conduct of government.

The expanded activities of a reinforced public tertiary mark the towns' scenery where federal workers and their families settle down carrying new values, with new private services and new businesses. These upgraded towns represent new poles structuring the regional space where networks and flows converge. The urban explosion of the new provincial capitals is certainly spectacular. A similar expansion of the same scope took place in the cities in the highest urban and administrative hierarchy. The strengthening of the public's training and control function has benefited Rabat-Sale.

The management of a complex and diversified system (economic and spatial) in the Casablanca metropolis has created multiple supports for equipment and infrastructure with the help of modern techniques of information. For example, in 1985, 54 percent of the public subscribers to the telex in Morocco were there. This has led to the establishment of high-level services and companies specializing in the needs of industry. Most financial institutions are grouped in Casablanca, and most industries have their head offices there. The concentration of all this industrial might makes this Atlantic conurbation the pivot of national space organization.

Regional Imbalances

Spatial implications of the growth patterns are that the regional disparities are deepening. One of the industrialization's objectives was to correct the inherited imbalances. However, after years of efforts, results are very disappointing. Industry's diffusion remains unequal, for investments and job opportunities are still concentrated in the central Atlantic zone, which remains very strong. The low degree of industrial integration increases the government's difficulties in trying to energize the regional economy. The authorities are prisoners of a fundamental contradiction: how to attract private capital (domestic or foreign) while avoiding taking coercive measures that discourage investments. Furthermore, in the current period, characterized by a weakening of the interventionist capacity, the government is not inclined toward the implementation of measures advancing industrial deconcentration.

Although the factory has not penetrated the regional peripheral environment, the diffusion of "modernity" and new practices turns out to be without limitation and stimulates profound changes. The generalization of the market economy, the improvement of roads, the rapid increase in the number of vehicles, the tightening of administrative controls—everything works toward a change in the traditional relations. In this context, the traditional regional organization is disappearing. Rural areas are more and more tied to the nearest city and, through its mediation, more closely integrated to the market. Rural society is organized into a hierarchy including a fringe of relatively well-to-do landowners, transportation contractors, shopkeepers, and a mass of marginalized cut off from the means of production. Just as the information revolution helped people realize that living conditions were mediocre for the majority, sociospatial inequality is more and more difficult to tolerate. New demands, particularly for equipment (school, dispensaries, water, electricity), cannot be fulfilled, so the propensity to emigrate to the cities is increasing. Migrations also reveal the social destructuring process and regional imbalances.

Evolution of the Moroccan Urban System

The Atlantic megalopolis of Casablanca and its Mohammedia appendix has about 26 percent of Morocco's city dwellers: there were 2.2 million inhabitants in 1982 and perhaps 4.6 million inhabitants by the year 2000 according to a daring projection (United Nations, 1989). Unquestionably, the urban concentration may appear to be less than in many other Arab countries. The spatial dissociation between the state control of Rabat-Sale and the economic power of Casablanca has avoided frequent macrocephalization of the central coastal zone. The megalopole Casablanca-Mohammedia-Rabat-Sale and Kenitra crushes the urban national network by its demographic, economic, social, political, and cultural weight and distorts the territorial organization. No counterweight capable of slowing down the coastal concentration exists.

Weaknesses of Intermediate Cities

The stratum of cities with regional vocations is well represented (16 cities between 100,000 and 500,000 inhabitants in 1991), showing major regional capitals (Fez, Marrakesh) and the emergence of other major poles. Yet intermediate cities have seen the weakening of their hold on the regional space and of their command power. In losing their autonomy of decision making and their control of regional production and being unable to perform as service and distribution centers of wealth, these cities have merely become relays of the central metropolitan space. The strengthening of the political power, the beefing up of superior activities, and the development of national executives, all have contributed to the bypassing of regional cities.

Regions have become more accessible with increasing speed in transportation, which facilitates the direct shipping of regional production through exportation and transformation centers. The tendency toward the concentration of industrial activities and the requirement to combine on the same space the high-level services have led to a strong opposition between the "metropolis" and the ''intermediate'' city. The former gets the riches and the latter endures the phenomenon of disinvestment strongly illustrated in the case of Fez and Marrakesh. Thus, the development of productive forces and modernization ends up, thanks to a cumulative process, to the establishment of a system of flux where space implications are exceptionally regional.

The Recent Transformation of the Model

The following three main features of the model stand out: the spatial broadening of the urban scene, the increasing proliferation of small and average-size towns, and the relative weakening of the growth of big cities.

All regions are now affected by urbanization, but the peripheral underurbanized zones have recorded the steadiest growth rates, such as the mountainous and arid regions south of Agadu at Figuig and the central plateau of the Middle-Atlas. Numerous flows run through most of these regions—capital from emigrés, industrial goods, innovations, men (rural exodus and descending migration)—and form converging points that crystallize urban functions. The new centers innervate the entire regional spaces.

The regional centers of attraction absorb the rural exodus and partially reduce the flow to the cities. This pattern reveals a new social and economic dynamism rooted in the heart of the Moroccan space and perhaps some new forms of mobility induced from the changes of its way of life. However, the strained rate of growth of small and average-size towns demonstrates its own economic dynamism as well as a critical situation in the rural world: the arrival of the rural people, which creates many problems in the labor market.

Between 1971 and 1982 there was a relative weakening of the dynamism of big cities—only Agadir and Khouribga had above-average net migration rates. These changes occurred at the advantage of small and average-size towns. The development of migrants by categories of centers reveals noticeable changes in these tendencies.

In the sixties the large cities were draining three-quarters of the migrants, the Atlantic conurbation more than half in its area and the economic metropolis three-tenths, as they represented for most migrants the only places of efficient urbanization, offering the best chances of employment. For example, the 1971–82 period demonstrates that the small and average-size towns attracted 55 percent of the total migrants. Cities of 20,000 to 50,000 inhabitants had spectacular gains of more than 12 percentage points, far superior to the Casablanca metropolis.

Some regional towns like Marrakesh and Tangiers recorded increases in the number of net migrants, while others such as Fez, Meknes, Safi, and Khourigba suffered sharp losses, one major factor being the development of the Atlantic conurbation (Casablanca-Rabat-Kenitra). While this conurbation's economic potential remains powerful—with three-fourths of the nation's wholesale business, the majority of the bank headquarters, and some tertiary activities at a superior level centered there—this Atlantic conurbation received fewer migrants in 1971–82 than in 1960–71, a considerable decline. Certainly, this is an important shift.

The weakening of the power of attraction reflects certain regional readjustments to national development policies. However, the dynamics of towns located in irrigated zones, of regional centers with strong emigration, and of several provincial capitals suggest definite population shifts. One must also consider the sociospatial homogenization to the plan of equipment and services and the difficulties of integration for migrants lacking the favorable adjustment characteristics within the economics of the big cities.

THE NEW URBAN ECONOMY

During the colonial phase cities were exclusively at the service of the dominant European group. They had a totally extroverted supervision of the colonial agricultural system. There were collection centers for farm products and mineral resources but rarely for centers of transformation. At that time the urban network configuration was closely tied to farming and mining exploitation zones, and the urbanization of the "useful Morocco" contrasted with the backwardness of the urban scene in peripheral zones.

The postcolonial urbanization phase revealed the effects of the demographic transition and of the restructuring of rural societies. Since colonial cities did not enjoy some fundamental new initiatives in the economic domain, they faced a strong eruption of unemployment and underemployment. The current phase of urbanization corresponds to the implantation of new activities generated by national construction and economic growth; however, the diversification and intensification of the task have not obliterated the imbalance between job suppliers and demands.

In the cities pressures on the labor market are very high. They increase as young people reach working age, a result not only of the demographic transition but also of the eviction of youth from school and the progress of women in the workplace. The rate of feminization of the economic population increased from 11 percent in 1971 to 26 percent in 1986. The unemployed population is very young, with nearly a third of those out of work in the ages of 15–24. The unemployment rate of 16 percent in 1986 has been relatively stable over the years although it increased noticeably among women and among youths. This has resulted in delayed female participation in urban work activities and an increased number of applicants for jobs. Beyond a certain threshold the unemployment curve levels, whereas the underemployment curve straightens. The weight of unemployment, waiting for work, seeking a temporary job, the precariousness of employment with low wages and poor working conditions—these deeply characterize the insecurity of all urban life, all the more so since the image of privileged people enjoying a "modern" job, well paid with access to a plentiful supply of consumer goods, is everywhere present.

Work has lost its social significance and fails to reward the artisan, the workman, and the apprentice with the meaning of his position within the organization. The heterogeneousness of all forms of activity is evidence of a generalized underemployment. Unemployment "in disguise" reflects all aspects of the tertiary sector of low productivity and revenue.

The lightness of industrial employment and the inability of the economy to integrate the city dwellers of active age into modern productive structures explain the formation of a large unstructured and informal sector which accounts for nearly 60 percent of the active population. Its characteristics include an inflexibility to adapt, an uneasiness of mobilizing savings, and a reluctance in balancing a good functioning of the urban system. Without doubt this unstructured sector reflects one of the most pertinent explanations of resistance of the Moroccan social formation to the urban crisis.

THE MODERN URBAN SECTOR

From a functional point of view the urban model of organization corresponds to the booming of the metropolitan area, accumulating all the functions of a space macro-organization and bearing a marked influence on the whole Moroccan territory. Obviously, the small towns guarantee the social training and supervision of local populations and provide the service needs of rural producers. The establishment of new activities such as public tertiary and various other activities induced in small towns justifies this logic. Therefore, the number of people, businesses, and private services expands rapidly, and the flows of transportation accelerate in the new subregional centers. However, this urban "administrative" development appears to be a bit fragile for centers whose only foundations are the public tertiary and its by-products. As public investments spread out quickly toward limited thresholds, the employment situation is likely to deteriorate further unless other productive activities are introduced to support the economic foundation.

The management of the geosystem is imposing to the main cities of the urban hierarchy and the reinforcement of the commanding and decision-making functions which beef up the high-level specialized activities. The central functions—political, commercial, and economic management including reception, communication, and leisure—are accountable for the creation of a multitude of public and private jobs, particularly the highly qualified positions (legal counsellors, research consultants, engineers, and computer specialists). Thus, the number of positions for the superior tertiary increased considerably in Casablanca, with the "fundamental" tertiary in 1984 growing by more than 110,000 people (Kaioua, 1985). This rapid increase in social categories of high income create consumption needs that continuously grow and weigh on the evolution of society and the space in large cities. In comparison, the activities of regional towns lack diversification especially, and the negative effect of the nonexistence of industrialization is added to the lack of investments.

In 1976 the Department of Industry announced that there were 6,674 industrial jobs in Marrakesh. A survey taken at the same time revealed that the traditional craft industry employed 17,225 artisans (30 percent of the active population). Indeed, the situation in Marrakesh appears exceptional, especially when the report indicates a large underestimation of craft industry employment in such surveys. The traditional craft industry still represents a relatively powerful sector of employment for many Moroccan towns.

Production in the craft industry has also changed on the organizational level with the dismantling of corporations and the marginalization of the regulatory agent's ability. In spite of attempts from authorities to generate confidence—for example, encouraging measures like administrative and financial aid (certain of production cooperatives for all transactions)—the craft industry is experiencing major difficulties and fails to provide decent incomes to the mass of its workers.

The technical production organization gives prominence to its dependence vis-à-vis the industry for the supply of raw materials as well as machinery (in many instances simple transfers of the obsolete material from the industry area to the artisan area). With the exception of a few branches, conditions are such that most artisans, because of insufficient funds, find themselves subordinate to merchants. These merchants, as intermediaries, have monopolies of raw materials and fix the retail prices of finished products. Caught in the trap, production artisans encounter great difficulty in developing common strategies that would enable them to chart the economic survival of their businesses.

Clearly the social hierarchy is no longer based on tradition and the respect of codified rules. Now the relations between employers and workers (often just simple apprentices) are mostly subject to a despicable type of exploitation. Frequently underage children work, frequently employers lack insurance coverage, and without formal codification, workers are paid by the piece and discharged when new orders are insufficient. Craft industry work does not provide the numerous immigrants incomes that guarantee them a satisfactory economic and social integration. More often the escape of the craft industry to its former model becomes "junk like" or gets diluted in the urban space to become another form of the invading informal sector.

The expanding nonstructured sector now accounts for 57 percent of all jobs in Morocco. Small production workers (including traditional artisans) hold 52 percent of the jobs, with retail businesses accounting for 23 percent and services 21 percent. However, there is no comparable survey similar to the 1981 Tunisian study which would measure the share of the added value to the manufacturing branches of small retail businesses and services in Morocco. Certainly, it is important that authorities in the National Accounting Office recognize this reality (Charmes, 1986).

The informal sector "residual," with its characteristically low income, illustrates the weight of "marginal" social categories (Escallier, 1984). Nevertheless, this subsistence sector cannot hide its dynamics. For instance, recently published monographs in small towns revealed that the income received from nonprestigious activities (such as jobber nonsedentary activity) was substantially higher than commonly believed. As the income of "modern" contractors (in textiles, clothing, leather, wood, and furniture) is generally much higher than the average of those in the structurized sector, it is urgent that authorities reconsider the role of this sector within the urban economy. Finally, is it better to consider it as a simple "regulator" of the "urban crisis" or to analyze it in terms of development potential in a phase of "transitional" urbanization?

REFERENCES

Centre d'Etudes et de Recherches Démographiques. (CERED). 1986. *Analyses et tendances démographiques au Maroc.* Centre d'Etudes et de Recherches Démographiques. Direction de la Satistique. Rabat.

———. 1987. *La dynamique des centres urbains au Maroc 1960–1982.* Direction de la statistique. Rabat.

Charmes, J. 1986. *Emplois et revenus dans le secteur non structure des pays du Maghreb et du Machrek.* Social Science Research Council. Near and Middle East Committee. Tutzing République Fédérale Allemande (RFA).

Enquète Demographique Nationale (EDN). 1990. *Enquête démographique Nationale 1986–1988. Rapport préliminaire.* Direction de la Satistique. Rabat.

Escallier, R. 1984. *Citadins et espace urbain au Maroc.* Urbanisation du Monde Arabe (URBAMA). Centre National de la Recherche Scientifique (CNRS) Tours: Fasc de Recherches 8 et 9.

Kaioua, A. 1985. "Casablanca: Gestion économique et polarisation de l'espace. Essai d'analyse du pouvoir de commandement." *Bulletin de la Societe languedocienne de Geographie. Actes de Colloque* "Les metropoles du Monde Arabe." No. 2–3:249–276.

United Nations. 1989. *Prospects of World Urbanization, 1988.* Population Studies No. 112. New York: United Nations.

16

Nigeria

S. I. Abumere

Nigeria is clearly one of the leaders on the African continent in terms of urbanization. In the first place, unlike in many countries in Africa, urbanization in Nigeria dates back far before the colonial period. When urbanization is defined by the number of African settlements with populations above certain thresholds, Nigeria is far and away the most urbanized. Even when we look at other indicators of urbanization such as percentage of total population which is urban or the rate of growth of the urban population, the country ranks among the very top leaders.

A large body of literature exists on urbanization in Nigeria (Mabogunje, 1965, 1968; and Ayeni, 1983). This chapter provides new insights and interpretations even in view of enormous data problems. The only Nigerian census which provided meaningful data for urban analysis was in 1952 and was elaborately utilized by A. L. Mabogunje (1968). The 1963 census provided very little urbanization information. It was, of course, the last census held in the country, and it serves as the source of the data currently being used by the government and researchers.

This chapter also explores the temporal and spatial patterns of Nigerian urbanization. Explanations for the contrasting structure and characteristics of Nigerian cities will be considered. Finally, the chapter will discuss the categorization of Nigerian centers by utilizing different criteria. Then, the enormous problems posed by increasing urbanization in Nigeria will be considered. This last issue warrants attention because Nigeria is a country where urbanization evidently went wrong.

TEMPORAL PATTERNS

One of the remarkable features of Nigerian urbanization is its antiquity. Many urban centers existed in the precolonial era of Nigeria. One must, however, recognize three distinctive periods of urbanization, namely, the precolonial, colonial, and postcolonial. The size, distribution, causal factors, and structure of the urban centers differ significantly in these periods.

Precolonial Urbanization

Northern and southwestern Nigeria were the main areas of precolonial urbanization, with urbanization in the southeast dating mainly back no further than the colonial period.

In northern Nigeria, the origins of the urban centers can be traced back to the ninth, sixteenth, seventeenth centuries during the great Sudanese empires of Ghana, Mali, and Songhai, respectively (Mabogunje, 1968). Such towns as Kano, Zaria, Katsina, Kukawa, Yerwa (Maiduguri), and Daura prospered from the trans-Saharan trade of the period by exporting handicraft goods, dyed cloths, and leather goods to north Africa and in turn importing salt and metals, especially copper. The Fulani *Jihad* of the nineteenth century added two important urban centers, Sokoto and Gombe, which served as headquarters of the military campaigns.

Just as the growth of northern Nigerian precolonial towns resulted from the trans-Saharan trade, growth of the southwestern towns was traceable to the Atlantic trade of the Europeans, first of slaves but later of such legitimate merchandise as palm oil and kernels. However, the southwestern towns originated from the waves of migrants in the area from the seventh century onwards. These towns grew through the depopulation of surrounding villages and forced movement of their populations into towns (Mabogunge, 1968). The advent of the transatlantic trade, which promoted the growth of southern towns, also brought the decline of the northern towns. Indeed, the reorientation of trade from the north (north Africa) to the south (Europe) brought about all sorts of socioeconomic consequences in Nigeria, among them the present-day disparity in levels of economic development between north and south Nigeria.

The populations of these precolonial towns, in the absence of census figures, may be garnered from the notebooks of early explorers who visited some of the urban centers at the time. Mabogunje (1968) has done extensive work in this regard, collating the figures of these European explorers. From the records of such explorers as Richard Lander (1825–27), Bath (1851–55), Clapperton (1825–27), Hinderer (1857), and Reverend Mann (1853), Mabogunje (1968) estimated the mid-nineteenth-century populations of selected Nigerian precolonial towns (Table 16.1).

Defining an urban center as a settlement with at least 20,000 population, Table 16.1 shows 25 towns in Nigeria by the middle of the nineteenth century, with

Table 16.1
Mid-Nineteenth Century Populations of Precolonial Nigerian Towns

Town	Population (000)	Town	Population (000)
Sokoto	120	Argonu	30
Ibadan	100	Addo	20
Abeokuta	100	Deegoa	30
Ilorin	70	Kiama	30
Zaria	40-50	Oke-Odan	24
Iwo	50	Baebarjie	20-25
Oyo	40	Dikwa	25
Ijebu-Ode	35	Isehin	20
Kano	30-40	Koso	20
Ijaiye	30	Epe	20
Ogbomosho	30	Wawa	20
Ede	30-40	Tabra	20
		Lagos	20

Source: Mabogunje, 1968.

the populations ranging from about 20,000 to 120,000. The relative sizes of the towns have changed significantly since. For instance, Sokoto, which once ranked first in the urban hierarchy, now ranks no higher than 22nd in the current urban hierarchy of the country. Lagos, which previously ranked among the lowest, now ranks first.

The combined population of the 25 urban centers in Table 16.1 is about 975,000 (see Mabogunje, 1968).

The Colonial Period

The immediate impact of the British colonial administration in Nigeria was the reinforcement of urbanization and economic development in the southern areas as a whole. This development occurred in three ways: through its ordering of Nigerian cities, through its preoccupation with the export and import trade, and through its distribution of amenities and developmental infrastructures. These three are not necessarily mutually exclusive and will be discussed together.

In 1917, the colonial administration passed the Township Ordinance, which provided for the creation, constitution, and administration of all towns in Nigeria (Mabogunje, 1968). Three categories of towns were created—first class, second

Figure 16.1
Distribution of First- and Second-Class Towns Classified by the British Colonial Administration in 1919

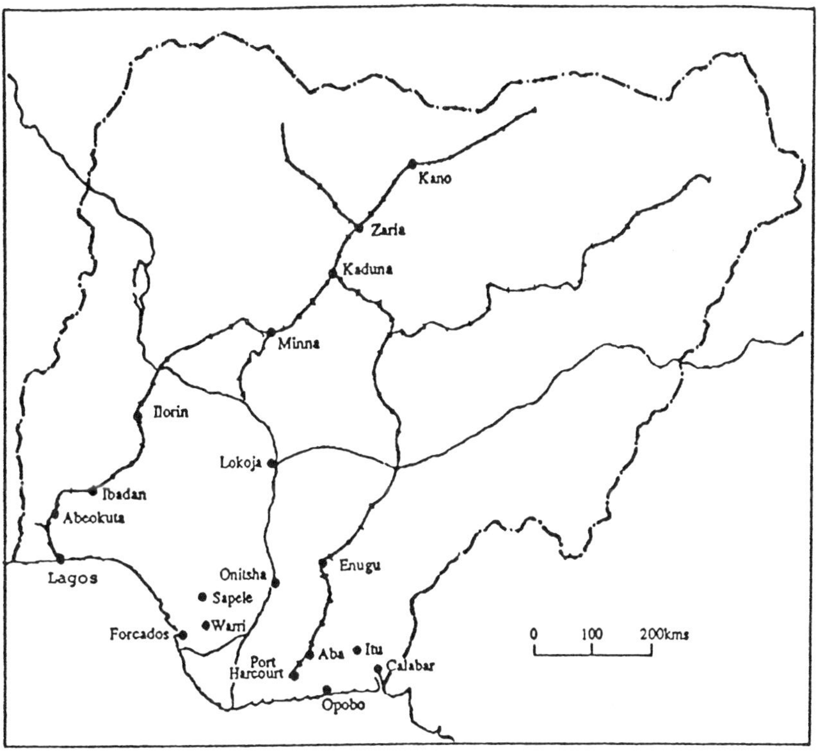

class, and third class. Lagos, the Nigerian capital at that time, was the only first-class town. There were 18 second-class towns, 12 in southern Nigeria and 6 in northern Nigeria. Of the 50 third-class towns, 38 were in the south and 12 in the north. Most towns accorded status in the classifications were either along or close to the coast or along the railway lines which had just then been constructed (Figures 16.1 and 16.2).

It is difficult to pinpoint the factors that may have influenced the colonial administration in developing this township classification. Certainly it was not population size alone; otherwise many third-class towns such as Ijebu Ode and Benin would have been at least second-class towns while unclassified towns such as Ogbomosho and Oshogbo would have qualified as second-class towns. The presence of small centers like Forcados, Itu, and Opobo in Figure 16.1 and Burutu, Koko, Kwale, Brass, Degema, Bonny, Eket, Ankpa, and Ibi in Figure 16.2 means that factors other than population size guided the township ordering. Certainly the traditional status of the towns was not the determining factor, otherwise Ife, Sokoto, and Benin would have qualified as first-class towns.

Figure 16.2
Third-Class Towns Classified by the British Colonial Administration in 1919

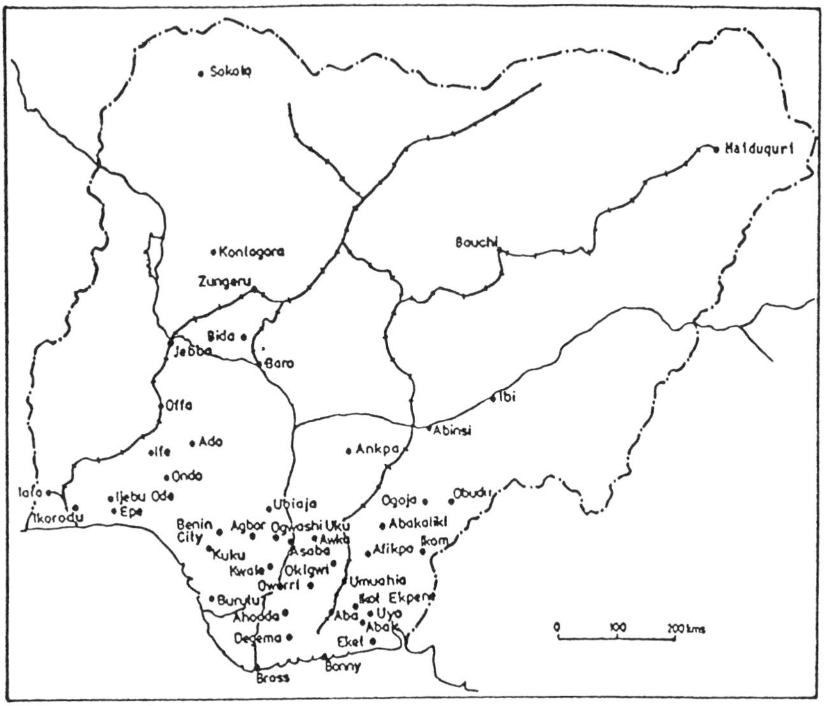

Apparently, proximity to coastal ports was crucial in determining the rating system, which was probably based on the location of the towns with respect to the British export and import trade. For example, Forcados, a small second-class coastal town (Figure 16.1), was so important during the colonial period that until 1914 goods for Lagos, the Nigerian capital, were transshipped from it (Church, 1968). Consequently, proximity to the coast and also a contribution to the export trade were critical factors in the ranking. This contribution may have been measured by the actual production of the exported raw materials, which then were mainly palm oil and kernels obtained from palm oil trees grown only in the rain forest of the south. Also, the rating system was based upon the roles played by collecting centers for raw materials, as well as their roles in the evacuation of these materials through ports or other means of transport. Finally, the roles that centers served, whether as base or headquarters of either the colonial administration officials or indeed the officials of the merchant firms, were other factors that favored southern locations more than northern ones.

Importantly, the township classification guided the colonial administration in the distribution of amenities and other developmental infrastructures. Thus Lagos, the only first-class town, was the first to get electricity in 1896, followed, in turn, by the second-class towns of Port Harcourt, Enugu, and Kaduna in 1929, and Kano and Abeokuta in 1930. Indeed, by 1950, Lagos was the only first-class town with electrical power. Of the 18 second-class towns, 12 had electricity, but only 3 of the 50 third-class towns did.

The same pattern is true of the provision of piped water where, by 1932, 9 of the 12 towns having reasonably good water schemes were either first- or second-class towns. Eight other centers, mostly third-class townships, had smaller water schemes (Mabogunje, 1968:114). The first- and second-class towns also were given high priorities in the distribution of health, educational, and transport facilities. Later, even the distribution of colonial investments in basic industries followed this pattern.

It is therefore clear that the colonial government's emphasis on export trade with the building of roads and communications networks to facilitate it, and its distribution of amenities and infrastructures on the basis of the township classification, resulted in the tremendous growth of southern towns. Thus the colonial period in Nigeria had at least three distinctive consequences for urban growth and development. First, it led to the growth of southern towns at the expense of northern ones. For instance, Sokoto declined from about 120,000 inhabitants in the 1850s to no more than 52,000 by 1952. Second, railway lines were constructed to strategically link areas producing exportable crops. Many flourishing towns not on rail lines such as Oyo and Ijebu Ode declined, while new towns sprang up along the lines such as Kaduna, Port Harcourt, Aba Enugu, and Jos. Third, the colonial period witnessed major changes in the demographic structures of several towns. Those towns on railway lines were found, according to the 1952 census, not just to have gained population through migration but also to have a population with more males than females (Table 16.2), with adult males dominating the population (Ayeni, 1983). Indeed, clearly the old towns off the railway lines not only lost population but also had a population structure with more females than males and more old men than women.

Of tremendous importance during the colonial period was the rise of urbanization in southeastern Nigeria, which hitherto was essentially rural. Four major urban centers emerged during this period in this area, namely, Port Harcourt, Enugu, Aba, and Owerri. Since this modest beginning, urbanization has accelerated in the southeast.

Postcolonial Period

Since independence there has been a reinforcement of the urban patterns of the colonial era. For instance, the advantages which coastal port and southern towns had during the colonial period continued. Industries and other employment-generating activities continued to be concentrated in southern towns, a situation which increased migration into these towns. The Nigerian civil war of 1967–70 again reinforced the existing regional urbanization patterns. Before and during

Table 16.2
Demographic Characteristics of Cities on and off the Railways, 1952

Type of City	Name of City	Total Population	Males as Percent of Total Population	Adult Males as of Percent Total Male
New	Engu	62,764	62.10	63.45
	Aba	57,787	63.40	58.45
	Kaduna	44,540	51.10	61.70
	Jos	38,527	58.40	68.10
Old Towns on Railway Lines	Ibadan	459,196	51.62	45.60
	Oshogbo	122,728	46.10	32.90
	Kano	127,204	50.60	63.78
	Zaria	53,974	51.10	61.78
Old Towns off Railway Lines	Benin City	53,753	52.60	54.50
	Ogbomosho	139,535	45.50	63.10
	Sokoto	51,986	49.00	48.40
	Maiduguri	56,740	51.30	66.30

Source: Compiled from Census Reports, 1952.

Table 16.3
Urban Population Growth in Nigeria, 1850–1963

Population '000	1850s	1921	1931	1952	1963
Total	NA	18,631	19,928	30,403	55,670
Urban (20,000+)	939	1,345	1,431	3,237	10,627
Percent Total	NA	7.2	7.2	10.6	19.1
No. of Centers	25	29	27	56	183

Source: Compiled from Census Reports, 1952, 1963.

the civil war, many southerners fled northern towns, which increased the population of many southern towns.

Table 16.3 summarizes the overall temporal pattern of urbanization in Nigeria from the precolonial to the postcolonial period.

The urban population rose from just under one million in 1850 to about 11 million in 1963, by which time nearly 20 percent of the total population was urban. Correspondingly, the number of urban centers increased from about 25 in 1850 to 183 in 1963. The projected urban population is expected to comprise just over 45 percent of the projected national population of about 130 million by the year 2000, and the number of urban centers may reach 250.

From 1990 projections, it is clear that Nigeria had at least 14 cities with populations of over a million with Lagos, the national capital, topping the hierarchy with about 9 million. There are expected to be at least 18 cities of one million inhabitants by 2,000. Surely, for a developing economy with limited resources, such rapid rates of urbanization must have serious consequences.

Some new towns have been created during the postcolonial period as a result of economic development projects, such as the construction of dams and lakes. The towns of New Bussa (from Kainji dam) and Bakalori (from the Bakalori dam) have been created in this way. Elsewhere in the country, some towns have been created as a result of the establishment of major industrial concerns. Bacita was so created for the sugar industries, while Ajaokuta rose from a steel plant. The construction of the capital city Abuja displaced several villages whose resettlement elsewhere in the country created the towns of New Wuse, New Karu, and New Karshi. In addition to reinforcing the urbanization patterns of the colonial period, the postcolonial period also witnessed the creation and construction of new towns.

SPATIAL PATTERNS OF NIGERIAN URBANIZATION

Urbanization is very unevenly distributed in Nigeria. Whether we define urban centers as settlements with at least 5,000 population (Table 16.4) or at least 20,000 population, it is clear that southwestern Nigeria is by far the most urbanized, followed by northern Nigeria. The same pattern is true when we utilize figures from the 1963 census. Urbanization in eastern Nigeria dates back no further than the colonial period, and the dominant type of settlement here before was rural. The area has recently experienced rapid urbanization, but without census data after 1963, it is difficult to measure it.

The spatial distribution of urban centers in Nigeria conforms to certain aspects of Christallerian hierarchies. For example, the spatial distribution of northern Nigeria towns fitted Walter Christaller's $K = 7$ administrative principle (1933). The regularity noted by Mabogunje is the fact that the smallest urban centers average 20 kilometers apart, while longer distances separated the larger or higher-order urban centers. With respect to spatial or regional planning, this type of urban distribution is of tremendous advantage as it facilitates the spread of economic development across the national space.

SOME ASPECTS OF THE CHARACTERISTICS AND STRUCTURE OF NIGERIAN URBAN CENTERS

Three distinguishing features of Nigerian urbanization will be highlighted in this section: (1) the remarkable size distribution of the urban centers, which

Table 16.4
Regional Distribution of Urban Centers, 1952 (Urban Centers with at Least 5,000 Population)

Urban Size Classes	Western Nigeria	Eastern Nigeria	Northern Nigeria	Total	Total Percent
Over 80,000	7	5	1	8	2.40
40,000-80,000	5	5	7	17	5.12
20,000-40,000	21	5	5	31	9.40
10,000-20,000	26	19	28	73	22.12
5,000-10,000	76	50	74	200	60.80
Total Number	135	79	115	329	100.00
Total Percent	41.3	24.00	34.50	100	

Source: Compiled from Census Reports, 1952.

Table 16.5
Size Classes of Nigerian Urban Centers, 1963

Population size Classes	No. of Cities	Percent
20 - 40,000	115	62.8
40 - 80,000	37	20.2
80 - 160,000	21	11.5
160 - 320,000	8	4.4
Over 320,000	2	1.1
Total	183	100.0

Source: Compiled from Nigerian Population Census, 1963.

certainly conforms to the rank-size rule; (2) the prevalence of a type of duality in several Nigerian cities consisting of a mixture of modernity and traditionalness; and (3) a unique urban structure.

The size distribution of Nigerian cities is shown in Tables 16.4 and 16.5. Smaller towns are much more numerous than larger towns, and city sizes tend to follow in close succession without any gaps. These are the hallmarks of an urban distribution which is truncated lognormal and fits the rank-size rule approximately.

Unlike several African countries with primate cities dominating the entire urban system, there is a clear absence of primacy in Nigeria. Perhaps the administrative decentralization of the country which dated back to the early colonial period played a great role in ensuring that several centers grew simultaneously across the country. Nigeria is a clear case of a developing country whose size distribution of urban centers is truncated lognormal and therefore approximates the rank-size rule.

In many Nigerian cities, duality, as represented by modern and traditional sectors, exists. The modern sector is characterized by employment in industries and other wage-paid employment. Most employment, however, is found in the traditional sector, which some writers have called a "bazaar" sector. It includes casual labor, petty trading, and primary activities such as agriculture and fishing. Indeed, the extraordinary situation in many Nigerian cities, especially in the precolonial cities, is the presence of large proportions of person engaged in primary activities. According to the 1963 census, 30 percent of the population of the city of Ibadan of at least 2 million were engaged in farming. The traditional sector of many Nigerian cities is therefore marked by the prevalence of rural-type activities and practices clearly absent in advanced Western cities.

However, much of the work which passes for employment may in fact be disguised unemployment or underemployment. As economic development occurs in Nigeria, the traditional sector will decrease in size, while the modern sector will expand considerably.

The typical structure of a Nigerian city possesses some unique characteristics which distinguish it from cities in the advanced countries, as well as from cities in other African countries. In models and theories of urban structure, it is generally accepted that low-class residential areas and slums are found in the inner cities in close proximity to the city center or central business district (CBD). These analytical concepts tend to show that fashionable residential areas develop at the city fringes or suburbs, as transportation improves along with income levels to enable middle- and upper-class citizens to live far away from work and noise and then to commute daily. In this respect, the existence of the "fashionable suburbia" is a common feature of many cities in the advanced economies. In many Nigerian cities, however, there is a reversal of this pattern. The suburbs are not high-class residences but slums (Abumere, 1983, 1986). This is true of such important cities as Enugu, Sapele, Jos, Kano, Warri, Lagos, Ibadan, Benin, and Sagamu.

Another distinctive feature of the Nigerian urban structure is the existence of two centers within the cities. The first is the traditional market center, usually in close proximity to the house of the traditional ruler, who may be an Emir or an Oba (Ayeni, 1983). This is the city center, or CBD, of the traditional sector discussed above. The second center is the CBD proper of the modern sector as popularized by the classical urban ecologists (Burgess, 1928).

A third duality is represented by the existence of two sections within the city, namely, old and new sections. In almost all Nigerian cities, the old section of town is occupied by the indigenes, or what Nigerians popularly call "sons of the soil." In this section, land is not regarded as a commodity which can be bought and sold. No matter how much money a prospective buyer offered, he could not buy land in this section unless he were an indigene himself. This, of course, means that today, in many Nigerian cities, it is extremely difficult to find a nonindigene residing in this traditional old section. The indigenes themselves are also often reluctant to move. The result is that the old section of town is often congested. Besides, it is poorly planned with narrow streets and inadequate arrangements for sewage, waste disposal, and general sanitation (Abumere, 1983). If any epidemic were to break out in the city, there is a high probability that it may have started in the old section. In northern Nigeria, this old section where the indigenes live is called *Tudun Wada,* and in many of these cities such as Kano, Zaria, and Bauchi the *Tundun Wada* is enclosed by a high wall to separate it from the rest of the town.

Unlike the old section, the new section is inhabited mainly by migrants, or what Nigerians often call "strangers." The new section of the city is usually better planned and with lower densities than the old section. Moreover, the inhabitants are generally better educated and enjoy a much higher standard of living. Also, the new section usually contains what are called Government Reservation Areas (GRAs), which were creations of the British colonial administration.

The creation of GRAs in Nigeria by the colonial administration is a piece of legislation whose origin properly belongs to the social and environmental events in Europe. In the late eighteenth century in Europe, rapidly increasing urban populations and urban densities resulted in alarming increases in the deleterious impact of infectious diseases on the health, morbidity, and mortality among the people. High incidences of disease infection were generally related to certain districts of the urban area, and this probably gave rise to the theory that diseases were associated with environmental and behavioral conditions among specific social classes, notably the poor and lower classes, which needed to be curbed. These developments in British society and their responses were transferred almost wholesale to British colonies, with the natives cast in the mold of the British lower classes. Thus in 1904, the Cantonment Proclamation, which gave guidelines for the layout, sanitation, and administration of the areas where British administrators and merchants should live, known as the GRA, was issued. The proclamation specified, among other things, how the GRA should be located and segregated from the native areas. When the British left, after independence, wealthy Nigerian administrators and business executives moved into the GRAs. The GRAs in all Nigerian towns have now expanded and prospered far more than they ever did during the colonial period.

It is possible to identify neighborhoods in several Nigerian cities. However, it is impossible to identify class-based neighborhoods common to many Western cities. Even in both the old and new sections of the Nigerian towns discussed above, high, middle, and low classes live in the same neighborhoods, and the only apparent differentiating mark is the size and quality of their residential building. A mansion which would certainly not shame any palace anywhere may be seen side by side with a low-class tenement structure barely passing for a house. Indeed, even in the GRA which approaches the status of a high/middle-class neighborhood, houses of lowly paid public servants are often found along with those of top business executives and multimillionaires. Apparently, social classes have not yet crystallized in Nigeria as in the advanced capitalist societies. Class identity is therefore not yet strong enough to serve as a basis for pursuing common interests or for neighborhood differentiation.

CATEGORIZATION OF NIGERIAN URBAN CENTERS

Nigerian urban centers may be categorized in various ways on the basis of such criteria as age, function, population and areal sizes, form, site and situation, architecture and building materials, culture, proximity to the seacoast, influence fields, and lastly, demographic and socioeconomic characteristics.

With respect to the age criterion, it is possible to identify old or new towns, precolonial, colonial, and postcolonial towns. Using the criteria of population and areal sizes, one may identify isolated dwellings, hamlets, small villages, large villages, small towns, large towns, cities, conurbations, and megalopolises in an ascending order. A functional categorization reveals Nigerian settlements providing mainly industrial, commercial, educational, administrative, and other services. When the criteria of site and situation were used, then one would identify settlements based on the characteristics which they have by virtue of their surroundings (site), whether coastal, highland, swamp, or marshland, or the characteristics they have by virtue of their location in relation to other settlements (situation).

In the literature, the categorization of urban centers has been restricted to two main criteria—population sizes and functions. As a result of the peculiar characteristics of many Nigerian precolonial towns, the use of population sizes might be misleading. There are many Nigerian towns such as Ife, Zaria, and Okene with large populations but with relatively few functions. If a town is to grow and fulfill its role, it must have functions which serve not only its citizens but also those of surrounding rural areas. A town with a large population but without major functions is no more than a large village. In the categorization attempted here, functions will be used rather than population size.

In studies of urban functions, it is usual to identify the basic and nonbasic functions. The basic city-forming functions are usually defined as export-oriented economic activities covering all industries in which the final product is exported out of the particular city. Usually the relative prosperity of a city depends critically on the size of its basic activities. Among such basic functions which a city performs to serve itself and others are industrial services of various kinds especially manufacturing, tertiary education, wholesaling, and specialized medical care services.

The nonbasic or city-serving functions include all locally oriented industries in which the final product is used or consumed within the particular city. Among such nonbasic functions which a city performs for its own residents are food retailing, hair cutting services, and petty trading.

To obtain the urban categories based on functions, data on the availability of 19 basic and nonbasic functions were obtained for the major urban centers in Nigeria. The functions ranged from petrol stations through health and educational facilities to banks and other higher-order functions but excluded manufacturing industries. These functions were then scored from 1 to 5 based on the degree of availability. Finally, total functional scores were obtained for all urban centers of interest. On the basis of these scores, towns were classified into six categories. Only Lagos, the current national capital, and Port Harcourt, a major seaport and the center of petroleum activities in Nigeria, belong to the first category. A second categorization was based on the levels of industrialization, as levels of urban incomes and modernization are heavily influenced by levels of industrialization. Examples of new industrializing countries have shown that industrialization, far more than any other sector, represents one of the fastest ways to achieve rapid economic development. Therefore, the categorization of urban centers on the basis of industrialization is probably the best way to identify which cities will grow rapidly with respect to population and overall economic performance.

To obtain the categorization desired, data on the number of industries in all important Nigeria towns were obtained. A weighting system was derived for the industrial classes such that towns manufacturing capital goods were given more weight than those producing intermediate goods, which were in turn given more weight than those producing consumer durable and nondurable goods. The manufacturing of capital and producer (intermediate) goods was considered the most crucial aspect of industrialization with tremendous capacity for rapid economic development. After the weighting, the total scores obtained for each urban center on all the industrial classes were obtained.

Lagos and Port Harcourt centers in category 1 are highest in the urban hierarchy in Nigeria and constitute the highest-order centers in the Christallerian formulation. Those in category 6 are the lowest-order centers. As one moves from the lower- to the higher-order centers, the number of functions performed by the towns increases rapidly (Table 16.6).

Urban centers were next ranked on population size, functions, and unweighted manufacturing industries. Spearman rank correlation coefficients were obtained, using these rankings. The hierarchies obtained through population size and functions in Nigeria are more highly related than those through population size and manufacturing industries. However, because all correlation coefficients are very high and statistically significant, the results do not differ significantly.

PROBLEMS OF URBANIZATION IN NIGERIA

The rapid urbanization in Nigeria in the last four decades has obviously brought many problems. The problems can be placed in their proper perspective if we

Table 16.6
Relationships between Urban Hierarchies Obtained through Population Sizes, Functions, Unweighted and Weighted Manufacturing Industries

	Population	Functions	Unweighted Mean	Weighted Mean
Populations	1.00	0.84	0.74	0.78
Functions		1.00	0.80	0.82
Unweighted Mean			1.00	0.97
Weighted Mean				1.00

recall that in terms of size and number of urban centers, Nigeria ranks among the most highly urbanized countries in the world. This means that the country has as many urban centers as several advanced economies but only has the resources of a typical developing country. The country's rate of urbanization far exceeds its rate of economic growth. The situation is not enhanced by the fact that many of these cities are preindustrial and thereby require high levels of maintenance. The overall results have been clear for all to see: the country just cannot cope.

A cursory look at many Nigerian urban centers quickly reveals shortages of almost every facility that makes urban living worthwhile. These shortages will increase by the year 2000 when the urban population is projected to be at least 60 million, the number of urban centers with at least 20,000 population at 250, and the number of cities with at least a million inhabitants at about 18. All these major expansions will be happening at a time when virtually all economic indicators will be declining. Already, the downturn in the economy which started a decade ago shows every sign of getting worse. It is usual for many Nigerians to "ignore the colonial litany" and trace all Nigerian urban problems back to the British. Thirty years after independence, however, such passing of the buck is unacceptable.

As far back as 1974, Mabogunje identified four main problems of the Nigerian urban centers. These included employment, liveability, manageability, and serviceability. These problems still exist, but they have since increased in severity. The extraordinary situation is that the resources to cope are fast declining while the magnitudes of the problems are increasing.

With respect to urban unemployment the problem has reached the point of alarm. By 1971, O. Falae (1971) estimated urban unemployment in Nigeria between 5 and 20 percent. Although no recent reliable figures are available, there is probably about 40 percent urban unemployment or more. The problem here, of course, is that since most urban employment in Nigeria is in the informal sector, it is not easy to estimate the magnitudes of employment and unemployment. Already, the consequences of this high urban unemployment have started to be seen in the form of high incidences of crime such as robberies, murders, and proliferation of adulterated goods including patent drugs.

The problem of serviceability is seen in the ever-increasing inability to provide effective urban services such as health, recreation, education, and social services in almost all Nigerian towns. One of the major problems here is insufficient and inadequate housing. The insufficiency is reflected in the extremely high room densities in many Nigerian cities. Overall, for the entire country, the average room density was about 2.4 persons. In Lagos, the national capital, it was as high as 3.5 persons per room, while in other cities such as Benin, Onitsha, and Warri, room densities were at least 3.0 persons. Indeed, of the 40 cities studied, as many as 27 (68 percent) had room densities greater than 2 persons. Since the Nigerian national standard is 2 persons per room, this means that a considerable proportion of Nigerian cities are actually above the national standard. Clearly, the rate of urban population increase far outstrips the rate of housing provision, and the situation will worsen.

Housing shortages, however, are not as serious in Nigeria as are other shortages. Most of the city amenities that people take for granted elsewhere in the world can no longer go around. Apart from the new capital city of Abuja, there is no other city in Nigeria with adequate water supply. The same is true of electricity, telephones, and several other basic necessities.

Luckily, Nigerians have not yet started to worry about the problems of the environment, important though these are especially elsewhere in the world. Otherwise, the heaps of uncleared solid and nonsolid wastes in several Nigerian cities would have been enough to bring a government down. The same is true of air and water pollution and slums, whose magnitudes have probably put them beyond solution this side of the twenty-first century.

Urban management problems in Nigeria center around finance and personnel. For instance, lacking money and personnel, Nigerian cities have been unable to face up to the problem of development control. In city after city, the level of squatter and unauthorized settlement at the city outskirts is extraordinarily high. Many low-income people who cannot afford to live in the city proper simply move to the outskirts and build themselves a shanty. In many cases, the houses consist of walls and roofs made of iron sheets. Without effective development control, these shanties grow at rates even faster than those of the city proper. In the cases of Ibadan and Lagos, such squatter settlements at city outskirts contain no less than 20 percent of the entire city population. Even in the brand-new city of Abuja, which is still being built as Nigeria's future capital city, squatter settlements have already emerged and are growing at such rates that if care is not taken, they may soon engulf the young city.

These shortages can only be resolved if resources are improved or there is a slowdown in the rates of urban growth. Nigeria, however, has never really worried about the problem of rapid urbanization. Policies to slow down the rates of urban growth through slowing down rural-urban migration or directing migrants to small or intermediate cities have never even been thought of. The growth of most Nigerian cities is accounted for mainly by rural-urban migration. In the case of Lagos, 75 percent of its growth is accounted for by this rural-urban migration alone. Migration policies should therefore be helpful. Also helpful would be population redistribution policies that consider the important issue of the mismatch between population distribution and the distribution of resources. At the root of all policies, however, will be the problem of money. In this regard, there is very little that many developing countries like Nigeria can do to solve the problems of rising urban populations and dwindling resources.

CONCLUSION

Urbanization, as the literature shows, is very good for economic development. Indeed, to spread the fruits of economic development across the national space, the role of urbanization can hardly be overemphasized. However, if the growth of urbanization is so high that a considerable proportion of the nation's resources and talents are diverted to solving urban problems, then, clearly, urbanization is an impediment to economic development.

Developing countries must constantly evolve policies which strike a favorable balance between the level of urbanization and the level of economic development. Unless this is done, urbanization may, in the end, spell doom for the country's prospects for economic development. African countries can hardly cope if the rates of urbanization greatly exceed the rates of resource accumulation. In the particular case of Nigeria, urbanization policies are obviously required if the country is to escape massive urbanization problems as well as current debt problems.

REFERENCES

Abumere, S. I. 1983. "City Surface Solid Waste in Nigerian Cities." *Environment International* 9:391–396.

———. 1986. "The Nigerian Urban Environment and the Problem of Slums." *Journal of Environmental Management* 23:125–137.

Ayeni, M. A. O. 1983. "Patterns, Processes and Problems of Urban Development." In *A Geography of Nigerian Development,* edited by J. S. Oguntoyinbo, O. O. Areola, and M. O. Filani, 190–210. Ibadan: Heinemann.

Berry, B. J. L. 1961. "City Size Distribution and Economic Development." *Economic Development and Cultural Change* 9:573–588.

Burgess, E. W. 1928. "The Growth of the City: An Introduction to a Research Project." In *The City,* edited by Robert E. Park, Ernest W. Burgess, and Roderick D. McKenzie, 47–62. Chicago: University of Chicago Press.

Christaller, Walter. 1933. *Die Zentralen Orte in Suddeutschland.* Jena: Fischer.

Church, H. 1968. *West Africa: A Study of the Environment and of Man's Use of It.* New York: Wiley.

Church, Ronald J. H. 1968. *West Africa: A Study of Man's Environment and Man's Use of It.* New York: Wiley.

Falae, O. 1971. "Unemployment in Nigeria." *Nigerian Journal of Economic and Social Studies* 13:59–75.

Hillery, G. A. 1968. *Communal Organizations*. Chicago: University of Chicago Press.

Mabogunje, A. L. 1965. "Urbanization in Nigeria: A Constraint on Economic Development." *Economic Development and Cultural Change* 13:415–438.

———. 1968. *Urbanisation in Nigeria*. London: University of London Press.

———. 1974. "Towards an Urban Policy in Nigeria." *Nigerian Journal of Social and Economic Studies* 16:85–97.

17

Senegal

Philippe Antoine and Gora Mboup

Senegal had about 7.7 million inhabitants in 1992 (6.88 million at the last census in 1988); more than 40 percent of the population live in cities, with one-half in Dakar, the capital. Essentially Sahelian, the country is in the middle of an economic and social crisis. Its economy depends very much on the exportation of raw products such as peanuts and phosphate. Urbanization does not rely on industrialization.

Agriculture, dominated by the production of peanuts, was particularly affected by the drought of recent years and by the fluctuation of the world prices of peanuts; therefore, income in the rural areas has become scarce. Without the diversification of crops, food production is insufficient to feed the population. Rice is a food of first necessity in Senegal and remains mostly imported. The local production of rice fails to meet the needs of the population. The phenomenon of rural exodus is still going on, and the rural population continues to migrate forced by the deterioration of their natural, economic, and social environment.

Data from Dakar, organized by the Office de la Recherche Scientifique et Technique d'Outre-Mer (ORSTOM) and the Institut Fondamental d'Afrique Noire (IFAN), provide an important quantitative inquiry. This inquiry was implemented on a stratified sample of residences (2,100 households spread out in the whole city) to obtain a comprehensive picture of the migratory system and of the economic activities in the city. The inquiry has provided the gathering of migratory, professional, and family biographies of 1,550 individuals (men and

Translated from the original French text by Sarah G. Browning and John Giron.

Figure 17.1
Major Cities in the Republic of Senegal

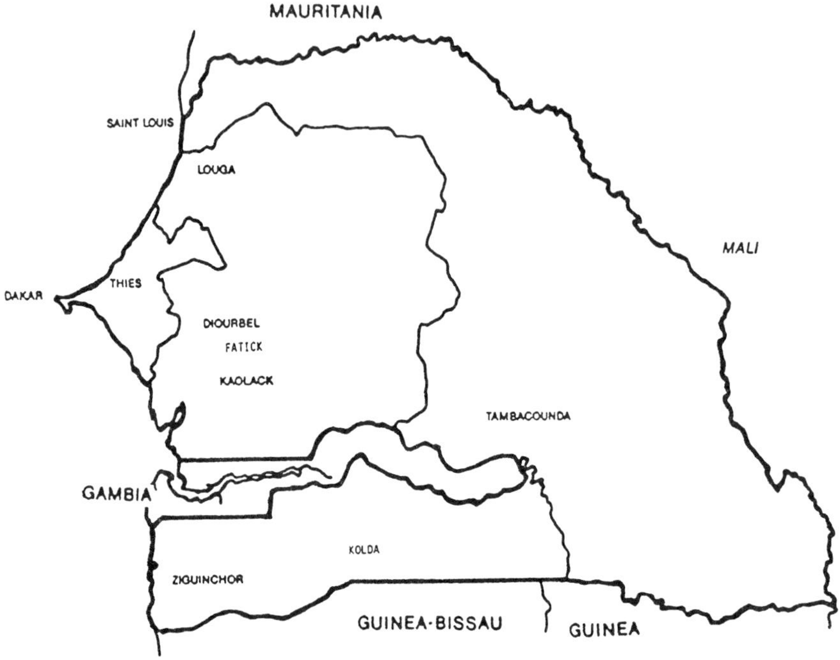

Source: Adapted from Ministére de l'Economie et de Finances, Direction de la Statistique, Division de Enquêtes et de la Démographie and Demographic and Health Surveys, IRD/Westinghouse, 1988: *Enquête Demographique et de Santé au Sénégal, 1986*.

women) to underscore interrelations between moving, the acquisition of employment, and the creation of a home (Antoine et al., 1992).

URBANIZATION IN SENEGAL

The Steps of Urbanization

Colonization gave urbanization the character it still has today. The large cities of today were founded by the former colonial authorities in chosen sites, with functions linked to its needs, and the localization of large urban centers had a great impact: Dakar constitutes the perfect prototype (Figure 17.1).

Urbanization in Senegal went through several phases linked to colonial history (Champaud, et al., 1985). First of all, the towns on the river Senegal, the ports of call, developed along this artery of communication and have carried on particularly the rubber trade (Saint-Louis founded in 1659, Podor, Matam, Bakel). The next phase was marked by the colonization of the whole country, the developing of the culture of peanuts, and the expansion of towns near railroads (between 1885 and 1924). Peanut trading led to a pyramid-like urban network composed of multiple collecting centers and three port outlets: Dakar, Rufisque, and Kaolack.

Independence in 1960 ended the peanut trade, roads supplanted railways, and urban functions were modified. The urban system lost its balance, and through the years, a whole series of factors combined to make Dakar the main urban development pole of the whole country. Dakar's history shows a progressive monopolizing of activities spread out in various parts of the century; the Dakar harbor supplanted those of Saint-Louis and Rufisque. In 1930, Kaolack's port activities were transferred to Dakar. In 1958, Saint-Louis was stripped of its function as Senegal's capital to the benefit of Dakar. Little by little, starting in 1960, Dakar began to monopolize the country's industrial activities, including the peanut oil factories and the wholesale businesses (large business companies shut the doors of their branches located in the inland towns).

The Growth of Dakar

Dakar is the oldest French-speaking city of black Africa. For a long time (seventeenth and eighteenth century or during the whole period of the slave trade) Europeans stayed on the Isle of Goree, facing Cape Verde. In 1857, the French took control of the Senegal coast, and Dakar was established as an urban district, independent of Goree. In 1866, Goree had 3,400 inhabitants and Dakar only a few hundred. By 1891, Dakar already had 18,000 inhabitants and Goree hardly 1,200. In 1885, the railroad from Saint-Louis to Dakar was completed. The great construction works at the Dakar harbor and public buildings were completed during the 1898–1914 period, and Dakar became the capital of the French Western Africa federation. From this time on colonial authorities decided to separate European districts from African descent. In 1915, the native district of the Medina, next to the Plateau, was created. Later, the town expansion took place by consecutive operations of housing developments, especially at the end of World War II, when an attempt was made to implement a new urban policy favoring the integration of the communities.

Dakar's demographic growth rate was 5.8 percent annually between 1921 and 1951; it increased substantially between 1951 and 1961 to 8 percent. Capital of the French West African nations until 1958, Dakar lost its political role in French-speaking Africa at the time of its independence. But the transfer of Senegal's capital from Saint-Louis to Dakar has allowed Dakar to reinforce its prominence among the other towns of Senegal. Between 1955 and 1961 its growth reached a rate of 9 percent.

As Dakar continued to grow, it generated its own replica: Pikine (according to M. Verniere's expression). In 1955 the administrative quarters in Dakar began expanding, resulting in people moving to Pikine. Although Pikine was not as well equipped as Dakar and most of its habitat was irregular in land values, but its buildings had definite qualities.

In spite of a slowing down in the demographic growth—4 percent annually between 1976 and 1988 (Mbodj, 1989), Dakar still has an increase of 55,000 people per year, the size of an average regional capital. This concentration of population goes together with a variety of activities such as administration, services, and industries. The city contributes 67 percent of the industrial production and 73 percent of the national added value.

The Urban Network

Dakar monopolizes numerous functions, and its relative weight in the urban population increases. In 1955, the Senegal urban population was 545,000 people in 24 cities, 16 of them with less than 10,000 inhabitants (Mainet, 1988). At present, out of the 37 districts classified as cities, the number with over 100,000 inhabitants went from 4 in 1976 to 7 in 1988, including Dakar and Pikine. Two districts have less than 5,000 inhabitants; by contrast, 16 districts have more than 5,000 inhabitants. According to the criteria, all districts or cities of more than 5,000 inhabitants, the urban population varies between 2,650,000 and 2,890,000 inhabitants (Ba and Sarr, 1990), which demonstrates that 40 percent of Senegal's population live in cities.

On the whole, internal migrations have little effect on some interior cities. For example, Saint-Louis (115,372 inhabitants in 1988 and 2 percent annual growth between 1976 and 1988), Longa (2 percent), and some smaller towns of the country's interior regions have lower growth rates. The two main cities of the interior, Thiès (175,465 inhabitants in 1988 and 3.6 percent annual growth) and Kaolack (152,007 inhabitants and 3.2 percent annual growth), have slightly higher rates. The cities of the interior rarely show a substantial demographic growth: typical average cities that became major centers of their regions are Fatick (18,416 inhabitants and 5.2 percent growth) and Kolda (34,337 inhabitants and 5.1 percent growth). Mbour (6.3 percent growth) and Ziguinchor (124,283 inhabitants and 4.9 percent growth) also represent high population gains which rest on real economic dynamism.

The urban hierarchy of the ancient interior town of Richard Toll changed very little. Thanks to sugar cane plantations and sugar mills, it grew from 1,000 inhabitants in 1970 to nearly 30,000 in 1988 (and became the 12th largest city). On the whole, the imbalance of the urban network is increasing to the benefit of the capital, which receives about one Senegalese migrant out of every five.

THE DEMOGRAPHIC COMPONENTS OF URBAN GROWTH

The main factors of urban growth are, of course, mortality, fertility, and migration. The Senegalese fertility survey (ESF, 1981) and the Senegalese demographic and health survey (EDS, 1988) are sources for mortality and fertility estimates; for migration data the results come chiefly from the 1988 census.

Mortality on the Decline

For the last two decades mortality has declined significantly, particularly at the child level (from birth to age 5). At the national level, the infant death rate (from birth to the fifth birthday), between 1963 and 1985, dropped from 287 per thousand to 191 per thousand, a decrease of 32 percent. This decline is relatively larger after than before the first birthday: the risk of dying from birth to the first birthday declined from 103 per thousand to 86 per thousand at the national level (a decrease of 17 percent), while the risk from the first to the fifth birthday dropped from 190 per thousand to 114 per thousand (a decline of 40 percent). During this period, child mortality remained higher in the rural zones than in cities, particularly in the capital city.

Child mortality in urban areas is now 68 percent as high as in rural areas (70 per thousand compared to 102 per thousand) (EDS, 1986). This inequality of mortality becomes higher when children have reached their first birthday. The likelihood of an urban one-year-old dying before its fifth birthday is, indeed, less than twice that in the rural area (71 thousand versus 164 per thousand). The crude death rate at the national level dropped from 27 per thousand in 1960 to 19 per thousand in 1978, then to 16 per thousand in 1981 and 1985. In Dakar, where the mortality level is the lowest, the mortality rate was estimated to be 12.7 per thousand in 1981 and 1985.

As an indication of the excellent state of health of the population, the decline of infant and childhood mortality reflects the proliferation of health programs, the improvement of sanitary infrastructures, and the better knowledge people have of hygiene conditions and children nutrition. In Dakar, there are concentrations of sanitary units (more than 50 percent of health centers, centers of child and maternity care, and hospitals), and an increasing propagation of public health counseling, which have contributed to lowering the mortality rate of infants and children. The most highly educated women live in Dakar, and the training of young mothers contributes significantly to the lowering of child mortality—eliminating deaths due to the lack of hygiene, encouraging better care for nursing and feeding the newborn, and eliminating poor interpretations of symptoms or use of medicines.

In 1986 only 9 percent of the females 15–49 years of age had a secondary education, whereas 21 percent of those living in urban areas studied in secondary schools. Twenty-five percent of the urban Senegal women had a primary education, compared to only 14 percent in the entire Senegal population. In the urban areas slightly over half of the urban women never attended school, whereas almost 80 percent of them in the République of Senegal had no formal schooling (Ministère de l'Economie et des Finances, 1988).

The demographic and health survey (1986) demonstrated that children whose mothers had an elementary or a secondary school education had two or three times more chances to reach their fifth birthday than those whose mothers never attended school (140 or 225 vs. 72 per thousand) (Ministère de l'Economie et des Finances, 1988).

Deaths due to measles, diarrhea, and malaria are decreasing rapidly in the cities. Children of women who have a high school education, or whose husband or partner is working for the modern sector, are better protected against malaria, diarrheic diseases, and malnutrition than others. In Dakar and other urban areas respectively, 10 to 15 percent of all children suffer severe malnutrition versus 25 percent in rural areas.

Children living in the capital city are not only better protected against these diseases, but are also better taken care of when they are affected by them (Ministère de l'Economie et des Finances, 1988).

The low level of mortality of children living in the capital does not apply to poor families, although their mortality rates are not as high as in rural areas. In fact, the EDS data (1986) demonstrate that the children of Dakar women whose husbands or partners work for the informal sector have less chance to survive than those employed in the modern sector.

Fertility

For the first twenty years after independence, fertility remained high in both rural and urban areas. The Senegal fertility survey (ESF, 1981) shows that Dakar families have as many children as rural families. The offspring of women 45–49 with completed families is over seven children for each woman. Urbanization does result in a decrease in fertility, but at present the opposite is true, as the social transformations taking place in cities are favorable to an increase. Dakar women marry young: more than half before the age of 19. The ESF (1981) and EDS (1988) estimate the average age at marriage is respectively 18.3 years old and 18.6 years old (MBDUP, 1992), close to the national average. Therefore, Dakar women start their maternity very early, at an average age of 19.

Urbanization, while bringing improvements in sanitation and a better knowledge of hygiene, decreases the risks of miscarriages and involuntary abortions and therefore increases fertility. Moreover, it contributes to the decline of traditional beliefs related to sexual taboos and lengthy nursing. Indeed, Dakar women breast-feed and abstain during the postpartum period not as long as rural women (respectively 16.5 months versus 20; 5 months and 6.7 months versus 8.4 months). The reduction in the duration of postpartum and nursing abstinence is not accompanied by a concomitant increase of contraception. Less than 5 percent of city women use contraceptive methods. Thus, intervals between birth are shorter for Dakar women than for those living in rural areas. There is an increase in potential of children, that is to say in natural fertility, as demonstrated by B. A. Easterlin and M. C. Crimmins (1982) and J. Bongaarts (1982).

At the present time, urbanization, instead of reducing fertility as it does mortality, tends to increase it or to maintain it at its high level.

The lack of synchronization between mortality and fertility in Dakar shows that the only ''urbanization'' criteria is insufficient to explain the demographic regime specific to Senegalese cities. It is important to integrate other dimensions such as the level of education and the family's social position in the economic life and in the modern sector.

Fertility levels depend, indeed, on the conditions of production and reproduction specific to each social group, according to its degree of involvement in the urban active life (Locoh, 1988; Mboup, 1992). A decrease in the fertility of women with higher education or a husband employed in the modern sector occurred. However, those constitute a minority in the Dakar female population (less than 10 percent.) In 1986 Senegal women 45–49 years old with no formal education had 6.8 children, those with a primary education had 5.7 children, while women with a secondary education had only 3.8 children (Ministère de l'Economie et des Finances, 1988).

The majority of the women in urban Senegal (79 percent) are either illiterate or have only an elementary level of education, and belong to poor families: their employment is precarious (informal sector), their salary is very low, and they do not have pension or retirement benefits. This is the reason that their behavior vis-à-vis procreation has no significant impact in lowering the fertility of all women of Dakar. For those families, a child remains a very important economic value (security in old age and labor). The ESF (1978) and the EDS (1986) demonstrate, as a matter of fact, that city women seek large families (more than 6 children per woman).

Finally, bearing in mind that the evolution in fertility has not followed the decrease in mortality, city women, particularly those in the capital, have more surviving children than their rural counterparts. The EDS data show that, indeed, for women of 15–19 years of age, 89 percent of the urban children at birth survive compared to 75 percent in the rural areas; at 45–49 years of age the gap is even wider: 81–55 percent.

Migration Patterns

According to the 1988 results (Ba and Sarr, 1990), out of a population of 6,881,919 individuals born in Senegal and residents in 1988, there were 999,060 lifetime migrants who had changed their region of residency. They are migrants who reside in a different region from their birthplace; this does not take into consideration the length of residency, nor the number of migrations; finally, it hides return migrations. The areas of Saint-Louis and Louga constitute genuine poles of emigration. These two regions supplied 277,180 lifetime migrants, that is, 31 percent of migrants from inside the country. The Dakar region, which constitutes the main pole of destination, received 462,090 migrants, 46 percent of the total. The Kaolack, Fatick, and Thiès regions are other poles of destination, but not comparable with Dakar. If one takes in consideration the "soldes migratoires" migratory balances among the ten regions of Senegal, only two showed a positive balance: Tambacounda with a slightly positive balance of +2,740 (this region has a low migration but it is helped by the cultivation of cotton); and Dakar, which has a net gain of 325,580 lifetime migrants. Of the 889,550 lifetime migrants who migrated within the country, 462,090 or 52 percent settled in Dakar.

The main migratory flow toward Dakar originated from Thiès (105,940 persons in Dakar were originally from that region); then from Saint-Louis (86,190), and natives of three regions, Ziguinchor (58,440), Dourbel (55,020) and Louga (52,290); and finally, migrants from Kaolack (39,630) and Fatick (38,400).

The proportion of lifetime migrants in the departure area was reported. In relative weight, Ziguinchor provided the most migrants to Dakar.

The 1988 results provide the regional direction to Dakar, in the last five years. For the entire Senegal, only three regions have positive balances: Dakar (+19,260), Ziguinchor (+6,660), and Tambacounda (+150). The Ziguinchor region is a paradox insofar as it supplies an important share of Dakar immigrants (15.2 percent) and receives migrants from neighboring regions. Of the internal migrants to Dakar, the main flux was of natives of Thiès followed by those of Saint-Louis and Ziguinchor. Emigrants from these three regions went essentially to Dakar since 62 percent of emigrants from Saint-Louis, 61 percent of the emigrants from Ziguinchor, and 57 percent from Thiès went to the capital.

The migratory flux continues, but it is not a rural exodus. On the contrary, the diversity of the flux shows (IFAN-ORSTOM survey) that a large number of the rural-urban migrants were originally from an urban milieu or else passed through an urban milieu. The important urban migrations to Dakar suggest the evolution of a Senegalese urban network.

APPRAISAL OF THE DEMOGRAPHIC GROWTH

The decline in mortality, much faster than that for fertility, results in a natural increase of the population at the national level at 2.9 percent. The latter is higher when one considers the capital, which has the lowest mortality rate (between 10 and 15 per thousand), and a birthrate identical with the national average (46 per thousand). The rate of natural increase in Dakar is between 3 and 3.6 percent.

According to the IFAN-ORSTOM study, the yearly immigration rate is approximately 3 percent. The difference between the annual growth (4 percent) and the natural growth in Dakar (between 3 and 3.6 percent) gives an estimate of the migratory remainder, between 0.4 and 1 percent. Therefore, each year, between 2 and 2.6 percent of the population leaves Dakar. These emigrants (approximately 30–37,000 people) are for the most part migrants returning to their homeland; the others are international immigrants who are leaving Senegal either for other African countries or for Arab countries, Europe, or North America. International migrations are becoming more and more diversified and represent one of the strategies used to escape the crisis.

Even if the demographic growth of Dakar has slowed down, the city continues to welcome a great number of interurban migrants from Senegal. The migratory phenomenon is particularly evident with the active age-group, and even a low migratory growth can hide important fluxes with certain age-groups. For instance, in Dakar, in 1989, 30 percent of the men and 24 percent of the women between the ages of 25 and 29 arrived after 1980. Regardless of the generation, arrivals are concentrated between 15 and 25 years of age. Migration affects especially adolescents and young adults, who must face new responsibilities in unknown surroundings.

Migrations have an impact on the age and sex structure in Dakar; 48 percent of male migrants are between 20 and 39 years of age, and 47 percent of female migrants are between 15 and 34 years. Women migrate at a younger age than men, but the women represent a slightly smaller percent at each age than male migrants. This infusion of younger blood in Dakar, which shows for 1989 a relatively regular age profile, contrary to that of 1955 which showed a narrowing at the 10–15 age level, and a definite increase at the 25–30 level, along with an overrepresentation of men beyond 30 years of age. This reflects the typical profile of an expanding city welcoming migrants.

Despite the slowdown in urban growth, the situation remains very alarming: urban equipment and employment are not keeping up with the rhythm of demographic growth.

LIVING CONDITIONS IN DAKAR

Varied living conditions are found in Dakar; villas, buildings from the end of the colonial era, developments which are more or less socially oriented, more traditional concessionaire evolutive dwellings, and sheds.

The dwelling is an indication of social differentiation. Three large categories of dwellings can be identified in the city of Dakar. The first constitutes the dwellings of high and middle standing: villas, apartment buildings, and apartments in housing developments Habitat à Loyer Modéré (HLM) and Société Immobilière du Cap Vert (SICAP). The middle class remains the principal beneficiary of urban planning. The SICAP (Cap Vert Real Estate Corporation) was created in 1950, and the OHLM (Low Income Housing Office) in 1959. Since their creation, the real estate corporations have built more than 11,000 housing units for SICAP (mostly between 1960 and 1980), and around 8,000 units for HLM (mostly between 1960 and 1970).

The second category includes the rather low-income style of housing: multistory houses, houses with terraces, and houses with corrugated iron or tile roofs. The third category includes the sheds.

Several modes of housing construction are possible. One part of the construction is a direct consequence of the cleaned lots development project (particularly the project dealing with the clean-up of 10,500 land lots in Cambarene which have not yet all been completed). Construction can also be private, but with the help of loans (BHS [The Construction Bank]). Yet the greatest part of today's construction comes from ''self-construction'' and jobber's projects. Habitations of the HLM or SICAP type represent only 14 percent of all dwellings. The second category is the most often seen in the city of Dakar; it includes multistory houses, houses with terraces (24 percent of available dwellings), and houses with corrugated iron or tile roofs, which by themselves represent 53 percent of all dwellings. Finally, the sheds are few (8 percent). One finds more sheds in Dakar (10 percent) than in Pikine (5 percent).

From the results of the IFAN-ORSTOM study, and comparisons with the adjusted figures from the 1955 census, one can describe the evolution of the living modes of the dwellings, and the consequences of the increase of the family size on residential strategies.

The nature of the dwellings changed between 1955 and 1990. The 1955 census provides eloquent information on the topology of habitations and the composition of households. Of all traditional constructions, only 13 percent were made of concrete, 54 percent were made of wood, and 33 percent were made of straw. Constructions made of traditional material (straw) or salvaged materials (boards) are being replaced by concrete.

The improvement of dwelling conditions is above all the result of judicial constraints and the evolution of urban developments during the past thirty years. Before independence, construction with temporary building materials was authorized in the ''African Quarters,'' but ''the inhabitant only obtained a final property title when built out of permanent materials'' (Sinou, 1990). Rather quickly, in the fifties, authorities were overwhelmed by the arrival of new migrants, and many shantytowns appeared on the nondeveloped urban fringes. It was at that time that a new policy of massive exodus of the ''illegals'' toward the periphery began. This policy was intensified after independence. Although, the 1967 urbanization plan did not have the means necessary for its implementation, it represented a turning point. Spontaneous urbanization is no longer considered ''an urban perversion which must be eliminated'' (Sinou, 1990). Dwelling norms are being lowered to allow more people to find a minimal habitation and to avoid the emergence of shantytowns. As far as the latter is concerned, the plan did succeed because no real shantytowns exist, and there are very few districts of only sheds, since these are rather scattered in various districts, sometimes hidden behind concession walls.

This construction topology is independent of the land status of the dwelling: a spontaneous habitation can be of good quality, and a shed can occupy a lot which has been divided and registered for a long time. Probably, 17 percent of all dwellings come from state construction companies, 5 to 6 percent are private dwellings subsidized by the state (loans), 22 percent result from private real estate transactions, and 53 to 56 percent of the dwellings have no official origins (CCCE, 1991).

The proportion of homeowners is relatively high in Dakar, where 48 percent of heads of families own their dwellings. The proportion of homeowners increases from the center to the periphery, and it goes from 38 percent in the downtown area, where renters are in the majority, to 49 percent in the nearby suburbs (Yoff, Patte d'oie, Camberene, Parcellas) and to 58 percent in the more remote suburbs of Pikine. Among those who call themselves "homeowners," half have property titles, or lodging permits, while the other half are living without property titles, especially when the lots have been obtained from tribal chiefs.

Homeowners have large families. If we take into consideration the population as a whole (and not just heads of families), 67 percent of the population lives in families whose head is a homeowner, and 28 percent are renters. We should emphasize the large number of dependents who live with the heads of households. More than 30 percent of the population lives with a parent.

The family composition has undergone major changes, and several assessments can be made of its evolution between 1955 and 1989. The average family size went from 4.2 persons in 1955 to 8.3 in 1989. The second assessment deals with the decrease in the number of women who are heads of households (15 percent in 1989 and 18 percent in 1955), although the trend is reversed in other African capitals. The two most striking evolutions deal with the aging of the male heads of households and the increase in the number of polynuclear households. In 1955, 21 percent of male heads of households were over 49 years of age, and in 1989 this number has reached 37 percent. On the other hand, the proportion of polynuclear households has increased from 7 to 24 percent of all households.

One may wonder about the consequences of the increase in size of households and its effects on the living conditions of the residential space. As far as the concessions, or lots, are concerned (in general 200 to 400), one or more households often live together (1.5 households on the average in 1989). There is a densification of the concessions, especially in the downtown districts of Dakar; but the overpopulated concessions do not increase; 5 percent of concessions had more than 30 inhabitants in 1955, and 4.9 percent in 1989. If the increase in the size of households has resulted in a very relative densification of the concessions, the density per room has evolved. Whereas in 1955, 29 percent of all households and 45 percent of the population lived with more than 3 persons per room, the situation worsened by 1989 when 44 percent of households and 54 percent of the population lived in more than 3 persons per room. Accordingly, the density jumped from 2.1 to 2.9 persons per room. Obviously, the increased size of households had repercussions on the living conditions of the house space available to households.

URBAN EQUIPMENT

The access of households to drinking water (faucet in the home) and electricity has markedly improved. In 1955, two major types of habitations are considered:

the ''European'' dwellings (18 percent of the population lives in them, of which only a little more than a quarter are Africans), and the ''African'' habitation (housing 82 percent of the population). This dichotomy no longer has much meaning today. But, in order to allow for comparisons, we have for 1989 (IFAN ORSTOM study) grouped, in the same category, high-standing habitations and the constructions completed by real estate corporations, and on the other hand, habitations in the concessions.

The first category sheltered 15 percent of the population in 1989, and the second category sheltered 85 percent. The first category, regardless of the time period, is connected in 93 percent of cases to the network of running water and electricity. In the 1989 concessions, the situation improved: nearly 40 percent of households have both water and electricity at their disposal; still 57 percent are without water (91 percent in 1955) and must gather it mostly at public fountains, while 40 percent (80 percent in 1955) have no electricity.

The fight against shantytowns has turned out to be relatively effective; the dwellings made of temporary building materials have given way to dwellings constructed of concrete. However, that doesn't mean that everyone has a decent place to live. As far as the water and electricity supply is concerned, successful efforts have been carried out, but more than half of the population of working-class districts do not have running water in their homes, with all the consequences for hygiene and health which result from problems linked to the stocking of water.

The city of Dakar is better equipped than the rest of the country in community equipment but, nevertheless, suffers from a lack of infrastructure. The city budget is approximately 6,700 cfa francs per inhabitant (1 U.S. dollar = 300 FCFA).

Without spending much time on major equipment with a national orientation, what does neighborhood equipment consist of? There are three primary classes for each 1,000 inhabitants in Dakar, only one in Pikine, and only one health station for each 23,000 people in Dakar and one for 19,000 in Pikine. The sewer network is insufficient, and many districts in Dakar and all of Pikine have no sewer system. Equipment and budgets for its upkeep remain too small to meet the needs of the population of a city with more than one and a half million people.

ECONOMIC ACTIVITY

To analyze employment, it is necessary to distinguish between the modern sector (such as jobs in businesses with accounting services) and the nonstructured sector. Employment statistics show that the modern sector, exclusively developed in cities, has undergone a growth of more than 6 percent during the first two decades of the independence of Senegal. But since the eighties it has declined. The work force has gone from 86,500 in 1971 to 173,000 in 1982, and 169,000 in 1986 (Bocquier, 1991).

Government employment represents 40 percent of the modern sector. During the seventies, the administration work force increased, and the supervising ratio (number of government workers per 1,000 habitants) went from 8 to 11. On the other hand, during the 1980s, the supervising ratio decreased 4 percent (Bocquier, 1991).

The decrease in the employment of the modern economy during the 1980s had an impact on the private sector which, after an 11 percent growth, went through a slower evolution of 2 percent. The private-sector share went from 18 percent in 1971 to 30 percent in 1988. Business in the modern sector had a spectacular drop: its share declined from 14 percent in the 1970s to less than 7 percent in the 1980s. Industrial production, after a 14 percent growth in the 1970s, had a very slow growth rate of 3 percent in the 1980s. In 1974, it represented 26 percent of the modern sector, and in the 1990s, less than 20 percent (Valette, 1990).

This decrease in the activity of the modern sector is also felt in the capital where the public and parapublic sectors account for 51,200 salaried employees, including 78 percent male, 67 percent in government jobs, and 29 percent working for private businesses. Its share in salaried employment was 44 percent (Zarour, 1989; Bocquier, 1991).

The private sector represents an important part of the modern sector (18 percent in 1971 and 30 percent in 1988). Employment in the private sector has jumped from 42,209 in 1960 to 107,164 in 1980, or a 5 percent yearly increase.

Industrial production, mostly concentrated in the capital, includes products derived from peanuts, phosphates, and fishing, as well as exports from Senegal. The harshness of climatic conditions limits peanut production. The low productivity and competitiveness of local industrial products, the deterioration of the exchange rate, the technological and energy-related production costs represent as many road blocks against investments, which are essentially foreign. Thus, the industry employs only 11 percent of salaried workers. This percentage is highly insufficient to support an urbanization that is qualitatively sufficient. The rates of workers from the industrial sector and the whole population reached its lowest level in the 1980s (1.7 percent, compared with 2.4 percent in previous years).

The modern sector represents less than 25 percent of the total employment in the great Dakar area, and is unable to meet the needs of new job seekers. During the last decade, the total number of active workers increased 4 percent, which corresponds to 98,723 new job seekers. The private sector has been able to absorb only 5,144 of them, or 5 percent, and the public sector 17 percent. The remainder, or 78 percent, must look to the informal sector (Bocquier, 1991).

Given the low absorption capacity of the modern, public, and private sectors, the majority is forced to work in the activity sector called "nonstructured." In production activities (woodwork, sewing) or services (mechanics, tailors) or commercial activities, it is still difficult to determine exactly the number of jobs in the nonstructured sector, these usually being temporary, in production, qualification, and income.

According to the IFAN-ORSTOM study, apprentices and family helpers, unpaid for the most part, represent 27 percent of all jobs, and 46 percent of the unstructured sector. Self-employed workers represent 45 percent of the unstructured sector. In the subdivisions of production and services, the independents, the apprentices, and the family helpers represent 71 percent (90,300) of the men and 25 percent of the women (18,000).

Building construction belongs for the most part to the nonstructured sector, and the number working is widely underestimated. The IFAN-ORSTOM study estimates the independents at 6,000, the apprentices at 1,800, and the salaried employees in the modern sector at 3,200, a total number of 11,000.

An important segment of the active population in the unstructured sector is engaged in commercial activities. Also, there are more women than men there: 40,000 compared to 31,000. Among employed women (109,600), only 15 percent are salaried workers in a business. Among the employed men, 39 percent work for a business. Thus, women are not as well represented as men in the modern sector.

Not all unemployed active people in the modern sector succeed in finding jobs in the nonstructured sector. The general population census of 1988 indicated an unemployment rate of 27 percent for males and 31 percent for females. In Dakar, an employed person supports an average of 3.4 other persons. The high level of unemployment is explained particularly by massive layoffs and the closing of private businesses. Industry is the sector of activity which accounts for the largest number of unemployed: 22 percent and 15 percent in the services and production sectors, and 19 percent of women in commercial activities. For men, the unemployment rate is approximately 14 percent in the industry sector.

Unemployment is worsened by structural adjustment programs (Diouf, 1992). In order to reduce its expenditures and lower the national debt, the state, which is the main employer in the modern sector (40 percent of administrative jobs), is forced to limit new recruiting and lay off government workers. With the use of custom and fiscal measures, the revision of work laws, the abolition of restrictions on the importation of products, and the liberalization of prices, the government of Senegal is attempting to rejuvenate industry and make it more competitive internationally. The limits of the modern sector in its ability to employ the urban population, along with lesser involvements from the state, have resulted in a progressive development of the sector of independent workers, family helpers, and apprentices. These are usually rural migrants and laid-off workers who have sought a new type of employment. The decline of the industrial and administrative sectors has had a great impact on temporary jobs generally held by rural migrants without an education.

The unstructured sector is dealing primarily with survival tactics in which all family members are involved, particularly women and children. The necessity of the participation of all members in production leaves unchanged the life cultural pattern of poor populations in the cities. Polygamy, fertility, the reproduction of social and identity alliances are integral parts of the process of survival tactics (Antoine et al., 1992).

The participation of members in family production takes place along varied pathways: children and women head mostly for the unstructured sector. Independent male workers and apprentices represent 71 percent in the subdivisions of production and services, and women 25 percent. The estimated number in independent businesses is 31,300 men and 40,000 women.

AN IMPOVERISHED URBAN POPULATION

There is little available information on revenues in Dakar. The net industrial income per person in Senegal has gone from 214,000 cfa francs in 1960 to 143,000 cfa francs in 1985 (in 1985 cfa francs). In 1980, the average monthly family income was estimated at 83,300 cfa francs in Dakar, and 51,200 cfa francs in Pikine (Ministère de l'Urbanisme, 1986). The official minimum wage in 1969 of 50.6 cfa francs an hour increased to 201.06 cfa francs in 1988, which is insufficient to offset inflation (the price index being 492.2 in 1989, with a base of 100 in 1967); with a constant currency value, the official 1988 minimum wage declined 13 percent since 1969. Some workers earn a salary below the official minimum wage.

In the IFAN-ORSTOM study (1992), seven questions dealt with the ownership of domestic goods, including radios and automobiles. Despite these structural imperfections, this variable reflects a standard of living scale going from 0 to 5. At both extremes, we find those who have no domestic goods, or at the very least a radio; such a situation is the norm for more than half of households (52 percent), and indicates the poverty which strikes an important proportion of households in Dakar. At the other extreme, 4 percent of households own almost all types of domestic goods. Between the two extremes are approximately 23 percent of the households (category 1 and 2), which own comparatively little equipment. Those in category 3, "average equipment" (16 percent), and category 4, "rather good equipment" (5 percent), own a minimum level of equipment which includes in most cases radios, refrigerators, televisions, and living room furniture.

Heads of households who have a satisfactory level of equipment belong for the most part to the categories of management level personnel (48 percent), important independent businessmen (7 percent), manual workers (8 percent), and retired people (10 percent). The majority in several active categories have no goods. Thus, 83 percent of unskilled laborers, 67 percent of independent businessmen, and 67 percent of the manual workers fall in this situation. Even among the heads of households who are salaried workers of service industries, 45 percent have no domestic goods. Eighty-five percent of the management-level personnel have average or higher quality equipment. Except for management personnel, retired individuals enjoy a relatively better situation than other professionals.

When equipment is considered by type of household, one category stands out very clearly: households with one or more nonrelated individuals, most of whom own no domestic goods. The percentage for men is 81, and for women, 76. These households take in other people (mononuclear households with children and other parents), and polynuclear households own most of the goods. Does this relative affluence result from sharing common goods with one another, or do the wealthier heads of households assume the responsibility for a greater number of persons? One is inclined to choose the second hypothesis, which corroborates our previous analyses. Usually, the households with female heads are poorer than those headed by men, particularly single-parent families.

Most people with good equipment live in high-standard dwellings (81 percent) or in good-quality dwellings made of concrete (19 percent). The poorest reside either in inadequate dwellings or in concrete dwellings of inferior quality; also a large proportion (41 percent) of people in high-quality concrete dwellings are impoverished. The poor live in poor dwellings, but a few households without many goods also live in better dwellings. Eighty-three percent of the heads of households with good equipment are owners (83.3 percent).

LIMITS OF APPLIED PROJECTS

As a sign of the rapid growth of cities, the government has included in its official population planning a national and regional development program. The regional integrated development projects aim to centralize modern activity (Ministère de l'Economie et des Finances 1988:10).

Among the stated objectives were the decentralization of industrial and administrative infrastructures to enhance the value of other cities and decrease the migratory flow to the capital. The progressive elaboration of regional poles of cultural, social, and economic development will enhance the production activities, stabilize the local population, and slow migration toward the Dakar area. The objectives also include the adoption of incentive measures for the implementation of small and mid-size businesses inside the country, and new activities in secondary cities to achieve a balanced distribution of national manpower; and the restructuralization of urban equipment, of sewer systems and water networks in the spontaneous dwelling district of Dakar and in the suburbs to improve sanitary conditions. The implementation of these objectives is being hampered by demographic constraints and problems linked to the long- and mid-term structural adjustment programs Programme d'Ájustement à Long et Moyen Terme) (PALMT).

The natality rate remains high in Dakar, and this shows that the redistribution policy would not itself reduce the rapid population growth of the capital. While continuing its sewer and hygiene policies, the state must instill new blood in its policies concerning the natality rate.

The priority investment and action programs dealing with the population, which were elaborated in 1989, have a tendency to revitalize the family plan programs, by integrating them within the health programs aimed at mothers and children. The communication, education, and information programs (Information, Education et Communication [IEC]) concerning populations are also financed to increase information concerning family planning (Ministère de la Sante Publique, 1989). The association between mortality and natality is not linear. The decrease in the mortality rate does not necessarily entail the adoption of family planning which leads to a decline in natality rates.

Despite the repeal in 1980 of the 1920 law forbidding contraception publicity and the use of contraceptives, and the integration of programs and modern services of family planning Planification Familiale (PF) within the health services for mothers and children Santé Maternelle et Infantile (SMI), the use of contraceptives remains low in the country (EDS, 1986).

Family planning programs are in fact inseparable from the economic conditions which prevail in the country. Among the most impoverished social groups, who operate according to survival tactics in which the participation of large numbers of individuals is indispensable to increase family production, the improvement of living conditions constitutes a prerequisite to the acceptance of family planning.

The structural adjustment program resulted in important negative social impacts on the job market, which are linked to the policy of deregulation from the state, to new industrial and agricultural policies, and to a clean-up in public finances.

Despite the creation of the insertion and reinsertion delegation Délégation à l'Insertion et à la Réinsertion (DIRE), whose function is to direct young and old workers "removed" from government jobs to other development sectors and regions, unemployment is at the most critical level of its history: not only are the young without jobs, but their parents occupy an unstable position in the job market. Administrative measures are rarely sustained by very concrete financial and economic programs: the distance between laws and regulations and facts still remains very important. This means that policies are rarely translated into concrete actions. The solutions to revitalize the economy are correctly identified, but the organizational and financial abilities necessary for their implementation are absent. The payment of the national debt and the drain of capital constitute an obstacle to the accumulation of capital on a national scale.

CONCLUSION

The employment crisis manifests grave consequences: the modern sector is no longer a career prospect for young people, the unstructured sector has insufficient abilities to offer jobs to the unemployed, and Senegal offers few opportunities of reconversion in agriculture, despite hopes generated by the development of the Senegal River valley.

Within this context of vanishing employment, the responsibilities of the heads of households increase, and are aggravated by low revenues and resources. The heads of households contribute to the maintenance of the entire household by assuming responsibility for household expenditures. The crisis enhances the dependence of young people on their elders. Besides the progressive densification of dwellings, the increase in the size of households results especially in the delayed departure of youths from their parental homes. The system of family concessions which is reproduced in the city lessens the tensions of the real estate market. But how long will one segment of the population be able to shelter another?

Demographic perspectives do not foresee any important slowdown of urbanization, given the natality rate which constantly remains high. The results from family planning programs remain mediocre. In fact, reproduction is inseparable from the economic conditions of production. The acceleration of migratory movements results in the rapid development of the unstructured sector, which will eventually reach its saturation point.

The 1990s began in Dakar with a saturated job market because of a lack of job opportunities and with a real estate market poorly adapted to the requirements of the population. The inequalities of access to resources are accentuated even within households. The orientations of the Structural Adjustments Plan of Senegal, compressing the resources from the modern sector, do not herald a positive solution to the crisis.

REFERENCES

Antoine, Philippe, O. Barbary, Philippe Bocquier, A. S. Fall, Y. M. Guisse, J. Nanitelamio, and A. Diop. 1992. *L'Insertion Urbaine: Le Cas de Dakar*. Dakar: IFAN-ORSTOM.

Ba, A., and I. Sarr. 1990. *Migration et Urbanisation au Sénégal. A Paraître au CERPOD*. Dakar.

Bocquier, Philippe. 1990. "Un Exemple d'Analyse Statistique des Biographies: l'Entree Dans la Vie Active à Dakar." In *Les Cahiers Pratiques Sociales et Travail en Milieu Urbain*. No. 14, Department ORSTOM-SUD. Paris.

———. 1991. "Les Mutations du Marche du Travail a Dakar (Sénégal) et l'Access au Premier Emploi." *Cahier 11–91. Villes et Développment*. Montreal: Groupe Interuniversitaire de Montreal.

Bongaarts, J. 1982. *The Proximate Determinants of Natural Marital Fertility*. New York: Population Council.

CCEE (Caisse Centrale de Cooperation Economique). 1991. *Evaluation des Politiques et Programmes Urbains au Sénégal*. Dakar.

Champaud, J., J. Lombard, and M. Sivignon. 1985. Villes Secondaires et Développement Regional au Sénégal. Convention. Dakar.

Diouf, M. 1992. "La Crise de l'Adjustement." *Politique Africaine* 45:62–85.

Easterlin, R. A., and M. C. Crimmins. 1982. *An Exploratory Study of the "Synthesis Framework" of Fertility Determinants with World Fertility Survey Data*. World Fertility Survey Scientific Reports, no. 40. Voorburg: The Netherlands.

Locoh, T. 1988. "Structures Familiales et Changements Sociaux." In *Population et*

Sociétés en Afrique au suo du Sahara, edited by D. T. Butin, 441–478. Paris: L'Harmattan.

Mainet, G. 1988. *La dynamique demographique des villes Senegalaises,* Departement de géographie (Multiligraphed), université de Dakar. Dakar.

Mbodj, F. G. 1989. "Interpretation des Resultats Préliminaires du Recensement Général de la Population et de l'Habitat de 1988 au Sénégal." *Historiens Géographes du Sénégal* 4–5:12–12.

Mboup, G. 1992. "Recherche des Determinants Socio-Economiques et Culturels au Sénégal a Partir de l'ESF (1978) et l'EDS (1986)." Ph.D. diss., University of Montreal.

Ministère de L'Economie et des Finances, Direction de la Statistique, Division des Enquetes et de la Demographíe. 1981. *Enquete Senegalaise de Fecondité, 1978.* Dakar.

Ministère de L'Economie et des Finances, Direction de la Statistique, Division des Enquetes et de la Demographie, et DHS-Institute for Resource Development/ Westinghouse. 1988. *Enquête Demographique et de Santé au Senegal, 1986.* Dakar.

Ministère de l'Urbanisme, Direction de la Statistique. 1986. *Enquête Urbanisme au Senegal, 1986.* Dakar.

Ministère de la Sante Publique, Ministère du Développement Social, OMS. 1989. Centre Pour la Population et la Sante Familiale. Université de Colombia. Dakar. *Projet de Prevention de la Mortalité Maternelle au Sénégal.* Dakar.

République du Sénégal, Presidence de la République-Secretariat Général, Delegation au Plan et aux Politiques Economiques, Direction de la Prevision et de la Statistique. 1989. *Les Principaux Resultats provisoires du Recensement de la Population et de l'Habitat du Sénégal—1988.* Dakar.

Sinou, A. 1990. *Dakar, Bulletin d'Informations Architecturales, Institut Français d'Architecture. Supplément au Numero 141.* Dakar.

Valette, A. 1990. "Emploi et Nouvelle Politique Industrielle au Sénégal." *Les Cahiers—Pratiques et Sociales et Travail en Milieu Urbain,* Numero 13. Paris: ORSTOM.

Zarour, C. 1989. *Etude du Secteur Informel de Dakar et Ses Environs Phase III.* Final Report. Senegal: USAID.

18

Sierra Leone

Toma J. Makannah and Mohamed Bailey

When the Portuguese explorers arrived in Sierra Leone in the middle of the fifteenth century, they gave the country its name. They also started trading in slaves and ivory. In fact, they sold thousands of slaves each year until the British parliament abolished slave trading by British subjects and in British colonies in 1807.

The traditional pattern of settlement during the precolonial period was one of fairly sizable villages surrounded by connecting hamlets. Trade in gold, rubber, and other commodities from Sudan by caravans was responsible for the growth of towns on its route even though sporadic civil disturbances acted as constraints on their growth.

By 1787, the small settlement of Freetown had only 350 inhabitants. In 1808, Freetown and its surrounding area became a British crown colony. Freetown had a steady population growth as a port city with a natural harbor which attracted west coast merchant shipping. Also, it became the seat of an admiralty court established in 1808 where owners of captured slave vessels were brought and their slaves freed.

Its population was about 2,100 in 1811 and 10,000 in 1833 (Harvey and Dewdney, 1968). Thousands of recaptive slaves were brought to Sierra Leone in the 1820s and 1830s (Harvey, 1972). The residents of Freetown were known as creoles. They were descendants of freed slaves captured in transit across the Atlantic by the British navy, then liberated and settled in the British crown colony. They had the status of British subjects and an anglicized culture (McKay, 1972).

Freetown's population was around 20,000 inhabitants in 1860 and 1870. Exports from Freetown increased sharply in the 1850s and 1860s, with palm oil, palm kernels, groundnuts, gold, and hides being the principal exports. Throughout Freetown's history, agricultural products dominated the export economy.

In 1896 a British protectorate was established over the hinterland of Sierra Leone, and it was administered separately from the crown colony. Sierra Leone was divided into small independent chiefdoms, with land being in communal ownership. A railway constructed during 1885–1915 connected the colony with the protectorate and served as a catalyst for the growth of towns along its route. In 1898, a hut tax was imposed. It was violently resisted by the Africans, but they were defeated.

Freetown's population continued to increase in its colonial days to 1961. The 1963 census gave a population of 128,000. The 1950s were prosperous years based upon diamond mining and high-grade iron ore, but the economy began to deteriorate in the 1970s.

Different sets of population estimates have been made for Freetown during the last 200 years. While they differ somewhat, they all show a rather impressive growth, and the city is now more than a half million population (Table 18.1).

RECENT URBAN DEVELOPMENTS

The patterns of urbanization in Sierra Leone reflect the large disproportionate share of the large cities, especially Freetown, the primate city, of the urban population as well as the rapid growth of the urban population (United Nations, 1991). Relatively few people are urbanites, and the uneven spatial distribution of the population is a problem.

The urban population of Sierra Leone—of places 5,000 and above—during the two census periods, 1963–74 and 1974–85, grew at annual average rates of 6.0 and 4.7 percent respectively, three and two times respectively of the total population. Freetown's share of the urban population increased from 31 percent in 1963 to 41 percent in 1985. Also, by 1963, Freetown's population was almost five times that of the second most populous town, Bo; and by 1974 and 1985 was nearly four and six times that of the second most populous town, Koidu-New Sembehun.

These features of emerging urbanization in the country seen against problems such as urban poverty, unemployment and underemployment, stress on social amenities, and the proliferation of slum and squatter settlements complicate the pursuit of economic development on the basis of equity, efficiency, and social justice (Pacione, 1990).

To tackle some of these problems, urbanization strategies have been proposed in national development plans and programs (Simon, 1992). Periodic monitoring of such policies would show their efficacy or otherwise.

The data utilized come from both historical information and from the country's three modern censuses, those of 1963, 1974, and 1985 (Sierra Leone, 1965; Sesay, 1989) and unpublished preliminary data from the 1985 population census

Table 18.1
Population of Freetown, Sierra Leone, 1792–2000

Year	By Fyfe and Jones	Hance	United Nations
1792	1,000		
1833	10,000		
1870	20,000		
1914	33,000	33,000	
1921		44,000	
1930		55,000	
1931	55,358		
1944	87,312		
1947		65,000	
1950			50,000
1954		90,000	
1960			100,000
1963	127,917[1]	128,000	
1966		148,000	
1970			210,000
1974	276,247[1]		
1980			400,000
1985	469,776[1]		
1990			690,000
2000			1,120,000

[1]Actual census counts in 1963, 1974, and 1985.

Compiled from Fyfe and Jones, 1968; Hance, 1970; United Nations, 1989.

(Sesay, 1989). No official definition of *urban* currently exists, although the threshold 2,000 is increasingly used (e.g., Byerlee et al., 1976; Okoye, 1981). Here, however, the threshold value 5,000 is employed in order to implicitly accommodate some of the economic criteria of urbanization. In justification of this choice, it has been pointed out that some of the localities considered as urban in the past were "really large villages which do not provide any services."

The plan of the chapter is to first discuss the historical and economic setting; to review the patterns of urbanization from 1963 to 1985; and then to examine the emergence of an urban hierarchy in Sierra Leone in 1963–85.

SETTING

With a land area of 28,000 square miles, Sierra Leone had a population of 4,151,000 in 1990. The annual, average rates of growth of the population during 1985–90, along with 1963–74 and 1974–85, the periods emphasized in this study, were 2.49, 1.79, and 2.24 percent, respectively.

The country became independent in 1963 after almost seventy years of British rule of the two constituent parts of the country, the then colony and protectorate. The colonial development strategy of polarized development based on core/periphery lines has left its imprint on postindependent urbanization. With the intention of acquiring the products of smallholder farmers in the interior, the colonial government built basic infrastructures, especially a network of transportation and communication systems focusing on Freetown and major towns. After independence, the advantages colonial rule gave these localities became entrenched, further enhancing their positions as major towns. Other factors that have influenced contemporary urbanization include mining, in particular alluvial diamond mining, commercial rice cultivation, export cropping, and commercial fishing (see Gleave, 1982, 1988).[1]

In the context of urbanization, the Sierra Leone economic system is built around two activities, agriculture and mining. The economic and social dominance of the Western Area is based on its location of the industrial, commercial, and administrative capital of the country as well as the main port, Freetown. Thus this region has more than her fair share of nonagricultural activities of manufacturing, services, and commerce. In contrast, in the provinces, agricultural pursuits are by a wide margin the most important economic activity.

The Eastern Province's economy is built around diamond mining in the Kono and Kenema districts, and cash-cropping in the Kenema and Kailahun districts. The Southern Province is also a largely agricultural region. Other important economic activities include fisheries in the Moyamba District and alluvial diamond mining in the Sewa Valley, rutile and bauxite mining in the Moyamba District as well as swamp rice cultivation in the Bonthe District.

Agriculture is also the mainstay of the economy of the Northern Province. The western coastal zone especially around the estuary of the Great and Little Scarcies is the major swamp rice cultivation area in the country.

Table 18.2
Percentage of Total Population in Urban Localities above Various Thresholds in 1963, 1974, and 1985 and Rates of Growth

Population Threshold	1963	1974	1985	Annual 1963-74	Rate of growth 1974-85
2,000	19.0	27.5	32.2	5.2	3.7
5,000	13.0	20.9	27.2	6.0	4.7
10,000	9.9	18.4	22.6	7.2	4.2
20,000	7.1	16.4	20.3	9.1	3.7
50,000	5.9	12.9	18.9	8.7	5.8
100,000	5.9	10.1	13.4	6.6	4.8

Source: Compiled from Sierra Leone Census, 1985.

THE PATTERNS OF URBANIZATION

Urban localities in Sierra Leone can be classified into three main categories (Okoye, 1981). The first group encompasses towns like Freetown, Kodiu-New Sembehun, the provincial headquarter towns of Bo, Makeni, and Kenema along with other localities such as Lunsar, Yengema, and Magburaka. These towns are the main centers of social, economic, and political activities in their various regions, and thus are among the fastest growing urban areas in the country.

The second group of towns include Kabala, Kailahun, Moyamba, Bonthe, and Kambia, whose major functions as administrative headquarters are locations of district offices, magistrate courts, banks, and post offices, which have been the basic reasons for their growth in recent years.

The third type of urban localities, which is not analyzed in this chapter, includes those within the size group 2,000–4,999. They consist of locations of missionary or government establishments, trading centers, and former railway stations. Some of these localities will grow to larger urban centers.

The distributions of these various types of towns differ from district to district (Sesay, 1989).

Level and Growth of Urbanization

The levels of urbanization experienced a remarkable expansion during 1963 to 1985, irrespective of the urban population threshold used (Table 18.2). Thus, in the 2,000 and 20,000 size groups urbanization increased from 19.0 and 7.1

percent in 1963 to 32.2 and 20.3 percent in 1985. When the threshold value 5,000 is employed, as is done in this chapter, the level of urbanization increased from 13 percent in 1963 to 27 percent in 1985.

During 1963–74, the urban population of all six threshold values grew, on the average, in excess of 5 percent per annum, with the fastest growth rates, 9.1, 8.7, and 7.2, occurring in 20,000, 50,000, and 10,000 thresholds, respectively. By 1974–85 rates of urban growth had dampened somewhat, ranging from 5.8 percent in the threshold 50,000 to 3.7 each in the thresholds, 2,000 and 20,000 (Figure 18.1). The growth rates for the threshold 5,000 were 6 percent in 1963–74 and 4.7 in 1974–85.

How do Sierra Leone's levels of urbanization and rates of urban growth compare with those of other West African countries? According to United Nations' medium variant estimates (ECA, 1989), which are based on national definitions of urban localities (a consideration that complicates international comparison), the level of urbanization for the West African subregion varied in 1985 from 8 percent in Burkina Faso to Cape Verde's atypical value of 53 percent. The overall level of 29 percent for the subregion is slightly higher than that of Sierra Leone.

Relative to urban growth rates, Sierra Leone's rate of 6 percent for 1963–74 is almost the same as the West African subregion's 5.9 for 1965–75. However, Sierra Leone's urban growth rate of 4.7 for 1974–85 is lower than the subregion's 5.9 for 1975–85.

Urbanization at the Regional Level

Regional urbanization trends of the four provinces are shown in Table 18.3 and those of the urban localities in Tables 18.4 and 18.5. Also, the urbanization patterns of the 12 districts are discussed but not presented in tabular form.

Eighteen localities qualified as urban in 1963, 20 in 1974, and 35 in 1985, with the largest expansion of urban localities and population occurring in the Eastern and Northern provinces. In 1963 and 1985, the three regions which had levels of urbanization equal to or more than the national levels were the Western Area, Kono and Bo districts, and in 1974 the Western Area and Kono District. It should be pointed out, however, that the Western Area's levels of urbanization, over 70 percent during the whole period, were well above those of Kono and Bo districts.

After these three regions the other districts with relatively high levels of urbanization during 1963–85 were Kenema, Bombali, and Bonthe districts. However, the levels of urbanization were relatively low for most of this period in Moyamba, Tonkolili, Koinadugu, and especially Pujehun districts, with the latter being the only wholly rural region of its size by 1985. Also, the insignificant percentage urban in the Moyamba District, despite its being the location of the rutile and bauxite mines, reflects to the highly capitalized and localized nature of these mining activities, unlike alluvial diamond mining.

Figure 18.1
Population in Localities with 5,000 or More Persons as Percentage of Total Population, 1985

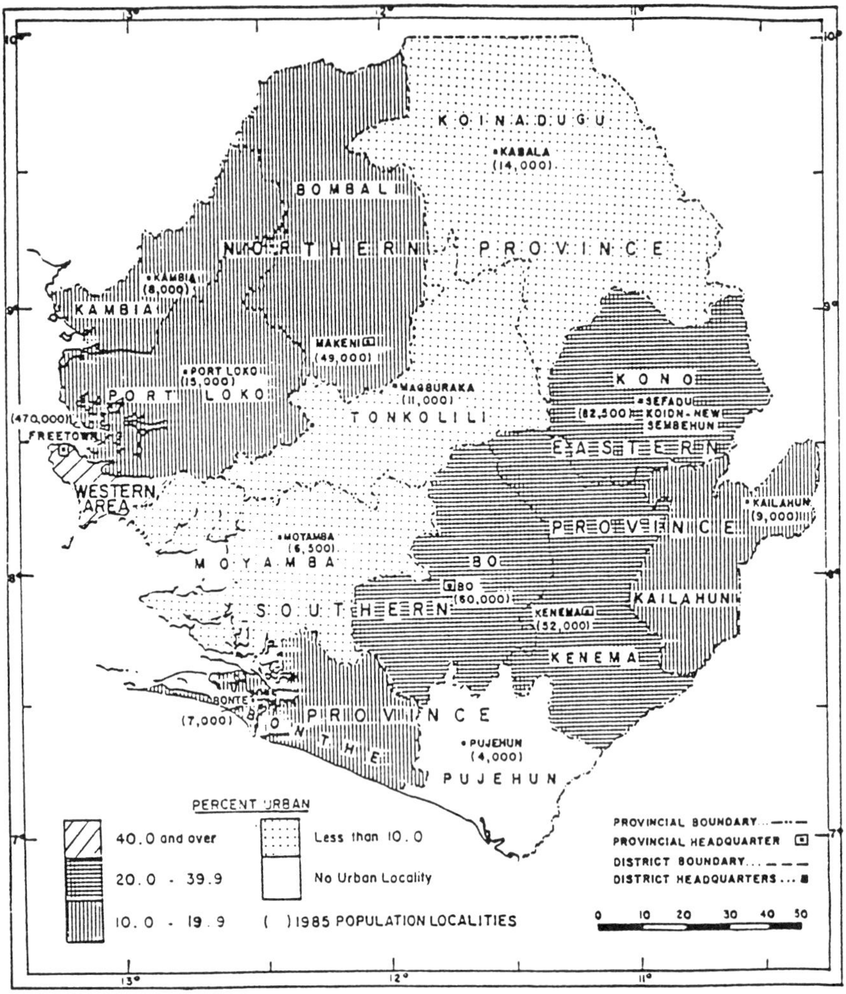

Urban Population by Size-Class of Locality

The number of localities in Sierra Leone was inversely related to size, with between 63 and 73 percent of the number of localities in 1963–85 in the size-class 2,000–4,999 (Table 18.4). This dominance was not, however, translated to the share of the urban population, for which the higher size-classes, such as 100,000 and above, 50,000–99,000, and 5,000–9,999, were clearly the leaders. The most rapid growth of urban localities and population between 1963 and 1985 took place in the higher size-classes, namely, 100,000 and above and

Table 18.3
Urban Population (5,000 and above) by Provinces, 1963, 1974, and 1985, and Growth Rates, 1963–74 and 1974–85

Province	1963	1974	1985	Annual Rate of Growth 1963-74	Annual Rate of Growth 1974-85
	- Urban Population -				
SOUTHERN	32,843	52,196	79,087	4.0	3.8
EASTERN	65,828	159,906	246,765	7.6	3.9
NORTHERN	36,618	82,713	145,103	7.0	5.1
WESTERN	148,010	276,248	486,540	5.3	5.2
TOTAL	283,297	572,062	957,495	6.1	4.7

Source: Compiled from Sierra Leone Census, 1985.

50,000–99,9999, along with the two lower size-classes, 2,000–2,999 and 5,000–9,999.

Population centers of 100,000 and above, which contain only Freetown, expanded twofold between 1963 and 1974, and almost fourfold between 1974 and 1985, relative to those 5,000–9,999, while the number of localities remained almost the same, more than doubled in 1974–85. Similarly, the population for this size-class barely grew in 1963–74, but increased more than 200 percent between 1974 and 1985.

Growth of Individual Localities

The urban landscape of Sierra Leone is obviously dominated by Freetown, given the high concentration of the country's economic and social infrastructures there. This is reflected by the extraordinarily high levels of urbanization of the Western Area, the location of the city: 76, 87, and 88 percent in 1963, 1974, and 1985, respectively. Between 1963 and 1974 this area grew at the annual average rate of 6.6 percent, largely through net in-migration and reclassification of localities (Table 18.5). Between 1974 and 1985 the population of Freetown grew at the reduced rate of 4.8 percent per annum. This was one of the highest growth rates of the large towns during this period. Net in-migration and natural increase made almost equal contributions to this growth.

One of the most dramatic developments in urbanization in 1963–74 was the meteoric rise of the combined localities Koidu-New Sembehun to second position

Table 18.4
Distribution of Urban Localities (Population 5,000 and above) by Size-Class, 1963, 1974, and 1985

Size of locality	No. of localities			Population		
	1963	1974	1985	1963	1974	1985
2,000-2,999	24	28	42	59,705	67,249	101,331
3,000-3,999	11	11	14	37,615	38,999	48,643
4,000-4,999	7	16	6	31,637	73,816	26,303
5,000-9,999	11	11	25	66,236	69,999	163,834
10,000-19,999	5	4	6	62,531	52,363	80,132
20,000-29,999	1	1	-	26,613	26,781	-
30,000-39,999	-	2	-	-	70,826	-
40,000-49,999	-	-	1	-	-	49,038
50,000-99,999	-	1	3	-	75,846	194,715
100,00 and over	1	1	1	127,917	276,247	469,776
TOTAL	60	75	98	412,254	752,129	1,133,772

Source: Compiled from Sierra Leone Census, 1985.

in the hierarchy of cities. Net in-migration as a result of diamond-mining activities in the area was the main reason for the expansion, after discounting the growth due to reclassification. Between 1974 and 1985, despite the fact that the town maintained its number two position, it experienced only insignificant population growth, no doubt, a reflection of declining diamond-mining activities during the period (Gleave, 1988). Other diamond-mining towns such as Jaiama Sewafe, Motema, and Yengema that enjoyed population expansion in 1963–74 suffered the same fate.

Bo Town, second largest in 1963, but third in 1974 in the hierarchy of towns, after Freetown and Koidu-New Sembehun, also maintained its number three position in 1985. It grew at the rate of 3.8 percent per annum in 1974–85, implying that natural increase rather than net in-migration was the main factor for the population increase.

Kenema and Makeni were among the fastest growing cities of the five most populous localities during 1974–85, 4.6 and 5.5 percent per annum, respectively. Net in-migration, related to diamond-mining activities in the case of the former,

Table 18.5
Population of the 25 Most Populous Localities in 1974, Population in 1963 and 1985, and Annual Growth Rates, 1963–74 and 1974–85

Locality	Population 1963	1974	1985	Annual Growth Rate 1963-74	1974-85
Freetown	127,917	276,247	469,776	6.6	4.8
Koidu-NewSembe.	11,706	75,846	82,474	16.0	0.8
Bo Town	26,613	39,371	59,768	3.4	3.8
Kenema	13,246	31,458	52,473	7.4	4.6
Makeni	12,304	26,781	49,038	6.7	5.5
Lunsar	12,132	16,723	16,073	2.8	-0.4
Yengema	7,313	14,493	12,938	6.0	-0.1
Port Loko	5,809	10,500	15,248	4.9	3.6
Magburaka	6,371	10,347	11,006	4.2	0.6
Kabala	4,610	7,847	13,923	4.6	5.2
Yomandu	5,469	7,488	6,208	2.7	-0.1
Kailahun	5,419	7,184	9,054	2.4	2.1
Segbwema	6,258	6,915	8,267	0.9	1.6
Moyamba	4,564	6,425	6,483	2.9	0.1
Bonthe	6,230	6,398	7,032	0.2	0.9
Rokupr	4,151	5,780	8,283	2.8	3.3
Kambia	3,700	5,740	7,631	3.8	2.6
Motema	1,124	5,501	6,312	13.6	0.1
Jaiama Sewa.	6,064	5,367	5,249	-0.1	-0.2
Koindu	2,130	4,956	8,238	7.2	4.6
Kamakwie	3,572	4,837	6,287	2.6	2.4
Lungi	2,170	4,796	5,319	6.8	0.9
Bumpeh-Kono	1,332	4,707	7,556	10.8	7.4
Tokpombu	1,524	4,647	10,944	10.7	7.8
Panguma	3,100	4,559	5,435	3.3	1.6

Source: Compiled from Sierra Leone Census, 1985.

and return migration from the diamond-mining areas for the latter, was the principal component of their growth.

The patterns of growth and decline of towns between 1963 and 1985 underlined the increasing contribution of natural increase to urban population growth especially during 1974 to 1985 in Sierra Leone's largest towns, Freetown, Koidu-New Sembehun, and Bo.

EMERGENCE OF AN URBAN HIERARCHY

The Sierra Leone economy is characterized by uneven regional patterns of development. According to a review of this regional problem, the Sierra Leone economy is marked by great polarities:

> the usual inequality between the agricultural and town population is compounded by an additional inequality: the existence of diamond-mining . . . as a high-income enclave, its process dependent on external forces and its local impact confined to the creation of employment. (ILO, 1981:25)

Government economic policies over the years have accentuated these inequalities. The most notable is the economic policy, whose origin could be traced to the colonial period, responsible for the skewed location of industrial and commercial enterprises in favor of urban areas, especially Freetown. That these same centers have been favored in the distribution of social services has led some authors to speak about an urban bias in resource allocation in the country (Levi, 1976:307; ILO, 1981:ix–xxxv; Gleave, 1988:353–354).

Compounding this rural-urban resource disparity gap have been the two aspects of government's policy toward the agricultural sector, namely the withholding from farmers of a substantial portion of agricultural revenues earned from the sale of export crops and the maintenance of superficially low prices for locally produced rice (Levi, 1976). The emerging urban hierarchy has played a role in this inequality.

Urban Size Distribution and the Rank-Size Rule

When urban localities are classified according to size, a mathematical relationship exists between the rank and the population size by the rank-size rule.[2] The rank-size rule holds when the population of the largest city is equal to the product of the population of the *i*th city and its rank. Despite the finding that this rule does not accurately fit all urban distributions, it is useful in examining urban structures and assessing trends in urban systems.

The rank-size rule can be expressed by the following equation:

$$R_i/P_1^{-q} = P_i \qquad (1)$$

where P_i and R_i are the population and rank of the *i*th city; P_l the population of the largest city; and q is a constant. The rank-size rule holds when q is 1; a q

Table 18.6
Rank-Size and Primacy Indexes, 1963, 1974 and 1985

Year	Rank-size Index a/	Primacy Index 1 PI(1) b/	Primacy Index 2 PI(2) c/
1963	.956	4.81	2.45
1974	.795	3.64	1.88
1985	.830	5.70	2.41

a/ The rank-size index is q in the equation below:

Log (Ri/P1) = a - q(log Pi)

where q is the regression coefficient, a is the intercept, Ri is the rank of the ith town, and Pi is the population of the ith city.

b/ PI(1) = P1/P2

c/ PI(2) = P1/(P1 + P2 + P3)

where Pi = population size of city with rank i.

value less than 1 denotes deviations from the rule in the direction of primacy, the smaller the q value the greater the deviation from the rule. A q value over 1 shows that major intermediate cities feature prominently in the city distribution pattern (Beckman, 1959; Sawers, 1989).

To estimate q the following equation was utilized (Table 18.6):

$$\log(R_i/P_1) = a - q(\log P_i) \qquad (2)$$

The population of places 2,000 and over were used for the preliminary evaluation of the rank-size rule. It is noticeable that the rise of Koidu-New Sembehun along with the reclassification of Kissy and Wellington, among other localities, to form Greater Freetown during 1963–74 have essentially stabilized the ranking of the intermediate towns. Thus, since 1974 the ten most populous localities and the ranking of the first six among them have remained the same. The population of Freetown in 1963, 1974, and 1985 was inordinately large compared with those of other bigger towns.

The applicability of the rank-size rule in describing city-size distribution during the period 1963 to 1985 was formally tested by means of three regression models. The pertinent results from the estimation using equation (2) are given in Table 18.6.[3] These results do not portray a consistent trend: according to q, the rank-size index, the 1963 pattern of urban distribution shows a lesser deviation than 1974's and 1985's. These differences from the rank-size rule can mainly be explained, as has been noted above, by the inordinately larger population of Freetown during the entire period. Second, because intermediate-sized towns like Bo, Kenema, Makeni, and Koidu-New Sembehun (during 1963–74) enjoyed population growth rates higher than most of the lower hierarchy towns as well as rates comparable to or even higher, in some cases, than those of Freetown. From a graphical analysis of the rank-size rule for 1963 and 1974, M. Peil and P. Sada (1984:85–86) detected two rank-size lines, one for the large towns and another for the rest of the system.

These deviations from the rank-size rule are indicative more of polarization than convergence, features displayed by urban systems characterized by primacy. Thus, the patterns, trends, and determinants of primacy in Sierra Leone are next assessed.

Urban Primacy

Primacy, as originally conceptualized by M. Jefferson (1939), refers to a situation where the size of the first city in a country is disproportionately larger, at least two or more times larger than the second city. This measure of primacy is referred to as the two-city primacy index. To make up for the shortcoming of the two-city primacy index in not taking into account size distribution beyond the first two cities, an additional measure is sometimes estimated, for example, in this chapter, the four-city primacy index, the population of the first city divided by the combined populations of the second, third, and fourth cities.

These two indexes of primacy have been estimated for 1963, 1974, and 1985 (Table 18.6). The results indicate that according to the two-city index, primacy decreased between 1963 and 1974, from 4.81 to 3.64. This was obviously due to the rise of Koidu-New Sembehun, which substantially reduced the population gap between the first city, Freetown, and the second, Koidu-New Sembehun. During the intercensal interval 1974–85, while the population of Freetown grew at 4.8 percent per annum, Koidu-New Sembehun's population grew at less than 1 percent per annum. The faster rates of growth of the third and fourth city, 3.8 and 4.6, which were below that of Freetown, did not make up for the lost population suffered by Koidu-New Sembehun. The two-city primacy index increased from 3.64 in 1974 to 5.7 in 1985 and the four-city index from 1.88 in 1974 to 2.41 in 1985.

Hence, by the two-city index, primacy is very high in Sierra Leone, along with Benin, Côte D'Ivoire, Mali, and Togo in the West African subregion, according to a recent study by the Economic Commission for Africa (ECA, 1989).

But a classification of selected West African countries based on the four-city index ranked Sierra Leone along with Burkina Faso, Ghana, Mali, Niger, and Senegal as medium primacy countries. Benin, Côte d'Ivoire, and Togo were classified as high primacy countries, and Nigeria and Gambia as low primacy countries (ECA, 1989).

The population dominance of Freetown in the emergent urbanization system of Sierra Leone is revealed in its disproportionate and growing share of the urban population: 31, 37, and 41 percent in 1963, 1974, and 1985, respectively. This trend, combined with the area's high concentration of economic and social infrastructure, has fostered primacy in the country.

Relative to economic primacy, it has been estimated that by 1974–75, 66 percent of manufacturing activities, 57 percent of doctors, 30 percent of banks, 71 percent of electricity generated, and 82 percent of telephones in the country were located in the Western Area, mainly Freetown (Campbell, 1986:table 4).

National planners have called attention to this phenomenon: "the most important facts about the regional situation in Sierra Leone are: (i) the primacy of the national capital, Freetown, and (ii) the marked disparities in the levels of economic, social and political-administrative development of the national capital, Freetown and its environs, . . . the Western Area, on the one hand, and the rest of the country, . . . the Provinces on the other" (Sierra Leone, 1974). Available evidence confirms that this pattern of resource allocation has remained unchanged (Sierra Leone, 1986b).

Among the determinants of primacy, the following are of special interest with respect to the recent development of urbanization in Sierra Leone, namely, ex-colonial status, the level of economic development, and the size of the country.[4]

Ex-colonial Status: In an ex-colonial country like Sierra Leone, the genesis and continuance of primacy are related to the concentration of administrative functions, transportation, political, and other modernization facilities in the capital and other major cities. In addition, capital cities like Freetown in Sierra Leone act as "head links" with the colonial capital and the world. With the advent of independence, the privileged position of these cities has become entrenched, thereby further engendering primacy.

The Level of Economic Development: At the initial stages of economic development, only a limited surplus is produced by the state, hardly enough to support fairly large urban centers with the needed basic physical and socioeconomic infrastructure. This exacerbates primacy: "polarization, regional inequality or primacy are normal aspects of the early stages of development" (Alonso, 1968:8). What is debated is the view that with development, convergence on the lines of the rank-size rule would occur. Authors like S. El-Shakhs (1972) contend that this will be the case, while others like J. R. Friedmann (1966:14) disagree: "disequilibrium is built into traditional societies from the start. . . . [T]hus regional convergence will not automatically occur in the course of a nation's development history." The evidence from Sierra Leone points to the fact that at least by 1985, divergence rather than convergence patterned on the rank-size rule was still taking place.

Size of the Country: According to central-place theory, the number of production centers should be selected in order to minimize total production and access costs to consumers for goods and services. These various cost items are determined by plant- or site-specific economies of scale. All things being equal, in small countries like Sierra Leone, because of insignificant access costs to consumers and limited within plant economies of scale due to the circumscribed industrial environment, there is a tendency for the concentration of production in one or very few localities.

CONCLUSIONS

This chapter has traced the evolution of urbanization patterns and trends in Sierra Leone since precolonial days. Freetown, the capital city, grew from a tiny settlement of no more than 350 people in 1787 to about 125,000 at independence in 1961, then to 690,000 in 1990, a very impressive gain in the 200-year period. Freetown is projected to have 1.12 million inhabitants by 2000 and the total Sierra Leone urban population may reach 2.17 million at that time (United Nations, 1989).

Despite the country's relatively low level of urbanization—27 percent in 1985—the urban population grew rapidly in 1974–85 and especially in 1963–74. The concentration of the urban population and development in the Western Area, the site of Freetown, the capital, has engendered primacy.

This resulting spatial pattern of uneven population distribution is perceived as a problem by planners. To this end regional policies have been proposed to ameliorate some of the adverse consequences of uneven population distribution. For example, *The Outline of the National Development Plan, 1981/82–1985/86* emphasizes rural development programs as one of the strategies for reducing regional imbalances in the country (Sierra Leone, 1986a).

The plan also envisages the "creation of a wide range of growth poles in the villages" among its regional development policies, although the actual mechanics of this strategy, especially the important issue of the selection of villages to act as growth poles, were not discussed. In this connection, drawing from the experience of Kenya, which in the 1970s also had a growth pole strategy, it is necessary to bear in mind in the formulation of a future growth pole strategy in Sierra Leone that villages should be selected on the criterion that they form part of an overall national spatial system rather than on their individual merit (Richardson, 1980).

More generally, solutions of problems of Sierra Leone's emergent urban system should be viewed holistically within the overall context of urban bias development (Drakakis-Smith, 1992). This implies that attention should be paid to issues such as future location of industries and other development infrastructures along with the correction of past policies inimical to agricultural production and directly and indirectly responsible for the widening of the rural-urban gap.

NOTES

1. For a useful historical overview of urbanization in the precolonial and colonial periods, see Harvey (1975) and Harvey and Dewdney (1968).

2. The rank-size rule employed to measure skewness in city distribution produces a distribution that is very similiar to the lognormal distribution as well as the Pareto distribution, although for the latter rank rather cumulative percentage of cities is utilized.

3. According to the three regression models estimated, the adjusted R square values varied between .894 in 1963 and .935 in 1974, and the t-statistics from −11.63 in 1963 to −20.75 in 1985. The three equations had roughly the same goodness of fit. Also note that only the populations 5,000 and above were used for the estimation (18 in 1963, 20 in 1974, and 35 in 1985).

4. For a more comprehensive discussion of the determinants of primacy, see Mutlu (1989).

REFERENCES

Alonso, W. 1968. "Urban and Regional Imbalances." *Economic Development and Cultural Change* 17:1–14.

Beckman, M. 1959. "City Hierarchies and the Distribution of City Size." *Economic Development and Cultural Change* 6:243–248.

Byerlee, D., J. L. Tommy, and Habib Fatoo. 1976. "Rural-Urban Migration in Sierra Leone: Determinants and Policy Implications." *African Rural Economy Papers,* No. 13. East Lansing: Michigan State University.

Campbell, E. K. 1986. "Internal Migration in the Western Area of Sierra Leone." *African Urban Quarterly* 1:86–101.

Drakakis-Smith, David, ed. 1992. *Urban and Regional Change in Southern Africa.* London: Routledge.

ECA (Economic Commission for Africa). 1989. *Patterns, Causes and Consequences of Urbanization in Africa.* Addis Ababa.

El-Shakhs, S. 1972. "Development, Primacy and Systems of Cities." *Journal of Developing Areas* 7:11–35.

Friedmann, J. R. 1966. *Regional Development Policy.* Cambridge, Mass.: MIT Press.

Fyfe, Christopher, and Eldred Jones. 1968. *Freetown: A Symposium.* Freetown: Sierra Leone University Press.

Gleave, M. B. 1982. "Population Redistribution in Sierra Leone 1963–74." In *Redistribution of Population in Africa,* edited by J. I. Clarke and L. A. Kosinski, 79–84. London: Heinemann.

———. 1988. "Changing Population Distribution in Sierra Leone, 1974–85." *Geography* 73:351–354.

Hance, William A. 1970. *Population, Migration, and Urbanization in Africa.* New York: Columbia University Press.

Harvey, M. 1972. "Town Size." In *Sierra Leone in Maps,* edited by J. I. Clarke, 48–49. New York: Africana Publishing Corporation.

———. 1975. "The Nature and Movement of the Population." In *Population Growth and Socio-Economic Change in West Africa,* edited by J. C. Caldwell, 455–472. New York: Columbia University Press.

Harvey, Milton, and John Dewdney. 1968. "Planning Problems in Freetown." In *Freetown: A Symposium,* edited by Christopher Fyfe and Eldred Jones, 179–95. Freetown: Sierra Leone University Press.

International Labour Organization. 1981. *Ensuring Equitable Growth: A Strategy for*

Increasing Employment, Equality and Basic Need Satisfaction in Sierra Leone. Addis Ababa: Jobs and Skills Program for Africa.

Jefferson, M. 1939. "The Law of the Primate City." *Geographical Review* 29:226–232.

Levi, J. F. S. 1976. *African Agriculture: Economic Action and Reaction in Sierra Leone.* Slough: Commonwealth Agriculture Bureaux.

McKay, J. 1972. "Freetown." In *Sierra Leone in Maps,* edited by J. I. Clarke, 58–59. New York: Africana Publishing Corporation.

Mutlu, S. 1989. "Urban Concentration and Primacy Revisted: An Analysis and Some Policy Conclusions." *Economic Development and Cultural Change* 37:611–639.

Okoye, C. S. 1981. *Population Distribution, Urbanization and Migration in Sierra Leone.* Freetown: Central Statistics Office.

Pacione, Michael. 1990. *Urban Problems: An Applied Analysis.* London: Routledge.

Peil, M., and P. Sada. 1984. *African Urban Society.* Chichester: John Wiley.

Richardson, H. W. 1980. "An Urban Development Strategy for Kenya." *Journal of Developing Areas* 15:97–118.

Sawers, L. 1989. "Urban Primacy in Tanzania." *Economic Development and Cultural Change* 37:841–859.

Sesay, L. M. 1989. "Urban Growth in Sierra Leone: Trends and Some Demographic Aspects." M.A. thesis Regional Institute for Population Studies (RIPS), University of Ghana, Legon.

Sierra Leone. 1965. *The 1963 Population Census of Sierra Leone,* vol. 2. Freetown: Central Statistics Office.

———. 1974. *National Development Plan 1974/75–1978/79.* Freetown: Government Printer for Ministry of Development and Economic Planning.

———. 1986a. *The Outline of the National Development Plan, 1981/82–1985/86.* Freetown: Ministry of Development and Economic Planning.

———. 1986b. *National Population Census: Provisional Figures.* Freetown: National Census Office.

Simon, David. 1992. *Cities, Capital and Development: African Cities in the World Economy.* London: Belhaven Press.

United Nations. 1989. *Prospects of World Urbanization, 1988.* Population Studies 112. New York.

———. 1991. *World Urbanization Prospects 1990.* Population Studies 120. New York.

19

South Africa

Anthony Lemon and Gillian P. Cook

Twentieth-century urbanization in South Africa reflects patterns of capitalist economic development and state policies. South African economic and geographical realities have long mirrored global north-south relationships of wealth and poverty (Lemon, 1987). Earlier use of the term *dual economy* gave the misleading impression that modern and subsistence economies existed side by side but quite apart from one another. The modern capitalist economy has exploited the labor supply of the traditional sector, in both the South African periphery and neighboring states, impoverishing and underdeveloping that periphery in the process.

In global terms, South Africa may be viewed as a semideveloped, secondary core which is both exploited by the core of the world capitalist economy and itself exploits the periphery (Wallerstein, 1974). South Africa may be viewed as consisting of three zones (Fair, 1984): the core zone of "installed capitalism" which encompasses the major enclaves of mining, manufacturing, and commercial activity; the "inner periphery" of commercial farming areas in white hands, which also includes mining areas, some of them relatively recent such as Phalaborwa in the eastern Transvaal and Sishen in the northern Cape; and the "outer periphery" which coincides with the bantustans, or homelands, based on the pattern of subsistence reserves established in the nineteenth century but modified and enlarged in a vain attempt to fit them for their intended apartheid role of independent states.

This simple model is reflected in the distributional and hierarchical characteristics of South African urbanization, and in the racially differentiated patterns of South African urbanization, leading I. J. van der Merwe (1973) to compare the relatively high levels of white, colored (mixed race), and Indian urbanization with those of developed countries, and the low levels of African urbanization with those of developing countries. Statistics alone, however, conceal the extent of the migrant labor system, the central feature of core-periphery exploitation whereby African labor has been imported to the mines and the cities on a temporary basis, leaving dependents in the outer periphery. Such a process has inevitably affected the age and sex profiles of urban populations.

In recent decades South Africa's major cities have experienced rapid growth similar to that of most Third World cities, but mostly unrecorded by official censuses because of its informal, periurban character and its spatial displacement across bantustan boundaries. So important is this phenomenon that even a quasi-official publication (the Development Bank of Southern Africa) publishes estimates of functional urbanization alongside official census figures (DBSA, 1990). This is but one problem which complicates the statistical analysis of urbanization in South Africa. Underenumeration, especially of urban Africans (not unconnected with their ''illegal'' status), was apparent in the 1980s, and its varying extent can invalidate simple comparison of censuses. This was further complicated by conferring nominal independence on four bantustans, beginning with Transkei in 1976 and ending with Ciskei in 1981. These so-called ''TVBC countries'' (Transkei, Venda, Bophuthatswana, and Ciskei) have been excluded from South African censuses. However, the DBSA, the South African Institute of Race Relations, and the Urban Foundation have prepared estimates to give a more complete picture.

THE SITUATION AT THE ACT OF UNION

One in four South Africans lived in towns by 1911 (Table 19.1). More than a quarter of the urban population lived in Johannesburg and Cape Town, the only two urban areas with populations of more than 100,000. Just over half of all whites were urbanized, with colored people and Indians not far behind. Only one in eight Africans was classified as urban, but already they constituted more than one-third of the total urban population of 1.5 million, an increase of more than 4 percent of their 1904 share.

Africanization of the towns was well underway even at the beginning of the century, a fact which points to the unreality of white attitudes to urban Africans over the ensuing decades. A high proportion of males reflected the importance of migrant labor, especially in the mines. Manufacturing had not yet developed significantly, and most Africans still relied on the rural economy for subsistence; mine wages below the cost of labor reproduction were made possible by the ability of dependents to support themselves from the land (Wolpe, 1972).

Indians who had come to work on the sugar plantations of Natal were initially offered land as an inducement to reindenture, but as their numbers increased this offer was withdrawn and they turned to market gardening and trading, mostly in periurban and urban areas. Many ''passenger'' immigrants, who had entered

Table 19.1
Increase in Urbanization Levels, 1904–85

	White	Per-cent	Colored/ Asian	Per-cent	African	Per-cent	Total	Per-cent
1904	599	53.6	263	46.5	361	10.3	1,222	23.6
1911	677	53.0	345	50.9	524	13.0	1,546	25.9
1921	908	59.7	385	54.3	658	14.0	1,950	28.2
1936	1,367	68.2	599	60.6	1,252	19.0	3,218	33.6
1946	1,793	75.6	788	65.0	1,902	24.3	4,482	39.3
1951	2,089	79.1	1,016	69.1	2,391	27.9	5,494	43.4
1960	2,575	83.6	1,428	71.9	3,471	31.8	7,474	46.7
1970	3,258	86.9	2,033	77.0	4,989	33.1	10,280	47.9
1980	3,955	87.9	2,692	78.8	6,660	32.5	13,307	45.1
1985	4,092	89.6	2,972	81.3	6,716	32.0	13,780	45.7

All population figures are in thousands.

Sources:

1904-70: Compiled from censuses of South Africa, 1980.

1985: Compiled from South Africa censuses.

the country independently in the 1880s and 1890s, had opened shops in the towns. Between 1891 and 1985 Indians were excluded from the Orange Free State, and other restrictions on their movement between provinces were lifted only in 1975.

The largest concentration of colored people has always been in the western Cape, notwithstanding the migration of many to towns in the Transvaal and elsewhere in search of employment prospects. Early this century coloreds were more highly urbanized than the recently arrived Indians, but this was reversed in 1921. A Cape Act of 1909 consolidated legal recognition of scattered rural areas and mission reserves for coloured people, and other areas, including semi-desert areas of the northwest Cape, were subsequently added. However, the majority of rural coloreds still work on white fruit, vegetable, and wine farms.

As A. J. Christopher and James D. Tarver showed in chapter 3 on urbanization in colonial days, the English-speaking inhabitants dominated the urban sector. The very word *Boer* means farmer, and these Afrikaners, as they gradually came to be known, proved reluctant urbanites. The initial impetus came from the Anglo-Boer War of 1899–1902, which, coupled with droughts and epidemics, compelled many Afrikaners to leave the land. English-speakers continued to dominate the urban capitalist economy; even today, after four decades of Afrikaner-dominated National party governments which have sought to increase Afrikaner participation, their share lags behind that of English-speakers.

URBANIZATION AND ECONOMIC GROWTH, 1911–51

The process of rapid white urbanization initiated by mining discoveries in the last three decades of the nineteenth century was temporarily halted in the first decade of the twentieth century after the Anglo-Boer War. In the next forty years the level of white urbanization rose from 53 percent to 79 percent only 10 percent short of its present level. Indian urbanization also rose rapidly, reaching virtually the same level as that of whites in the mid-1940s; by 1951 77 percent of the Indians were urban residents.

This urbanization process rested upon industrialization. South Africa's gold mines, unlike those in other countries, were sufficiently large and durable to sustain regional economic growth. The geological conditions required much machinery and equipment, and many backward linkages developed to supply the industry's needs, particularly during World War I when South Africa suffered from shipping difficulties and inflated costs of European suppliers. With coal nearby, the Witwatersrand was the natural location for heavy industrial development, while its growing population provided a large consumer market. The Transvaal overtook the Cape as the leading industrial area during the war, and continued to increase its share of industrial output until 1934–35, when it reached 47 percent; since then it has remained approximately stable. The port cities gradually became the servants of this virile industrial interior (McCrystal, 1969).

Tariff barriers, first erected in 1914, were strengthened after 1925, while the establishment of the parastatal Iron and Steel Corporation in 1928 and a higher gold price further assisted rapid manufacturing expansion in the late 1920s and in the postdepression 1930s. The number of workers in manufacturing increased from 115,000 in 1924–25 to 245,000 in 1939–40 (Bell, 1973:27).

The 1933–45 period was one of takeoff into self-sustained growth (Houghton, 1973, 16–17). Foreign capital was attracted, and domestic capital formation increased markedly. During World War II the manufacturing sector exceeded the share of mining in the national income. Manufacturing employment reached 361,000 by 1945, accelerating the movement of Africans out of the reserves. In terms of absolute numbers the African urban population surpassed that of whites between 1936 and 1946, by which time the functioning of the South African economy was irrevocably dependent on the economic integration of all races (Lemon, 1976:35).

Between 200,000 and 300,000 poor whites in the 1920s and 1930s were adversely affected by the legacy of the Anglo-Boer War and the reconstruction of agriculture as they were unable to produce for urban markets and export. Small farmers unable to carry on, and white farm laborers who lost their jobs, were forced into the towns.

This second wave of reluctant, predominantly Afrikaner, urbanites who possessed no industrial skills found mining and industry largely controlled by English interests, and were forced to compete with Africans and colored people whose wages were too low to support a European lifestyle. To lift these whites from degradation, the government introduced labor legislation to protect white workers, thereby laying the foundations on which subsequent apartheid policies were built. While there has been no repetition of the large exodus of poor whites since the 1930s, rural whites continued to decrease in numbers. White migration to urban areas had a profound effect on South Africa's racial demographic map. In a pioneering contribution to the geography of apartheid, H. C. Brookfield (1957) published two maps jointly entitled "the shrinkage of white South Africa." They showed that the areas in which whites constituted 40 and 25 percent respectively of the total population in 1951 were a mere skeleton of their 1911 extent. Huge areas of South Africa, chiefly in the semiarid Karoo and western Highveld, had far smaller white populations in 1951.

Colored people were also urbanizing during this period, but more slowly than Indians or whites; by 1951, 64 percent lived in urban areas, an increase of 18 percent since 1911. A number of reasons explain why the rural colored population remained relatively large. The extension of whites' fruit and vegetable growing, wine production, and mixed farming continued to provide employment in the winter rainfall area of the Cape. Seasonal workers often sought urban employment at other times of the year, but especially if living within commuting distance, they remained rural. African migration to the urban areas in the western Cape (prior to the adoption of an official colored labor preference policy in 1955) also explains why so many colored people remained on the land. The relatively slow provision of low-rent urban housing, with resultant squatting and overcrowding, also deterred rapid colored urbanization.

In 1960 for whites and Indians, and 1970 for colored people, urbanization reached such high levels that only small subsequent increases were possible. Thus, in recent decades urbanization has been essentially an African phenomenon, in both percentage and especially numerical terms.

AFRICAN URBANIZATION, 1921–51: SEGREGATION AND "STALLARDISM"

During the three decades, the level of African urbanization doubled, reaching 28 percent in 1951. Although this was just a third of the white level, it represented a larger absolute number of people, 2.4 million blacks compared to 2.1 million whites. This shift occurred despite official attempts to limit the urbanization of Africans and was accompanied by an increase in the proportion of Africans living in family units in contrast to predominantly male migrant labor conditions. The housing authorities built only 99,250 houses between 1920 and 1950, half for Africans.

Legislation to regulate the conditions of urban Africans was envisaged as early as 1912 of an African middle class with property rights in urban areas. Instead, the policies of the Stallard (Transvaal Local Government) Commission of 1922 won the day, with the assistance of white labor and urban commercial capital which saw their positions threatened by a growing African influx (Rich, 1978). The Commission wanted, *inter alia,* to restrict the number of urban Africans to minimize expenditures on locations. The essence of "Stallardism" is summed up in the oft-quoted dictum that

> the native should only be allowed to enter the urban areas, which are essentially the White man's creation, when he is willing to enter and minister to the needs of the White man, and should depart therefrom when he ceases so to minister. (Transvaal 1922, para. 42)

This doctrine constituted the official government policy for decades. It had far-reaching implications for the provision of services, property ownership, participation in administration, and the morphology of African townships (Smit and Booysen, 1977).

Stallardist principles were embodied in the 1923 Natives (Urban Areas) Act. The act empowered, but did not compel, local authorities to set aside land for African occupation in segregated locations, to house Africans living in the town or require their employers to do so, and to implement a rudimentary system of influx control. The importance of the act rests upon the precedents it established for future legislation (Maylam, 1990). This embodied the central principles of segregation (and hence relocation) and influx control, together with the expectation that African urbanization would be self-financing and the co-optation of Africans, initially in an advisory capacity, to help the system operate. All these principles were developed and strengthened in subsequent legislation, and in some respects including the Botha reforms of the 1980s.

Some of the large municipalities such as Johannesburg, Kimberley, and Bloemfontein, adopted the act almost immediately, although Durban did so only in the 1930s. Smaller towns were more cautious, fearing excessive financial responsibilities, but most African "locations" had been registered by 1937. However, few municipalities were willing to subsidize African housing from general revenue, most relying on profits from beer halls, and only 11 towns had systematically instituted influx controls by 1937 (Savage, 1986). More systematic influx control was introduced in the 1937 Native Laws Amendment Act, but its central measures—giving Africans coming to the towns 14 days to find work and making Africans liable to "rustication" if municipal returns showed a labor surplus—remained discretionary.

Rapid industrial growth in the war years led to some changes in attitude. Industrialists stressed the value of semiskilled Africans in manufacturing employment, and several official voices urged reform. J. C. Smuts himself viewed African urbanization realistically, urging that "you might as well try to sweep the ocean back with a broom" (1942:10). Yet his government sought to strengthen influx control through the 1945 Natives (Urban Areas) Consolidation

Act. This reduced the period allowed to search for work to three days. Section 10 allowed an African to claim permanent residence in an urban area only if he had resided there continuously since birth, had lawfully resided there for 15 years, or had worked there for the same employer for 10 years. Once again, however, this law was only applicable at the request of a local authority until the new Nationalist government made it mandatory in 1952.

In the early postwar years, squatter settlements mushroomed around the bigger cities. Most municipalities made some attempt to fill the African housing backlog, but the task was immense. The old reluctance to increase the rates to subsidize large-scale African housing was compounded by continuing doubts about the permanency of the Urban African population, encouraged by uncertainty over the life of some of the goldfields. Signs of a change in official attitudes to African urbanization were apparent in the report of the Fagan Commission (South Africa, 1948), which strongly criticized the migrant labor system and the inhumanity of the influx control. However, whites were alarmed by the dramatic growth of urban African numbers, which became a central issue in the 1948 election campaign, in which the National party's *swart gevaar* (black danger) arguments contributed to its unexpected victory. Had Smuts won, both urbanization and urban residential patterns would have been treated pragmatically rather than ideologically; instead controls on both were to be strictly reinforced under apartheid.

AFRICAN URBANIZATION UNDER APARTHEID

Apartheid ideologies continued to view urban Africans in essentially Stallardist terms, as a labor force whose workers (and their dependents) "belonged" in the bantustans, and as a necessary evil whose numbers should be minimized and whose presence should be tightly controlled.

The most fundamental measure affecting African urbanization was the 1952 Native Laws Amendment Act, which laid the basis for all state intervention to control the distribution of African labor between town and country and between towns. Section 10 of the 1945 act became mandatory and was extended to cover mine workers who had been previously exempted. The act also strengthened provision for the expulsion of Africans deemed surplus to labor requirements, and introduced *efflux control* by means of canalizing labor through labor bureaus in rural areas, from which permission to go to "prescribed" (mainly urban) areas had to be obtained. Similar controls were applied to movement between prescribed areas in relation to labor demands. Rigorous implementation of these measures, which were further strengthened in 1964, resulted in well over half a million prosecutions annually for transgressions of the pass laws in the late 1960s. Within urban areas and their environs, the central state assumed more and more power over the lives of urban Africans, at the expense of local autonomy. The 1951 Illegal Squatting Act was aimed at periurban squatting by Africans who were seeking or were already in employment in adjacent towns.

Within those towns, the Department of Native Affairs intervened with increasing frequency, ignoring municipal opposition to schemes such as the removal of long-established African communities in western Johannesburg. From 1954 onwards attempts were even made, especially in new townships, to segregate African ethnic groups from one another, in order to give substance to the policy of linking Africans with their respective bantustans (Pirie, 1984). In 1972 the municipalities surrendered control of urban Africans to 22 administration boards, which became responsible for housing, influx control, and the regulation of African labor (Bekker and Humphries, 1985).

In the late 1960s the policy shifted to one of providing accommodation in bantustans for Africans working in adjacent or nearby towns whenever possible. This was effected by General Circular no. 27 of 1967, in terms of which local authorities had to obtain government approval before initiating any African housing schemes. Extensions to existing townships in Pretoria, East London, and elsewhere were subsequently suspended, and the city councils, acting as agents of the South African Bantu Trust, began large-scale construction programs at Mabopane (Bophuthatswana, north of Pretoria), Mdantsane (Ciskei, near East London), and elsewhere in the bantustans. Such townships accommodated not only increased African population but also those removed from existing townships such as Duncan Village (East London) and Cato Manor (Durban). So began the damming up of African urbanization behind artificial boundaries which has continued ever since in both townships and informal settlements, creating increasingly disembodied apartheid cities or urban functional regions.

It is impossible to evaluate precisely the impact of these policies on the actual levels of African urbanization. Throughout the period 1921–51 the intercensal growth rate of the urban African population exceeded 4 percent annually, notwithstanding the controls operated by many local authorities in terms of the 1923, 1937, and 1945 acts. The much more stringent controls introduced after 1950 made little dent in this rate of growth in the first two decades, although it certainly would have been higher in the absence of controls. The level of African urbanization continued to grow steadily from 28 percent in 1951 to 33 percent in 1970, when the urban African population reached 5 million.

Thereafter, the statistical picture becomes complicated. Official census figures suggest that 38 percent of Africans were urbanized in 1980 and 40 percent in 1985, but these figures exclude Transkei, Bophuthatswana, and Venda, all "independent." Their inclusion reduces the African urbanization level in both years to about 33 percent, as in 1970, suggesting that apartheid was finally succeeding in halting the process of African urbanization. Such an impression is misleading. The 1980 census in particular underestimated the urban African population substantially, and to a greater extent than past censuses. Both the 1980 and 1985 censuses also excluded the growing numbers of Africans living in informal settlements in bantustan areas near Durban, East London, Newcastle, Pretoria, and elsewhere, who were clearly urban-oriented and dependent on incomes generated in an urban milieu. Many resettlement areas in the bantustans—the so-called dense settlements—are also urban in the sense of lacking agricultural support, although they possess few urban functions. Allowing for these and other factors, the level of African urbanization appears to have reached approximately 56 percent in 1980 and 65 percent in 1985, or 55 percent excluding the denser settlements. These figures exclude Transkei, Bophuthatswana, and Venda, all independent in 1980; Ciskei became independent shortly afterwards and was also excluded from the 1985 census. Given the deficiencies of the data on which these estimates are based, they should be treated only as indicative of the approximate magnitude.[1]

AFRICAN POPULATION DISTRIBUTION BY AGE, SEX, AND REGIONAL TYPE

The 1950s emerged as the last decade of substantial net migration to urban areas outside the bantustans, estimated at 307,000 to the metropolitan areas and 49,000 to other towns. C. Simkins (1984) attributes 28 percent of this migration to white rural areas, where farm mechanization was already reducing labor needs, and the rest to the bantustans. The percentage of domestic Africans in the towns and metropolitan areas rose from 25 to 30 in this decade, indicating that state controls were failing in their objective. Masculinity ratios dropped in both towns, where a figure of 1.04 indicated near normality, and metropolitan areas, where a substantial decrease still left a masculinity ratio of 1.39 (Table 19.2). The percentage of Africans in economically active age-groups declined in this decade, providing evidence of growing normalization of family structures among urban Africans in the 1950s.

Simkins's breakdown of migration by age cohorts shows a relatively strong migration to metropolitan areas in the 15–29 age group, but a greater tendency among both young and old to leave the metropolitan areas. This suggests a relatively unsettled urban African population during the 1950s, continuing to maintain strong rural links.

The 1960s were characterized as "the decade of the big state effort of population relocation," with a massive net inflow of 977,000 to the bantustans. This appears to be largely the result of an outflow from white rural areas, reflecting the extent of state-sponsored removals of "surplus people"—labor tenants and squatters from white-owned farms, and residents of "black spots," areas of African land, to which the inhabitants in many cases had legal title, in the midst of commercial farming areas (Baldwin, 1975; Platzky and Walker, 1985). These forced migrations were massive in scale, greatly disruptive, and usually reduced their victims to cruel poverty and dependence in euphemistically labelled "closer settlements" in the bantustans.

Significantly, there was also a net outflow of 195,000 Africans from the metropolitan areas and 8,000 from the towns in the 1960s. Here is the first clear indication that state policies were achieving their objectives, coinciding in the later years of the decade with both peak numbers of prosecutions under the pass

Table 19.2
Urban African Population, 1950–80 (in Thousands)

	Metropolitan			Towns		
	Male		Female	Male		Female
1950						
Percent of total	20.7		12.7	9.2		8.1
Masculinity ratio		1.66			1.16	
Percent 15-64 M	80		65	64		56
Percent 15-59 F						
1960						
Percent of total	23.8		17.1	9.3		9.0
Masculinity ratio		1.39			1.04	
Percent 15-64 M	73		59	58		52
Percent 15-59 F						
1970						
Percent of total	21.8		16.6	10.2		7.7
Masculinity ratio		1.29			1.31	
Percent 15-64 M	70		59	67		53
Percent 15-59 F						
1980						
Percent of total	21.0		16.3	9.4		6.7
Masculinity ratio		1.28			1.39	
Percent 15-64 M	74		66	67		60
Percent 15-59 F						

Source: Compiled from South Africa Censuses, 1951, 1960, 1970, 1980.

laws and the implementation of General Circular no. 27 of 1967. In the metropolitan areas the outflow had little effect on the masculinity ratio, which decreased further to 1.29, but in other towns it rose significantly to 1.31. The proportion of Africans in the economically active age-groups continued to decline slightly in metropolitan areas but rose in other towns, producing a convergence of profiles between these two urban environments.

A net emigration of children under 15 years of age occurred from both towns and metropolitan areas, and of all ages from metropolitan areas in the late 1960s. This out-movement of young people presumably consisted of children not permitted to live in prescribed (urban) areas, who were sent to live with family members in rural areas, whether on white farms or in the bantustans. The demand for adult labor was sufficient to induce net migration in the age-group (15–29), preponderantly male, to both metropolitan areas and towns. Emigration of both sexes was characteristic of older age-groups, for which the labor demand was reduced, but the rate of emigration was less than in the 1950s.

There was a continuing but slower net movement to the bantustans in the 1970s. The net migration from white rural areas was smaller but still over half a million. Net movement from metropolitan areas dropped to almost zero, but migration from other towns increased. This was influenced by the government program of wholly or partially closing small-town locations, relocating the inhabitants in the bantustans, and replacing settled labor with commuters. Masculinity ratios continued to rise in these towns, although much more slowly than in the 1960s, but they remained stable in the metropolitan areas. The proportion of economically active Africans rose slightly in the metropolitan areas, reverting to the 1960 figure, but remained stable in other towns.

Migration rates of people over 30 from metropolitan areas were further reduced in the 1970s, with some movement to other towns. Migration rates from metropolitan areas of those under 15 increased markedly, suggesting greater pressures on parents to send their children to the bantustans. The increasingly violent nature of township life, including the violence of political protest from 1976 (the year of the Soweto riots) and frequent disruption of education, contributed to such pressures.

The demographic complexities of the 1921–51 period may be attributed to three sets of pressures on rural Africans: the decline in employment on white farms, initially the rapidly increasing African population living on farms; population growth and increased rural overcrowding in the bantustans, with limited growth of employment opportunities, despite state-sponsored industrial growth points; and apartheid policies to minimize the African presence in both urban and rural areas outside the bantustans. The natural response to the first two pressures would have been migration to urban areas in search of better opportunities, but this was severely constrained by the third, state-induced pressure. This pressure had a limited effect in the 1950s, but since 1960 it resulted in a massive net movement of Africans to the bantustans; stalled urbanization outside the bantustans in notable contrast to other semideveloped economies; and destabilization of parts of what was an increasingly settled African population.

There has been not only a movement to the homelands, but movements within them. Homeland urbanization is a crucial part of the African urban experience in South Africa, and one whose spatial characteristics are largely a product of apartheid.

BANTUSTAN URBANIZATION SINCE 1960

Urban growth in the bantustans was very limited in 1960. The dramatic changes which have occurred since are largely a product of apartheid policies rather than pure economic forces. Thus despite the location of the bantustans in the periphery of the South African space economy, their share of the African population has increased sharply since 1960: for men, the percentage living in the bantustans rose from 33 in 1960 to 48 in 1980, and for women, who participate little in the migrant labor process, the percentage increased from 45 to 57 (Simkins, 1984:8). These increases result from relocation from both white rural areas and, since 1967, urban areas outside the bantustans; the rate of natural increase in the bantustans has also tended to be slightly higher than in metropolitan areas.

A normal hierarchy is absent (Cook, 1980a, 1980b), reflecting both the artificiality of the bantustans as political units and their peripherality within the South African space-economy. The largest urban settlements are characteristically appendages of white core areas across the border, forming politically and to varying extents physically detached parts of urban functional regions.

Several distinct forms of urban settlement may be recognized in the bantustans;

1. Capital "cities," all of them new urban places except Umtata (Transkei) and the old town of Mafeking, now Mafikeng, which has been incorporated into the new capital of Bophuthatswana, Mmabatho (see Drummond and Parnell, 1991).
2. Industrial growth points designated under present and previous decentralization programs. Under the 1982 strategy, 28 of the 48 industrial development points were located in the bantustans (Lemon, 1987; 186), although some have attracted very limited industrial capacity.
3. "Denser settlements," as mentioned above, currently estimated to house 3 million people.
4. Proclaimed towns which are functionally part of a wider urban system based on a white town, city, or metropolitan area.
5. Informal urban settlements which are also part of wider urban systems based on white urban areas, and which frequently adjoin townships in category 4.

These categories overlap considerably in practice. Thus five bantustan capitals—Mmabatho-Mafikeng, Umtata, Ulundi (KwaZulu), Phuthaditjaba (QwaQwa), and Thohoyandou (Venda)—are also industrial development points (Figure 19.1) So are many proclaimed towns which are part of urban functional regions based on white towns: examples include Babelegi and Garankuwa in Bophuthatswana, north of Pretoria, Madadeni/Osizweni, adjacent to the steel town of Newcastle in northern Natal, and Seshego in Lebowa, adjacent to Pietersburg in the northern Transvaal.

The divergence between officially recorded and functional urbanization is even greater in the bantustans than in the rest of South Africa (Table 19.3). This is particularly true of those bantustans with large informal urban settlements in

Figure 19.1
Population Centers of 20,000 Inhabitants and Homeland Areas, 1985

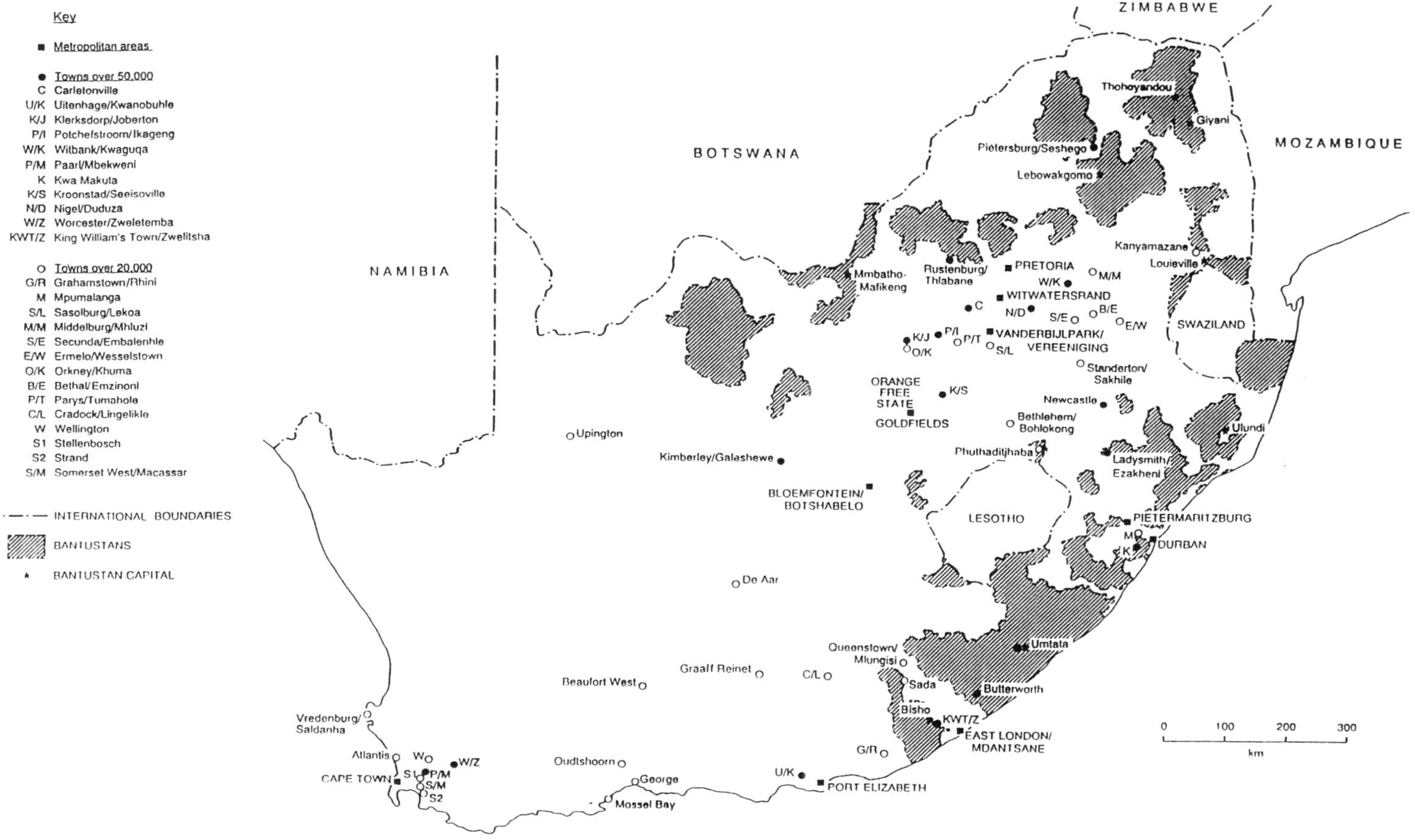

Table 19.3
South African Urbanization, 1980, 1985, 1989

Country		1980	1985	1989
South	(O)	13,057	15,512	17,547
Africa	Percent	53.7	55.9	57.1
	(F)	16,526	18,655	21,573
	Percent	68.0	67.2	70.2
Transkei	(O)	129	153	173
	Percent	4.9	5.3	5.8
	(F)	234	292	364
	Percent	8.9	10.2	11.7
Bophutha-	(O)	239	277	300
tswana	Percent	15.8	15.9	15.6
	(F)	1.083	1,198	1,341
	Percent	71.7	68.8	69.8
Venda	(O)	7	14	19
	Percent	1.9	3.0	3.6
	(F)	66	77	90
	Percent	17.3	16.7	17.1
Ciskei	(O)	242	268	283
	Percent	35.4	35.5	35.2
	(F)	458	557	680
	Percent	67.1	74.3	84.7
TOTAL	(O)	13,674	16,224	18,322
	Percent	46.4	48.3	49.4
	(F)	18,367	20,779	24,048
	Percent	62.3	61.9	64.8

Key: O = Official (census) figures

F = Functional urban population, which includes periurban (concentrations of people who commute to proclaimed urban areas for employment, shopping, etc.) and semiurban population concentrations of over 5,000.

Source: DBSA, 1990.

category 5 above: hence the extraordinary variations in the 1989 urbanization levels for Ciskei and Bophuthatswana in Table 19.3. Bantustans further removed from larger white towns characteristically display much lower levels of urbanization, but the tendency of capitals such as Umtata to generate their own rural-urban migration and periurban informal settlements helps to explain still significant differences between official and functional urbanization figures.

Within the bantustans, the pressures on migration identified above have led to a massive redistribution of population toward both formal townships and informal settlements in border areas which offer ''jumping off points'' for potential employment opportunities in white urban areas. Normal urbanization is thus displaced across bantustan borders, and ''frontier commuters'' must daily cross these borders in the course of their journey to work (Lemon, 1982). They numbered 773,000 in 1982, and perhaps 850,000 in 1990, for which no reliable data are available. Undoubtedly the increase in the number of commuters has been much slower than that of the periurban populations from which they are drawn. This reflects the stagnation of the South African economy in the 1980s, accompanied by increasing African unemployment; in such a situation those fortunate enough to live in white urban areas—those with ''section 10 rights'' until the repeal of the 1945 Natives (Urban Areas) Consolidation Act in 1986—had a better chance of keeping or finding urban employment than those in distant informal settlements.

This phenomenon affects the bantustans unequally. Transkei, Gazankulu, QwaQwa, and KaNgwane are too distant from white towns for significant daily movement, although widespread informal urbanization has occurred in some relatively remote bantustan locations, as in Kanyamazane (KaNgwane), which depends partly on employment on white tobacco farms in the White River area, and the settlement of Lonely Park on the fringes of Mmabatho. Small commuter flows occur from Venda to Louis Trichardt and from Lebowa to Pietersburg and Potgietersrus. By far the most important flows, however, are from KwaZulu to Durban, Pietermaritzburg, and Newcastle; from Bophuthatswana and KwaNdebele to Pretoria and the Eastern Rand; and from Mdantsane, Ciskei, to East London. These correspond to the major concentrations of urban and periurban population within bantustan border areas, which are discussed below.

KwaZulu was responsible for more than half of all ''frontier commuters'' in 1982. By 1990, the Urban Foundation estimated an informally settled population of 1.7 million in the Durban functional region, most of them living within the boundaries of KwaZulu, which included six town councils in the metropolitan core area and no less than 40 informal settlements without formal local authority structures in the distant periphery of the Durban functional region (Davies, 1991:84). Dense shack concentrations have tended to cluster near formal townships where some services are available and transport is more accessible. M. D. McGrath (1989) found that 63 percent of adults had no formal employment, underlining the growing dependence of such areas on informal employment. For those who do have jobs, journeys to work are long and often indirect, costly in money, time, and effort.

Pretoria is unusual in attracting "frontier commuters" from two bantustans, Bophuthatswana and KwaNdebele. The latter—characterized by A. Mabin (1989:9) as "no more than a recent and growing assemblance of land bought by the state and turned over to newly fashioned 'tribal authorities' who maximize income by renting residential sites"—grew from minimal population to 255,000 in 1988.

Bophuthatswana's commuting settlements are longer established, and remain far more important numerically. Behind the formal town of Mabopane, with its purpose-built commuter rail link to Pretoria, lies the Winterveld, an area of largely freehold land with a population of at least 600,000, about one-third of Bophuthatswana's total population. African landowners in this area have facilitated informal settlement by renting plots at considerable profit to themselves. People have moved here as a result of the rationalization and mechanization of white farming, evictions from "black spots" surrounded by white farmland, and removal from land in Pretoria designated as "group areas" for other race groups. Such is the pull of Pretoria that this population includes many non-Tswana people, who have resisted continued harassment from the Bophuthatswana authorities rather than return to the bantustans of the northern and eastern Transvaal (Lemon, 1987:229).

The containment of African urbanization has, in the case of Pretoria, led to extremely long travel distances, averaging 52 kilometers in one direction (Hattingh and Horn, 1991). Given the poverty of those who must commute, subsidy of travel costs is essential. In the case of KwaNdebele, whose commuters face some of the longest journeys to work anywhere in South Africa, the total cost of bus subsidies actually exceeds the gross domestic product (GDP) of this impoverished bantustan (Lelyveld, 1986). People from the most distant periurban outposts of both KwaNdebele and Bophuthatswana spend up to seven hours a day on traveling.

The third major concentration of urban population within the bantustans is found at Mdantsane, 20 kilometers northwest of East London. This huge township is a direct product of apartheid ideology. The failure of the East London City Council to improve the lot of its African population led to direct government intervention, designed not only to rectify the situation but more specifically to develop Mdantsane as an African township within an African homeland. Construction began in 1963 and has continued ever since, allowing for the relocation of Africans from East London between 1964 and 1983. The removal of the African populace was never fully achieved; removals were resisted and eventually halted following the refusal of Ciskei to accommodate any more people removed from East London (Fox et al., 1991).

The population of Mdantsane already exceeded that of East London by 1973. It has continued to grow through both natural increase and migration from rural areas in Ciskei. Today Mdantsane has become, *de jure,* not only the largest bantustan township, but also the second largest formal township in South Africa (after Soweto), with a population that now exceeds 250,000.

The halting of removals from East London to Mdantsane symbolizes the wider inability of apartheid planners to realize their grandiose ideals. This change in policy occurred at a time when the inevitability of African urbanization to meet the changing labor needs of a more sophisticated economy had become gradually apparent to the government. We shall now examine its responses in the face of this new awareness in the 1980s.

STATE RESPONSES TO AFRICAN URBANIZATION IN THE 1980s

Initially the government sought to deal with African urbanization through characteristic incremental reforms designed to optimize labor flows within a modified apartheid framework (Lemon, 1987:233). The basic strategy, embodied in the report of the Riekert Commission (South Africa, 1979) and a subsequent white paper, was to widen differentiation between "insiders" and "outsiders." By making the best use of those Africans who already possessed section 10 rights, allowing them spatial and job mobility, the need to admit more Africans to the cities could be minimized. Rural Africans (whether on white farms or in the bantustans) would thus be pushed firmly to the end of the labor queue.

Attempts to translate the Riekert proposals into legislation were rejected by Parliament, largely because of conservative drafting which failed to entrench, let along extend, urban residence rights in the spirit of Riekert. Forces outside the state apparatus seemed to be driving toward more fundamental changes than the Riekert proposals (Hindson and Lacey, 1983:104). Meanwhile, however, the legal definition of those who could potentially qualify for section 10 rights was actually narrowed by the independence of Transkei, Bophuthatswana, Venda, and Ciskei; children born after the independence of the bantustan to which they were officially assigned could never acquire these rights, regardless of where they were officially born or actually lived (Budlender, 1984).

In South Africa as a whole, some 3.9 million Africans qualified in their own right in 1985, and a further 1.7 million qualified as dependents. They were concentrated largely in Pretoria-Witwatersrand-Vereeniging (PWV), Port Elizabeth, Bloemfontein, and Kimberley (Bekker and Humphries, 1985). In Pretoria, the East Rand, and Bloemfontein their numbers were steadily eroded by the use of housing as a control, as people with section 10 rights were forced to accept offers of new housing in townships outside prescribed urban areas, at Soshanguve, Ekangala, and Botshabelo respectively. In Natal, the widening of KwaZulu's boundaries to include *de facto* townships of Durban left few people formally qualified, although those who had been previously, continued to be treated as "administrative section 10s" (Lemon, 1991:20). In the western Cape, application of the policy of colored labor preference between 1954 and 1984 meant that few Africans were able to qualify for section 10 rights.

In 1983, in the face of an unwelcome court judgment, the government attempted to limit the effect of amending section 10 so that the family of a man who had qualified by virtue of ten years continuous employment with his employer could only join him if he had a house of his own rented or bought, or married quarters provided by his employer. This appeared to close the door on any continuing legal urbanization process (Duncan, 1985).

The actual machinery of influx control and labor allocation changed considerably after 1980. The centralization of recruitment in new ''employment and guidance'' centers in or near African townships in larger cities gave preference to local work seekers, as Riekert had recommended, increasing their mobility. After the onset of recession in 1982, stricter controls were exercised over the entry of workers without section 10 qualifications into urban areas. In the bantustans, S. Greenberg and H. Giliomee (1985) document the breakdown of labor bureaus and mine recruitment as the labor market contracted and the labor surplus grew ever larger, with the result that vast areas and populations were virtually excluded from the urban labor market.

Notwithstanding this bureaucratic environment, many rural households had to find access to urban economies for sheer survival. They found various means of doing so, ranging from backyard shacks in formal townships to the periurban bantustan settlements described above. By the end of the 1980s, there were an estimated 7 million informal settlers in and around South African towns. Overcrowding of township housing had reached almost unimaginable proportions in many areas: densities of 15 or more persons per four-roomed house were widespread, with even higher figures in some areas. In the metropolitan fringe, people settled on whatever land they could find, including farms, smallholdings, and vacant land around the Witwatersrand and in Inanda, near Durban, and on church-owned land at St. Wendolin's, also near Durban. Many faced eviction and relocation, often repeatedly, but for some at least their persistence was eventually rewarded as new communities became established, albeit precariously (Mabin, 1989).

Hopes of more fundamental reform in response to increasing awareness of the desperate struggle for survival being waged in the bantustans were seemingly dashed by the 1985 Laws on Co-operation and Development Amendment Act, which was clearly influenced by the Riekert proposals. It allowed the transfer of section 10 rights outside the prescribed areas where they were obtained, and the accumulation of such rights during ten years of living and working in different prescribed areas. It also allowed Africans who settled in self-governing or independent bantustans, or on South African Black Trust land (which was officially destined for incorporation within the bantustans), or whose homes became part of these areas, to retain any section 10 rights they might have.

Such piecemeal tinkering left the situation of rural Africans unchanged, and seemed to indicate that the government had no intention of lifting influx control in the near future. Later the same year, however, the report of a President's Council committee reflected new thinking (South Africa, 1985). African urbanization was accepted not only as inevitable but as "an *opportunity* to utilize one of a country's greatest assets, namely its people, in such a way that the end result for all will be an improvement in the quality of life" (South Africa, 1985:26). The report proposed the elimination of discriminatory aspects of influx control and a shift to a positive strategy emphasizing the development role of orderly urbanization. This would involve the guidance and channelling of urbanization mainly by indirect incentives and disincentives, but also by "*direct control measures,* mainly through existing legislation" (South Africa, 1985:198), including that concerning racial group areas, squatting and slums, health, immigration and security.

In practice the new dispensation continued to be racially discriminatory in two major respects: the continuing allocation of the greater part of the cities to whites, colored people, and Indians under group areas legislation; and the simple fact that Africans were (and are) the only ethnic group still seeking to urbanize necessarily made them the prime targets of any constraints on urbanization.

The new approach was embodied in the 1986 Abolition of Influx Control Act, which provided for total repeal of the Natives (Urban Areas) Consolidation Act of 1945 and the partial or entire repeal of 33 other laws. These changes represented a significant reversal of some of the most hated apartheid policies including the pass laws and the migrant labor system, which had long forced the splitting of families, interrupted the urban experience of Africans, and made most of them insecure. But the new strategy still sought to control and channel African urbanization, using material constraints of land and housing as tools in distributing labor and population, and employing the decentralization and deconcentration programs developed under the regional development strategy which had been operative since 1982 (Tomlinson and Addleson, 1987). As Mabin (1989) argues, this strategy did much more than recognize the breakdown of Stallardist controls: it actually sought to take advantage of informal settlements on the metropolitan peripheries and further afield to fragment the African urban population in ways which facilitated indirect political control.

In the late 1980s the government continued to try to control urban growth in various ways, seeking to control both slums and squatting. The 1988 Prevention of Illegal Squatting Amendment Act included a series of punitive measures, intended largely as a deterrent, but open to farmers and local authorities to use if they wished. More positively, however, the act includes several measures allowing the provision of more land for squatting, particularly the establishment of "informal towns," in which normal regulations governing the establishment of towns would not apply. This was evidently intended as a major instrument to guide the process of informal urbanization.

These reforms of the Botha presidency in the 1980s were dramatically overtaken by the more fundamental changes wrought by President F. W. deKlerk in 1990 and 1991. In the latter year the repeal of the Group Areas, Land and Population Registration acts removed the continuing legal basis for a racially discriminatory urbanization policy, although controls on the availability and location of land for housing and informal settlement will continue to bear almost exclusively on the African population in practice. The next section examines the spatial and hierarchical distribution of South African urban settlements against which the postapartheid urbanization process must evolve.

THE DISTRIBUTION AND SIZE OF URBAN SETTLEMENTS IN 1985

Using the 1985 censuses of South Africa and Transkei, Bophuthatewana, Venda, and Ciskei ("the countries"), the official populations of all metropolitan areas listed in order of size in Table 19.4 and urban centers with more than 20,000 inhabitants are identified in Figure 19.1. Where the census gives separate figures for different parts of a contiguous urban area, often on an ethnic basis where black areas had acquired the status of independent local authorities, these are added together; in some cases, such as East London/Mdantsane, this entailed adding the figures from the censuses of two different "countries." The figures in Table 19.4 thus represent urban systems rather than single local authority areas. They are, however, far smaller in many cases than the functionally urbanized populations, for which the availability of published estimates is too fragmentary to be useful here.

The appellation "metropolitan areas" is arbitrary, and varies from one source to another. The big gap between the population of Pietermaritzburg and Newcastle justifies the recognition of ten metropolitan areas in Table 19.4. No less than 80 percent of all urban dwellers in towns of over 20,000 are found in these ten areas, indicating a very high degree of concentration. Even more pronounced is the collective dominance of Pretoria-Witwatersrand-Vereeniging, South Africa's megalopolis, which alone has 39 percent of urban dwellers in all the settlements appearing in Table 19.4. This area also generates 40 percent of South Africa's GDP.

The metropolitan areas have overshadowed other towns, limiting their growth, to the extent that only four others had more than 100,000 people, together accounting for a mere 4 percent of urban dwellers. Thirteen towns had between 50,000 and 100,000 people, and 31 towns between 20,000 and 50,000. During 1911–36, 77 percent of the positive net shift in South Africa's population occurred in the eight largest metropolitan areas plus Kimberley (Fair, 1965:65), notwithstanding the establishment of several new towns in this period, based on railway development (De Aar), agricultural intensification (eastern Orange Free State), coastal tourism (Margate), and resource development (Nigel). Between 1936 and 1960, 74 percent of the positive net shift was still in the same nine metropolitan areas, but in the 1960s the upward shifts of African population were more widely distributed (Board, 1973), reflecting *inter alia* both recent industrial development and new mining developments on the eastern highveld. All new towns established between the mid-1930s and 1970 were resource-based.

At a magisterial district level, the distribution of districts with an urbanization

Table 19.4
Metropolitan Areas in 1985, with a Summary of the Urban Population in Centers of Various Sizes

METROPOLITAN AREAS	POPULATION 1985
Witwatersrand	3,395,286
Greater Cape Town	1,911,521
Durban	1,482,127
Greater Pretoria	1,034,572
Port Elizabeth	501,804
Vanderbijlpark/Vereeniging	462,242
Greater East London	431,973
Greater Bloemfontein	328,609
Free State Goldfields	320,319
Pietermaritzburg	236,463

	TOTAL URBAN POPULATION	PERCENT OF TOTAL URBAN
Total Metropolitan Areas	10,074,196	72
Towns over 100,000	530,226	4
Towns over 50,000	889,507	6
Towns over 20,000	968,551	7
Other Urban Settlements	1,636,776	11
Total	14,078,652	100

Source: Compiled from South Africa Censuses, 1985.

level of more than 80 percent corresponds quite closely with metropolitan areas, but the 40 percent level divides the country into a relatively more urbanized southwestern part and a relatively less urbanized northeastern part (Van der Merwe, Van der Merwe, and de Necker, 1991). This appears surprising at first sight, given the far greater density of urban settlement in the northeastern half of the country. The explanation rests in the semiarid nature of much of the southwestern half, which supports only extensive grazing outside the winter rainfall area around Cape Town. All of the bantustans except western Bophuthatswana are in the better watered half of the country, although topography and soils limit their agricultural potential over wide areas (Pickles and Weiner, 1991). Outside the bantustans too there is a denser rural population in these northern and eastern parts of South Africa, and it is these areas which are potential reservoirs for future urbanization.

The high degree of metropolitan concentration has long been used by the South African government to justify its industrial decentralization policies, although the relationship of these to apartheid ideology, and in particular the concentration of as high a proportion of the African population as possible in the bantustans, has always been apparent. The urban hierarchy shows that industrial growth points have made a minimal contribution to the redistribution of the urban population. The proportion of urban population living in the 59 deconcentration and industrial development points earmarked in the 1982 strategy (many of which had enjoyed incentives under previous decentralization programs) was only 13 percent in 1980 and 15 percent in 1985 (Van der Merwe, Van der Merwe, and de Necker, 1991).

Umtata is the only freestanding growth point with more than 50,000 people in the bantustans. Apart from its capital city functions, it benefits from being, almost uniquely among bantustan towns, an established town with a rail connection long before Transkeian independence. The same is true of Butterworth, the second growth point to appear. The two freestanding urban places in Ciskei both began life as resettlement camps, thus the people were dumped there long before a degree of very low-wage employment was induced to follow. The same is true of the entire bantustan of QwaQwa, whose capital is Phuthaditjhaba. The only remaining bantustan settlement to appear, Kanyamazane, has already been mentioned for its unusual dependence on agricultural employment on white farms.

The distribution and size of urban settlements in South Africa pose considerable problems for postapartheid planners. Should there be an attempt to reduce the urban dominance of the metropolitan areas by concentrating on secondary cities? The relative absence of higher-order centers over large areas such as the western Karoo and northern Cape makes balanced regional development difficult to achieve, leading I. J. Van der Merwe, J. H. Van der Merwe, and P. H. de Necker (1991) to stress the need for strong regional centers to be identified. Also problematic will be the future of bantustan towns which owe their very existence to apartheid planning: should they be sustained by further assistance or allowed to decline? Underlying all these questions is the probable scale of both continuing urbanization and urban population growth in the next two decades, and the search for strategies to cope with change on the scale anticipated.

PROJECTED URBANIZATION, 1990–2010

If functional and density criteria are used, the urbanization level of South Africa's total population was approaching 60 percent in 1990, excluding denser settlements in the bantustans. This is only slightly below average for countries with similar levels of economic development, which suggests that decades of state control have largely displaced rather than prevented African urbanization. By 1990 about half the African population was urbanized (58 percent including denser settlements), with 39 percent in the functional metropolitan regions of PWV, Cape Town, Durban, Pietermaritzburg, Port Elizabeth, East London, Bloemfontein Botshabelo, and the Orange Free State goldfields (Simkins, 1990). Projections of future African urbanization must estimate the speed with which fertility is likely to drop (the African population was growing by 2.8 percent per annum in the late 1980s), and the extent of (informal) African in-migration from other countries, attracted by the perceived opportunities of a more developed economy (Lemon, 1991:209). The Urban Foundation (1990) projects growth of some 600,000 Africans each year in metropolitan areas, leading to an African population in these areas of about 17.7 million by the year 2000 and 23.7 million in 2010. Two-thirds of this growth will result from natural increase rather than migration, which suggests a limited role at best for regional policies designed to reduce pressures on metropolitan areas.

Already more than 7 million people live in informal housing, including 2.5 million in the PWV area, 1.7 million in greater Durban, and another 1 million split between the Winterveld of Bophuthatswana and KwaNdebele. Such deprivation derives both from the powerlessness of the poor (which can change slowly at best in a new political order), and the fact that South Africa is increasingly a labor-surplus economy (Tomlinson, 1990:13), with between 25 and 40 percent of the economically active urban African population formally unemployed. Policies which make well-located, affordable land available to the poor must be a priority in the 1990s (Tomlinson, 1990; Lemon, 1991). This will be made easier by the repeal in 1991 of the Group Areas Act, ending 40 years of legally entrenched segregation, but will not be achieved without measures to guide and where necessary intervene in the workings of the land market.

The future of South African cities will be affected by wider considerations of rural, regional, and economic policy. If allowed to do so, people live where they can work, thus rural development policies affect the nature and directions of urbanization. Any attempt to create economic agricultural units in the bantustans must displace many people from their current partial dependence on inadequate holdings, and it is most unlikely that the economic base of the bantustans will expand to absorb them. Indeed, the reincorporation of the bantustans into South Africa would remove the functions of their capitals, which could result in severe hardship unless these towns are given alternative functions, perhaps as regional capitals. The future of bantustan growth points, where even existing industries may leave when concessions cease to operate, appears bleak. Migration to bantustan towns is unlikely to cease altogether, but it is likely to be much exceeded by migration from both rural and urban areas in the bantustans to larger cities (Lemon, 1991:213).

The future of white farms also affects the demographic equation. Some degree of subdivision and transfer to African occupation seems inevitable, at least in the better-watered northern and eastern parts of the country. It should not be forgotten, however, that these farms already support (albeit at a miserably low level of living) a sizable African and colored labor force. It seems unlikely that changes of ownership, farm size, and tenure will allow these farms to support a significantly greater African population than at present. Future levels of African urbanization are thus unlikely to be much affected by what happens to these farms.

To what extent, if any, should postapartheid planners seek to control and channel future urbanization? They cannot but be mindful of the costly failures of apartheid decentralization programs, and the decades of African suffering under influx control policies which ultimately failed to achieve their objectives. Hitherto growth points have been too numerous and in many cases unattractively located, attracting only heavily subsidized, labor-intensive industries paying poverty wages. If there is any scope for constructive regional policy, it rests in the stimulation of secondary core areas with strong potential for regional growth (Bos, 1989; Lemon, 1990; Van der Merwe, 1990). At best, however, this is unlikely to do more than close the predicted gap between the growth rates of such secondary cities and those of metropolitan areas.

Even this degree of state intervention to modify the urban system should be critically appraised. In much of the Third World (and often also in the developed countries) efforts to plan the spatial configuration of the urban system as an instrument of regional economic policy have been unsuccessful (Rogerson, 1989a, 1989b). Urban planning in the new South Africa must be centered on the needs of all the people who live, and want to live, in the cities. In the foreseeable future, this means that the goal should be the optimal functioning of the urban system to support accelerated economic development and employment creation.

NOTE

1. These figures are calculated using census figures for white, colored, and Indian urbanization, DBSA (1990) estimates of overall functional urbanization, and an estimate by the Urban Foundation (n.d., c. 1990) suggesting that 6 percent of the total South African population lived in the "dense settlements" in 1985.

REFERENCES

Baldwin, A. 1975. "Mass Removals and Separate Development." *Journal of Southern African Studies* 1:215–227.

Bekker, S. B., and R. Humphries. 1985. *From Control to Confusion: The Changing Role of Administration Boards in South Africa, 1971–1983*. Pietermaritzburg: Shuter and Shooter.

Bell, R. T. 1973. *Industrial Decentralisation in South Africa*. Cape Town: Oxford University Press.

Board, C. 1973. ''Population Concentration in South Africa 1960–1970: A Shift and Share Analysis.'' *Standard Bank Review* supplement (September):5–13.

Bos, D. J. 1989. ''Prospects for the Development of Intermediate Cities as Part of a Decentralization Programme for South Africa.'' *Development Studies Southern Africa* 6:58–81.

Brookfield, H. C. 1957. ''Some Geographical Implications of the Apartheid and Partnership Policies in Southern Africa.'' *Transactions of the Institute of British Geographers* 23:225–247.

Budlender, D. 1984. *Incorporation and Exclusion: Recent Development in Labour Law and Influx Control.* Johannesburg: South African Institute of Race Relations.

Cook, G. P. 1980a. ''Scattered Towns or an Urban System?'' In *Ciskei: Economics and Politics of Dependence in a South African Homeland,* edited by Nancy Charton, 30–47. London: Croom Helm.

———. 1980b. ''Position in an Urban Hierarchy.'' In *Mdantsane: Transitional City,* edited by G. P. Cook and J. Opland, 73–88. Grahamstown: Institute of Social and Economic Research, Rhodes University.

Davies, R. J. 1991. ''Durban.'' In *Homes Apart,* edited by Anthony Lemon, 71–89. London: Paul Chapman.

DBSA (Development Bank South Africa). 1990. *SATVBC Countries: Statistical Abstracts 1989.* Headway Hill, Transvaal: Development Bank of South Africa.

Drummond, J. H., and S. Parnell. 1991. ''Mafikeng-Mmabatho.'' In *Homes Apart,* edited by Anthony Lemon, 162–173. London: Paul Chapman.

Duncan, S. 1985. ''Social and Practical Problems Resulting from the Law Relating to Urban Africans.'' In *Acta Juridica 1984,* 247–254. University of Cape Town: Juta for the Faculty of Law.

Fair, T. J. D. 1965. ''The Core-Periphery Concept and Population Growth in South Africa, 1911–1960.'' *South African Geographical Journal* 47:59–71.

———. 1984. ''The Urbanization Process in South Africa.'' In *Studies on Urbanisation in South Africa,* edited by E. A. Kraayenbrink, 1–5. Johannesburg: South African Institute of Race Relations.

Fox, R., E. Nel, and C. Rentges. 1991. ''East London.'' In *Homes Apart,* edited by Anthony Lemon, 58–70. London: Paul Chapman.

Greenberg, S., and H. Giliomee. 1985. ''Managing Influx Control from the Rural End: The Black Homelands and the Underbelly of Privilege.'' In *Up Against the Fences: Poverty, Passes and Privilege in South Africa,* edited by H. Giliomee and L. Schlemmer, 68–84. New York: St. Martin's Press.

Hattingh, P. S., and A. C. Horn. 1991. ''Pretoria.'' In *Homes Apart,* edited by Anthony Lemon, 146–161. London: Paul Chapman.

Hindson, D. and M. Lacey. 1983. ''Influx Control and Labour Allocation: Policy and Practice since the Riekert Commission.'' *South African Review One,* edited by South African Research Service, 97–113. Johannesburg: Ravan.

Houghton, D. H. 1973. *The South African Economy.* Cape Town: Oxford University Press.

Lelyveld, J. 1986. *Move Your Shadow: South Africa, Black and White.* London: Michael Joseph.

Lemon, A. 1976. *Apartheid: A Geography of Separation.* Farnborough: Saxon House.

———. 1982. ''Migrant Labour and Frontier Commuters: Reorganizing South Africa's Black Labour Supply.'' In *Living under Apartheid: Aspects of Urbanization and*

Social Change in South Africa, edited by David M. Smith, 64–89. London: Allen and Unwin.

———. 1987. *Apartheid in Transition.* Aldershot: Gower.

———. "Urban Policy Options to Prevent Rural and Urban Overcrowding: The Size and Location of Urban Settlement." Paper given at the Newick Park Conference, Sussex, July 26–29, 1989, substantially reprinted in *Towards an Urbanization and Housing Policy for South Africa.* Johannesburg: Christian Research and Education Information for Democracy (CREID).

———, ed. 1991. *Homes Apart: South Africa's Segregated Cities.* London: Paul Chapman.

Mabin A. 1989. "Struggle for the City: Urbanization and Political Strategies of the South African State." *Social Dynamics* 15:1–28.

McCrystal, L. P. 1969. *City, Town or Country: The Economics of Concentration and Dispersal with Particular Reference to South Africa.* Cape Town: A. A. Balkema.

McGrath, M. D. 1989. "Income Distribution, Expenditure Patterns and Poverty." Paper prepared for *The Durban Functional Region: Planning for the 21st Century.* Tongaat-Hulett Properties Ltd.

Maylam, P. 1990. "The Rise and Decline of Urban Apartheid in South Africa." *African Affairs* 89:57–84.

Pickles, J., and D. Weiner. 1991. "Rural and Regional Restructuring of Apartheid: Ideology, Development Policy and Competition for Space." *Antipode* 23:2–32.

Pirie, G. H. 1984. "Ethno-linguistic Zoning in South African Black Townships." *Area* 16:291–298.

Platzky, L., and C. Walker. 1985. *The Surplus People: Forced Removals in South Africa.* Johannesburg: Ravan.

Rich, P. B. 1978. "Ministering to the White Man's Needs: The Development of Urban Segregation in South Africa 1913–23." *African Studies* 37:177–191.

Rogerson, C. M. 1989a. "Managing Urban Growth in South Africa: Learning from the International Experience." *South African Geographical Journal* 71:129–133.

———. 1989b. "Rethinking National Urban Policies: Lessons for South Africa." *South African Geographical Journal* 71:134–141.

Savage, M. 1986. "The Imposition of Pass Laws on the African Population in South Africa 1916–1984." *African Affairs* 85:181–205.

Simkins, C. 1984. "The Distribution of the African Population of South Africa by Age, Sex and Region-Type, 1950–1980 and a Note on Projecting African Population Distribution and Migration to the year 2000." In *Studies on Urbanisation in South Africa,* edited by E. A. Kraayenbrink, 6–15. Johannesburg: South African Institute of Race Relations.

———. 1990. "People Power." *Leadership* 9:59–60.

Smit, P., and J. J. Booysen. 1977. *Urbanization in the Homelands—A New Dimension in the Urbanization Process of the Black Population of South Africa?* Monograph Series on Inter-Group Relations, no. 3. University of Pretoria: Institute for Plural Societies.

Smuts, J. C. 1942. *The Basis of Trusteeship.* New Africa Pamphlet no. 2. Johannesburg: South African Institute of Race Relations.

South Africa. 1948. *Report of the Native Laws Commission, 1946–1948.* UG 28/1948. Pretoria: Government Printer.

———. 1979. *Report of the Commission of Inquiry into Legislation Affecting the Utilization of Manpower.* RP 32/1979. Pretoria: Government Printer.

———. 1985. *Report of the Committee for Constitutional Affairs of the President's Council on an Urbanization Strategy for the Republic of South Africa.* PC 3/1985. Cape Town: Government Printer.

Tomlinson, R. 1990. *Urbanization in Post-Apartheid South Africa.* London: Unwin Hyman.

Tomlinson, R., and M. Addleson, eds. 1987. *Regional Restructuring under Apartheid: Urban and Regional Policies in Contemporary South Africa.* Johannesburg: Ravan.

Transvaal. 1922. *Report of the Transvaal Local Government Commission.* TP 1/1922.

Urban Foundation. n.d. (c.1990). *Policies for a New Urban Future: Urban Debate 2010 (2) Policy Overview: The Urban Challenge.* Johannesburg: Urban Foundation.

Van der Merwe, I. J. 1973. "Differential Urbanization in South Africa." *Geography* 58:335–339.

———. 1990. *Secondary Cities: A Literature Survey and Implications for an Urbanization Strategy in South Africa* [in Afrikaans]. Special report for the Department of Planning and Provincial Affairs, Pretoria.

Van der Merwe, I. J., J. H. Van der Merwe, and P. H. de Necker, 1991. "A Spatial and Socio-economic Profile of Urbanization in Southern Africa." *Africa Insight* 21:97–106.

Wallerstein, I. 1974. "Dependence in an Interdependent World: The Limited Possibilities of Transformation within the World Capitalist Economy." *African Studies Review* 17:1–26.

Wolpe, H. 1972. "Capitalism and Cheap Labour Power in South Africa: From Segregation to Apartheid." *Economy and Society* 1:425–456.

20

Zambia

Carole Rakodi

Zambia is one of the most urbanized countries in Africa. In 1963, 21 percent of the population lived in urban areas, a result of the colonial exploitation of the country's mineral resources. Following independence in 1964, with the relaxation of colonial controls over African urban residence and employment growth, rapid rural-urban migration resulted in 29 percent of the country's population being urban in 1969 and 36 percent in 1974. Thereafter the rate of urbanization slowed somewhat, with the 1980 census recording 40 percent of the population as urban and the 1990 census 42 percent.[1]

COLONIAL URBANIZATION

Until the nineteenth century, Zambia had a subsistence, largely agricultural economy.[2] Population density was low and settlements small and scattered. Following the routes of missionaries toward the end of the century, European farmers and traders settled in four areas (Figure 20.1): Fort Jameson, now Chipata; Abercorn, now Mbala; Livingstone; and Kalomo (Blankhart, 1981). The British South Africa Company, in accordance with its charter of 1889, had the right to negotiate with local chiefs for land for farming and mineral exploitation, and was also responsible for the administration of Northern Rhodesia from 1891 to 1924 (Rakodi, 1986).

Economic development in Northern Rhodesia was initially slow: only the lead and zinc deposits at Broken Hill (Kabwe) appeared to offer commercial promise. By 1909, however, the railway line from Capetown had reached Katanga in the Congo (Zaire), and by the 1920s copper mining had commenced in the Copperbelt

Figure 20.1
Urban Areas in Northern Rhodesia

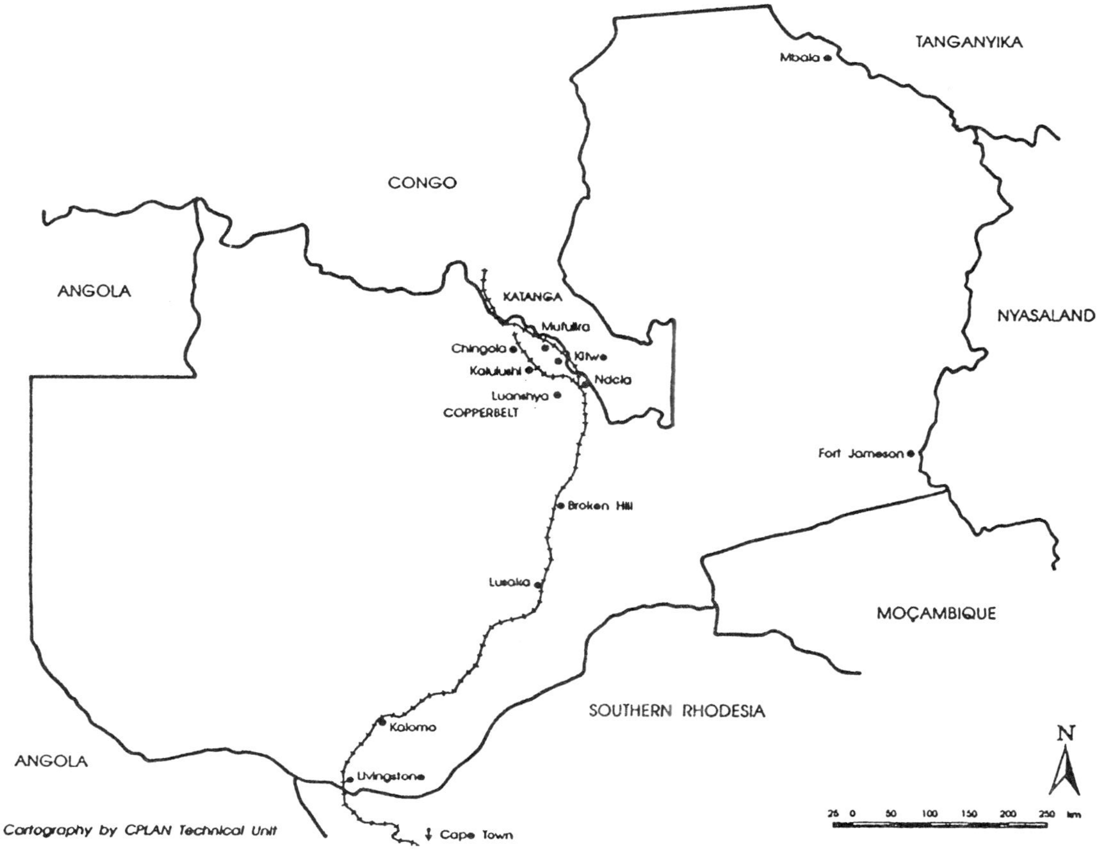

Cartography by CPLAN Technical Unit

of Northern Rhodesia. In 1924 the British government took over Northern Rhodesia as a protectorate. The development of copper mining led to an increased demand for labor. While recruitment of labor for the mining industries to the south continued until independence, by 1930 a majority of the migrant wage workers were employed within the country (Kay, 1967). In addition to the labor needs of the mines, about three million hectares of land was alienated at derisory prices, mainly along the length of the railway, to expatriate farmers.

Labor supply for the colonial enterprises and revenue for the colony's administration were assured by the imposition of taxes, which from 1905 had mostly to be paid in cash (Simons, 1979). A particular system of circulatory labor migration linked to a specific means of labor reproduction was thus developed to meet the needs of mining capital. In effect, the wage bill was divided into a direct wage, paid to migrant male workers at a level sufficient to entice them into urban employment, but insufficient to enable them to support their families in urban areas, and an indirect or social wage, met by the kin of the migrant work force, who continued to cultivate land in the migrant's area of origin (Rakodi, 1986).

Urban areas were established to provide a work force for the mining industry, services to the European population, and a base for administration. The territory was administered from Kalomo until 1907, when Livingstone became the capital. Once the protectorate was established, an administrative system based on indirect rule was considered appropriate for rural areas. However, this was unsuitable for the tribally and racially mixed urban areas, for which a separate administrative system was established (Rakodi, 1986). Town planning and public health regulations were introduced which were concerned primarily with the health and welfare of the European population, while conditions in African residential areas were poor (Simons, 1979).

The colonial policy was to discourage permanent urban residence by the African population, and this was enforced by requiring identification certificates and visitors' permits to provide a means of checking, by the use of police raids, the right to urban residence. Illegal residents and women and children not living under the protection of a legally resident man could then be repatriated to their villages, a danger which did not deter many women from migrating to urban areas (Parpart, 1986, 1988). Because the labor force was regarded as temporary, the responsibility for providing housing (for rent) was considered to rest with the employers. These included, above all, the mining companies, which were given the right to fund and develop townships on land in their ownership, initiating a parallel administrative system in urban areas which persists today (Tipple, 1976; Rakodi, 1986). Lusaka at the end of the 1920s was a small agricultural service center on a railway siding. The colonial government wished to select a more centrally located site than Livingstone for a capital for the newly established protectorate, closer to the now rapidly growing Copperbelt, but not too close to be dominated. Lusaka, near the geographical center of gravity of the country, was selected. The particular form which the growing urban center took was influenced by land ownership, topography, geology, colonial urban policy, and the government's consultant planner's adherence to "garden city" ideas (Rakodi, 1986). The subsequent colonial planning, development, and administrative history of Lusaka is analyzed in detail by C. J. Williams (1986) and C. Rakodi (1986).

By the 1940s, contradictions emerged in the system of low-wage circular migration and a policy of stabilization was adopted, first by the lead and zinc mine at Broken Hill in order to compete for labor with the more profitable Copperbelt mines. According to this policy of balanced stabilization, a minority of urban male workers could be joined by their families, provided they returned to the rural areas on retirement. The policy was reflected in new housing legislation in 1948, which imposed obligations on large employers to house their employees or pay rent on behalf of the employee for accommodation in local authority administered housing (Collins, 1980). The ordinance established African housing areas, subject to different building regulations and in which non-Africans were not allowed to live. The latter prohibition reinforced segregated housing, which was already well established by separate provisions of large plots for Europeans. Most plots were used for housing let at nominal or nil rents to employees of the colonial administration and foreign-owned companies. Plots were also allocated for the construction of houses by the Asian, mainly commercial, community (Rakodi, 1986).

The 1949 Local Government Act increased the power and privileges of local authorities, but at the same time, the consultative African organizations, which had since the 1930s been intended to be the vehicles for representation of otherwise disenfranchised African views, declined in importance. Instead, common national aims became more important to the indigenous population, and the struggles against the color bar and for better working conditions became more overtly political. Thus the local authorities evaded and diluted central government attempts to promote direct African participation in urban administration until the eve of independence in 1963.

At independence in 1963, a fifth of the country's population was living in urban areas, and 95 percent lived in the ten largest settlements. The largest Copperbelt mining town, Kitwe, had a population of 123,000, the same as the capital, Lusaka. Eight of the other nine largest towns, ranging in population from 21,000 to 93,000, were mining towns, all of them along the line of rail.

Towns, therefore, were unusually well developed, but were concentrated along railways especially in the mining areas, leaving the remainder of the country with a sparse distribution of small administrative centers. The urban spatial structure and built environment reflected the underlying ideology of separate development. Zambia inherited a relatively strong system of urban local government based on the British model, but subject to a number of contradictions. In particular, Africans were excluded from senior technical posts by the discriminatory education system and from full political participation by their disenfranchisement. Urban development was based on a complex land administration system.

As a result, even before independence, a significant proportion of the urban population (16 percent in Lusaka in 1963) had utilized unauthorized procedures to obtain access to land for the construction of housing (Rakodi, 1986:211). Official housing was largely provided for rent, almost invariably at a subsidized rate, leading to expectations with respect to desirable dwelling standards. In Lusaka, for example, 41 percent of the population in 1963 was living in low-cost rental housing units (Rakodi, 1986:211). The colonial legacy thus included a particular pattern of urbanization which had developed in response to colonial administrative and economic needs and an urban environment reflecting colonial urban policies. Although these concrete expressions of urban development are often portrayed as an enduring legacy, inherited policy assumptions and administrative structures and procedures are at least as important and possibly as enduring (Rakodi, 1986).

TRENDS IN URBANIZATION, 1963–90

National Economic Trends and Urban Population Growth

In the postindependence period, rapid growth in urban population occurred, in response partly to the removal of restrictions on freedom of movement, partly to the failure of development policies to equalize urban and rural income opportunities, and partly to the growth in employment opportunities in urban areas. Constraints on permanent urban residence had been lifted at independence.

Rapid national economic growth in the years following independence (10.6 percent per annum increase in gross domestic product (GDP) 1963–69), based on high copper prices on the world market and increased government investment, was accompanied by an increase in urban jobs. Thus formal employment in towns grew by 6 percent per annum between 1963 and 1969 (Wood, 1982:110). Policies to develop import substitution industry and growth in public sector employment associated with the extension of government functions and establishment of numerous parastatals (Turok, 1990) led to urban growth of 9 percent per annum between 1963 and 1969, 76 percent of which was probably due to in-migration (Zambia, 1981a) (Table 20.1).

By the early 1970s, Zambia was a relatively prosperous middle-income country. However, its economy was heavily dependent on copper, which accounted for 90 percent of its exports, as in 1964. In 1971 and again in 1974 copper prices fell dramatically. At the same time, the cost of imports rose, with the result that by 1982 Zambia was exporting more than four times as much copper to import the same volume of goods as it had in 1970 (Clark and Allison, 1989:6). Its economy was further damaged by oil price increases of the early and late 1970s and the struggle for independence and majority rule in adjacent countries.

Table 20.1
Urban Population Growth in Zambia, 1963–90

URBAN AREAS	URBAN AREAS WITH 50,000 INHABITANTS IN 1980						
	POPULATION				AVERAGE ANNUAL GROWTH RATE		
	1963	1969	1980	1990	1963 -1969	1969 -1980	1980 -1990
Lusaka	123,146	262,425	535,830	982,362	13.4	6.5	6.1
Kitwe	123,027	199,798	266,286	338,207	8.4	2.6	2.4
Ndola	92,691	159,786	250,502	376,311	9.5	4.0	4.0
Mufulira	80,609	107,802	135,535	152,944	5.0	2.1	1.2
Chingola	59,517	103,292	130,875	167,954	9.6	2.1	2.5
Kabwe	39,522	65,974	136,006	166,519	8.9	6.6	2.0
Luanshya	75,332	96,282	110,907	146,275	4.2	1.3	2.8
Livingstone	33,026	45,243	63,275	82,218	5.4	3.0	2.6
Chililabombwe	34,165	44,862	54,737	76,848	4.6	2.1	3.4
Kalulushi	21,303	32,272	52,146	75,197	7.2	4.3	3.6
Large Urban Areas	682,338	1,117,736	1,736,099	2,564,835			
Towns 5,000 to 50,000 in 1980	32,682	74,380	522,401	720,931			
Total Urban	715,020	1,192,116	2,258,500	3,285,766	8.9	5.8	3.7

Source: Compiled from Zambia Censuses, 1981, 1990.

Its transport routes through Mozambique, Angola, and Southern Rhodesia were disrupted by armed struggles and border closures, necessitating extra investment in alternative routes to the sea through Tanzania, while increases in defense spending and the cost of accommodating large numbers of refugees exacerbated the country's economic difficulties. Between 1975 and 1981 per capita GDP fell by over 20 percent in real terms. Formal-sector employment peaked in 1975 and in the following five years fell by 6 percent (Zambia, 1981b:1, 5).

The rate of urban growth fell in this period, especially in the larger urban areas, to 6.0 percent per annum, but the urban population increased by 89 percent

(Zambia, 1985:67). The volume of migration was reduced because of the decline in economic opportunities, and an increasing proportion of urban growth could be attributed to natural increase, but it was estimated that 58 percent between 1969 and 1980 was a result of net in-migration (Wood, 1982). In 1969, 44 percent of the population of Central Province (including Lusaka) were born in their district of enumeration and 37 percent in the Copperbelt Province. By 1980, these percentages increased to 51 respectively in Central Province and 50 in Copperbelt Province, with rural-urban migrants comprising 11 percent of the urban population of Copperbelt Province and 24 percent of Lusaka's population (Zambia, 1985:108, 110).

Zambia has been involved in a ''waltz with the international lenders'' since the mid-1970s (Burdette, 1988). In the early 1980s its economic position continued to deteriorate, with copper prices falling, except for small upturns in 1987 and 1989. However, copper reserves are being depleted, mining costs are rising, and Zambia has been unable to take advantage of price rises (Clark and Allison, 1989). Instead, real per capita GDP fell 2.3 percent between 1980 and 1988 (Kayizzi-Mugerwa, 1990:61), so that average real incomes in the mid-1980s were about half their 1976 level, production and employment declined, while debt increased and inflation rates rose to 47 percent in 1985, 60 percent in 1986, and 130 percent in 1990 (Loxley, 1990; Mwanza, 1991).

Since 1978 a series of stabilization programs has been agreed with the International Monetary Fund (IMF). Access to credit was dependent on restraining the growth of domestic demand, reducing debt repayment arrears, and increasing exports while reducing imports by means of devaluation (Mwanza, 1991). By 1984, 60 percent of Zambia's foreign exchange earnings were being absorbed by debt repayment (Clark and Allison, 1989). Price decontrols began in earnest in 1981, while wages were frozen. As a result, in the 1980–85 period, wage earners' real incomes fell at an annual rate of 13 percent whereas agricultural producer prices rose, turning the terms of trade against the urban population. Attempts to reduce the maize meal subsidy in 1986 led to food riots in the Copperbelt.

In 1987, the government reverted to a fixed exchange rate, reimposed the mealie meal subsidy, and limited debt service to 10 percent of export earnings (Mwanza, 1991). Economic performance was reasonably good in 1988 and 1989, as agricultural production rose in response to higher producer prices and good weather, and manufacturing output increased. However, mining output fell, all multilateral and some bilateral aid was suspended, and the debt burden increased, so that the government was forced to return to the International Monetary Fund/International Bank for Reconstruction Development structural adjustment program in 1989. Renewed attempts to reduce the subsidy on maize led to further food riots in Lusaka, Kafue, and Kabwe in mid-1990 and to the reintroduction of the subsidy for some sections of the population and increases in civil service salaries and housing allowances.

Nevertheless, economic liberalization has continued, with debt relief linked to fulfillment of the terms of the structural adjustment program and some funds being directed to counterbalance the effects of the policies insisted upon by the donors earlier in the 1980s (Mwanza, 1991). The attempts to achieve stabilization and structural adjustment have neither solved the balance of payments crisis nor resulted in economic restructuring.[3] They have, instead, increased the vulnerability of government to often contradictory foreign direction and had severe political repercussions and socially regressive effects (Burdette, 1988; Clark and Allison, 1989).

The overall rate of urban growth declined still further in the 1980s to 3.7 percent per annum (little above the rate of natural increase of 3.2 percent per annum), as Zambia's economic difficulties continued. This still represented an increment of 46 percent in the decade, or about a million urban residents (Zambia, 1990). Nevertheless, the decline in urban incomes and contraction in public- and private-sector employment, both of which have affected the urban low income population more adversely than the rich, have increased the proportion of the population living in poverty and reduced the attraction of living in urban settlements. Both the rapid growth in urban population and prosperity in the postindependence period, and the recent economic decline have, however, had a differential impact.

Trends in the National Settlement Size Distribution

In the first six years after independence, Lusaka grew rapidly; 13.4 percent per annum (Table 20.1). Although Lusaka did not continue as the fastest growing urban center it increased its dominance from 17 percent of the total urban population in 1963 to 30 percent in 1990. The four Copperbelt towns most dominated by mining, which grew rapidly immediately after independence, had smaller population gains between 1974 and 1980, as employment in mining and quarrying fell from a 1975 peak of nearly 65,000 to just over 52,000 in 1979 (Zambia, 1981b:5).[4] Growth in other large centers continued despite the recession because of increases in government administrative employment, investment in state industries and new mine plant, and boundary extensions (Wood, 1982). Kitwe and Ndola diversified their economies in manufacturing and services, by providing a range of services to other Copperbelt towns.

Population growth rates in the 1980s were similar to those of the later 1970s. Kabwe showed the most dramatic decline as its mine shed and major labor movements were not attracted to the town (Table 20.1). Chingola, Luanshya, and Chililabombwe grew somewhat faster, while Kitwe, Livingstone, and Kalulushi grew very slowly. Recently there have been migrant flows away from the Copperbelt to Lusaka and parts of Central Province, areas less badly hit by the recession, and to Northern and Luapula provinces, associated with return migration. The impact of the recession and structural adjustment measures on urban residents is reflected in a net migration from six of the ten largest towns, four of which are Copperbelt towns.

Table 20.2
Growth Rates of Urban Townships with Populations of 11,000 to 40,000 in 1980

SMALL URBAN AREAS	1980 POPULATION	AVERAGE ANNUAL RATE OF GROWTH		
		1963-69	1969-74	1974-80
Kasama	38,093	4.9	13.6	14.5
Mansa	34,801	5.5	-1.2	28.0
Chipata	32,291	9.0	4.3	11.7
Kafue	29,794	31.7	11.3	7.2
Mazabuka	29,602	3.5	11.6	18.2
Mpika	25,880	8.8	47.1	24.7
Mongu	24,919	11.5	4.3	13.2
Choma	17,943	9.8	-2.7	9.5
Solwezi	15,032	12.2	14.0	11.8
Kapiri Mposhi	13,677	12.8	31.7	25.1
Monze	13,141	4.3	5.0	17.0
Samfya-Mwanfuli	11,188	12.2	-1.0	11.9
Mbala	11,179	6.1	8.4	5.9

Source: Compiled from Zambia Censuses, 1969, 1974, 1980, 1990.

Small towns accounted for only 5 percent of the urban population in 1963 and 6 percent in 1969, but by 1980 they accounted for 22 percent of the urban population (Table 20.2).

Population growth occurred in towns along the Tanzania-Zambia railway, such as Kapiri Mposhi, Kasama, and Mpika, and in some provincial capitals (Figure 20.1). Centers such as Mongu, Chipata, Solwezi, Kasama, and Mazabuka benefited from government-sponsored rural industrialization projects (Zambia, 1985). Some settlements lost population in the early 1970s (Mansa, Choma, and Samfya-Mwanfuli), but their 1974–80 growth rates were similar to or greater than those of the 1960s. However, their figures should be treated with caution.

The rapid growth of many smaller settlements did not persist into the 1980s, which reflects improved opportunities for farmers following producer price increases and the lack of public investment in rural industrialization and urban infrastructure, which reduced opportunities in urban areas.

Changes in the growth rates of urban areas reflect a redirection of rural-urban migration from the line-of-rail and Copperbelt towns to small urban centers in more outlying areas. Nevertheless, the growth of the largest urban areas greatly exceeded the growth of smaller settlements. By 1990 one out of every three inhabitants lived in urban areas with populations of over 50,000.

The population of the Lusaka and Copperbelt provinces has been largely urban since 1969. Along with the Central Province, these line-of-rail provinces accounted for 94 percent of national urban population in 1969, but declined to 77 percent in 1980, and went back to 82 percent in 1990. Regardless, the urban population remains highly concentrated in precisely the areas which emerged during the colonial period.

NATIONAL SETTLEMENT POLICY AND ITS OUTCOMES

The distribution of settlements inherited at independence reflected the nature of Zambia's economy and its spatial expression. In 1964, despite the importance of mining, 70 percent of the population was engaged in subsistence agriculture. However, the contribution of agriculture to GDP remained static for many years at 10 percent. Large commercial farmers produced over two-thirds of the marketed maize and were concentrated along the line of rail. Infrastructure investment and higher order services were concentrated in the central provinces. The country was characterized by marked rural-urban income differentials, with average per capita annual incomes of rural Africans being about 8 percent of those in the towns (Simmance, 1972).

National development plans have attempted to diversify the economy from its dependence on copper, by industrialization and agricultural development, lessening interregional inequalities and reducing rural-urban income and service provision disparities. Measures to assist rural development emphasized the provision of services and infrastructure and encouragement of employment in non-line-of-rail urban areas. However, agricultural production has generally failed to grow consistently, and service levels were insufficient to attract other economic activities.

The failure of the rural economy was accompanied by an expansion of manufacturing output from a small base of 20 percent per annum between 1964 and 1969 and a real increase in urban wages of 50 percent compared to only 3–4 percent in rural areas. Capital investment continued to be disproportionately concentrated in urban activities and in the three line-of-rail provinces (Simmance, 1972; Kayizzi-Mugerwa, 1990). The gap between urban and rural incomes has, therefore, widened. In particular, large public-sector wage increases, free social services and subsidized housing, and food subsidies favored urban over rural residents and encouraged migration.

Rural economic diversification, to generate income and employment and discourage migration to urban centers, was to be achieved by industrial decentralization policies. The intended development of manufacturing never materialized because of the decline in government revenue after the mid-1970s and a faulty industrial development plan.

Most industrial production was for the urban market and generated few rural linkages. Thus by the end of the 1970s, the ''spatially lopsided pattern of development'' remained largely unchanged, with 98 percent of manufacturing, 84 percent of wage employment, and 91 percent of wages drawn concentrated in the three line-of-rail provinces (Zambia, 1979:79). Sporadic attempts to decentralize industry to smaller urban centers have had only limited success, and the measures so far devised are unlikely to make much difference to the pattern of investment or urban development (Rakodi, 1990).

A policy of ''decentralized concentration'' of investment resources was adopted and continued during the Fourth National Development Plan, with the aim of balancing economic growth with the reduction of inequalities, by selecting growth places in which investment would be concentrated, rationalizing the settlement pattern to increase the efficiency of investment, and effectively decentralizing planning and decision making. Settlements were classified into four types.

Growth Poles

Growth poles included the already urbanized regions of Lusaka and the Copperbelt, which were expected to develop further without special development efforts.

Centers of Development

The provincial capitals and other large towns were expected to be the main focal points for development at the provincial level. A range of services to be provided by such centers was listed. Kabwe and Livingstone were felt to be already performing such functions and were upgraded to growth poles in the Third National Development Plan (TNDP), despite symptoms of economic decline. In the Third National Development Plan the spatial framework for broader policies was developed in considerably more detail than previously. The policy of ''decentralized concentration'' of investment resources adopted in this plan was continued in the Fourth National Development Plan. The towns selected as centers of development in 1979 are shown in Figure 20.2. In 1989 this category was extended to include the five towns with populations of 10,000 and 50,000.

Subcenters of Development

Fifty centers at district level were selected and the services to be provided listed. In 1989 these comprised the remaining district centers and all other towns with a population of 5,000 to 10,000 (a total of 19).

Village Development Centers

On the basis of agricultural potential, density of population in the surrounding rural area, all-weather roads, and the presence of a primary school, 431 village

Figure 20.2
Third National Development Plan: Hierarchy of Development Centers

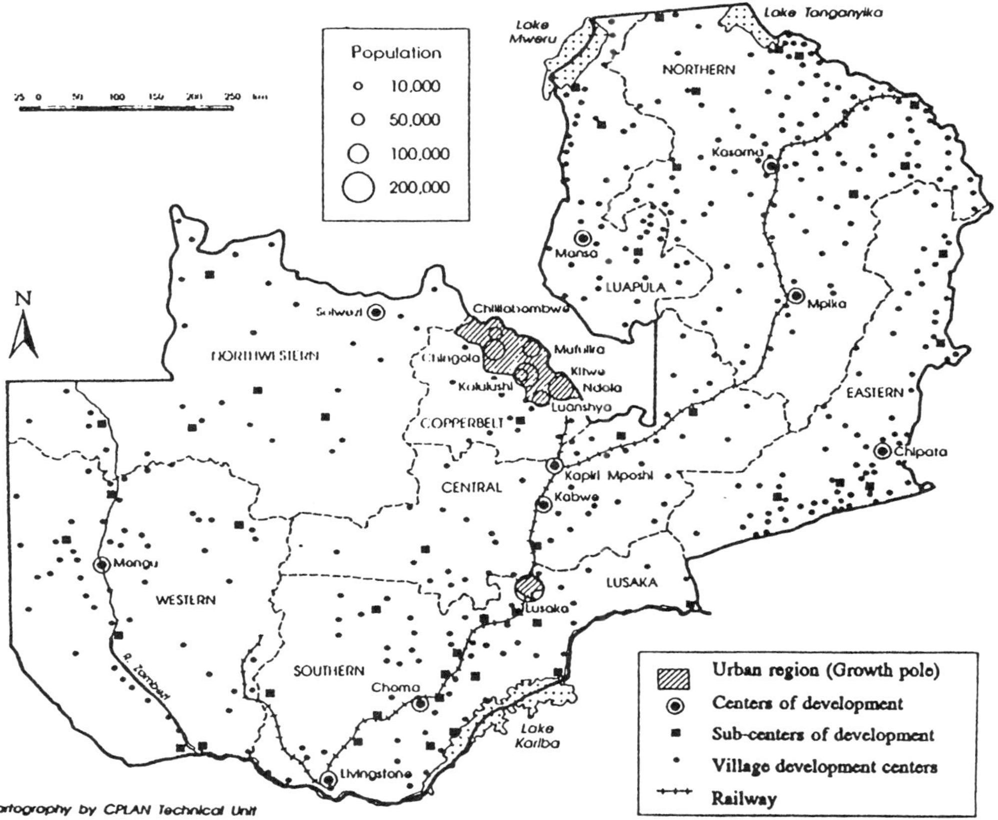

Cartography by CPLAN Technical Unit

development centers were to be selected. They were intended to serve as nuclei for rural development and locations for the lowest order social, agricultural, and marketing services. Although by 1983 over 100 villages had 50 percent of the desirable facilities, insufficient resources had been allocated to implement fully the program, and in the TNDP they were replaced by ward development centers, defined in administrative/population terms as "sub-bomas and other small urban settlements with populations ranging from 500 to 5,000 people" (Zambia, 1989:579), rather than in terms of development potential. Forty-three settlements were listed, and although the list is inconclusive, the intention is clearly greater selectivity.

Decentralization of planning and decision making was intended to encourage regional development. However, political administrative decision making has remained centralized because of changes in views about whether attention should be concentrated on building up capacity at the district or the provincial level.

The settlement policy incorporated in the third and fourth plans was sensible, but the resource implications were not considered. As Zambia struggled with its overwhelming economic problems, few investment or staff resources were available to promote greater interregional or intraregional equality, effective decentralization, or changes in the pattern of urban settlement.

CHARACTERISTICS OF URBAN AREAS

Much of the colonial urban legacy has been lasting, but many changes in the characteristics of the urban population have occurred in response to broader economic, social, and political changes and policy initiatives.

The Urban Political System

Enfranchisement of the African population at independence provided an opportunity for greater democratic control of the local state apparatus. In the absence of substantial research, the full implication of this is far from clear (Rakodi, 1988a). Through their access to the national and local state, higher income urban residents, who moved into previously European areas, have been able to protect their access to higher standards of infrastructure and services, and their entitlement to subsidized employer-provided housing. In the unauthorized housing areas, regarded as illegal by the government until 1972, and outside the jurisdiction, although not the boundaries of urban local authorities, the political parties established a strong base and took on some of the functions of local government, such as the granting of permission to construct houses. By the end of the 1970s, the demands of residents of these areas for infrastructure and security of tenure had been articulated through the political party. These were reinforced after the declaration of a one-party state, by the need of the single party to strengthen its position in areas formerly dominated by the opposition party, and the physical and financial impossibility of relocating all the residents of squatter areas into serviced plot schemes, and gave rise to a policy change which was incorporated in the Second National Development Plan (SNDP). In Lusaka, all major unauthorized housing areas were upgraded between 1974 and 1981 with the assistance of a World Bank loan, and the procedures further strengthened the position of their political party.

However, interest in local government in the urban areas waned as the powers of local councils were circumscribed by central government and their resources became increasingly inadequate in face of the demands of accommodating urban growth. Despite the avowed intention of the 1981 Local Administration Act to strengthen the administrative and financial capacity of local authorities, no serious attempts have been made (Rakodi, 1988a).

Some Demographic and Social Characteristics of the Urban Population

In 1964, Zambia's urban population, especially in the Copperbelt, was dominated by men of working age. Despite the colonial labor and urban residence policies, the majority of the national population were females, with a sex ratio in the Central Province in 1963 of 109 and 126 in Copperbelt Province. With the final removal of restrictions on migration, many women and children migrated to urban areas, mainly to join their husbands and fathers, although some migrated independently. The result was a decline in the ratio by 1969, especially in the Copperbelt, where it dropped from 126 to 109, but also in Central Province, to 105.

The parity between men and women in the main urban areas has been increasing throughout the postindependence period, and by 1990 the numbers were roughly equal. Although there were still relatively more men than women in urban than in rural areas, a long tradition of migration, the increasing contribution of natural increase to urban population growth, and the reduced opportunities for migrants to obtain wage jobs have contributed to the reduced dominance of men in the urban population.

The age structure figures in the 1985 Census Report for 1969 and 1980 are not ideally grouped for analysis. They do, however, indicate a smaller number of children of school age (5–14), larger proportions of working-age people (15–44) (especially men), and smaller proportions of older people (45+, especially in the Copperbelt) in the largely urban provinces than in the national population as a whole in 1969.

Influences on household[5] composition vary between urban and rural areas. In urban areas, the larger proportion of male migrants, who are either single or have left their families at home, exerts a downward pressure on household size. The pressure on urban households to accommodate rural-urban migrants during periods of job or house search is counteracted by their resistance to the inelastic nature of (declining real) urban wages. Nevertheless, the average 1980 urban household size of 5.6 was larger than the 4.7 in rural areas.

Owing to the greater longevity of women and increased marital instability, the proportion of households headed by women has increased from 24 percent in 1969 to 28 percent in 1980. Despite an increase in the average size of female-headed households (3.6 in 1969 to 4.1 in 1980), they were still smaller than those headed by men (5.0 and 5.3 respectively). A third of all rural households were headed by women, while in the urban areas, the proportion of female household heads is 18 percent of the total. There are a variety of reasons for these differences in household composition, especially the country's economic and migration history and the difficulties facing women in obtaining access to wage income to support their own households.

The Urban Economy

Most men in urban areas have always been economically active, with 73 percent in 1980 (Zambia, 1985:193).[6] In the Copperbelt, large proportions have been employed in the mining sector, which accounted for 15 percent of working men in all urban areas in 1980 (Zambia, 1985:197) and of all formal-sector employment in the later 1980s (Zambia, 1989:66). Exceeding this sector in size are business, community, social, and personal services, in which almost a third of all economically active men worked in 1980 (Zambia, 1985:197). Manufacturing, by contrast, was a relatively insignificant source of employment (10 percent of all urban working men in 1980).

The most prominent features of male employment in Zambian urban areas are that it is predominantly wage employment, even as recently as 1980 (87 percent), and it is predominantly in public- and private-sector services, with the exception of the Copperbelt. Open unemployment was low until the mid-1970s, but then increased, reaching 13 percent in Lusaka and 24 percent in the Copperbelt by 1980 (Zambia, 1985:204).

The economic activity rate of urban women has always been lower than that of men, understating their economic contribution in both cash income earning and household production terms. For example, the female activity rate in urban areas in 1980 was 33 percent of all women age 12+ (Zambia, 1985:193), ignoring much of their economic activity, such as food production (Bardouille, 1984; Rakodi, 1988b). A relatively low proportion of women are in wage employment (55 percent in 1980) and a high proportion (42 percent) in self-employment. R. Bardouille (1984:167) notes the small proportion of women in the formal-sector labor force (7 percent nationally in 1969) and their concentration in the service and retail trade sectors. By far the largest proportion of working women are self-employed petty traders in the informal sector, illustrating the difficulty which women have experienced in obtaining access to formal-sector wage employment because of educational disadvantage, sociocultural norms, and practical difficulties of child care. By 1986, a third of the labor force in urban areas were women. The proportion of men in formal-sector employment had shrunk to 72 percent, and the proportion of women increased to 26 percent as some were able to enter clerical, administrative, and professional occupations. Still, nearly three-quarters of the women were in informal-sector employment, including retailing and the provision of services which are extensions of their domestic skills, such as hairdressing, sewing and beer brewing. The more lucrative informal-sector activities, including manufacturing and the more profitable branches of retailing, are dominated by men.

The urban labor force and employment structure are not only differentiated by gender, but also by age. Youth unemployment is a particularly serious problem, with 55 percent of those in the economically active population age 15–24 unemployed in 1980, compared to relatively few age 30+ (Zambia, 1985:204).

Until the mid-1970s, the average urban real incomes were increasing. Although wage increases were generally restrained, controlled prices and food subsidies restrained inflation and dampened wage demands, with relatively limited proportions of the urban population below the poverty line. Since the early 1970s, the situation has deteriorated. Between 1973 and 1977 average real urban incomes fell 13 percent (ILO, 1981:33), as wage increases were restricted; prices, even of controlled commodities such as roller meal, bread, and cooking oil, rose; and many price-controlled goods were siphoned off and sold through the black market at higher prices. In 1980, 26 percent of the households had insufficient incomes to satisfy their minimum private consumption needs. The situation worsened following the introduction of "economic pricing" in 1983 (Burdette, 1988). Existing inequalities have been exacerbated by policy reforms since the late 1970s, which have favored large businesses in particular (Turok, 1990). The Structural Adjustment Programmes (SAPs) imposed since 1978 did not initially include poverty alleviation programs or measures to protect the poorest households from the effects of policy reforms (Mwanza, 1991). Malnutrition increased and health suffered (Clark and Allison, 1989). The regressive income effects of urban wage and employment policies in the last twenty years have exacerbated inherited inequalities.

The Urban Built Environment

The segregated and stratified urban environment inherited from preindependence days resulted in the political clout of higher income urban residents and enabled them to maintain these differentials in infrastructure and planning standards. The inherited housing system, in which most units were provided at subsidized rents for public- or private-sector employees, has also been highly regressive (Sanyal, 1981). Despite official statements threatening the introduction of economic rents for public-sector housing and policies to encourage home ownership, the vested interest of public-sector employees, who benefit greatly (and increasingly with increased seniority) from the existing system, has made it difficult to introduce radical changes.

In 1964 a relatively large proportion of the low-income employed population lived in good-quality municipal or mine rented housing, at relatively low rents.

As in most other newly independent countries, it was hoped to maintain or improve on these standards in new development, for rent, or, increasingly, by self-help for home ownership, even though it was very evident by the 1970s that the adoption of these were relatively high standards for lower-income households. The latter had no choice but to build or buy houses in unauthorized areas, which accommodated, for example, 40 percent of Lusaka's dwellings in 1973 and 42 percent in 1980 (Rakodi, 1986:196). In the later 1970s, in addition to the provision of serviced plots, the main unauthorized areas in Lusaka were upgraded by the provision of security of tenure and improved social and physical infrastructure.

In 1974 half of the urban dwellings had a private and a shared tap, while 18 percent used wells or less satisfactory sources of water. By 1980, following improvements in the 1970s as areas, especially in Lusaka, were upgraded, standards of access to physical and social infrastructure improved. However, deficiencies persisted and worsened in the 1980s, as reductions in expenditures led to a virtual halt in the provision of newly serviced areas or further upgrading, and to the poor operation and maintenance of infrastructure provided earlier, illustrated by, for example, cholera outbreaks. Urban inequalities in living standards have always been evident and, far from being ameliorated, have been exacerbated by subsequent events and policies too strongly influenced by the powerful within society.

CONCLUSION

Zambia inherited an economy heavily based on mining in 1964 and a national space in which commercial agricultural production, infrastructure, investment, and nonagricultural economic activity were all concentrated in the central part of the country along the north-south line of rail. Already highly urbanized at independence, the trend has continued, and it is anticipated that nearly 60 percent of the population may be urban inhabitants by the year 2000 (United Nations, 1991:107).

The political and economic characteristics inherited from colonial days, together with subsequent regional events and deterioration in the country's position in the global economy, have made it extremely difficult to achieve the structural changes in the economy needed to reduce Zambia's vulnerability. As a result, the inherited uneven patterns of regional development, urbanization, and income have also proved recalcitrant, despite a consistent political commitment to reducing interregional, intraurban, and urban-rural disparities. A complex set of external and internal factors explains the country's failure to achieve many of its aims.

Whether considering the colonial period of Zambia's history, the immediate postindependence of relative prosperity, or the seemingly inexorable economic decline of the last two decades, the picture which emerges with respect to urban patterns is one of continuity. The national settlement pattern has changed relatively little, despite some halfhearted policy attempts to decentralize away from Lusaka and the Copperbelt, because underlying economic trends and actual investment have favored continued concentration. The pattern within urban areas has also changed relatively little, partly because of the durability of the built environment, but also because of the power structure and the nature of policies adopted. Genuine commitment, at least among some decision makers, to meeting basic needs and devising affordable housing policies, together with a buoyant urban economy, led to improvements in the quality of life for many urban households in the 1960s and 1970s. However, these improvements have been overtaken by a deterioration in services provided and greater inequality and poverty among urban households as a result of the economic difficulties and SAPs of the late 1970s and 1980s.

Central government has had an ambivalent attitude toward urban local government. If the inevitable future urbanization is managed in such a way that towns and cities provide viable locations for economic activity while not absorbing a disproportionate share of national resources, local government must be given scope for developing greater administrative and fiscal capacity. At the same time, care must be taken to ensure that the effects of aspatial policies do not counteract the aims of national settlement and urban development policies. The extent to which these aims are practically, politically, and financially feasible remains to be seen.

NOTES

1. In the 1963 and 1969 censuses an urban place was defined as one with a population of 5,000 or more. For the 1980 census this definition was expanded and elaborated to include "(1) a locality of 5,000 and more inhabitants, at least half of whom are engaged in non-agricultural activities; (2) other settlements with less than 5,000 people but with urban attributes such as piped water supply, electricity, schools and hospitals, etc.; (3) administrative centers and other places with suitable population agglomerations which perform service functions; and (4) places of any size which perform primarily non-agricultural functions (e.g. railway sidings)" (Zambia, 1985:68). According to the 1963 and 1969 definition the urban population was 39.9 percent of the total in 1980, whereas according to the 1980 definition 40.7 percent of the total was urban.

2. This section draws heavily on Rakodi (1986), in which sources are more fully acknowledged.

3. For a detailed critique of the reasons for this failure, including structural constraints in the Zambian economy and the inadequate assumptions on which the recovery measures promoted by the IMF, the World Bank, and other donors have been based, see Loxley (1990).

4. Or from 64,800 in December 1977 to 61,980 in December 1979, according to the new series data (Zambia, 1981b: Supplement p. 1).

5. A household is defined as "a group of persons who normally live and eat together and these persons are called members of that household" (Zambia, 1985:209).

6. Information on the urban labor force is available from the 1986 Labour Force Survey to supplement 1980 census data, in which there are a number of unexplained discrepancies,

while employment structure tables for urban areas were never prepared from the 1969 census returns, except for Lusaka.

REFERENCES

Bardouille, R. 1984. "The Sexual Division of Labour in the Urban Informal Sector: A Case Study of Lusaka." In *Beyond Political Independence: Zambia: Development Predicament,* edited by K. Woldring with C. Chibaye, 161–182. Berlin: Mouton.

Blankhart, S. T. 1981. *The Settlement Pattern in Zambia.* Lusaka: Department of Town and Country Planning.

Burdette, M. M. 1988. *Zambia: Between Two Worlds.* Boulder, Colo.: Westview and London: Avebury.

Clark, J., with C. Allison. 1989. *Zambia. Debt and Poverty.* Oxford: Oxfam.

Collins, J. 1980. "Lusaka: Urban Planning in a British Colony, 1931–64." In *Shaping an Urban World,* edited by G. Cherry, 227–241. London: Mansell.

ILO (International Labour Office). 1981. *Zambia: Basic Needs in an Economy under Pressure.* Addis Ababa: International Labour Office.

Kay, G. 1967. *A Social Geography of Zambia.* London: University of London Press.

Kayizzi-Mugerwa, S. 1990. "Growth from Own Resources: Zambia's Fourth National Development Plan in Perspective." *Development Policy Review* 8:59–76.

Loxley, J. 1990. "Structural Adjustment in Africa: Reflections on Ghana and Zambia." *Review of African Political Economy* 47:8–27.

Mwanza, A. 1991. "Structural Adjustment Programmes in Tanzania and Zambia: Some Lessons for Late-Starters in SADCC." *Southern Africa Political and Economic Monthly* 4:4–11.

Parpart, J. L. 1986. "Class and Gender on the Copperbelt. Women in Northern Rhodesian Copper Mining Communities, 1926–1964." In *Women and Class in Africa,* edited by C. Robertson and I. Berger, 141–160. New York: Africana Holmes and Meier.

———. 1988. "Sexuality and Power on the Zambia Copperbelt: 1926–1964." In *Patriarchy and Class: African Women in the Home and the Workforce,* edited by S. B. Stichter and J. L. Parpart, 115–138. Boulder, Colo.: Westview.

Rakodi, C. 1986. "Colonial Urban Policy and Planning in Northern Rhodesia and Its Legacy." *Third World Planning Review* 8:193–217.

———. 1988a. "The Local State and Urban Local Government in Zambia." *Public Administration and Development* 8:27–46.

———. 1988b. "Urban Agriculture: Research Questions and Zambian Evidence." *Journal of Modern African Studies* 26:495–515.

———. 1990. "Policies and Preoccupations in Rural and Regional Development Planning in Tanzania, Zambia and Zimbabwe." In *Third World Regional Development: A Reappraisal,* edited by D. Simon, 127–153. London: Paul Chapman.

Sanyal, B. 1981. "Who Gets What, Where, Why and How: A Critical Look at the Housing Subsidies in Zambia." *Development and Change* 12:409–440.

Simons, H. J. 1979. "Zambia's Urban Situation." In *Development in Zambia,* edited by B. Turok, 1–25. London: Zed Press.

Simmance, A. 1972. *Urbanization in Zambia.* New York: Ford Foundation.

Tipple, A. G. 1976. "The Low-Cost Housing Market in Kitwe, Zambia." *Ekistics* 41:148–152.

Turok, B. 1990. *Mixed Economy in Focus: Zambia*. London: Institute for African Alternatives.

United Nations. 1991. *World Urbanization Prospects, 1990*. Population Studies No. 121. New York: Department of International Economic and Social Affairs.

Williams, G. J., ed. 1986. *Lusaka and Its Environs*. Handbook Series No. 9. Lusaka: Zambia Geographical Association.

Wood, A. P. 1982. "Population Trends in Zambia: A Review of the 1980 Census." In *Recent National Population Change*, edited by A. M. Findlay, 102–125. Durham: Institute of British Geographers, Population Geography Study Group.

Zambia, Government of. 1979. *Third National Development Plan 1979–1983*. Lusaka: Office of the President, National Commission for Development Planning.

———. 1981a. *1980 Census of Population and Housing. Preliminary Report*. Lusaka: Central Statistical Office.

———. 1981b. *Monthly Digest of Statistics*. Vol. 17, nos. 7–12. Lusaka: Central Statistical Office.

———. 1985. *1980 Population and Housing Census of Zambia (Analytical Report Volume II) Demographic and Socio-Economic Characteristics of Zambia Population*. Lusaka: Central Statistical Office.

———. 1986. *Human Settlement Policies in Zambia over the Past Decade 1976–1986*. Lusaka: Department of Town and Country Planning.

———. 1989. *New Economic Recovery Programme. Fourth National Development Plan 1989–1993*. Lusaka: Office of the President, National Commission for Development Planning.

———. 1990. *1990 Census of Population, Housing and Agriculture, Preliminary Report*. Zambia: Central Statistical Office.

Part III

Special Urbanization Topics

21

Urbanization Policy and Economic Growth in Sub-Saharan Africa: The Private Sector's Role in Urban Development

Dennis A. Rondinelli

Sub-Saharan Africa is one of the poorest and least urbanized regions in the world. Only about one-third of the population lives in urban places, and most live in relatively small towns and cities. Yet urban population growth is extremely high and will continue to be so for the rest of this century. From 1960 until 1988 urban population in the region grew at an average annual rate of 6 percent, and is projected to grow by more than 5 percent a year throughout the 1990s (UNDP, 1990).

Economic growth in sub-Saharan Africa has been sluggish for the past twenty years. Average annual growth of gross national product (GNP) per capita from 1965 to 1988 was negligible at 0.2 percent. During much of the 1980s the growth rate of both exports (−0.7 percent) and imports (−5.0 percent) was negative, as was that of gross domestic investment (−7.3 percent). From 1980 to 1988 gross domestic product (GDP) in the region grew by an average of less than 1 percent a year; agricultural production increased by only 1.8 percent and services by about 1.5 percent annually. Growth of industrial production fell by nearly 1 percent a year at a time when average annual rates of inflation exceeded 15 percent (World Bank, 1990).

The results of such disappointing economic performances were predictable: the World Bank (1990) estimates that more than 47 percent of the 480 million people in sub-Saharan Africa are poor and two-thirds of the poor live in extreme poverty. The United Nations Development Programme (UNDP, 1990) calculates that about one-third of the urban population and two-thirds of the rural population had incomes below the poverty level in the late 1980s. In 1988, the average per capita GNP for the region was about $330. Only the small oil- and mineral-rich country of Gabon reached a per capita GNP of more than $2,000 (Table 21.1). The growth rate of earnings per employee in sub-Saharan Africa declined by 3.5 percent between 1980 and 1986. As a result, the World Bank (1990) estimates that by the late 1980s living standards in much of the region had fallen to 1960s levels.

Economic and social characteristics of the population in sub-Saharan Africa not only reflect the region's poverty but reinforce low levels of economic growth. Less than half the population is literate. Only about 45 percent has access to basic health services, and only 37 percent is served by safe water supplies (UNDP, 1990). Sub-Saharan Africa has a high overall population growth rate—about 3.2 percent a year—and the United Nations estimates that population will continue to grow by more than 3 percent a year throughout the 1990s. The region has a high dependency ratio with almost 47 percent of the population younger than 15. The mortality rate for children under 5 is among the highest in the world, while life expectancy remains at about 50, and net primary school enrollments (56 percent) are the lowest of any developing region (World Bank, 1990).

Sub-Saharan countries face three critical problems that pose serious challenges for the rest of this decade and the early years of the next century. The first challenge is increasing and sustaining agricultural production to meet the expanding food needs of growing populations and to alleviate hunger and malnutrition. The second problem is generating employment for their growing labor forces. The third task is expanding and strengthening in urban areas private enterprises that can absorb more agricultural outputs and generate more employment.

Increasing and sustaining agricultural production will remain a crucial element of economic development during the 1990s. Agriculture still contributes about 34 percent of GDP in sub-Saharan Africa, more than industry and only slightly less than services. As Table 21.1 indicates, agriculture accounts for more than 40 percent of GDP in Benin, Burundi, the Central African Republic, Chad, Ethiopia, Ghana, Madagascar, Mali, and Sierra Leone, while in Tanzania, Somalia, Mozambique, and Uganda it contributes more than 60 percent. In many sub-Saharan countries agricultural goods are still the main export, and many of their governments receive large amounts of revenues from direct and indirect taxes on agriculture (Lele, 1981). Agriculture also employs about 70 percent of the population in the region.

But agricultural production has grown at rates far lower than those of population in most African countries. This, along with pervasive poverty, weak distribution and marketing channels, and civil strife, has contributed to severe food crises in some sub-Saharan countries and widespread malnutrition in others (Brown, 1987; UNDP, 1990). In Ethiopia, Mozambique, Angola, and the Sudan, a significant portion of the population is subject at regular intervals to crises of food scarcity (Reutlinger, 1985). Generating employment will be a second serious challenge facing sub-Saharan African countries. High rates of population growth

Table 21.1
Economic and Demographic Characteristics of Sub-Saharan African Countries

Country	Per capita GNP 1988 (dollars)	% of GDP From Agric. 1988	% Urban Population 1988	Av. Annual Urb. Pop. Growth Rate 1980-1988 (%)	% of Urban Pop. in Largest City	Total Population (in millions) 1990	2025
Angola	470	--	27	5.0	64	10.0	24.5
Benin	390	40	40	7.8	63	4.7	12.7
Botswana	1,010	3	22	8.4	--	1.3	4.2
Burkina Faso	210	39	9	5.4	41	7.9	20.1
Burundi	240	56	7	9.5	--	5.4	11.8
Cameroon	1,010	26	47	7.2	21	11.4	27.7
Cent.Afr.Rep.	380	44	45	4.9	36	2.9	6.3
Chad	160	47	31	7.4	39	5.7	12.4
Congo	910	15	41	4.8	56	1.9	4.7
Côte d'Ivoire	770	36	45	6.6	34	11.7	29.9
Ethiopia	120	42	13	5.2	37	50.1	122.3
Gabon	2,970	11	--	--	--	1.3	2.6
Gambia	--	--	--	--	--	0.7	1.5
Ghana	400	49	33	4.2	35	16.1	47.0
Guinea	430	30	24	5.7	80	6.9	15.6
Guinea-Bissau	--	--	--	--	--	0.9	2.0
Kenya	370	31	22	8.2	57	25.4	82.9
Lesotho	420	21	19	7.2	--	1.7	3.9
Liberia	450	37	43	5.8	--	2.6	7.5
Madagascar	190	41	24	5.9	36	11.6	28.1
Malawi	170	37	14	7.9	19	8.2	21.9

Table 21.1 (Continued)

Country	Per capita GNP 1988 (dollars)	% of GDP From Agric. 1988	% Urban Population 1988	Av. Annual Urb. Pop. Growth Rate 1980-1988 (%)	% of Urban Pop. in Largest City	Total Population (in millions) 1990	2025
Mali	230	49	19	3.5	24	9.4	24.1
Mauritania	480	38	40	7.8	39	2.2	5.9
Mauritius	1,800	13	42	0.8	--	1.1	1.6
Mozambique	100	62	24	11.0	83	15.9	37.2
Niger	300	36	18	8.0	31	7.1	18.9
Nigeria	290	34	34	6.3	17	113.3	338.1
Rwanda	320	38	7	8.2	--	7.2	20.2
Senegal	650	22	38	4.0	65	7.3	17.9
Sierra Leone	300	46	26	5.0	47	3.9	7.4
Somalia	170	65	37	5.6	34	5.2	12.2
Sudan	480	33	21	4.1	31	24.9	55.4
Tanzania	160	66	30	11.6	50	26.9	83.8
Togo	370	34	25	7.0	60	3.4	8.9
Uganda	280	72	10	5.1	52	18.4	55.2
Zaire	170	31	39	4.6	28	34.9	90.1
Zambia	290	14	54	6.7	35	7.9	23.8
Zimbabwe	650	11	27	6.2	50	10.5	32.7
Africa Total	--	--	34	4.9	--	642.1	1,596.9

Sources: Compiled from World Bank, 1990; United Nations, 1990.

are rapidly increasing the size of the region's labor force. The United Nations (1988) estimates that over the 35-year period between 1990 and the year 2025 the labor force in the 38 countries listed in Table 21.2 will more than double, from about 196 million to 540 million. In Kenya, Ghana, Mauritania, Nigeria, and Zambia, the labor force could more than triple in size. The absolute numbers of people that will be added to the labor force in some countries will be enormous: nearly 86 million in Nigeria alone; nearly 25 million each in Kenya, Ethiopia, and Tanzania; and more than 15 million each in Zaire and Zambia. Hence, economic development policies in the region can be successful only if they are tied closely to programs for employment generation.

Third, underlying food production and employment policies in African countries must be a recognition that governments alone cannot deal with them effectively. Most sub-Saharan African countries are deeply in debt. The region's aggregate external debt grew from about $6 billion in 1970 to about $126 billion in 1988 during a period when real GDP per capita fell by 11 percent (Green, 1989). As a result, sub-Saharan countries now depend heavily on external financial assistance and are under pressure from the International Monetary Fund and the World Bank to reduce public expenditures. Therefore, governments must build the capacity of the private sector to play a stronger role in meeting the challenges of expanding agricultural production and urban employment.

At the same time, sub-Saharan African countries must find ways of coping with the pervasive economic and social changes accompanying rapid urbanization. It was noted earlier that during the 1980s the region's urban population grew an average of more than 6 percent a year. But in Niger, Rwanda, Botswana, Burundi, and Kenya, urban places grew by more than 8 percent annually, and in Mozambique and Tanzania their populations expanded by more than 11 percent a year. The population of urban areas grew at least 5 percent a year in 18 other countries in the region. The capacity of governments in sub-Saharan Africa to fashion urbanization policies that provide an economic environment and settlement structure conducive to expanding private enterprise, employment, and agricultural production will largely determine how quickly their countries achieve higher rates of economic growth and social progress.

What is often overlooked by governments in sub-Saharan Africa is that urbanization policy will be crucial to dealing with all three challenges. Although much is already known about how to improve food production, generate employment, and stimulate enterprise development, far less is known about how these activities influence and are affected by urbanization. Increasing evidence suggests that strengthening urban-rural linkages will be crucial to coping effectively with all three challenges (Rondinelli and Ruddle, 1978; Rondinelli, 1983, 1985).

RELATIONSHIPS BETWEEN URBANIZATION AND AGRICULTURAL DEVELOPMENT

Historically, in much of the world, urbanization and agricultural development have been inextricably related. In both Western and more advanced developing

Table 21.2
Labor Force Growth in Sub-Saharan Africa

Country	Projected Size of Economically Active Population (in millions)	
	1990	2025
Angola	4.1	9.6
Benin	2.2	6.1
Botswana	0.5	1.5
Burkina Faso	4.2	9.7
Burundi	2.8	6.3
Cameroon	4.4	10.8
Cent.Afr.Rep.	1.4	2.9
Chad	1.9	4.7
Congo	0.8	2.2
Côte d'Ivoire	4.6	12.8
Ethiopia	21.2	48.4
Gabon	0.5	1.0
Gambia	0.3	0.6
Ghana	5.7	18.6
Guinea	3.1	6.5
Guinea-Bissau	0.5	0.9
Kenya	10.0	34.8
Lesotho	0.8	1.8
Liberia	0.9	2.7
Madagascar	5.0	12.0
Malawi	3.5	9.1
Mali	2.9	8.7
Mauritania	0.7	2.1
Mauritius	0.4	0.6
Mozambique	8.4	18.6
Niger	3.6	9.3
Nigeria	41.9	127.7
Rwanda	3.5	9.8
Senegal	3.2	7.1

Table 21.1 (Continued)

Country	Projected Size of Economically Active Population (in millions) 1990	2025
Sierra Leone	1.4	2.8
Somalia	2.1	4.9
Sudan	8.1	22.4
Tanzania	0.3	0.8
Togo	12.6	37.5
Uganda	1.4	3.6
Zaire	8.1	23.5
Zambia	13.1	36.4
Zimbabwe	3.9	12.1
Africa Total	242.8	649.6

Sources: Compiled from United Nations, 1988.

countries a large, domestically produced agricultural surplus was necessary for economic growth, urbanization, and modernization (Coleman and Nixon, 1978). Successful developing countries found it essential to increase the supply of land, labor, capital, and technologies such as fertilizers, pesticides, irrigation equipment, and higher yielding seed varieties to increase agricultural output. S. Kuznets (1961) noted that as agriculture became more productive, it contributed to economic development in three ways. Its *production contribution* was to make available to the nonagricultural population increased amounts of food, the demand for which rose with higher levels of urbanization. Its *factor contribution* was supplying the rest of the economy with labor and capital, both of which tended to expand with greater agricultural production. Its *market contribution* was the increasing internal demand for services and manufactured goods that accompanied rising incomes and revenues resulting from higher agricultural output. Rising incomes from increased agricultural production created internal demand for a wide range of manufactured goods produced in cities and towns. Where agricultural production increased beyond the subsistence level, demand increased rapidly among rural households, initially for basic consumption and household goods produced in local towns and later for durable consumption goods produced in larger cities (Johnston and Kilby, 1975).

As agriculture became more commercialized, linkages between the rural economy and urban centers became more crucial (Bairoch, 1988). First, maintaining high levels of production required manufactured inputs, including fertilizers, pesticides, farm implements, flood control and irrigation equipment, land clearance equipment, tractors, agricultural chemicals, storage and refrigeration facilities, and transportation equipment, much of which had to be produced in cities. Second, agricultural products provided inputs for expanding agroprocessing industries—those that milled grains and rice, processed meat and dairy products, and refined sugar, for example—many of which were located in small towns and cities. Third, agroprocessing in turn created demand for other manufactured goods such as milling equipment, machine parts, packaging materials, tin-plate and glass containers, and transportation equipment. Finally, agriculture provided inputs, such as natural fibers, to non-food-processing industries (UNIDO, 1972).

These relationships between agriculture and urban manufacturing and commerce slowly extended throughout the urban settlement system, from market towns and small cities to large metropolitan areas. Urban settlements grew from the expansion of private enterprises that generated off-farm employment to absorb the growing labor force displaced from agricultural jobs as productivity increased and labor-saving technology was introduced.

Growing towns and cities absorbed increasing amounts of surplus agricultural goods by providing markets and distribution networks for a wide range of food and other rural products (Hohenberg and Lees, 1985).

Moreover, as per capita income increased in urban areas, the composition of demand shifted significantly: from subsistence staples such as grains, starches, and tubers produced in traditional agriculture to commercially produced meats, vegetables, dairy products, and fruits. The percentage of dietary calories that came from complex carbohydrates and vegetable protein declined with rising incomes in cities, and the percentage from fats, sugar, and animal protein increased (Scrimshaw and Taylor, 1980).

Many characteristics of urbanization and economic development in sub-Saharan Africa are, of course, substantially different from those in other developing regions. In much of sub-Saharan Africa urbanization is proceeding more rapidly than commercialization of agriculture. Low levels of agricultural production encourage large numbers of the rural poor to migrate to cities, where employment opportunities and living standards are perceived to be better. They also prevent many sub-Saharan countries from earning larger amounts of foreign exchange from agricultural exports and inhibit the growth of industry because the rural population has insufficient purchasing power to consume manufactured goods. Moreover, the dominant forms of agricultural production in low surplus regions do not expand incomes fast enough or offer sufficient nonfarm economic opportunities to retain local population.

Rapid urbanization has also brought strong political pressures to keep the costs of food low, frequently resulting in government pricing policies that are adverse to farmers. The World Bank reports that agricultural development in much of sub-Saharan Africa has been adversely affected because "the perennial pressure for cheap food in urban centers led governments to hold producer prices for food crops below their border price equivalents" (Acharya, 1978). Government policies reflect the fact that "urban consumers in Africa constitute a vigilant and potent pressure group demanding low-priced food,'' R. H. Bates (1983:33) points out. In Africa, urban consumers spend between 50 and 60 percent of their incomes on food and thus pay close attention to food prices. They form a powerful political force because they are geographically concentrated, strategically located in national capitals, and can bring strong pressures on political elites to maintain cheap food policies. ''Political regimes that are unable to supply low-cost food are seen as dangerously incompetent and as failing to protect the interest of key elements of the social order,'' Bates (1983:34) notes. Food shortages and rising prices contributed to the coup against Busia in Ghana and led political unrest that threatened the government of Daniel Arap Moi in Kenya.

Pricing policies that subsidize food costs for urban residents depress the profit margins for rural farmers, an adverse consequence that is often exacerbated by wage policies that create large income disparities between urban and rural workers.

But the generation of food surpluses will remain an essential condition for agricultural development and economic transformation in sub-Saharan Africa for many years to come. The need for a widely dispersed system of efficiently functioning towns and cities to support agriculture will be as essential to economic development in sub-Saharan Africa as it was in other developing regions. Where they function effectively, small- and medium-sized cities in sub-Saharan Africa create demand for products of cottage industries in surrounding rural areas; provide employment opportunities for both urban and rural residents in a wide range of agricultural processing and trade activities; and function as agricultural supply centers, providing equipment, seeds, fertilizer, machinery, repair services and information needed for agricultural development (Rondinelli, 1985). Perhaps the single most important function of urban centers, however, is that they form an essential marketing network through which agricultural commodities are collected, exchanged, and redistributed and through which the products of urban enterprises are traded in rural areas (Bromley, 1984; Omer and Associates, 1986; Aradeon et al., 1986).

Where agriculture has become more commercialized in sub-Saharan Africa, both food and other agricultural products are sold by farmers in rural areas through cooperatives, itinerant traders, brokers, hullers, processors, and millers, or directly by farmers themselves in periodic markets. Food products are also sold in market towns to brokers and truckers, commission agents, and government marketing agents, or directly to consumers in marketplaces (Sherman, 1985). Often some portion of the agricultural products sold in towns is bulked by traders, brokers and truckers, processors and assemblers, and commission agents for resale to wholesalers and retailers in larger towns (Kore, 1985). Government marketing boards, wholesalers, and brokers often rebulk goods available in town and small city markets for sale to exporters, wholesalers, retailers, public institutions, supermarkets, informal-sector vendors, restaurants and hotels, grocery stores, and a wide range of other outlets in big cities. Thus, towns and cities not only facilitate the marketing of farm products, but are essential to the whole chain of exchange on which commercial agriculture depends (Okoso-Amaa, 1975; Riley and Weber, 1979).

Without a network of towns and cities, agricultural trade in a region is usually restricted to periodic markets in which subsistence farmers exchange goods among themselves. Studies of agricultural marketing systems in Guinea and Niger show that in regions with weak and unintegrated market centers there are few incentives for increasing production (Doan and Lewis, 1989; Aberg and Blacque-Belair, 1990). Analyses of agricultural marketing systems in Uganda indicate that under such conditions agriculture does not easily expand beyond subsistence or low-surplus production levels (Bendavid-Val et al., 1990). The incentives that come with the ability of farmers to market their goods competitively are lost.

Studies of poverty, food supply, and malnutrition in Zambia in the 1980s suggest that regional variations were closely associated with distance from urban centers or rail accessibility. The line-of-rail regions with good connections to urban centers tended to be more prosperous, more productive, and less subject to food shortages because they had better communications and easier access to urban markets, were more easily supplied with agricultural inputs and credit, and had better access to public services. Poverty, malnutrition, and food insecurity were more serious in the less favored regions—the western, northeastern, Copperbelt, northern, and parts of the eastern provinces—that were remote from cities and that had poor communications and little access to urban markets. The overwhelming majority of the farmers in the less favored regions were subsistence growers. R. Chambers and H. Singer (1981:24) point out that "there is a marked concentration of almost all the commercial farmers and a substantial majority probably at least 90 percent—of the emergent farmers in the more favored areas," near or with easy access to urban centers.

The low level of agricultural production in many African countries is due in part to the fact that market centers are not efficient in transmitting demand from urban to rural areas and the market towns are not accessible from production areas. A study of Uganda's marketing system found that in the areas around the towns of Wobulenzi and Kayunga, for example, the poor conditions of roads substantially increased the costs of moving agricultural commodities out of the farming areas to market towns (Bendavid-Val et al., 1990).

Studies of the Shaba region of Zaire point out that the low level of maize production during the 1980s was due in large part to ineffective marketing linkages between rural areas and towns and cities. "Due to poorly organized marketing systems and badly maintained roads, only a small number of merchants are able to transport food crops from the countryside to the major cities. This small group of merchants, therefore, controls the farm gate price in the rural areas," observers pointed out (Nsaku and Ames, 1984–85). Because of the lack of or delay in receiving information about market prices, and their inability to participate directly in marketing activities, most poor farmers were at the mercy of intermediaries. Itinerant traders paid a lower price for agricultural goods than the going market rate in order to cover their transport costs; but many also convinced farmers to sell their goods at below market prices by claiming that the floor prices were the fixed legal prices. After continuing to receive low prices for their goods year after year, farmers in the Shaba region were discouraged from increasing their output, and consumers in the towns and cities were compelled to pay higher prices for maize in the market. This forced the government to import maize to feed the growing urban population.

As a regional economy begins to diversify, and the marketing system becomes more integrated, the distinction between "urban" and "rural" begins to fade. The settlement systems in such regions may be more accurately seen as a continuum rather than as dichotomous. The commercialization of agriculture is reinforced by the emergence of marketing linkages between rural areas and towns and cities, and at the same time creates new possibilities for stronger and more numerous linkages. In their studies of Central Province, a commercializing agricultural region in Kenya, D. B. Freeman and G. B. Norcliff (1984) found a complex set of relationships emerging between rural and town economies that made them interdependent. In Kenya, these linkages became more complex and interrelated as agricultural production and urbanization increased. They included stronger relations between farms and urban production and commercial enterprises. Farms supplied products for processing in the towns, and urban enterprises provided transport and marketing services, tools, seed, fertilizer, and various types of repair services to farms. New relationships also emerged between farms and urban households. Rural households provided labor and capital; urban households provided wages, interest payments, and profits to rural households, and purchased food and other agricultural products from farmers or intermediaries.

Surveys of three districts in western Kenya found that as the regional agricultural economy developed there emerged a strong positive correlation between the level of agricultural production and the development of full-time nonfarming activities in both rural areas and towns (Carlsen, 1980). A positive relationship also emerged between the level of nonfarming activities and the level of disposable income, and between the ratio of manufacturing to trading activities and equality in the distribution of incomes. Carlsen (1980:220) found "no evidence that the growth in smallholder production has led to the formation of a non-accumulating class of 'middle peasants.' " Smallholders were able to save and invest a portion of their incomes, although much of the saving was done by the higher income peasant families.

URBANIZATION AND EMPLOYMENT

The inextricable relationships between urbanization and economic development are seen most clearly in the impact of rural emigration on the growth of urban areas in sub-Saharan Africa and the resulting need for cities to generate employment.

Because of the limited labor-absorbing capacity of agriculture in sub-Saharan

Africa, urban centers have had to play the major role in absorbing larger numbers of rural people who could not derive an adequate livelihood from agriculture. In low-surplus regions of Botswana, for example, the migration of household members has been essential because crop production simply could not supply adequate income or sufficient amounts of food to meet minimum caloric requirements. Migration to urban areas, however, had different effects for rural families in different income groups. C. Kerven (1982) found that for the poorest families migration brought a decline in agricultural production, especially when the migrant was the male household head. Female-headed groups with no adult males usually ended up worse off because absence of the male migrant forced households to hire labor, the cost of which offset or exceeded urban wage remittances.

For families who attained above-subsistence living conditions, however, migration generated remittances sufficient to cover the loss of labor and skills of the migrant and allowed the farm family to purchase capital goods or intermittent labor. For higher income families in poor regions, migration provided a wage supplement to agricultural activity that increased overall income and allowed the family to diversify into livestock raising as well as crop farming.

The attraction of towns and cities for migrants from rural areas where agriculture cannot adequately support the labor force is strong. The economic base of many towns and cities in Africa is dominated by retail and service activities and by agroprocessing and agribusiness enterprises.

Small-scale enterprises in towns and cities provide part-time employment and supplementary income for underemployed members of rural households, and full-time employment for townspeople in construction, service, transport, processing, commercial, and manufacturing activities (World Bank, 1978). Describing the function of medium-sized towns in southeastern Nigeria, F. C. Okafor (1985:155) points out that they "provide the first attraction to school leavers and migrants where they engage in several off-farm activities. Such towns facilitate the adaption of migrants from rural to urban life. The majority of the traders, taxi drivers and carpenters are usually people from within a radius of about ten kilometers from the urban base of their operations." He observed that many of these migrants work in the towns part-time to supplement their incomes while they continue to farm nearby lands. The secondary towns also provide employment for people from surrounding villages who take jobs as traders, or as casual or daily paid laborers.

Much of the urban employment in sub-Saharan countries is in the informal sector. Although informal-sector activities are sometimes considered ineffective employment generators, they do absorb the labor of the operators, and often of their family members, on a full- or part-time basis. They provide a crucial source of income, especially for poor urban households. While street vendors and hawkers often work alone, market vendors, small shop owners, and stall vendors usually work with their spouses, children, or members of their extended family. Many small food distribution and preparation enterprises engage the labor of from one to three family members and sometimes one or two full- or part-time employees (Cohen, 1984b). In Dar es Salaam, food shops require on average two full-time operators or several part-time employees. Many of the shops, however, are run by several members of the same family working part-time on different days of the week or at different times of the day (Sporrek, 1985). Moreover, many of the food vending and preparation activities in cities are operated by women and provide a source of employment that supplements family income. For example, studies of street food vendors in Ziguinchor, a secondary city in Senegal, reveal that 77 percent are women (Cohen, 1984a). Street food sales can be done part-time, leaving women time to take care of other household duties. Moreover, the skill requirements are relatively low. Often street food businesses can be operated on a small scale by women who simply add larger amounts of food to the family cooking pot.

In many sub-Saharan countries, the manufacturing and service sectors will have to expand at very high rates in order to provide enough jobs for the rapidly increasing labor force. Even in Kenya, which has been relatively successful in increasing production, the agricultural sector will not be able to absorb much of the expanding labor force over the next 20 years (Lewis, 1989). But in most sub-Saharan countries, neither manufacturing nor services are growing fast enough to employ surplus labor.

Thus, both sluggish agricultural production and continuing rural underdevelopment directly affect urbanization by pushing rural labor into towns and cities. The ability of towns and cities to absorb the growing labor force will be a critical factor in the pace of sub-Saharan development over the next two decades.

URBANIZATION AND PRIVATE ENTERPRISE DEVELOPMENT

The expansion of private enterprise, and especially of micro- and small-scale activities in urban areas, will be essential for developing agriculture and for generating employment in sub-Saharan Africa. Urban areas will also take on increasing importance as locations for enterprises that can produce and distribute goods and services needed for agricultural development. As noted earlier, the expansion of private enterprise not only contributes to the growth of the urban economy, but through linkages of exchange with rural areas creates demand for agricultural goods. Much of the urban household's prepared food purchases, for example, are from informal-sector stalls that are operated by people living in nearby rural areas or by urban residents who purchase their supplies from rural households or their intermediaries. A majority of poor urban families in African cities obtain their food and other household goods from informal enterprises. Finally, large cities house the wholesalers and exporters that absorb large amounts of agricultural commodities produced in rural regions.

The advantages of proximity and the economies of scale that towns and cities offer to private enterprise facilitate interaction among businesses and their suppliers, distributors, and consumers. This financial, service, and technological complex is especially crucial to the success of smaller enterprises that must maximize the use of their limited financial resources (Townroe, 1983). C. Liedholm and D. Mead (1986) found that for these reasons more than 75 percent of the manufacturing employment in Sierra Leone was located in towns, as was more than 60 percent in Zambia and Ghana. Small-scale enterprises in urban centers are also crucial because they are the foundation from which many indigenous enterprises grow. D. Anderson (1982:923) contends that established firms in developing countries almost always began "as very small entities, with low amounts of capital drawn from the savings of the owner or borrowings from friends and relatives; initial levels of employment are low, typically less than a dozen, though the figure varies with the nature of the business; the social and occupational backgrounds of the owners vary greatly; and the firms that expand into medium or large scale activities do so continually or in steps." In a sense, then, towns and cities act as incubators for urban enterprise.

Agroprocessing enterprises in towns and cities in sub-Saharan Africa absorb large amounts of agricultural goods produced in rural regions and generate significant employment opportunities. R. A. Obudho and P. Waller (1976) note that the town of Kisumu grew as a processing center for one of the most productive agricultural regions of Kenya. It benefited from its proximity to the tea plantations in Kericho; coffee farms in Abagusii, South Nyanza, Kakamega, Busia, and Bungoma districts; and the sugar cane processing industries in Muhoroni and Mwani. The industrial base of the city—composed of grain mills, groundnut crushing factories, hide and skin curing plants, timber yards, fishpacking plants, and agricultural equipment assembly plants—was closely related to the agricultural economy of the surrounding areas.

In Senegal, nearly half of the economic activity in secondary towns is related to agroprocessing. Agroprocessing accounts for about 46 percent of the commerce and provides more than 40 percent of the nonfarm jobs. In Kaolack, Ziguinchor, and Droubel, oil mills offer employment to rural workers, as do sugar and rice processing activities in Richard Toll, tomato processing in Dagana, fish processing in Saint-Louis and M'bour, and shrimp processing in Zinguinchor (Republic of Senegal, 1984).

Urban wholesalers and assemblers also play an important role in African food marketing systems. For example, in Tanzania, farmers from the hinterlands of Dar es Salaam and Morogoro, and the Coast Region of Mbeya, Arusha, and Lushoto all supply the major wholesale market in the city of Dar es Salaam (Sporrek, 1985). The largest amounts of food are bulked at rural assembly points by truckers, middlemen, and small-scale wholesalers. The intermediaries travel to various market towns until they have enough to fill a lorry and then proceed to Dar es Salaam to sell the produce at the wholesale department of the city's Kariakoo market. The wholesale market then distributes food to the major outlets, including a small number of supermarkets and numerous provision and food stores, small groceries or "dukas," and special shops. The dukas are located throughout the city in small shop-houses in which the owners live on the second floor or in the back. About 60 percent of the food in Dar es Salaam is marketed through dukas and special shops, and about 25 percent is sold by street and market vendors or by the producers themselves. Street food vendors and street food preparers make up a large portion of the food distribution system in urban areas. It is estimated that about 85 percent of all food purchases in Accra, Ghana, for example, are made from market and street vendors. One street vendor exists for every 35 inhabitants of the city (Sporrek, 1985).

Informal-sector enterprises in most cities in sub-Saharan Africa are also closely linked to formal-sector firms. Many hawkers and vendors buy their products from retailers, wholesalers, and groceries, then break bulk and sell the products in small lots. In Dar es Salaam, most market and street sellers obtain their supplies from the Kariakoo Market Corporation, the government-controlled national food procurement and wholesaling center. Indeed, the corporation depends on the purchases of these informal-sector participants for a large portion of its sales (Sporrek, 1985).

Thus, the growth of private enterprises in towns and cities depends heavily on increased agricultural production and rural income as well as on the availability of urban infrastructure and efficient interurban and rural transport linkages. Anderson (1982:926) concluded from his review of small-scale enterprise development in Africa that "the nature of agricultural development strategy is exceedingly important in determining both the size and the regional distributions of industrial development." The success of efforts to expand small enterprise and employment opportunities, however, also depends on the existence of, or ability to provide, preconditions for their efficient operation in towns and cities. The World Bank's (1978) research on small-scale enterprises found that although they depend on the growth of agriculture and on rural development for their markets, they tend to locate in towns that offer the infrastructure and services they need to operate economically. Thus, nonfarm enterprises are both the beneficiaries of and contributors to urban development. If more rural households are to benefit from small enterprise and employment expansion in towns and cities, the physical linkages between those settlements and surrounding rural areas must be better developed.

URBANIZATION POLICIES FOR ECONOMIC GROWTH: CREATING AN EFFICIENT URBAN MARKETING SYSTEM

The analysis presented here suggests that in sub-Saharan Africa urban centers and rural areas do not grow or decline independently of each other; they are inextricably related parts of the spatial economy in which production, distribution, and exchange must take place. Economic activities operate in physical space through settlement systems that either facilitate or retard their efficiency.

The most important set of linkages between urban and rural areas, and among agriculture, employment, and enterprise development, are marketing channels.

Although macroeconomic and pricing policies are important, agricultural production will not expand in subsistence or low surplus areas unless farmers have access to markets at which they can sell their surplus production at a fair price (Mellor, 1986). The commercialization of agriculture depends on rural households having access to inputs, services, information, and infrastructure—all of which require the existence of vertically coordinated marketing channels based in towns and cities to distribute modern inputs and services. Given the pervasive relationships between urban and rural development, the pattern of urbanization emerging in sub-Saharan Africa is likely to cause serious economic problems in the future. In most African countries the urban population is largely concentrated in a few cities; urban settlements tend to be few in number, economically weak, and unevenly distributed geographically (Rondinelli, 1988). The physical and economic linkages between market towns and larger urban centers, and with their rural hinterlands, also tend to be weak (Aberg and Blacque-Belair, 1990; Doan and Lewis, 1989; Bendavid-Val et al., 1990).

Thus, urbanization policies in sub-Saharan Africa must recognize and address these deficiencies in the market system.

Urbanization policies should be tailored to regional conditions and needs. In order to address more effectively the problems of food production, employment, and private enterprise development, urbanization policies must be based on an analysis of, and offer solutions that are tailored to, specific regional conditions. Although national economic and political factors strongly affect agricultural output, food production problems occur in well-defined ecological zones. Problems of food production in highland regions differ drastically from those in savanna and forest regions. "This great natural diversity, sometimes reinforced by cultural influences, has also produced great variation in the dominant and secondary food crops produced in different areas within a country," S. N. Archaya (1978:82) observed in his review of agricultural problems in sub-Saharan Africa, "and this further complicates the problems of crop improvement."

Food crises and the problems of food instability are also primarily regional in nature. In an extensive study of food insecurity for the World Bank, E. J. Clay (1981b:84) concluded that "the regional dimensions of poverty and malnutrition, which are again country specific, reflect classic problems of location and remoteness from the metropolis; environmental and technological factors limit agricultural productivity growth and market demand for agricultural commodities." Many analysts of food security issues argue that problems of famine and malnutrition can best be solved through policies and programs aimed at overcoming deficiencies in regional economies (Clay, 1981b). As one study concludes, for the majority of the rural poor, "food security can best be achieved by enabling them to grow more, eat more, and sell more at better prices, building up from the resources they already have where they are" (Chambers and Singer, 1981:22).

A regional context for analysis is also important because the impacts of many investments in private enterprise are area-wide. The linkages between towns and cities and their rural hinterlands have distinct geographic patterns. It is the synergy among economic activities in close physical proximity in towns or cities that creates new stimuli for urban economic growth, greater demand for agricultural products, and the expansion of employment opportunities (Rondinelli, 1985).

Urbanization policies in sub-Saharan Africa must recognize the importance of, and create economic conditions conducive to, expanding private enterprise in towns. Informal enterprises are likely to be the most important components of the food distribution system in sub-Saharan cities and the major sources of off-farm employment for a long time to come. The International Labor Office (1988) reports that in most sub-Saharan countries urban wage employment accounts for less than 10 percent of total employment and that over the past decade opportunities for formal employment have declined. In Niger, for example, only about 2 percent of the population was employed in the modern sector, and manufacturing accounted for only a little more than 1 percent of GDP at the end of the 1980s (Doan and Lewis, 1989).

Large wholesaling, retailing, and manufacturing firms are most likely to be able to provide for themselves, but small-scale enterprises and informal-sector vendors face a myriad of problems that are sometimes caused by government policy and that often can be ameliorated through policy reforms and technical assistance programs. Experience suggests that the most critical problems for micro and informal enterprises are lack of capital; lack of business skills; restriction, regulation, and harassment by local authorities; and lack of reliable sources for raw materials and supplies (Farbman, 1981).

Informal enterprises have often been harassed by African governments that have tried to clear vendors from the streets or to confine them to restricted areas. Some municipal governments have passed laws against hawking, imposed high license fees on vendors, and enacted sanitary standards for food preparation that vendors and hawkers could not possibly meet and that consumers did not want. Street vendors have often been subjected to harassment by police or local government officials who solicit bribes for allowing them to operate (Bromley, 1985).

No amount of harassment or restriction has reduced or eliminated informal-sector activities. Nor is such a result particularly desirable given the segmentation of urban food markets and the crucial role that vendors, hawkers, and small shops play in providing food at prices that most low- and middle-income urban families can afford.

Assistance to small-scale enterprises can take a number of forms, including credit, technical and production assistance, management assistance, marketing assistance, and provision of common facilities. Programs of financial and technical assistance to small-scale enterprises often have been plagued with administrative problems, however, and new programs need to be designed more carefully. Liedholm and Mead (1986) found that successful financial assistance programs for small enterprises have had three important characteristics: first, loans were provided for working rather than fixed capital; second, loans were screened by local organizations on the basis of the borrowers' character rather than technical criteria of project feasibility; and, third, loans were made for small amounts and for relatively short periods of time to encourage and ensure high repayment rates.

Experience also suggests that assistance programs must be tailored to the specific needs of small-scale enterprises and to the capital, skill, and resource requirements of individuals and families involved in informal sector activities. Governments in sub-Saharan countries can benefit from experience with small enterprise development programs in other developing regions (Liedholm and Mead, 1986; Kilby, 1979). Programs that helped existing enterprises were usually more effective and successful than those attempting to promote new enterprises. They were most effective when they provided only a single ''missing ingredient'' to firms that could otherwise operate effectively. Programs that were task-specific and tailored to the needs of particular industries or product groups were more successful than those attempting to help large numbers of disparate enterprises. Those that were formulated on the basis of industry surveys that gauged effective demand for assistance also tended to be more successful. Help provided by nongovernmental or private organizations with a proven record of effectiveness in delivering nonfinancial assistance to small enterprises was more successful than that provided by public bureaucracies.

When properly designed and implemented, the combination of credit and technical assistance for small enterprises can contribute significantly, along with investments in basic social services and physical infrastructure in towns and cities, to creating a more efficient and effective rural-urban marketing system.

Urbanization policy in sub-Saharan Africa should give much more attention to strengthening the market linkages between urban and rural areas. Any marketing system is composed of three elements: market functions, market processes, and market centers. Marketing is usually defined as the set of business activities affecting the flow of goods and services from producer to consumer, excluding only those activities that change the form of goods (Gupta, 1975). Marketing includes three sets of functions: *exchange* functions include buying, assembling, and selling goods; *physical* functions involve transporting, storing, and warehousing goods; and *facilitative* functions include classification and grading financing, market information, and risk bearing.

The marketing process also involves three sets of activities related to these functions. Through *concentration or assembly* the marketable surpluses of individual producers are bulked at one point in sufficient quantity to allow marketing functions such as transportation, storage, grading, and processing to be carried on efficiently and economically. Through *equalization* activities the flows of supplies are matched with the rate of demand by wholesalers, processors, and retailers who store, release, and distribute adequate stocks of seasonally produced goods at appropriate times and places to meet demand. Through distribution, arrangements are made to supply commodities in appropriate volume and quantity for use by intermediaries and consumers.

Towns and cities serve as market centers where these functions and processes are performed. As noted earlier, market centers often form an integrated hierarchy ranging from periodic markets, bulking centers, market towns, distribution centers, and terminal markets in large cities or ports, each performing increasingly diverse, complex, and more numerous marketing activities.

The acceleration of economic growth requires policies that focus on improving both the processes and functions and the spatial aspects of market systems. H. J. Mittendorf (1981:141) correctly concluded that future strategies for the development of marketing systems in developing countries should include more systematic planning of food marketing systems to serve urban areas. Plans should be aimed at improving the vertical coordination of marketing functions among rural areas, market towns, and intermediate and large cities, and the training of marketing personnel at all levels of the settlement hierarchy. This requires testing alternative forms of marketing organization at the farm level to meet the needs of farmers at different levels of income and with different size landholdings, and testing marketing services for various types of commodities in different regions. These improvements require training programs in food marketing, agro-processing, and agribusiness that are tailored to sub-Saharan economies.

Both substantive and spatial improvements in marketing systems must be considered in planning and implementing urbanization policies aimed at promoting economic development in sub-Saharan Africa. The marketing linkages between rural and urban areas will grow stronger only if investments in facilities, services, and infrastructure are well chosen and appropriately located in those towns and cities that form crucial nodes in the marketing network.

Urbanization policies in sub-Saharan African countries should encourage investments in public services, facilities, infrastructure, and productive activities in a pattern of "decentralized concentration." To be effective in strengthening the urban market system in sub-Saharan Africa, investments in infrastructure and facilities must be located in settlements with large enough concentrations of people and with a sufficient hinterland population to support them economically. Moreover, investments must be made first in areas with strong economic growth potential and with transport linkages to other market centers. Mittendorf (1981:137) correctly points out that "the mere building of new markets and their regulation is not enough. A rural market has to be coordinated vertically with the next wholesale market or with the wholesale supply agent in the case of agricultural input supply. The form and degree of forward and backward linkages of the rural market must be determined with accuracy."

When they are properly located, investments in physical infrastructure and marketing facilities can also support processing, bulking, and distribution functions in urban centers. Studies of farm-to-market road investments, for example, indicate their pervasive impacts on both agriculture and urban development (Anderson and Vandervoort, 1982; Cobb et al., 1980). Among the most important benefits have been: lower transportation costs for farmers to get their produce to market; significant agricultural production increases and changes in crop composition along the road corridors; higher rates of adoption of commercial inputs that increased food production; more effective agricultural extension; the spread of processing activities in towns and cities along the roadways; increases in land values along new access roads, encouraging more intensive land use and more extensive cultivation of high-value commercial crops; the emergence of new and more effective marketing patterns; increased access to off-farm employment; and greater access to social and public services.

Strengthening the marketing functions of towns and cities in sub-Saharan Africa should be done selectively, incrementally, and strategically. Not all towns and cities, however, can or should have a full range of marketing services, facilities, and infrastructure. In most sub-Saharan African countries governments must allocate their resources carefully and should start in areas with the potential for strong agricultural production or where agriculture is already commercialized. One of the benefits of developing an integrated system of towns and cities is that it provides access to a wide range of functions for a large number of people without each settlement having to provide all of them.

CONCLUSIONS

In sum, rapid urbanization is inevitable and irreversible in sub-Saharan Africa. Attempts to slow the pace of urbanization or to prevent the growth of cities in other developing regions have been futile (Rondinelli, 1991). They are equally unlikely to work in sub-Saharan Africa. The real opportunities for governments in the region lie in using public resources effectively to create conditions that will allow private enterprise to expand in cities and towns and to create effective systems of urban market centers that facilitate trade and generate employment for a rapidly expanding labor force.

REFERENCES

Aberg, J. A., and P. Blacque-Belair. 1990. *The Role of Market Towns in Guinea.* Research Triangle Park, N.C.: Research Triangle Institute.

Acharya, S. N. 1978. *Perspectives and Problems of Development in Low Income, Sub-Saharan Africa.* World Bank Staff Working Paper No. 300. Washington: World Bank.

Anderson, D. 1982. "Small Industries in Developing Countries: A Discussion of Issues." *World Development* 10:913–948.

Anderson, G. W., and C. G. Vandervoort. 1982. *Rural Roads Evaluation Summary Report.* Program Evaluation Report No. 5. Washington: U.S. Agency for International Development.

Aradeon, D., T. A. Aina, and J. Umo. 1986. "South West Nigeria." In *Small and Intermediate Urban Centers,* edited by J. E. Hardoy and D. Satterthwaite, 225–278. London: Hodder and Stoughton.

Bairoch, P. 1988. *Cities and Economic Development: From the Dawn of History to the Present.* Chicago: University of Chicago Press.

Bates, R. H. 1983. *The Regulation of Rural Markets in Africa.* AID Evaluation Special Study No. 14. Washington: U.S. Agency for International Development.

Bendavid-Val, A., J. E. Littlefield, and G. R. McDowell. 1990. *Market Towns in Uganda: Recovery and Development.* Blacksburg, Va.: Virginia Polytechnic Institute and State University.

Bromley, R. 1984. "Market Centres, Marketing Policies and Agricultural Development." *Regional Development Dialogue* 5:149–165.

———, ed. 1985. *Planning for Small Enterprises in Third World Cities.* London: Pergamon Press.

Brown, L. R. 1987. "Food Growth Slowdown: Danger Signal for the Future." In *Food Policy,* edited by J. P. Gittinger, J. Leslie and C. Hoisington, 89–102. Baltimore: Johns Hopkins University Press.

Carlsen, J. 1980. *Economic and Social Transformation in Rural Kenya.* New York: Holmes and Meier.

Chambers, R., and H. Singer. 1981. "Poverty, Malnutrition and Food Insecurity in Zambia." In *Food Policy Issues in Low Income Countries,* edited by E. Clay, R. Chambers, H. Singer, and M. Lipton, 20–47. World Bank Staff Working Paper No. 473. Washington: World Bank.

Clay, E. J. 1981a. "Food Policy Issues in Low Income Countries: An Overview." In *Food Policy Issues in Low Income Countries,* edited by E. Clay, R. Chambers, H. Singer, and M. Lipton, 1–19. World Bank Staff Working Paper No. 473. Washington: World Bank.

———. 1981b. "Poverty, Food Insecurity and Public Policy in Bangladesh." In *Food Policy Issues in Low Income Countries,* edited by E. Clay, R. Chambers, H. Singer, and M. Lipton, 48–84. World Bank Staff Working Paper No. 473. Washington: World Bank.

Cobb, R., R. Hunt, C. Vandervoort, C. Bledson, and R. McClusky. 1980. *Liberia: Rural Roads.* Project Impact Evaluation No. 6. Washington: U.S. Agency for International Development.

Cohen, M. 1984a. *Informal Sector Activity in Regional Urban Areas: The Street Food Trade.* Washington: Equity Policy Center.

———. 1984b. *The Urban Street Foods Trade: Implications for Policy.* Washington: Equity Policy Center.

Coleman, D., and F. Nixon. 1978. *Economics of Change in Less Developed Countries.* New York: Wiley.

Doan, P., and B. D. Lewis. 1989. *Niger Market Town Development Study.* Research Triangle Park, N.C.: Research Triangle Institute.

Farbman, M. 1981. *Assisting the Smallest Economic Activities of the Urban Poor,* edited by M. Farbman, 1–56. Washington: U.S. Agency for International Development.

Freeman, D. B., and G. B. Norcliff. 1981. "The Rural Nonfarm Sector and the Development Process in Kenya." In *Planning African Development,* edited by G. Norcliff and T. Pinfold, 62–78. Boulder, Colo.: Westview Press.

———. 1984. "Relations between the Rural Nonfarm and Small Sectors in Central Province, Kenya." *Tijdschrift voor Economische en Sociale Geografie* 75:61–73.

Green, J. 1989. "The Debt Problem of Sub-Saharan Africa." *Finance and Development* 26:9–12.

Gupta, A. P. 1975. *Marketing of Agricultural Products in India.* Bombay: Vora and Company Publishers.

Hohenberg, P. M., and L. H. Lees. 1985. *The Making of Urban Europe 1000–1950.* Cambridge, Mass.: Harvard University Press.

International Labor Office (ILO). 1988. *World Labor Report*. Vol. 3. Geneva: ILO.
Johnston, B. F., and P. Kilby. 1975. *Agriculture and Structural Transformation*. New York: Oxford University Press.
Kerven, C. 1982. *The Effects of Migration on Agricultural Production*. Gaborone, Botswana: Central Statistics Office.
Kilby, P. 1979. ''Evaluating Technical Assistance.'' *World Development* 7:309–323.
Kore, H. 1985. ''Aspects of the Grain Trade in Western Niger.'' In *Agricultural Markets in the Semi-Arid Tropics*, 61–67. Patancheru, India: International Crops Research Institute for the Semi-Arid Tropics.
Kuznets, S. 1961. ''Economic Growth and the Contribution of Agriculture: Notes on Measurement.'' *International Journal of Agrarian Affairs* 3:56–75.
Lele, U. 1981. ''Rural Africa: Modernization, Equity and Long Term Development.'' *Science* 211:547–553.
Lewis, D. B. 1989. ''Secondary Cities in Kenya.'' In *The Urbanization Revolution*, edited by R. May, Jr., 141–147. New York: Plenum.
Liedholm, C., and D. Mead. 1986. *Small-Scale Industries in Developing Countries: Empirical Evidence and Policy Implications*. East Lansing, Mich.: Michigan State University.
Mellor, J. W. 1986. ''Agriculture on the Road to Industrialization.'' In *Development Strategies Reconsidered*, edited by J. P. Lewis and V. Kallab, 67–89. Washington D.C.: Overseas Development Council.
Mittendorf, H. J. 1981. ''Useful Strategies for Developing Countries Striving to Improve Food Marketing Systems.'' In *Rural Change*, edited by G. Johnson and A. Marender, 131–144. Totowa, N.J.: Allenheld and Osmun.
Nsaku, N., and G. C. W. Ames. 1984–85. ''Constraints on Maize Production in Zaire.'' *Journal of African Studies* 11:156–163.
Obudho, R. A., and P. Waller, ed. 1976. *Periodic Markets, Urbanization and Regional Planning: A Case Study of Western Kenya*. Westport, Conn.: Greenwood Press.
Okafor, F. C. 1985. ''The Functional Role of Medium-Sized Towns in Regional Development.'' *Third World Planning Review* 7:143–159.
Okoso-Amaa, K. 1975. *Rice Marketing in Ghana*. Uppsala: Scandinavian Institute of African Studies.
Omer, A., and Associates. 1986. ''The Gezira Region, The Sudan.'' In *Small and Intermediate Urban Centers*, edited by J. E. Hardoy and D. Satterthwaite, 80–130. London: Hodder and Stoughton.
Republic of Senegal. 1984. *The Senegalese Experience in Urbanization: The Role of Secondary Towns in Economic and Social Development*. Dakar: Ministry of Urbanism and Housing.
Reutlinger, S. 1985. ''Food Security and Poverty in LDCs.'' *Finance and Development* 22:7–11.
Riley, H. M., and M. T. Weber. 1979. ''Marketing in Developing Countries.'' Working Paper No. 6, MSU Rural Development Series. East Lansing, Mich.: Department of Agricultural Economics, Michigan State University.
Rondinelli, D. A. 1983. *Secondary Cities in Developing Countries*. Beverly Hills, Calif.: Sage.
———. 1985. *Applied Methods of Regional Analysis*. Boulder, Colo.: Westview Press.
———. 1988. ''Giant and Secondary City Growth in Africa.'' In *The Metropolis Era:*

A World of Giant Cities, edited by Mattei Dogan and John D. Kasarada, Vol. 1, 291–321. Newbury Park: Sage.

———. 1991. "Asian Urban Development Policies in the 1990s: From Growth Control to Urban Diffusion." *World Development* 19:791–803.

Rondinelli, D. A., and K. Ruddle. 1978. *Urbanization and Rural Development: A Spatial Policy for Equitable Growth.* New York: Praeger.

Scrimshaw, N. S., and L. Taylor. 1980. "Food." *Scientific American* 243:78–88.

Sherman, J. R. 1985. "Food Grain Marketing in Burkina-Faso." In *Agricultural Markets in the Semi-Arid Tropics,* 81–95. Patancheru, India: International Crops Research Institute for the Semi-Arid Tropics.

Sporrek, A. 1985. *Food Marketing and Urban Growth in Dar es Salaam.* Lund Studies in Geography No. 51. Lund, Sweden: Royal University of Lund.

Townroe, P. M. 1983. *Location Factors in the Decentralization of Industry.* World Bank Staff Working Paper No. 517. Washington: World Bank.

UNDP (United Nations Development Programme). 1990. *Human Development Report 1990.* New York: Oxford University Press.

UNIDO (United Nations Industrial Development Organization). 1972. *Industrial Development Survey.* Vol. 4, ID-83. New York: United Nations.

United Nations. 1988. *World Demographic Estimates and Projections: 1950–2025.* New York: United Nations.

World Bank. 1978. *Employment and Development of Small Enterprises: Sector Policy Paper.* Washington: World Bank.

———. 1990. *World Development Report 1990.* Washington: World Bank.

22

Economic Aspects of Rural-Urban Migration

John Weeks

With some exceptions, notably in West Africa, urbanization came to Africa south of the Sahara[1] as a phenomenon of colonial rule. Wage labor, initially for plantations, mines, and public works, began and grew in response to the needs of colonial administration and commerce. When the 1960s brought independence to most of the region (Ghana earlier and the Portuguese colonies later) no sub-Saharan country had more than a minority of its population in cities, and except for a few mining enclaves, in no city did wage labor account for a majority of the labor force. Though cities and towns grew far faster than the population as a whole during the ensuing decades, as the end of the century approached still no sub-Saharan country had reached 50 percent urban, and no urban labor force had a wage labor majority.[2]

While the colonial period brought a substantial process of urbanization, rarely did observers attribute this to disproportionate material attractions of city life, which would later become the analytical emphasis. The wealth and privileges of city life were overwhelmingly enjoyed by the colonialists, with the urban-rural division a transparent derivative from the enormous inequality between Europeans and Africans (with Asian immigrants making up a substantial intermediate class in some colonies, especially in East Africa). Faced with this contrast between privileged Europeans and impoverished Africans, the concept of a urban-rural income gap had little relevance.

With independence there occurred in every country a process of "Africanization," in which Europeans and Asians in some cases were replaced with African nationals, in the civil service, the universities, and, to a lesser degree, in the Westernized private sector. In some countries, Ghana and Tanzania being examples, an attempt was made to compress the racist colonial pay scales.[3] But everywhere the difference between what a common laborer earned and the salaries of professionals and managers remained enormous; only now it represented an inequality among Africans rather than between Africans and Europeans. Since all but a few of the newly independent countries lacked an African landed elite, those earning high incomes, comparable to the salaries in the former colonial centers, were concentrated in the major cities, as was the small but emerging class of indigenous capitalists.

Thus, the income differences passed down as a colonial legacy changed the perception of the distributional dichotomy from European-African to urban-rural. Central in this new class structure and its normative interpretation were the wage earners, overwhelmingly concentrated in urban areas except for the mining and plantation enclaves. During the colonial period wages remained low, probably comparable alternative income-earning opportunities, both rural and urban (though the absence of quantitative information for the period makes this only a qualitative assessment). Indeed, in British East Africa what was judged as excessive labor turnover in the Westernized sector (''labor instability'') prompted the colonial government to institute a ''high wage policy,'' whose stated goal was to provide a level of pay such that an African employee could support a family in urban areas (Weeks, 1971e).

In most sub-Saharan countries trade unions, which grew rapidly in number and membership during the late colonial period, played a prominent role in pressuring for independence. Once independence was achieved, workers' organizations represented a substantial political force beyond their relative numbers in the labor force, though commentators greatly exaggerated that influence. With their prestige high and influence at its peak, trade unions achieved substantial wage increases in the immediate post-independence period, particularly in former British East Africa. Because most wage workers were employed in towns and cities, the transitory inflation of trade union power enhanced the appearance of a fundamental division of wealth and privilege between urban and rural areas.

The urban-rural division also seemed fundamental to the development strategy of the postindependence governments. With rare exceptions, the colonial authorities did not encourage manufacturing in Africa, and quite the contrary occurred in some cases. Both as an economic strategy of modernization and a nationalist desire to redress this delayed development, the new governments embarked upon programs of import substitution and large-scale public works. By their nature, most of these projects tended either to be located in urban areas or to have their benefits concentrated there. These projects characteristically drew a major proportion of their finance from external donors, so it seemed that foreign aid served the towns and did little for the countryside.

The manner by which governments raised the domestic portion of development expenditure also supported the growing perception of an excessive urban focus to African development strategy. In consequence of their extremely underdeveloped nature, African countries were overwhelmingly agricultural. Except for the countries with important mining sectors, both government taxation and foreign exchange earnings, the domestic sources of development expenditure, would necessarily come from agriculture. Given the virtually insurmountable difficulties in administering direct taxes on farm income in underdeveloped countries (difficulties not insignificant in developed countries), fiscal revenues in African countries overwhelmingly derived from indirect levies on monetary exchanges. Even more, governments faced the practical impossibility of systematically taxing the exchanges carried out in the countless markets of domestic exchange.

Therefore, for reasons of necessity and convenience rather than principle or grand strategy, governments taxed imports and exports, which for exports, in the absence of mining and expatriate plantations, meant that agricultural producers disproportionately carried the burden to finance the state. Governments taxed with *ad valorem* or physical quantity levies, but more important in many countries were produce marketing boards.[4] These institutions virtually without exception were creations of the former colonial administrations. Governments granted them monopsony power[5] in the trading of the major export crops, the most important of which were cocoa, coffee, cotton, and groundnuts. Though these marketing boards provided services to facilitate exports, transport, and storage, their *raison d'être* seemed the extraction of a surplus from export producers by purchasing crops well below the prevailing world price, then applying the extracted surplus to urban-focused projects. As with other state functions, the fiscal system appeared to be a vehicle for the transfer of resources from countryside to town.

Independently of fiscal transfers, the development strategy of import substitution industrialization (ISI) could be interpreted as prejudicial to the countryside. The tariffs that protected manufacturers themselves altered the returns in favor of industry and insofar as domestic manufacturing replaced cheaper imports (the point of the tariffs), farmers suffered real income reduction through terms of trade losses.[6] By stressing only the negative aspects of protection and ignoring its longer-term dynamic effects, critics of development policy implied that manufacturing, indeed the entire urban economy, existed only by virtue of the explicit and implicit losses of agriculture, its growth largely the result of its semiparasitic relationship to the countryside. This critique of the prevailing development strategy of African governments might have traced its philosophical roots back to the eighteenth-century French Physiocrats, whose analysis concluded that all value arose from agricultural production. Notwithstanding its emphasis on "free markets," this position shared much with the analysis of the nineteenth-century French agrarian socialists, who considered the rise of industrial capitalism to be the result of unequal exchange between peasant agriculture and capitalist manufacturing.[7] However, as description this critique provided important empirical insights, highlighting the tensions and contradictions inherent in the transition from agrarian to industrial society and its associated process of urbanization.

URBAN BIAS AND THE ANALYSIS OF MIGRATION

The antiurban, anti-industrialization critique created a stylized analytical model of the typical African country, in which society was starkly divided between an urban modern sector (later to be distinguished by the modifier ''formal''),[8] where urban elites and wage earners enjoyed extravagant privileges, and the rural sector, where a vast undifferentiated peasantry lived in poverty; and the latter were the producers of the wealth that maintained the former. As simplistic and stylized as this vision was, it provided the basis for the policies of the major aid donors for several decades.[9]

Within this perspective rural-to-urban migration was treated almost exclusively as a ''pull'' phenomenon. It was alleged that the concentration of resources in urban areas induced rural people to abandon the countryside for the towns. In the absence of the urban-rural gap, which was seen as an arbitrary creation of government policy, rural society would provide an adequate source of livelihood appropriate to the stage of development of African countries. This stylized impression, that migration derived from the material advantages of city life, found formal expression in the Todaro model of rural-urban migration,[10] in which urbanization was reduced to the phenomenon of migration, and the latter to the expected income to be enjoyed in cities. The hypothesis that the movement of people responded overwhelmingly to income differentials had a long tradition in the literature of neoclassical economics. In an analytical context which took institutions, including access to land, as given, choice of livelihood and the location of that livelihood would be based upon ''opportunity cost'': the comparison of the returns to alternative forms of employment. This approach to labor allocation was at the heart of the extremely influential Lewis model of ''economic development with unlimited supplies of labor.''[11]

In the 1960s there arose a considerable literature on the tendency in Africa for modern-sector employment to grow slower than the urban labor force, a consequence of which was said to be ''unemployment.''[12] In the African context the concept of unemployment was problematical in the extreme, as numerous authors pointed out. However, when employed uncritically in the opportunity cost model, it provided an ingredient in a powerful policy message. If one takes rural income (itself complex in the concrete) as given and institutions unchanged, then the decision to migrate could be treated as the result of a hedonistic comparison between that rural income and the expected value of the return from urban employment. If one then treats the urban labor force as divided between the employed (the modern sector) and the unemployed, the expected value would not be the urban wage itself, but rather that wage discounted by the probability of obtaining modern-sector employment. The next analytical step was to formalize the commonsense notion that more unemployment implies less chance of finding a job, by making the probability of gaining employment inversely related to the rate of unemployment. One could then conclude that migration would continue as long as the urban wage multiplied by the employment rate (one minus the unemployment rate) exceeded rural income; or formally, if

$$(W_u)(1 - e) > W_r$$

where W_u = the modern sector wage, e = the unemployment rate, and W_r = the average rural income.

This simple formulation, based upon problematical analytical categories, embodied a powerful and unexpected policy message: other things equal, an increase in urban employment (decrease in the unemployment rate) would *increase* migration, since its *ceterus paribus* result is to raise the expected value of urban employment. The model said that policy measures to increase urban employment were "self-defeating," for they generated the very unemployment they sought to reduce.[13] This message of the elaborated opportunity cost model carried profoundly antiurban and anti-working-class policy implications. The cause of the migration problem was high urban wages, and these high wages the result of the disproportionate power of urban workers. In response to this power, African governments unwisely adopted the trappings of developed country labor relations, including minimum wage laws. The application of these inappropriate measures resulted in wages far above what "free markets" would have dictated, with migration the inevitable result.[14]

In terms of formal logic, the opportunity cost model was fraught with difficulties. As noted, central to the argument was the use of "unemployment" in the sense it is applied in developed market economies: people seeking work and without jobs. Given the nature of African societies, especially the absence of state support for the unemployed, this direct transference of the developed country category was singularly inappropriate. To deal with this difficulty, the model might be reformulated in terms of three sectors, the rural, the urban modern ("formal"), and the urban traditional ("informal"). Then, the argument became that migrants first entered into the low-wage, low-productivity informal sector, where they awaited their luck at the lottery of high-wage formal employment. However, the informal sector itself was not without serious analytical problems,[15] rendering it a thin reed upon which to hang a theory of migration.[16] Even were one to accept unemployment as a relevant category (or the informal sector in its place), the argument then turns on the job search/selection process being random. If ethnicity, political patronage, and other noneconomic factors influence access to formal-sector employment, as is certainly the case, then the probabilistic approach breaks down. Finally, the opportunity cost model is based upon a strict dichotomy between rural and urban areas. Derivative from this, it presumes that residence in urban areas gives the job seeker an increased likelihood of obtaining employment. While this may be the case in a random job selection world, it need not be when clientage and patronage play a major role. Perhaps more fundamental, it may be incorrect to conceive of African societies as divided between townspeople and country people. Given the important role of the extended family, the appropriate approach may be to treat households as spanning rural and urban areas. The common practice of semiurban farming also casts in doubt the validity of the rural-urban dichotomy and the welfare judgments derived from it.[17]

The growth of towns, by stimulating the market demand for foodstuffs, may actually foster agricultural development and incomes.[18] The discussion takes up this point in the next section.

Notwithstanding the conceptual problems, the model gained great influence, in part because its overall message complemented well the neoclassical critique of structural transformation via protectionist measures (import substitution industrialization). It implied that unemployment would only be reduced through a development strategy that focused on rural areas rather than purposeful interventions in favor of industrialization. In the 1980s this quintessential neoclassical position[19] would pass from academic critique to the basis of policy for multilateral and bilateral aid donors, with little reflection upon its long-term implications. The emphasis on rural development as the route to solving the problem of development found its most sophisticated analytical and polemical expression in the work of Michael Lipton, which enshrined the term "urban bias" into the development literature.[20] For Lipton, migration represented but one of a broad range of destructive consequences for rural people of the misallocation of resources to urban areas. Further, the redressing of the urban bias would not only facilitate development but also spread more widely the benefits of growth. While Lipton's book made only passing reference to African countries, casual empiricism suggested that it applied (if at all) more to Africa than elsewhere. Unlike in Latin America and much of Asia, Africa south of the Sahara lacked the extreme rural inequality that might result in the benefits from growth being concentrated in the hands of a few large landlords and capitalist agroenterprises.[21]

While casual impression suggested that urban bias was a common phenomenon, empirical verification proved much more elusive. J. B. Knight's work on Ghana (1972), one of the few attempts in the 1970s to calculate the "urban-rural gap," showed that the income differential relevant to migration was negligible. In the same vein, J. F. S. Levi (1973) attempted to verify the opportunity cost hypothesis for Sierra Leone and found that it failed to explain rural/urban migration patterns. These results were subsequently supported by a series of studies commissioned by the Jobs and Skills Program for Africa (regional body of the International Labor Office). The comparison of over a dozen case studies indicated a quite varied pattern, with no consistent urban bias in income levels.[22] This finding was consistent with the argument that urban bias should not be viewed as a general phenomenon of African countries (or underdeveloped countries elsewhere), but rather as the superficial manifestation of specific historical and class characteristics of various societies and inherent in the development process itself.[23]

A critique of the concept of urban bias lies beyond the scope of this chapter, but one can note that the empirical evidence for Africa indicated a pattern of rural-urban income differentials associated with colonialism and decolonialism. In West Africa, where the colonial authorities pursued a low-wage policy, the income differentials between urban workers and farm families after independence were slight and in some cases favored agriculturalists.[24] The few instances of a wide income gap between these two groups could be found in East and Central Africa, reflecting the colonial wage policy of establishing a stable urban labor force[25] or the transitory reaction to racist wage scales (e.g., the mines in Zambia).

THE COLLAPSE OF URBAN REAL WAGES

The stereotype of African countries divided between the wealth of the large cities and the poverty of the countryside corresponded to a brief moment in the history of the region, at most from about 1960 to the mid-1970s. During this decade and a half favorable external conditions allowed the implementation of import substitution policies, supported by foreign exchange reserves accumulated before independence, relatively stable terms of trade, and the inflow of concessionary finance. However, with the sharp increase in oil prices in 1973–74, the external environment turned much more hostile. As is well documented, the sub-Saharan countries as a group suffered greater terms of trade losses than any other region of the Third World, particularly acute for 1978–81.[26] This fall in the terms of trade and the associated decline in export earnings resulted in a drop in government revenues that intensified the pressure for wage restraint that had characterized policy since independence. Balance of payments pressure also depressed manufacturing growth, which placed downward pressure on private-sector wages. After the first set of oil price increases, urban wagcs in Africa south of the Sahara came under increasing pressure.

The accumulation of evidence in the late 1970s and 1980s showed clearly a continuous and in some cases catastrophic fall in urban real wages. There were several aspects of this fall which affected migration. First, where relevant statistics were available, they showed that unskilled workers in the modern (formal) sector fared worse than skilled workers. This implied that the relevant income opportunity luring most migrants (urban unskilled jobs) became decreasingly attractive. Second, urban real wages fell by so much that a growing proportion of wage earner households dropped below poverty level as measured, for example, by the ability to purchase a minimum diet.[27] Third, despite the fall in real wages, migration from rural to urban areas appears not to have abated, and urban labor markets if anything were in greater excess supply in the late 1980s than ten years before (see below). Fourth, falling wages did not clear urban labor markets, contrary to the prediction of the orthodox economic theory behind the opportunity cost model. Fifth, the fall in wages did result in a blurring of the distinction between the formal and informal sectors in urban areas, a distinction key to the wage-differential hypothesis about migration. The difference in incomes decreased, and along with this decrease lifestyles and living conditions

Table 22.1
Urban Real Wages for Selected Sub-Saharan African Countries, 1970–86 (1978 = 100)

COUNTRY	YEAR								
	1970	1979	1980	1981	1982	1983	1984	1985	1986
Burundi	-	99	95	102	101	131	134	129	127
Cameroon	-	94	94	92	92	-	-	-	-
Ghana	208	77	85	48	46	35	38	71	-
Kenya	122	100	100	98	93	85	81	81	80
Malawi	-	97	96	96	100	86	66	69	-
Nigeria	99	82	85	82	77	72	59	63	-
Sierra Leone	149	96	113	94	87	53	41	30	29
Somalia	128	98	57	-	-	-	-	-	10
Swaziland	-	103	65	78	77	112	120	120	-
Tanzania	125	-	-	72	-	49	-	-	-
Uganda	313	-	16	22	-	-	41	-	-
Zimbabwe	-	87	108	103	96	83	69	108	99

Note: Average earnings in nonagricultural activities, usually establishments hiring ten or more workers.
Source: Compiled from International Labour Office, 1987.

of households deriving their primary incomes from formal and informal activities became similar. All of this went along with the income gap between rural and urban areas narrowing sharply. So great was this last shift that, in some countries by the mid-1980s, incomes received by farm families exceeded urban wage earner incomes. Below the most important of these five for migration are treated in greater detail.

Evidence of the fall in real wages is presented in Table 22.1.[28] In the case of every country for which there were data back to the early 1970s, real urban wages fell sharply during that decade. This was even true for Nigeria, which went through a tremendous boom due to the increase in oil prices. In the 1980s urban wages fell much more. It is analytically useful to take 1978 as the base year, since it marked the second oil price "shock," which ushered in a period of severe economic crisis for many African countries. From this base year until the mid-1980s, real wages fell by more than half in five countries (Ghana, Sierra Leone, Somalia, Tanzania, and Uganda). In Kenya, Malawi, and Nigeria the declines were less, but still substantial, from 20 to 35 percent. In two countries urban real wages rose, but both cases involve circumstances so particular as not to contradict the rule. Real wages rose by over 20 percent in Burundi, but this country had perhaps the smallest wage labor force relative to its population of any in the table. In the case of Swaziland the urban labor market was governed by the demand for migrant labor to South Africa, not domestic conditions.

One does not have to calculate rural incomes to deduce that rural-urban differentials must have fallen. Even in those countries with the poorest growth performances (e.g., Ghana), the fall in real wages far surpassed the decline in per capita gross domestic product (GDP). Since for every country in the table the rural population exceeded the urban, it follows that wage incomes must have fallen more than farm incomes. The implication of the table is that urban wage labor came under extreme pressure of falling incomes in the 1970s and 1980s, and in some countries may have disintegrated as a coherent economic group. In the more populous countries of the region, where a working class emerged in the postcolonial period, a wage income was no longer sufficient to support a family in the 1980s. In some countries it was insufficient to support a worker on her/his own (e.g., Uganda, Ghana, Tanzania, and Somalia).[29]

Despite the decline in urban real wages, rural-to-urban migration showed no tendency to decline (Table 22.2). In the table, rates of urban growth are divided into two periods, 1965–73 and 1973–84. The time periods coincide with the dramatic change in the international economic environment confronting the African countries and the resultant regional development crisis. The earlier period includes the postindependence years up to the first oil "shock." It was during these years that per capita incomes in most Sub-Saharan Africa (SSA) countries rose, when most would say that development strategy had its greatest "urban bias," and the gap between rural and urban incomes was the widest. During the second period economic growth slowed, with most countries suffering per capita declines.[30] The purpose of this table is to inspect whether the decline in urban wages seemed associated with a reduction of rates of migration. The information is not ideal, since the urbanization rates in some cases are projections, rather than being based on census data. Further, the impact on migration of wages may be masked by other changes, such as civil strife.[31] However, so extreme was the decline in urban economies that one would expect some abatement of migration if the opportunity cost model captured the primary determinants of labor allocation.

The table provides rates of urban growth and urban real wages[32] for 31 countries, and the statistics show a mixed pattern. For 10 countries, the rate of urban population growth declined, but for 16 it rose. In the case of 5 others, the measured rates were virtually the same for the two periods (Angola, the Central African Republic, Niger, Togo, and Zambia). The simple average across countries was virtually the same for both periods (6.4 percent). The most dramatic change occurred in Uganda, and this could be explained by catastrophic economic and political events in that country.[33] It may well be that the reduction in the rate of migration in some SSA countries during 1973–84 was the result of a narrowing of rural-urban income differentials. Given the small decline in the former compared to the massive drop in the latter, the relationship between the two appears at most to be tenuous.

Table 22.2
Rate of Growth of Urban Population, and Wage Trends in Sub-Saharan African Countries, 1965–84

Country	Rate of Growth 1965-73	Rate of Growth 1973-84	Direction of change	Urban real wages
I. Consistent with predicted outcome (9)				
Botswana	19.0	11.3	decline	decline
Ethiopia	7.4	6.1	decline	decline
Lesotho	7.8	20.1	increase	increase
Malawi	8.2	7.3	decline	decline
Senegal	4.2	3.8	decline	decline
Sierra Leone	5.0	3.5	decline	decline
Somalia	6.4	5.4	decline	decline
Sudan	6.3	5.5	decline	decline
Uganda	8.3	-0.1	decline	decline
II. [Borderline] (3)				
Burundi	1.4	3.3	increase	stable
Cameroon	7.3	8.2	increase	stable
Zimbabwe	6.8	6.1	decline	stable
III. Contrary to predicted outcome (7)				
Burkina Faso	6.5	4.8	decline	increase
Ghana	4.5	5.3	increase	decline
Kenya	7.3	7.9	increase	decline
Liberia	5.3	6.0	increase	decline
Nigeria	4.7	5.2	increase	decline
Tanzania	8.1	8.6	increase	decline
Zambia	8.2	8.3	increase	decline
IV. No wage data (12)				
Angola	5.9	6.0	no change	
Congo	4.4	5.4	increase	
Benin	4.5	5.0	increase	
Central African Rep	4.4	4.6	no change	
Côte d'Ivoire	8.2	8.3	increase	
Congo	4.4	5.4	increase	
Guinea	5.0	6.2	increase	
Mali	5.4	4.5	increase	
Niger	7.0	7.1	no change	
Rwanda	6.0	6.6	increase	
Togo	6.4	6.5	no change	
Zaire	5.9	7.1	increase	

Sources: Compiled from World Bank, 1986, 1987; ILO/JASPA, 1984, 1991.

The countries are divided into three groups, the first comprised of the nine countries for which one observes the outcome predicted by the opportunity cost model: a decline in the rate of urban growth was associated with a decline in urban wages (or in the case of Lesotho, an increase in both). For three more countries the result is borderline: urban real wages were more or less stable and the change in urban growth mixed (up in two cases, down in the third). These three countries would seem neither to confirm nor to contradict the predictions of the model. For seven countries the relationship between urban wages and urban population growth appeared contrary to the prediction of the model: wages fell, but the rate of urban growth increased (and vice versa for Burkina Faso). For the last twelve countries in the table the rate of urban growth increased in each case or remained virtually the same. While there were no wage data for these twelve countries, it was certainly the case that urban incomes fell sharply in some of them.

The statistical evidence demonstrates a substantial contraction of urban incomes relatively to rural ones in Africa south of the Sahara after the mid-1970s. This trend was in contrast to the previous fifteen years, when African countries enjoyed modest to strong rates of economic growth, a disproportionate amount of which occurred in urban areas. During the earlier period it was not an unreasonable inference that the growth of urban activity stimulated rural-to-urban migration. However, the proposition that the expected income gap between rural and urban occupations represented the primary attraction for immigrants went unverified. Nevertheless, it was treated as fact rather than hypothesis. In the 1970s and 1980s, urban incomes (and especially wages) fell sharply relative to rural incomes, yet statistics suggest that rural-to-urban migration continued at the same rate. One can conclude that an alternative to the opportunity cost model was required to explain migration.

MIGRATION AND HOUSEHOLD STRATEGIES

Since the early 1970s the most important factor influencing income distribution and migration in SSA countries has been economic decline itself. The impact of economic decline was uneven, partly due to the substantial proportion of output in the region which represented nonmonetized subsistence production.[34] Decline depressed the monetary sector of SSA economies more than the subsistence sectors, a general law of economic cycles in underdeveloped countries. However, its operation is not obvious, for the truth in the law is that among self-employed producers consuming their own output, a form of "Say's Law" holds in the strict sense.[35] If one has access to the means to produce and is not greatly engaged in exchange, supply and demand must coincide since the decision to produce and the decision to consume are one and the same.

Subsistence production should be viewed in its relationship to activities which bring cash incomes, with subsistence production representing a choice when the monetary sector contracts. When the demand for cash crops declines, as during the 1980s for African farmers, agricultural households may have no alternative but to apply their surplus land and labor to subsistence production. Where conditions permit (i.e., access to land), erstwhile wage earners may take up agriculture to survive (Uganda represented an extreme example). Thus, the tendency for monetary income to decline relative to subsistence income during an economic crisis is in part due to the basic difference between the two (the latter is immune to demand failures), and also the shift of the labor force from monetary to nonmonetary activities to survive in periods of economic decline. While farm households maintained subsistence production during the African development crisis of the 1980s, the decline of the monetary sector generated downward pressures on subsistence income, by increasing competition over land.

As monetary sectors contracted relative to subsistence sectors, the economic decline in SSA countries shifted income in favor of the rural sector. For both urban and rural areas these shifts were quite complex. While virtually all urban dwellers derive their livelihoods from monetary exchange, the typical labor force was divided among entrepreneurs, government employees, private-sector wage earners, and informal-sector workers whose economic activities are extremely diverse and whose incomes vary from the extremely low to the highly remunerated.[36] A decline in aggregate demand directly impacts upon private-sector entrepreneurs and wage earners, as well as on informal-sector operators. For government employees, the consequence is less direct, working through government revenues. The result throughout Africa of budgetary pressure was to drive down real wages in the public sector as inflation outpaced nominal pay increases.

In the rural sector the contraction of the monetary economy resulted in declines in real incomes, but livelihoods of farmers were cushioned by subsistence production. In general, cash-crop producers may incur debts, and the ability to survive indebtedness until market conditions improve is positively related to producers' accumulated wealth.[37]

Where land was *de facto* alienable, indebtedness resulted in the loss of farms and permanent exclusion from the market for smaller producers. Limited evidence suggests that landlessness became a significant phenomenon in SSA countries, though certainly not as widespread as in Latin America or Asia.[38] The development of a market for land was not sufficiently advanced in SSA countries for economic pressure alone to generate bankruptcies and landlessness.[39] However, policies to privatize land could generate such a result. Under land tenure systems characterizing the region in the 1980s,[40] rural households in SSA countries retreated into subsistence when market conditions deteriorated. As a result, market shares of large producers rose relative to the shares of small producers during the economic crisis of the 1980s.[41]

Discussion of rural income shifts in response to the economic contraction should not be confined to on-farm livelihoods. Rural nonfarm activities represented a substantial and growing contribution to household incomes, occupying perhaps 20 percent of the rural labor force in SSA countries in the mid-1980s, particularly important for the poorer segments of the population (Advisory Committee on Rural Employment, 1983). Most nonfarm activities were linked to cash-crop agriculture. While little information is available, it is reasonable to assume that rural nonfarm incomes, because they involved monetary exchange, contracted along with cash-crop earnings. Thus, when rural cash incomes fell, all sources of money income contracted in rural areas, with important consequences for rural-urban migration.

Migration is both the theoretical and actual link between rural and urban incomes, though in a much more complex way than suggested by opportunity cost models. These are general equilibrium theoretical systems constrained from reaching full employment by a rigid urban wage. Such analysis derives its inspiration from the general neoclassical one-sector model in which a full employment solution with all markets cleared is the consequence if all variables are free to seek their market clearing levels. In this formulation, unemployment and migration are wage or income gap phenomena, never demand phenomena. That is, urban employment is constrained by the wage being too high (not by insufficient demand for output), and migration is the result of greater expected earnings in urban areas (not push factors in agriculture). During the 1960s this was a useful simplification, for most SSA economies grew at rates that kept them pressing against crucial constraints such as skilled labor, rather than product demand. Urban employment could not have been increased to any great extent by an expansion of aggregate demand alone, even had there been no foreign exchange constraint on growth or structural scarcities, such as skilled labor that limited employment growth. However, even in the context of the 1960s, it was questionable to believe that flexible wages could have cleared the labor market. That belief involves a number of dubious assumptions which have been subjected to severe criticism within mainstream economic theory,[42] and only rescued by the more conservative and orthodox climate of opinion during the 1980s.

Abandoning the conclusion that wages can equilibrate labor markets yields important conclusions in the African context. In a demand-constrained situation a falling urban-rural income differential can induce urban migration, contrary to the predictions of the wage-constrained general equilibrium model. If the relevant decision unit is the extended family (as research on SSA countries suggests) and if families seek to maintain themselves above some target minimum poverty level, then falling incomes in either rural or urban areas can induce rather than discourage migration even to where the relative reward to labor has fallen. This would be the case even more in the context of rural households losing access to land. The apparently "perverse" behavior, more seeking urban work when urban incomes fall, results because the availability of different forms of livelihood making is constrained by nonprice factors. In this circumstance, households must take what is available and cannot make their choices solely on the basis of relative rates of return.

In a demand-constrained economy with access to land being limited, a falling urban-rural income gap may not have any predictable impact on the evaluation by agents of the advantages of seeking urban and rural livelihoods. If cash-crop production is limited by product demand, then a rise in rural incomes relative to urban incomes is of limited relevance to urban workers even if they have access to land appropriate for cash crops. In a demand-constrained situation, the consequence of urban workers shifting to agriculture is either an increase in subsistence production or an expansion of cash-crop output which drives down price and reduces the return to rural work.

CONCLUSION

In the 1960s and 1970s, the economic analysis of African rural-to-urban migration focused on relative incomes as the major determinants of labor allocation. This reflected the tendency in orthodox economics to take institutional structures and social relations as given, as well as to view rising per capita incomes as the norm and declines as exceptions. By the late 1970s this economic approach no longer bore close relation to the realities of African towns and countryside. As the monetary economies contracted and land came under pressure to be commercialized, the complexity of migration to towns became increasingly clear.

The fundamental problem with the opportunity cost approach to urban migration was its ahistorical character. Explicit in the analysis was the idea that rural-to-urban migration was strictly a symmetrical process; when urban-rural income ratios were less than one, de-urbanization resulted. No country has ever experienced such reverse migration except under conditions of extreme social strain (to the point of chaos and anarchy). By the 1990s African rural-to-urban migration represented an irreversible process associated with profound structural changes in towns and the countryside.[43]

NOTES

1. This chapter refers to the continental African countries south of the Sahara, and when ''Africa'' is used it is employed as a shortened reference to that set of countries.

2. For labor force statistics and description, see Doctor and Gallis (1986) and Rimmer (1984:ch. 3).

3. The definitive study of wage levels and employment conditions in the African civil service is Robinson (1990).

4. The role of marketing boards is given a balanced assessment in Helleiner (1964).

5. A monopoly is a single seller, and a monopsony a single buyer.

6. In the logic of neoclassical economics, under appropriate assumptions, markets not subject to state intervention produce an outcome optimal in terms of economic efficiency. This conclusion, special case though it may be, is ideologically important, since it provides an apparently objective, value-free critique of import substitution.

7. Byres (1979) characterized the entire ''urban bias'' approach as ''neo-populist.''

8. The concept of ''informality'' derives from two articles in the early 1970s, Hart (1973) and Weeks (1971a).

9. See, for example, World Bank (1981, 1989a:29).

10. The original formulation of the model is found in Todaro (1969), though Todaro (1971) is less technical and captures the essence of the argument. Considerably more nuanced, with less emphasis upon "pull" factors, is the treatment of migration in Todaro (1990).

11. See Lewis (1954), and for a critique, Weeks (1971c).

12. A seminal article was Frank (1970).

13. In formal terms, the rate of unemployment is the equilibrating variable. Given W_u and W_r, the unemployment rate is unique, for it establishes the equality of the expected incomes in the two sectors.

14. This position was argued by Kilby (1967), who also maintained that the Anglo-Saxon model of labor relations provoked political strife. For a contrary view, see Weeks (1971b).

15. The literature on the informal sector is reviewed in Turnham, Salome, and Schwartz (1990). See especially the chapters by Charmes and Fields.

16. Lachaud was quite negative about the utility of the concept for labor market analysis: "Including the concept of the informal sector in analysis of the urban labor market seems to run into a double difficulty, largely due to the nature of the reference paradigm: inadequate assessment of the heterogeneity of forms of production and labor, and an incomplete analysis of their mode of integration into the economic and social environment" (Lachaud, 1990:118).

17. In a review of the literature on urban and semiurban farming, Swindell (1988:99) writes;

> [U]rban sub-regions [in tropical Africa] are characterized by a mosaic of production and exchange relations with considerable connectivity between urban and rural areas. . . . [T]he notion of an urban/rural divide and the impoverishment of rural people by a privileged class of urban dwellers seems open to question. . . . While the urban/rural division may identify spatial differences in wealth, it also obscures important interrelationships between town and countryside.

18. "Rapid urbanization and the rising market for foodstuffs have given a considerable fillip to agriculture [in tropical Africa]" (Swindell, 1988:112).

19. Quintessentially so because it derived from static comparative advantage theory, in which countries are advised to do what they currently do best, without regard for future (dynamic) possibilities, which would require policy interventions to realize.

20. Much of the evidence for "urban bias" offered by Lipton referred to India, but the analysis was enthusiastically applied to Africa. See Lipton (1977) and the detailed critique in Byres (1979).

21. A key argument in Lipton's plea for a rural-based strategy was the assertion that income distribution tended to be more equally distributed among the rural population than the urban. Byres challenged this assertion on the basis of data cited by Lipton. However, for Africa, the rural distribution did seem to be more equal, though comparable statistics are rare and unreliable. For what is available, see Jain (1975); and, more rigorously done, van Ginneken and Jong-goo Park (1984), whose work includes among its 23 countries Kenya, Sierra Leone, the Sudan, Tanzania, and Zambia.

22. The case studies were summarized in ILO/JASPA (1982, 1984). Among these case studies (released separately) were three by Vali Jamal (Nigeria [1986], Uganda [1985], and Tanzania [1989]).

23. Ellis (1984) argues for Tanzania that to the extent that resources flowed dispro-

portionately to urban areas, this could not be interpreted as reflecting a purely rural-urban division of those resources.

24. This was particularly the case for Sierra Leone (Weeks, 1992: ch. 5; Jamal, n.d.). Rimmer noted the relatively low urban wages in West Africa even after independence: "since 1960 West African governments have restrained wage increases and the real value of wages has tended to fall in the face of more or less pronounced inflation" (Rimmer, 1984:93–94).

25. This policy is discussed in Weeks (1971e).

26. An excellent, if not very accessible, review of the impact of the terms of trade on African countries is found in Saigal (1990). The evidence is briefly reviewed in Weeks (1992; ch. 2). In a World Bank paper, Singh (1983:6–7) comments, "In the past decades, world prices of agricultural commodities relative to world prices of manufactured productions have tended to fall. . . . Terms of trade losses (in percentages) were particularly large [during 1978–81] for Ethiopia (27), Kenya (19), Madagascar (26), Tanzania (16), Ghana (36), Ivory Coast (30), and Sudan (21)." Note that all percentages are negative.

27. For example: Weeks (1992: ch. 5), Sierra Leone; Jamal (1986), Nigeria; and Jamal (1989), Tanzania.

28. A brief but useful survey of wage trends is found in United Nations (1990:162–165).

29. This assertion is documented in Jamal and Weeks (1988, 1992).

30. According to the World Bank, for sub-Saharan Africa as a whole the annual rate of growth of gross domestic product in constant prices for the first period was 8.5 percent and 1.6 percent for the second period. Since population in the region grew at about three percent a year, the statistics imply that per capita income declined during 1973–84 (World Bank, 1986:182). Countries in which per capita income rose during the first half of the 1980s were: Chad, Guinea-Bissau, Burkina Faso, and the Gambia. For all other countries included in World Bank tables, per capita income fell (World Bank, 1989b:221).

31. The impact of war and insurrection on demographic patterns in sub-Saharan Africa cannot be overstated, notably in Ethiopia, the Sudan, Chad, Mozambique, Angola, Uganda, Somalia, and Liberia.

32. The last column in the table draws on the statistics in Table 22.1, and also from other sources whose information on wages was insufficiently precise to include in Table 22.1. See notes to Table 22.2.

33. The Ugandan case is treated in detail in Jamal (1985).

34. Throughout this discussion "subsistence" production refers to output which is directly consumed by the farm household, or used directly in the farm production process. Thus, the term does not necessarily refer to a standard of living of the farm family.

35. In the nineteenth century the French economist J. B. Say argued that a general overproduction of commodities ("a glut") was not possible because the motivation of production is consumption: someone produces a commodity with the purpose of using the revenue from the sale of that commodity to purchase another commodity. The "law" is frequently epitomized in the phrase "supply creates its own demand." To the extent that there is truth in this argument, it applies most strictly to production for the direct use of the producer.

36. An extensive literature exists on the characteristics of informal-sector employment. A number of case studies are summarized in ILO (1991: ch. 3).

37. For a theoretical treatment, see Weeks (1971d); and for a survey of empirical evidence, Michael Lipton (with Richard Longhurst) (1985).

38. African land tenure systems and evidence of landlessness are treated in FAO (1985) and Lipton (1982).

39. However, a number of case studies have documented the development of a market in land and the associated landlessness. Swindell (1988:112) comments, "[I]f a researcher is looking for landless or land-poor people and their exploitation by a rising class of capitalist farmers, urban peripheries and hinterlands may be better places to look." See particularly the path-breaking study by Hill (1977). For an analytical discussion of the development of a land market in Africa, see Sender and Smith (1986).

40. A useful review of African land tenure systems is found in Bruce (1986).

41. Economic differentiation in the rural sector was particularly advanced in Kenya. For a detailed discussion of farm size in that country, see Livingstone (1986: ch. 11).

42. The most important of these is that no "false trading" can occur; that is, no exchanges at disequilibrium prices (Hahn, 1989; Taylor, 1983; Weeks, 1989).

43. Commenting on the impact of the economic crisis of the 1980s, the Economic Commission for Africa (1989:16) wrote:

> The African social structure is currently undergoing severe strains and stresses due to uncontrolled urbanisation, erosion of social sanctions and values and initiative modernism. . . . Today, more than ever before, the African social fabric is in danger of collapse as a result of the cumulative impact of deteriorating economic crisis.

Many African economies moved from stagnation to declining growth; food deficits reached alarming proportions; unemployment mounted; underutilization of industrial capacity became widespread; and environmental degradation threatened the very survival of the African people.

REFERENCES

Advisory Committee on Rural Development. 1983. *Promotion of Employment and Incomes for the Rural Poor, Including Rural Women, through Non-farm Activities.* Geneva: ILO.

Bruce, John W. 1986. "Land Tenure Issues in Project Design and Strategies for Agricultural Development in sub-Saharan Africa." LTC Paper 128, Land Tenure Center, University of Wisconsin–Madison.

Byres, T. J. 1979. "Of Neo-populist Pipe-dreams: Daedalus in the Third World and the Myth of Urban Bias." *Journal of Peasant Studies* 6:210–244.

Colclough, Christopher. 1982. "Wage Flexibility in Sub-Saharan Africa: Trends and Explanations." In *Towards Social Adjustment: Labour Market Issues in Structural Adjustment,* edited by Guy Standing and Victor Tokman, 211–232. Geneva: ILO.

Doctor, K. C., and H. Gallis. 1966. "Size and Characteristics of Wage Employment in Africa: Some Statistical Estimates." *International Labour Review* 93:149–173.

Economic Commission for Africa. 1989. *African Alternative Framework to Structural Adjustment Programmes for Socio-Economic Recovery and Transformation.* Addis Ababa: Economic Commission for Africa.

El-Bagir, Ibrahim, Jenny Dey, Ali Abdel Gadir Ali, Tony Barnett, Jayati Ghosh, and Albert Wagner. 1984. *Labour Markets in the Sudan.* Geneva: ILO.

Ellis, Frank. 1984. "Relative Agricultural Prices and the Urban Bias Model: A Comparative Analysis of the United Republic of Tanzania and Fiji." *Journal of Development Studies* 20:28–51.

FAO (Food and Agricultural Organization). 1985. *Report of the Round Table on the Dynamics of Land Tenure and Agrarian Systems in Africa.* Rome: FAO.

Frank, Charles R. 1970. "The Problem of Urban Unemployment in Africa." In *Problems of Employment and Unemployment in the Near East and South Asia,* edited by L. Ridker and H. Lubell, 783–818. New Dehli: Vikas.

Hahn, Frank. 1984. *Equilibrium and Macroeconomics.* Oxford: Basil Blackwell.

Hart, Keith. 1973. "Informal Income Opportunities and Urban Employment in Ghana." *Journal of Modern African Studies* 11:61–89.

Helleiner, G. K. 1964. "The Fiscal Role of the Marketing Boards in Nigerian Economic Development, 1947–61." *Economic Journal* 74:582–610.

Hill, P. 1977. *Population, Prosperity and Poverty: Rural Kano 1900 and 1970.* Cambridge: Cambridge University Press.

ILO (International Labor Organization), World Employment Program. 1991. *The Urban Informal Sector in Africa in Retrospect and Prospect: An Annotated Bibliography.* International Labour Bibliography No. 10. Geneva: ILO.

ILO/JASPA (International Labor Office and Jobs and Skills Program for Africa). 1982. *Rural-Urban Gap and Income Distribution in Africa: The Synthesis Report of Six Countries.* Addis Ababa: JASPA.

———. 1984. *Synthesis Report of 17 countries.* Addis Ababa: JASPA.

———. 1987. *Yearbook of Labour Statistics 1987.* Geneva: ILO.

———. 1991. *African Employment Report, 1990.* Addis Ababa: JASPA.

Jain, Shail. 1975. *Size Distribution of Income: A Compilation of Data.* Washington, D.C.: World Bank.

Jamal, Vali. 1985. "Structural Adjustment and Food Security in Uganda." Photocopied. Geneva: ILO.

———. 1986. "Poverty and Inequality in Nigeria." Photocopied. Geneva: ILO.

———. 1989. "The Demise of the Labor Aristocracy in Africa: Structural Adjustment in Tanzania." In *Debt Disaster,* edited by John Weeks, 175–191. New York: New York University Press.

Jamal, Vali, and John Weeks. 1987. "Rural-Urban Income Trends in Sub-Saharan Africa." World Employment Programme Working Paper, Labour Market and Employment Analysis, Working Paper No. 18. Geneva: ILO.

———. 1988. "The Vanishing Rural-Urban Gap in Sub-Saharan Africa." *International Labour Review* 127:271–292.

———. 1992. *Africa Misunderstood.* London: Routledge.

Kilby, Peter. 1967. "Industrial Relations and Wage Determination: Failure of the Anglo-Saxon Model." *Journal of Developing Areas* 1:489–519.

Knight, J. B. 1972. "Rural-Urban Income Comparisons and Migration in Ghana." *Bulletin of the Oxford University Institute of Economics and Statistics* 34:199–228.

Lachaud, J. P. 1990. "The Urban Informal Sector and the Labour Market in Sub-Saharan Africa." In *The Informal Sector Revisited,* edited by David Turnham, Bernard Salome, and Antoine Schwartz, 111–130. Paris: OECD Organization for Economic Cooperation and Development Centre.

Levi, J. F. S. 1973. "Migration from the Land and Urban Unemployment in Sierra Leone." *Bulletin of the Oxford University Institute of Economics and Statistics* 35:309–326.

Lewis, W. Arthur. 1954. "Economic Development with Unlimited Supplies of Labour." *The Manchester School of Economic and Social Studies* 22:139–191.

Lipton, Michael. 1977. *Why Poor People Stay Poor. A Study of Urban Bias in World Development*. London: Temple Smith.

———. 1982. "Labor and Poverty." World Bank Staff Working Paper. Washington, D.C.

Lipton, Michael (with Richard Longhurst). 1985. "Modern Varieties, International Agricultural Research, and the Poor." Consultative Group on International Research World Bank Study Paper Number 2. Washington, D.C.

Livingstone, Ian. 1986. *Rural Development, Employment and Incomes in Kenya*. Aldershot, UK: Gower.

Rimmer, Douglas. 1984. *The Economies of West Africa*. New York: St. Martin's Press.

Robinson, Derek. 1990. *Civil Service Pay in Africa*. Geneva: ILO.

Saigal, Reshma. 1990. *Policy Reforms in Sub-Saharan African in the 1980s and Implications for the Agricultural Sector*. Rome: FAO.

Sender, John, and Sheila Smith. 1986. *The Development of Capitalism in Africa*. London: Methuen.

Singh, Shamsher. 1983. "Sub-Saharan Agriculture: Synthesis and Trade Prospects." World Bank Staff Working Papers, Number 608. Washington, D.C.

Swindell, Ken. 1988. "Agrarian Change and Peri-urban Fringes in Tropical Africa." In *Rural Transformation in Tropical Africa*, edited by Douglas Rimmer, 98–115. Athens: Ohio University Press.

Taylor, Lance. 1983. *Structuralist Macroeconomics: Applicable Models for the Third World*. New York: Basic Books.

Todaro, M. P. 1969. "A Model of Labor Migration and Urban Unemployment in Less Developed Countries." *American Economic Review* 59:138–148.

———. 1971. "Income Expectations, Rural-Urban Migration and Employment in Africa." *International Labour Review* 104:387–413.

———. 1990. *Economic Development in the Third World*. 3rd ed. New York: Longman.

Turnham, David, Bernard Salome, and Antoine Schwartz, eds. 1990. *The Informal Sector Revisited*. Paris: OECD Development Centre.

United Nations. 1990. *World Economic Survey, 1990*. New York: United Nations.

van Ginneken, Wouter, and Jong-goo Park, eds. 1984. *Generating Internationally Comparable Income Distribution Estimates*. Geneva: ILO.

Weeks, John. 1971a. "Does Employment Matter?" *Manpower and Unemployment Research in Africa* (Montreal: Center for Developing Area Studies) 4:67–70. Reprinted (1973) in *Third World Employment*, edited by Richard Jolly, Emanuel de Kadt, Hans Singer, and Fiona Wilson, 61–65. Harmondsworth: Penguin Books.

———. 1971b. "The Impact of Institutional Factors and Economic Forces on Urban Wages in Nigeria." *Nigerian Journal of Economic and Social Studies* 13:313–339.

———. 1971c. "The Political Economy of Labor Transfer." *Science and Society* 35:463–480.

———. 1971d. "Uncertainty, Risk and Wealth and Income Distribution in Peasant Agriculture." *Journal of Development Studies* 7:28–36.

———. 1971e. "Wage Policy and the Colonial Legacy: A Comparative Study." *Journal of Modern African Studies* 9:361–387.

———. 1989. *A Critique of Neoclassical Macroeconomics*. London: Macmillan.

———. 1992. *Development Strategy and the Economy of Sierra Leone*. London: Macmillan.

World Bank. 1981. *Accelerated Development in Sub-Saharan Africa*. Washington: World Bank.

———. 1986. *World Development Report 1986*. New York: Oxford University Press.

———. 1987. *Country Economic Memorandum*. Washington: World Bank.

———. 1989a. *Sub-Saharan Africa: From Crisis to Sustainable Growth*. Washington: World Bank.

———. 1989b. *World Development Report 1989*. New York: Oxford University Press.

23

Urbanization and National Capitals in Africa

A. J. Christopher

Capital cities have evolved with the emergence of the modern state system in Africa. It is difficult to define the functional threshold at which a village, the seat of a chief, becomes the capital city of a state, and the seat of the government. In northern Africa the state and city systems are of considerable antiquity, although substantially modified in the nineteenth century under the impact of colonialism. However, it is suggested that over large parts of Africa, south of the Sahara, it was the European colonial powers, with their desire to establish fixed hierarchical systems of administration, which led to the foundation of the first recognizable capital cities (Simon, 1992). Consequently, the African state and urban systems which are in operation today largely reflect the decisions and priorities of the European colonial powers rather than the needs of indigenous polities.

The capital city in any state fulfills a number of significant functions, which separate it from other towns and cities in the state territory. The capital is the focus of the administration and is vested with an aura of sovereignty. Throughout most of history this has been expressed as the location of the residence of the king or his vice-regent. As a result the capital has been the place from which political power has been exercised over a state area. Frequently this has also involved the wielding of religious and economic power as the boundaries between the three were often blurred. It is notable that with the concentration of such power in one place, the capital is usually the largest city in the state in terms of population and physical extent and the focus of conspicuous consumption (Scholler, 1978). The most prominent example of this is the position of Cairo, which has steadily increased its level of primacy in the present century (Khalifa and Moheiddin, 1988; United Nations, 1990). However, significant exceptions to this generalization occur, notably where modern industrial development has taken place subsequent to the evolution of the political system. Nevertheless, there has been a general tendency in Africa for the political system to adapt to changing circumstances, with the result that shifts in the site of the capital have been frequent. It is proposed to examine the changes in the distribution of capitals in Africa, with particular reference to the impact of the colonial era and subsequent adjustments.

THE PRECOLONIAL ERA

The precolonial state structure in Africa varied substantially, ranging from the extensive centralized empires of North Africa to the kinship groupings of Central Africa. The form and functions of capitals were equally wide-ranging. The capitals of Egypt, ranging from Memphis and Heliopolis in Pharaonic times through Greek-founded Alexandria to Moslem Fustat and Cairo represent a degree of continuity unequalled anywhere else on the continent (Abu-Lughod, 1971). The strategic location of Cairo, and its predecessors, at the head of the Nile Delta, gave it political significance, which coastal Alexandria or upstream Karnak was only able to rival for restricted periods of Egyptian history. Other empires, notably those based at Carthage in North Africa and Meroe in Nubia, lasted for several centuries, and successor states have adopted similar strategic locational decisions in more recent eras. Other countries in medieval times were ruled from several cities. The shifting capitals of Ethiopia and Morocco reflect not only the continuity of the states, but also the personal preferences of the rulers and the varying fortunes of the empires subject to foreign invasion and economic changes (Horvath, 1969).

The state structure south of the Sahara was less stable than that in the north. Furthermore, southern capitals were liable to sudden and often permanent abandonment. The great medieval West African empires established cities and capitals including Gao and Tombouctou, but status was often linked with the fate of a particular dynasty. Later the Moslem states based at Kano, Sokoto, and Bamako held sway as a series of rulers strove for the supremacy of the region (Fage, 1978). Urban Moslem traditions were reproduced on the East African coast, where the Swahili city-states controlled the commercial links between the interior of the continent and the Indian Ocean trading system. They failed to achieve any degree of lasting unity until the rise of Oman in the seventeenth century. Zanzibar finally assumed these functions with the division of the Omani Empire in the mid-nineteenth century. Central Africa was remarkably devoid of towns and cities until medieval times. The major Yoruba cities, of which Ibadan was the most prominent, founded and expanded in the precolonial era, were significant exceptions to this generalization (Mabogunje, 1962). The development of long-distance trade and the emergence of more coherent state structures in central and southern Africa from the sixteenth century onwards resulted in the establishment of other capitals including Kampala in Buganda and Bulawayo in Matabeleland (Hirst, 1972). The emergent preliterate states in southern Africa lacked the organizational elements which characterized the more northerly states, and hence capitals tended to be temporary, reflecting the shifting nature of the system. The lack of the impedimenta of public records and treasuries together with permanent buildings, which deterred frequent changing of sites in more organizationally advanced societies, allowed the Zulu and other monarchies to move to new sites at the decree of the king. Significantly, it was only with the destruction of the last precolonial capital at Ulundi in 1879 that that particular site became especially significant for the Zulu nation.

COLONIAL CAPITALS

Following the intervention of the European colonial powers, new approaches to imperial and trading systems were evolved. Two basic approaches were adopted to control the flow of trade which was the main link between African and European societies. The first approach was the direct or indirect cooperation with, and influence of, the precolonial system. An early example was related to the attempt to convert existing polities to Christianity. The Portuguese missions to the Congo kingdom based at São Salvador were the forerunners of the policy of indirect rule evolved with most success by the British in the late nineteenth century. Thus the Portuguese, as a result of their weak demographic position and the adverse disease environment of much of the African continent, were not intent on the conquest of large territories as the Spanish had been in the Americas, but on influencing existing states. The second approach was the creation of a series of headquarters for the systems of trading bascs established around the African coastline. The castle at Elmina acted as the headquarters for the entire Portuguese, later Dutch, West African trading enterprise. Similarly Cape Coast and Christianborg were the capitals for the English (later British) and Danish enterprises respectively on the Guinea Coast (Van Dantzig, 1980). All three came under British control in 1872, and Christianborg at Accra, on account of its healthier record, was selected for the continued use of the British administration.

These two forms of colonial capital, the indigenous city and the coastal headlink, were replicated throughout the colonial era. The conquest of indigenous polities in the nineteenth century was often followed by the adoption of the preexisting capital by the European conquerors. Nevertheless, the practice was by no means universal, as the designated city needed to be either well established, without rivals, or itself in a suitable headlink position. In 1830 the French inherited the structures of the previous Turko-Arab Algerian bureaucracy, including its capital, as they did the royal administration in Madagascar based at the inland city of Antananarivo. In both these cases no obvious rival cities were available for the colonial government. However, many indigenous capitals were not suitable for use as centers of colonial administration. For example, Tombouctou had declined economically and demographically since medieval times as a result of realignments in trading relationships, and it was considered too peripheral to the areas under secure French control. Bamako proved to be better located with regard to French military lines of communication from the base on the coast of Senegal. Symbolically, the French moved the capital of Morocco from inland Fez to coastal Rabat with the proclamation of the protectorate. The shift reflected the changed economic and political circumstances of the country as it was absorbed into the colonial system. French trading patterns were aligned with external, not internal trade, while the large interior cities were regarded as less secure militarily than sites subject to seapower.

The majority of capitals established in the course of the initial scramble for Africa were situated on the coast at the point of entry and export. It was as transshipment points for men and materials that they became vital to the establishment and extension of colonial rule. By 1900 when the partition of the continent had been effectively completed, some 28 of the 44 colonial capitals were located on the coast, a situation that was closely bound up with the pattern of European conquest (Figure 23.1).

Changing Colonial Capitals

When it is considered how rapid the selection of the sites of the initial colonial capitals had been, often with little detailed prior survey, it is surprising how enduring they proved to be. Thus 28 of the 44 colonial capitals in existence in 1900 still retain that status in 1991 (Figure 23.2). This is not to suggest that stability had been achieved by that date. Unsuitable sites were abandoned for a variety of reasons. Three basic processes were at work promoting change, namely the administrative rearrangements of the colonial powers, the quest for healthier sites, and the recognition of changing economic circumstances. It is instructive to examine these changes in some detail, as the process of change virtually ceased at independence.

Changing Administrative Patterns

The administrative patterns of the colonial era were remarkably fluid. Large colonial units were fragmented for ease of administration, while some colonies were incorporated into their neighbors for reasons of economy. Federations were established and abolished, while the colonial powers fought among themselves and annexed the territories of the vanquished.

The administrative pattern that emerged from the partition of Africa in the last quarter of the nineteenth century included many extensive colonies which had been acquired rapidly and with limited appreciation of the problems of governing extensive units with ethnically diverse populations. The division of the large French entities such as the Senegal began in 1895, while the extensive territories of the British Royal Niger Company were partitioned in 1899. Other

Figure 23.1
Colonial Capitals in Africa, 1900

large colonies that were subdivided at intervals were the French Sudan, French Congo, and Rhodesia. The French West African territories acquired their current outlines only in 1947 with the redesignation of Upper Volta as a separate colony after its earlier suppression in 1933 as an economy measure.

The creation of landlocked colonies necessitated the selection of inland sites for capitals. In some instances the major indigenous cities or capitals such as Bamako and Ougadougou were designated, while in others new forms of head-links were adopted on a river through which the movement of men, materials, and trade was concentrated. Thus Bangui on the Congo River system and Livingstone, on the Zambesi at the crossing of the railway line from the south, operated as interior ports of entry. Even the initial military choice of Zinder in Niger was abandoned in favor of the riverine location of Naimey (Sidikou, 1975).

Parallel with the process of fragmentation went that of unification and fede-

Figure 23.2
Changes in National Capitals, 1900–1991

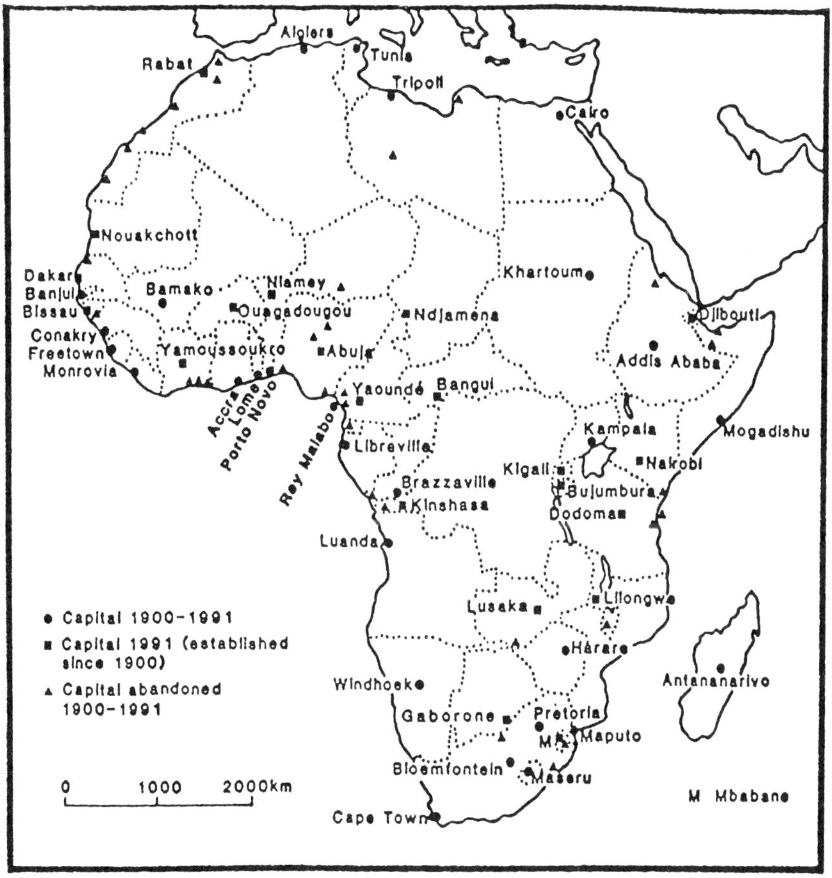

ration, whereby groups of colonies were linked for administrative purposes. The federations of French West Africa and French Equatorial Africa were designed to maintain close supervision and standardized procedures in spheres where broad regional services could be profitably integrated. The choice of the federal capital usually ended with the selection of the capital of the most important component colony in the federation, for example, Saint-Louis in West Africa or Brazzaville in Equatorial Africa. However, the French West African capital was shifted from Saint-Louis to Dakar in 1904, some fifty years before the Senegalese administration did the same (Seck, 1970). The temporary shift of the Middle Congo administration from Brazzaville to Pointe-Noire also demonstrated the attempt to separate federal and individual colonial functions spatially.

The Union of South Africa in 1910 presented a particularly difficult problem as the four component colonies enjoyed self-governing status at the time of federation and therefore decisions had to be taken by local consensus rather than by imperial decree. The formula adopted provided for the capital functions to be dispersed among three of the colonial capitals. Cape Town became the seat of the legislature; Pretoria the center of the administration; and Bloemfontein the seat of the judiciary. In contrast, Salisbury, the capital of the politically dominant member, also served as the capital of the last significant colonial federation, Rhodesia and Nyasaland from 1953 to 1963 (Wood, 1976). This pattern prevailed in two-unit mergers at or immediately after independence, including Ethiopia, Somalia, Tanzania, Equatorial Guinea, and Cameroon.

Federal arrangements were not confined to groupings of colonies. Sometimes an intermediate level of administration was introduced to fragment an existing colony into smaller autonomous administrative units. The Portuguese divided Mozambique into six, subsequently seven, separate autonomous units in the 1890s. Chartered commercial companies based at Beira, Porto Amelia, and Quelimane controlled three of the new colonies. Beira retained capital status until 1942, when the charter of the Mozambique Company expired. Additionally, Lourenco Marques, Mozambique, Inhambane, and Tete achieved the status of colonial capitals until the arrangement was abolished in 1920. A governor-general stationed in Lourenco Marques after 1895 exercised supervisory powers over the entire group. At the same time a Portuguese Congo colony based in Cabinda was separated from Angola, but this arrangement too was ephemeral. Similarly, in the Western Sahara, the Spanish created a series of colonies variously divided as Rio de Oro, La Angra, Cabo Juby, and Ifni, each governed from its main urban center. Sidi Ifni continued as a separate administrative enclave until it was reincorporated into Morocco in 1969.

Territorial realignments associated with the two world wars resulted in the establishment of temporary capitals. The portions of Cameroon and Togo mandated to Great Britain were administratively incorporated into neighboring Nigeria and Gold Coast respectively after a brief period of separate existence. Buea was revived temporarily prior to reincorporation into Cameroon at the end of the colonial era. The partition of German East Africa between Belgium and Great Britain after World War I resulted in the elevation of Usumburu to the status of capital for Ruanda-Urundi, then the mandated territory of Belgium. During World War II, separate administrations for Cyrenaica and Fezzan in Libya were established with capitals at Benghazi and Murzuk, but the division was short-lived as Libya was reunited as an independent state in 1951 (Rossi, 1973). Temporary capitals for ephemeral colonies were not solely associated with the immediate aftermath of a war. Great Britain transferred Jubaland to Italy in 1925, and it was subject to a separate administration based at Kismayo until it was formally incorporated into Somalia.

The government of Morocco probably experienced the most complex political arrangements imposed during the colonial era. France proclaimed a protectorate over most of the country in 1912 and transferred the capital from Fez to Rabat (Abu-Lughod, 1980). Spain established capitals for the northern and southern zones of its protectorate at Tetouan and Cabo Juby respectively. Subsequently, Tangier became an international city with its own administration. The country maintained nominal integrity under the sultan but only regained sovereignty in 1956 when Rabat became the administrative capital of the reunited country.

Considerations of Health

In the period before the late nineteenth century, European personnel suffered from diseases and high mortality rates in tropical Africa. The colonial powers, therefore, made efforts to locate administrative centers at localities perceived to be healthy. Italy located its administration for Eritrea at upland Asmara rather than at the Red Sea port of Massawa. Similarly the Germans selected Buea on the slopes of Mount Cameroon rather than the port at Douala. However, with Buea under British occupation after 1914, the French temporarily returned the administrative headquarters of their section of Cameroon to coastal Douala but later moved to the relative comfort of inland Yaoundé. In the search for healthier sites, the shifts were not always from the coast to the interior. Unhealthy Grand-Bassam in the Côte d'Ivoire was abandoned in favor of Bingerville in 1900, and the Portuguese finally abandoned Bolama in favor of Bissau in 1942. This trend was observable even in landlocked countries. In Swaziland, the administration moved from centrally located Manzini to eccentrically situated, but upland, Mbabane.

Health might have been the officially stated motive, but in many locational shifts other factors were important. Thus the transfer of the British East African administration from the port of Mombasa to Nairobi might have been prompted by economic and developmental considerations, but local officials emphasized the departure from the unpleasant coastal climate. Successive British administrations in Lagos repeatedly but unsuccessfully investigated the practicability of moving the capital of Nigeria from the island to a more congenial site (Gale, 1979; Peil, 1991). An independent government eventually made the decision to move to the interior, but the reasons advanced were significantly different from those debated by the British.

Changing Economic Conditions

Changing economic circumstances, including new developmental priorities and changes in transportation systems, accounted for the relocation of several capitals. The capital of Northern Rhodesia was shifted to Lusaka to be more central on the axis of economic growth along the main railroad (Williams, 1986). Nairobi was selected as part of an effort to promote European colonization in a highland environment that promised to become the main center of economic activity in the country (Morgan, 1967). Relocation for economic reasons did not necessarily mean transfer to a centrally placed site. The Portuguese moved the capital of the East African possessions from the historic site on the island of

Mozambique to the new center of economic activity in the south at Lourenco Marques.

Changes in transportation technology and systems led to the relocation of other colonial capitals. The administration of German East Africa initially occupied the site of the terminus of mainland porterage routes at Bagamayo on the Zanzibar Channel opposite the city of Zanzibar. However, new intercontinental trade links led to the selection of the large harbor at Dar es Salaam where facilities for deep draft vessels could be constructed. The historical Senegalese capital at Saint-Louis on the Senegal River, although suitable for the ships of the sailing era, was inaccessible for large steam vessels. Hence, the capital was shifted to the new deep-water harbor constructed at Dakar. Engineering considerations made Abidjan, not Bingerville, the terminus of the Côte d'Ivoire railway, and the new port soon became the capital of the colony. The problems of navigation on the lower Congo River influenced both the French and Belgian Congo administrators to leave the coastal sites for locations above the rapids on the main navigable section of the river at Brazzaville and Leopoldville.

In all these instances the administrators either anticipated or followed economic trends and actively sought to locate a capital city at the hub of the colonial economy. Abandoned centers either withered or were superseded by a new capital city in the urban hierarchy. Creating a capital as a primate city in a colonial urban structure appears to have been an objective inherited from the general European experience. But there were exceptions to this generalization. Capital functions sometimes remained in small urban centers for historical reasons. The French administration in Morocco rejected both Fez, the then largest city, and Casablanca, the rapidly growing commercial port, in favor of Rabat, a small center that would be exclusively devoted to administration. Similar historical associations allowed Porto Novo to remain the capital of Benin and Dahomey despite the economic dominance of Cotonou. In South Africa, the rural-based Afrikaner settler government resisted any attempt to transfer the administration from Pretoria to industrial Johannesburg, with its British business connotations.

INDEPENDENCE

Independence, which was generally achieved within a few years on either side of 1960, brought practical problems of selecting capitals as well as opportunities for African national self-expression (Hamdan, 1964). The most immediate problems were the anomalous positions of the Mauritanian and Bechuanaland capitals, Saint-Louis and Mafeking, situated beyond their national boundaries. These problems offered a new approach to capital location, which involved an increased African participation in decision making and planning. Although the government of Bechuanaland considered regional ethnic groupings in its decision, water supply, as in the case of Mauritania, determined the final choice (Best, 1970). This factor had been a significant consideration for the initial location of the administration outside the colonial territory. Consequently, Nouakchott and Gaborone were still highly peripheral in the state territory. Another problem associated with independence was the partition of the Belgian trust territory of Ruanda-Urundi into two sovereign states and the designation of Kigali as the capital of the former (Nwafor, 1981). State territorial changes, which had been so frequent in the colonial era, virtually ceased with independence as the Organization of African Unity held its members to respecting the boundaries inherited at the time of independence. Thus one source of the demand for new capitals no longer operates.

Independence, however, brought about a reappraisal of the inherited colonial capitals with their foreign images. The bold moves by Brazil and Pakistan to abandon inherited capitals in favor of new nationally conceived and designed cities at Brazilia and Islamabad respectively evoked an immediate political and emotional response among many African leaders. Yet for financial reasons it proved to be impossible in most cases to emulate the Brazilian and Pakistani examples. Only four countries, Malawi, Nigeria, Tanzania, and the Côte d'Ivoire, pressed ahead with plans to change the location of the capital in the thirty years after independence. This is in marked contrast to the fluidity of the previous colonial system. Financial considerations have been of major importance in preventing any wholesale relocation. Indeed the Tanzanian transfer has been suspended as a result of budgetary difficulties. Thus the inertia imposed by the accumulated investment in colonial capitals has inhibited postindependent governments from undertaking ambitious projects. In addition, the size of the national bureaucracies has swollen dramatically, making the transfer of thousands of officials and their dependents, rather than a few hundred, often with limited numbers of dependents, a more formidable undertaking. Thus the majority of African leaders had to content themselves with the Africanization of a colonial structure, through the building of new governmental quarters, and the more symbolic renaming of the cities after precolonial leaders, events, or places (Davies, 1972). Accordingly, Bathurst became Banjul, Lourenco Marques became Maputo, and Salisbury became Harare, thereby satisfying national honor at minimal cost.

The four transfers of site deserve examination as they illustrate a set of priorities which differ markedly from those in operation in the colonial period. The new Nigerian capital is possibly the most complex in motivation (Nwafor, 1980). Lagos had been regarded as unhealthy and overcrowded since early colonial times, and a transfer elsewhere, even to the Northern Nigeria regional capital at Kaduna, had been projected but never implemented. The independent federal government was able to force the decision as a measure to achieve greater national unity in the wake of the civil war. The main objective was to remove the federal government from the direct influence of one of the three principal regional ethnic groupings to an area perceived as being politically neutral. Abuja satisfied most of the requirements for both territorial centrality and political neutrality. Thus the model of Washington or Canberra within a federal state structure was sought and implemented.

Malawi, despite its poverty at independence, was able to achieve economic growth and foreign, largely South African, investment to contemplate leaving colonial Zomba in the south for a centrally situated location at Lilongwe (Connell, 1972). In contrast, the shift from Dar es Salaam to Dodoma was part of the presidential aspiration to develop and implement the philosophy of African Socialism in Tanzania. It thus represented a radical departure from European concepts in planning which were dominant in both the colonial and postcolonial periods (Hoyle, 1978). Yammoussukro in the Côte d'Ivoire was developed to transfer the capital to the interior, in this case to the presidential birthplace, where the new city could be built as a monument to the founder of the state (Armstrong, 1985). In all four cases sites central to the national territory were selected. However, only Dodoma was located on the main transportation arteries and so avoided the high costs of installing new communications links which have been major developmental costs in the cases of the other three.

The establishment of new capitals and their relocation was a notable feature of the colonial era. In contrast, relative stability in capital sites has prevailed since independence. Between 1900 and 1959, 27 new capitals were established in Africa, a rate of almost one every two years. Only six were established from 1960 to 1990, a rate of one every five years. Of the six, four were new capitals chosen as national alternatives to the colonial image, while the other two were associated with the immediate forced preindependence shifts of administration headquarters for Botswana and Rwanda.

South Africa

South Africa is an exception to many generalizations about the African continent. Two points are of importance to the theme of capital cities. First, the colonial era was longer and the European imprint more dominant than elsewhere on the continent (Christopher, 1982). The complex history of the colonial period involved the creation of a multiplicity of European-controlled colonies and independent frontier republics, each with its ephemeral capital, mostly dating from the nineteenth century (Christopher, 1976). Second, the South African government's policy of apartheid resulted in the emergence of new functional capitals, although the sovereignty of the states involved has not been internationally recognized. The implementation of apartheid was directed toward the maintenance of European control over the core of the South African state through a policy of state partition, by establishing a series of ethnically defined African states which would be excluded from the national central political process. To this end a number of African language groups were distinguished and states established based on the lands which had been designated as tribal reserves in colonial times. The end product was the creation of a series of "nation-states" (Christopher, 1982).

A problem facing the planners was the provision of capital cities for the new states. Because the states had been rural reserves, few possessed urban centers of any size. The South African government drew up guidelines for the establishment of new capitals (Best and Young, 1972). These included the selection of an open unused site, away from European influence, without historic ties, in the center of the territory and with the prospect of economic development. The implementation of these guidelines presented a number of difficulties. The fragmented nature of the new states, with unknown future boundaries and the large-scale population transfers associated with the policy, was not conducive to stability. Only rarely was the historic site available, notably in Umtata in Transkei or Ulundi in KwaZulu, to overcome the South African government's guidelines stipulating a lack of historic ties. In others an African residential area outside a European-occupied town was developed. Thus after many vicissitudes the Ciskei capital was established at Bisho, adjacent to King Williams Town. The Ciskei government had wished to incorporate this city as it had been the capital of the ephemeral nineteenth-century British colony of British Kaffraria and therefore possessed the basic infrastructure required by an administration. However, the South African government retained the town within its borders, although it is virtually surrounded by Ciskeian territory. Similar problems were apparent in the transfer of Mafeking, renamed Mafikeng, to Bophuthatswana (Parnell, 1986). Although internationally unrecognized, some of the states operate as independent entities, even to the extent of maintaining diplomatic missions among themselves and South Africa. The current reform initiative in South Africa indicates that the country will be reunited, but the final form is open to debate. The South African homeland capitals will then join the list of capitals of other ephemeral postindependence states including Elisabethville (Katanga) and Enugu (Biafra).

FORM AND FUNCTION

It is the function of the capital which distinguishes it from other cities. As the seat of government it plays a key role in the activities of the state, whether colonial or independent. The government may range in complexity and size from a governor, assisted by a number of officials, to a fully fledged executive, legislative, and judicial complex. The form of the city thus is influenced by the form of the government and by its previous heritage. In all cases the extent of the bureaucracy is often the most significant aspect of the city's development. Where the city is also the main industrial and commercial center of the state, the government functions may occupy a distinct quarter. This is particularly true of many of the twentieth-century layouts, influenced by West European segregatory land use planning theory. However, in the absence of major industrial and commercial complexes in many African countries the economy of the capital remains heavily dependent upon government functions.

Government ideology is firmly implanted upon the capital cities. Colonialism as a system and an urban image has already been examined. However, replanning the colonial city may take many forms. In South Africa the ideology of apartheid was systematically stamped upon Cape Town and Pretoria after the election of the National party government in 1948 (Olivier and Hattingh, 1985; Western, 1981). The results were massive forced movements of people as the indigenous population, Asians, and persons of mixed descent were moved to the periphery of the cities, leaving all-European centers. The imminent change of government in South Africa suggests that the capitals are about to be reshaped in the image of yet another ideology.

Apart from the historic cities of North Africa, few capitals had initial problems of inadequate space, although these have subsequently developed as population growth has taken place and congestion has occurred (United Nations, 1991). Thus many of the central governmental quarters of cities planned as capitals are spacious, even if the more recent suburbs are crowded (Winters, 1982). In examining the building blocks by which the capital is put together, the governor's or presidential palace is symbolically often centrally situated. Here the contrast between the British and continental styles is evident, with the former more likely to be a suburban mansion and the latter a central city edifice. The parliamentary buildings are usually of more recent origin, reflecting the late introduction of direct participation in government by the local population, and hence they occupy a less significant place in the city plan. The ministries, frequently in a ministerial complex with the extensive offices attached, are more ubiquitous features of the government quarter. Finally, major extensive users of space are the peripheral army, air force, and police bases which have politically dominated so many African cities both before and after independence. Because of the disproportionate conspicuous spending which takes place in the capital, the layout of avenues is grander than in other cities; there are more monuments and greater attention to beautification. It is often in the capital that an attempt has been made to present a national image through such aspects as architecture and statuary. Thus in the nineteenth century Algiers was gallicized, in an attempt to create the image of a French provincial town. Since 1962 this process has been reversed to re-create the image of an Arab and Moslem city. A significant feature of African states has been the meeting of the Organization of African Unity in various capitals, necessitating the construction of convention centers often in excess of the requirements of the country, lending a certain pan-African image.

CONCLUSION

Capital cities form an integral part of the state system in Africa, as the centers of national government and usually of economic development. As such they have distinctive land use patterns, and a disproportionate part of the national budget is spent within them. Accordingly, they are usually the subject of massive in-migration by those seeking economic and political opportunities not available elsewhere. Thus capitals tend to be the primate cities within the national urban hierarchy. Surprisingly, the majority of capitals are European colonial foundations, as few date from precolonial times, and only a small number have been established since independence. Hence even after over thirty years of independence the capitals of Africa tend to reflect the styles and locational preferences of the colonial powers.

REFERENCES

Abu-Lughod, J. L. 1971. *Cairo: 1001 Years of the City Victorious.* Princeton: Princeton University Press.

———. 1980. *Rabat: Urban Apartheid in Morocco.* Princeton: Princeton University Press.

Armstrong, A. 1985. "Another New Capital for Africa." *Geography* 70:72–74.

Best, A. C. G. 1970. "Gaberone: Problems and Prospects for a New Capital." *Geographical Review* 60:1–14.

Best, A. C. G., and B. S. Young. 1972. "Capitals for the Homelands." *Journal for Geography* 3:1043–1055.

Boxer, C. R. 1969. *The Portuguese Seaborne Empire 1415–1825.* New York: Alfred Knopf.

Christopher, A. J. 1976. *Southern Africa: Studies in Historical Geography.* Hamden, Conn.: Archon.

———. 1982. *South Africa.* New York: Longman.

———. 1984. *Colonial Africa.* New York: Barnes and Noble.

———. 1985. "Continuity and Change in African Capitals." *Geographical Review* 75:44–57.

Connell, J. 1972. "Another New Capital for Africa." *East African Geographical Review* 10:89–92.

Davies, D. H. 1972. "Lusaka: From Colonial to Independent Capital." *Proceedings of the Geographical Association of Rhodesia* 5:14–21.

Fage, J. D. 1978. *A History of Africa.* London: Hutchinson.

Gale, T. S. 1979. "Lagos: The History of British Colonial Neglect of Traditional African Cities." *African Urban Studies* 5:11–24.

Hamdan, G. 1964. "Capitals of the New Africa." *Economic Geography* 24:239–253.

Hirst, M. A. 1972. *Essays on the Social Geography of Kampala, Uganda.* Perth: University of Western Australia.

Horvath, R. J. 1969. "The Wandering Capitals of Ethiopia." *Journal of African History* 10:205–219.

Hoyle, B. S. 1979. "African Socialism and Urban Development: The Relocation of the Tanzanian Capital." *Tijdschrift voor Economische en Sociale Geografie* 70:207–216.

Khalifa, A. M., and M. M. Moheiddin. 1988. "Cairo." In *The Metropolis Era: Mega-Cities,* edited by M. Dogan and J. D. Kasarda, 2:235–267. Newbury Park: Sage.

Mabogunje, A. L. 1962. *Yoruba Towns.* Ibadan: University of Ibadan Press.

Morgan, W. T. W. 1967. *Nairobi: City and Region.* Nairobi: Oxford University Press.

Nwafor, J. C. 1980. "The Relocation of Nigeria's Federal Capital: A Device for Greater Territorial Integration and National Unity." *GeoJournal* 4:359–366.

———. 1981. "Some Aspects of Urban Development in Tropical Africa: The Growth toward Urban Status of Kigali, Capital of Rwanda." *African Urban Studies* 9:39–56.

Olivier, J. J., and P. S. Hattingh. 1985. "Die Suid-Afrikaanse stad as funksioneelruimtelike sisteem.'' In *Verstedeling in Suid-Afrika,* edited by F. A. van Jaarsveld, 45–61. Pretoria: University of Pretoria.

Parnell, S. 1986. ''From Mafeking to Mafikeng: The Transformation of a South African Town.'' *GeoJournal* 12:203–210.

Peil, Margaret. 1991. *Lagos: The City Is the People.* Boston: G. K. Hall.

Potts, D. 1985. ''Capital Relocation in Africa: The Case of Lilongwe.'' *Geographical Journal* 151:182–196.

Rossi, G. 1973. ''Le Colonie Italiane all Conferenze di Potsdam.'' *Africa* 28:507–544.

Scholler, P. 1978. ''The Role of the Capital City within the National Settlement System.'' *Geographia Polonica* 39:223–234.

Seck, A. 1970. *Dakar: Metropole Quest-Africaine.* Dakar: Institut Fondamental d'Afrique Noire.

Sidikou, A. H. 1975. ''Naimey.'' *Cahiers d'Outre-Mer* 28:201–217.

Simon, David D. 1992. *Cities, Capital and Development: African Cities in the World Economy.* London: Belhaven Press.

United Nations. 1991. *World Urbanization Prospects 1990.* Population Studies 121. New York.

———. 1990. *Population Growth and Policies in Mega Cities, Cairo.* Population Policy Paper No. 34. New York.

Van Dantzig, A. 1980. *Forts and Castles of Ghana.* Accra: Sedco Publications.

Western, J. 1981. *Outcast Cape Town.* Minneapolis: University of Minnesota Press.

Williams, G. J. 1986. *Lusaka and Its Environs.* Lusaka: Zambia Geographical Association.

Winters, C. 1982. ''Urban Morphogenesis in Francophone Black Africa.'' *Geographical Review* 72:139–154.

Wood, R. 1976. ''Siting the Capital of the Central African Federation.'' In *Studies in Local History,* edited by J. A. Benyon, 71–79. Cape Town: Oxford University Press.

24

African HIV/AIDS and Urbanization

Peter O. Way

Acquired Immune Deficiency Syndrome (AIDS) and the Human Immunodeficiency Virus (HIV) that causes it have been spreading in African countries for more than a decade (WHO, 1992). However, because of the variety of manifestations of AIDS and the inadequacy of public health and medical systems in Africa, much of the impact of AIDS up to this time has gone unreported and unquantified.

The World Health Organization (WHO) estimates that by 1992 there have been up to 1 million AIDS cases in sub-Saharan Africa, and 6.5 million African adults may currently be infected with HIV (WHO, 1992). Our current knowledge of HIV and AIDS provides little hope that those infected will live much beyond the current estimate of approximately 8 to 10 years after infection, on the average. Much publicized medications, such as AZT, are too expensive and are not widely available. Vaccine research, while providing promising results, may be of more help to future generations than the current one.

The impact of AIDS on populations and societies is more substantial than that of some other diseases because of the age-groups affected. Deaths from AIDS are concentrated in the young- and middle-adult years, age-groups that have low expected mortality in the absence of AIDS. The investment in the upbringing, education, and training of these young adults and their potential future contribution to economic and family life make their loss a greater societal blow than the loss of either the very young or the very old—the groups typically hardest hit by other illnesses. AIDS also increases the levels of infant and child mortality, which have been a major target of international population and health development programs over the last several decades.

Although we do not have a firm understanding of the impact of AIDS upon societies to date, there is little question that the future impact will be even more substantial. Those that have died up until now were infected in the relatively early years of the AIDS epidemics in countries throughout Africa. As epidemics continue to grow in some countries which have had slow growth to date, and as they mature in countries which have experienced more rapid growth, the number of AIDS cases and AIDS deaths will increase exponentially.

African urbanization patterns over the past several decades have played a role in facilitating the spread of HIV in Africa. With urbanization, traditional behavioral patterns change, migration and population movement throughout the country increase, and greater reliance is placed on a cash economy. As described in the following discussion, all of these factors contribute to the spread of HIV infection and AIDS.

DATA SOURCES AND ISSUES

Our knowledge of the infection and spread of HIV and AIDS in sub-Saharan Africa is based on a variety of reports and studies which are known to be incomplete and nonrepresentative. AIDS case reporting, for example, from African countries to the World Health Organization has been estimated to be about 10 percent complete, due to a variety of factors, including inadequate country reporting systems, particularly in the early years of the AIDS epidemic, and a reluctance on the part of countries to report AIDS cases to an international organization. A knowledge of AIDS cases alone, moreover, is not sufficient for an understanding of the dynamics of the epidemic, due to the extended incubation period between initial infection and later development of HIV-related illness. Thus, even the most accurate AIDS case data would only provide a picture of the epidemic of infection as it existed as many as ten years ago.

As a result, there has been considerable attention paid to the collection of data on HIV infection among various population groups. In the early years of the epidemic, many of these studies were conducted in a nonscientific manner, and may have provided results that were not representative even of the population group that was targeted by the study. More recently, increasing attention has been paid to such issues as increased sample sizes, representativeness of the sample selection, geographic coverage, and confirmatory testing of HIV positive results. Consequently, both the quantity and the quality of seroprevalence data have improved markedly in recent years. Nevertheless, many biases still remain, and caution must be used in the interpretation of the results.

Only a handful of nationally representative seroprevalence surveys have been conducted in sub-Saharan Africa, largely due to cost, diversion of skilled manpower, and an understanding that a nationally representative sample may not provide much useful information about the groups of greatest risk for HIV infection. Thus, in recent years sentinel surveillance programs have been developed to monitor defined populations for changes in HIV infection levels. For example, countries may develop programs that monitor infection among antenatal women attending government clinics, patients receiving treatment for sexually transmitted diseases, and women engaged in commercial sex activities. Results from these studies can provide rapid feedback on infection levels and trends in populations at various levels of risk without the time and effort required to mount a national survey.

Data presented in this chapter were taken from the *HIV/AIDS Surveillance Data Base,* developed and maintained at the U.S. Bureau of the Census, with funding support from the U.S. Agency for International Development. Data are regularly compiled from the scientific and technical literature as well as presentations at major international conferences. The *HIV/AIDS Surveillance Data Base* currently contains over 12,000 data records drawn from over 1,700 publications and presentations.

MODES OF TRANSMISSION IN SUB-SAHARAN AFRICA

The World Health Organization Global Programme on AIDS (Mann and Chin, 1988) has developed a typology to describe the various patterns of infection and spread of AIDS around the world. Within this typology, Africa is characterized as a Pattern II region, with a predominance of heterosexual transmission and substantial vertical (mother to child) transmission. As of 1992, WHO estimated that along with 6.5 million adult infections, 750,000 HIV-infected infants had been born in Africa (WHO, 1992). Infected blood is thought to account for only about 10 percent of all HIV infections. Homosexual transmission and transmission through intravenous drug use are generally considered to have minimal impact on the epidemic in sub-Saharan Africa.

TRENDS IN SELECTED POPULATION GROUPS

The following discussion focuses on four groups at varying levels of risk for HIV infection, namely, commercial sex workers, patients at sexually transmitted disease (STD) clinics, pregnant women, and blood donors. The purpose is to describe the HIV/AIDS epidemic in Africa as it has been documented in these groups. Most of these studies have been conducted in urban settings.

This categorization into the following four risk groups is based on a desire to track infection patterns in populations at elevated risk of infection (prostitutes and STD patients), as well as to describe infection in samples which may be more representative of the general population (pregnant women and blood donors). Due to the lack of large numbers of surveys of the general population, this description is also determined by the availability of data.

Commercial Sex Workers

Given the predominant role that heterosexual transmission plays in the HIV epidemic in Africa, it should be no surprise that prostitutes and their

Figure 24.1
HIV Seroprevalence for Commercial Sex Workers in Sub-Saharan Africa Circa 1990

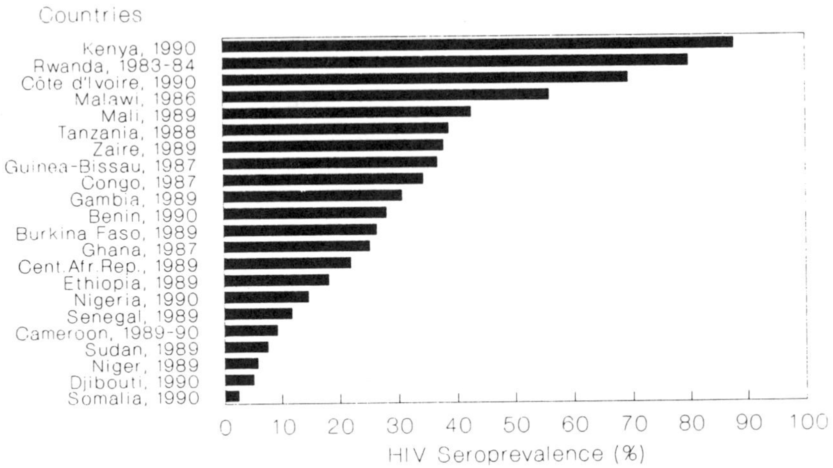

clients play a central role in this epidemic (Padian, 1988). As A. Larson (1989) has described, the organization of the commercial sex industry and the availability of casual sex partners can play a key role in the spread of HIV infection in a country. Modelers in the field of sexually transmitted diseases have documented the importance of "core groups" in the spread of infection (Hethcote and Yorke, 1984). Prostitutes, because of the number of sexual partners, are in many countries the group most at risk for HIV infection. Unfortunately, in many African cities, this risk has resulted in infection levels approaching 50 percent. In some, and especially, among low Socioeconomic status (SES) prostitutes (who tend to have more clients), infection has become nearly universal.

In Africa, as elsewhere, prostitution is not exclusively an urban phenomenon. The commercial sex industry thrives along major transportation routes in Africa and is evident, for example, in rural township trading centers. Nevertheless, urban prostitution has contributed to the extremely rapid spread of infection in African cities.

Data are available on HIV infection among samples of urban prostitutes in the *HIV/AIDS Surveillance Data Base* for 22 countries in sub-Saharan Africa (Figure 24.1). In 10 of these 22 countries, the most recent data show infection levels over 30 percent. In several countries more than half of these women are infected. Data from other population groups indicate that infection levels in many countries are increasing and there is no guarantee that, for example, the five countries in Figure 24.1 with infection levels under 10 percent will for long continue at such low levels. Although data on commercial sex workers are not available for all countries, based on these 22 it could be safely said that infection levels in this population group is much higher than in the general population.

STD Clinic Patients

Knowledge of levels of HIV infection among the population with frequent casual sexual contacts is of high priority. But the selection of such a sample is understandably problematic. However, patients attending STD clinics can be considered a sample of that population, since they or their partners are likely to have had sexual contact with others. They are at elevated risk due both to the presence of multiple partners and to the potentially enhanced risk of HIV infection among those with various other STDs (Wasserheit, 1990). Various studies, for example, have estimated those with a recent STD to be at several times higher risk for HIV infection than those with no such exposure.

Several factors, on the other hand, may result in the data on HIV infection among STD patients not being representative of the total population with casual sex behavior. Among these are biases in the propensity to seek treatment at public facilities and variation (e.g., by sex) in the presence of symptomatic infections. Nevertheless, such studies provide valuable information on a potentially large population at high risk of HIV infection at a time when surveys of AIDS Knowledge, Attitudes, Behaviors, and Practices (KABP) are beginning to shed some light on sexual contacts outside of marital partnerships (Caraël et al., 1991). Several of these studies have shown, as expected, that urban residents are more likely to have casual or commercial sex partners, on the average, than their rural counterparts.

Patterns of increase in HIV infection among large samples of STD patients for several sub-Saharan African countries are shown in Figure 24.2. Quite rapid increases are noted recently in Kenya, Côte d'Ivoire, and Ethiopia. Infection levels in the capital cities of these countries have reached over 20 percent for STD patients. Although both Gabon and South Africa (results are for black females) show relatively low levels of infection, the increases noted in the most recent data are ominous. In contrast with these other countries, Nigeria has documented only a slow increase in infection among this population group.

Studies of STD patients in several other countries have documented HIV infection levels over 50 percent (Figure 24.3). Patterns of sex differentials in HIV infection are inconsistent. In some cases (Burundi, Zambia), males have higher HIV infection levels than females, while in others (CAR [Central African Republic], Ethiopia, South Africa) the reverse situation was found. The stage of the epidemic or patterns of treatment in public facilities may contribute to these observed differences.

Figure 24.2
HIV Seroprevalence for STD Patients in Urban Areas of Selected African Countries: 1982–90

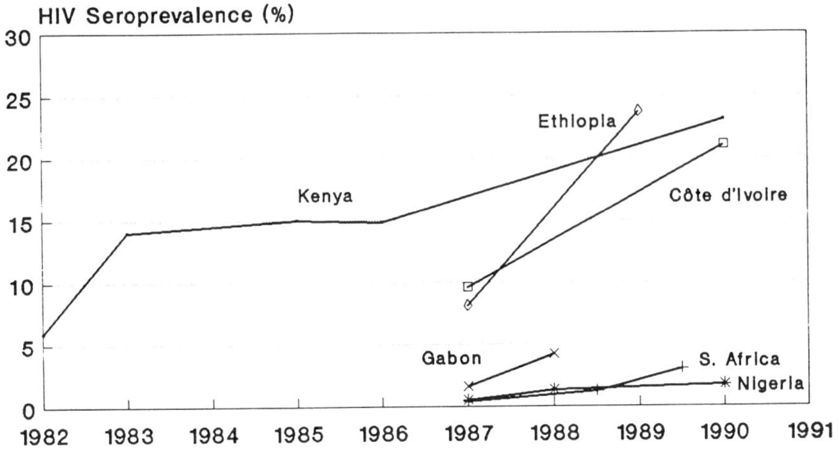

Note: Includes infection from HIV-1 and/or HIV-2.

Figure 24.3
HIV Seroprevalence for STD Patients by Sex in Selected African Countries

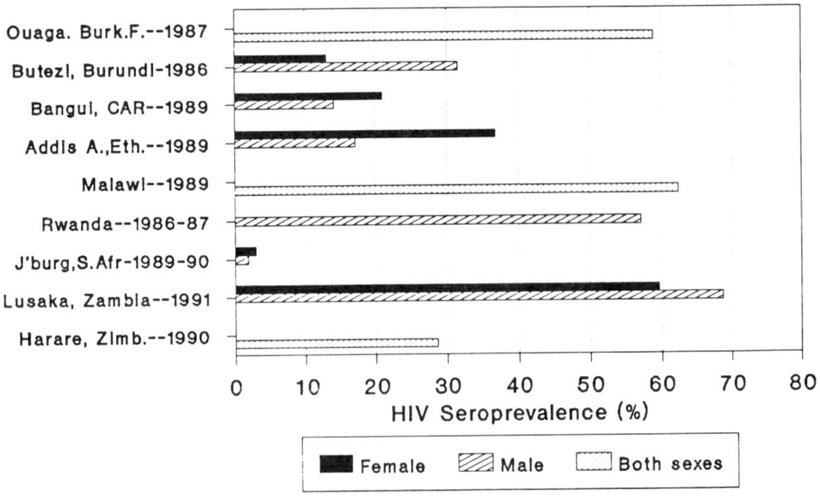

Note: Includes infection from HIV-1 and/or HIV-2.

Figure 24.4
HIV Seroprevalence for Pregnant Women in Selected Urban Areas of Africa, 1985–91

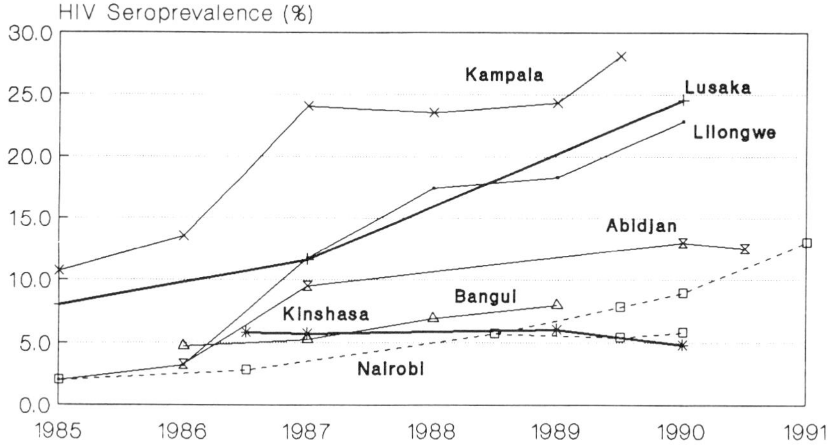

Note: Includes infection from HIV-1 and/or HIV-2.

Pregnant Women

Samples of pregnant women are often used as surrogates for the general population. This is convenient, since in many countries women attend government clinics to receive antenatal care. To some extent, pregnant women can be considered to be at somewhat higher risk that the general population, since they are sexually active. On the other hand, they also are drawn from a limited age range, may be biased toward those in marital (formal or informal) unions, and tend to be younger than adult women in general, given typical age-specific fertility rate patterns. Nevertheless, for many countries, data on pregnant women provide the most representative picture of HIV infection in the general population.

Since 1985, HIV seroprevalence studies of pregnant women have been conducted in a number of African countries. Seroprevalence data from those studies provide an initially confusing picture of regional trends (Figure 24.4). A variety of studies over the past six or more years in Uganda, Zambia, and Malawi show a consistent and rapid increase in HIV infection levels among pregnant women in the capital cities of these countries. By 1990, more than 20 percent of the samples of pregnant women in those areas were infected, while in 1986 infection levels in both Lusaka and Lilongwe were well below 10 percent. Kigali, Rwanda, with a reported infection rate of over 30 percent in 1989, is another major urban area with high levels of infection.

In contrast, pregnant women in Nairobi and Bangui have shown quite moderate

Figure 24.5
HIV Seroprevalence for Blood Donors by Age, Sex, and Type of Donor, Uganda: 1990

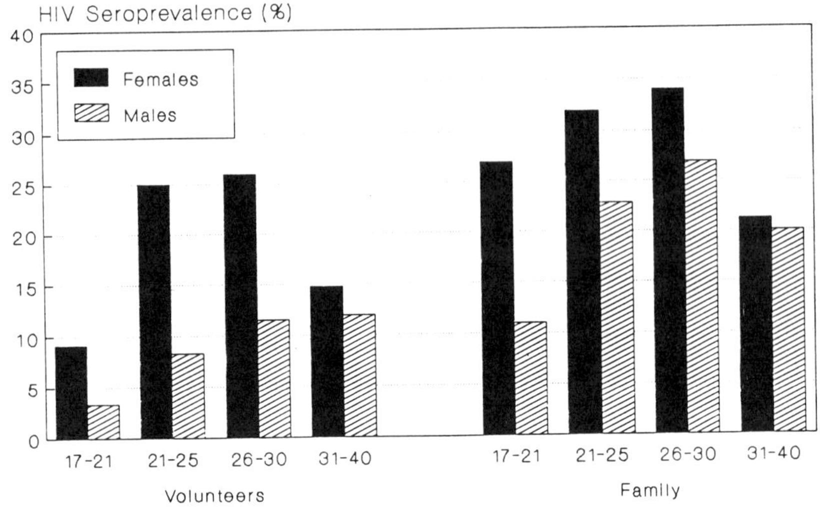

increases, and infection levels in Kinshasa have been relatively stable at 5 to 6 percent. Infection levels for pregnant women in Abidjan increased rapidly to around 10 percent by 1987, but appear to have plateaued by 1990.

Blood Donors

HIV seroprevalence data from blood banks for many countries represent readily accessible samples for use in monitoring changes in HIV infection in the population. However, comparisons with general-population samples in several areas raise questions regarding the representativeness of the blood donor samples (Torrey et al., 1990). Donors tend to be predominantly urban, male, and in their young adult ages. In addition, female donors appear to be a higher-risk group than the general population or male donors. Screening and self-selection processes may act to further bias the sample. An example of such processes can be seen in data from blood donors in Uganda (Figure 24.5). Female volunteer donors are about twice as likely to be HIV positive as their male volunteer counterparts, while family donors, perhaps more representative of the population, are more evenly balanced. Studies in Zaire and other countries have confirmed this tendency for family donors to be more infected than volunteers.

Obviously, issues related to the quality of the blood supply influence decisions regarding the monitoring of blood donors. But, from the available data to date, it does not appear that this group represents a valid proxy for the general population.

ISSUES

Age and Sex Patterns of Infection

Although the precise values are not yet known, there is increasing evidence that women are more at risk of HIV infection than are men, when considered either on a per contact or per partnership basis. In this respect, HIV is no different from other STDs where a similar relation exists. On the population level, however, the risk of HIV infection for women will be a result of the sexual behavior of those women and (secondarily) the behavior of their sexual partners. Available data from several African countries in the latest round of sexual behavior surveys (Caraël et al., 1991) suggest that a differential in sexual behavior exists such that males are more likely to engage in casual sexual contacts than females. This will tend to counterbalance the female's biologically higher susceptibility to infection. The result is that, as the WHO has suggested, the overall sex ratio of HIV-infected population in Africa is not far from 1:1.

This does not mean that in every African country one can expect equal levels of infection, as the timing of the epidemic and sexual behavior patterns will differ. Several serosurveys in Uganda, for example, yield sex ratios for infected respondents of 1:1.4 (Berkley et al., 1990). In Côte d'Ivoire, on the other hand, nationally representative rural seroprevalence levels applied to the population, by age and sex, imply nearly 2 infected males per infected female in the rural area.

Another factor of importance is age-mixing—the tendency for males to choose a younger female as a spouse (as well as a casual sexual partner). This behavior results in HIV infection levels in younger women tending to be higher than males in the same age cohort, while older males tend to have higher infection levels than females of the same age. This pattern is shown in Figure 24.6 for Uganda, and has been documented in a number of other settings.

Urban/Rural Differentials

Available data from sub-Saharan Africa have tended to show a large differential in HIV infection levels between urban and rural areas of a country. A representative population survey in Rwanda in 1986, for example, found 17 percent of the adult population in Kigali to be infected, while only 2 percent of the rural population sampled were HIV positive. This urban bias is evident throughout Rwanda in the data by prefecture (Figure 24.7). Data from Côte d'Ivoire demonstrate both the typical age pattern of infection and urban-rural differentials in infection levels (Figure 24.8).

Such urban biases are likely to result from differences in the timing of the introduction of HIV into the population, and differences in patterns of sexual behavior between urban and rural populations. However, exceptions to this generalization can be identified. For example, the Rakai district in rural Uganda

Figure 24.6
HIV Seroprevalence for the Population of Uganda, by Age and Sex: 1987–88

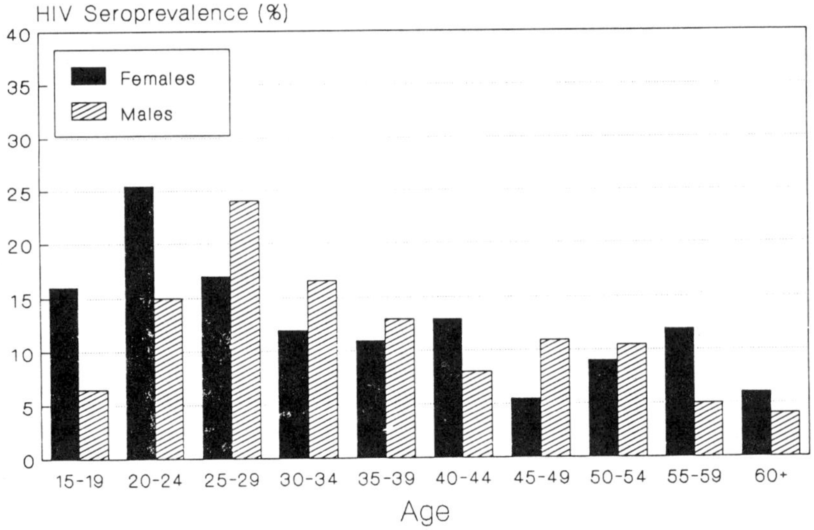

Figure 24.7
HIV Seroprevalence for the Population of Rwanda, by Prefecture: 1986

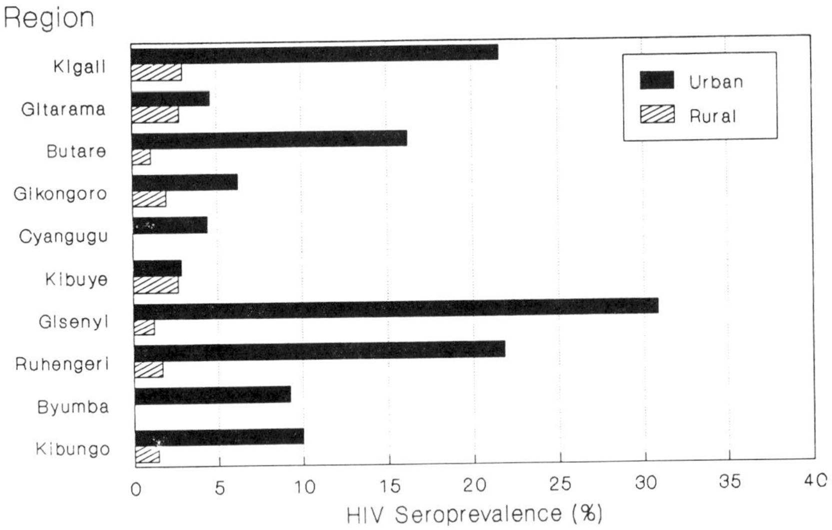

has recorded HIV infection levels that equal those in Kampala, while rural infection levels are about one-half of the urban (Figure 24.9). Across the border in Tanzania, the Bukoba district has a higher HIV seroprevalence than Dar es Salaam. However, within the Bukoba district, urban areas exhibited higher rates

Figure 24.8
HIV Seroprevalence for the Population of Côte d'Ivoire, by Age, Sex, and Urban/ Rural Residence: 1989

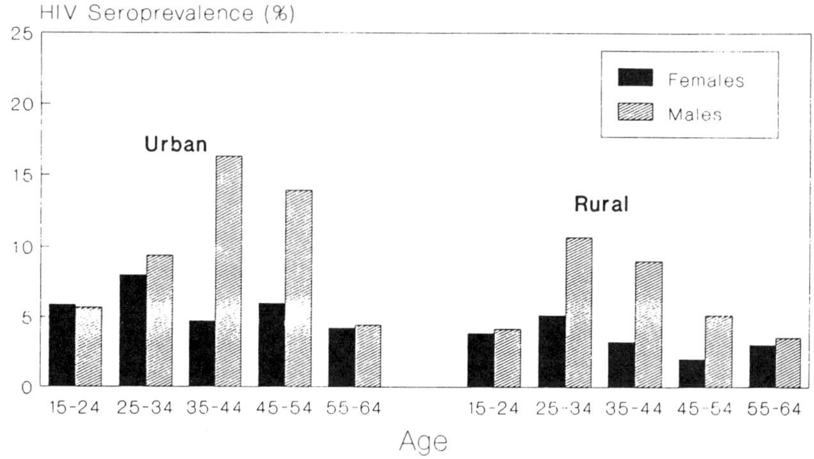

Note: Includes infection for HIV-1 and/or HIV-2.

Figure 24.9
HIV Seroprevalence for the Population of Uganda, by Region: 1987–88

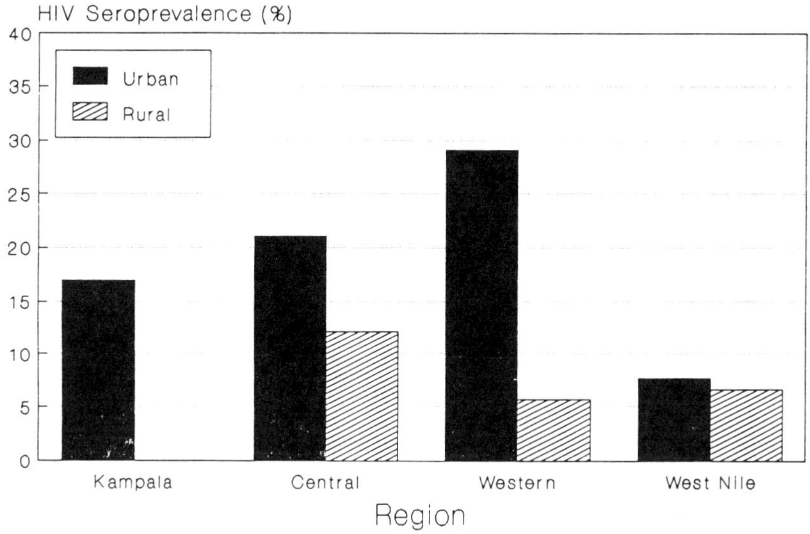

Figure 24.10
African HIV-1 Seroprevalence for Low-Risk Urban Populations

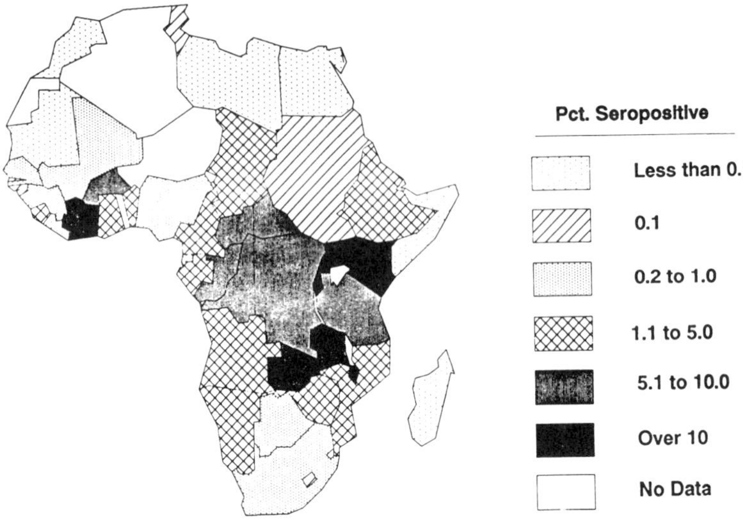

of infection than did rural areas (24 percent vs. 5 percent, respectively). The availability of adequate transportation routes to and through rural areas and the level of rural-urban migration both contribute to the speed of the spread of HIV infection to these rural areas. Thus, countries with well-developed transportation infrastructures and high levels of rural-urban migration may experience rapid spread of HIV infection to rural areas.

Geographic Variation

Results from seroprevalence surveys presented above have tended to highlight the trends in particular population groups and focus on the differentials among populations at different levels of risk. It is equally important to emphasize the geographic variation in current levels of HIV infection between countries, based on a comparison of low-risk urban population groups. Figure 24.10 shows the most recent available data by country for Africa. Factors that can be shown or hypothesized to contribute to the observed variation include the timing of the introduction of the HIV virus to the population; marriage practices and sexual behavior before and outside of marriage; prevalence of STDs in the population; and male circumcision practices. This geographic pattern will be changing over time, as HIV infection levels continue to increase in some countries, while others experience some plateauing of infection.

WHAT THE FUTURE HOLDS

The patterns and trends presented above allow some extrapolation to the future, however tentative, based on the brief documented history of HIV/AIDS in Africa and borrowing from the experience of those countries most affected in the region. This extrapolation provides the following glimpses of the future:

- HIV infection and the impact of AIDS will continue to increase in most African countries in the near future. Infection will spread into rural areas for which little information currently exists.
- The population will continue to be exposed to varying degrees of risk, depending on their behavior and that of sexual partners. Differentials in HIV infection levels will persist, reflecting the variation in risk.
- AIDS will have an increasing impact on the African population, primarily through increased mortality in the population under age 5 and between 30 and 50 years of age. In many countries, gains in infant and child survival and in life expectancy, hard-won over the past several decades, will be reversed (Valleroy et al., 1990).
- The majority of African epidemics will continue to be predominantly urban epidemics, despite some spread into rural areas. Urban areas will experience the greatest impacts, in terms of increased morbidity and mortality. To the extent that significant numbers of those with HIV-related illness return to their rural homelands, some of this impact will be hidden from urban view.
- Unfortunately, due to the weak systems for demographic data collection and reliance on indirect measures of mortality, the documentation of much of this impact will be handicapped by delays in data collection and the inability of current methods to provide precise dating of events. Current measures of adult mortality in Africa are particularly weak and subject to these limitations.
- Efforts to implement interventions to limit the spread of HIV will challenge behavioral scientists working in the region both in terms of measuring relevant behaviors as well as identifying their determinants.
- The need to evaluate interventions will further challenge researchers to identify relevant proximate and intermediate outcome measures, estimate these measures with accuracy and efficiency, and provide adequate linkages to program interventions to demonstrate program efficacy to donor agencies.

AIDS is rapidly becoming a fact of life in Africa. Over the next decade AIDS and its impact will become a fact of life for demographic and behavioral researchers working in Africa, if it has not already. Despite the medical and biological emphasis in much of AIDS research, AIDS is, at its roots, intrinsically bound to social and sexual patterns of behavior. Therefore, social and behavioral scientists have much to contribute to addressing the roots of this epidemic.

AIDS AND URBANIZATION

The process of urbanization has clearly contributed to the spread of HIV and AIDS in Africa over the past decade. As populations increasingly abandon their

Table 24.1
Urban Population and Percent Urban, 1990

Region	Urban Population (Thousands)	Percent Urban
Sub-Saharan Africa	154,745	30.9
Eastern Africa	42,860	21.8
Middle Africa	26,458	37.8
Southern Africa	22,465	54.9
Western Africa	62,962	32.5

Source: Compiled from United Nations, 1991; tables A.1 and A.2.

rural roots and head for the bright lights of the city, they frequently have adopted a lifestyle and behaviors that have placed them at increased risk for HIV infection.

As Table 24.1 shows, however, the majority of population in sub-Saharan Africa still resides in rural areas. Thus, according to United Nations estimates, less than one-third of the population of Africa south of the Sahara was living in urban areas in 1990. By region, this figure varies from under 22 percent in eastern Africa to nearly 55 percent for southern Africa.

However, current African urbanization patterns represent a two-edged sword with regard to the regional AIDS pandemic. On the one hand, the current level of HIV infection in Africa has undoubtedly been kept below potential levels by low levels of urbanization and, in many cases, a national transportation infrastructure that restricts rather than fosters internal movement. On the other hand, the large proportion of population that still resides in rural areas represents potential fuel for the AIDS epidemic.

Continued spread of HIV infection will occur both among those drawn to the cities and among those who remain behind, though perhaps to a lesser degree. Thus, the number of HIV infections in Africa can continue to grow, even if peak infection levels do not increase.

Because AIDS epidemics tend to be concentrated in urban areas, they will have a disproportionate impact on the more educated and the more highly skilled workers. This will result from the concentration of such populations in urban areas. Even if AIDS epidemics are not selective of those with higher SES in an urban area, nationally, those with higher SES will be disporportionately affected due to their urban status. Moreover, there is some evidence to suggest that HIV infection indeed varies by SES, although the results are far from conclusive and regional variation exists. For example, studies in Rwanda, Zaire, and Zambia have all found the level of HIV infection in the highest SES category to be 2 to 4 times the level found among those in the lowest category (Allen et al., 1991; Melbye et al., 1986; and Ndilu et al., 1988).

What opportunity is there for urban programs and policies that hinder, rather than foster, the continued spread of HIV? Several possibilities come to mind:

- Create opportunities in urban areas that are gender balanced, avoiding the excess population of young males that supports a large commercial sex industry.
- Develop programs that support the migration of family groups rather than individuals.
- Support rural development programs that provide a viable alternative to rural-urban migration.
- Target young adults for AIDS education and prevention materials, not only in large cities, but also in the provincial towns and trading centers that often serve as intermediate stops for migrants.

Policy makers must keep in mind, however, that urbanization is not the cause of the spread of HIV and AIDS in Africa. Those working in the field of AIDS prevention long ago recognized that the individual risk of HIV infection is related to specific behaviors and not group identification, sexual preference, or place of residence.

Results of mathematical modeling (Stanley et al., 1991; Way and Stanecki, 1991) have shown that behavioral change, including consistent condom use, prompt and appropriate treatment of sexually transmitted diseases, and a reduction in the number of casual partners, can substantially modify the potential path of an epidemic in a population. Strong and effective intervention programs can limit the spread of HIV infection in Africa, even as these societies struggle to develop modern economies and provide opportunities to their population.

REFERENCES

Allen, S., C. Lindan, A. Serufilira, P. Vande Perre, A. C. Rundle, F. Nsengumuremyi, M. Caraël, J. Schwalbe, and S. Hulley. 1991. ''Human Immunodeficiency Virus Infection in Urban Rwanda: Demographic and Behavioral Correlates in a Representative Sample of Childbearing Women.'' *Journal of the American Medical Association* 266:1657–63.

Berkley, S., W. Naamara, S. Okware, R. Downing, J. Konde-Lule, M. Wawer, M. Musagaara, and S. Musgrave. 1990. ''AIDS and HIV Infection in Uganda–Are More Women Infected Than Men?'' *AIDS* 4:1237–42.

Caraël, M., M. Carballo, B. Ferry, A. Mehryar, and G. Slutkin. 1991. ''Prevalence of High-Risk Sexual Behaviors in Some African Countries: Evidence from Recent Surveys.'' Poster Session presented at the VII International Conference on AIDS, Florence, Italy.

..ncote, H., and J. Yorke. 1984. *Gonorrhea Transmission Dynamics and Control.* Lecture Notes in Biomathematics, No. 56. New York: Springer-Verlag.

Larson, A. 1989. "Social Context of HIV Transmission in Africa: Historical and Cultural Bases of East and Central African Sexual Relations." *Review of Infectious Diseases* 11:916–931.

Mann, J., and J. Chin. 1988. "AIDS: A Global Perspective." *New England Journal of Medicine* 319:302–303.

Melbye, M., A. Bayley, J. K. Manuwele, S. Clayden, W. A. Blattner, R. Tedder, E. K. Njelesani, K. Mukelabai, F. J. Bowa, A. Levin, R. A. Weiss, and R. J. Biggar. 1986. "Evidence for the Heterosexual Transmission and Clinical Manifestations of Human Immunodeficiency Virus Infection and Related Conditions in Lusaka, Zambia." *Lancet* 2:1113–1115.

Ndilu, M., D. Sequeira, S. Hassig, R. Kambale, R. Colebunders, M. Kashamuka, and R. Ryder. 1988. "Medical, Social and Economic Impact of HIV Infection in a Large African Factory." IV International Conference on AIDS, Stockholm: Poster 9583.

Padian, N. 1988. "Prostitute Women and AIDS: Epidemiology." *AIDS* 2:413–419.

Stanley, A., S. Seitz, P. Way, P. D. Johnson, and T. F. Curry. 1991. "The United States Interagency Working Group Approach: The IWG Model for the Heterosexual Spread of HIV and the Demographic Impact of the AIDS Epidemic." In *The AIDS Epidemic and Its Demographic Consequences,* 119–136. New York: United Nations Department of International Economic and Social Affairs.

Torrey B., M. Mulligan, and P. Way. 1990. "Blood Donors and AIDS in Africa: The Gift Relationship Revisited." Staff Paper No 53. Washington, D.C.: U.S. Bureau of the Census, Center for International Research.

United Nations. 1991. *World Urbanization Prospects 1990: Estimates and Projections of Urban and Rural Population and of Urban Agglomerations.* New York.

Valleroy, L., J. Harris, and P. Way. 1990. "The Impact of HIV-1 Infection on Child Survival in the Developing World." *AIDS* 4:667–672.

Wasserheit, J. 1990. "Epidemiological Synergy: Interrelationships between HIV Infection and Other STDs." Paper prepared for the International Workshop on AIDS and Reproductive Health, Bellagio, Italy.

Way, P., and K. Stanecki. 1991. "The Demographic Impact of an AIDS Epidemic on an African Country: Application of the IWG AIDS Model." Working Paper No. 58. Washington, D.C.: U.S. Bureau of the Census Center for International Research.

WHO (World Health Organization) 1992. *Current and Future Dimensions of the HIV/AIDS Pandemic: A Capsule Summary, January, 1992.* Geneva: Global Programme on AIDS.

25

Africa's Urban Future: From Nation-States to a System of Regions

Brian J. L. Berry

Africa is a continent of ancient, diverse, and discontinuous urban traditions across which the Four Horsemen still ride. Natural disasters, wars, famines, and plagues continue to wreak havoc as new nations seek to establish growth directions that free them from the spatial tyrannies imposed by selective colonial development and control. Old enmities and new drives from power render that task all the more difficult: there is a vicious circle in which political instability produces poor economic performance, and poor economic performance engenders further political strife.

Elsewhere, we are accustomed to the idea that productivity differences between urban and rural areas draw in migrants and feed city growth in an upward spiral of increasingly efficient performance. In Africa the story is one of push from rural distress, even when there are no discernible urban advantages. As Akin Mabogunje so graphically points out in the Introduction, it is these new urbanites who are crafting new urban economies and lifestyles in the seedbed of their "informal sector." The very notion of "informality" is an externally imposed residual category, relating to activities not counted in received census practice, but it is a false one. Mabogunje rightly calls for a new paradigm of urban development in Africa, one that reflects the fact that in these very informalities people are evolving institutions and social structures to facilitate and mediate their access to factors of production, notably urban land, credit, and technical know-how.

Given the corpus of this reference book, how close, we might ask, are we to such a paradigm? The book recounts a long and fascinating but problematic journey. What are its high points? Can we now see the shape of the paradigm for which Mabogunje calls? These are the issues that I will address in this concluding chapter.

Let us begin by skimming the highlights:

• Cities were born as capitals, centers of religion-secular authority, five millennia ago in Menes's Egypt. A key need was to survive with a fluctuating water regime. Key inventions were the calendar and writing. Distinctive urban economies developed, creating new professions, and trading networks emerged. Egyptian ideas diffused along these networks, and cities were established elsewhere. The first city in what Tertius Chandler terms "Negrodom," for example, was an Egyptian colonial transplant.

• With the decline of Egypt, successive urbanizing influences have been imposed by sources external to the continent.

—There was Graeco-Roman urbanization on the northern littoral.

—There also was an Islamic overlay on northern Africa, with penetration into Negrodom via Arab trading networks and the planting of slave-trade entrepôts.

—There was a distinctive European colonial structuring of African space that centered on peripheral ports, with radiating access routes to exploitable resources and, later, to environments deemed suitable for European settlement. Town-centered exploitation and settlement were accompanied by a patchwork of boundaries that ignored Africa's ethnic map yet became its nation-states, guaranteeing conflicting claims to power that have fed the vicious circle of political instability and poor economic performance. Sustained urbanization first appeared in the colonial period and helped structure African development as part of the European periphery. Whereas capital and "head-link" cities grew relatively large, administrative and other centers remained relatively small. Colonial policy held rural-to-urban migration in check, and separated European from African and from external (Arab, Indian) traders.

• With independence and the removal of colonial constraints, urbanization has surged from its 15 percent level in 1950 (33 million people). The first fruits of death control have pushed up the rate of natural increase, while rural-to-urban migration has accelerated. Whereas the overall level of urbanization remains low—29 percent (129 million people) in 1980—it is expected to rise very steeply to 52 percent (765 million people) in 2025. Urban growth rates in excess of 4 percent annually imply doubling times of 17 years or less. To date, much of the urban growth has reinforced patterns of the colonial era.

• Distinctive differences are, however, emerging between five great regions (North Africa, West Africa, East Africa, Middle Africa, and Southern Africa), separated by cultural heritage, economic base, and by significant differences in lifetime migration propensities. Whatever the region, urban primacy has increased: the largest cities are growing more rapidly than those beneath them, concentrating the continent's urban population in a limited number of increasingly dominant foci, and sharpening the perceived differences between urban and rural

Africa. Among the regions there are, however, important differences in political objectives that are coming into play.

- Some exceptions to primate-city-led growth have emerged, notably in such countries as Algeria where the postindependence surge in rural-to-urban migration was absorbed by cities that would otherwise have been depopulated by a European withdrawal of close to 1 million persons, and by a vigorous counter-urban socialist regional planning strategy. Elsewhere, most aspire to more balanced urban growth and regional development.
- With the departure of the Europeans, the expulsion of Asian traders, and the acceleration of rural-to-urban migration, urban labor markets and social structures have been transformed in the newly Africanized cities. Major distinctions have emerged in these cities between the modern urban sector and a massive and frequently denigrated "informal" sector. The former is protected and externally oriented; the latter is indigenous and continually innovative in its ways of ensuring survival.
- In all of this, South Africa remains the exception, with its division into a core zone of installed capitalism, an inner periphery of commercial farming and mining areas in white hands, and an outer periphery based on the system of subsistence reserves established in the nineteenth century. This exceptional status will surely change as the African National Congress (ANC) assumes power.
- Whatever may be thought of the social problems of massed populations,
  —Giant cities remain the engines of African growth.
  —There is "overurbanization" when viewed from the perspective of Western models of industry-led urban development, but this notion may be fallacious under a reconsideration of the role of the informal sector.
  —In part, problems of poor economic performance have been the consequence of the rush of postcolonial governments to concentrate growth in massive state monopolies which have facilitated corruption but constrained competition and held innovation in check in the protected sectors.
  —It is clear that the potential links between agricultural development and urban growth have largely been ignored.
- An antiurban anti-industrialization critique has emerged in Africa, based upon a model of an African country divided between an urban modern sector, where elites and workers enjoy many privileges, and a rural sector, where the peasantry live in poverty. In this model
  —Rural-to-urban migration is viewed as a "pull" phenomenon, the attraction of city life.
  —Cities are viewed as growing too rapidly.
  —Policies have been instituted to restore regional balance.

However, throughout Africa urban wages have collapsed and rural-urban differentials have fallen, yet migration has not declined. The reason is that profound structural transformations are underway, in which institutional structures and social and economic relations are no longer given. Migration reflects this process of restructuring, and chains of relationships that have yet to be fully forged.

As a geographer, I have missed in the foregoing a set of maps to help tie the changes since World War II together and to place change in Africa in a global context, but perhaps since pulling things together is the role of a concluding essay, that gap can be filled here.

African nations began their postcolonial experience with levels of urbanization that, in the 1950s, were among the lowest in the world—levels that were shared with much of Asia (Figure 25.1). During the 1960s and 1970s in North Africa, and in the 1970s in Middle Africa, the levels of urbanization shot up, however, differentiating the continent both internally and from Asia.

To accomplish this, rates of urban growth in Africa have been the highest in the world (Figure 25.2). In part, these rapid urban growth rates have been fed by the rising tide of natural increase, which escalated in the 1960s and by the 1970s served to differentiate North and East Africa from other parts of the continent, reaching rates equalled only in Middle America (Figure 25.3).

Not only were Africa's urban growth rates high because of rising rates of natural increase, however; the contributions of migration to urban growth also have been among the highest in the world, again setting Africa's experience apart (Figure 25.4). The migration story is more complicated than revealed by Figure 25.4, however. We need to differentiate between rural-to-urban migration within nations, and transnational urbanward migration which shifts urban growth from one nation to another. In closed national societies urban growth has only two sources, natural increase and rural-to-urban migration, but in an open system of interacting nations, not all of a given nation's rural surplus may be translated into domestic urban growth. Some emigrate, and some of the emigrants may contribute to urban growth elsewhere. For sending nations, *ceteris paribus,* urban growth is less than it would have been under conditions of closure; for receiving nations, there is a more rapid rate of urban growth.

We know surprisingly little about these transnational flows, and thus of rural-to-urban migration corrected for transnational exits and entries, because they have not been a matter of systematic reporting. The only broad-based information on international migration comes from individual countries' reports on landed immigrants by country of origin. These data record only inflows of official migrants, not the ruralward-urbanward breakdown of their destinations. To derive estimates of the contributions of transnational migrants to urban growth in receiving countries and of the magnitude of urban growth forgone because these emigrants have left sending countries, we must resort to demographic analysis.

To understand the demographic analysis consider Figures 25.5 and 25.6, which chart an Algerian example. Figure 25.5 shows the average annual urban growth rate in each censal interval, 1951–81, and the contribution of natural increase to this growth. The difference between the two is the contribution to growth of migration from all sources, a contribution that is charted in Figure 25.6, together with estimates of what the contribution of rural-to-urban migration to the urban growth rate would have been if all Algerians leaving the countryside had moved into that country's urban areas.

Figure 25.1
Levels of Urbanization, 1950–59, 1960–69, and 1970–79

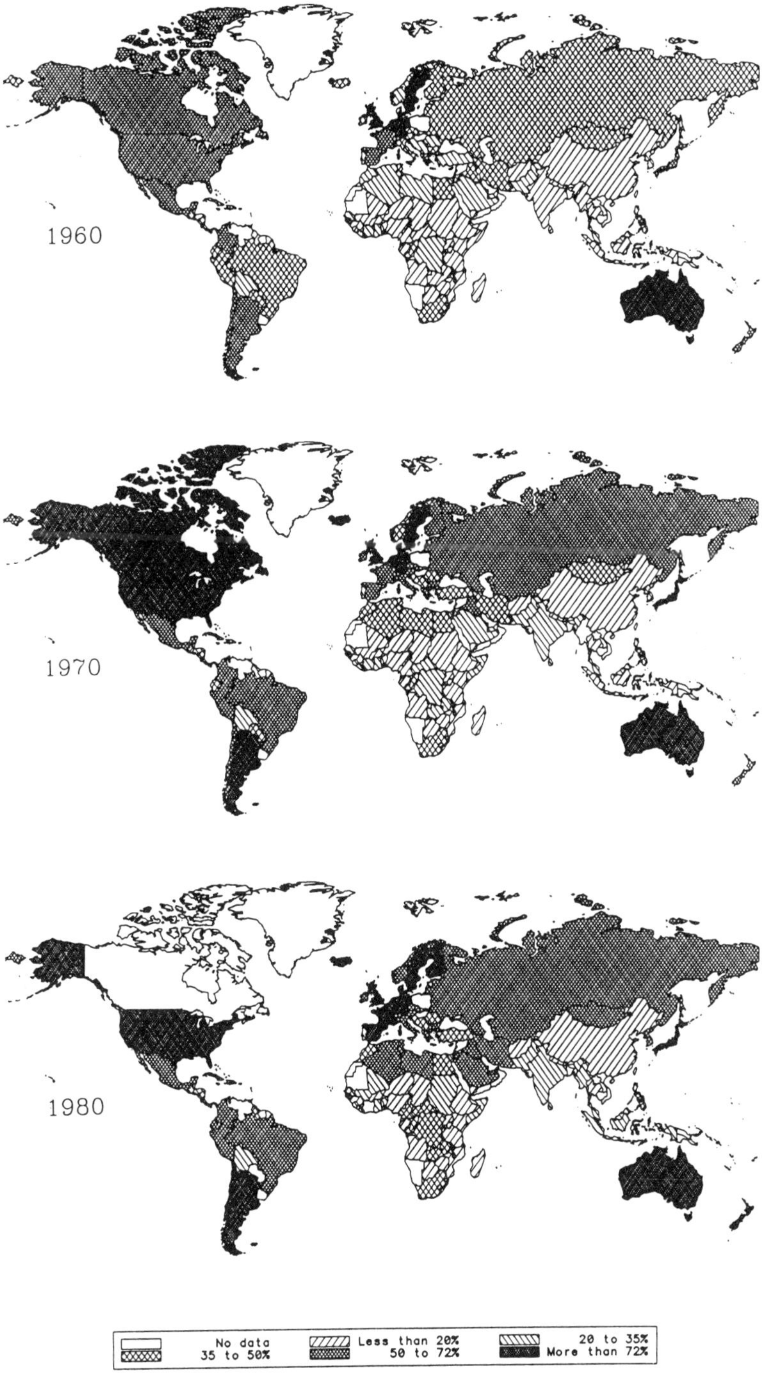

Figure 25.2
Urban Growth Rates, 1950–59, 1960–69, and 1970–79

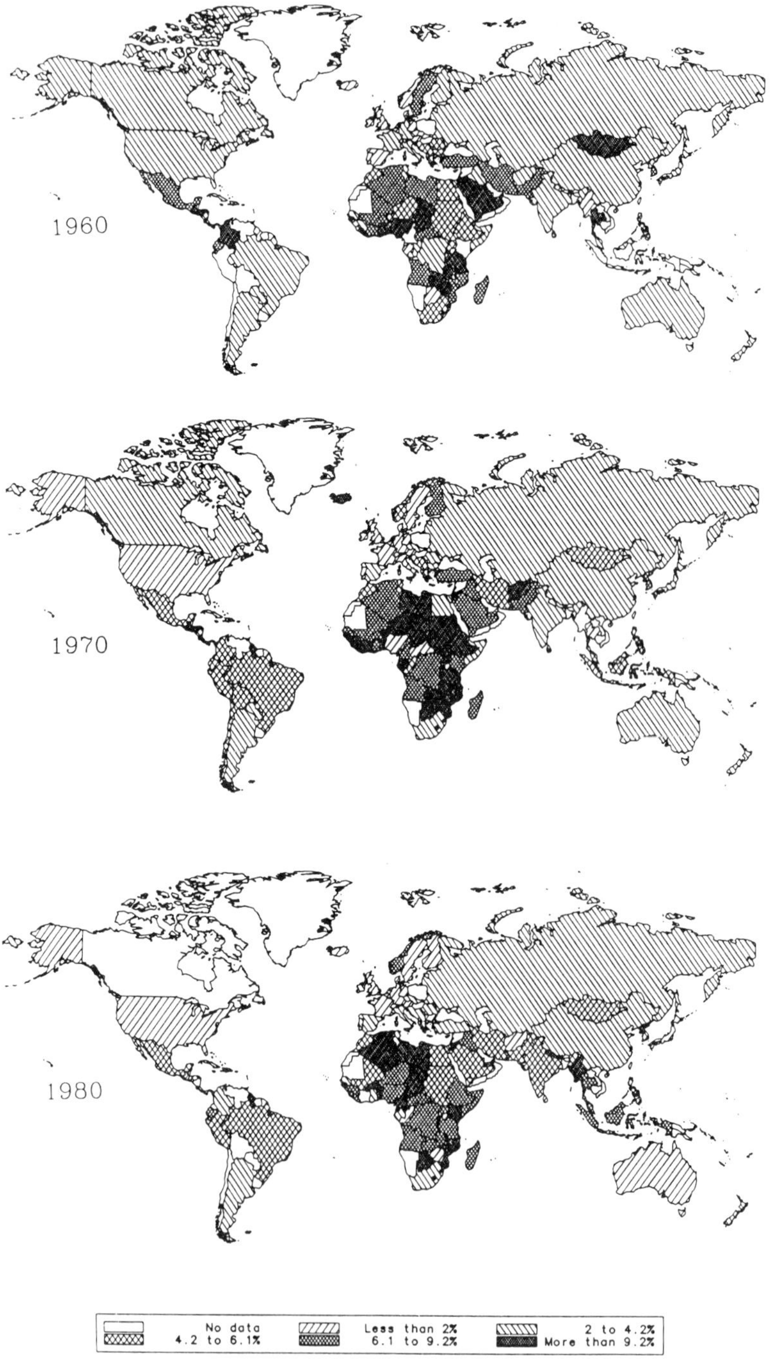

Figure 25.3
Natural Increase: Percentage-Point Contributions to Urban Growth Rates, 1950–59, 1960–69, and 1970–79

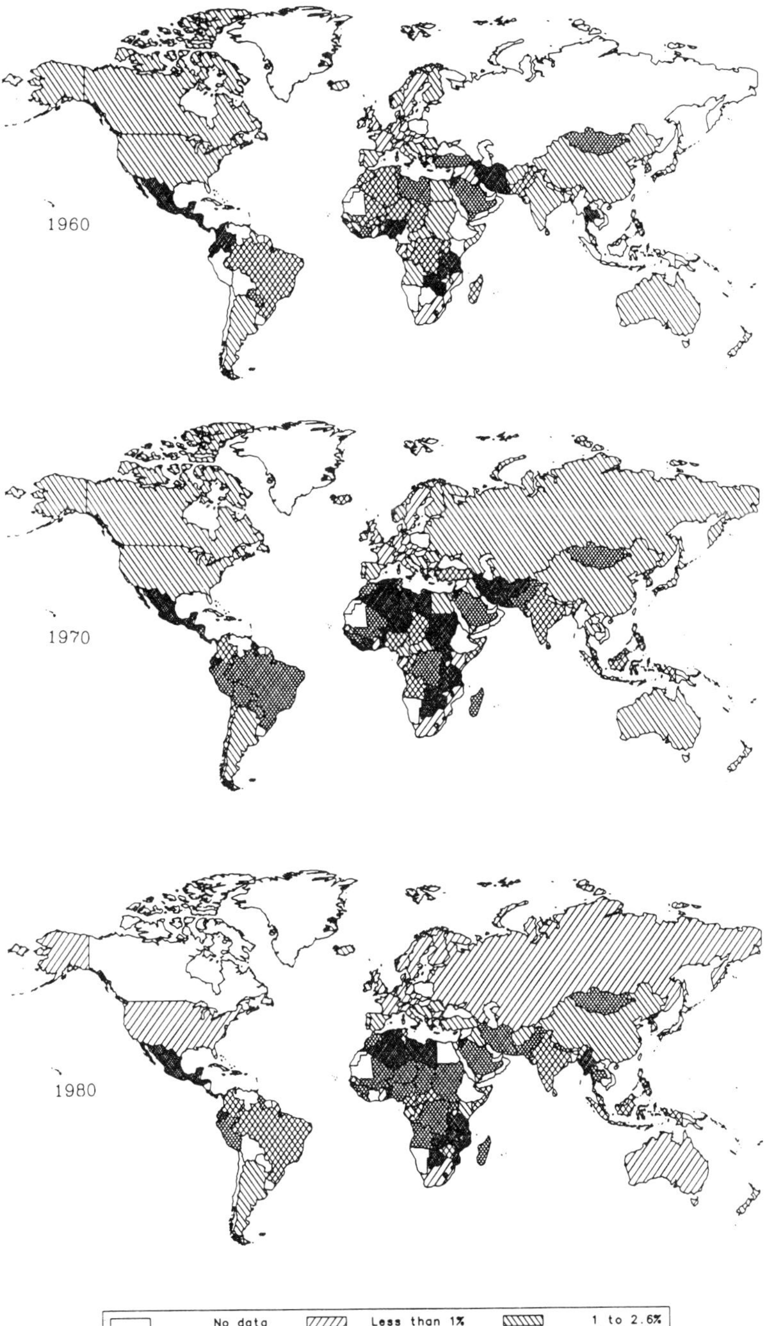

Figure 25.4
Migration: Percentage-Point Contributions to Urban Growth Rates, 1950–59, 1960–69, and 1970–79

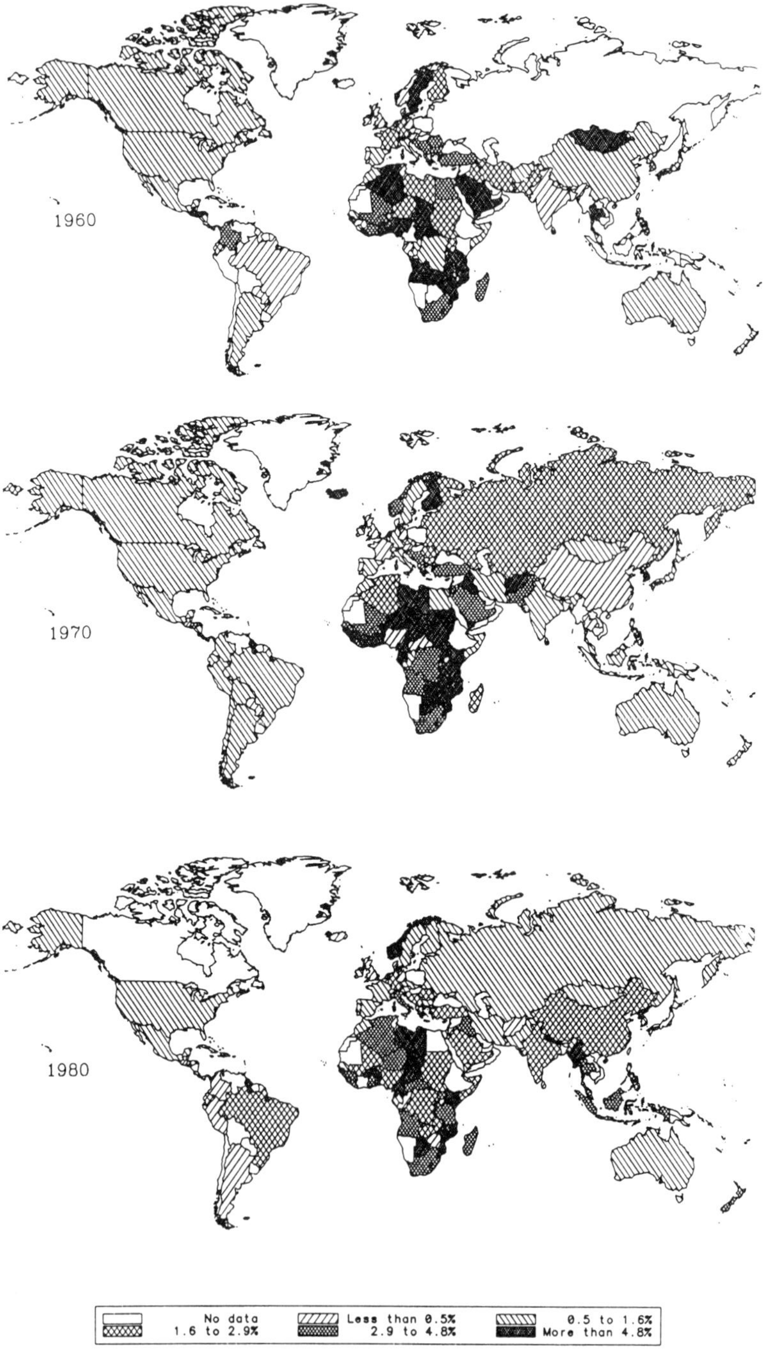

Figure 25.5
Algeria: Urban Growth Rate and the Contributions of Natural Increase and Net Migration

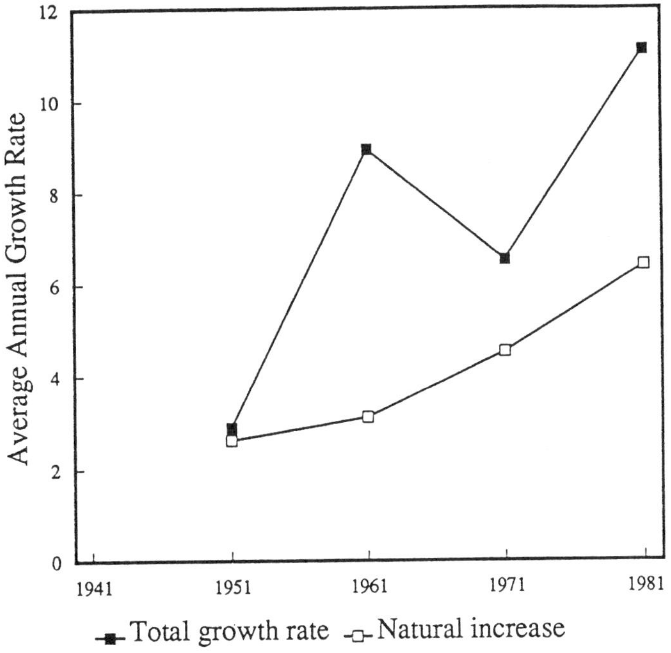

To obtain these estimates, we first calculated the difference between rural population growth and the magnitude of natural increase in rural areas. The surplus of natural increase over growth was assumed to translate into domestic rural-to-urban migration, and the numbers of migrants in each time interval therefore were converted into an imputed contribution to the urban growth rate. Comparison of the two curves (the growth percentage due to all migration, and that which might have resulted from domestic rural-to-urban flows) reveals an excess of rural emigrants over net growth due to migration in the period 1961–81. This implies that there was a net outflow from Algeria in this time period.

If we turn to another example, that of South Africa, as charted in Figure 25.7, the situation is reversed, however: transnational urbanward migration contributed to the South African urban growth rate at the expense of urbanization in the migrants' countries of origin. As Figure 25.8 shows, this enabled South Africa to constrain domestic rural-to-urban migration to levels beneath those of Algeria.

The calculations that produced Figures 25.6 and 25.8 yield both the numbers of transnational urbanward immigrants/emigrants by time period, and their contributions to the urban growth rate. I have made such calculations for every country and for every time period for which data are available. In each case, basic data were derived from national censuses, from statistical bureaus' esti-

Figure 25.6
Algeria: Contributions of Rural-to-Urban and Transnational Urbanward Migration to the Urban Growth Rate

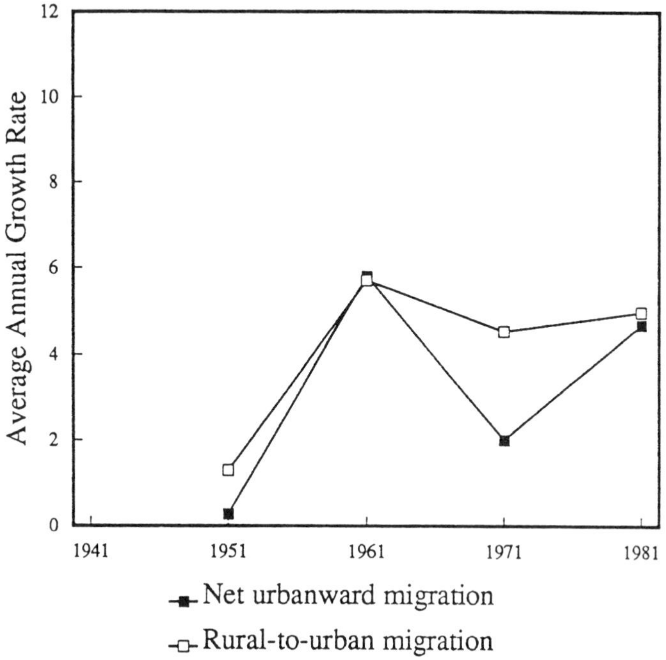

mates of natural increase in urban and rural areas, and failing these, from a wide range of secondary demographic analyses of urban growth. No attempt was made to standardize urban/rural definitions: each country's official definitions were used. Nor was it possible to adjust for the changing political map, except as reflected in the expanding data set over time. Finally, because countries' censuses have varied in timing and frequency, country-by-country estimates of transnational urbanward migration were interpolated to yield a standardized decadal data set in which the 1950s represent 1951–60 and other periods.

The summary results of these calculations for Africa appear in Table 25.1. The numbers reveal that Algeria's annual urban growth rate was 2.5 percentage points slower in 1961–70 (−2.52 in the table) than it would have been if there had not been net emigration. South Africa's urban growth rate was 2.7 percentage points higher in 1971–80 (2.73 in the table) than it would have been if, *ceteris paribus,* there had been no transnational urbanward migration.

The resulting world maps of shares of urban growth due to transnational urbanward migration (Figure 25.9) differ substantially from the maps of raw migration-produced growth (Figure 25.4). Elsewhere in the world, major global destinations for transnational urbanward immigrants such as North and South America and Australia stand out, but so do certain regions within Africa, where

Figure 25.7
South Africa: Urban Growth Rate and the Contributions of Natural Increase and Net Migration

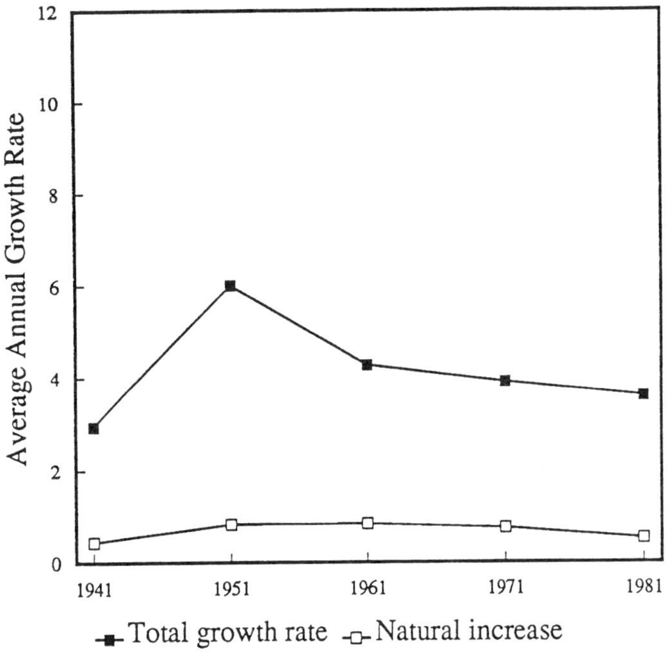

urban growth rates of nations in the Sahel and in Middle Africa are significantly less than they might have been under conditions of closure, a share of their potential urban growth transferred to gainers in West and Southern Africa.

This transnational redistribution of the potential urban population was slower 1951–60 than in the succeeding decades, with the big gainers Mozambique, Zambia, Zimbabwe, Ghana, Togo, South Africa, and Swaziland. The 1960s saw a broad-based exodus from North Africa. What is readily apparent is that both globally and within Africa, the urban growth experiences of individual nation-states are not independent of the experiences of others: regional and global networks are busy transferring urbanization from one area to another. Less and less can we analyze urbanization in Africa within the context of individual nation-states: the future framework must be that of larger regional systems.

Many of the transnational flows clearly were pushed by one or another of the Apocalyptic Horsemen: from the margins of the Sahel to the coastal cities of West Africa by natural calamity; by war and revolution in many other places. The effects of AIDS, the new plague, are, however, not yet in evidence in the available censuses.

Other urbanward transnational migration flows may well reflect the search for opportunity, as when large numbers of West Africans flocked to Nigeria during

Figure 25.8
South Africa: Percentage-Point Contributions of Rural-to-Urban and Transnational Urbanward Migration to the Urban Growth Rate

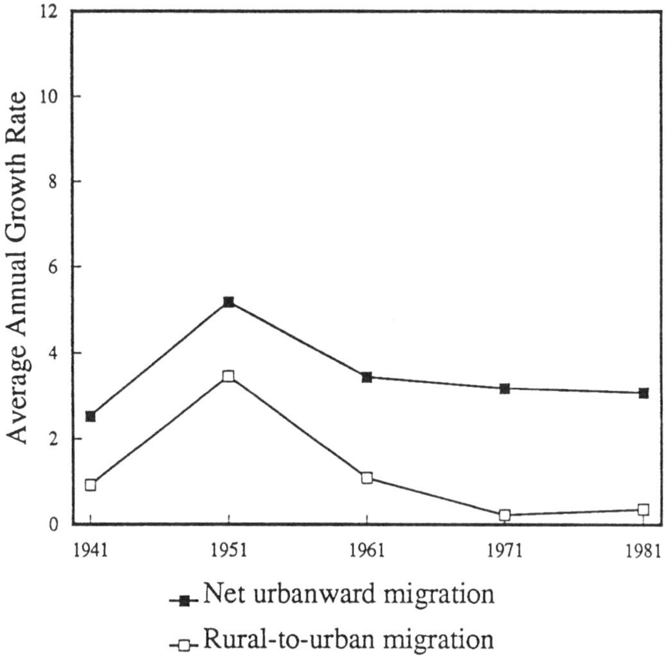

the oil boom and were expelled when boom turned to bust. If such economics-driven migration is selective of the young, the better-educated, and the most creative, what also is implied is another kind of vicious circle: losses are of the most desirable human resources in the sending countries, making development all the more difficult; gains enhance both factor supplies and productivity in the receiving countries, making it more likely that creative change can occur.

Clearly, such circles are linked at a regional scale, but what regional systems are emerging across Africa to redefine the continent's cores and peripheries? Some hints are given in Table 25.1, but the message it conveys is broader and more profound. To reiterate: urbanization in Africa is a continent-wide process and individual nation-states do not stand alone. Potential urban growth is being redistributed across the continent in a complex and dynamic web of gainers and losers.

Adjusted for transnational movements, the maps of the contributions of rural-to-urban migration to the urban growth rate also change substantially (compare Figures 25.4 and 25.10). Whereas there was transnational emigration that reduced urban growth rates in North Africa in the 1960s, rural-to-urban migration remained a potent source of urban growth southward from that region into Middle and East Africa, a pattern that continued into the 1970s. On either side of this

Table 25.1
Average Annual Percentage Change in Urban Population Due to Foreign Migration in African Countries by Decade, 1951–60 through 1971–80

Region	Country	1951-1960	1961-1970	1971-1980
North Africa	Algeria	0.09	-2.52	-0.30
	Egypt	1.21	0.34	0.38
	Mauritania	-1.92	-1.06	1.32
	Libya	1.20	-1.02	2.86
	Morocco	-0.05	-0.84	-0.76
	Sudan	0.19	-1.27	1.12
	Tunisia	-1.04	-2.00	-0.87
East Africa	Ethiopia	-0.68	-1.31	2.32
	Kenya	na	4.11	4.58
	Madagascar	0.45	0.09	-0.42
	Malawi	na	-0.34	-0.53
	Mauritius	0.22	-0.45	-0.47
	Mozambique	3.06	3.54	3.52
	Somali	-0.66	0.26	-0.36
	Tanzania	0.34	-0.10	0.89
	Uganda	0.47	2.31	-0.29
	Zambia	4.27	-0.01	-0.23
	Zimbabwe	5.57	2.56	-0.25
Middle Africa	Angola	0.53	-0.77	-1.26
	Burundi	na	-1.73	-1.71
	Cameroon	na	2.71	0.59
	Central African R.	-0.20	1.36	2.33
	Chad	0.40	1.90	-0.16
	Congo	-0.74	1.72	0.11
	Equatorial Africa	na	-0.21	-0.48
	Rwanda	0.86	0.11	1.09
West Africa	Benin	-0.03	0.42	-1.29
	Burkina Faso	1.98	-0.21	-1.40
	Cape Verde	-0.38	0.18	-1.70
	Gabon	0.11	9.85	0.15
	Gambia	-3.36	5.74	0.23
	Ghana	7.56	2.99	2.37
	Guinea	1.26	0.61	1.07
	Guinea-Bissau	na	-1.30	5.92
	Côte d'Ivoire	-0.32	3.08	3.29
	Liberia	0.30	0.23	0.57

Table 25.1 (Continued)

Region	Country	1951-1960	1961-1970	1971-1980
West Africa	Mali	na	-0.30	0.81
	Niger	0.48	1.80	-0.84
	Nigeria	2.39	-0.02	0.61
	Senegal	-0.21	-1.08	3.77
	Sierra Leone	-1.91	-0.67	0.46
	Togo	3.88	0.45	-0.44
Southern Africa	Botswana	na	-6.96	3.28
	Lesotho	-0.33	1.77	2.58
	South Africa	2.37	2.96	2.73
	Swaziland	4.43	7.41	0.28

Source: Computed from National Population Censuses, 1951-80.

belt, it is transnational immigrant flows that have been the most potent sources of growth, suggesting a continued rapid rural exodus along this central axis that is both firing urban growth within the axial belt and contributing streams of migrants who help elevate urban growth rates around the continental margins.

It is the major cities of these emergent migration-fed development zones, arrayed around the continental margins, that are becoming the seedbeds of change, out of which distinctive African urban economies and cultures are evolving. Simultaneously, significant differences are emerging between the big cities along cardinal regional lines: North, South, East, and West, with an axis in Middle Africa hollowed out not simply by natural calamity and continuing warfare, but now also by the diffusion of AIDS.

The texture of urban life, already well established in the North, will be conditioned by Islam and differentiated by the outcome of secular-fundamentalist conflicts. That in the South, with the continent's strongest Western-style urban-industrial cores, will be shaped by the end of apartheid, the transfer of rule from a minority of whites to an ANC-led majority, and a reconnection of periphery and core that will let loose an urbanward flood and perhaps produce a white exodus of dimensions that equal the French withdrawal from North Africa.

It is in West and East Africa that I believe that "informalization" will produce the greatest shifts in the nature of urban growth and in the interpenetration of urban and rural lifestyles and folkways to which many of the writers in this book have alluded. Extended family networks, arrayed within class and ethnic groups, extend from village to city and provide multiple bases of economic support and individual safety nets, while educating selected representatives to be parts of the worlds of formal-sector business and of public administration. As a result, increasing shares of national product go unreported; Western-based measures of wealth and poverty, and Western-favored methods of redistribution all prove

Figure 25.9
Transnational Urbanward Migration: Percentage-Point Contributions to Urban Growth Rates, 1950–59, 1960–69, 1970–79

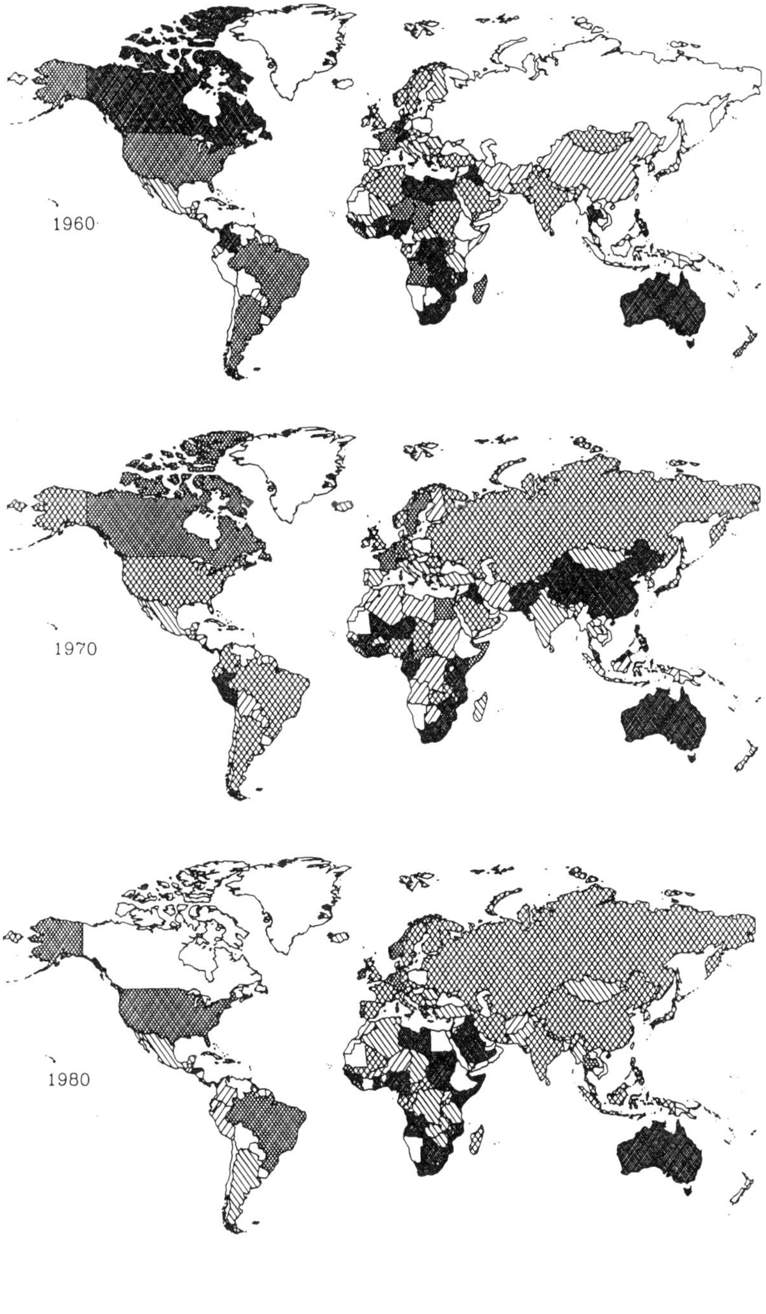

Figure 25.10
Rural-to-Urban Migration: Percentage-Point Contributions to Urban Growth Rates, 1950–59, 1960–69, and 1970–79

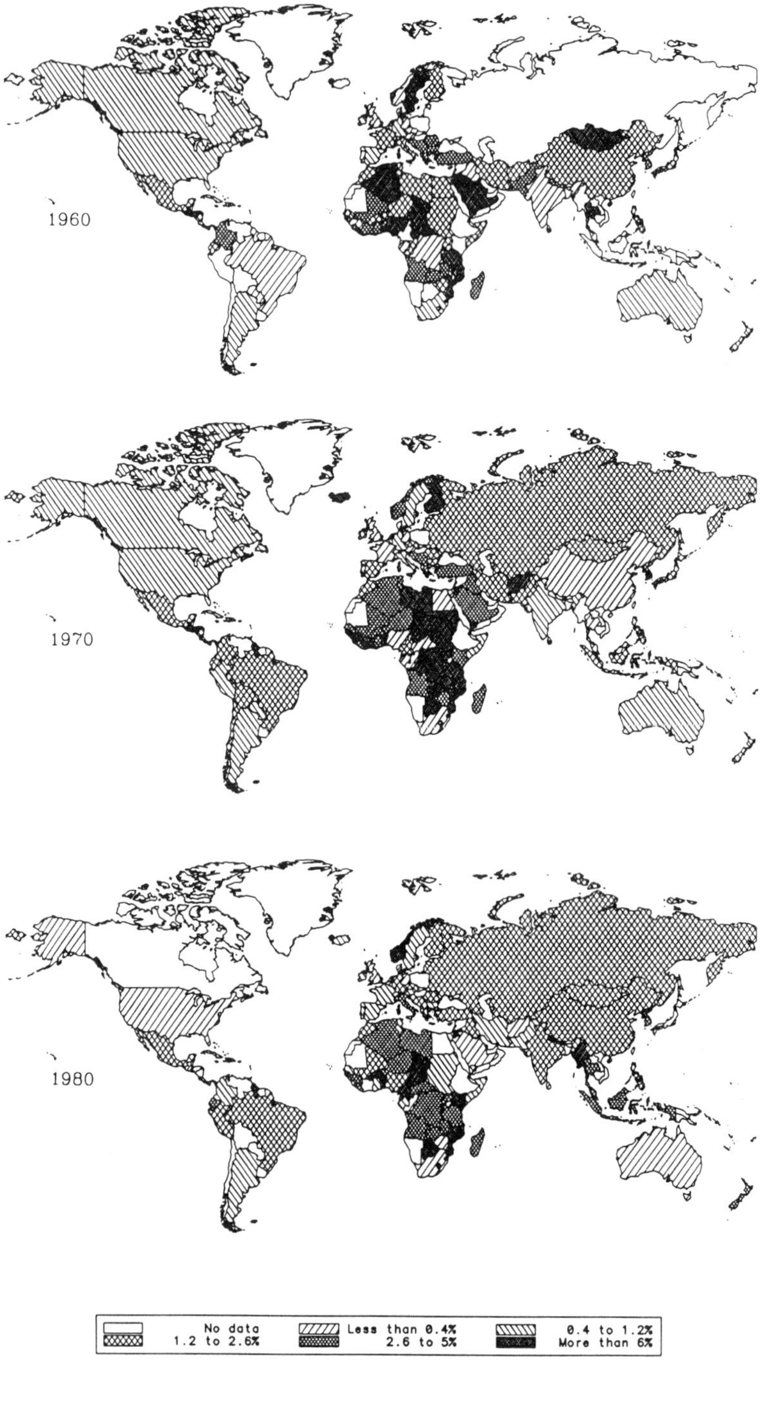

fallacious. Received urban theory provides few, and at best only poor, guides to the restructuring that is underway—restructuring occurring under conditions of more rapid urban growth than elsewhere in the world, with as widespread a volume of transnational redistribution as seen elsewhere. These shifts mean that a fertile ground exists for continuing research that will produce the new rounds of social theory that are needed to comprehend the urbanization that is coming to characterize an increasingly dynamic African urban scene.

Bibliography

Abu-Lughod, Janet. 1965. "Urbanization in Egypt: Present State and Future Prospects." *Economic Development and Cultural Change* 13:313–343.

———. 1976. "Development in North African Urbanism: The Process of Decolonization." In *Urbanization and Counterurbanization,* edited by Brian J. L. Berry, 191–211. Newbury Park: Sage.

Adam, Andre, Mario Cataudella, and Mariagiovanna Riitand. 1981. *Decolonizzazione e spazio urbano: il caso del Maghreb.* Milano: F. Angeli.

Alawar, M. 1982. "Urbanization in Libya: Present State and Future Prospects." In *Social and Economic Development of Libya,* edited by E. G. H. Joffe and K. S. McLachlan, 331–353. London: Means Press.

Ankerl, Geza. 1986. *Urbanization Overspeed in Tropical Africa, 1970–2000: Facts, Social Problems, and Policy.* Geneva: INU Press, Institut Universitaire CP 55 1211 Geneve.

———. 1987. *Urbanisation rapide en Afrique tropicale faits, conséquences et politiques societales, 1970–2000.* Paris: Berger-Levrault.

Antoine, Philippe. 1988. "Demographic Indicators and Urbanization in Abidjan." *Espace, Populations, Sociétés* 2:227–243, 171–172.

———. 1983. "The Population of Abidjan within Its Walls: Urban Dynamics and the Development of Demographic Structures between 1955 and 1978." *Cahiers ORSTOM: Série Sciences Humaines* 19:371–395.

Augel, Johannes, Peter Hillen, and Luiz Ramalho. 1986. *Die Verplante Wohnmisere: urbane Entwicklung und "armutsorientierter" Wohnungsbau in Africa and Lateinamerika.* Saarbrucken: Breitenbach.

Belachew, Haliu. 1983. "Towards an Understanding of Urban Growth in Ethiopia." In *Studies in African and Asian Demography,* 287–323. Cairo Demographic Centre Monograph Series No. 11. Cairo.

Benoist, Pere J. P., et al. 1979. *Le Village piège: urbanisation et agro-industrie sucrière en Côte d'Ivoire*. Paris: Presses universitaires de France.

Bessat, Collette. 1983. *Développement urbain en Afrique noire: quel habitat promouvoir? expériences et perspectives*. Paris: République française. Ministère des relations extérieures.

Brennan, Ellen M., and Harry W. Richardson. 1986. "Urbanization and Urban Policy in Sub-Saharan Africa." *African Urban Quarterly* 1:20–42.

Bricas, N., et al., eds. 1985. *Nourrir les villes en Afrique sub-saharienne*. Paris: L'Harmattan.

Brule, J. C., and G. Mutin. 1982. "Industrialisation et Urbanization en Algérie." *Maghreb-Machrek* 96:41–66.

Cairo Demographic Centre (CDC). 1973. *Urbanization in Some Arab and African Countries*. Research Monograph Series, No. 4. Cairo: CDC.

Carr, W. J. P. 1990. *Soweto: Its Creation, Life, and Decline*. Johannesburg: South African Institute of Race Relations.

Centre national de la recherche scientifique. 1984. *Villes et problèmes urbains Contemporains en Afrique noire*. Paris: L'Harmattan.

Chandler, Tertius. 1987. *Four Thousand Years of Urban Growth*. Lewistown, N.Y.: St. David's University Press.

Cidonio, Gianfranco. 1981. *Squilibri e prospettive dell'Africa nuova: problemi di economia politica e processi di urbanizzazione in Africa dopo l'indipendenza*. Roma: Bulzoni.

Cilliers, S. P. 1982. *Urban Growth in South Africa. 1936–2000: A Demographic Overview*. Stellenbosch: University of Stellenbosch.

———. 1989. *Managing Rapid Urbanisation*. Stellenbosch: University of Stellenbosch.

Coquery-Vidrovitch, Catherine, ed. 1988. *Processus d'urbanisation en Afrique*. 2 vols. Paris: L'Harmattan.

Dewar, David, Alison Todes, and Vanessa Watson. 1983–84. "Urban Pressures and Policies in Africa: Lessons from Kenya, Tanzania, Zambia, and Zimbabwe." *Journal of Contemporary African Studies* 3:79–107.

Dogan, Mattei, and John D. Kasarda, eds. 1988. *The Metropolis Era*. 2 vols. Newbury Park: Sage.

Drakakis-Smith, David, ed. 1992. *Urban and Regional Change in Southern Africa*. London: Routledge.

Ela, Jean Marc. 1983. *La ville en Afrique noire*. Paris: Editions Karthala.

Goldstein, Sidney, and David F. Sly. 1977. *Patterns of Urbanization: Comparative Country Studies*. 2 vols. Dolhain: Ordina Editions.

Gugler, Josef, and William G. Flanagan. 1978. *Urbanization and Social Change in West Africa*. Cambridge: Cambridge University Press.

Haeringer, Philippe, ed. 1984. *De Caracas à Kinshasa: bonnes feuilles de la recherche urbaine a l'ORSTOM, 1978–1983*. Paris: Editions de l'ORSTOM.

Haines, Richard, and Gina Buigs, eds. 1985. *The Struggle for Social and Economic Space: Urbanization in Twentieth Century South Africa*. Durban: University of Durban–Westville.

Hakim, M. S. Abdel, and Wassin A. Hamid. 1982. *Some Aspects of Urbanization in Egypt*. Durham, England: University of Durham.

Hance, William A. 1970. *Population, Migration, and Urbanization in Africa*. New York: Columbia University Press.

Hanna, William John. 1981. *Urban Dynamics in Black Africa: An Interdisciplinary Approach.* 2nd rev. ed. New York: Aldine Publishing Company.

Hayuma, A. M. 1983. "The Growth of Population and Employment in the Dar es Salaam City Region, Tanzania." *Ekistics* 50:255–259.

Hindson, D. 1987. *Pass Controls and the Urban African Proletariat in South Africa.* Johannesburg: Ravan Press.

Hull, Richard W. 1976. *African Cities and Towns before the European Conquest.* New York: W. W. Norton.

Kuper, Hilda. 1977. *Urbanization and Migration in West Africa.* Westport, Conn.: Greenwood Press.

Le Bris, Emile. 1987. *Famille et résidence dans les villes africaines: Dakar, Bamako, Saint-Louis, Lomé.* Paris: L'Harmattan.

LeSourd, Michel. 1985. "The Rural Exodus of the Baoule and Urbanization in the Ivory Coast." *Espace, Populations, Sociétés* 1:62–69.

Levtzion, Nchemia, and Humphrey J. Fisher. 1987. *Rural and Urban Islam in West Africa.* Boulder, Colo.: L. Rienner Publishers.

Liauzu, Claude, et al., eds. 1985. *Enjeux urbains au Maghreb: crises, pouvoirs et mouvements sociaux.* Paris: Editions L'Harmattan.

Mabogunje, Akin L. 1969. *Urbanization in Nigeria.* New York: Africana Publishing Corporation.

———. 1977. "The Urban Situation in Nigeria." In *Patterns of Urbanization: Comparative Country Studies,* edited by Sidney Goldstein and David F. Sly, 2:569–641. Dolhain: Ordina Editions.

Marlin, John, Immanuel Ness, and Stephen T. Collins. 1986. *Book of World City Rankings.* New York: Free Press.

Mashabela, Harry. 1990. *Mekhukhu: Urban African Cities of the Future.* Johannesburg: South African Institute of Race Relations.

Mitchell, J. Clyde. 1987. *Cities, Society, and Social Perception: A Central African Perspective.* Oxford, England: Clarendon Press.

Mokkadem, A. 1989. "L'Urbanization en Algérie." *Revue Statistiques* (Office National des Statistiques) 23:1–5.

Muwonge, Joe Wamala. 1980. "Urban Policy and Patterns of Low-Income Settlement in Nairobi, Kenya." *Population and Development Review* 6:595–613.

Nouschi, A., et al., eds. 1980. *Système urbain et développement au Maghreb: travaux du séminaire international de Hammamet.* Tunis: Ceres productions.

Obudho, Robert A. 1985. *Demography, Urbanization, and Spatial Planning in Kenya.* Westport, Conn.: Greenwood Press.

———. 1985. "Multivariate Analysis of Kenya's Urban Systems." *Geojournal* 13:385–399.

Obudho, R. A., and Salah El-Shakhs. 1979. *Development of Urban Systems in Africa.* New York: Praeger.

O'Connor, Anthony. 1981. *Urbanization in Tropical Africa, an Annotated Bibliography.* Boston: G. K. Hall.

———. 1983. *The African City.* New York: Africana Publishing Company.

Onokerhoraye, Andrew G. 1986. *Urban Systems and Planning for Africa.* Benin City, Nigeria: University of Benin.

Pacione, Michael. 1981. *Problems and Planning in Third World Cities.* New York: St. Martin's Press.

———. 1990. *Urban Problems: An Applied Urban Analysis.* London: Routledge.

Panzac, Daniel. 1983. "Espace et Population en Égypte." *Méditerranée* 4:71–80.

Peel, J. D. Y. 1980. "Urbanization and Urban History in West Africa." *Journal of African History* 21:269–277.

Peil, Margaret. 1981. *Cities and Suburbs: Urban Life in West Africa.* New York: Africana Publishing Company.

———. 1984. *African Urban Society.* Chichester, England: J. Wiley.

———. 1991. *Lagos: The City Is the People.* Boston: G. K. Hall.

Rafig, Muhammad, and Assefa Hailemariam. 1987. "Some Structural Aspects of Urbanization in Ethiopia." *Genus* 43:183–204.

Richardson, H. W. 1980. "An Urban Development Strategy for Kenya." *Journal of Developing Areas* 15:97–118.

Roden, Hanne. 1984. *The World Bank: Introduction to Its Involvement in Urbanisation in the 3rd World: The Case of Botswana.* Copenhagen: School of Architecture.

Rondinelli, Dennis A. 1985. "Population Distribution and Economic Development in Africa: The Need for Urbanization Policies." *Population Research and Policy Review* 4:173–196.

———. 1988. "Giant and Secondary Cities in Africa." In *The Metropolis Era: A World of Giant Cities,* edited by M. Dogan and J. Kasarda, 1:291–321. Beverly Hills: Sage.

Sandbrook, Richard. 1982. *The Politics of Basic Needs: Urban Aspects of Assaulting Poverty in Africa.* Toronto: University of Toronto Press.

Schneider, Karl-Gunther. 1983. *Die Stadte des sudlichen Afrika.* Berlin: Gebr. Borntraeger.

Schwarz, Alf. 1983. *Les dupes de la modernisation: développement urbain et sous-développement en Afrique.* Montreal: Nouvelle optique.

Sembajwe, I. S. L. 1985. *Urban Population Growth Rates in Africa with Special Reference to Lesotho.* Roma, Lesotho: National University of Lesotho.

Sierig, Jörg. 1988. *Spontansiedlungen in Afrika.* Stuttgart: IRB Verlag (IRB-Literaturauslese, Nr. 2318).

Simon, David. 1992. *Cities, Capital and Development: African Cities in the World Economy.* London: Belhaven Press.

Smith, David M., ed. 1992. *The Apartheid City and Beyond: Urbanization and Social Change in South Africa.* London: Routledge.

Soja, Edward W., and C. E. Weaver. 1976. "Urbanization and Underdevelopment in East Africa." In *Urbanization and Counterurbanization,* edited by Brian J. L. Berry, 233–266. Beverly Hills: Sage.

Stren, Richard E., and W. R. White. 1989. *African Cities in Crises.* Boulder, Colo.: Westview Press.

Swilling, Mark, Richard Humphries, and Khehla Shubane, eds. 1991. *Apartheid City in Transition.* Cape Town: Oxford University Press.

Tesfaghiorghis, Habtemariam. 1986. "The Growth of Urbanization in Ethiopia, 1966–1984." *Eastern Africa Economic Review* 2:157–67.

Tomlinson, Richard. 1988. "South Africa's Urban Policy: A New Form of Influx Control." *Urban Affairs Quarterly* 23:487–510.

———. 1990. *Urbanization in Post-Apartheid South Africa.* London: Unwin Hyman.

United Nations. 1987. *The Prospects of World Urbanization, Revised as of 1984–85.* New York.

———. 1989. *Prospects of World Urbanization, 1988*. Population Studies No. 112. New York.

———. 1990. *Population Growth and Policies in Mega-cities, Cairo*. Population Policy Paper No. 34. New York.

———. 1991. *World Population Prospects 1990*. Population Studies No. 120. New York.

———. 1991. *World Urbanization Prospects 1990*. Population Studies No. 121. New York.

United Nations, Economic Commission of Africa. 1983. *Population Distribution and Urbanization, ECA Member States*. African Population Studies Series No. 7. Addis Ababa.

———. 1989. *Patterns, Causes, and Consequences of Urbanization in Africa*. Addis Ababa.

Vincent, Maurice. 1984. "Urbanisation et Développement au Cameroon." *Revue Tiers Monde* 25:427–436.

Wane, A. A. Oumar. 1985. "Urban Growth in Senegal: Urbanization and the Spread of Dakar." *Mondes en Développement* 13:553–580.

Wessels, Elizabeth. 1984. *Urbanisation in Africa*. Pretoria: Africa Institute of South Africa.

World Bank. 1979. *Urban Growth and Economic Development in the Sahel*. Working Paper No. 315. Washington, D.C.

———. 1986. *Population Growth and Policies in Sub-Saharan Africa*. Washington, D.C.

Zachariah, K. C., and Julien Condé. 1981. *Migration in West Africa: Demographic Aspects*. New York: Published for the World Bank [by] Oxford University Press.

Name Index

Subject Index

About the Editor and Contributors

JAMES D. TARVER, the author of over 100 publications, was Demographic Consultant for the United Nations, Professor of Demography and Acting Dean, Faculty of Social Sciences, University of Botswana, and Professor of Sociology and Director, Demographic Research and Training Center, University of Georgia. He also taught at Catholic and Howard universities, Washington, D.C. He is the author of *The Demography of Africa*.

S. I. ABUMERE is Professor of Geography and Dean, Faculty of the Social Sciences, University of Ibadan, Nigeria. He has papers on population movements and development and has co-authored papers with Akin L. Mabogunje.

FILIPE R. AMADO is Director of the Planning Cabinet of Agostinho Neto University, Luanda, Angola, and Lecturer in the Department of Economics and the Law School.

PHILIPPE ANTOINE is Director of Research at the French Institute of Scientific Research for the Development in Cooperation (ORSTOM) and has worked in Algeria, the Côte d'Ivoire, and Senegal. Currently, he is studying migrants in the urban milieu of Dakar in collaboration with the Fundamental Institute of North Africa (IFAN). Formerly, he was a Visiting Researcher at the Department of Demography, University of Montreal.

MOHAMED BAILEY is a faculty member at Los Medanos College, Pittsburg, California. He lectured at the University of Sierra Leone and published on the fertility and mortality of Sierra Leone and has recently published articles in *Journal of Tropical Pediatrics, Social Science and Medicine,* and *Canadian Studies in Population.*

BRIAN J. L. BERRY is Lloyd Viel Berkner University Professor and Director, Bruton Center for Development Studies at the University of Texas, Dallas. He is a member of the National Academy of Sciences, a Fellow of the American Academy of Arts and Sciences and of the British Academy, and the past president of the Association of American Geographers. He received the Victoria Medal from the Royal Geographical Society. Professor Berry is the author of more than 300 books and articles and is the editor of *Urban Geography.*

ALAIN-MICHEL CAMARA is a demographer in the National Direction of Statistics and Information in the Mali Ministry of Planning, Bamako, Mali.

TERTIUS CHANDLER, a historian and demographer, has written two standard reference books: *3,000 Years of Urban Growth* and *4,000 Years of Urban Growth,* as well as articles on Moses and on education. He ran for Congress twice and resides in Berkeley, California.

A. J. CHRISTOPHER is Professor and Head, Department of Geography, University of Port Elizabeth, South Africa. He has published a number of books and articles on the historical and political geography of southern Africa, Africa, and the British Commonwealth. His most recent book, *The Atlas of Apartheid,* was published in 1994.

GILLIAN P. COOK, is Lecturer in Geography, La Sainte Union College, University of Southampton, U.K. Formerly she lectured at Rhodes University, Grahamstown, and at the University of Cape Town in South Africa and has observed the urbanization process in that country firsthand. Her publications focus on South African urban and settlement geography as reflected in the recent contributions to *Homes Apart,* edited by Anthony Lemon and *The Apartheid City and Beyond,* edited by David M. Smith.

FAUSTO CRUZ teaches economics at Agostinho Neto University, Luanda, Angola, and has served as a consultant for the United Nations Development Program and the World Bank.

SEKOUBA DIARRA is a demographer in the National Direction of Statistics and Information in the Mali Ministry of Planning, Bamako, Mali.

MOHAMED EL-ATTAR is Professor of Sociology at Mississippi State University. He has served twice with the United Nations as a senior migration and urbanization expert. He has published articles on internal migration, fertility, family planning, and occupational studies in such professional journals as *Social Biology, Journal of Biosocial Science, Growth and Change, The Gerontologist, Demography-India, The Egyptian Population and Family Planning Review, l'Egypte Contemporaine, The Arab Journal of Social Sciences, International Journal of Contemporary Sociology,* and *Contemporary Sociology.*

ROBERT ESCALLIER is Professor of Geography, University of Nice-Sophia-Antipolis, and Director, Center of Modern and Contemporary Mediterranean. Also, he is editor of *Cahiers of the Mediterranean* and a member of the Center for the Study and Research on Urbanization of the Arab World: Urbanisation du Monde Arabe (URBAMA) by the Centre National de la Recherche Scientifique (CNRS). He has published many articles, chapters, and other works about urbanization of the Maghreb, particularly *Citadins et Espaces Urbains au Maroc* (1984), and is a prominent scholar of urbanization in Northwest Africa.

THOMAS J. GOLIBER is Senior Scientist and Director of the RAPID IV population policy project at The Futures Group in Washington, D.C. Since 1979 he has worked on projects to provide technical assistance to African leaders in the analysis of population issues and the development of population policies and programs. He authored *Sub-Saharan Africa: Population Pressures on Development* and *Africa's Expanding Population: Old Problems, New Policies* in the Population Bulletin series of the Population Reference Bureau.

RALPH HAKKERT, formerly of Agostinho Neto University, Luanda, Angola, is a consultant for the United Nations and is in Honduras. His research interests are demographic methods, statistical demography, projections, and demographic computer applications.

SAAD KEZEIRI is Associate Professor, Urban Planning and Urban Geography, Garyounis University, Benghazi, Libya. His professional interests are urbanization, urban planning, and regional planning in the Middle East. His publications include papers on urban planning and economic development in Libya.

AKA KOUAME, formerly a researcher in the Department of Demography, University of Montreal, is now at the Institut de Formation et de Recherche Démographiques (IFORD), Yaoundé, Cameroon.

ANTHONY LEMON is a Lecturer in Geography, University of Oxford, and Fellow of Mansfield College. His publications are concerned with the geography of apartheid and the transition to a post-apartheid society. Among his books are *Apartheid: A Geography of Separation* (1970), *Apartheid in Transition* (1987), and *Homes Apart: South Africa's Segregated Cities* (1991).

AKIN L. MABOGUNJE is a distinguished demographer and one of the most prominent Africans to write about urbanization in Africa, beginning in the early 1960s. His contributions are truly vast. In 1962, he wrote about Yoruba towns, in 1968 about urbanization in Nigeria, in 1976 about cities and African development. Formerly, he was Professor of Geography at the University of Ibadan. Now, he devotes most of his efforts to such worthwhile endeavors as World Hunger Programs and related humanitarian achievements.

TOMA J. MAKANNAH is Chief, General Demography Section, Population Division, United Nations Economic Commission for Africa (UNECA), Addis Ababa, Ethiopia. He has published articles and monographs on African urbanization and data collection systems as well as on the demography of Sierra Leone, where he formerly served as a demographic statistician at the Central Statistics Office. He and Thando D. Gwebu co-authored *Patterns, Causes, and Consequences of Urbanization in Africa* (UNECA, 1989).

RICHARD MARCOUX is a researcher in the Department of Demography, University of Montreal. He is a member of the ''Population et développement au Sahel'' (Population and development in the Sahel) research group and is working in the area of the insertion of migrants in urban zones. During 1991–92 he conducted a demographic survey in Bamako, Mali. His doctoral dissertation examined child labor in urban Mali, and his major research interests include migration and housing, family structure and urbanization, nuptiality, and women's activity in West Africa.

GORA MBOUP has been awarded a Ph.D. in demography at the University of Montreal. Formerly, he was a Ford Foundation researcher, worked at the Direction of Statistics in Senegal during the 1988 census, and at the University of Dakar. He is currently at the Westinghouse Institute for Development.

H. MAX MILLER is Associate Professor of Sociology, University of Georgia, Athens. He has published papers on the demography of Africa, community development, and rural sociology in *African Studies, Rural Africana, African Urban Quarterly, African Population Studies,* and in the *Handbook on International Migration* (Greenwood Press, 1990).

ROBERT A. OBUDHO is Senior Lecturer in Geography, University of Nairobi; Associate Professor of Geography, Urban and Regional Planning, State University of New York at Albany, U.S.A.; and Editor, *African Urban Quarterly.* His research includes urbanization and regional planning in developing countries, particularly Africa. His articles and reviews have appeared in the *Annals of the Association of American Geographers; African Studies Review Journal; African Urban Studies; African Urban Quarterly; Cahier Etudes Africanise; Social Indicators Journal; Geojournal;* and *Third World Planning Review.* He is the author of *Urbanization in Kenya: A Bottom-up Approach to Development Plan-*

ning; editor and contributor to *Urbanization National Development and Regional Planning in Africa;* co-author of *Periodic Markets, Urbanization and Regional Planning: A Case Study from Western Kenya;* and editor and contributor to *Urbanization and Development Planning in Kenya* and *Demography, Urbanization and Spatial Planning in Kenya.*

ROSE A. OBUDHO co-authored *Precolonial Urbanization in East Africa,* a publication by the Urban Center for Research, Nairobi (1988).

CAROLE RAKODI is a Senior Lecturer, Department of City and Regional Planning, University of Wales, Cardiff, U.K. She was an urban planner in Zambia, has taught, undertaken consultancy work, and researched in India, Malaysia, China, and Zimbabwe. She has published on urban planning and on housing policy in developing countries, and is the joint editor of and contributor to *Managing Fast Growing Cities: New Approaches to Urban Planning and Management in the Developing World* (1993).

DENNIS A. RONDINELLI is Professor of International Business, Kenan-Flagler Business School, and Director of the International Private Enterprise Development Research Center in the Kenan Institute of Private Enterprise, University of North Carolina, Chapel Hill. Professor Rondinelli has published 11 books and more than 140 articles and monographs on international economic development, urban and regional planning in developing countries, development management and privatization, and private enterprise development. His most recent book is the second revised edition of *Development Projects as Policy Experiments: An Adaptive Approach to Development Administration.*

RAM N. SINGH is a Senior Research Associate, Office of Research, U.S. Department of Education. Before joining the Department, he was a Professor of Sociology and taught courses in demography, research methods, and statistics at both undergraduate and graduate levels. In addition, he has published articles on fertility and migration.

KEITH SUTTON is a Senior Lecturer in Geography, University of Manchester, teaching courses on the geography of Third World economic development, with particular reference to Algeria and the rest of the Maghreb. He has visited the Maghreb for over twenty years and published on Algeria's population, rural settlement, agrarian reform, and regional development. Formerly, he was secretary of the Maghreb Studies Association and is currently researching the Casbah of Algiers.

GABRIEL TATI is a researcher at the Institut de Formation et de Recherche Démographiques (IFORD), Yaoundé, Cameroon. His research deals with the demographic and socioeconomic aspects of the urban growth in Africa. He has contributed to the project "Migration, Urbanization and Development in Central Africa" conducted by IFORD and Centre Français sur la Population et le Développement and is the author of a forthcoming book. Also he has presented papers at international seminars on the social aspects of Structural Adjustment Programs in Africa.

HABTEMARIAM TESFAGHIORGHIS is a research fellow in Graduate Studies in Demography at the National Center for Development Studies, Australian National University. He has published on Aboriginal demography and socio-economic status. He was the Team Leader of the Demography and Housing Experts, which conducted the first-ever Population and Housing Census of Ethiopia in 1984. His research interests include fertility and mortality studies, population projections, and urbanization; and his regional interests are Africa, Australian Aboriginal demography, and Micronesia.

PETER O. WAY is Senior Research Analyst at the Center for International Research, U.S. Bureau of the Census. He has authored numerous publications and presentations on the current AIDS situation, particularly in developing countries, and on the current and future demographic and economic impact of AIDS epidemics. He was recently invited to give the state-of-the-art presentation on the Demographic Impact of AIDS at the VIII International AIDS Conference in Amsterdam. He has published in a variety of journals such as *AIDS, AIDS and Society, Society,* and *The New England Journal of Medicine.*

JOHN WEEKS is Professor of Development Economics and Director of the Center for Development Studies at the School of Oriental and African Studies at the University of London. He has published numerous articles and books on the economic problems of Africa, most recently *Development Policy and the Economy of Sierra Leone* (London: Macmillan, 1992), and with Vali Jamal, *Africa Misunderstood* (London: Macmillan, 1993). He has served as a consultant in Africa for many international organizations, including the FAO and ILO.